GLENCOE
BUSINESS AND PERSONAL
FINANCE

Jack R. Kapoor
Professor of Business and Economics
Business and Services Division
College of DuPage
Glen Ellyn, Illinois

Les R. Dlabay
Associate Professor of Business
Department of Economics and Business
Lake Forest College
Lake Forest, Illinois

Robert J. Hughes
Professor of Business
Dallas County Community Colleges
Dallas, Texas

New York, New York   Columbus, Ohio   Woodland Hills, California   Peoria, Illinois

Business and Personal Finance Program Components

Program Resources
Student Edition
Teacher's Annotated Edition

Reinforcement
Student Activity Workbook

Teacher's Resource Binder
Student Activity Workbook (TAE)
Lesson Plans
Reproducible Tests
Internet Resources
Blackline Masters
Your Personal Financial Planner

Technology-Based Resources
Assessment Package
Financial Planner Software
Interactive Lesson Planner
PowerPoint Presentations
Virtual Business

Enrichment
Standard & Poor's Extension Activities
Money Matter: Personal and Family Financial
   Management Simulation

NOTICE. Information on featured companies, organizations, and their products
and services is included for educational purposes only, and it does not present
or imply endorsement of the *Business and Personal Finance* program.

Glencoe/McGraw-Hill

*A Division of The **McGraw·Hill** Companies*

Printed in the United States of America.

Send all inquiries to:
Glencoe/McGraw-Hill
21600 Oxnard Street, Suite 500
Woodland Hills, California 91367-4906

ISBN 0-02-644128-4 (Student Text)
ISBN 0-07-823766-1 (Teacher's Annotated Edition)

1 2 3 4 5 6 7 8 9   027   06 05 04 03 02 01 00

Table of Contents

Chapter 11 Real Estate and Other Investment Alternatives   350

UNIT ④ PROTECTING YOUR FINANCES   376

Chapter 12 Planning Your Tax Strategy   378

Go Figure...

How can you get the most from your reading? Effective readers are active readers. As they read, they have conversations with themselves about the text; they get involved. Don't be a passive reader! Use the strategies below to help you read actively and effectively.

1 Predict

what the section will be about.

Make educated guesses about what the section is about by combining clues in the text with what you already know. Predicting helps you anticipate questions and stay alert to new information.

Ask Yourself

- What does this section heading mean?
- What is this section about?
- How does this section tie in with what I have read so far?
- Why is this information important in understanding business and personal finance?

2 Connect

what you read with your own life.

Draw parallels between what you are reading and the events and circumstances in your own life.

Ask Yourself

- What do I know about the topic?
- How do my experiences compare to the information in the text?
- How could I apply this information in my own life?
- Why is this information important in understanding business and personal finance?

3 Question

as you read to make sure you understand the content.

Ask yourself questions to help you clarify the reading as you go along.

Ask Yourself

- Do I understand what I've read so far?
- What is this section about?
- What does this mean?
- Why is this information important in understanding business and personal finance?

4 Respond

to what you read.

React to what you are reading. Form opinions and make judgments about the section while you are reading—not just after you've finished.

Ask Yourself

- Does this information make sense?
- What can I learn from this section?
- How can I use this information to start planning for my financial future?
- Why is this information important in understanding business and personal finance?

PLANNING PERSONAL FINANCES

Unit 1 provides the foundation for studying and using personal financial planning techniques. The next four chapters will describe the steps in the financial planning process, the relationship between career planning and financial fulfillment, ways to assess your current financial situation, and the importance of wise buying decisions.

READING STRATEGIES

To get the most out of your reading

- **PREDICT** what the section will be about.
- **CONNECT** what you read with your own life.
- **QUESTION** as you read to make sure you understand the content.
- **RESPOND** to what you've read.

START TODAY

Setting Goals

By setting goals that are important to you, you can achieve your financial dreams. Goal setting is like a compass to guide you in the right direction. What can you do today that will help you have a successful financial future?

Personal Financial Planning

STANDARD
&POOR'S

Q&A

Q: I'm just a student. What difference does it make how I spend my money?

A: Even when you're in high school, financial planning can help you decide how to spend, save, and invest your money so that you can use it for purchases or activities that really matter to you. You won't always be a student. Learning to save and use money wisely now will increase your chances of having financial security in the future. In other words, when you're older, you won't have to struggle to pay your bills.

Decisions and Goals in Personal Finance

Laura Diaz is 17 and works part-time at a local supermarket, where she earns $120 a week. She enjoys traveling and eating in trendy restaurants. Laura dreams of buying a house before she's 30 and hopes to retire by the time she's 55. To make these desires a reality, Laura needs to earn and invest her money wisely.

John Preston is 16 and earns $100 a week baby-sitting his younger sister and a neighbor's son after school. He enjoys quiet weekends with his friends and plans to rent a small apartment when he graduates from college. His most immediate desire is for a mountain bike. Although his tastes are simpler than Laura's, he'll still need to manage his money.

The financial decisions Laura and John make will determine whether they'll fulfill their dreams for the future. Unfortunately, most people are never taught how to manage their money. As a result, many adults can barely pay their bills each month. They run up thousands of dollars of debt and never get ahead financially. The time to learn how to manage your money is now.

Making Personal Financial Decisions

What is personal finance? It's everything in your life that involves money. *Personal financial planning* means spending, saving, and investing your money so you can have the kind of life you want as well as financial security. Everyone has different financial goals. *Goals* are the things you want to accomplish. Getting a college education, buying a car, or starting a business are some examples of goals. Planning your personal finances is important because it will help you reach your goals, no matter what they are.

It's up to you to make and follow a financial plan. Some of the benefits of planning are:

- you have more money, know how to use money to achieve your goals, and are financially secure;
- you have less chance of going into debt you can't handle;
- you can help your partner and support your children.

Whether you're spending, saving, or investing money, planning can help you with big or small financial decisions. The financial planning process has six steps.

PREDICT

Identify at least five strategies that you think will help you achieve your financial goals.

What's Your Financial ID?

YOUR SPENDING PROFILE

Whether you're a saver or a spender is part of your personality. Being a saver or a spender isn't good or bad on its own, but either personality can cause problems if not managed properly. Here's a chance to test your financial personality.

If someone gave you $200, what would you do with it? Read the options below and choose three.

___ Take my closest friends out to eat and to the movies (5 points)
___ Spend $50 on fun items and save the rest (3 points)
___ Put the money toward my next car payment (1 point)
___ Buy new clothes for school (3 points)
___ Hit the nearest record store and buy several CDs (5 points)
___ Buy a portable CD player (3 points)
___ Get a cell phone (5 points)
___ Buy a savings bond (1 point)
___ Put it in a savings account for future education (1 point)
___ Buy the hottest new concert tickets (5 points)

What do your choices say about you?

Big saver: If you scored 3–5, you're willing to give up things today so you can buy something you want more tomorrow.

Middle of the roader: If you scored 7–11, you know how to use your money for current needs while keeping an eye on the future.

Big spender: If you scored 13–15, wow, do you like to spend money!

MONEY MATTERS Your values affect the ways in which you spend money. *What are some reasons people might shop at a flea market or swap meet?*

Step 1   Determine Your Current Financial Situation

To figure out your current financial situation, make a list of your savings, monthly income (money you receive, such as job earnings, allowance, gifts, and interest on bank accounts), monthly expenses (money you spend), and debts (money you owe to others). A good way to estimate your expenses is to keep a careful record of everything you spend your money on for one month. You might want to use a small notebook to track the cost of all your purchases. Once you've determined your financial situation, you'll be able to start planning.

Step 2   Develop Your Financial Goals

To develop clear financial goals, you'll need to think about your attitude toward money. Is it more important to you to spend your money now or to save for the future? Would you rather get a job right after high school or continue your education? What role do your personal values play in your financial decisions? *Values* are the beliefs and principles you consider important, correct, and desirable. Different people value different things.

Another important aspect of developing financial goals is being able to distinguish between your needs and your wants. A need is something you must have to survive, such as food, shelter, and clothing. A want is something you desire or would like to have or do. For example, if you live in an area where the winter is cold, you need a coat. You may want a leather jacket, but other types of coats could also keep you warm.

Only you can decide what goals to pursue, and it's important to make them as specific as possible. For example, you might decide to save $50 every month or 15 percent of every paycheck.

Step 3 Identify Alternative Courses of Action

It's impossible to make a good decision unless you know all your options. Generally, you'll have several possible courses of action. Suppose that you're saving $50 a month. Your options might include the following:

- Expand the current situation. You may decide to increase the amount you save every month to $60.
- Change the current situation. You could invest in stocks instead of putting your money into a savings account.

FIGURE 1.1

Get the Facts

Information on financial planning can come from many sources:

1 *Financial specialists (accountants, bankers, financial planners, insurance agents, tax attorneys, and tax preparers)*

2 *Computer software and the Internet*

- Start something new. You could use the $50 to pay off your debts.
- Continue the same course of action. You may choose not to change anything.

In each case, however, be aware that the costs of your decision may outweigh the benefits.

Step 4 — Evaluate Your Alternatives

When you evaluate your alternatives, use the many sources of financial information that are available. Look at where you are in your life, your present financial situation, and your personal values. Be sure to consider the consequences and risks of each decision you make.

SOURCES OF FINANCIAL INFORMATION   It's important to keep up-to-date with social and economic conditions. A company that manufactures the latest technology or designs the trendiest clothes may be a good investment. On the other hand, if you learn that a corporation is being sued, would you want to invest in it? How do you keep track of everything? Many sources of information are available to help you with your financial decisions. (see **Figure 1.1**)

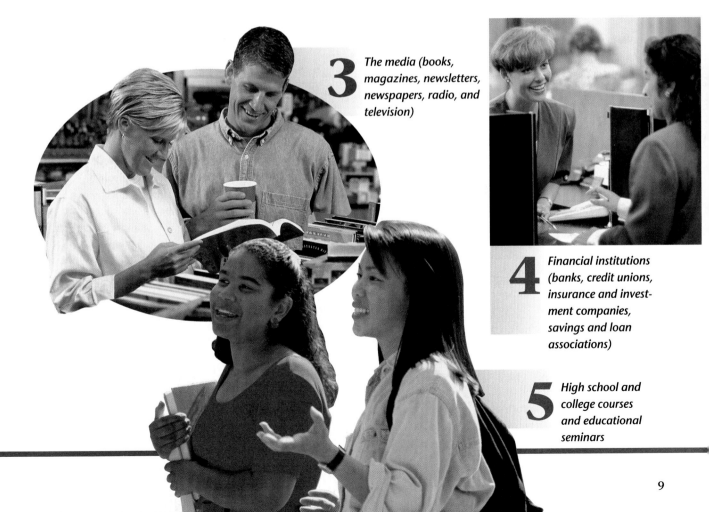

3 The media (books, magazines, newsletters, newspapers, radio, and television)

4 Financial institutions (banks, credit unions, insurance and investment companies, savings and loan associations)

5 High school and college courses and educational seminars

CONSEQUENCES OF CHOICES You can't have it all. When you choose one option, it eliminates other possibilities. Suppose that you want to become a full-time college student. You also want the income you would earn at a full-time job. In choosing to pursue your education, you give up the opportunity to work full-time, at least for the moment. An *opportunity cost*, sometimes called a trade-off, is what you give up when you make one choice instead of another. The opportunity cost of going to college is working at a full-time job. Choosing between the alternatives involves more than just knowing what you give up. It also involves knowing what you gain.

UNDERSTANDING RISKS If you decide to ride your bicycle on a busy city street, you're taking a risk that a car may hit you. When you make a financial decision, you also accept certain risks. Some types of financial risks include:

- **Inflation risk.** If you wait to buy a car until next year, you accept the possibility that the price may increase.
- **Interest rate risk.** Interest rates go up or down, which may affect the cost of borrowing or the profits you earn when you save or invest.

*C*areers in Finance

PERSONAL BANKER

If you have money to invest but don't know what your options are, you might be surprised to know that you can turn to your local bank for help. Most banks have employees called personal bankers who are trained to help customers put their money to best use. In addition to setting up savings and checking accounts, personal bankers explain all the financial products and services the bank offers, such as insurance, trusts, investments, estate planning, and mortgages. Most personal bankers only sell products offered by their banks.

Skills	Communication, computer, interpersonal, math, sales ability
Personality	Good judgment, likes working with people, tactful
Education	Suggested bachelor's degree with a major in business administration or economics
Pay range	$23,000 to $42,000 a year, depending on experience, location, and bank

Research Search the classified ads in your local newspaper for personal banker ads. What qualifications do banks look for? How much experience do they want? Are personal bankers in demand?

 For more information on personal bankers visit finance.glencoe.com **or your local library.**

- **Income risk.** You may lose your job due to unexpected health problems, family problems, an accident, or changes in your field of work.
- **Personal risk.** Driving for eight hours on icy mountain roads may not be worth the money you would save on airfare.
- **Liquidity risk.** *Liquidity* is the ability to easily convert your financial resources into cash without a loss in value. Some long-term investments, such as a house or an antique doll collection, can be difficult to convert to cash quickly.

Step 5   Create and Use Your Financial Plan of Action

A plan of action is a list of ways to achieve your financial goals. If your goal is to increase your savings, a plan of action could be to cut back on spending. If you want to increase your income, you could get a part-time job or work more hours at your present job. You could use the extra money you earn to pay off debts or to purchase stocks or make other investments.

Step 6   Review and Revise Your Plan

Financial planning doesn't end when you start to follow your plan. As you get older, your finances and needs will change. That means that your financial plan will have to change, too. You should reevaluate and revise it every year.

Developing Personal Financial Goals

Why do so many people have money problems? The main reason is that they don't plan how they'll use their money. You can avoid money problems by planning with clear financial goals in mind.

Types of Financial Goals

Two factors will influence your planning. The first is the time frame in which you would like to achieve your goals. The second is the type of financial need that inspires your goals.

COMMON Cents

Pay Yourself First

When you receive your paycheck, pay yourself first. This means before you pay bills or buy anything, put something into your savings account, even if it's only a small amount. Think of it as paying yourself. Try saving 1 percent of your take-home pay or allowance the first month, 2 percent the second month, and so forth. At the end of the year, you'll be saving 12 percent. Then sit back and watch your money grow.

STANDARD &POOR'S

CASE STUDY

$\mathcal{M}$eet Dylan Shaw. He's a typical teen who hangs out with friends, goes to movies, teases his sisters, and tries to get out of chores around the house. Dylan wants to go to college to study computer science, so he's been working part-time for a couple of years and saving his money. He has saved about $2,000 so far. Some of the savings are from gifts, but Dylan has earned most of his money. At his current job, he earns $6.75 an hour cleaning and drying cars at a car wash. He works 20 hours a week and gets about $35 in tips. During the summer he works full-time at the car wash.

Dylan puts his money in a savings account at a local bank. The money earns 2.75 percent interest a year. Dylan has been thinking about other ways to invest his money so it will earn more. He turned to the experts at Standard & Poor's for advice.

STANDARD &POOR'S **Analysis:** Many teens don't realize that a financial plan can help them, even at this early stage in their lives. Dylan has a clear goal of going to college, and he knows that he will have to help with his education expenses. Instead of waiting until the last minute and hoping to find a good part-time job that will help pay his college costs, Dylan is planning ahead. He wants to work fewer hours his first year in college so he can adjust to student life and have some fun. Saving money now will help him meet these goals.

STANDARD &POOR'S **Recommendation:** Dylan is right to be concerned with the earnings on his savings. A higher return could mean a big difference in the amount of money he has when he's ready for college. Dylan could place his current savings in a certificate of deposit. It's a low-risk investment that earns a higher interest rate than a regular savings account. He should keep at least half his money in a low-risk or risk-free investment. As Dylan saves more money, he might consider buying shares of a mutual fund or an individual stock. Over a period of years, stocks generally earn a higher return than savings accounts, although there's also a higher risk of loss if the price of the stock purchased decreases in value.

Critical Thinking Questions

1. Why do you think the advisor wants Dylan to keep at least half his money in a low-risk investment?
2. What is the relationship between risk and the potential return on a stock or mutual fund investment?
3. How do you think a savings and investment plan could help you meet your goals?

TIMING OF GOALS   Goals can be defined by the time it takes to achieve them:

- Short-term goals are those which you'll reach in one year or less (saving to buy a computer).
- Intermediate goals take two to five years to reach (saving for a down payment on a house).
- Long-term goals take more than five years to reach (planning for retirement).

It's best to start with short-term goals that may lead to long-term ones. Some goals, such as being able to pay your taxes in April or having money for the holidays, occur every year. Other goals, such as buying a car, may come up only occasionally. What are some of your short-term, intermediate, and long-term goals?

GOALS FOR DIFFERENT FINANCIAL NEEDS Having your hair cut at a salon is different from buying a new car. A haircut is a *service*, a task that a person or a machine performs for you. A new car is a *good*, a physical object that is produced and can be weighed or measured.

You may buy a soda every day. You'll probably buy a new car every five or six years. How you establish and reach your financial goals will depend on whether a goal involves consumable goods (such as a soda), durable goods (such as a car), or intangible items (such as an education):

- Consumable goods are purchases that you make often and use up quickly. Food and products such as shampoo and conditioner are in this category. Although the cost of such items may not equal that of a car, they do add up.
- Durable goods are expensive items that you don't purchase often. Most durable goods, such as cars and large appliances, will last three years or more when used on a regular basis.
- Intangible items cannot be touched and are often important to your well-being and happiness. Examples of intangibles include your personal relationships, health, education, and free time. Intangibles are often overlooked but can be expensive.

Guidelines for Setting Goals

How can you make sound financial decisions? You must know what your goals are. However, these will change as you go through life. The financial goals you set as a student will be different from

$AVVY SAVER

Financial Tips That Work

1. Save money every time you get paid.
2. Spend less than you make.
3. Work out a budget and stick to it.
4. Pay your bills and taxes on time.
5. Balance your checkbook every month.

QUESTION

Why might intangible items be expensive? For example, why might happiness be expensive?

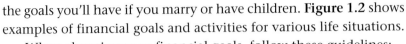

the goals you'll have if you marry or have children. **Figure 1.2** shows examples of financial goals and activities for various life situations.

When choosing your financial goals, follow these guidelines:

1. Your financial goals should be realistic.
2. Your financial goals should be specific.
3. Your financial goals should have a clear time frame.
4. Your financial goals should help you decide what type of action to take.

Influences on Personal Financial Planning

Angela just graduated from high school and will be going to college in the fall. She will move out of her parents' house and live in the college dorm. Angela is beginning a new and exciting stage in her life. She'll experience more personal freedom, but with her new independence also comes more financial responsibility. Many influences will affect Angela's day-to-day financial decisions. The three most important are life situations, personal values, and economic factors.

Life Situations and Personal Values

As you enter adulthood, you will experience many changes. You may start a new career, get married, have children, or move to a new city. Such events will affect your financial planning. Your personal values also influence your financial decisions.

Economic Factors

Economics is the study of the decisions that go into making, distributing, and using goods and services. The *economy* consists of the ways in which people make, distribute, and use their goods and services. To understand economics and the economy, you will need to be aware of market forces, financial institutions, global influences, and economic conditions. Each of these factors plays a role in day-to-day financial decision making.

MARKET FORCES   The forces of supply and demand determine the prices of goods and services. *Supply* is the amount of goods and services available for sale. *Demand* is the amount of goods and services people are willing to buy. When there is a high demand for an item such as a popular toy, or when a company cannot manufacture enough of a certain good to keep up with the demand, the price of the good rises. When there is little demand for a product, or when a company produces more than it can sell, the price of the product drops.

FINANCIAL INSTITUTIONS   Most people do business with financial institutions, which include banks, credit unions, savings and loan associations, insurance companies, and investment companies. Financial institutions provide services that increase financial activity in the economy. They handle savings and checking accounts, provide loans, sell insurance, and make investments for their clients.

Among the various government agencies that regulate financial activities, the Federal Reserve System has significant responsibility in the U.S. economy. The *Federal Reserve System*, or the Fed (as it is more commonly called), is the central banking organization of the

Figure 1.2
Financial Goals and Activities for Various Life Situations

Life Situation	Financial Goals and Activities
Young single adult	Become financially independent. Obtain career training. Develop a savings plan. Carefully manage your use of credit.
Young couple with no children	Create an effective financial record-keeping system. Implement a budget. Carefully manage your use of credit. Develop a savings and investment program.
Couple with young children	Purchase a home. Obtain adequate health and life insurance. Start a college fund. Make a will and name a guardian for your children.
Single parent with young children	Obtain adequate health, life, and disability insurance. Make a will and name a guardian for your children. Establish an emergency fund.
Middle-aged, single adult	Contribute to a tax-deferred retirement plan. Evaluate and select appropriate investments. Accumulate an adequate emergency fund. Review will and estate plans.
Older couple with no children at home	Plan retirement housing, living expenses, and activities. Obtain health insurance for retirement. Review will and estate plans.

CHANGING TIMES   As you get older, your financial needs and goals will change. *What are some goals you may have ten years from now that you don't have today?*

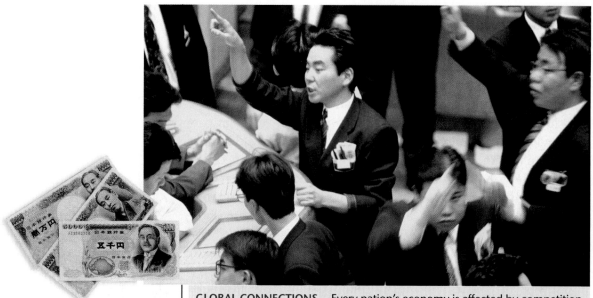

GLOBAL CONNECTIONS Every nation's economy is affected by competition with other nations. *What happens when other countries sell more goods to the United States than American companies can sell in those markets?*

United States. Its primary role in the U.S. economy is the regulation of the money supply. The Fed controls the money supply by determining interest rates and by buying or selling government securities. Its decisions affect the interest rate you earn on your savings, the interest rate you pay when you borrow money—and to some extent—the prices of the products you buy.

GLOBAL INFLUENCES Choose five items in your home or classroom. Where were they made? Some of the products were probably made in another country. You are part of a global marketplace.

The economy of every nation is affected by competition with other nations. Each country wants consumers in other countries to buy their products. When other countries sell more goods to the United States than U.S. companies can sell in those markets, more money leaves the United States than enters it. Then less money is available for spending and investing, so interest rates may rise.

ECONOMIC CONDITIONS Current economic conditions will also affect your financial decisions. **Figure 1.3** shows how economic conditions can influence financial planning. The three most important conditions are consumer prices, consumer spending, and interest rates.

Consumer Prices Over time, the price of just about everything goes up. This rise in the level of prices for goods and services is called *inflation*. During times of inflation, it takes more of your money to buy the same amount of goods and services. For example, if the rate of inflation is 5 percent, then a computer that cost $1,000 last year would now cost $1,050.

Inflation can be especially hard on certain groups, such as retired people whose income may not increase. The inflation rate affects consumer prices and varies from year to year. In the early 1960s, the annual inflation rate was between 1 and 3 percent. In the late 1970s and early 1980s, the inflation rate climbed to 10–12 percent each year. It slowed to 3 percent or less per year in the 1990s.

Consumer Spending A *consumer* is a person who purchases and uses goods or services. You are a consumer whenever you buy anything—a CD, books, clothes, lunch, or even a haircut.

Consumer spending helps create and maintain jobs. When people increase the amounts of products or services that they purchase,

Figure 1.3

Economic Conditions and Financial Planning

Economic Condition	What It Measures	How It Influences Financial Planning
Consumer prices	The value of a dollar; changes in inflation	If consumer prices increase faster than wages, the value of the dollar decreases—a dollar buys less than it did before. Consumers tend to buy fewer goods and services. Lenders charge higher interest rates.
Consumer spending	Demand for goods and services by individuals and households	Increased consumer spending usually creates more jobs and higher wages. Reduced consumer spending causes unemployment to increase.
Interest rates	Cost of money, cost of credit when you borrow, and the return on your money when you save or invest	Higher interest rates make borrowing money more expensive and make saving more attractive. When interest rates increase, consumer prices tend to increase.
Money supply	The dollars available for spending in our economy	The Federal Reserve System sometimes adjusts interest rates in order to increase or decrease the amount of money circulating in the economy. If the Fed lowers interest rates, the money supply increases. If the Fed raises interest rates, the money supply decreases.
Unemployment	The number of people without jobs who are willing and able to work	Low unemployment increases consumer spending. High unemployment reduces consumer spending.
Gross domestic product (GDP)	Total dollar value of all the goods and services produced in a country in one year	The GDP provides an indication of how well people are living in a country.

ECONOMIC CONDITIONS Economic conditions you can't control will affect your financial planning. *Choose a condition listed above, and explain how it affects your life today.*

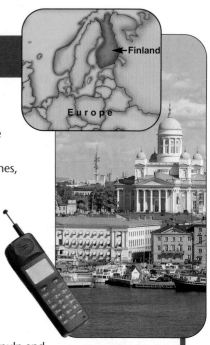

Finland

Europe

$\mathcal{D}$o you know which is the most "wired" nation in the world? The answer might surprise you if you chose the United States with its high-speed, technology-driven economy. Finland is currently the most wired nation. More than 60 percent of its residents have cell phones, and at least 35 percent are connected to the Internet. Most teenagers in Finland have their own cell phones, and the world's leading cellular phone-maker, Nokia, is based there. Here's a snapshot of Finland.

Geographic area	130,558 sq. mi.
Population	5,170,000
Capital	Helsinki (pop. 532,100)
Language	Finnish, Swedish
Currency	markka
Gross domestic product (GDP)	$102.1 billion
Per capita GDP	$20,000
Economy	Industry: metal products, shipbuilding, pulp and paper. Agriculture: cereals, sugar beets, potatoes, cattle, fish. Exports: paper and pulp, machinery, chemicals, metals, timber.

View of Helsinki, capital of Finland

Thinking Critically

Conversion Check in your local newspaper or on the Internet for the current exchange rate between the Finnish markka and the U.S. dollar. If you bought a cell phone for $100, how much would it cost in Finnish markkas?

For more information on Finland visit finance.glencoe.com or your local library.

companies have to hire extra employees to meet the demand. This situation leads to a higher rate of employment, making jobs easier for people to find. More people work, and in turn, they have more money to spend. However, when consumers buy fewer goods and services, companies have to produce less and lay off workers. Then unemployment rises, making jobs harder to find.

Interest Rates Like everything else, money has a price, and this price is called interest. *Interest* is the price that is paid for the use of another's money. When you deposit your paycheck in a savings account, for example, the interest you receive is money the bank or other financial institution pays you for the use of your money. The bank, in turn, uses your money to make loans to people who want to purchase items such as houses and new businesses. Borrowers who receive the loans must pay a fee, also called interest, for the use of the money.

Interest rates demonstrate the cost of money. When consumers increase their savings and investments, the supply of money that is available for others to borrow grows, and interest rates go down. When consumers borrow more money, the demand for money increases, and interest rates rise.

Interest rates on loans also rise during times of inflation. Interest rates will affect your financial planning. The earnings you receive from your savings account, or the interest you pay on a loan, depend on the current interest rates.

SECTION 1.1 ASSESSMENT

CHECK YOUR UNDERSTANDING

1. Name the six steps used to create a financial plan.
2. What is the relationship between the timing of your goals and the type of good or service that you seek?
3. Describe two economic factors that affect financial decisions. How might these factors influence your financial planning?

THINK CRITICALLY

4. Why is it important to distinguish between your needs and your wants?

USING COMMUNICATION SKILLS

5. **Left to Chance?** You're talking to a friend who says that she never sets any financial goals and that her financial success or failure happens by luck.
   Role-Play With a partner, role-play a response to your friend's philosophy. Explain how planning, more than luck, determines financial success or failure.

SOLVING MONEY PROBLEMS

6. **Financial Planning Process** Rosa and her best friend, Linda, live in Chicago and want to drive cross-country next year. Both work part-time and earn $97 a week after taxes. They'll need to save at least $500 each to pay for the trip. They plan to visit Rosa's aunt, who lives in Denver, and Linda's brother in Los Angeles.
   Analyze Help Rosa and Linda apply the six steps of the financial planning process to reach their goal.

What You'll Learn

- How to **determine** the opportunity costs associated with each of your financial decisions
- How to **identify** strategies for achieving your financial goals for the different stages of your life

Why It's Important

By recognizing the trade-offs of financial decisions and learning to use your money wisely now, you'll be able to satisfy your values and meet your financial needs and goals throughout your life.

KEY TERMS

- time value of money
- principal
- future value
- annuity
- present value

Opportunity Costs and Financial Strategies

Opportunity Costs and the Time Value of Money

Whenever you make a choice, you have to give up some of your other options. When making your financial decisions, consider both the personal and financial opportunity costs carefully.

Personal Opportunity Costs

Like financial resources, your personal resources—your health, knowledge, skills, and time—require management. Do you eat a lot of junk food and avoid exercise? Do you get enough sleep each night? The decisions you make about your health can have serious consequences as you age. In much the

TIMING YOUR FUN   Managing your time is as important as managing your money. *How can you use your time more efficiently when studying so you'll also have time to do things you enjoy?*

same way, the financial decisions you make today will affect your financial health in the future.

Suppose that you and your friends have tickets to a sold-out concert this Thursday night. On Thursday afternoon your algebra teacher announces that she's giving you an important test on Friday. You're going to have to decide whether you'll go to the concert, study for the test, or somehow do both. You'll have to decide how to use your time to meet your needs, achieve your goals, and satisfy your values.

Financial Opportunity Costs

You make choices about money almost all the time. Will you buy the $100 pair of sneakers you saw at the mall or save that money? You can't do both. Consider the *time value of money*, which is the increase of an amount of money as a result of interest or dividends earned. If you decide to save or invest the $100 instead of buying the sneakers, that money will be worth more later on because you'll earn interest or dividends on it. On the other hand, perhaps your sneakers are worn out. In that case, your needs right now make the trade-off of interest earnings necessary and worthwhile.

Every time you spend, save, or invest money, try to think about the time value of that money as an opportunity cost. For example, starting early in life to save money for retirement means that you'll probably be able to live comfortably in the future.

Calculating Interest

You can calculate the time value of your savings by figuring out how much interest you'll earn. To do this, you'll need to know the principal, the annual interest rate, and the length of time your money will be in the account.

In the case of a savings account, the *principal* is the amount of money you deposit and on which interest is paid. (In the case of a loan, the principal is the amount that you borrow.) When you open a savings account, the bank or financial institution will inform you of the interest rate on your account. This is usually given as an annual percentage so that you know how much you'll earn on a yearly basis. By comparing interest rates at several financial institutions, you'll be able to figure out which one will make your money grow the fastest.

You can figure out how much interest your money will earn in the first year by multiplying the principal by the annual interest rate (see the Go Figure box on the following page).

RESPOND

Do you ever find yourself tempted to spend money on items that you don't really need, such as electronic gadgets or trendy clothes? Imagine that you decided not to buy such things. What would you do with the money you saved as a result of your decision?

ANNUAL INTEREST

Example: You deposited $1,000 in a savings account. The bank is paying you 5% annual interest. How much interest will you earn if you keep your money in the bank for one year?

Formula: Principal × Annual Interest Rate = Interest Earned for One Year

Solution: $1,000 × 5% = $50
You will earn $50 in interest.

FUTURE VALUE OF A SINGLE DEPOSIT *Future value* is the amount your original deposit will be worth in the future based on earning a specific interest rate over a specific period of time. You can figure out how much your savings will grow by multiplying the principal by the annual interest rate and then adding that interest amount to the principal.

You can determine the future value for two years, three years, and so on. Each year, interest is earned on the original amount of your principal and on any previously earned interest.

To calculate the interest earned for the second year, you would add any interest earned in the first year to the principal. Then you would take that amount and multiply it by the annual interest rate.

THE FUTURE VALUE OF A SINGLE DEPOSIT

Example: You deposited $1,000 in a savings account that pays you 5% annual interest. You earned $50 in interest after the first year. How much interest would you earn if you kept your money in the bank for two years?

Formula: (Principal + Previously Earned Interest) × Annual Interest Rate = Interest Earned for the Second Year

Solution: ($1,000 + $50) × 5% = $52.50
You will earn $52.50 in interest. You would add this earned interest to your previous amount ($1,050 + $52.50 = $1,102.50). The future value of your original $1,000 deposit would be $1,102.50 after two years.

Future value computations are also called compounding. With compounding, your money increases faster because you are paid interest on your original deposit and on previously earned interest.

Future value tables simplify the process of figuring out the effect of compounding. The table in part A of **Figure 1.4** shows the future

Figure 1.4

Future and Present Value Tables

A. Future Value of a Single Deposit

	Annual Interest Rate				
Year	5%	6%	7%	8%	9%
5	1.276	1.338	1.403	1.469	1.539
6	1.340	1.419	1.501	1.587	1.677
7	1.407	1.504	1.606	1.714	1.828
8	1.477	1.594	1.718	1.851	1.993
9	1.551	1.689	1.838	1.999	2.172
10	1.629	1.791	1.967	2.159	2.367

B. Future Value of a Series of Equal Annual Deposits

Year	5%	6%	7%	8%	9%
5	5.526	5.637	5.751	5.867	5.985
6	6.802	6.975	7.153	7.336	7.523
7	8.142	8.394	8.654	8.923	9.200
8	9.549	9.897	10.260	10.637	11.028
9	11.027	11.491	11.978	12.488	13.021
10	12.578	13.181	13.816	14.487	15.193

C. Present Value of a Single Deposit

Year	5%	6%	7%	8%	9%
5	0.784	0.747	0.713	0.681	0.650
6	0.746	0.705	0.666	0.630	0.596
7	0.711	0.665	0.623	0.583	0.547
8	0.677	0.627	0.582	0.540	0.502
9	0.645	0.592	0.544	0.500	0.460
10	0.614	0.558	0.508	0.463	0.422

D. Present Value of a Series of Equal Annual Deposits

Year	5%	6%	7%	8%	9%
5	4.329	4.212	4.100	3.993	3.890
6	5.076	4.917	4.767	4.623	4.486
7	5.786	5.582	5.389	5.206	5.033
8	6.463	6.210	5.971	5.747	5.535
9	7.108	6.802	6.515	6.247	5.995
10	7.722	7.360	7.024	6.710	6.418

TIME IS MONEY

Future value tables can save you time and reduce errors when computing interest over a long period of time. Present value tables can help you figure out how much you need to deposit now in order to have a certain amount of money in the future. *How much money would you have if you save $2,000 a year for 10 years at 9% interest?*

QUESTION

Why would you want to know the future value of a deposit when making financial plans?

value of a single deposit of $1. To use the table, find the annual interest rate that your money is earning. Then see what the future value is at Year 5, Year 6, and so on. Multiply the future value figure by the amount of your deposit. For example, if you deposit $1 in a 7 percent account, at the end of Year 7, you would have $1.61 ($1 × 1.606 = $1.606).

The sooner you begin to make deposits, the more time you'll give your money to compound, and the more it will increase. Depositing $1,000 in a 5 percent account at age 40 will give you $3,387 when you reach age 65. However, if you make the same $1,000 deposit in a 5 percent account at age 25, you'll have a total of $7,040 when you reach 65.

FUTURE VALUE OF A SERIES OF DEPOSITS Some savers and investors like to make regular deposits into their savings. A series of equal regular deposits is called an *annuity*. Using part B of **Figure 1.4**, which shows the future value of a series of equal yearly deposits, can you find what the future value would be if you deposited $1,000 a year at 5 percent annual interest for six years? At the end of the six years, you will have $6,802 ($1,000 × 6.802 = $6,802).

PRESENT VALUE OF A SINGLE DEPOSIT You can also calculate the *present value*, which is the amount of money you would need to deposit now in order to attain a desired amount in the future. For example, if you want to have $1,000 in five years for a down payment on a car, and your savings account pays 5 percent annual interest, how much money will you need to deposit now in order to earn enough interest to accumulate $1,000? Part C of **Figure 1.4** will help you find the answer. Find Year 5 in the left column, and look across to the 5 percent interest rate column. The value given is 0.784. Multiply this value by the amount of money you want to have in five years ($1,000 × 0.784 = $784). You'll need to deposit $784 now in order to have $1,000 in five years.

PRESENT VALUE OF A SERIES OF DEPOSITS You can also use present value calculations to determine how much you need to deposit so you can take a specific amount of money out of your savings account for a certain number of years. If you want to take $400 out of your account each year for nine years, and your money is earning interest at 8 percent a year, how much money will you need to deposit now? Part D of **Figure 1.4** will help you find the answer. Find Year 9 in the left column and look across to the 8 percent interest rate column. The value given is 6.247. Multiply this value by the amount of money that you want to take out every year ($400 × 6.247 = $2,498.80). You'll need to deposit $2,498.80 now to be able to take out $400 each year for nine years. This type of calculation is often used to estimate how much money you'll need for retirement.

Achieving Your Financial Goals

Throughout your life you'll have many different financial needs and goals. By learning to use your money wisely now, you'll be able to achieve many of those goals. This book is designed to give you a framework to help you learn how to make financial decisions. Financial planning involves first choosing a career and then learning how to protect and manage the money you earn. By using the following eight strategies, you can avoid many common money mistakes:

1. **OBTAIN** You obtain financial resources by working, making investments, or owning property. Obtaining money is the foundation of financial planning because you'll use that money for all other financial activities.

2. **PLAN** The key to achieving your financial goals and financial security is to plan how you'll spend your money.

3. **SPEND** Many people buy more than they can afford. Others buy too many things they can afford but don't need. Spending less than you earn is the *only* way to achieve financial security.

4. **SAVE** Long-term financial security starts with a savings plan. If you save on a regular basis, you'll have money to pay your bills, make major purchases, and cope with emergencies.

5. **BORROW** When you use a credit card or take out another type of loan, you are borrowing money. Borrowing wisely—and only when necessary—will help you achieve your financial goals and avoid money problems.

6. **INVEST** People invest for two main reasons: to increase their current income and for long-term growth. To increase current income, you can choose investments that pay regular dividends or interest. For long-term growth, you'll choose stocks, mutual funds, real estate, and other investments that have the potential to increase in value in the future.

7. **MANAGE RISK** To protect your resources in case you are ever seriously injured, get sick, or die, you'll need insurance coverage. Insurance will protect you and those who depend on you.

8. **RETIRE** When you start to plan for retirement, it's important to consider the age at which you would like to stop working full-time. You should also think about where you'll want to live and how you'll want to spend your time: at a part-time job, doing volunteer work, or enjoying hobbies or sports.

RISKY BUSINESS Accidents happen when you least expect them. *What are some ways to manage the risks associated with sports?*

Getting Your Own Wheels

Are you dreaming of buying your own car? Olivia Johnson is. So far she's saved $3,000. Olivia has her eye on a used car that costs $9,000. Olivia figures she can afford a monthly car payment of no more than $200. Using the interest-rate table below, Olivia calculates the monthly payment needed to repay her car loan by multiplying the amount of the loan by the interest factor. She wants to pay off her loan in three years.

Olivia's Loan Story

Cost of car	$9,000.00
Less the down payment	−3,000.00
Amount of loan	$6,000.00
Multiply loan amount by interest factor (0.03133) for 36 months	
$6,000 × 0.03133 =	**$187.98**

Interest Rate of 8%

Months	Interest Factor
12 (one year)	0.08698
24 (two years)	0.04522
36 (three years)	**0.03133**
48 (four years)	0.02441

Olivia will pay $187.98 a month if she decides to borrow $6,000 for three years.

Calculate Now decide what your dream car is. Look in your local newspaper for a car you would like to buy. How much will it cost? Suppose you can afford 25 percent of the total price for a down payment. How much money will you need to borrow to pay the complete cost of the car you want? In your workbook or on a separate sheet of paper, calculate how much money you'll need for your monthly car payment. Calculate what your monthly payment will be if you paid off your loan in 1, 2, 3, or 4 years. (1) What is the total amount you will pay for your car if you pay it off in 1, 2, 3, or 4 years? (2) How much interest will you pay on your loan? (3) Which payment plan would enable you to pay the least amount of money for your car? (4) Which payment plan would have the lowest payments?

Developing and Using Your Financial Plan

A good personal financial plan includes assessing your present financial situation, making a list of your current needs, and deciding how to plan for future needs. You can design a plan on your own, hire a financial planner, or use a good money-management software program. Making your financial plan work takes time, effort, and patience, but you'll develop habits that will give you a lifetime of satisfaction and security.

SECTION 1.2 ASSESSMENT

CHECK YOUR UNDERSTANDING

1. What are the opportunity costs associated with financial decisions?
2. Name the eight strategies you can apply to achieve your financial goals.
3. How can investing your money help you achieve your financial goals?

THINK CRITICALLY

4. Using the concept of the time value of money, write an argument in favor of shopping for a good interest rate.

USING MATH SKILLS

5. **Saving Strategies** Tanya wants to open her own pet-grooming business after she graduates from high school. However, after doing research, she realizes that she needs to save $18,000 for the start-up capital for her business. Tanya plans to make a series of deposits of $3,000 every year for five years. She estimates that she'll earn an annual interest rate of 5 percent on her savings.
   Calculate Using the tables in **Figure 1.4**, calculate what amount Tanya will have available in five years to start her business. How much more money will she need to save?

SOLVING MONEY PROBLEMS

6. **Saving Versus Spending** Omar received $545 in gifts when he graduated from high school. His parents want him to save the money for college, but Omar wants to buy new clothes, a watch, some CDs, and a video game. He also needs new tires because the ones on his car are badly worn. Omar asks you for advice. How should he spend his graduation money?
   Debate Working in a small group, help Omar decide what to do with his money. Consider the various financial opportunity costs and the time value of money.

CHAPTER 1 ASSESSMENT

CHAPTER SUMMARY

- Personal financial planning means managing your money (spending, saving, and investing) so that you can achieve financial independence and security.

- The six steps of financial planning are: (1) Determine your current financial situation; (2) Develop your financial goals; (3) Identify alternative courses of action; (4) Evaluate your alternatives; (5) Create and use your financial plan of action; (6) Review and revise your plan.

- Your financial goals should be realistic, specific, set within a clear time frame, and help you decide what type of action to take.

- The most important influences on personal financial planning are your life situations, your personal values, and outside economic factors.

- For all your financial decisions, you must make choices and give up something. These trade-offs, or opportunity costs, can be personal or financial.

- The eight strategies for achieving your financial goals and avoiding money problems are: obtain, plan, spend, save, borrow, invest, manage risk, and retire.

Understanding and Using Vocabulary

Using 8–12 of the key terms below, write an imaginary conversation between you and a younger person. Explain to this person why it's important to have a financial plan.

personal financial planning	economy
goals	supply
values	demand
opportunity cost	Federal Reserve System
liquidity	inflation
service	consumer
good	interest
economics	time value of money
	principal

future value   present value
annuity

Review Key Concepts

1. What questions should you ask yourself before you develop your financial goals?
2. Explain the differences between short-term, intermediate, and long-term goals.
3. Name four guidelines for setting financial goals.
4. What economic factors and conditions might influence a person's financial planning?
5. Describe the differences between future value and present value of a single deposit.

CHAPTER 1 ASSESSMENT

Apply Key Concepts

1. List five of your personal values. How might they affect your financial goals?
2. List three short-term, three intermediate, and three long-term goals you have. How can your short-term and intermediate goals assist you in achieving your long-term goals?
3. Following the recommended guidelines for setting goals, choose two financial goals for yourself.
4. Name an item you bought on sale recently. Why do you think the price was reduced? Think of an item for which you paid more money than you had in the past. Why do you think the price increased?
5. Using **Figure 1.4**, calculate the future value of $1,000 deposited in a 6 percent account for seven years.

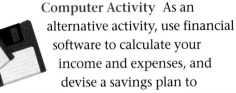 **Computer Activity** As an alternative activity, use financial software to calculate your income and expenses, and devise a savings plan to achieve your goal.

Real-World Application

CONNECT WITH ECONOMICS

Leon and Alice both enjoy well-paying jobs, and they spend almost everything they earn. Last year they adopted their son, Casey. Now they want to buy a house. Neither of them has ever saved for such a large expense, so they don't know how to begin.

Think Critically Leon and Alice come to you for financial advice. What do you say to them?

? Problem Solving Today

COMPUTERS AND COSTS

You've decided to buy a computer to help you with your studies. To get the one you want, you'll need to save $1,350 in the next year. You work part-time and make $119.50 a week after taxes. Each week you put $50 into your college tuition fund. You spend the rest of the money on school supplies, clothes, CDs, movies, and eating out with friends.

Analyze 1) How much money will you need to save each week for a computer? 2) If you decide to skip a week, how will that affect your savings plan? 3) What trade-offs might you need to make in order to buy your computer?

FINANCE Online

INFLATION RELATION

You want to determine how much inflation has affected the value of a dollar.

Connect Using various Internet search engines, look for the inflation rate for the year you were born. Then find the following information:

1. How much would $100 in today's money have been worth in that year?
2. If you work after school or on weekends, how much would your present hourly wage have been worth? (If you are not working, use $6 per hour.)
3. How much would the same wage have been worth 25, 50, and 100 years ago?

Financial Aspects of Career Planning

STANDARD
&POOR'S

Q&A

Q: I just want a job where I can make lots of money. Why should I bother with a career action plan?

A: Money, and lots of it, may be your motivation for work, but you need to consider many other factors as well. Since you will probably spend the majority of your life working, the old adage, "Choose a career you love and the money will follow," might be something to think about. Your personal values, goals, and interests are the basis for any career decision.

Decisions in Planning Your Career

Isabel Barbado is a math whiz. Despite a heavy course load, she finds time to carry out the record-keeping duties for her school's student council and junior class. Because she has a natural ability with numbers, she's considering a career in accounting. She knows that she'll need to study hard to earn her college degree. Nevertheless, Isabel believes that being an accountant would be a rewarding and satisfying career for her. She might even be able to get a job with one of her favorite nonprofit organizations. Isabel plays an active part in her community's efforts to save the wetlands in her state.

Bill Chan is fascinated with sports, especially soccer and baseball. He spends his free time playing on school and community teams, and he never misses a game on television. Bill is considering a sports-related career. He's been investigating possibilities such as becoming a fitness trainer, a physical education teacher, or a sportscaster.

Although Isabel and Bill have different ideas about their career goals, they have something in common. They will need to make informed decisions about their careers to achieve personal satisfaction and financial security.

Choosing a Career

Some people find true satisfaction in their work, whereas others work just to make money. Like many people, you may decide to get a *job*—work that you do mainly to earn money. On the other hand, you may decide to prepare for a career. A *career* is a commitment to work in a field that you find interesting and fulfilling. It's likely to be a lifelong challenge that will call for continued training and provide you with opportunities for growth. Choosing the right career is an important financial decision that you'll need to make. It will affect your personal life, too. Ensuring that your career will fulfill your personal and financial goals requires planning.

Trade-offs of Career Decisions

Many factors influence the way you live and your financial condition. Your choice of career will affect the amount of money you make, the people you meet, and how much spare time you have. Some people don't develop a strong connection between the type of work they do and who they are. They work to maintain a *standard of living*, a measure of quality of life based on the amounts and

What's Your Financial ID?

FIND YOUR PERSONALITY TRAITS

Learning more about your own personality will help you choose a career. Read the characteristics below that describe people's personalities. On a separate piece of paper write down the five traits that best describe you, then answer the question that follows.

Personality Traits

outgoing	ambitious	patient
studious	kind	thoughtful
neat	strong	intelligent
quiet	trustworthy	respectful
playful	warm	happy
energetic	persistent	spontaneous
serious	organized	worried
easygoing	rebellious	sensitive
caring	stubborn	sociable
loyal	responsible	creative
confident	fair	talkative
cheerful	calm	inquisitive
dependable	brave	funny
generous	helpful	athletic
shy	imaginative	competitive

Keeping in mind the five traits that best describe your personality, what kind of work do you think would suit you? For example, if you're persistent, outgoing, and assertive, you might work in sales. If you're inquisitive and creative, you might enjoy a career in writing. List the jobs or careers that you think fit best with your personality.

kinds of goods and services a person can buy. They also work to pay for the hobbies and activities they enjoy. Others pursue careers that provide them with both money and personal fulfillment. They select careers that reflect their interests, values, and goals.

As with any other decision you make, choosing a career will involve trade-offs, or opportunity costs. Traditionally, people devote most of their time and energy to their work. Sometimes their family lives and personal satisfaction suffer as a result. Recent *trends*—developments that mark changes in a particular area—indicate that some people are making career decisions that allow them to spend more time with their families or to enjoy their hobbies and interests. Perhaps you will marry and have children someday. When these and other important changes occur, you will have to make trade-offs between your personal and social life and your work life.

You may prefer a career that is challenging and offers you the chance to grow, even if it doesn't earn you a large salary. On the other hand, you may choose to work in a job that's less satisfying but offers more money. If you work for a large company, you might turn down a transfer or a promotion (and the extra money that comes with it) because it would mean moving to a new place or having less free time. You may look for part-time work or work situations with flexible hours so that you'll have more time to spend with your family. You could also decide to give up the security of working for someone else to take on the challenge of running your own business.

The more you know about your own interests, values, needs, and goals, the better you'll be able to choose a career that will provide a balance between personal satisfaction and financial rewards.

WEIGHING YOUR OPTIONS Choosing a career involves trade-offs. Some parents will decline a job with a higher salary for a job that offers a flexible schedule. *What other trade-offs might a parent have to make?*

Career Training and Skill Development

Obtaining as much education as possible will help you meet your financial goals. The more you know, the greater your chances for success. Having a college degree doesn't mean you'll definitely reach your goals and make a lot of money. However, more education increases your *potential earning power*, the amount of money you may earn over time. In addition to your level of education, your field of study will affect your salary. Some careers, such as law and medicine, generally offer higher salaries than others, such as education and the fine arts. In any case, it's your choice.

Imagine yourself 10 or 15 years from now. What would be the ideal job or career for you? How would that job or career fulfill your personal goals?

Education isn't the only ingredient for success in your job or career. You'll need to adapt to each individual work situation. By developing certain habits, you will become an asset to any employer. For example, most successful people are able to work well with others. They always strive to do their best. They don't allow conflict with other employees or changes in their duties to affect the quality of their work. They're creative when it comes to solving problems. They read a variety of materials and know how to express themselves well. They understand themselves and other people. These basic qualities and skills make success more likely in most job situations. How do you measure up to this checklist for success? If you think that you might fall short in some areas, what might you do to improve?

Personal Factors

You can take special tests to learn more about your own abilities, interests, and personal qualities. These tests—called aptitude tests

---

INTERNATIONAL FINANCE | Belize

*S*and and surf mean fun and relaxation, especially in Belize, where the crystal-clear Caribbean Sea laps the country's eastern border. The major tourist magnet along the coast is the spectacular barrier reef, the longest in the Western Hemisphere. Stretching 175 miles, the reef provides a spectacular environment for sea life and humans alike. Each year growing numbers of tourists dive into its deep caves, snorkel above flowerlike sea anemones, swim with brightly colored fish, or watch watermen net lobsters. Here's a snapshot of Belize.

Belize's barrier reef

Geographic area	8,867 sq. mi.
Population	248,000
Capital	Belmopan (pop. 6,800)
Language	English, Spanish, Mayan, Carib
Currency	dollar
Gross domestic product (GDP)	$649 million
Per capita GDP	$2,960
Economy	Industry: garment production, food processing, tourism, and construction. Agriculture: bananas, coca, citrus, lumber, fish, cultured shrimp. Exports: sugar, citrus fruits, bananas.

Thinking Critically

Analyze List some of the ways you think the barrier reef contributes to Belize's economy.

 For more information on Belize visit finance.glencoe.com or your local library.

and interest inventories—may give you an edge in choosing a career. You can usually find out more about such tests in your school's guidance office. Public libraries, bookstores, and the Internet also offer materials of this kind if you would rather test yourself.

WHAT DO YOU DO BEST? *Aptitudes* are the natural abilities that people possess. No two people are alike, but everyone has one or more special talents. For example, you may have a beautiful singing voice, excel at working with numbers, or be able to solve puzzles easily. These are all natural aptitudes. Try taking an aptitude test to find out what you do best.

WHAT DO YOU ENJOY? *Interest inventories* are tests that help you identify the activities you enjoy the most. Then they match your interests, likes, and dislikes with various kinds of work. Someone who enjoys nature and the outdoors could become a science teacher, wildlife biologist, nature photographer, or landscape designer. A person who likes to make things could become a carpenter, clothes designer, architect, or engineer. Try listing some of your interests. What types of careers can you think of that would match your interests?

DOES YOUR DREAM JOB EXIST? Taking aptitude tests and interest inventories probably won't lead you to the ideal career. They can only point you in the right direction. Another important issue to consider when thinking about your career goals is your personality. For example, do you enjoy large parties, or would you rather stay at home and read a book? Do you like to take chances or prefer to play it safe? Do you work well under pressure, or do you need a lot of time to do a job well?

The goal is to find a job or career that gives you the right balance between financial rewards and personal satisfaction. Some people adapt easily to any work environment. Others are always on the lookout for something better. One thing is certain: Your work situation will never stop changing. The key is to remain flexible.

NATURE LOVER If you enjoy being outdoors, observing the habits of wildlife, or looking at the stars, you might choose a career in zoology or astronomy. *Name at least two of your interests that might be related to a career.*

Making Career Decisions

Before you make any decision about your career, you should first review your situation. Changes in your personal life and in society will affect your work life, and the reverse is also true. **Figure 2.1** on page 36 shows the stages of career planning, changes, and advancement. If you are getting ready to enter the workforce, you will probably start at stage 1. That stage will involve determining your personal and career interests.

Figure 2.1

Stages of Career Planning, Changes, and Advancement

2 Identify job opportunities in chosen field.

1 Assess personal goals, abilities, and interests. Research careers.

3 Develop a résumé and cover letter. Apply for jobs.

4 Interview for available positions. Improve interviewing skills.

5 Consider job offers. Accept the job that meets financial and personal requirements.

6 Plan and implement a program for career development.

Career Entry

Change to a Different Career

Change Job Within Same Career

Career Advancement

STARTING OVER If you have chosen a career and are dissatisfied with the work that you are doing, you have the option of changing to a different career. *What are some ways to make a wise choice?*

This diagram is only a framework. The way you use it will depend on your opportunity costs, the choices that are available to you, and your career area. If you're unsure about the direction you should take, talk to people in your field of interest. Ask them what they like and don't like about their work. How did they get into this field? They can help you with your career planning. **Figure 2.2** on page 38 shows how to develop a career plan of action.

Career Opportunities: Now and in the Future

Before you begin your job search, you should think about how the following factors might affect you.

Social Influences

Demographic trends are ways in which groups of people change over time. These developments can affect your employment opportunities. Some recent demographic trends that have affected the job market include:

- More working parents. This trend expands the supply of jobs in child care and food services.
- More leisure time. This change boosts interest in health, physical fitness, and recreational products.
- More elderly people in the overall population. This development produces a greater need for workers in retirement facilities, health care, and travel services.
- Greater demand for ongoing employment training. This trend increases career opportunities for teachers and trainers within business organizations.

What other employment opportunities might be influenced by these trends?

Geographic trends are changes that happen when people move from one area of the country to another and as financial centers shift location. In recent years, some of the fastest-growing job markets have included cities in Arizona, Colorado, Florida, Georgia, Nevada, North Carolina, and Texas.

Geographic location also influences earning level. Remember to consider differences in earning levels as you decide where to look for employment. Big cities, such as San Francisco, New York, and Chicago, usually offer higher salaries, but the cost of living—the cost

academic Connection

HEALTH

Experts predict that there will be 3.1 million new jobs in the health care industry over the next few years. Interestingly, many of these jobs will be in the field of finance. With a partner, list as many financial services careers as you can think of that might be found in the health field. If possible, contact hospitals, nursing homes, doctors' offices, and managed care facilities. Choose one career from your list and find out more about it.

1 *Personal and Career Interests: Make a list of things you enjoy doing. Think about how you could turn an activity that you like into a career.*

2 *Career Skills: Think about work experiences you've already had. Which ones did you like? Which ones didn't go so well? What skills did you learn?*

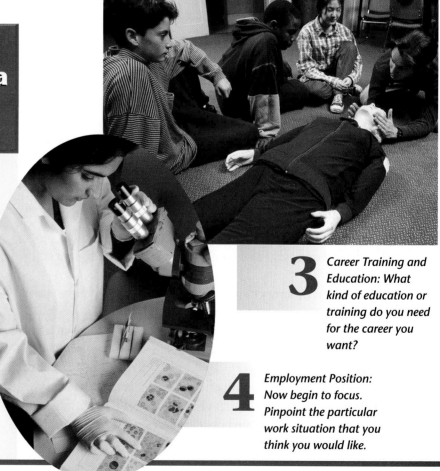

FIGURE 2.2

Developing a Career Plan of Action

If you want your career to start off on the right foot, you need a plan of action. You need to know where you are, where you want to go, when you want to arrive, and how you're going to get there.

3 *Career Training and Education: What kind of education or training do you need for the career you want?*

4 *Employment Position: Now begin to focus. Pinpoint the particular work situation that you think you would like.*

of food, housing, transportation, and other expenses—is also higher in such areas.

If you accept a high-paying position in a big city, you may actually have a lower standard of living than you would in an area where income levels and the cost of living are lower.

PREDICT

List some possible trends that will influence your future job or career prospects.

Economic Factors

High interest rates, price increases, or decreased demand for certain goods and services can reduce career opportunities. You can't control the effects of economic factors on employment trends. You can, however, understand that these factors affect some businesses more than others. For example, high interest rates reduce employment in housing-related industries, such as construction and real estate, because people are less likely to buy houses when interest rates are high.

Trends in Industry and Technology

Changes in industry and technology also affect the job market. In recent years, the need for manufacturing workers has decreased as a result of several notable trends. First, increased competition from other countries has reduced demand for American-made products. Second, automation has taken over many tasks that used to be done by factory workers.

Perhaps you have chosen a career in the fast-paced field of electronics technology. You know that your skills are valuable, but you also know that constant technological advances can quickly outdate products and jobs. As a result, you must accept some financial uncertainty.

While opportunities have dwindled in some areas of the economy, opportunities in other areas have grown. *Service industries*, those that provide services for a fee, will offer some of the greatest employment potential in coming years. Careers in these industries include the following:

Career Center

Does your school have a career center? You'll find a variety of free information there that can help you with college choices, job opportunities, and career counseling. Drop by there soon.

- Computer or telecommunications technology—systems analysts, Web site developers, repair personnel, service technicians
- Health care—medical assistants, physical therapists, home health workers
- Business services—employee benefit managers, trainers
- Social services—child-care workers, elder-care coordinators
- Hospitality services—travel agents, food service managers
- Management—employment service workers, recruiters
- Education—teachers for elementary, secondary, and postsecondary schools, teachers in adult education

STANDARD &POOR'S

CASE STUDY

*T*rina Brown is a junior majoring in finance at an out-of-state college. She studies hard and has maintained a 3.4 grade point average. Trina is president-elect of her sorority and serves as chairman of the school-wide community service committee. She feels that these experiences will provide an opportunity to polish her leadership and organizational skills as she prepares for the business world. In addition, Trina works part-time in the financial aid department to help pay for her tuition. Trina will have to make some career planning decisions as early as this spring. Right now she thinks becoming a stockbroker could be the right career and maybe a summer internship in this field might help her make up her mind. However, paid internships are hard to find in her community. Trina usually works full-time during the summer in order to pay for school. She has turned to the experts at Standard & Poor's for advice.

STANDARD &POOR'S **Analysis:** Many college students don't understand that career planning should start even before they begin college. Trina has been working hard maintaining her grades, developing leadership skills, and volunteering in the community. These are excellent first steps, but Trina needs to plan her career path and develop some short- and long-term career goals. Trina should sample a variety of careers in the financial services industry through job shadowing, internships, or even tours of various companies.

STANDARD &POOR'S **Recommendation:** Career planning should be a very important part of Trina's college life. Although Trina seems happy with her chosen major, she should take a aptitude test as well as an interest inventory. Based on the results, Trina can develop her short- and long-term career goals. She must consider her personal values and needs when setting these goals. A summer internship in the financial services field would also help Trina. Although she might not be paid for the internship, the experience would be invaluable. Through the internship, Trina might be able to find a mentor and even secure a position upon graduation. If Trina needs to earn extra money, a part-time job during the evenings would help with the expenses.

Critical Thinking Questions

1. Why is it important for Trina to set long-term goals even though she hasn't even begun her career?
2. How can a mentor help Trina in her career development?
3. What are some ways Trina can assess the future potential of the careers she might choose?

- Financial services—insurance agents, investment brokers

Whatever career area you choose, knowledge of a variety of computer programs and the Internet will be essential. In our global economy, knowing more than one language will also put you ahead of the game.

SECTION 2.1 ASSESSMENT

CHECK YOUR UNDERSTANDING

1. List at least three characteristics of successful people. Describe how each characteristic might be an asset at school or work.
2. How can you learn more about your own abilities, interests, and personal qualities as they relate to career planning?
3. Discuss three factors that influence employment opportunities.

THINK CRITICALLY

4. Why do you think that the increase in the number of working parents has contributed to a higher demand for food services? Why do you think that an increase in leisure time boosts interest in personal health?

USING COMMUNICATION SKILLS

5. **New Career Choices** Service industries will offer some of the greatest potential for jobs in the coming years.
   Conduct a Survey Are your classmates planning to explore the types of careers mentioned in the section "Trends in Industry and Technology"? With a partner, conduct a survey of five students, and identify the most popular career choices among them.

SOLVING MONEY PROBLEMS

6. **Social Influences** Tyrell has worked his way up from sales associate to department supervisor for a large suburban discount store. Now he has the offer of a higher position at the company's headquarters in Atlanta. Currently, Tyrell earns about $18,000 annually, which covers the cost of food, housing, transportation, and other living expenses. If he accepts the new job, his salary will increase 20 percent, but the cost of living in Atlanta is much higher than it is in the suburbs. By doing some research, he has found out that the rent for a one-bedroom apartment averages $800 per month and that the round-trip train ride to work will cost about $4 per day. Food will probably cost $65 per week.
   Analyze Assuming Tyrell works five days a week and 52 weeks a year, help him calculate what these expenses would total annually if he moved to Atlanta.

What You'll Learn

- How to **apply** effective strategies to obtain employment
- How to **identify** the financial and legal issues to consider when looking for employment
- How to **analyze** methods that will help you grow and develop in your career

Why It's Important

Effective strategies will help you get the job or career that meets your personal and financial goals. Managing your career over time will help you deal with the changes that will occur in your life.

KEY TERMS

- **internship**
- **cooperative education**
- **networking**
- **informational interview**
- **résumé**
- **cover letter**
- **cafeteria-style employee benefits**
- **pension plan**
- **mentor**

Obtaining Employment and Developing a Career

Employment Search Strategies

Meg filled out dozens of job applications but never received a call for an interview. Douglas went to many interviews and found a challenging and satisfying job. What are the differences between these two people? The answer has to do with how well they communicated the value of the experience they already had and how effectively they used proven employment strategies.

Obtaining Employment Experience

Many young people who are entering the world of work worry that they don't have enough experience. Are you, too, overlooking the importance of work-related training?

PART-TIME WORK Summer and part-time jobs can provide valuable experience. If you've been a camp counselor during the summer, you may decide that you really enjoy working with children and would like to get a job in a day-care center. Perhaps you're a cashier at a drugstore after school and on weekends. You may want to pursue a career in pharmacology or business administration.

Many companies use temporary workers to fill some positions. Working as a "temp" is a good way to gain experience and find out what a particular field is like. For the same reasons, part-time and temporary work can be worthwhile for people who are changing careers.

VOLUNTEER WORK You can learn new skills, develop good work habits, and make professional contacts by volunteering. Nonprofit community organizations and some government agencies often include volunteers on their staffs. You might collect funds for a disaster relief project or build houses with Habitat for Humanity. Volunteering can help you develop skills that you can apply to other work situations. Where could you volunteer in your community?

INTERNSHIPS AND COOPERATIVE EDUCATION In very competitive fields, an internship may give you the experience you need to obtain employment. An *internship* is a position in which a person receives training by working with people who are experienced in a particular field. Sometimes it can lead to permanent employment. Because applying for an internship is similar to applying for a job, you get a chance to practice your application and interviewing skills.

High schools, colleges, and universities offer cooperative education programs. *Cooperative education* programs allow students to enhance classroom learning with part-time work related to their majors and interests. For example, you take your high school classes in the morning, and in the afternoon you work at a local business to apply the workplace skills you learned in class. Among the many participating employers in Northeastern University's cooperative education program are Massachusetts General Hospital, Merrill Lynch, and the Boston Symphony Orchestra.

CLASS PROJECTS OR AFTER-SCHOOL ACTIVITIES
Don't forget that class assignments and school activities can be sources of work-related experience. They can help you gain valuable career skills such as these:

- Managing, organizing, and coordinating people
- Public speaking
- Goal setting, planning, and supervising
- Financial planning and budgeting
- Conducting research

Using Career Information Sources

Just as with any other financial decision, you need up-to-date information to make the best career decisions. Many sources of information are available to you.

LIBRARIES   Most school and public libraries offer a variety of references on careers. You might want to start with such guides as the *Occupational Outlook Handbook*, the *Dictionary of Occupational Titles*, and the *Occupational Outlook Quarterly*.

MASS MEDIA   Most newspapers feature business and employment sections with articles on job hunting and career trends.

THE INTERNET   Log on to the Internet for a wealth of information about jobs and employment. You'll find tips and suggestions on everything from filling out applications to job interviewing.

SCHOOL GUIDANCE OFFICES   Visit your school guidance office for materials and advice on career planning. Take advantage of any placement services your school may offer.

COMMUNITY ORGANIZATIONS   Almost every community has business and civic groups that can help you in your career search. Attending their meetings gives you an opportunity to meet local businesspeople.

VOLUNTEER   Volunteering for a local or national non-profit organization can provide work-related experience. *What types of skills might you gain by helping participants in a Special Olympics event?*

PROFESSIONAL ORGANIZATIONS Many professions have organizations dedicated to sharing information. The *Encyclopedia of Associations* can help you find organizations representing careers that interest you.

CONTACTS Family, friends, coworkers, teachers, professors, former employers—the people you already know can help you to prepare for your career. Even people whom you don't know yet can assist you in a job search. That's why it's never too late to begin networking. *Networking* is a way of making and using contacts to get job information and advice.

The contacts you make may not be people who can hire you, but they may know someone who can. They may be able to arrange an *informational interview*, a meeting with someone who works in your area of interest who can provide you with practical information about the career or company you're considering.

CONNECT

List any job-related experience you've had with part-time employment, volunteer work, internships, cooperative education, class projects, and after-school activities. What sources did you use to find each particular experience?

Identifying Job Opportunities

If you're going to find employment that's right for you, you need to know where the job openings are. The sources listed here can help.

Job Advertisements

All newspapers have classified ads that include help-wanted listings. Although most advertise only jobs that are available locally, some major newspapers such as the *Wall Street Journal* list jobs from a wide geographic area.

The Internet is now one of the most valuable sources for job opportunities. If you're interested in working for a particular company, you can use a search engine to find its Web site and learn more about it. Sometimes you can also find lists of current job openings the company may have. In addition to Web sites, the Internet offers newsgroups and bulletin boards that may assist you.

Job Fairs

At a job fair, recruiters from local and national companies set up tables or booths where you can discuss job opportunities and submit your résumé. To make the most of a job fair, be prepared to make your best impression on several recruiters in a short span of time. They may call you for an in-depth interview at a later date.

Employment Agencies

Employment agencies are businesses that match job hunters with employers. Sometimes the company that hires you pays the fee that the employment agency charges. In other instances, you pay the fee, or you and your new employer share the cost. Don't get involved with agencies that ask you to pay a fee without promising you a job in return. The government also supports employment services. To find out more about them, contact your state's employment service or department of labor.

Other Ways to Find a Job

Your ability to find a job is limited only by your imagination and energy. Don't forget about these sources:

- Visit or call specific companies where you would like to work and ask to speak to someone who might help you.
- Check your local telephone directories for the names of businesses in your field of interest, and contact them.
- Talk to people with similar interests who have already graduated from your school. They may be able to help you focus your career search.

Remember, finding a job is a job in itself. For the best results, work as many hours a week seeking a job as you expect to work each

ANOTHER APPROACH Take your job search beyond the classified ads in the Sunday paper. *What might be some of the benefits of contacting companies even if they aren't advertising a job opening?*

week on the job. Don't hesitate to check in often with your contacts. Situations may change from one day to the next.

Applying for a Job

This morning the personnel director of a company to whom Christopher had sent his résumé and cover letter many weeks ago called him. In only two days, he has an appointment for a job interview. He's excited, but he knows that he has a lot to do to prepare.

Making the best possible presentation of your skills and experience is the key to landing a job. Your résumé is your most important tool. A *résumé* is usually a one- or two-page summary of your education, training, experience, and qualifications. It provides prospective employers with an overview of the special contribution you may be able to make to their companies.

The two basic types of résumés are the chronological résumé and the skills résumé. The chronological résumé outlines your education, work experience, and related information, year by year (or in longer periods). This format is useful for job hunters who have continuous work experience. A skills résumé highlights your skills and abilities in specific categories, such as communications, supervision, and research. If you are a recent graduate or are changing careers, a skills résumé might be the better choice for you.

Whether you send your résumé to an employer by regular mail or via e-mail, you will want to include a cover letter. A *cover letter* is the personal letter that you present along with your résumé. While the résumé serves as an overall summary of your qualifications, a cover letter tells a potential employer why you are interested in a particular job and why you think that it would be worthwhile to interview you.

See **Figure 2.3** for examples of a chronological résumé, a skills résumé, and a sample cover letter.

The interview is your chance to shine. It is a formal meeting with your potential employer that allows you to express why you think you are the best person for the job. If you are granted an interview, you should obtain as much information as you can about the company or industry before your interview. Possible resources include the library, the Internet, and informal interviews with people who are familiar with that company or industry. Here are some typical questions an employer might ask in an interview:

- What education and training qualify you for this job?
- Why are you interested in working for this company?

QUESTION

Why would a skills résumé be a better choice for a recent high school graduate? Why is it necessary to include a cover letter when submitting a résumé to a potential employer?

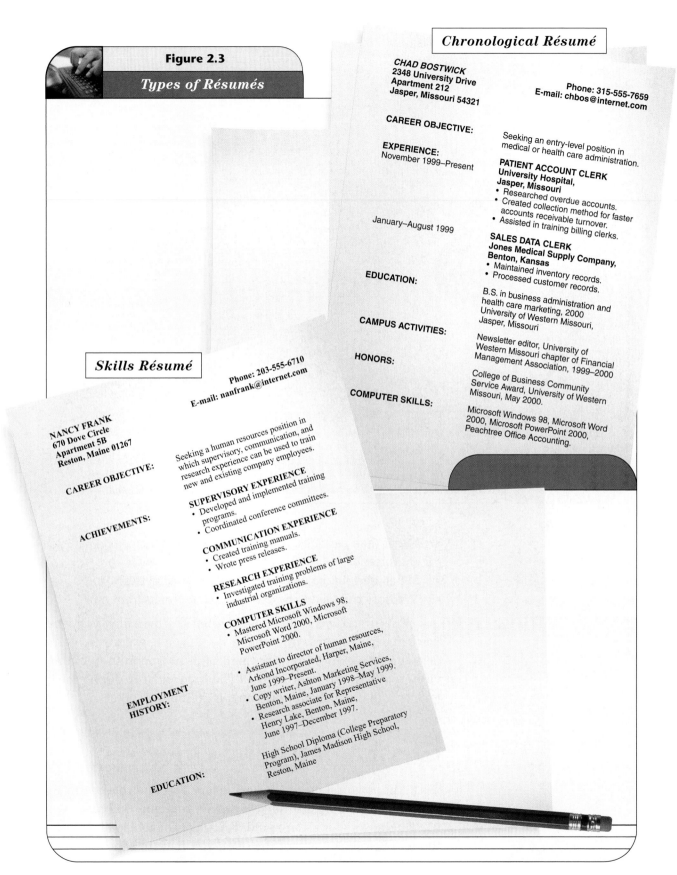

Figure 2.3

Types of Résumés

Chronological Résumé

CHAD BOSTWICK
2348 University Drive
Apartment 212
Jasper, Missouri 54321

Phone: 315-555-7659
E-mail: chbos@internet.com

CAREER OBJECTIVE:

Seeking an entry-level position in medical or health care administration.

EXPERIENCE:
November 1999–Present

PATIENT ACCOUNT CLERK
University Hospital,
Jasper, Missouri
• Researched overdue accounts.
• Created collection method for faster accounts receivable turnover.
• Assisted in training billing clerks.

January–August 1999

SALES DATA CLERK
Jones Medical Supply Company,
Benton, Kansas
• Maintained inventory records.
• Processed customer records.

EDUCATION:

B.S. in business administration and health care marketing, 2000
University of Western Missouri,
Jasper, Missouri

CAMPUS ACTIVITIES:

Newsletter editor, University of Western Missouri chapter of Financial Management Association, 1999–2000

HONORS:

College of Business Community Service Award, University of Western Missouri, May 2000.

COMPUTER SKILLS:

Microsoft Windows 98, Microsoft Word 2000, Microsoft PowerPoint 2000, Peachtree Office Accounting.

Skills Résumé

Phone: 203-555-6710
E-mail: nanfrank@internet.com

NANCY FRANK
670 Dove Circle
Apartment 5B
Reston, Maine 01267

CAREER OBJECTIVE:

Seeking a human resources position in which supervisory, communication, and research experience can be used to train new and existing company employees.

ACHIEVEMENTS:

SUPERVISORY EXPERIENCE
• Developed and implemented training programs.
• Coordinated conference committees.

COMMUNICATION EXPERIENCE
• Created training manuals.
• Wrote press releases.

RESEARCH EXPERIENCE
• Investigated training problems of large industrial organizations.

COMPUTER SKILLS
• Mastered Microsoft Windows 98, Microsoft Word 2000, Microsoft PowerPoint 2000.

EMPLOYMENT HISTORY:

• Assistant to director of human resources, Arkond Incorporated, Harper, Maine, June 1999–Present.
• Copy writer, Ashton Marketing Services, Benton, Maine, January 1998–May 1999.
• Research associate for Representative Henry Lake, Benton, Maine, June 1997–December 1997.

EDUCATION:

High School Diploma (College Preparatory Program), James Madison High School, Reston, Maine

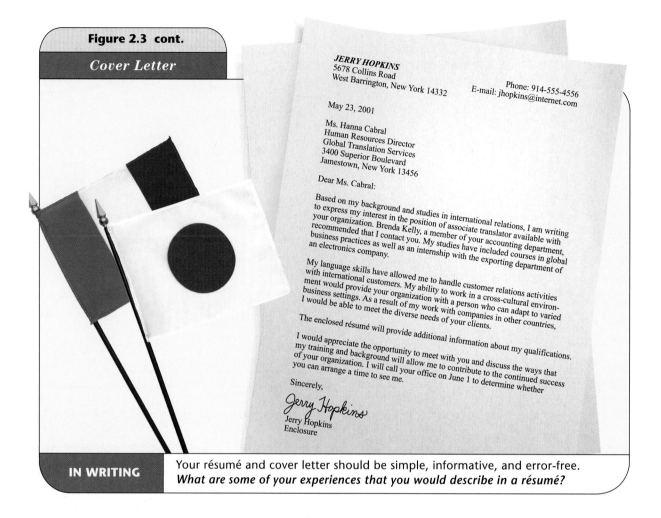

Figure 2.3 cont.

Cover Letter

JERRY HOPKINS
5678 Collins Road
West Barrington, New York 14332

Phone: 914-555-4556
E-mail: jhopkins@internet.com

May 23, 2001

Ms. Hanna Cabral
Human Resources Director
Global Translation Services
3400 Superior Boulevard
Jamestown, New York 13456

Dear Ms. Cabral:

Based on my background and studies in international relations, I am writing to express my interest in the position of associate translator available with your organization. Brenda Kelly, a member of your accounting department, recommended that I contact you. My studies have included courses in global business practices as well as an internship with the exporting department of an electronics company.

My language skills have allowed me to handle customer relations activities with international customers. My ability to work in a cross-cultural environment would provide your organization with a person who can adapt to varied business settings. As a result of my work with companies in other countries, I would be able to meet the diverse needs of your clients.

The enclosed résumé will provide additional information about my qualifications.

I would appreciate the opportunity to meet with you and discuss the ways that my training and background will allow me to contribute to the continued success of your organization. I will call your office on June 1 to determine whether you can arrange a time to see me.

Sincerely,

Jerry Hopkins

Jerry Hopkins
Enclosure

IN WRITING Your résumé and cover letter should be simple, informative, and error-free.
What are some of your experiences that you would describe in a résumé?

- Other than past jobs, what experiences have helped prepare you for this job?
- What are your major strengths? Major weaknesses?
- What do you plan to be doing five or ten years from now?

Most interviewers will end the interview by telling you when you can expect to hear from them. While you're waiting, send that person a note expressing your thanks for the opportunity to interview. You may also want to recall your performance during the interview and think about how you might improve.

Considering a Job Offer

Perhaps you'll go on several interviews and meet with disappointment. Sooner or later, however, someone will say: "We'd like you to work for us." You did it! You got the job! Wait a minute, though. Before you accept the offer, you have to consider several factors. Be sure that you know all you can about the company, the job you're being offered, the salary, and any other financial benefits.

The Work Environment

In the same way that your personality is unique, every workplace has its own unique style. As you go on interviews, you'll notice differences in the ways that managers deal with employees. The pace and pressure of the work will vary. Even the way people behave with one another when they're at work will depend on the company. Do the values, goals, and lifestyles of the people who already work there seem similar to yours?

Ask about official company policies. How does the company handle pay increases? How does it measure the quality of employees' work? How does it decide which employees to promote?

Factors Affecting Salary

Your beginning salary will depend on your education and experience, the size of the company, and the average salary for the job you're considering. To make sure that you're starting with a fair salary, talk to people with similar jobs at other companies, or look for related information on the Internet.

Raises and promotions are a direct result of how well you do your job. Once you've accepted a job offer and started to work, meet regularly with your supervisor. Ask for feedback on your performance and any suggestions for improvement. Let your supervisor know that you are interested in increased responsibility. Meeting—or exceeding—your supervisor's expectations should bring the reward of a raise. If it doesn't, you might want to look for another job.

Measuring Employee Benefits

You'll also want to evaluate what types of benefits the company offers besides a paycheck. Pay particular attention to health care, retirement benefits, and the specific needs of your family.

WORK CULTURE The pace and pressure of the work differs from company to company. *What type of pace might be most appropriate for your personality and work habits?*

MEETING EMPLOYEE NEEDS   Changes in society have brought about changes in the types of benefits that employees receive. Today, single-parent families and households in which both parents work are common. Businesses have responded to these changes in a variety of ways.

Cafeteria-style employee benefits are programs that allow workers to choose the benefits that best meet their personal needs. A married employee with children may want more life and health insurance, whereas a single parent may also be interested in child-care services.

Because people today live longer, retirement programs are more important than ever. In addition to Social Security benefits, some companies contribute to a *pension plan*, a retirement plan that is funded at least in part by an employer. The features of pension plans vary among several basic types. Some plans provide you with a fixed amount of money at retirement. If a business uses a profit-sharing plan, it makes an annual contribution to a retirement fund each year. The money in this fund builds up until you reach retirement age. A third type of pension plan is a 401(k). You set aside a portion of your salary from each paycheck to go into your 401(k) fund. Your employer will often match a percentage of your contribution.

Careers in Finance

CASHIER

Being a cashier is a good way to start your career because you usually don't need any previous experience. A neat appearance, solid math skills, and attention to detail are all the basics you need. Most companies give their cashiers on-the-job training. Cashiers handle money, total bills, receive payments, make change, and give receipts. They may do other tasks as well, such as handling returns and exchanges. A cashier must also know the store's policies and procedures for accepting various forms of payments, such as cash, credit card, and personal check. If you're juggling a busy school schedule, part-time positions are plentiful. Movie theaters, supermarkets, drugstores, department stores, restaurants, and many other businesses hire cashiers.

Skills	Communication, computer, dexterity, math
Personality	Detail oriented, honest, likes working with people, neat
Education	High school student; on-the-job training
Pay range	Minimum wage or higher, depending on experience, location, and business

Research   Look through the classified ads in your local newspaper for cashier positions. What types of businesses advertise for cashiers? Why would a cashier position be a good way to start to a career?

 For more information on cashiers visit finance.glencoe.com or your local library.

COMPARING BENEFITS You can compare the dollar value of employee benefits in several ways. The market value of a benefit is what the benefit would cost if you had to pay for it yourself. For example, the market value of free health insurance is what it would cost you to buy the same coverage. The market value of one week's (five days') vacation is 1/52 of your annual salary.

Taxes should also play a part in your decisions about employment benefits. A tax-exempt benefit is one on which you won't have to pay taxes. A free life insurance policy is an example of a tax-exempt benefit. A tax-deferred benefit is a benefit for which you will have to pay income tax sometime in the future, most likely after you retire. A 401(k) plan is an example of a tax-deferred benefit.

Your Rights as an Employee

As an employee you have certain legal rights. You also have certain legal rights during the hiring process:

- An employer cannot refuse to hire a woman, or terminate her employment, because she is pregnant. A female employee who stops working because she is pregnant must be given full credit for previous service as well as credit for any retirement benefits and seniority that she has accumulated.
- An employer cannot discriminate against a person for any reason related to age, race, color, religion, gender, marital status, national origin, or any mental or physical disabilities.
- In certain cases, an employer must pay the minimum wage set by the government as well as a certain amount for overtime work.
- An employer must pay for Social Security benefits, unemployment insurance, and worker's compensation funds in case of a work-related injury or illness.

Long-Term Career Development

A job is for today, but a career can last for a lifetime. Will you always enjoy the work that you do today? Will you be successful in the career you select? You can't predict the future, but you can develop skills and attitudes that will increase your chances of being satisfied with your work in years to come. Here are some basic guidelines to follow:

$AVVY SAVER

Where to Find Money for College

1. Ask your school counselor about student loans, grants, and scholarships.
2. Check the Internet, using the keywords "college scholarships."
3. Ask for money for college instead of gifts.
4. Apply for scholarships offered by your parents' employers.
5. Get a part-time job and save as much as possible.

- Make a point of improving your communication skills. Do your best to get along with your coworkers. Remain flexible and open to new ideas.
- Develop good work habits. Use lists, short-term and long-term goals, note cards, and other time-management techniques. When you have a task to complete, do it as well as you can.
- Be aware that problems may arise, and be ready to take action when they do. Be creative in solving your own problems, and don't hesitate to help other people solve theirs.

Training Opportunities

Advances in technology are changing the world of work at an ever increasing pace. Many careers that people have today did not exist just a few years ago. These rapid changes will surely continue. A key to your ongoing success will be your ability to keep up with changes in technology and to adapt to the global economy. Remember that you will always be learning new skills and ideas.

How can you make sure that your skills remain up-to-date? Many companies offer regular training programs, encourage attendance at professional seminars, or help pay for college courses. Read as much as possible on your own. Take advantage of the wealth of information on business, economic, and social trends on the Internet and in newspapers, magazines, and professional journals. Talk with others in your field. Informal meetings with coworkers and associates from other companies can be a valuable source of new information.

Career Paths and Advancement

As time goes by, you'll experience changes in your personal interests, values, and goals. Outside factors, such as economic conditions and social trends, will also affect you. These changes will influence your career choices and other financial decisions that you make. You will probably go through a series of career stages like those shown in **Figure 2.4,** each with specific tasks and challenges.

One way to make sure that your career develops as you want it to is to gain the support of someone with more experience and knowledge. A *mentor* is an experienced employee who serves as a teacher and counselor for a less experienced person. A mentor can give you one-on-one training and help you to meet other knowledgeable people. He or she can also provide you with emotional support during difficult times at work. Many organizations have formal mentoring programs. Some of the best mentors are retired people who are eager to share a lifetime of knowledge and experience.

YOUR RIGHTS An employer cannot discriminate against a person during the hiring process for any reason related to age, race, color, religion, gender, marital status, national origin, or any mental or physical disabilities. *What would you do if your legal rights were not honored?*

Changing Careers

Most workers change jobs several times over the course of their lives. Some seek a better position within the same field. Others move into a whole new career. In some cases, you may see signs that it's time to move on:

- You feel bored or depressed at work.
- Your job affects you in a negative way physically or emotionally.
- You receive a series of poor performance evaluations.
- You have little opportunity to win a raise or promotion.
- You have a poor relationship with your supervisor or coworkers.

Sometimes switching jobs will mean that you'll just have to make a few minor adjustments in your life. At other times, it will mean that you need more training and may have to start again from scratch. There is no exact formula for deciding whether you should make a career change. However, you may consider how the financial and personal costs and benefits of changing careers will affect your needs and goals.

Figure 2.4

Stages of Career Development

Stage	Characteristics	Concerns
Pre-entry and career exploration	• Assess personal interests • Obtain necessary training • Find an entry-level job	• Matching interests and abilities to job • Dealing with disappointment
Career growth	• Obtain experience, develop skills • Concentrate on an area of specialization • Gain respect of colleagues	• Developing career contacts • Avoiding career burnout
Advancement and midcareer adjustment	• Continue to gain experience and knowledge • Seek new challenges and expanded responsibility	• Finding continued satisfaction • Maintaining sensitivity toward colleagues and subordinates
Late career and preretirement	• Make financial and personal plans for retirement	• Determining professional involvement after retirement • Planning participation in community activities

NEW HORIZONS

Each stage of career development brings new tasks and new concerns. *Why might you decide to seek new challenges and responsibilities during the midcareer adjustment stage?*

Applying for a Job

Mark Cortez was interested in working at his neighborhood grocery store as a clerk. He wanted to work part-time after school and on weekends to earn money for his personal expenses. He filled out the application at the store and was called back for an interview. Mark interviewed with the store manager and got the job.

Complete Before you interview for a job, you will probably have to fill out an application. Take time to practice "the art" of completing application forms. Always fill out a job application as neatly and accurately as possible. Write "N/A" in any blank for which an answer is not required. N/A means "Not Applicable" and tells the employer that you saw the question, but it does not apply to you. Fill out the application in your workbook, being sure to fill it out completely. Use a pencil before you complete the application in ink, or use a rough copy.

Were there any questions that you could not answer? If so, list the questions.

APPLICATION FOR EMPLOYMENT

SUPERIOR MARKETS

DIRECTIONS: Please use a pen and print.
Answer all sections completely and accurately.

NAME			SOCIAL SECURITY NUMBER
LAST Cortez	FIRST Mark	MIDDLE A.	032 —32 —2712

HOME ADDRESS

NUMBER 134	STREET North Avenue	CITY Indianapolis	STATE IN	ZIP 46268

TELEPHONE #	ALTERNATE #
(317) 555-2492	

POSITION APPLIED FOR	SPECIFY DAYS AND HOURS AVAILABLE	PAY DESIRED
Clerk	evenings and weekends	negotiable

EDUCATION

	NAME AND ADDRESS OF SCHOOL	COURSE	DATE LEFT
ELEMENTARY	Valley Middle School Indianapolis, IN 46266	N/A	June 6, 1999
MIDDLE SCHOOL	Northwest High School Indianapolis, IN 46244	N/A	N/A
HIGH SCHOOL	N/A	N/A	N/A
VOCATIONAL SCHOOL	N/A	N/A	N/A
COLLEGE OR UNIVERSITY	N/A	N/A	N/A
OTHER			

LAST EMPLOYMENT

NAME OF COMPANY	ADDRESS	SUPERVISOR	JOB	PAY
Cameron's Business Supply	1217 Sheldon Ave Indianapolis, IN 46244	Jill Lambert	Clerk	$6.00/hr
DATE BEGAN	DATE LEFT	REASON FOR LEAVING		
June 2001	September 2001	Summer position only		

Additional qualifications applicant has to offer for consideration. These may include job-related interests, experiences, or volunteer activities.

Volunteer one night a week to help deliver meals-on-wheels on weight-lifting team and run track at school.

The facts set forth on my application are true and complete.

DATE October 8, 2001   SIGNATURE Mark A Cortez

Analyze: What do you think a neatly prepared application would tell a prospective employer about you?

Understand that you may find yourself out of a job through no fault of your own. This situation can cause great emotional and financial stress for you and your family. Here are some ways to cope with the situation while looking for another job. Continue to eat, sleep, and exercise as usual. Stay involved in family and community activities; you may find new career contacts anywhere. Improve your career skills through personal study, formal classes, or volunteer work. Think about opportunities with nonprofit organizations, government agencies, temporary employment, or consulting work.

SECTION 2.2 ASSESSMENT

CHECK YOUR UNDERSTANDING

1. Describe three ways that you might obtain employment experience.
2. What factors will affect your salary? What issues other than salary should you consider when evaluating a job offer?
3. Discuss two methods that you might use to grow and develop in your career.

THINK CRITICALLY

4. Compare the advantages and disadvantages of using the career information sources discussed in this section.

USING MATH SKILLS

5. **Employee Benefits** Gustavo has received a promising job offer from XYZ Company. He would earn $25,000 a year. In addition, he would receive two weeks of paid vacation, five paid personal days, and five sick days. He would also receive a free health insurance plan that has an equivalent market value of approximately $5,000.
   Calculate Considering the dollar value of employee benefits, how much will Gustavo's employment package be worth if he accepts this job offer?

SOLVING MONEY PROBLEMS

6. **Measuring Employee Benefits** Suzanne is a single mother who works full-time and pays a sitter to take care of her two children. She recently moved to another state and found a new job. The company offers a variety of employee benefit plans. Suzanne needs to determine which benefits will be best for her family.
   Identifying Alternatives Based on the information in the section on measuring employee benefits, what alternatives might Suzanne have? What will she have to consider in making her decision?

CHAPTER 2 ASSESSMENT

CHAPTER SUMMARY

- By understanding your own interests, values, needs, and goals, you will be able to plan a career that provides personal satisfaction and financial rewards.

- To make the right career decisions, you will have to assess your education, your abilities, and your interests.

- You can evaluate the employment opportunities that are available to you by studying demographic and geographic trends, the economy, and changes in industry and technology.

- Effective strategies for obtaining employment include gaining experience, using career information sources, and identifying job opportunities.

- The key to getting hired is to make the best possible presentation of your skills and experience in your résumé, your cover letter, and interviews.

- Before accepting a job offer, consider the work environment, the salary, and the benefits.

- You have basic legal rights, both during the hiring process and as an employee.

- You can grow and develop in your career by sharpening your skills, taking advantage of training opportunities, gaining the support of a mentor, and being willing to change jobs or careers if necessary.

Internet zone

Understanding and Using Vocabulary

With a partner, role-play an imaginary job interview. Take turns being the interviewer and the job applicant. Use as many key terms in your discussion as you can.

job
career
standard of living
trends
potential earning
   power
aptitudes
interest inventories

demographic trends
service industries
internship
cooperative education
networking
informational
   interview
résumé

cover letter
cafeteria-style
   employee benefits

pension plan
mentor

Review Key Concepts

1. What is the connection between education and potential earning power?
2. What can you do to learn more about your own abilities and interests?
3. What is the main goal in choosing a career?
4. How can changes in industry and technology influence the job market?
5. How can a mentor help you develop your career?

CHAPTER 2 ASSESSMENT

Apply Key Concepts

1. Predict what might happen to your financial situation if you decided not to pursue your education beyond high school, compared to what might happen if you decided to go to college for a bachelor's degree.
2. Go to your school guidance department and ask a counselor to administer an aptitude test or interest inventory to you. What did you learn about your abilities and interests?
3. Describe one factor that you feel is particularly important in choosing a career.
4. Identify three ways in which current social or economic trends could affect your own career goals and financial planning.
5. Write down four ways in which you might need help to develop your career.

 ## Problem Solving Today

RUNNING YOUR OWN BUSINESS

Last summer you designed your own Web site. You have talked to the owners of several local businesses that are interested in hiring you to develop sites for them. To begin this business adventure, you'll need computer equipment and a reliable car. These items will cost about $8,000. You want to determine how quickly you'll be able to recover your investment.

Analyze 1) If you have four customers; charge each one $35 per hour for the development of a Web site; and spend an average of 50 hours working on each site, how much money will you earn? 2) If you update each Web site every six months and charge a flat fee of $125 for this task, how soon can you reach your goal?

 **Computer Activity** As an alternative activity, use financial software to calculate your potential income and devise a plan to recover your investment.

Real-World Application

CONNECT WITH LANGUAGE ARTS

Imagine that you are looking for a job. You want to prepare a list of employers that you might target. Then you plan to call each company to find out if they have job openings. **Think Critically** Using the Internet and your local telephone directory, prepare a list of potential employers. Next, develop a script for your telephone call. Your script should include what you would say to the person who answers the telephone and what you might say to the person who has the power to hire you.

 **FINANCE** *Online*

LOOKING AHEAD

You are looking for help in developing a professional résumé.

Connect Using different search engines, look for information about careers and résumés. Find out the following:

1. What careers will be in the greatest demand in the next five years?
2. What are the most important aspects of a résumé that an employer looks for?
3. What are some questions that an employer might ask in an interview?

CHAPTER 3
Money Management Strategy

STANDARD &POOR'S

Q&A

Q: I've got a great job and no bills. I still live at home. Why do I need an emergency fund?

A: Emergency funds are for those unexpected things that happen to us, and also those "rainy day" great ideas that we want to pursue. There's no guarantee that your job will always be there for you. If you become sick or injured, you may have to take time off from work. Even if you have disability insurance, it may only pay a fraction of what you earned. If you own a car, you may have unexpected repair bills.

Organizing Your Personal Financial Records

*T*om McDaniel worked all summer at the local Food Barn and saved a lot of money. However, shortly after school started in the fall, he quickly ran out of cash. Yesterday he borrowed money from his friend Sean to go to the movies and for dinner afterward. Today Tom asked his father for a loan because he had a date, needed gas for his car, and had to make a car insurance payment. Worried about his son's spending habits, Mr. McDaniel suggested that Tom think about managing his money.

Money management is planning how to get the most from your money. Good money management can help you keep track of where your money goes so that you can make it go farther.

Opportunity Costs and Money Management

Every time you make a decision, you're choosing one thing and rejecting another. This is true no matter how major or minor the decision may be. Perhaps you decide to go to the movies instead of reading a book for your English homework assignment. On a Saturday afternoon, you may choose to play ball with the neighbor's dog rather than watch television or surf the Internet. Every decision you make represents a trade-off, or opportunity cost.

Trade-offs are especially common when it comes to making decisions about money management. You may have had to make a few of these financial trade-offs yourself:

- Should you spend your whole paycheck on clothes, or should you put some of it in the bank so that it will earn interest?
- Is it a good idea to shop around and see if another store has this CD player at a lower price, or is that a waste of your time?

Trade-offs can be very hard to resolve because usually you can think of good reasons for making either choice. In the first example above, the first option would increase the amount you can spend now. The alternative, depositing some money, would contribute to your long-term financial security. In the second example, you might be able to save some money by checking prices at other stores downtown or at a different mall, but you'd also be using up something you can never replace: your time.

What's Your Financial ID?

MONEY MANAGEMENT QUIZ

Imagine you were living on your own. How would you handle your money? On a separate sheet of paper take this money management quiz.

1. I would create a budget for my income and expenses.
   a. Always
   b. Sometimes
   c. Never

2. I would pay the rent or mortgage payment and utility bills on time.
   a. Always
   b. Sometimes
   c. Never

3. I would keep three months of my living expenses in reserve for emergencies.
   a. Always
   b. Sometimes
   c. Never

4. I would save 10 percent of my take-home pay.
   a. Always
   b. Sometimes
   c. Never

5. I would set money aside for large expenses.
   a. Always
   b. Sometimes
   c. Never

6. I would save to buy what I want.
   a. Always
   b. Sometimes
   c. Never

7. I would use credit only when I have money to cover the charge.
   a. Always
   b. Sometimes
   c. Never

8. I would balance my checkbook every month.
   a. Always
   b. Sometimes
   c. Never

How did you score? Give yourself 2 points for each "always," 1 point for each "sometimes," and 0 points for each "never."

If you scored 12–16, you're practicing good money management skills.

If you scored 6–11, with a little more effort you could improve your money management skills.

If you scored 0–5, it's time to start developing money management skills.

How can you be sure of making the right decisions when you're faced with tough opportunity costs? Although you may never be sure, you can become a better judge. You can consider the factors that influence your decision making by compiling a mental list of your options. Then consider how these options fit your values and your current financial situation.

Thinking about your values, your goals, and the state of your bank account can make many of your spending decisions easier. For example, if your goal is to save as much money as you can for college, then you'll probably choose to borrow a book from the library rather than buy it from a bookstore. On the other hand, if your goal is to put aside only a certain amount of your paycheck each month, you may choose to buy the book with the money you have left.

Benefits of Organizing Your Financial Documents

PREDICT

Why is it important to keep your financial records organized?

The first step in effective money management is to organize your personal financial documents. The category of "personal financial documents" includes a variety of materials, such as bank statements

HALF OFF Some people would rather wait to buy an item they want until it goes on sale. *When might this be a wise money management strategy? When might it make more sense to go ahead and buy the item, even if it's not on sale?*

and paycheck stubs. These documents tell you how much money you have. The receipt for the shirt you bought last week counts too.

Personal financial documents also include records that are not directly related to your day-to-day use of money. Car titles, birth certificates, and tax forms are all personal financial documents. Together, these records present a clear picture of your finances.

Creating an organized system for handling your personal financial documents has several specific advantages. Most obviously, such a system helps you find any document you may need in a hurry. Organizing your documents also helps you:

- plan and measure your financial progress;
- handle routine money matters, such as depositing paychecks in the bank and paying bills on time;
- determine how much money you'll have available to spend now and in the future;
- make effective decisions about how to save money.

Once you have organized your financial records, you'll have a better handle on your needs, your wants, and your current financial position.

Where to Keep Your Financial Documents

You can keep your financial documents in any of several different places—in a home file, in a safe-deposit box, or on a computer. To organize your documents as effectively as possible, you may want to use all three. Each method has advantages and disadvantages, depending on the types of records.

Home Files

One choice is to keep financial documents in a home file. Such a file is simple to set up and doesn't take up much space. You can use a file drawer, a series of folders, or even a cardboard box. Whatever method you use, your home file should be simple and allow quick access to your documents.

You may already have the beginnings of a home filing system. For example, you may have been keeping a savings account passbook in the back of a bureau drawer ever since you were ten, or maybe you have an accordion file folder where you store all your receipts. To make good use of a home filing system, you'll need to sort through all your personal financial records. Next, arrange them according to the nature and type of each document, and label all folders or boxes. Train yourself to file your receipts and other financial papers as soon as possible after receiving them.

What types of financial documents should you keep in a home file? If you have a checking account, you'll want to keep your bank statements so that you can determine how much money you have in your account or verify your checkbook against the statements. However, do not keep hard-to-replace documents, such as a car title or paperwork related to a mortgage loan, in a home file. A cardboard box does not protect against fire, water, or theft.

Safe-Deposit Boxes

You should keep such important documents as car titles and mortgage loan papers locked away in a *safe-deposit box*—a small, secure storage compartment that you can rent in a bank, usually for $100 a year or less. Other items commonly kept in safe-deposit boxes include rental agreements, birth certificates, adoption papers, and valuable collectibles, such as coins or stamps.

Safe-deposit boxes are usually kept in a locked, fireproof room that is accessible only while the bank is open for business. Each box has two individual locks. You, the holder of the box, have one key; the bank keeps the other. The box can be opened only when both keys are used together.

Safe-deposit boxes offer more security for your valuables than your home file because at a bank, loss from fire and other disasters is extremely rare. Moreover, the financial institution that owns the box usually (though not always) has insurance to cover such losses. Nevertheless, it is probably a wise idea to keep copies at home of all the financial records in your safe-deposit box.

Home Computers

Rental agreements and canceled checks can't be stored on a home computer. Still, if you have a personal computer, it can be a great place to keep certain types of financial records. It's also a terrific tool to use in planning your financial future.

You can use a software program specifically designed to keep a running summary of checks you've written. You enter any checks that you've written, and the computer automatically calculates the

Figure 3.1

Where to Keep Your Financial Records

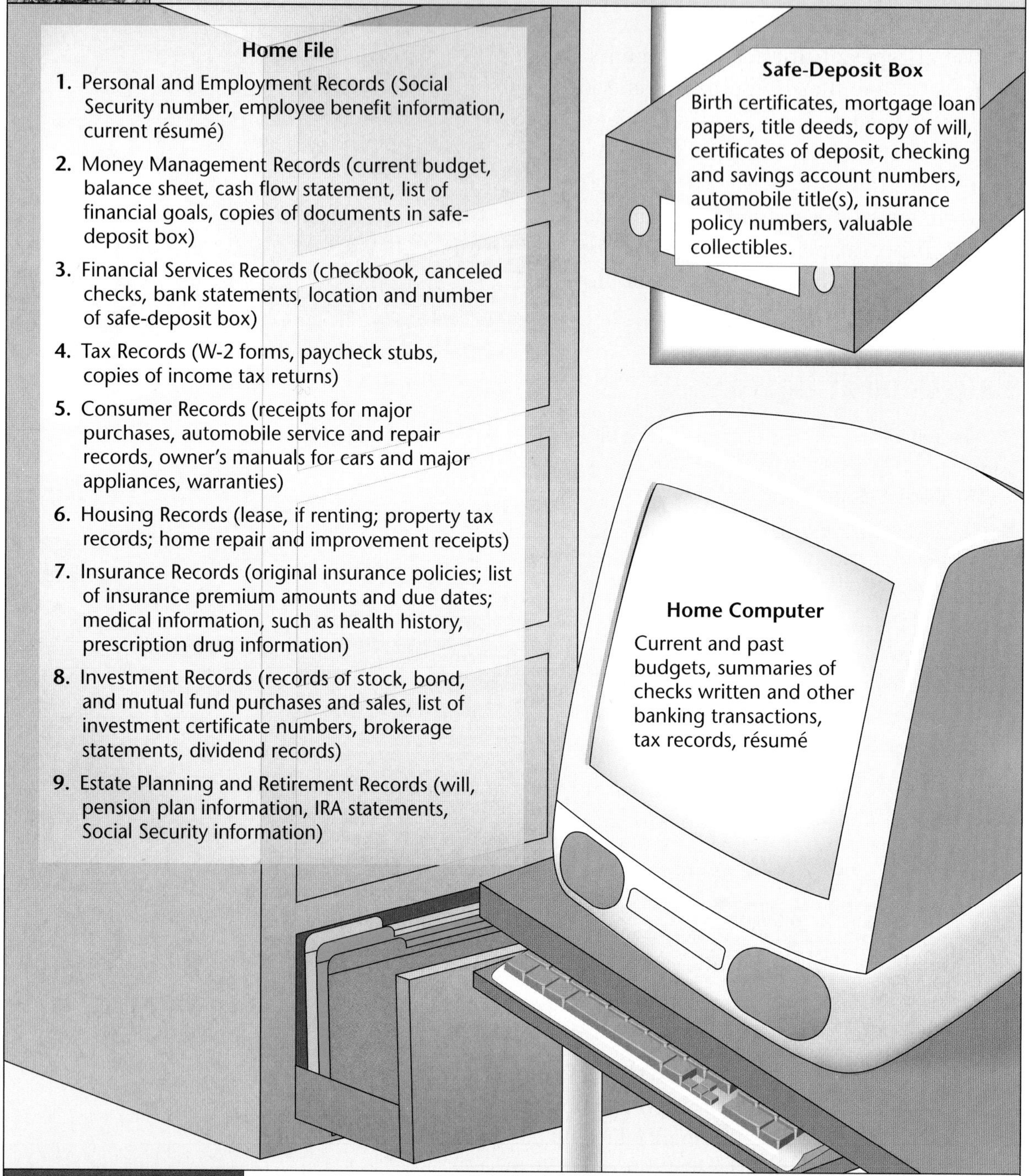

Home File

1. Personal and Employment Records (Social Security number, employee benefit information, current résumé)

2. Money Management Records (current budget, balance sheet, cash flow statement, list of financial goals, copies of documents in safe-deposit box)

3. Financial Services Records (checkbook, canceled checks, bank statements, location and number of safe-deposit box)

4. Tax Records (W-2 forms, paycheck stubs, copies of income tax returns)

5. Consumer Records (receipts for major purchases, automobile service and repair records, owner's manuals for cars and major appliances, warranties)

6. Housing Records (lease, if renting; property tax records; home repair and improvement receipts)

7. Insurance Records (original insurance policies; list of insurance premium amounts and due dates; medical information, such as health history, prescription drug information)

8. Investment Records (records of stock, bond, and mutual fund purchases and sales, list of investment certificate numbers, brokerage statements, dividend records)

9. Estate Planning and Retirement Records (will, pension plan information, IRA statements, Social Security information)

Safe-Deposit Box

Birth certificates, mortgage loan papers, title deeds, copy of will, certificates of deposit, checking and savings account numbers, automobile title(s), insurance policy numbers, valuable collectibles.

Home Computer

Current and past budgets, summaries of checks written and other banking transactions, tax records, résumé

SAFE AND SOUND A home file, safe-deposit box, or personal computer will enable you to organize your financial documents. *Where do you currently store important financial documents? Name at least three of your personal financial documents that you might store in a home file.*

new balance in your account. Another option is to track your monthly spending on a computer. You can see at a glance how much money you're spending, and you can easily compare your expenses from one month to the next.

Figure 3.1 lists the types of financial documents that you might keep in a home file, safe-deposit box, or on a computer.

SECTION 3.1   ASSESSMENT

CHECK YOUR UNDERSTANDING

1. How will organizing your financial documents help you manage your money?
2. What steps would you take to create a home filing system?
3. What are the advantages of using a safe-deposit box to store your personal financial documents?

THINK CRITICALLY

4. List three examples of money-related opportunity costs you've faced in the last two months. Write a sentence explaining what decision you made and why.

USING COMMUNICATION SKILLS

5. **Organizing Financial Records** To become a member of an Internet video library, Maritza has to put down a deposit of $100, using her credit card. When and if Maritza chooses to discontinue her membership, the library will refund her deposit only if she has returned all her rented videos, has paid the annual membership fee, and presents her membership agreement.
   Give Advice Suggest some places Maritza might store the agreement to ensure her claim to the deposit.

SOLVING MONEY PROBLEMS

6. **Financial Documents** Martin is sitting in his bedroom, surrounded by dozens of papers— gas receipts for his car, a checkbook, a couple of unopened and unpaid bills, paycheck stubs from his work at the day-care center, and much more. He wants to organize his financial documents in a shoebox, but he is completely overwhelmed by the amount of paper.
   Evaluate Help Martin prioritize this job. Give him some suggestions about breaking it down into parts, starting with the most important tasks.

Personal Financial Statements

The Personal Balance Sheet: What Are You Worth Now?

What You'll Learn

- How to **develop** a personal balance sheet and cash flow statement
- How to **analyze** your personal financial situation

Why It's Important

Personal financial statements can give you a good idea of where you're headed financially and where you are now in relation to your financial goals.

KEY TERMS

- **personal financial statements**
- **balance sheet**
- **net worth**
- **assets**
- **liquid assets**
- **real estate**
- **market value**
- **liabilities**
- **insolvency**
- **cash flow**
- **income**
- **take-home pay**
- **discretionary income**
- **surplus**
- **deficit**

Most of the documents mentioned in the previous section are issued by banks, the federal and state governments, and businesses. However, such documents reveal only a part of your financial picture. For a complete look at your financial situation, you should create a personal balance sheet and a cash flow statement. These reports are known as personal financial statements. *Personal financial statements* are documents that provide information about your current financial position and present a summary of your income and spending.

Personal financial statements can help you:

- determine what you own and what you owe;
- measure your progress toward your financial goals;
- track your financial activities;
- organize information that you can use when you file your tax return or apply for credit.

To evaluate your financial situation, you first need to create a balance sheet. A *balance sheet*, also called a net worth statement, is a financial statement that lists the items of value that you own, the debts that you owe, and your net worth. Your *net worth* is the difference between the amount that you own and the debts that you owe. Net worth is a measure of your current financial position. To create a personal balance sheet, follow these steps.

Step 1   Determine Your Assets

Your *assets* are any items of value that you own, including cash, property, personal possessions, and investments. To determine your assets, you need to consider four categories of wealth.

LIQUID ASSETS The first category is called liquid assets. *Liquid assets* are cash and items that can be quickly converted to cash. The money in your savings and checking accounts is a liquid asset. If Bharat has $500 in his savings account and $35 in cash, his liquid assets are worth $535 ($500 + $35 = $535). This money is immediately available for Bharat to spend. Although he may be able to convert other assets into cash, the process is not quite as easy or as fast.

REAL ESTATE   The second category is *real estate*, land that a person or family owns and anything that is on it, such as a house or any other building. The amount recorded on the real estate portion of your balance sheet is the property's *market value*, or the price at which you could sell the property. Suppose that the Shah family owns a house and a cottage whose market values are $135,000 and $84,000, respectively. They would list the sum of those figures—$219,000—under the heading "Real Estate" on their balance sheet.

PERSONAL POSSESSIONS   Personal possessions make up the third category, which includes cars and any other valuable belongings that are not real estate. The emphasis here is on "valuable"—no old clothes or used CDs. Joyce might choose to list her new $800 electric guitar, her television, her skis, and several pieces of fine jewelry.

Although you may list personal possessions on the balance sheet at their original cost, you will get a better idea of your financial situation by recording their current market value. For example, Joyce's television is almost certainly worth less now than it was when she purchased it five years ago. In contrast, collectible items, such as old baseball cards and comic books, may increase in value over time. Although determining current values for some items may be difficult, doing so will give you a more accurate picture of your net worth. You may have to look up comparable items in classified ads or visit thrift stores. If you have access to the Internet, you can also check Web sites where people buy and sell such items.

INVESTMENT ASSETS   The fourth category of wealth is investment assets. Investment assets include retirement accounts and securities such as stocks and bonds. Typically, you would set aside such assets for long-term financial needs, such as paying for college, saving to buy a house, or retirement. The amount you record should reflect the value of the assets at the time when you prepare the balance sheet.

Step 2   Determine Your Liabilities

When you prepare a personal balance sheet, you must also record your *liabilities*, or the debts that you owe. Suppose that Marlene borrows $200 from her mother to buy a new printer for her computer. She would record the printer as an asset, but she would also have to record $200 as a liability on her personal balance sheet.

CURRENT LIABILITIES   Current liabilities are short-term debts that have to be paid within a year or so. Most medical bills, cash loans, taxes, and insurance payments fall under this heading.

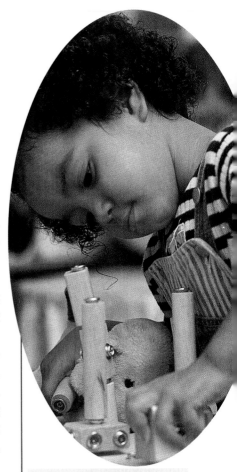

PLAY TIME Perhaps you've saved a favorite toy or other item from your childhood. *Which ones do you think might be valuable? How can you find out?*

LONG-TERM LIABILITIES Long-term liabilities are debts that don't have to be fully repaid for at least a year. Car loans, student loans, and mortgage loans are examples of long-term liabilities. Note that the term "liabilities" includes only money that you will owe for longer than a month. For example, a telephone bill doesn't qualify as a liability.

Step 3 ## Calculate Your Net Worth

Once you know the amounts of your assets and liabilities, you can calculate your net worth. Here's a formula you can use to determine your net worth. Subtract your liabilities from your assets; the difference is your net worth.

Go Figure... **NET WORTH**

Example:	What is Janine's net worth if her assets are worth $3,000 and her liabilities total $700?
Formula:	Assets − Liabilities = Net Worth
Solution:	$3,000 − $700 = $2,300 Janine's net worth is $2,300.

RESPOND

Using the formula in the Go Figure box, calculate your net worth.

It's also important to understand the meaning of net worth. If the Romano family has a net worth of $62,300, that doesn't mean that they have $62,300 to spend. Much of their wealth may be in stocks, real estate, and personal possessions, which can't be easily converted to cash. As a rule, net worth is only an indication of your general financial situation.

Although you may have a high net worth, you can still have trouble paying your bills. This is especially true when most of your assets are not liquid and you don't have enough cash to meet your expenses. That can happen if you purchase a more expensive car than you can afford or spend all of your savings to buy a house. **Figure 3.2** shows an example of a personal balance sheet.

If you are unable to pay all of your debts, you may experience insolvency. *Insolvency* is the condition that occurs if your liabilities are greater than your assets. Suppose that Brad owes $4,000 and that his assets (a ten-year-old car and an old computer) are worth $1,800. Even if Brad sold all his assets and put his whole $1,500 paycheck toward paying his debts, he would still be insolvent.

Figure 3.2

Creating a Personal Balance Sheet

Melinda and Carroll Durbin
Personal Balance Sheet as of October 31, 2002

Assets

Liquid Assets

Checking account balance	$1,450	
Savings account balance	550	
Total liquid assets		$2,000

Real Estate

Market value of house		$105,000

Personal Possessions

Market value of car	4,250	
Furniture and appliances	2,500	
Electronic equipment	2,000	
Collectibles	750	
Total personal possessions		$9,500

Investment Assets

Retirement accounts	15,000	
Stock investments	3,300	
Total investment assets		18,300
Total Assets		$134,800

Liabilities

Current Liabilities

Medical bills	$1,250	
Credit card balances	2,300	
Total current liabilities		$3,550

Long-term Liabilities

Mortgage	92,500	
Student loan	3,500	
Car loan	2,500	
Total long-term liabilities		98,500
Total Liabilities		$102,050
Net Worth (assets minus liabilities)		$32,750

TRUE OR FALSE? The Durbin's personal balance sheet indicates that they have a positive net worth of $32,750. *Does this figure reflect their true financial situation? Explain your answer.*

Step 4 **Evaluate Your Financial Situation**

You can use a balance sheet to track your financial progress. Update your balance sheet, or make a new one, every few months, and chart changes over time. Is your net worth increasing? Good! Keep doing whatever it is you're doing to make that happen. Is it decreasing—or just holding steady? Changes might be in order. As a rule, you can increase your net worth by increasing your savings, increasing the value of your investments, reducing your expenses, and/or reducing your debts.

The Cash Flow Statement: Income Versus Expenses

The money that actually goes into and out of your wallet and bank accounts is called *cash flow*. It's divided into two parts: cash inflow and cash outflow. Cash inflow is the money you receive, or your

Careers in Finance

FINANCIAL SOFTWARE DESIGNER

More than ever technology can help solve problems, especially financial problems. Do you enjoy solving problems using computers? That's what financial software designers do by creating programs that help companies collect and analyze vital financial information. To improve their products, designers spend time talking to clients and experimenting with other products on the market. They read about the latest technology, always trying to figure out how new ideas can help their customers. They take advantage of any opportunity to work with new software or equipment. The best financial software designers have learned about accounting or business first, and they understand how finance fits into the business world.

Skills	Accounting, analytical, communication, computer programming language, math, time management, problem solving
Personality	Ability to evaluate information, good judgment
Education	Bachelor's degree in accounting or business plus computer experience
Pay range	$40,000 to $100,000 a year, depending on experience, company, and location

Critical Thinking Why are financial software designers who understand business more valuable to employers?

 For more information on financial software designers visit finance.glencoe.com **or your local library.**

Figure 3.3

Creating a Cash Flow Statement

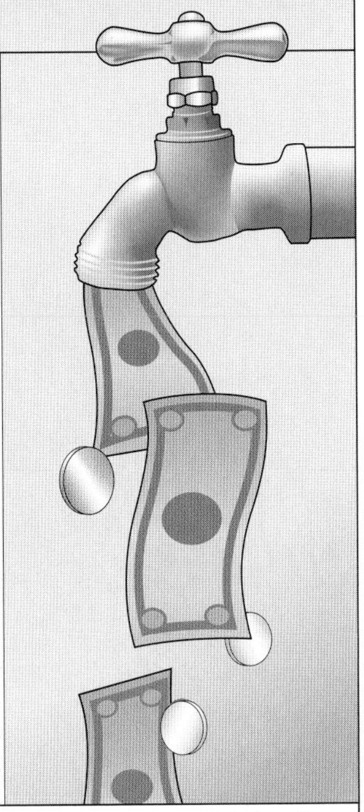

Amy Grossman
Cash Flow Statement for the Month Ending July 31, 2002

Income (Cash Inflow)	
Take-home pay	$450
Allowance	100
Savings account interest	12
Total income	$562

Expenses (Cash Outflow)	
Fixed expenses (cable TV, train commuter tickets, etc.)	$ 80
Variable expenses (recreation, clothing, take-out food)	320
Total expenses	$400
Net Cash Flow	**$162**

MONEY SUPPLY Amy's cash flow statement indicates that her net cash flow is $162. *How might she increase her net cash flow?*

income. That may mean a paycheck from a job, an allowance from your parents, or interest earned in your savings account. Cash outflow includes all of the money you spend.

A cash flow statement is simply a summary of your cash flow during a particular period, usually a month or a year. This summary gives you important feedback on your income and spending patterns. To create a cash flow statement, such as the one shown in **Figure 3.3**, follow these steps.

Step 1 Record Your Income

List all of your sources of income during a given month, and record the amounts as your cash inflow. Make sure that you record the exact amount that is available to you to use. Most paychecks, for instance, reflect various deductions for federal and state taxes. These taxes are withheld from the total amount of money you have earned, or your gross pay. Your *take-home pay*, or net pay, is the amount of income left after taxes and other deductions are taken out of your gross pay.

QUESTION

Why is it necessary to distinguish cash flow from net worth?

Joshua earns $1,000 a month, but he doesn't receive the entire amount. After taxes, his take-home pay is $700. Your take-home pay—not your pay before deductions—should be listed on the cash flow statement. This amount plus your interest earnings on investments and savings is your cash inflow.

Some financial experts evaluate the strength of a person's income by using a measurement called discretionary income. The money left over after you have paid for the essentials—food, clothing, shelter, transportation, and medication—is your *discretionary income*. You can spend this amount at your discretion, or according to your wants. The higher your discretionary income, the better off you are.

Step 2 Record Your Expenses

Expenses fall into two basic types: fixed and variable. Fixed expenses are those that are more or less the same each month. Cable television charges, rent, and bus fare for commuting to work or school are all examples of fixed expenses.

Variable expenses are those that may change from month to month. Food and clothing are variable expenses. During some months you may need to buy new sweaters and pants, but during other months, you may have no clothing expenses at all. Electricity, medical costs, and recreation are also examples of variable expenses. The total of your fixed and variable expenses is your cash outflow.

Step 3 Determine Your Net Cash Flow

You can determine your net cash flow by subtracting your expenses from your income.

Go Figure...	NET CASH FLOW
Example:	What is Jason's net cash flow if his income for the month is $1,500 and his expenses add up to $1,350?
Formula:	Income − Expenses = Net Cash Flow
Solution:	$1,500 − $1,350 = $150. Jason has a positive net cash flow of $150.

Because Jason's net cash flow is positive, he has a *surplus*—extra money that can be spent or saved, depending on a person's financial goals and values. If his net cash flow were negative, though, he would have a deficit. A *deficit* is the situation that occurs if you spend more than you earn or receive.

Analyzing Your Financial Position from Your Personal Financial Statements

When your net cash flow changes, so does your net worth. Every time you create a deficit by spending more than you earn, your net worth declines. To make up for the deficit, you can either borrow money (increasing your liabilities) or draw from your savings (decreasing your assets). In either case, your net worth declines.

On the other hand, if you end a month with a surplus, your net worth will probably go up. That's because you can choose to save the money, adding to your assets, or you can use it to pay off previous debts, reducing your liabilities. Whichever path you select, your net

	Figure 3.4		
	Evaluating Your Financial Progress		
Ratio	**Calculation**	**Example**	**Meaning**
Debt ratio	liabilities divided by net worth	$25,000 ÷ $50,000 = 0.5	Compares your liabilities to your net worth. A low debt ratio is desirable.
Liquidity ratio	liquid assets divided by monthly expenses	$10,000 ÷ $4,000 = 2.5	Indicates number of months you would be able to pay your living expenses in case of a financial emergency, such as the loss of your job. The higher the liquidity ratio, the better.
Debt-payments ratio	monthly credit payments divided by take-home pay	$540 ÷ $3,600 = 0.15 = 15%	Indicates how much of a person's earnings goes to pay debts (excluding a home mortgage). Most financial experts recommend a debt-payments ratio of less than 20 percent.
Savings ratio	amount saved each month divided by gross monthly income	$600 ÷ $5,000 = 0.12 = 12%	Most financial experts recommend a savings ratio of at least 10 percent.

EXPERT ADVICE Suppose that you earned $2,200 gross monthly income and you were paid twice a month. *What would be your savings ratio if you saved approximately $60 from each paycheck? Would you be saving enough?*

worth will increase. As a general rule, if you have a surplus cash flow, your net worth increases; if you have a deficit, your net worth decreases.

However, net worth doesn't quite give you an accurate idea of your finances. You can use your balance sheet and cash flow statement to determine your financial situation in other ways as well. See **Figure 3.4** on page 73 for details.

SECTION 3.2 ASSESSMENT

CHECK YOUR UNDERSTANDING

1. How do you calculate your net worth when you prepare a balance sheet?
2. Explain how you should record your income on a cash flow statement.
3. If your personal financial statements indicate that you have a deficit, what might you do to change your financial situation?

THINK CRITICALLY

4. List the three most valuable items that you own that would fall into the category of personal possessions.

USING MATH SKILLS

5. **Finding the Net** Tameka's income for the month of January was $2,375. Her fixed expenses during that same month were $750, and her variable expenses totaled $1,750. **Calculate** What was Tameka's net cash flow during January? Be sure to indicate whether she had a surplus or a deficit.

SOLVING MONEY PROBLEMS

6. **Spending Wisely** Larry's personal balance sheet shows $1,200 in credit card debts; a savings account of $550; and personal property amounting to $3,700 in rare stamps. Recently he was promoted at his part-time job. Because of that, and because he made an effort to reduce his expenses, he had a positive cash flow of $600 last month. He asks what you think he should do with the surplus cash.
Present a Plan Evaluate Larry's possible choices and come up with a specific plan of action for his use of the surplus. Be prepared to defend your recommendation.

Budgeting to Achieve Your Financial Goals

Preparing a Practical Budget

A *budget* is a plan for using your money in a way that best meets your wants and needs. It is essential to intelligent money management. By using a budget, you'll learn how to live within your income and how to spend your money wisely. You will also develop good money management skills that will help you reach your financial goals.

Step 1   Setting Your Financial Goals

Your financial goals are the purposes you want to accomplish with your money. What you do with your money today will affect your ability to achieve your financial goals in the future. To meet those financial goals, you'll need to plan your savings, your spending, and your investments.

How should you set your financial goals? That depends on your lifestyle and on your hopes for the future. Perhaps you would like to get a pilot's license after you graduate from college. Flying lessons are expensive, and you may need to log several hundred hours of flying time before you can obtain a license. The type of job you choose determines your income and your ability to save to reach your financial goals. Your values will influence your spending and saving habits as well.

It's important to make your financial goals as specific as possible. A definite time frame is a good idea, too. You may find it helpful to separate your goals into short-term, intermediate, and long-term goals.

Step 2   Estimating Your Income

Once you've set your goals, you can begin working on a budget that's practical for you. Start by recording your estimated income for the next month. Include all sources of income that you know you'll be receiving, such as your take-home pay and income on investments and savings. Do not include money you may or may not get,

---

SCIENCE

Imagine that you are a scientist at a large university in Florida. You have spent the last several years studying the declining wildlife in the Everglades. This year you need to apply for a financial grant of $100,000 to help continue your research. Prepare a detailed budget of how you will spend the money over the next 12 months. Include your salary, equipment, supplies, transportation, and any other expenses you might have.

such as bonuses and gifts. In **Figure 3.5**, the Thompsons have estimated that their income for next month will be $3,550.

Estimating income is easier in some cases than in others. Ryan always works 12 hours each week and gets paid on the 15th of every month. In contrast, Rachel works irregular hours at two part-time jobs. During some weeks, she earns only $75, but there are weeks when her earnings are four times that amount. Rachel should estimate her income based on her best guess about what will happen in the coming month. Alternatively, she might make her estimate a little lower than she thinks it will actually be. That will help her avoid overspending. Whatever your estimate, record that amount. Remember that a budget should always be a written document.

Step 3   Budgeting for Unexpected Expenses and Savings

The Thompsons have decided to put aside a little money each month to help with unexpected expenses as well as to reach their financial goals. Every month they place $100 in an emergency fund. One of their financial goals is to save three to six months' worth of living expenses in case someone in the family becomes unemployed, needs medical attention unexpectedly, or encounters some other financial problem. They keep their emergency fund in a separate savings account that will earn interest.

The Thompsons are also trying to meet three other financial goals, some short-term, others long-term. They deposit money in their vacation fund each month, hoping that they'll soon have enough to take a trip to Jamaica. They also have a college fund for their young children and an investment fund to buy stocks. In all, they put $150 into these other special savings accounts each month, bringing their total monthly savings to $250.

Step 4   Budgeting for Fixed Expenses

Next, the Thompsons list all their monthly expenses. They start by listing their fixed expenses, or those that don't change from month to month. For the Thompsons, that includes their mortgage, automobile and student loan payments, and insurance premiums. Their budgeted total for fixed payments comes to $1,200.

PREDICT

What are some examples of variable expenses?

Step 5   Budgeting for Variable Expenses

Planning for variable expenses—those that vary from one month to the next—is not as easy as budgeting for fixed expenses. Such items

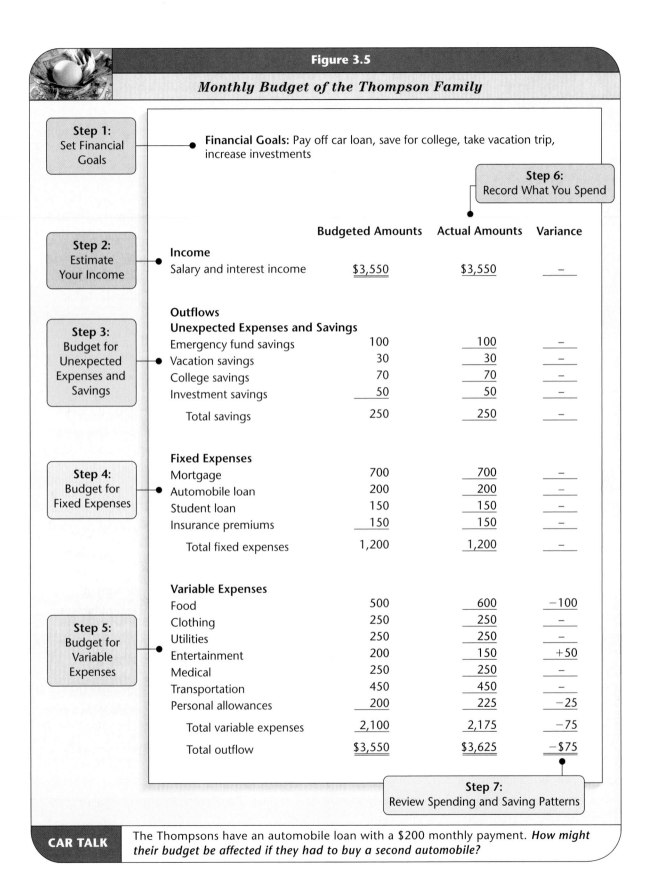

Figure 3.5

Monthly Budget of the Thompson Family

Step 1:
Set Financial Goals

Financial Goals: Pay off car loan, save for college, take vacation trip, increase investments

Step 6:
Record What You Spend

	Budgeted Amounts	Actual Amounts	Variance
Income			
Salary and interest income	$3,550	$3,550	–
Outflows			
Unexpected Expenses and Savings			
Emergency fund savings	100	100	–
Vacation savings	30	30	–
College savings	70	70	–
Investment savings	50	50	–
Total savings	250	250	–
Fixed Expenses			
Mortgage	700	700	–
Automobile loan	200	200	–
Student loan	150	150	–
Insurance premiums	150	150	–
Total fixed expenses	1,200	1,200	–
Variable Expenses			
Food	500	600	–100
Clothing	250	250	–
Utilities	250	250	–
Entertainment	200	150	+50
Medical	250	250	–
Transportation	450	450	–
Personal allowances	200	225	–25
Total variable expenses	2,100	2,175	–75
Total outflow	$3,550	$3,625	–$75

Step 2:
Estimate Your Income

Step 3:
Budget for Unexpected Expenses and Savings

Step 4:
Budget for Fixed Expenses

Step 5:
Budget for Variable Expenses

Step 7:
Review Spending and Saving Patterns

CAR TALK The Thompsons have an automobile loan with a $200 monthly payment. *How might their budget be affected if they had to buy a second automobile?*

STANDARD &POOR'S

CASE STUDY

*B*en and Yolanda Bazo have been married for two years. They've tried to stick to a budget, but they always end up arguing about money because they never have enough of it. Yolanda wants to track every expense so they have some idea of where their money goes. Ben dislikes the thought of writing down every penny he spends. Yolanda is very frustrated with their situation. Last year they owed $4,500 on their credit cards; this year they owe $7,000. They don't have any savings, and Yolanda would love to buy a house.

Yolanda finally convinced Ben to organize their check stubs, receipts, and credit card statements to see where their money was going. It turns out that last year they spent more than $2,000 in restaurants and charged $800 on their vacation. Their car cost them $1,650 for upkeep, and they donated $500 to the homeless shelter. Now that they've figured out how they're spending their money, Ben and Yolanda want to know what to do next. They've turned to the experts at Standard & Poor's for advice.

Analysis: Ben and Yolanda are spending more than they earn. They use credit cards to pay their expenses, and the amount of their debt is growing each year. As more of their income goes toward paying the interest on their debt, they'll have even less money available to spend and to save for things they want. To get back on track, they need to agree on some financial goals and work together toward them.

Recommendation: Ben and Yolanda need to stick to a budget that reflects their current expenses and also allows them to save. They can cut their expenses by spending less on entertainment, using public transportation whenever possible, and donating time rather than money to charities. Their first priorities should be to build a cash reserve for emergencies and to reduce their debt. Ben and Yolanda can start by locking up their credit cards and putting at least 10 percent of each paycheck in a savings account or money market fund. When they've built emergency savings equal to three months' living expenses, they can begin paying more each month on their credit cards and setting aside savings to invest for long-term goals, such as buying a house and retirement.

Critical Thinking Questions

1. Why is it important for Ben and Yolanda to reduce their credit card debt?
2. How can Ben and Yolanda create a budget that will allow them to have some fun and still save money?
3. Why should Ben and Yolanda plan now for long-term goals such as retirement when they are so young?

as medical costs are often unexpected. Heating and cooling costs can vary with the season. As with income, you should make your best guesses based on costs from previous months. When in doubt, guess high. The Thompsons budgeted $2,100 for these expenses.

How can you determine reasonable expense levels? Financial experts publish guidelines that tell what proportion of income should go for various expenses. Another guide is the *consumer price index (CPI)*, a measure of the changes in prices for commonly purchased goods and services in the United States. Comparing the CPI to your actual budget can indicate when you're spending too much on various items. A third source of information is your friends and relatives. If you eat out more often than any of your friends or buy many more clothes than your friends or siblings, that's an indication that your budget may be in trouble.

Step 6   Recording What You Spend

Although your budget is prepared, your work is still incomplete. You must now begin to keep track of your actual income and expenses. Remember, many budgeted items are only guesses. Maybe your old car will continue to run through the month. Then again, maybe it will break down next week and need $400 worth of repairs. To find out how practical your budget is, you'll need to keep track of your expenses during an entire month and revise your budget if necessary.

In **Figure 3.5**, the Thompsons have used a second column to record the actual amounts they spent. In some cases, their expenses were the same as they had expected. In other cases, they weren't. Your spending will not always work out as planned. The difference between the budgeted amount and the actual amount that you spend is the *budget variance.* This figure can be either a surplus or a deficit. It's a surplus if you spend less money than you had expected, but it's a deficit if you spend more. Budget variances can also occur in the income category. Earning more than you anticipated creates a surplus, whereas earning less results in a deficit.

Although the Thompsons have no budget variance on the income side, they have a surplus in their expense section. They spent $50 less than they had expected they would on entertainment. However, they spent more than they had budgeted in the other variable expense categories, creating a deficit in those categories. The overall result was a total monthly deficit of $75.

Step 7 ## Reviewing Spending and Saving Patterns

Budgeting is a continual process. You may need to review your budget each month and consider making changes based on the nature of your expenses.

REVIEWING YOUR FINANCIAL PROGRESS If you find yourself falling behind on bill payments, or if you're left with a lot of money at the end of the month, you may need to revise your budget. Even if your budget generally seems to be on target, it's a good idea to prepare an occasional budget summary to review your progress. See **Figure 3.6**.

REVISING YOUR GOALS AND ADJUSTING YOUR BUDGET If you always seem to have deficits, ask yourself where you can cut your expenses. Review your spending patterns carefully to see where the shortfalls occur. Could you rent videos instead of going to the movie theater every week? Could you take a bag lunch

FIGURE 3.6

A Budget Summary

You can prepare an annual budget summary to compare your actual spending with the amounts that you have budgeted. Completing an annual budget summary will be vital to both successful short-term money management and long-term financial security.

1 *To begin, make a clean copy of your monthly budget.*

2 *Next, record your actual expenses in each category over a period of several months.*

to school instead of buying cafeteria food? Perhaps you don't really need a car to get around. Doing without it might sometimes be inconvenient, but it certainly would be cheaper.

To decide which expenses to cut, it might help to take another look at your financial goals. Which purchases fit into your overall plan for the future? The answer can help you in deciding what to cut. How quickly are you progressing toward your objectives? Are your goals changing? Maybe your goals are outdated. In that case, revise your goals to meet your needs.

How to Budget Successfully

Simply preparing a budget will not solve your financial problems, nor will keeping track of every expense down to the last penny. You have to take care to follow a practical spending plan to make it work.

Money management experts agree that a budget should have several important characteristics. First, a good budget is carefully planned. Your estimates cannot be wild guesses, and your spending categories must cover all expenses. Second, a good budget is practical. If your first full-time job pays you $1,500 a month, don't expect to buy a sports car anytime soon.

Third, a good budget is flexible. Throughout your life, you will encounter unexpected expenses and probably unexpected shifts in

3 *Highlight areas where your spending consistently goes over your budget. Also highlight areas for which you have spent less than you budgeted. This will help you to see where you might have to make changes in your budget.*

*I*f you were a teenager living in Israel, you might be a kibbutznik. A kibbutznik is a volunteer who lives, works, and shares common property in a communal settlement known as a kibbutz. Called the nation's conscience, kibbutzniks work without pay for the good of the country. In return all their needs are met by the kibbutz, from food to medical care. In some settlements jobs rotate. On any given day you might plant crops, tend the settlement's children, or wait tables in a trendy restaurant. Although farming once provided the major income for the kibbutz, today tourism, high-tech industries, and small businesses have become the economic focus. Here's a snapshot of Israel.

Geographic area	8,019 sq. mi.
Population	6,135,000
Capital	Jerusalem (pop. 702,000)
Language	Hebrew, Arabic, English
Currency	new shekel
Gross domestic product (GDP)	$96.7 billion
Per capita GDP	$17,500
Economy	Industry: food processing, diamond cutting and polishing, textiles and apparel, chemicals. Agriculture: citrus and other fruits, vegetables, beef, poultry. Exports: machinery and equipment, cut diamonds, chemicals, textiles, and apparel.

A kibbutznik working on a farm

Thinking Critically

Evaluate What do you think would be some of the positive aspects of living on a kibbutz? What would be some of the drawbacks?

 For more information on Israel visit finance.glencoe.com or your local library.

income as well. Your budget needs to be easy to revise when changes like these occur. Finally, a good budget must be written and easily accessible. Use a notebook, folder, or computer to store your budget, but don't try to keep the information in your head or on loose scraps of paper—the odds are you will forget or lose the information.

Ways to Increase Your Savings

Increasing your savings is the key to establishing a sound financial future. The more you save, the better you'll be able to handle unexpected emergencies and the sooner you'll be able to meet your financial goals. If you save large amounts, it may be possible for you to retire comfortably and to send your children to college. Best of all, money that is saved earns interest income.

However, learning to save is not easy. Many Americans are often tempted to buy whatever they want, whenever they want it. Moreover, when your income is low, saving anything at all can be especially hard. According to January 1999 figures released by the U.S. Department of Commerce, Americans save less than a penny for every ten dollars they earn. Fortunately, you can improve your savings rate by using several savings strategies.

One method you can adopt is to set aside a fixed amount as savings before you sit down to pay your bills. Tyronne, for instance, considers his savings as a fixed expense. He writes himself a check for $75 before he pays his bills; then he sends the check for immediate deposit into his savings account. Tyronne has set a specific dollar amount, but you can also set aside a percentage of your monthly income.

Your employer may offer a similar option called a payroll savings deduction. A payroll savings deduction is a portion of your earnings that is automatically taken out of your paycheck and put into your savings or retirement account. Teresa has authorized her employer to deduct $50 from each paycheck. Although that arrangement reduces her take-home pay to $750, she can rest assured that she's on her way to meeting her financial goals.

Pay or Save?

Be a smart consumer and pay off your credit card bills first. The interest rate charged on credit cards is usually higher than the interest you can earn from your savings account.

SAVE Bringing your lunch to school or work is one way to spend less money than you would eating out. *On an average day, how much money do you spend on food? How might you save in this area?*

Your Financial Portfolio

What's Your Net Worth?

Roberto plans to go to Europe next summer with the school band. He probably will be able to save enough money by working all year at his part-time job. However, he's prepared to sell some of his possessions if he needs to, so he made a list of his assets and liabilities to determine his net worth.

Roberto's Balance Sheet

Assets

Checking account balance	$ 150
Savings accounts	635
Savings bonds	600

Personal Possessions

Market value of automobile	$2,300
Stereo, TV, and video equipment	1,600
Computer	1,350
Watch	330
Total Assets	**$6,965**

Liabilities

Balance due on car loan	$1,527
Total Liabilities	**1,527**
Net worth (assets – liabilities)	**$5,438**

Calculate Determine your net worth. In your workbook or on a separate sheet of paper, list all your assets, personal possessions, and liabilities (what you owe). Are you surprised that your net worth is as much (or as little) as it is? How much would you like your net worth to be in ten years? When you retire?

A third way is to start small. Make an effort to spend less each day. If you read a magazine in the library, count out the purchase price of the magazine and place it in a jar. If you go to the $4.50 matinee movie instead of the $7.75 evening show, pat yourself on the back and pay the jar the $3.25 difference. You can also put your spare coins, and even an occasional bill, into the jar. Before long you'll have enough cash to start up a savings account or make a substantial deposit into an existing one.

How you save, though, is less important than the action of saving. The earlier you start, the better. Even small amounts of savings can grow faster than most people realize. These savings can help you reach your financial goals.

SECTION 3.3   ASSESSMENT

CHECK YOUR UNDERSTANDING

1. What are some practical ways to budget for variable expenses?
2. If you continually experience budget deficits, how can you decide which expenses to cut?
3. Name three methods you might use to increase your savings.

THINK CRITICALLY

4. List three of your variable expenses. Estimate the amounts for each of these expenses for one month.

USING COMMUNICATION SKILLS

5. **No Cuts!** Tara complains that she just can't seem to get ahead financially. Every time she receives a paycheck, it seems to disappear. All her expenses, she adds, are absolutely necessary.
   Explain Alternatives Persuade Tara that cutting some of her expenses is not only possible but also critical if she wants to meet her financial goals.

SOLVING MONEY PROBLEMS

6. **Budgets** Hiroko earns $2,000 a month. Her monthly expenses are about $1,850, leaving $150 for savings. She now has $1,000 in her emergency savings account and another $300 in an account for a new computer. Hiroko has been offered a job that will pay her an extra $200 a month, but she will need to buy a car to travel to the new job.
   Analyze What financial factors should Hiroko consider as she decides whether to accept the job?

CHAPTER 3 ASSESSMENT

CHAPTER SUMMARY

- Organizing your financial documents can help you achieve your money management goals.

- Balance sheets and cash flow statements are two personal financial documents that show where your money comes from and where it goes.

- Personal financial statements enable you to analyze your current financial situation.

- By preparing a practical budget, you will learn how to live within your income and how to spend your money wisely.

- Increasing your savings will help you meet your financial goals.

Understanding and Using Vocabulary

Write eight to ten sentences, using as many of these terms as possible. Then rewrite the sentences, leaving a blank line in place of the key word or words. Working with a partner, see how many of each other's sentences you can complete correctly.

money management
safe-deposit box
personal financial
   statements
balance sheet
net worth
assets
liquid assets
real estate
market value
liabilities

insolvency
cash flow
income
take-home pay
discretionary income
surplus
deficit
budget
consumer price index
   (CPI)
budget variance

Review Key Concepts

1. Explain the difference between fixed and variable expenses.
2. Name the main places to store and organize financial documents.
3. What are the four types of assets a person can own?
4. What are the seven steps in preparing a budget?
5. Explain the difference between a surplus and a deficit.

Apply Key Concepts

1. Suppose that your actual variable expenses for a particular month are almost double what you had anticipated. Predict how this might affect your budget.
2. Write down two ways in which you might use a computer to manage your financial documents.

CHAPTER 3 ASSESSMENT

3. Argue for or against this statement: People with a large amount of assets also have many liabilities.
4. Which step in budgeting do you think is the most difficult? Explain your answer.
5. How might popular culture encourage people to have cash flow deficits?

 ## Problem Solving Today

SAVING FOR THE SENIOR TRIP

Suppose that the senior class is offering a trip to Florida that costs $600 per student. You plan to save the money for the trip over the next five months. Your variable expenses (clothes, CDs, gas, and DVD rentals) average $290 each month, and your fixed expenses (car insurance, piano lessons, monthly payment for new speakers) are $210. You have a part-time job teaching elementary school students to use computers. That job pays you $18 an hour, but you can only work 20 hours a month. You also have a job at a deli, where you earn $7 an hour and can work as many hours as you want.

Compute 1) How many hours per month will you have to work at the deli to save the money for the school trip? 2) Review your budgeted expenses to see how you might reduce the number of hours you have to work at the deli. 3) Describe how you approached the problem.

Computer Activity As an alternative activity, use a spreadsheet program to draw up your personal budget and calculate your expected earnings. Prepare a savings plan to achieve your goals. Revise your budget if necessary.

Real-World Application

CONNECT WITH SOCIAL STUDIES

In this chapter, you learned that Americans tend to have a very low savings rate. Do the citizens of other industrialized nations have better money management habits than Americans do?

Conduct Research Using the Internet and your public library, choose an industrialized country and investigate the spending and saving habits of its citizens. If they have better money management skills, suggest how Americans can adopt some of their techniques.

BUDGETING FOR COLLEGE

You plan to attend college next year. Your parents would like to determine which institution is better suited to the family budget, and they need some advice about how to get started.

Connect Using several search engines, look for information about budgeting for a college education. Then answer the following:

1. Name the general categories of expenses a college student will have?
2. How is the cost of college affected if you are a resident of the state in which the school is located?
3. What financial programs might colleges offer to help families budget for the cost of education?

CHAPTER 4

Consumer Purchasing Strategies and Legal Protection

STANDARD & POOR'S

Q&A

Q: I love to shop at the mall. It's close to my house and all my friends hang out there. Is it really that important to comparison shop? It's easier to just go to one place and buy what I need.

A: Prices and quality can be very different from one store to another. If your favorite mall has several department stores, compare prices on similar items to see if one has a lower price than the others. On expensive items it's definitely worth it to check prices at other stores. If you write down the manufacturer and style information, you can do this legwork by phone.

Consumer Purchasing

ikko and his friends love to watch and analyze movies. Every Friday night they go to a theater, where they each spend a total of about $13 on tickets, popcorn, and soda. In 1998 the 30.9 million teens in the United States spent $141 billion on goods and services.

No matter what your age, income, or household situation, whenever you buy anything, you are a consumer. Your buying decisions will depend on many influences in your life. For Nikko and his friends, an interest in entertainment—movies in particular—plays a big part in how they spend their money.

Factors that Influence Buying Decisions

You may enjoy shopping and do it often, or maybe you don't go to the mall until you need to buy something. In either case, wise buying decisions will help you get the most out of the products and services you buy now as well as enable you to meet your long-term financial goals. To get the most for your money, you need to recognize the elements that affect your buying habits. **Figure 4.1** shows some of the economic, social, and personal factors that influence the purchases you make.

The following example shows several of these factors at work. Fran is thinking about buying a new backpack. Economic factors will play an important role in her decision. She'll be more likely to spend her money on a backpack that seems well made, is not too expensive, and can be repaired easily if it rips. Social factors may also affect Fran's choice. She may be more likely to buy a certain brand if it's in style and if she could use it for her hobby—painting. In addition, personal factors may be at work. Fran will have to determine how much of her income will be used to pay for the backpack.

In order to make the most of your buying power, you'll also have to consider trade-offs. Suppose that you buy a stereo with a credit

What You'll Learn

- How to **determine** the factors that influence your buying decisions
- How to **use** a research-based approach to buying goods and services
- How to **apply** strategies to make wise buying decisions

Why It's Important

If you understand the factors that influence your buying decisions and recognize the choices that are available to you, you will be more likely to buy quality products and get the best value you can for your money.

KEY TERMS

- **down payment**
- **cooperative**
- **impulse buying**
- **open dating**
- **unit pricing**
- **rebate**
- **warranty**
- **service contract**

Figure 4.1

Influences on Consumer Buying Decisions

Economic Factors

Prices
Interest rates
Product quality
Supply and demand
Convenience
Product safety
Brand name
Maintenance costs
Warranty

Social Factors

Lifestyle
Interests
Hobbies
Friends
Culture
Advertisements
Media (magazines, radio,
television, newspapers)

Personal Factors

Gender
Age
Occupation
Income
Education
Family size
Geographic region
Ethnic background
Religion

MAKING A DIFFERENCE Economic, social, and personal factors influence consumer buying decisions. *How might a family's size and income affect the type of house that they buy?*

card instead of waiting until you've saved enough money to pay cash for it. You get the pleasure of having the stereo now. However, you may pay a higher price in the long run because of fees and interest the credit card company charges for use of the card.

Perhaps you choose a jacket because it's the cheapest one available. Within a few days, you may discover that it's poorly made or difficult to repair. You may save time by ordering a sweater from a catalog or online. However, if you decide that you don't want it for any reason, you may have to pay postage to return it to the company. You probably won't get your money back for the initial shipping and handling charges. By keeping in mind that buying decisions always involve trade-offs, you'll be better prepared to make wise choices.

Consumer Purchasing: A Research-Based Approach

Taking time to do research and evaluate items you want to buy will enable you to get more value for your money. Following a research-based approach to buying goods and services can help you buy a high-priced item, such as a treadmill or a gym membership, more intelligently. In addition, it will give you useful practice in making ordinary purchasing decisions about low-cost items, such as toothpaste. A research-based approach to buying has four phases.

Phase 1   Before You Shop

Before you can begin to construct the walls of a house, you need to lay its foundation. In the same way, before you begin to shop, you need to do some background work. A good start to successful shopping involves three steps: identifying your needs, gathering information, and becoming aware of the marketplace. Completing these steps will enable you to get what you really want.

IDENTIFYING YOUR NEEDS   Suppose that your VeryKool jeans are worn out, and you would like to buy a new pair. You think that your problem is a "need for a new pair of VeryKool jeans," when the actual problem is a "need for new jeans." Some people always buy Brand A when Brand B sells for the same price. They may not even consider Brand C, which is cheaper than either A or B and could also serve their needs. If you define your needs clearly, you'll be more likely to make the best buying decisions.

GATHERING INFORMATION   Suppose that Sarah loses her watch on a white-water rafting trip. She might be able to borrow a watch from a friend for a day or two, but eventually she'll need to buy a new watch. To begin her search, she should gather information on the different models and prices of watches.

Information for buying decisions usually falls into three categories: costs, options, and consequences. Sarah might consider questions related to cost, such as "What do watches cost at various locations?" Her options will depend on the brands that the manufacturers produce and on where those brands are available. Sarah will also have to consider consequences—in this case, how the purchase of a new watch might affect her financial situation.

Some people don't spend enough time gathering and evaluating information. Others do so much research that they become confused and frustrated. Simple, routine purchases probably don't require much more research than your own experience can provide. For more expensive items, it's worthwhile to talk to people you know.

CONNECT

Have you ever purchased a big-ticket item, such as a stereo or a car? What research did you do before you purchased the item?

IDENTIFYING NEEDS It's important to identify your real needs before making a buying decision. For example, taking public transportation to school or work may be a better financial option than buying a car. *What are some questions you might ask yourself to help identify your real needs?*

Other resources include product advertising and labeling, media-sources, consumer publications such as *Consumer Reports*, government agencies, or the Internet. **Figure 4.2** illustrates some of these resources. As you research and gather information, take notes on what you learn. Keeping a written record of the information you collect can be helpful in making comparisons later.

BECOMING AWARE OF THE MARKETPLACE Knowledge is power. Once you have done research, you'll be aware of sources of the item you want to buy. In addition, you'll be able to identify the brands and features from which you can choose, average prices for the item, and where you can obtain reliable information about similar products.

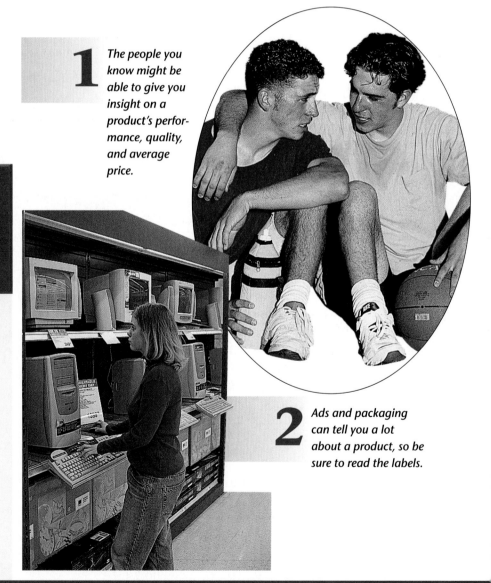

FIGURE 4.2

Sources of Consumer Information

You can gather information to help with purchasing decisions from a number of different sources. Just remember to make sure that they're reliable, complete, relevant, and impartial.

1 The people you know might be able to give you insight on a product's performance, quality, and average price.

2 Ads and packaging can tell you a lot about a product, so be sure to read the labels.

As you gain more knowledge about the marketplace, it's wise to become familiar with some of the common myths that consumers believe about sales, returns, and credit. **Figure 4.3** describes some common myths.

Phase 2 Weighing the Alternatives

Every consumer decision may be approached in several acceptable ways. Instead of buying an item, for example, you might decide to rent it, borrow it, or do without it. You also have alternatives to spending cash for a product. You might take advantage of special deals that allow you to delay payment, or you might choose to pay with a credit card.

3 *Reports issued by the media and independent testing organizations on the quality of products and services are usually valuable, easily available, and inexpensive.*

4 *Most companies, magazines, newspapers, consumer organizations, and government agencies have Web sites with product information and shopping suggestions.*

Figure 4.3

Common Consumer Myths

The National Association of Consumer Agency Administrators recently identified a list of common consumer myths. These include:

"I can return my car within three days of purchase." While many people would say that this statement is true, there is no such time period.

"It says right here that I've won; it must be true." Fake prize notifications continue to become more convincing. Some consumers actually go to company offices to try to pick up their prizes.

"If I lose my credit cards, I'm liable for purchases." Federal laws limit charges on lost or stolen cards to $50. Most major credit card companies will not even charge you the $50 if you make a reasonable effort to notify the company quickly of lost or stolen cards.

"An auto lease is just like a rental; if I have problems with the car or problems paying, I can just bring it back." Most leases require payments for the duration of the contract. Early termination of the contract can often result in various additional charges.

"You can't repossess my car; it's on private property." While state laws vary, the general rule is that repossession cannot occur if it involves force or entry into a dwelling. However, vehicles in driveways and unlocked garages are usually fair game.

Source: "Ten Top Consumer Law 'Urban Myths,'" National Association of Consumer Agency Administrators, 1010 Vermont Avenue NW, #514, Washington DC 20005; (202) 347-7395; Web site: www.nacaanet.org.

FACT OR FICTION? These are some typical myths that consumers believe about sales, returns, and credit. *How can such myths affect you as a consumer?*

DECIDE WHAT'S IMPORTANT TO YOU   As Sarah considers the selection of watches in a department store, she decides that a light-up dial and an alarm are two features that she would use. In terms of performance, she prefers a model that can withstand rugged outdoor activities. She wants a watch that has big numbers and a stainless steel wristband.

As you evaluate alternatives, decide which characteristics of the product—such as features, performance, or design—are important to you. As you research the available brands, you'll recognize the characteristics that most closely match your needs. You can judge a potential purchase on the basis of the following factors: your personal values, available time for research, the amount of money you have to spend, the convenience of buying the item immediately, and the pros and cons of a particular brand.

COMPARE PRICES   The price of an item is an important consideration. Prices can vary for all types of products. For example, Sarah's watch may cost as little as $15 or as much as $500.

Differences in price may be related to quality, but price does not always equal quality. When the quality and quantity are basically the same—as in items such as aspirin, sugar, or salt—the lowest price is likely to be the wisest choice.

When prices and quality vary, you have two options. If you can afford all choices, you can buy the highest-quality item. If you can't afford all choices, you should consider buying the item that gives you the best value per dollar that you spend.

DO SOME COMPARISON SHOPPING Comparison shopping involves comparing prices and features of similar items at different stores. Many people consider comparison shopping a waste of time. However, it can be very useful when:

- you're buying complex or expensive items, such as a computer or a mountain bike;
- you're buying items you purchase often, such as shampoo or school supplies;
- you can comparison shop easily, perhaps using the Internet, advertisements, or mail-order catalogs;
- different sellers offer different prices and services;
- product quality or price varies greatly.

Phase 3   Making the Purchase

After you've completed the research and evaluation process, some other activities and decisions may be appropriate. These include negotiating the price (if possible), deciding whether to use cash or credit, and determining the real price of the product.

CAN YOU NEGOTIATE THE PRICE? Certain purchases, such as real estate or cars, may involve price negotiation. To negotiate, you'll need as much information as possible about the product and the buying situation. You must also make sure that you're dealing with a person, such as the owner or store manager, who has authority to give you a lower price or additional features.

SHOULD YOU USE CASH OR CREDIT? When making a purchase, you generally have two options—pay cash or use credit. In deciding which of these payment methods to use, you need to consider the costs and benefits of each one.

Credit is an arrangement to buy something now and pay for it later. It's a type of loan. To repay the loan, you'll have to make monthly payments that often include additional fees. The advantage of paying cash is that you don't have to pay these extra fees or make continuing payments. However, because the money is no longer in your bank account, you lose the opportunity to earn interest on it. Moreover, the money is no longer available for emergencies.

Before deciding to use credit, you need to evaluate its various costs, such as interest rates and fees. These costs will differ depending on:

- the source of the loan (for example, your parents, a bank, a credit card company);

What's Your Financial ID?

ARE YOU A SMART SHOPPER?

With so many places to shop and a wide variety of products to buy, it takes skills and practice to get the most from your money. On a separate sheet of paper, test your shopping know-how.

1. When I want something, I
   a. Go to the nearest store that has it and buy it. (1 point)
   b. Locate where I can buy it at the lowest cost today and buy it. (2 points)
   c. Wait for the item to go on sale. (3 points)

2. I like to
   a. Buy what looks good to me at the time. (1 point)
   b. Look at consumer guides to help me choose the best buy. (2 points)
   c. Compare all the brands and decide which offers the most value. (3 points)

3. When buying an item in the drugstore, I
   a. Always buy name brands. (1 point)
   b. Always buy generic brands. (2 points)
   c. Calculate the best price per weight or unit and buy accordingly. (3 points)

4. When shopping for clothes, I
   a. Buy what strikes my fancy. (1 point)
   b. Only buy what's on sale. (2 points)
   c. Only buy what I know I will wear. (3 points)

5. I use coupons whenever I can.
   a. Never (1 point)
   b. Sometimes (2 points)
   c. Always (3 points)

6. When eating out, I
   a. Order what I want, regardless of cost. (1 point)
   b. Sometimes am more concerned about cost but sometimes order expensive dishes. (2 points)
   c. Always look at prices and order accordingly. (3 points)

7. Whenever I can, I borrow books and videos from the library.
   a. Never (1 point)
   b. Sometimes (2 points)
   c. Always (3 points)

8. When buying CDs or videos, I
   a. Get what I want as soon as it comes out. (1 point)
   b. Try to wait for a sale but get what I want if I really want it. (2 points)
   c. Wait for a sale. (3 points)

If you scored:

21–24: You're a smart shopper. However, be sure you treat yourself occasionally, too.

16–20: You sometimes make choices that cost more, but you're usually aware of them.

Less than 16: Try to practice a few more smart shopping skills and see how much you save.

- the type of credit account;
- the payment period;
- the amount of the down payment. The **down payment** is a portion of the total cost of an item that must be paid at the time of purchase.

DO YOU KNOW WHAT THE REAL PRICE IS? Sometimes you may discover that what appears to be a bargain is not such a good deal after extra costs are added to the price. Stores may charge you a fee for such services as installation or delivery. To protect yourself, find out exactly what the purchase price includes, and get all costs and conditions in writing.

Phase 4 ## After the Purchase

After making a purchase, you may have other costs or tasks. A car, for example, will require additional maintenance and ownership costs, such as gasoline and insurance. You may have to learn how to use it correctly to improve its performance and minimize the need for major repairs. If your car requires repair service, you should follow a process similar to the one you used in making the original purchase—investigate, evaluate, and negotiate a variety of servicing options.

In some cases, you may be dissatisfied with a purchase and want to return or replace it. When that happens, you need to know how to handle your complaints effectively. The next section of this chapter explains how to resolve consumer complaints.

Finally, remember that the purchasing process is an ongoing activity. You'll continually need to rethink and reevaluate your decisions. The information that you gather before you shop as well as your previous buying experiences will help you make decisions in the future. Also, be sure to consider changes in your lifestyle, values, goals, and financial resources. These changes make every purchasing decision a new experience with different alternatives and opportunity costs.

Smart Buying Strategies

People have a variety of buying styles. Gordon looks for ways to save on the brands he regularly buys. Anita and Roger buy the lowest-priced brands or look for the best bargains. Whatever your style, several strategies can help you get the most value for your dollar.

BEST BUYS Timing your purchases to get the best buys is not limited to clothes. *Why do you think that September, October, and November are the best months to buy apples?*

Figure 4.4

Types of Retailers

	Benefits	Limitations
Traditional Stores		
Department stores	Wide variety of products grouped by department	Possible inexperience or limited knowledge of sales staff
Specialty stores	Wide selection of a specific product line; knowledgeable sales staff	Prices generally higher; location and shopping hours may not be convenient
Discount stores	Convenient parking; low prices	Self-service format; minimal assistance from sales staff
Contemporary Retailers		
Convenience stores	Convenient location; long hours; fast service	Prices generally higher than those of other types
Factory outlet	Brand-name items; low prices	May offer only "seconds" or "irregulars"; few services; returns may not be allowed
Hypermarket	Full supermarket combined with general merchandise discount store	Clerks not likely to offer specialized service or product information
Warehouse, Superstore	Large quantities of items at discount prices	May require membership fee; limited services; inventory items may vary

SHOP AROUND Consumers have a choice of many different types of stores, each of which has pros and cons. *How can competition among stores benefit consumers?*

Timing Purchases

Whether you're looking for a coat or a swimsuit, you're more likely to find a bargain at certain times of the year. Stores traditionally offer reduced prices for seasonal clothing and other items about midway through a particular season. You can also find reduced prices at "back-to-school" sales, "white" sales, and other special sales. Timing your purchases to take advantage of sales can result in big savings.

In recent years competition to attract consumers has become more intense. As a result, some stores now offer discounts and sales throughout the year.

The law of supply and demand can also affect the timing of purchases. For example, if you wait a few months before buying a popular new CD or video, the price may be lower than it was when it first came out because the demand for the item has decreased. When businesses want to reduce the supply of a product, they often feature clearance sales. Clearance sales—which offer low prices to clear, or get rid of, excess stock—are ideal opportunities to buy items you use regularly.

Selecting the Store

The quality and variety of goods at a store may influence your decision to shop there. You may also choose a store because of its hours, location, prices, reputation, policies, and services such as parking and delivery. **Figure 4.4** provides an overview of the major types of retailers—businesses that sell directly to consumers.

Over the years, several alternatives to store shopping have emerged. One of these is the *cooperative*, a nonprofit organization owned and operated by its members for the purpose of saving money on the purchase of goods and services. Because a cooperative buys large amounts, it's able to lower costs for its members. The main drawback to cooperatives is that they offer few customer services.

Another alternative to store shopping is direct selling, which includes mail order, TV home shopping, and online shopping. An advantage of shopping this way is the convenience of not having to leave home. Online shopping sometimes offers lower prices, and you may find excellent product information on the Internet. The possible disadvantages of direct selling are paying for shipping and handling, and difficulty in returning purchases and receiving refunds.

Comparing Brands

Most items are sold under a number of well-known brand names that identify the products and their manufacturers. National-brand

DON'T LEAVE HOME Mail order, telephone sales, TV home shopping, and the Internet have made it possible for consumers to get many of the products they want without setting foot in a traditional store. *What are the advantages of this shopping option?*

Chapter 4 *Consumer Purchasing Strategies and Legal Protection* ▒▒ 99

products are widely advertised and available in many stores. Although they are usually more expensive than nonbrand products, national brands usually offer consistent quality.

A store-brand product is usually sold by one chain of stores and carries the name of that chain on its label. Examples of these products include paper and canned goods and dairy foods. Because store-brand products are often made by the same companies that make national-brand. products, the quality is high. However, because they don't carry a brand-name label, they're often cheaper.

When comparing brands, remember to consider price and quality. You should also be sure to plan what you're going to buy before you shop, and take a list of what you need. Displays may attract your attention and lead to *impulse buying*—purchasing items on the spur of the moment. Impulse buying may be fun, but it often ends up costing you more than you had planned or expected. Also, you often end up buying products that you don't really need.

Label Information

Labels on product packages typically contain a great deal of advertising. However, federal laws also require some labels to include factual information. Food labels, for example, must indicate the common name of the product, the name and address of the manufacturer or distributor, the net weight of the product, and a list of the ingredients in decreasing order of weight.

In addition, labels on almost all processed foods must have nutrition information, such as the number of calories in one serving and the specific amounts of nutrients and food substances in the product. Some foods are advertised as being "low in fat" or "light," "low in sodium," or "high in fiber." Foods must meet government criteria to be labeled with such terms. Some labels describe benefits that a food, or a nutrient in it, provides. Manufacturers can include such health claims on product packages only if they have scientific evidence to support the claims.

To help consumers determine the freshness of some foods, manufacturers print dates on the labels. *Open dating* indicates the freshness or "shelf life" of a perishable product, such as milk or bread. Labels indicate open dating with phrases such as "Use before May 2001" or "Not to be sold after October 8."

Product labels for appliances, such as refrigerators, air conditioners, washing machines, and dryers, include information about operating costs, which can help you select the most energy-efficient models.

NUTRITION FACTS Some food labels claim that the product is "low in fat" or "light." Foods must meet government criteria to be labeled with such terms. *Why do you think this type of regulation is necessary?*

Comparing Prices

Claudia went to the drugstore to buy a bottle of mouthwash and noticed that her favorite brand is offered in two sizes at different prices. The best way for her to determine which one is the better buy is to use unit pricing. **Unit pricing** is the use of a standard unit of measurement to compare the prices of packages that are different sizes. Most grocery stores and drugstores provide the unit pricing information for the products they sell. If a store does not provide this information, you can calculate the unit price by dividing the price of the item by the unit of measurement (weight, volume, or quantity). For example, an 8-ounce can of frozen orange juice that costs $1.60 has a unit price of 20 cents per ounce.

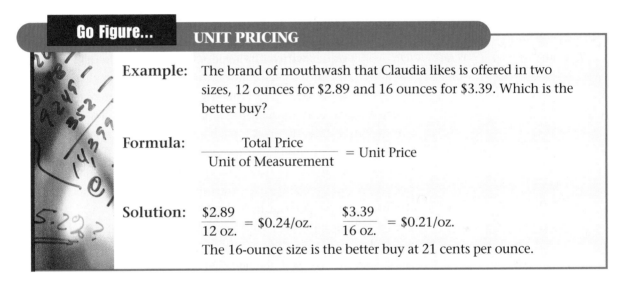

Go Figure...   **UNIT PRICING**

Example: The brand of mouthwash that Claudia likes is offered in two sizes, 12 ounces for $2.89 and 16 ounces for $3.39. Which is the better buy?

Formula:
$$\frac{\text{Total Price}}{\text{Unit of Measurement}} = \text{Unit Price}$$

Solution:
$$\frac{\$2.89}{12 \text{ oz.}} = \$0.24/\text{oz.} \qquad \frac{\$3.39}{16 \text{ oz.}} = \$0.21/\text{oz.}$$
The 16-ounce size is the better buy at 21 cents per ounce.

Once you know how to calculate the unit price, you can compare the unit prices for various sizes, brands, and stores. Keep in mind that the package with the lowest unit price may not be the best buy for your situation. For example, a 10-pound bag of potatoes might have the lowest unit price, but if you don't eat potatoes often, they may spoil before you can use them.

Two common ways to save money are to take advantage of discount coupons and manufacturers' rebates. By using discount coupons, you save money on products at the time you purchase them. A **rebate** is a partial refund of the price of a product. To obtain a rebate, you usually have to submit a form, the original receipt, and the package's UPC symbol, or bar code.

When comparing prices, the following guidelines can be very helpful:

Too much impulse buying can ruin anyone's budget. When you're tempted to buy clothes, CDs, or anything else that you really don't need, give yourself a two-day cool-down period. If you decide you really want it, you can go back to the store and buy it. Chances are, though, that most things won't seem as necessary to have a few days later.

- More convenience (location, hours, sales staff) usually means higher prices.
- Ready-to-use products (frozen prepared dinners, preassembled toys) usually have higher prices.
- Large packages are usually the best buy, although you'll need to use unit pricing to compare brands, sizes, and stores.
- "Sale" may not always mean that you save money; the sale price at one store may be higher than the regular price at another store.

Evaluating Warranties

Many products come with a guarantee of quality called a warranty. A *warranty* is a written guarantee from the manufacturer or distributor that states the conditions under which the product can be returned, replaced, or repaired. Federal law requires sellers of products that cost more than $15 (and that have a warranty) to make the warranty available to customers before purchase. The warranty is often printed directly on the package.

Warranties are divided into two basic types: implied and express. Implied warranties are unwritten guarantees that cover certain aspects of a product or its use. An implied warranty of merchantability, for example, guarantees that a product is fit for its intended use—a toaster will toast bread, or a CD player will play CDs.

Express warranties, which are usually written, come in two forms. A full warranty states that a defective product will be fixed or replaced at no charge during a reasonable amount of time. A limited warranty covers only certain aspects of the product—such as parts—or requires the buyer to pay a portion of the shipping or repair charges.

Warranties help to assure you that the products you buy meet certain standards and perform properly in normal conditions. However, they do not offer protection against regular wear and tear. They also do not protect you from poor buying decisions.

When you buy some products, you may be offered a *service contract*, a separately purchased agreement by the manufacturer or distributor to cover the costs of repairing the item. Service contracts are sometimes called extended warranties, but they aren't really warranties. You have to pay extra to obtain a service contract. Such contracts are generally offered on large, expensive items, such as cars and home appliances. The cost of such a contract can be quite high. Sometimes it's not worth the cost; it might be wiser to set aside money for needed repairs instead.

QUESTION

Rank the importance of a good warranty for the purchase of the following items: a CD player, a wool blazer, a baseball glove, a car. Explain your reasoning.

STANDARD &POOR'S

CASE STUDY

Francine Martin was working part-time and attending college full-time. She often ran short of money to pay all her bills, so she began charging everything, even her tuition and food. Within three years she was forced to declare bankruptcy. To get her finances back on track, Francine started working full-time. She needed a car, but because of her poor credit rating no one would loan her the money. She bought a car from "Norman's Used Cars—Pay By the Week." Although the car ran a little rough, it did come with a 90-day warranty. Unfortunately the car was in the shop for repairs more often than it was on the road. Francine made her payments each week, but the car was almost useless. After two months she decided to return it to Norman and ask for her money back. Norman refused, stating that the warranty did not provide for refunds. Francine is extremely angry. She doesn't know what to do, so she has turned to the experts at Standard & Poor's for advice.

Analysis: Investments in big-ticket items need to be made with care. Manufacturer's and dealer's warranties are a valuable part of the purchase and must be read carefully. Buying from reputable dealers and selecting brand name products will provide additional protection, as these companies value their good name. Francine's financial distress led her to buy a car from a dealer she would otherwise have avoided. Now she may be forced to take legal action to get relief.

Recommendation: Francine is right to recognize that her investment hasn't provided the value she sought. The terms of the warranty require that the dealer fix specific problems with the car. There may also be a lemon law in her state that would require the dealer to replace the car or refund the purchase price. Francine can start by consulting a legal professional familiar with the laws in her state. Consumer advocacy groups can often provide a referral to an attorney who will provide a consultation for little or no charge. At a minimum Francine should have the car checked by another dealer or garage and obtain a written estimate of repair costs. It's possible that the repairs will cost more than the car is worth. Francine can use this estimate to negotiate with Norman, either directly or in small claims court, to pay for the repairs or to refund some of the purchase price.

Critical Thinking Questions

1. What other choices might Francine have made rather than buying a car from Norman?
2. How might Francine have better protected herself when purchasing the car?
3. What might happen if Francine decides to sell the car to someone else?

Smart shoppers know when to buy, where to buy, what to buy, how much to pay, and how to make sure that the products they buy will perform as advertised. In the next section, you'll learn some additional rules for smart shoppers: how to resolve consumer complaints and how to use the law to ensure that your rights as a consumer are protected.

SECTION 4.1 ASSESSMENT

CHECK YOUR UNDERSTANDING

1. What are three economic factors that influence what people buy?
2. Suppose that you're considering buying a pair of in-line skates. What steps might you take before you shop and as you weigh your alternatives?
3. Identify and explain at least five strategies followed by smart shoppers.

THINK CRITICALLY

4. **Create** a scenario in which someone is considering a purchase. Discuss the economic, social, and personal factors that will play a role in this buying decision.

USING MATH SKILLS

5. **Cat Food Costs** Gilda would do anything for Midnight, her 11-year-old cat. Until recently, she's been paying an animal hospital $22.50 every 2 weeks for a 10-pound bag of vitamin-enriched organic cat food designed especially for older cats. On Wednesday, Gilda called a local pet store and discovered that it stocks a brand of cat food similar to the one she buys at the animal hospital, except that it's not organic. The pet store sells 25-pound bags of the food for $59.55 and 50-pound bags for $99.50.
   Calculate Using the formula for unit pricing, calculate the best buy among the three different-size bags of cat food. Would the lowest-priced cat food necessarily be the best choice for Gilda? Why or why not?

SOLVING MONEY PROBLEMS

6. **Getting the Best Buy** Marta loves shopping for holiday gifts for her friends and family. This year she's decided to start looking for gifts early, in June. She hopes that the extra time will allow her to find the perfect gift for everyone on her shopping list. Some of her friends have said that by shopping so early she might also get some good bargains.
   Apply Using the information in the section on smart buying strategies, explain how Marta can shop wisely to make the best choices for gifts and get good bargains.

Resolving Consumer Complaints

Sources of Common Consumer Complaints

When you purchase a product, you usually don't expect to have any problems with it, especially if you've done research and weighed the alternatives. Unfortunately, every purchase involves some degree of risk.

Most customer dissatisfaction results from products that are defective or of poor quality. Consumers also complain about unexpected costs, deceptive pricing, and poor repair service. Another source of consumer complaints is *fraud*—dishonest business practices that are meant to deceive, trick, or gain an unfair advantage.

CLINICAL STUDIES SHOW: FASTEST WEIGHT LOSS PROGRAM EVER

"I Lost 142 Pounds Fast! Eating 5 and 6 Meals a Day of All My Favorite Foods!!"

'This Is The Easiest Diet That I Had Ever Tried!"

YOU CAN EAT ALL YOU WANT
HESE GREAT FOODS WHILE
A WEIGHT DISAPPEARS:

)N, EGGS, ROAST PORK,
ST BEEF, SPARE RIBS,
:KEN, SHRIMP, LOBSTER
PPING IN BUTTER) AN
H MORE...

Users Have Lost Over 5 Million Pounds!"

Available at most nutrition centers and other fine stores

SHIPPED CONFIDENTIALLY

BEFORE
From a
54" Waist
to a
34" Waist   LARRY HALEPE

BEFORE
Lost
55 lbs.
and went
from Size

BUYER BEWARE Many advertisements appeal to the emotions of consumers. *How might this ad influence someone to buy the product?*

BACK TO THE STORE If you have a problem with a product or service and are going to attempt to resolve it, remember to document each step. *What types of records should you keep?*

Common Types of Fraud

Every year millions of consumers become victims of unethical people who use dishonest business practices to trick or cheat buyers. Experts estimate that fraud costs consumers tens of billions of dollars annually.

As a consumer, you must be aware of various types of fraud. Telephone and mail scams may offer you phony free prizes, travel packages, work-at-home schemes, and investment opportunities. Fraudulent diet products and other remedies attract consumers with phrases such as "scientific breakthrough" or "miraculous cure."

The best way to protect yourself from consumer fraud is to recognize it before you become a victim—and to report it if you see it happening.

Resolving Differences Between Buyers and Sellers

If you're dissatisfied with a product or service and decide to make a complaint, remember to document the process. Keep a file of receipts, names of people you talk to, dates of attempted repairs, copies of letters you wrote, and any fees that you have had to pay.

Resolving complaints with a business can usually be handled in five different ways.

Return to the Place of Purchase

Most consumers can resolve their complaints at the original location of the business transaction. Businesses generally care about their reputation for honesty and fairness and will do what's necessary to settle reasonable complaints. Remember to bring sales receipts and other relevant information. It's also best if you keep calm and avoid yelling or threatening the salespeople or managers. Explain the problem as clearly as possible, and ask them to help you resolve it.

Contact Company Headquarters

If you can't resolve your problem at the local store or business, contact the company headquarters. Sending a complaint letter like

INTERNATIONAL FINANCE   Canada

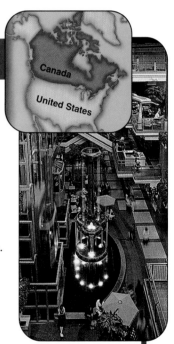

Canada

United States

*G*oing underground doesn't always mean hiding out. In Montréal, Canada's largest city, it means a trip to the Underground, a thriving social and commercial complex beneath the city's streets. In a region famous for frigid winters and howling winds, the Underground provides a climate-controlled environment with year-round entertainment. Each day tourists and locals drop in to shop at trendy boutiques and department stores, catch the latest movie, or simply hang out with friends in one of the many public squares. Connected by miles of walkways, this city under the city claims the largest protected pedestrian network in the world. It's said that you could wander here for days. Here's a snapshot of Canada.

Geographic area	3,849,670 sq. mi.
Population	30,589,000
Capital	Ottawa (pop. 314,000)
Language	English, French (both official)
Currency	dollar
Gross domestic product (GDP)	$658 billion
Per capita GDP	$21,700
Economy	Industry: minerals, food products, wood and paper products. Agriculture: wheat, barley, dairy products, forest products, commercial fisheries. Exports: newsprint, wood pulp, timber.

The Underground in Montréal

Thinking Critically

Analyze Why would the Montréal Underground be a good location for a business?

For more information on Canada visit finance.glencoe.com or your local library.

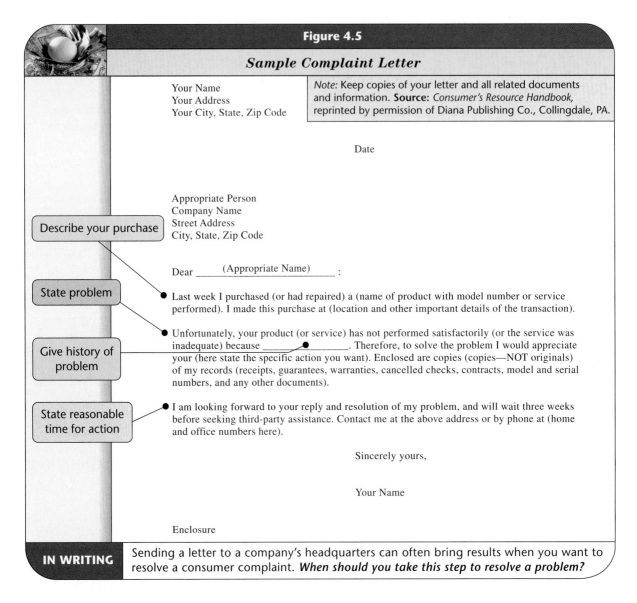

Figure 4.5

Sample Complaint Letter

Your Name
Your Address
Your City, State, Zip Code

Note: Keep copies of your letter and all related documents and information. **Source:** *Consumer's Resource Handbook,* reprinted by permission of Diana Publishing Co., Collingdale, PA.

Date

Describe your purchase

Appropriate Person
Company Name
Street Address
City, State, Zip Code

Dear _____ (Appropriate Name) _____ :

State problem

Last week I purchased (or had repaired) a (name of product with model number or service performed). I made this purchase at (location and other important details of the transaction).

Give history of problem

Unfortunately, your product (or service) has not performed satisfactorily (or the service was inadequate) because _____. Therefore, to solve the problem I would appreciate your (here state the specific action you want). Enclosed are copies (copies—NOT originals) of my records (receipts, guarantees, warranties, cancelled checks, contracts, model and serial numbers, and any other documents).

State reasonable time for action

I am looking forward to your reply and resolution of my problem, and will wait three weeks before seeking third-party assistance. Contact me at the above address or by phone at (home and office numbers here).

Sincerely yours,

Your Name

Enclosure

IN WRITING Sending a letter to a company's headquarters can often bring results when you want to resolve a consumer complaint. *When should you take this step to resolve a problem?*

the one shown in **Figure 4.5** often will be effective. To find a company's address, check the *Consumer's Resource Handbook*. Your library may have other useful references as well, and company Web sites are a good place to look, too. If you would rather talk to someone in the company's customer service department but don't know the telephone number, call 1-800-555-1212, the toll-free information number. Your library may also carry a directory of toll-free numbers. Some companies print their toll-free numbers on their packages.

Get Help from a Consumer Agency

If the company isn't providing the answers you seek, you can try to get help from various consumer, business, and government organizations. These include national organizations that deal with issues such as nutrition and automobile safety. Local organizations also handle complaints, do surveys, and provide legal assistance.

Among the best-known consumer agencies is the Better Business Bureau, a network of offices around the country sponsored by local business organizations. These bureaus deal with complaints against local merchants. However, the merchants are under no obligation to respond to those complaints. Therefore, the bureaus are most valuable before you buy a product. They can tell you about the experiences other consumers have had with a certain store or company.

A large network of local, state, and federal government agencies is also available. These agencies handle all sorts of problems, from false advertising to illegal business activities. One federal agency is the Food and Drug Administration, which sets safety standards for food, drugs, chemicals, cosmetics, and household and medical devices. The Consumer Product Safety Commission, another federal agency, helps protect consumers against unsafe products. If you don't know which consumer protection agency to choose, contact your U.S. representative in Washington, D.C.

Dispute Resolution

Dispute resolution programs offer another way to settle disagreements about a product or service. Working out a complaint may involve mediation. *Mediation* is the attempt by a neutral third party to resolve a conflict between a customer and a business through discussion and negotiation. A decision made in mediation is not legally binding. Sometimes manufacturers and industry organizations will turn to the arbitration process to resolve consumer complaints. *Arbitration* is a process where a conflict between a customer and a business is resolved by an impartial third party whose decision is legally binding.

Settling a dispute through one of these methods can be quicker, less expensive, and less stressful than going to court. To find out what programs are available in your area, contact local or state consumer protection agencies, state attorneys general, small claims courts, local chapters of the Better Business Bureau, trade associations, and local bar associations.

Take Legal Action

If none of these methods produces the results you want, you may choose to take legal action.

academic **c**onnection

LANGUAGE ARTS

Warranties should be written in clear language, but many consumers find them very difficult to understand. Sometimes the print is so small that people don't even try to read them. Find an example of a warranty on a big-ticket item you would like to purchase, such as a computer, VCR, or DVD player. Rewrite the warranty in your own words, then see if a classmate can easily read and understand it.

Legal Options for Consumers

Perhaps you've tried to settle your dispute by going to the place of business, contacting the company headquarters, or getting help from a consumer agency, but you're still unhappy with the outcome. Your final alternative is to turn to the law.

Small Claims Court

Every state has a system of courts to settle minor disagreements. A *small claims court* is a court that deals with legal disputes that involve amounts below a certain limit. The amount varies from state to state, ranging from about $500 to $10,000. Disputes that are brought to small claims courts usually do not involve juries or lawyers, so the cost of this type of legal action is relatively low. The decision of the judge is final.

Before you take a dispute to small claims court, visit the court and watch other cases to learn about court procedures. When you

PREDICT

What are some ways a consumer can use the legal system to resolve a dispute?

Careers in Finance

RETAIL SALES ASSOCIATE

If you're thinking of a job in retail sales, you could become a sales associate. Sales associates help customers with their purchases—from clothes to pet supplies. They can work in small, family-run stores or large chains. Sales associates answer customers' questions, deal with customers' problems, stock merchandise, handle money, run cash registers, and take inventory. Many work irregular hours and weekends and stand for long periods of time. Retail sales associates don't need a college degree. If you work hard, show sales ability, and are willing to take on more responsibility, you could be promoted to a manager or buyer.

Skills	Communication, computer, math, sales ability
Personality	Able to work under stress, detail oriented, honest, likes working with people, neat
Education	High school diploma; accounting, business, and marketing courses may help you advance into management.
Pay range	Minimum wage to $15 an hour, depending on experience and skill; sometimes includes commissions

Evaluate   What might be some of the advantages and disadvantages of working as a retail sales associate?

 For more information on a career as a retail sales associate visit finance.glencoe.com or your local library.

present your case, you should be calm and polite and stick to the point. You'll need to submit your own evidence, such as receipts, contracts, and photographs. You may use witnesses if you know people who can testify on your behalf and support your claim. The whole process usually takes only a few weeks. Generally, it's not difficult to get a judgment in your favor.

Class-Action Suits

Occasionally a number of people all have the same complaint. For example, several people may have been injured by a defective product or overcharged by a utility company. Such a group may qualify for a class-action suit. A *class-action suit* is a legal action on behalf of all the people who have suffered the same injustice. These people are called a "class" and are represented by one lawyer or a group of lawyers working together.

If a situation qualifies for a class-action suit, all affected parties must be notified of the suit. An individual may decide not to participate and file a separate lawsuit instead. If the court rules in favor of the class action, the money awarded is generally divided among all those involved or put into public funds for government use.

A MATTER FOR THE COURT To resolve a consumer complaint, it may sometimes be necessary to take your case to small claims court. *How is a small claims court different from a trial court?*

Hiring a Lawyer and other Legal Alternatives

If you don't want to go to small claims court or join in a class-action suit, you may seek the services of a lawyer. You might try to get a lawyer's name from someone you know. In addition, you can find the names of lawyers in newspapers, in the yellow pages of the phone book, or by calling a local branch of the American Bar Association (ABA), a professional organization of lawyers. It's important to make sure that the lawyer you choose has experience in handling your type of case. You should also ask about fees and payment policies. Lawyers can be expensive. You may decide that your problem is not worth spending a lot of time and money.

Perhaps the cost of lawyers and other legal services is too high for you. If so, you may seek help from a *legal aid society*, one of a network of community law offices that provide free or low-cost legal assistance. Supported by public funds, these offices provide a variety of legal services. Not everyone is eligible for help from a legal aid society. Your income must fall below a certain amount, which varies from state to state.

Your Budget

David wants a $2,500 laptop computer. At his part-time job at Computer Warehouse, he earns $7 an hour and works an average of 16 hours a week. For 10 weeks in the summer he works 40 hours a week. He also makes money on the side by setting up and troubleshooting computers. By keeping track of his expenses he has figured his monthly budget.

Budgeting for Spending Bucks

Income:		Average Monthly Income
	Monthly take-home pay from Computer Warehouse	$502.50
	Income from setting up and troubleshooting computers	50.00
	Other income	20.00
	Total Income	**$572.50**

Expenses:		Average Monthly Expenses
	Fixed Expenses	
	Online services	$ 20.00
	Car loan and insurance	135.00
	Variable Expenses	
	Entertainment and personal	90.00
	Gifts and contributions	25.00
	Total Expenses	**$270.00**

(Total Income − Total Expenses = Savings)
($572.50 − 270.00 = $302.50)
David can save $302.50 a month.

If David sticks to his budget, in a year's time he can save $3,630. ($302.50 × 12 = $3,630.00) That would be more than enough to buy the computer he wants.

Calculate What is your budget? A budget can help you see where you are spending your money and assist you in determining how long it will take to save for a special purchase.

In your workbook or on a separate sheet of paper, calculate your income and expenses for one month. How much can you save in one month? What is the cost of your desired purchase? How long will it take you to save for what you want?

Many tools are available to protect your rights. They will not be valuable, however, unless you use them. You'll be less likely to encounter consumer problems if you do business only with companies that have a good reputation, avoid signing contracts and other documents you don't understand, and watch out for offers that seem too good to be true.

SECTION 4.2 ASSESSMENT

CHECK YOUR UNDERSTANDING

1. What are some basic things you should do when trying to resolve a difference with a business?
2. Identify the five methods of resolving consumer complaints.
3. What are some of the advantages and disadvantages of taking a consumer dispute to small claims court?

THINK CRITICALLY

4. Write a brief paragraph describing a product or service with which you were dissatisfied, and explain what the problem was. Did you complain? If so, what specific steps did you take, and what was the outcome?

USING COMMUNICATION SKILLS

5. **Too Good to Be True?** You recently received a letter offering a four-day vacation trip to the Bahamas for only $350. According to the letter, the price includes transportation, a hotel room, and all meals. To take advantage of the offer and reserve a space, you must send a check for half the cost—$175—within ten days. The offer sounds too good to be true, and you suspect that it's a fraud.
   Roundtable Discussion With your classmates, brainstorm various types of fraud. Discuss ways to avoid becoming a victim of fraud.

SOLVING MONEY PROBLEMS

6. **Resolving Consumer Complaints** Eduardo and Ana recently bought a new dining room table that they saw advertised on a furniture manufacturer's Web site. When the table arrived and they opened the box, they discovered long, deep scratches on the top of the table. The company is located thousands of miles from where they live. The box had no directions about how they could return the product.
   Summarize Describe the steps Eduardo and Ana should take to resolve their situation and get either a refund or a new table.

CHAPTER 4 ASSESSMENT

CHAPTER SUMMARY

- Economic, social, and personal factors influence your buying decisions.

- By following a research-based approach to purchasing goods and services, you can get more value for your money.

- Smart buying strategies include timing your purchases, selecting the store carefully, comparing brands, reading labels, comparing prices, and evaluating warranties.

- The five ways to resolve consumer problems are to return to the place of purchase; contact company headquarters; get help from a consumer agency; investigate dispute resolution programs; or take legal action.

- Legal options available to consumers include bringing a case to small claims court, joining in a class-action suit, hiring a lawyer, and seeking help from a legal aid society.

Internet zone

Understanding and Using Vocabulary

Knowing these terms will help you speak the language of a smart consumer. Write a brief paragraph about consumer protection, using at least seven of these terms.

down payment
cooperative
impulse buying
open dating
unit pricing
rebate
warranty

service contract
fraud
mediation
arbitration
small claims court
class-action suit
legal aid society

Review Key Concepts

1. Why does a person buy some products and not others?

2. What factors influence the choices that consumers make when they select a store?

3. How can comparison shopping help you make wiser buying decisions?

4. How can consumer agencies help you avoid and resolve problems?

5. What legal alternatives do you have when you need to resolve a consumer problem?

Apply Key Concepts

1. Identify which factors play the greatest role in your own buying decisions.

2. Visit three local stores to compare prices, policies, and services. Summarize your findings.

3. List some of the factors you might look for in comparison shopping. Rate the importance of each in relation to your own shopping experiences.

CHAPTER 4 ASSESSMENT

4. Choose three local stores or businesses and contact the local Better Business Bureau to find out about them. Compare the three places in terms of customer satisfaction.

5. Using the phone book, locate at least two lawyers who handle consumer complaints. What services do they provide? Write a brief report on your findings.

Problem Solving Today

USING YOUR MONEY

For your birthday, your parents gave you $100 in cash. You could use the money to buy the pair of $100 snowshoes you've wanted; every winter you go to the mountains four times with friends, and you rent snowshoes for $6 each time. On the other hand, you could also pay off the $100 you owe on your credit card and avoid paying the 18 percent annual interest charge, which amounts to $1.50 per month.

Analyze 1) How much money would you save in one year if you bought the snowshoes? 2) How much interest would you pay in a year if you didn't repay what you owe on the credit card? 3) Which is the better option?

Computer Activity As an alternative activity, use financial software to calculate which option would be the best use of your money.

Real-World Application

CONNECT WITH SOCIAL STUDIES

Jacob and Marie Hauser are involved in a class-action suit against an automobile company. Several years ago a number of people around the country were involved in fatal accidents because a safety device in a particular model of car did not work properly. The Hausers' son was killed in such an accident. The legal rights of the parties involved in the lawsuit are protected, in part, by the National Traffic and Motor Vehicle Safety Act of 1966.

Do Research Using the library and Internet resources, investigate other federal laws passed after the 1930s that are related to consumer safety. Summarize how each of these laws helps consumers.

FINANCE Online

ONLINE SHOPPING

The Internet offers a variety of buying services to help you make informed decisions about the products that you want. Some of these services may help you save money by letting you name your own prices. Others provide updates on the latest deals.

Connect Using various Internet search engines, find sites that provide information on shopping for bargains and consumer buying services. Then answer the following questions:

1. How might you save money by making your travel arrangements online?
2. How can you determine which stores have the best prices for computers?
3. If you were in the market for a new car, what online methods might you use to evaluate your choices?

Get a Financial Life!

CASE STUDY

Career Planning and Decision Making

Overview

Karla Cunningham will be graduating from high school this year. She is facing a variety of important decisions—from developing her personal financial goals to planning her career strategy.

When you make decisions, you're taking control of your life. You can shape your future in ways that are important to you. To make sound decisions, you should know what your goals are and understand the ways in which your personal values and life situations will influence your choices. If you are prepared to make decisions—rather than leave your future to chance or allow others to tell you what to do—you'll be able to achieve personal satisfaction and financial security.

Develop a process to help plan your own career; then share it with Karla so that she can plan hers.

Resources

- Career center/guidance office at school
- Career development book
- Crayons, markers, colored pencils
- Internet (optional)
- Portfolio (ring binder or file folder)
- Poster board
- Presentation software (optional)
- Public or school library
- Word processor

Procedures

Step A   THE PROCESS

In order to develop a career plan, you must set goals, understand your abilities and interests, and conduct research. By following this process, you'll have a head start into the future. In addition, you'll be able to share what you've learned with Karla or your friends so that they can be prepared as well.

1. Develop five to seven financial goals. You should have at least one short-term, one intermediate, and one long-term goal. Your selected career will help you meet your goals.

2. Take an aptitude test and/or interest inventory. You can find these in your school's guidance office or career center, or even on the Internet.

3. Research a career that you are interested in learning more about. Make sure that you find out about the educational requirements, skills needed, pay range, duties and responsibilities, opportunities for advancement, and future trends in the field.

4. Conduct an informational interview with someone who is working in your area of interest to gather practical information about the career that you're considering, or arrange to "job shadow" someone who is working in your selected field. (To job shadow means to follow a person on the job for a day to learn about a particular career.)

5. Obtain catalogs from colleges or other postsecondary institutions where training is offered in the field you are researching. Try to locate at least one institution in your community, one other in your state, and one out of state.

6. Using a word processor, create templates for a résumé and cover letter.

Step B — CREATE YOUR PORTFOLIO

As you work through the process, save the results so that you can refer, review, and refine. Divide your portfolio into six sections. Label the sections: (1) Goals, (2) Tests, (3) Career Research, (4) Live Work, (5) Education, and (6) Résumé.

1. Using a word processor, type your goals in a large font (16–18 point). These will be your guiding principles. Place them in section 1.

2. Place the results of your aptitude test or interest inventory in section 2.

3. Type a two- or three-page (double-spaced) career report based on your research, and place it in section 3.

4. Write about your informational interview or job shadowing experience. Include pictures, brochures, or other materials that you might have received. Place these items in section 4.

5. Place the catalogs that you collect in section 5.

6. Place the templates that you create in section 6.

Step C — PRESENTATION

One of the most important skills that employers look for in a good employee is the ability to communicate. This is a skill that you can develop in class through oral presentations.

1. Read a book on career development. Examples include:
   - *What Color Is Your Parachute? 2000* by Richard Nelson Bolles;
   - *Who Moved My Cheese?* by Spencer Johnson;
   - *Job Interviews for Dummies* by Joyce Lain Kennedy;
   - *Cool Careers for Dummies* by Marty Nemko, Paul Edwards, Sarah Edwards;
   - *I Could Do Anything If I Only Knew What It Was* by Barbara Sher, with Barbara Smith.

2. Using either presentation software or poster board with markers, crayons, or colored pencils, create a five-minute presentation that summarizes the book.

3. Include your opinion of the book, stating whether or not you would recommend it to Karla.

UNIT 2

BANKING AND CREDIT

Unit 2 describes a wide range of services that can help you plan, manage, and save in order to achieve your financial goals. The next three chapters will discuss the selection and use of financial services, the role of credit in your buying decisions, and the finances of housing.

READING STRATEGIES

To get the most out of your reading

- **PREDICT** what the section will be about.
- **CONNECT** what you read with your own life.
- **QUESTION** as you read to make sure you understand the content.
- **RESPOND** to what you've read.

118

START TODAY

Be Credit Smart

Establishing and maintaining good credit will impact your entire adult life. What can you do today to start developing a good credit history?

Banking

Q&A

Q: Why do I need the services of a bank? I only make $75 a week and use most of it for movies, food, and CDs.

A: You may not need a bank if you have only a small amount of money to take care of. However, $75 a week is a large sum to spend on entertainment. You should open a savings account and try to save at least $10 a week. After three months you'd have $130, and after a year you'd have more than $500.

US SAVINGS BONDS

CHECKS SAVE

CDs

Selecting Financial Services and Institutions

When Michelle started her part-time job as a sales associate at a local drugstore, her boss, Mr. Fried, asked her if she wanted to sign up for direct deposit. He explained that the company could deposit her paycheck into her checking or savings account electronically. Michelle decided to find out more about this at her bank. The customer service representative at the bank assured her of the safety and convenience of direct deposit. She also gave Michelle information on other services that the bank offered. Michelle decided to check out other financial institutions as well to see which one would give her the best rates on savings and charge the lowest fees for services.

What You'll Learn

- How to **identify** available financial services
- How to **distinguish** among various types of financial institutions

Why It's Important

Understanding the features of financial services and institutions will help you choose those services and institutions that best meet your needs.

KEY TERMS

- **automatic teller machine (ATM)**
- **debit card**
- **point-of-sale transaction**
- **commercial bank**
- **savings and loan association (S&L)**
- **credit union**

How to Manage Your Cash

With more than 11,000 banks, 2,000 savings and loan associations, and 12,000 credit unions in the United States, you have a wide array of financial services from which to choose. A "trip to the bank" may be a visit to an automatic teller machine (ATM) in the mall or a quick look at your savings account balance on the Internet. Your choice of financial services will depend on your daily cash needs and your savings goals. (See **Figure 5.1**.)

Daily Cash Needs

Your daily cash needs may include buying lunch, going to the movies with friends, filling the car with gasoline, or paying for other routine activities. Of course, you can carry currency—bills and coins—to pay for these items. You can also use a credit card or go to an ATM, also known as a cash machine.

As you decide which payment method to use for your everyday needs, consider the pros and cons of each one. For example, ATMs

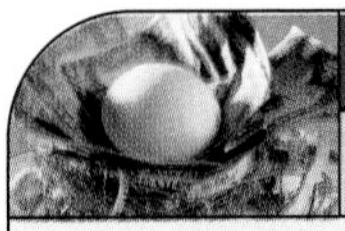

Figure 5.1

Financial Services

Financial Services for Short-Term Needs
- Daily purchases
- Living expenses
- Emergency fund

Daily Cash Needs
- Check cashing
- Automatic teller machines (ATMs)
- Prepaid cards

Savings
- Regular savings account
- Money market account

Checking
- Regular checking account
- Online payments
- Automatic preauthorized payments
- Payment by phone
- Cashier's checks
- Money orders

Credit Cards

Financial Services for Long-Term Goals
- Major purchases
- Long-term financial security

Savings
- Certificates of deposit (CDs)
- U.S. savings bonds

Credit Services
- Cash loans for cars, education
- Home loans

Investment Services
- Mutual funds
- Financial advice

Other Services
- Tax preparation
- Insurance
- Budgeting

PLANNING AHEAD You may think that you need only cash and perhaps checking services at this point in your life. *Why would it be a good idea to start now to save even a small amount regularly?*

often charge a fee for each use. Think about it: If you pay a $1 fee at an ATM each time you take out cash, and you do this twice a week, you spend $104 on fees each year.

In addition to your short-term cash needs, you'll want to consider your long-term financial goals. Resist the temptation to overspend and don't buy on impulse or overuse credit cards. Try not to dip into your savings to pay current bills. Do put any extra money you have to work for you—in a savings account or investment plan.

Sources of Quick Cash

Regardless of how well you plan, you may sometimes discover that you need more cash than you have available. You have two options: use your savings, or borrow the money. Remember that either choice requires a trade-off. Although you will have immediate access to the funds you need, your long-term financial goals—such as paying for college, buying a car, or starting your own business—may have to be postponed.

What's Your Financial ID?

ORALLY

BASIC BANKING QUIZ

How much do you know about basic bank services and terms? Take this quiz before you read the chapter, then try it again after studying the chapter to see how much you've learned. Write your answers on a separate sheet of paper.

1. A bank CD is a _____.
   a. cash deposit
   b. compact disc
   c. certificate of deposit
   d. compact deposit

2. To borrow money from the bank, you need to ask for a _____.
   a. loan
   b. money market account
   c. safe-deposit box
   d. transfer

3. You can store valuables in the bank's vault if you have _____.
   a. permission
   b. a money market account
   c. a safe-deposit box
   d. an ATM card

4. You keep money in a bank account to _____.
   a. keep it safe
   b. earn interest
   c. learn financial responsibility
   d. all of the above

5. The total amount of money in your bank account is called _____.
   a. the statement
   b. the interest
   c. the balance
   d. peanuts

6. The amount of money your bank account earns depends on the _____.
   a. type of account you have
   b. balance in your account
   c. interest rate
   d. all of the above

7. When you make a purchase and have the funds taken directly from your checking account, you use a _____.
   a. credit card
   b. note from your mother
   c. debit card
   d. driver's license

8. To set up a savings plan that requires a low minimum balance and allows you to withdraw funds at any time, you would _____.
   a. buy a CD
   b. buy a U.S. Savings Bond
   c. put the money under your mattress
   d. open a savings account

BE SMART. INVEST YOUR MONEY IN THE FUTURE.

Types of Financial Services

In order to stay competitive in today's marketplace, banks and other financial institutions have expanded the range of services that they offer. These services can be divided into three main categories: savings, payment services, and borrowing.

Savings

Safe storage of funds for future use is a basic need for everyone. Money that is going to be left in a financial institution for months or years is called a time deposit. Examples include money that you keep in savings accounts and certificates of deposit.

Payment Services

The ability to transfer money from your account to businesses or individuals for payments is a necessary part of day-to-day financial activity. The most commonly used payment service is a checking account. Money that you place in a checking account is called a demand deposit because you can withdraw the money at any time, or on demand.

Careers in Finance

BANK TELLER

Many careers in banking start at the teller's window. Bank tellers cash checks, accept deposits and loan payments, handle withdrawals, and sell traveler's checks. They may do other tasks, depending on the type of banking institution where they work. Because tellers deal with customers' money, they must pay close attention to their work, verifying names, dates, numbers, and identities. Most tellers use calculators and computers as well as other types of electronic equipment.

Skills	Communication, computer, interpersonal, math
Personality	Detail oriented, discreet, honest, likes working with people, tactful
Education	High school diploma and on-the-job training; associate of arts or bachelor's degree; certification from the Institute of Financial Education or the American Institute of Banking may help you advance into management.
Pay range	$12,000 to $25,000 a year, depending on experience, location, and bank

Research   Invite a bank manager to your class to discuss the opportunities available to tellers. Ask questions about the training, experience, and education that a bank teller needs.

 For more information on bank tellers visit finance.glencoe.com or your local library.

Borrowing

Most people use credit at some time during their lives. If you need to borrow money, financial institutions offer many options. You can borrow for the short term by using a credit card or taking out a personal cash loan. If you need to borrow for a longer term, such as to buy a house or car, you may apply for a mortgage or auto loan. Chapter 6 discusses the types and costs of credit.

Other Financial Services

Financial institutions may also offer insurance protection; stock, bond, and mutual fund investment accounts; tax help; and financial planning services.

Electronic Banking Services

CONNECT

Do you currently use electronic banking services? What are the pros and cons of the services you use?

When Jeff was in high school, he had to be sure to get to his bank by 3 P.M. on Friday, or he would have to wait until 9 A.M. on Monday to cash his paycheck. Now Jeff's bank is open for longer periods on weekdays as well as on Saturday and Sunday. For more convenience, Jeff can use his bank's electronic services 24 hours a day. He can check the status of his account or make a transaction from an ATM, by telephone, or online.

Direct Deposit

Today many businesses offer their employees the option of having their pay deposited directly into a designated bank account. Instead of a paycheck, employees receive a statement that lists deductions and other information about their earnings. State and federal government checks, such as those for Social Security and public assistance, can also be deposited electronically into the recipient's bank account. Direct deposit saves time, money, and effort. It also offers safety because you don't have to worry about your check being lost or stolen.

Automatic Payments

An increasing number of utility companies, lenders, and other businesses allow customers to use an automatic payment system. With your authorization, your bank will withdraw the amount of your monthly payment or bill from your bank account. It's a good idea to make sure you always have enough money in your account for the

payment. Try to stagger these payments according to when you receive your paycheck, so that you maintain an even cash flow. Check your bank statements each month to make sure that the payments were made correctly.

Automatic Teller Machines (ATMs)

Cash machines, or *automatic teller machines (ATMs)*, are computer terminals that let you withdraw cash from your account, make deposits, and transfer money from one account to another. Not only do ATMs allow you to handle routine banking tasks, but many also sell bus passes and postage stamps, among other things. ATMs are located in banks, shopping malls, grocery stores, and even sports arenas.

To use an ATM for banking, you must apply for a card from your financial institution. This card, called a *debit card* or cash card, allows you to withdraw money or pay for purchases from your checking or savings account. The card also allows you to access the machine for other purposes. Some financial institutions may charge a small fee for the use of the card. Unlike a credit card, a debit card enables you to spend only the money that you have in your account.

When you use your debit card, the computer will ask you to enter your personal identification number (PIN). Do not give this number to anyone else. It is a good idea to memorize it rather than write it down. Never keep your PIN with your debit card. If your card is lost or stolen along with your PIN, anyone could take money from your account!

ATM FEES The fees that financial institutions charge for the convenience of using an ATM can add up over time. You may feel that the benefit is worth the cost. However, you might consider these suggestions:

- Compare ATM fees before opening an account. Be sure to get the list of fees in writing.
- Use your own bank's machines to avoid the additional fees that other banks charge when you use their machines.
- Consider using personal checks, traveler's checks, credit cards, and prepaid cash cards when you are away from home.

LOST DEBIT CARDS If you lose your debit card, or if it is stolen, let your bank know immediately. If you notify the institution within two days of losing your card, you can be held responsible for only $50 of any unauthorized use. If you wait longer, you may be held responsible for as much as $500 for its unauthorized use for up to 60 days. Beyond that time, your liability may be unlimited. Some card issuers, however, may hold you responsible for only $50, regardless of when you report it. Check with your card issuer.

Plastic Payments

Although cash and checks are still very common methods of paying for goods and services, various access cards are also gaining acceptance.

POINT-OF-SALE TRANSACTIONS In a *point-of-sale transaction*, you use a debit card to purchase an item or a service at a retail store, in a restaurant, or elsewhere.

Financial institutions offer two types of cards for these transactions: online and offline. An online card works like an ATM card. You have to use your PIN to authorize the payment, and the money is transferred from your account instantly. Charges made with the offline card don't require a PIN, and the funds to cover the payment are deducted from your account within a day or two.

STORED-VALUE CARDS Prepaid cards that you can spend for bus or subway fares, school lunches, long-distance phone calls, or library fees are becoming common. Some of these cards, such as phone cards, are disposable. Others, called stored-value cards, are reloadable, or "rechargeable."

For his birthday, Jackie gave her brother a $25 stored-value card from his favorite music store. When he used the card to buy a CD that was on sale for $15, the price of his purchase was subtracted by an electronic card reader. The remaining cash value was stored in a microchip in the card.

ELECTRONIC CASH Some companies are working to develop electronic money. They plan to create electronic versions of all existing payment systems—paper money, coins, credit cards, and checks. Perhaps a day will come when you won't have to handle currency at all.

PLASTIC PAYMENT
Debit cards are convenient, cashless ways to make purchases. *What might be one drawback to using a debit card?*

Opportunity Costs of Financial Services

When you're making decisions about saving and spending, try to find a balance between your short-term needs and your future financial security. Also, consider the opportunity costs, or trade-offs, of each choice you make as you select financial services. Think about these examples:

- Is a higher interest rate on a certificate of deposit worth giving up liquidity, the ability to easily convert your financial resources into cash without a loss in value?
- Would you trade the convenience of getting cash from the ATM near your office for lower ATM fees?
- Is it worth opening a checking account that has no fees but doesn't earn interest if you have to keep a minimum balance of $500?

Remember to consider the value not only of the money you are saving but also of your time. Reevaluate your choices occasionally—you may find a new financial institution that offers you more of the services you need, or offers them more cheaply.

Types of Financial Institutions

After you have identified the services you want, you can choose from among many types of financial institutions. You may select an institution that offers a wide range of services or one that specializes in certain services. Many institutions provide the option of "cyberbanking," or banking via the Internet. In 1995 some banks began to operate exclusively on the Internet.

Federal Deposit Insurance Corporation

One criterion that should guide your selection of a financial institution is its safety record. During the Great Depression, many banks failed, and the people and businesses that had made deposits in these institutions lost their money. In 1933 the federal government created the Federal Deposit Insurance Corporation (FDIC) to protect deposits in banks. The FDIC insures each account in a federally chartered bank up to $100,000 per account. The FDIC also administers the Savings Association Insurance Fund (SAIF) for savings and loan associations. Like the FDIC, the SAIF insures deposits up to $100,000. All federally chartered banks must participate in the FDIC program. Banks that are not federally chartered may choose to enroll in the program.

Deposit-Type Institutions

Most people use deposit-type institutions to handle their banking needs. These institutions include commercial banks, savings and loan associations, mutual savings banks, and credit unions.

COMMERCIAL BANKS A *commercial bank* is a for-profit institution that offers a full range of financial services, including checking, savings, and lending. Commercial banks serve individuals and businesses. These banks are authorized to conduct business through a charter, or license, that is granted by either the federal government or a state government.

SAVINGS AND LOAN ASSOCIATIONS A *savings and loan association (S&L)* traditionally specialized in savings accounts and mortgage loans. Today this type of financial institution also offers many of the same services as commercial banks, including checking accounts, business loans, and investment services. S&Ls have either a federal or a state charter.

MUTUAL SAVINGS BANKS Mutual savings banks specialize in savings accounts and mortgage loans. Some offer personal and automobile loans as well. The interest rates on loans from a mutual savings bank may be lower than those that a commercial bank charges. In addition, mutual savings banks sometimes pay a higher interest rate on savings accounts.

CREDIT UNIONS A *credit union* is a nonprofit financial institution that is owned by its members and organized for their benefit. Traditionally its members have some common bond, such as membership in the same labor union or church or employment by the same company. Most credit unions offer a full range of services, including checking accounts, loans, credit cards, ATMs, and investment services. Their fees and loan rates are generally lower than those at commercial banks.

CONVENIENCE   Many people use commercial banks because these banks offer a full range of financial services. *What might be some of the specific attractions of a large commercial bank?*

Nondeposit-Type Institutions

Financial services are also available from institutions such as life insurance companies, investment companies, finance companies, and mortgage companies.

LIFE INSURANCE COMPANIES   Although the main purpose of life insurance companies is to provide financial security for dependents, many policies also contain savings and investment features. In addition, some insurance companies offer retirement planning ser-vices. You'll learn more about life insurance in Chapter 14.

INVESTMENT COMPANIES   These firms combine your money with that of other investors in order to buy stocks, bonds, and other securities. The investment company then manages these combined investments, which are called mutual funds and are discussed in detail in Chapter 10.

FINANCE COMPANIES   The main business of finance companies is to make loans to consumers and small businesses. Often finance companies provide loans to people who cannot borrow

FIGURE 5.2

Selecting a Financial Institution

When you're ready to choose a financial institution, plan so that you'll have the services you need and won't pay for those you won't use. Do your banking homework.

1 Stop by the bank branch to pick up brochures about the bank's services. While there, speak to a customer service representative about the bank's services.

2 Take the brochures home with you and study them. Discuss the features with your parents.

elsewhere because they have a low income or few assets. As a result, these companies' rates are often higher than those of most other lenders. Some finance companies offer other financial planning services as well.

MORTGAGE COMPANIES Mortgage companies specialize in loans for the purchase of homes. Chapter 7 discusses the finances of housing in detail.

Comparing Financial Institutions

Figure 5.2 provides some tips for selecting a financial institution. When you compare financial institutions, you should also ask these important questions:

PREDICT

What information would you need to know before deciding on the best financial institution for your needs?

3 *Go online, if the bank has a Web site, to get complete information on the institution's benefits, fees, and charges.*

4 *Open your checking and savings accounts and start managing your money.*

- Where can you get the highest rate of interest on your savings?
- Where can you obtain a checking account with low or no fees to write checks?
- Will you be able to borrow money from the institution—with a credit card or another type of loan—when you need it?
- Do you need an institution that offers free financial advice?
- Is the institution FDIC or SAIF-insured?
- Does the institution have convenient locations?
- Does it have online banking services?
- Does it have any special banking services that you might need?

SECTION 5.1 ASSESSMENT

CHECK YOUR UNDERSTANDING

1. What three main categories of services are offered by financial institutions?
2. Describe the types of electronic banking services that are available.
3. Which institutions fall under the category of deposit-type institutions? Which are classified as nondeposit-type institutions?

THINK CRITICALLY

4. Explain what financial services you use now, and discuss how your needs might change in the next five years.

USING MATH SKILLS

5. **Wise Use of ATMs** Margaret uses an ATM three times a week. It isn't her bank's machine, but it's convenient to the store where she works part-time. For every transaction, Margaret pays a fee of $1.50.
   Calculate What is Margaret's annual spending for the use of this ATM?

SOLVING MONEY PROBLEMS

6. **Choosing a Financial Institution** Dakota is thinking about changing banks. He has a part-time job at a supermarket. Sometimes he works late hours, and he would like the convenience of being able to make deposits and withdrawals at any time. He needs cash for food and gas, and he writes only two checks a month—to his compact disc club account and to his credit card company. Soon he'll need to take out a loan to buy a car. He also wants to put aside some money to pay for technical school.
   Select Help Dakota select the type of financial institution that offers the features that would be most useful to him.

Savings Plans and Payment Methods

Types of Savings Plans

In order to achieve your financial goals, you'll need a savings program. Among your alternatives are regular savings accounts, certificates of deposit, money market accounts, and U.S. Savings Bonds (See **Figure 5.3**).

Regular Savings Accounts

Regular savings accounts, traditionally called passbook accounts, are ideal if you plan to make frequent deposits and withdrawals. They require little or no minimum balance and allow you to withdraw money quickly. The trade-off for this convenience is that the interest you earn will be low compared with other savings plans.

You may receive a passbook that records deposits and withdrawals, but often you will get a monthly or quarterly statement in the mail. Commercial banks, savings and loan associations, and other financial institutions offer regular savings accounts. At credit unions they are called share accounts.

Certificates of Deposit

A *certificate of deposit (CD)* is a time deposit that requires you to leave your money in a financial institution for a set amount of time. This fixed period of time is called the term. The date when the money becomes available to you is called the maturity date. This savings plan is a relatively low-risk way to invest your money. It offers a higher interest rate than a regular savings account, but you will have to accept a few trade-offs.

To earn the higher interest rate paid by CDs, you must accept three key limitations. First, you may have to leave your money on deposit anywhere from a month to five or more years. Second, you will usually have to pay a penalty if you take the money out before the maturity date. Third, financial institutions require that you deposit a certain minimum amount to buy a CD. This amount is usually larger than the balance a regular savings account requires.

What You'll Learn

- How to **compare** the costs and benefits of different savings plans
- How to **evaluate** savings plans
- How to **compare** the costs and benefits of different types of checking accounts
- How to **use** a checking account effectively

Why It's Important

Recognizing the types of savings plans and payment methods that financial institutions offer can help you make wise use of your money.

KEY TERMS

- **certificate of deposit (CD)**
- **money market account**
- **rate of return**
- **compounding**
- **annual percentage yield (APY)**
- **overdraft protection**
- **stop-payment order**
- **endorsement**
- **bank reconciliation**

Figure 5.3

Savings Alternatives

Type of Account	Benefits	Drawbacks
Regular savings accounts	• Low minimum balance • Ease of withdrawal • Insured	• Low rate of return
Certificates of deposit (CDs)	• Guaranteed rate of return for time of CD • Insured	• Possible penalty for early withdrawal • Minimum deposit
Money market accounts	• Good rate of return • Some check writing • Insured	• Minimum balance • No interest and possible service charge if below a certain balance
U.S. Savings Bonds	• Good rate of return • Low minimum deposit • Guaranteed by the government • Free from state and local taxes	• Lower rate of return when cashed in before bond reaches maturity date

SO MANY CHOICES Each of the main types of savings plans has pros and cons that you should consider. *Which types would be best for a person who wants to save frequently but with small amounts?*

Here are some tips for investing in CDs:

- Find out where you can get the best rate. You don't need to bank in your neighborhood. You can put your savings in a bank anywhere in the United States. You can use the Internet to find out what rates banks all over the country are offering.
- Consider the economy as you decide what maturity date to choose. You may want to buy a long-term CD if interest rates are relatively high. Then, if interest rates go down because of changes in the economy, your money will continue to earn the higher rate.
- Never let a financial institution "roll over" a CD—that is, reinvest it at maturity—unless you have checked current interest rates and know that you will continue to get the best rate possible.
- Consider when you will need the money. If you plan to use the money in two years to help pay for college, then buy a CD with a term of two years or less.

Money Market Accounts

A *money market account* is a savings account in which the interest rate varies from month to month. The rates float, or go up and down, as market rates change. Although the interest rate of a money market account is usually higher than that of a regular savings account, a money market account also requires a higher minimum balance, typically $1,000. It generally allows you to write a limited number of checks to make large payments or to transfer money to other accounts. The FDIC insures money market accounts that are managed by banks against loss.

U.S. Savings Bonds

For Meagan's high school graduation in 1990, her aunt gave her a U.S. Savings Bond. Her aunt paid $250 for the bond, but it has a face value of $500. This means that if Meagan keeps the bond long enough, it will eventually earn enough interest to be worth $500 or even more.

One savings option is to purchase Series EE Savings Bonds from the federal government in amounts that range from $25 to $5,000 (face values of $50 to $10,000, respectively). The government limits total purchases per year to $15,000 ($30,000 face value) per person.

The maturity date, or the date a bond reaches its face value, depends on the issue date and the interest rate the bond is earning. For some bonds the rate changes every six months. Because interest rates vary, no official maturity date exists for Series EE Savings Bonds. Bonds purchased after April 1997 and cashed after less than five years are subject to a three-month penalty—that is, you will not receive

MEETING GOALS Most people save for many years to pay for college. *Why might certificates of deposit be a good investment for someone who is saving for such a long-term goal?*

STANDARD &POOR'S

CASE STUDY

*C*arter Yuma works in a large office building downtown. The building has an ATM in the lobby so employees can make deposits and withdrawals with ease. Lately Carter has been withdrawing cash from the ATM two or three times per week. When Carter received his bank statement this month, it included a few surprises. Withdrawing cash from his checking account caused his balance to fall below the minimum. The bank charges $7.50 when this happens. He was charged fees for the 11 cash withdrawals he made during the month. Carter had one overdraft, which cost him $25. Carter didn't know that banks charged these kinds of fees. Nor did he realize that having easy access to the ATM could lead to overspending. Not knowing what to do next, Carter turned to the experts at Standard & Poor's for advice.

STANDARD &POOR'S **Analysis:** Carter is right in wanting to keep an eye on transaction fees, as they can add up to a surprisingly large bill. Using an ATM is not necessarily a bad thing; many people prefer to carry only as much cash as they need. It's important, though, to write down ATM withdrawals and keep track of checking account balances. With a little thought about his spending needs and habits, Carter can find an inexpensive solution that will work for his situation.

STANDARD &POOR'S **Recommendation:** Carter can first look for a bank that will base his monthly fees on the total of all the balances in his checking and savings accounts with that bank rather than on individual accounts. Then he can open several accounts, each for a different purpose. The first is Carter's main checking account, used to pay his regular monthly bills. The second should be a savings account that pays interest. Carter can deposit his paycheck into the checking account and then write a check or transfer money to his savings account. To make it easier to limit his cash expenditures, Carter can deposit his weekly spending money in a third account. This is the account from which Carter would make ATM withdrawals, using a machine from his bank in order to avoid extra transaction fees and remembering to record his withdrawals.

Critical Thinking Questions

1. Why do you think Carter finds it easier to overspend when he withdraws cash from an ATM than when he writes a check for purchases?

2. What factors should Carter consider when selecting a bank with which to do business?

3. What other strategies might Carter use to avoid the temptation of withdrawing more from his account than he'd planned to spend?

any interest for the last three months before you cashed it. For example, if you cash a bond after 18 months, you receive only 15 months' worth of interest.

A Series EE Savings Bond continues to earn interest for 30 years if you do not cash it in. The longer you hold it, the more it is worth. Its value may even exceed the face value if it is held past maturity.

Meagan kept her bond for ten years. In 2000 she decided to cash it in to help her make a down payment on a condominium. She found out that it was worth a little more than $450. Your bond's worth will depend on current interest rates and on the month and year in which the bond was issued.

The interest you earn on Series EE Bonds is exempt from, or free of, state and local taxes. You don't pay federal taxes on the earnings until you cash in the bond. Once a Series EE Bond has reached maturity, you can choose to defer federal taxes further by exchanging it for a Series HH Bond. Low- and middle-income families who use the money from redeemed Series EE Bonds to pay for education—college or a qualified technical school—pay no taxes on the interest.

Evaluating Savings Plans

Your selection of a savings plan will be influenced by several factors, including the rate of return, inflation, tax considerations, liquidity, restrictions, and fees.

Rate of Return

Earnings on savings can be measured by the rate of return, or yield. The *rate of return* is the percentage of increase in the value of your savings from earned interest. For example, when Emisha put the $50 she earned baby-sitting on New Year's Eve into a regular savings account last year, she earned $1.50 in interest. Therefore, her rate of return was 3 percent. To calculate the rate of return, she divided the total interest earned by the amount she had deposited in her account ($1.50 ÷ 50 = 3%).

COMPOUNDING   The yield on your savings will usually be greater than the stated interest rate. *Compounding* is the process in which interest is earned on both the principal—the amount you deposited—and on any previously earned interest. It is a multistep process for computing interest. First, the interest on the principal is computed. That interest is added to the principal. The next time interest is computed, the new, larger balance is used. These steps may take place every year, every quarter, every month, or even every day.

If you had the choice, would you want your savings account interest compounded daily, monthly, or yearly? Explain your reasoning.

How much interest would your account earn in one year if the interest were compounded monthly? To make this calculation, you would first multiply the principal by the annual interest rate. Divide that figure by 12, the number of months in a year. This is the interest you would earn after the first month.

To calculate the interest earned for the second month, you would add any interest earned in the first month to the principal. Then you would take that amount and multiply it by the annual interest rate. Next you would divide that number by 12. This is your interest earned in the second month. After you have repeated this calculation for all 12 months, you would add the monthly interest totals. The sum of the monthly interest amounts is the interest your account would earn in one year if the interest were compounded monthly.

Go Figure...

INTEREST COMPOUNDED MONTHLY

Example: You deposit $100 in a savings account. The bank is paying you 6%, which is compounded monthly. How much interest will you earn for the year?

Formula: A. Find the interest earned for the first month.

$$\frac{\text{Principal} \times \text{Annual Interest Rate}}{12} = \text{Interest Earned for First Month}$$

B. $$\frac{(\text{Principal} + \text{Previously Earned Interest}) \times \text{Annual Interest Rate}}{12}$$

= Interest Earned for a Given Month

Solution:

Month	Calculation
1	$(100.00 \times 6\%) \div 12 = \$0.50$
2	$(100.50 \times 6\%) \div 12 = \$0.50$
3	$(101.00 \times 6\%) \div 12 = \$0.51$
4	$(101.51 \times 6\%) \div 12 = \$0.51$
5	$(102.02 \times 6\%) \div 12 = \$0.51$
6	$(102.53 \times 6\%) \div 12 = \$0.51$
7	$(103.04 \times 6\%) \div 12 = \$0.52$
8	$(103.56 \times 6\%) \div 12 = \$0.52$
9	$(104.08 \times 6\%) \div 12 = \$0.52$
10	$(104.60 \times 6\%) \div 12 = \$0.52$
11	$(105.12 \times 6\%) \div 12 = \$0.53$
12	$(105.65 \times 6\%) \div 12 = \underline{\$0.53}$
	$6.18

At the end of the year, you will have $106.18 ($100.00 + $6.18 = $106.18). You earned $6.18 in interest for the year.

The more frequently your balance is compounded, the greater your yield, or rate of return, will be. For example, if you deposited $100 in an account with a 6 percent annual interest rate that was compounded annually (once a year), after one year you would earn $6 ($100 × 6% = $6). Your rate of return is 6 percent. If you had put that same $100 in an account that was compounded monthly at an annual interest rate of 6 percent, your rate of return would be higher. Remember, your rate of return is the total interest earned divided by the amount of your original deposit.

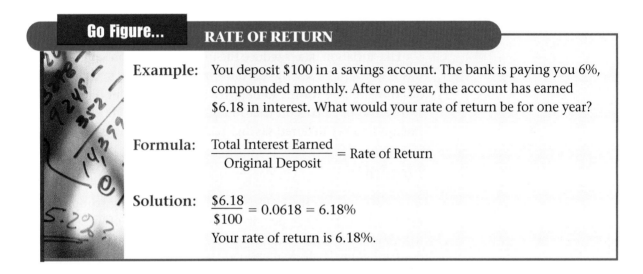

Go Figure...   **RATE OF RETURN**

Example: You deposit $100 in a savings account. The bank is paying you 6%, compounded monthly. After one year, the account has earned $6.18 in interest. What would your rate of return be for one year?

Formula: $\dfrac{\text{Total Interest Earned}}{\text{Original Deposit}} = \text{Rate of Return}$

Solution: $\dfrac{\$6.18}{\$100} = 0.0618 = 6.18\%$

Your rate of return is 6.18%.

The difference may not seem like much, but compounding can have a great impact on large amounts of money that are held in savings for long periods.

TRUTH IN SAVINGS According to the Truth in Savings Act, financial institutions have to inform you of the terms and conditions of all savings accounts, including fees, interest rates, and the annual percentage yield (APY).

The *annual percentage yield (APY)* tells you how much interest a financial institution would pay on a $100 deposit for one year. If the APY is 4 percent, the bank pays $4 interest ($100 × 4% = $4). The interest is based on the annual rate and the frequency of compounding for a 365-day period. The higher the APY, the better the return.

The APY helps you determine the amount you can expect to earn on your money. Because it is stated as a percentage and as an annual rate, it enables you to compare savings plans that have different rates and compounding frequencies.

Inflation

You should compare the rate of return you earn on your savings with the rate of inflation. If you open a savings account that offers 5 percent interest, and inflation rises to 10 percent, you will experience a loss in the buying power of your money. Usually, however, the interest rates offered on savings accounts increase if the rate of inflation increases. The biggest problem with inflation occurs if you are locked into one interest rate for a long period, as with a certificate of deposit.

Tax Considerations

Like inflation, taxes reduce the interest earned on savings. Karim was glad to find a savings account that was paying 4 percent interest. However, he wasn't so happy when he filled out his tax return and had to pay taxes on that interest. He decided to look into tax-exempt and tax-deferred savings plans for some of his money.

Liquidity

Check the savings plans you are considering to determine whether they charge a penalty or pay a lower rate of interest if you withdraw your funds early. If you need to be able to withdraw your money readily, you may want to put it in a liquid account, even though it may earn lower interest. On the other hand, if you're saving money for long-term goals, liquidity is not as important as a high rate of return.

Restrictions and Fees

Be aware of any restrictions on savings plans, such as a delay between the time when interest is earned and when it is actually paid into your account. Also check for fees you may be charged for making deposits and withdrawals. Find out about any service charges you may have to pay if your balance drops below a certain amount, or if you don't use your account for a certain period. These fees and service charges can add up.

Types of Checking Accounts

Checking accounts can be divided into three main categories: regular, activity, and interest-earning accounts.

*F*or anyone opening a bank account in Switzerland, the likely question is: Which bank? It's said that the country has more banks than dentists. Once the hub of European trade routes, Switzerland has been a major banking center since the 16th century. Swiss neutrality during wartime and the expertise of its bankers attract customers from all over the world. Depositors also like the banks' secrecy. Customers can ask to be identified by number only. At one time individuals could stash huge fortunes, no questions asked. In 1991 total secrecy became impossible; now banks must report anything suspicious about a deposit's origin to the authorities.

Geographic area	15,941 sq. mi.
Population	7,119,000
Capital	Bern (pop. 128,900)
Language	German, French, Italian, Romansch
Currency	franc
Gross domestic product (GDP)	$172.4 billion
Per capita GDP	$23,800
Economy	Industry: machinery, chemicals, watches, textiles.
	Agriculture: grains, fruits, vegetables, meat.
	Exports: machinery, chemicals, metals.

Switzerland is a major banking center.

Thinking Critically

Apply   If you were planning to open a savings account in one of your hometown banks, what services would prompt you to choose one bank over another?

For more information on Switzerland visit finance.glencoe.com **or your local library.**

Regular Checking Accounts

Regular checking accounts usually don't require you to keep a minimum balance. However, if the account does require a minimum balance and your account drops below that amount, you will have to pay a monthly service charge. A $7 or $8 charge every month can take quite a bite out of your funds. Usually this can be reduced or eliminated by having your pay directly deposited. Some institutions will waive the service charge if you keep a certain balance in your savings account.

Activity Accounts

If you write only a few checks each month and are unable to maintain a minimum balance, this type of account may be right for you.

The financial institution will charge a fee for each check you write, and sometimes a fee for each deposit, as well as a monthly service charge. However, you don't need to maintain a minimum balance.

Interest-Earning Checking Accounts

A cross between checking and savings, these accounts usually pay interest (a very low rate) if you maintain a minimum balance. If your account balance goes below the limit, you may not earn interest, and you may also have to pay a service charge.

Evaluating Checking Accounts

How do you decide which type of checking account will meet your needs? You'll need to weigh several factors.

RESTRICTIONS The most common restriction is the requirement that you keep a minimum balance. Other restrictions may include the number of transactions allowed and the number of checks you may write in a month.

FEES AND CHARGES Checking account fees have increased in recent years and continue to rise. You may pay not only a monthly service charge but also high fees for check printing, overdrafts, and stop-payment orders.

INTEREST Interest rates, frequency of compounding, and the way in which interest is calculated all affect an interest-bearing checking account.

SPECIAL SERVICES Commonly used checking account services include ATMs and banking by telephone and online. Financial institutions are also looking for ways to reduce the paper and postage costs associated with checking accounts. One solution is not to return canceled checks to customers. The financial institution stores the checks on microfilm and sends detailed statements to the customer. If a customer requests a copy of a canceled check, the institution makes a copy from the microfilm—for a fee.

As a checking account customer, you may also receive *overdraft protection*—an automatic loan made to you if you write a check for more money than you have in your account. The institution will charge interest on that loan, but the amount may be less than the fee it would charge if you overdrew on your account. Your bank also may offer an overdraft protection service that transfers money from your savings to your checking account. The bank charges a small fee for this service.

Using a Checking Account

After you've selected the type of checking account that best fits your needs, you'll need to know how to use it effectively.

Opening a Checking Account

Before you open a checking account, you'll have to decide whether you want an individual or joint account. An individual account has one owner; a joint account has two or more. Personal joint accounts are usually "or" accounts, which means that only one of the owners needs to sign a check. You'll sign a signature card at the bank so that your signature on a check can be verified.

Writing Checks

Before you write a check, write the date, the number of the check, the name of the party who will receive the payment, and the exact amount in your check register. A check register is a small booklet that you use to record activity in your account; it is usually sent to you with your supply of checks. Record all checks that you write, deposits, ATM withdrawals, debit card charges, interest earned (if any), any fees, and other transactions in your check register. Be sure to keep a current balance by deducting from or adding to your balance the amount of any transaction. Otherwise, you'll lose track of how much you actually have in your account. **Figure 5.4** shows a sample check register.

The correct way to write a check, shown in **Figure 5.5**, consists of the following steps:

1. Write the current date.
2. Write the name of the party that will receive the check.
3. Record the amount of the payment in figures.
4. Write the amount in words.
5. Sign the check in the same way you signed your signature card at the bank.
6. Make a note of the reason for the payment. This is a good place to record any account number if the payment is for a credit card or service, such as electricity or cable television.

If you make a mistake when writing a check, don't try to erase the error. Write a new check, tear up the old check, and write "Void"

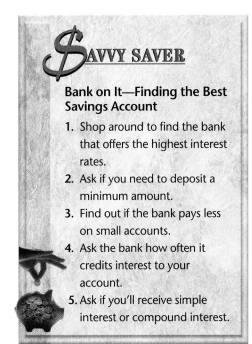

$AVVY SAVER

Bank on It—Finding the Best Savings Account

1. Shop around to find the bank that offers the highest interest rates.
2. Ask if you need to deposit a minimum amount.
3. Find out if the bank pays less on small accounts.
4. Ask the bank how often it credits interest to your account.
5. Ask if you'll receive simple interest or compound interest.

in your check register. If the mistake is small you may be able to correct the check and write your initials next to the error.

If a check is lost or stolen, or if you want to take back your payment for a business transaction, you may ask the bank to issue a stop-payment order. A **stop-payment order** is a request that an institution not cash a particular check. When Mason realized that he had accidentally sent his credit card payment to the telephone company, he asked the bank to stop payment on the $100 check he had written. Fees for this service can range from $10 to $20, so you should make sure that it is worth the charge.

Making Deposits

To add money to your checking account, you'll fill out a deposit ticket. Tickets usually include room to list four or five checks and any amount of cash that you are depositing. You'll have to endorse, or sign, the back of each check you've received. The **endorsement** is the signature of the payee, the party to whom the check has been written.

Here are some tips to follow when endorsing a check:

• Don't endorse a check until you're ready to cash or deposit it.
• Write your signature on the left end of the back of the check, on the lines printed for endorsement.

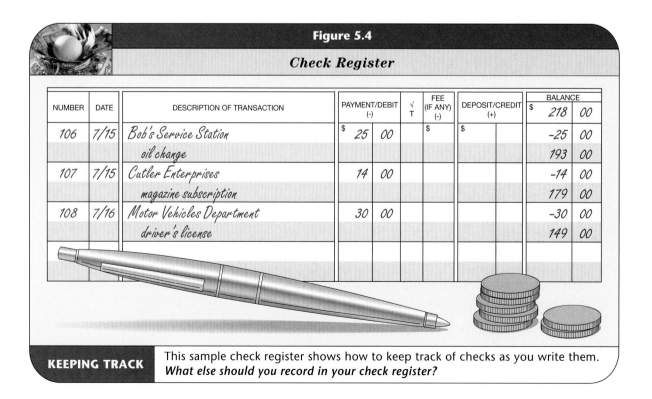

Figure 5.4

Check Register

NUMBER	DATE	DESCRIPTION OF TRANSACTION	PAYMENT/DEBIT (-)		√ T	FEE (IF ANY) (-)	DEPOSIT/CREDIT (+)		BALANCE $ 218	00
106	7/15	Bob's Service Station	$ 25	00	$	$			-25	00
		oil change							193	00
107	7/15	Cutler Enterprises	14	00					-14	00
		magazine subscription							179	00
108	7/16	Motor Vehicles Department	30	00					-30	00
		driver's license							149	00

KEEPING TRACK This sample check register shows how to keep track of checks as you write them. *What else should you record in your check register?*

144 ▓▓ Unit 2 *Banking and Credit*

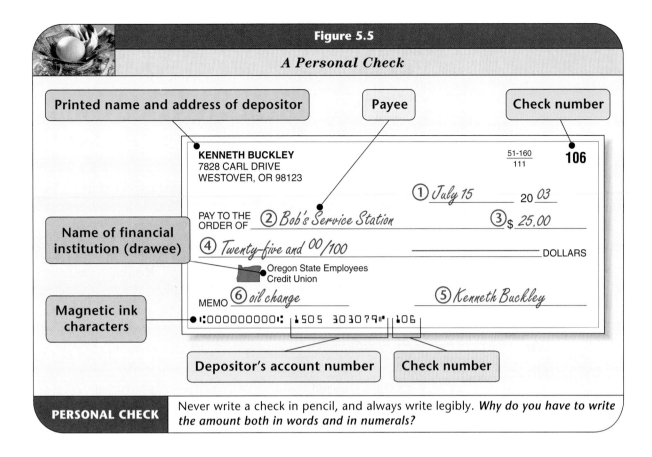

Figure 5.5

A Personal Check

- Printed name and address of depositor
- Payee
- Check number
- Name of financial institution (drawee)
- Magnetic ink characters
- Depositor's account number
- Check number

KENNETH BUCKLEY
7828 CARL DRIVE
WESTOVER, OR 98123

51-160 / 111

106

① July 15 20 03

PAY TO THE ORDER OF ② Bob's Service Station ③ $ 25.00

④ Twenty-five and 00/100 ————————— DOLLARS

Oregon State Employees Credit Union

MEMO ⑥ oil change ⑤ Kenneth Buckley

⑈000000000⑈ 1505 303079⑈ 106

PERSONAL CHECK Never write a check in pencil, and always write legibly. *Why do you have to write the amount both in words and in numerals?*

- Use only a pen so that your signature cannot be erased.
- If you are depositing a check by mail, write "For deposit only" directly above your signature.
- Sign your name exactly as it is spelled on the front of the check. If your name has been misspelled on the front, the endorsement should include the incorrect spelling, followed by your correct signature.

Check Clearing

Check clearing is a system that ensures that the money you deposited in the account is available for withdrawal. For example, if you deposit a check for $50 into your account, your bank usually holds that $50 until it clears with the bank on which it was drawn. During this time you cannot withdraw that money. By law, institutions are limited to holding funds from checks drawn on local banks no more than two business days, and from checks drawn on nonlocal banks to no more than five business days. Check clearing rules vary by bank, so check with your bank for specifics.

Maintaining a Checking Account

Each month your bank will send you a statement that shows your checking account activity for the month. It will list:

- deposits,
- checks that you have written that have come into the bank to be charged against your account (usually listed by check number),

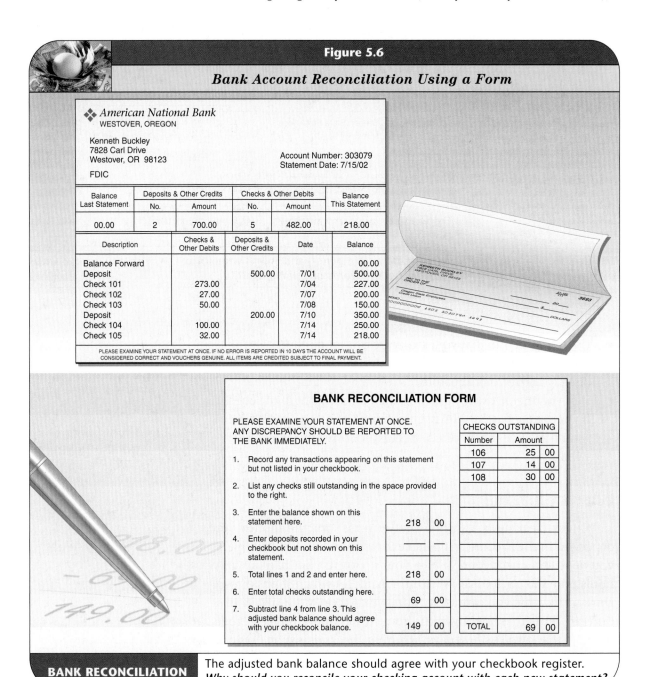

Figure 5.6

Bank Account Reconciliation Using a Form

❖ *American National Bank*
WESTOVER, OREGON

Kenneth Buckley
7828 Carl Drive
Westover, OR 98123

FDIC

Account Number: 303079
Statement Date: 7/15/02

Balance Last Statement	Deposits & Other Credits		Checks & Other Debits		Balance This Statement
	No.	Amount	No.	Amount	
00.00	2	700.00	5	482.00	218.00

Description	Checks & Other Debits	Deposits & Other Credits	Date	Balance
Balance Forward				00.00
Deposit		500.00	7/01	500.00
Check 101	273.00		7/04	227.00
Check 102	27.00		7/07	200.00
Check 103	50.00		7/08	150.00
Deposit		200.00	7/10	350.00
Check 104	100.00		7/14	250.00
Check 105	32.00		7/14	218.00

PLEASE EXAMINE YOUR STATEMENT AT ONCE. IF NO ERROR IS REPORTED IN 10 DAYS THE ACCOUNT WILL BE CONSIDERED CORRECT AND VOUCHERS GENUINE. ALL ITEMS ARE CREDITED SUBJECT TO FINAL PAYMENT.

BANK RECONCILIATION FORM

PLEASE EXAMINE YOUR STATEMENT AT ONCE. ANY DISCREPANCY SHOULD BE REPORTED TO THE BANK IMMEDIATELY.

1. Record any transactions appearing on this statement but not listed in your checkbook.

2. List any checks still outstanding in the space provided to the right.

3. Enter the balance shown on this statement here. **218 | 00**

4. Enter deposits recorded in your checkbook but not shown on this statement. **— | —**

5. Total lines 1 and 2 and enter here. **218 | 00**

6. Enter total checks outstanding here. **69 | 00**

7. Subtract line 4 from line 3. This adjusted bank balance should agree with your checkbook balance. **149 | 00**

CHECKS OUTSTANDING	
Number	Amount
106	25 00
107	14 00
108	30 00
TOTAL	69 00

BANK RECONCILIATION   The adjusted bank balance should agree with your checkbook register. *Why should you reconcile your checking account with each new statement?*

- ATM withdrawals,
- debit card charges (usually identified by the business or organization to whom you made the payment),
- interest earned (if any),
- and any fees.

The balance reported on the bank statement will probably be different from the balance in your check register. You may have written checks that have not yet cleared your bank, or maybe you deposited money into your account after the statement was prepared.

To determine your true balance, you should fill out a bank reconciliation form. A *bank reconciliation* is a report that accounts for the differences between the bank statement and your checkbook balance. Carrying out this process is often called "balancing your checkbook."

To reconcile your account, follow these steps. (A simplified version of a reconciliation form is shown in **Figure 5.6**.)

1. Compare the checks you have written during the month with those that are listed on the bank statement as paid, or cleared. List all outstanding checks—those which you wrote but that have not cleared. Subtract the total amount of outstanding checks from the balance on the bank statement.
2. Determine whether any recent deposits are not on the bank statement. If so, add the amounts of those deposits to the bank statement balance.
3. Subtract fees and charges listed on the statement from your checkbook balance.
4. Add any interest earned to your checkbook balance.

Once you have followed these steps, compare the balance in your check register and the adjusted bank balance on the reconciliation form. They should be the same. If the balances don't match, check your math, and make sure that all checks and deposits are entered correctly in your check register and on the statement. If the bank has entered a wrong amount for a check, you must report the error as soon as possible.

Other Payment Methods

You may make payments by methods other than by personal check. A certified check is a personal check with a guaranteed payment. The financial institution deducts the amount from your account when it certifies the check. You can purchase a cashier's check

Money Toss

Empty the change from your pocket or wallet every night and throw it into a jar. At the end of each month, deposit all your "throwaway" money in your savings account. That loose change can really add up.

QUESTION

Why is it important to balance your checkbook?

Comparison Shopping for Banking Services

Enrique is ready to open some bank accounts and is looking for the bank that best suits his needs. He is deciding between the local bank and the credit union where he works.

Enrique's Savings Search

Name of Institution	Kensington Bank	Acme Credit Union
Savings		
Annual interest rate	1.8%	2.5%
Minimum balance required	$100	none
Certificate of Deposit (CD) interest rate 1 year	6.40%	6.70%
Checking		
Monthly service charge	$8.50	$6.00
Minimum balance for "free" checking	$3,000	$1,000
Fees for ATM	Free	no ATMs
Cost of checks	$10.00	$8.75
Overdraft protection	yes	none
Banking hours	Mon.–Sat. 9–6, Closed Sun.	Mon.–Fri. 9–6, Closed Sat. & Sun.

Enrique decided to open a checking account at the bank because he needed the convenience of using the ATM. He opened a savings account at the credit union because it pays higher interest. When he has enough money, he will also purchase a CD at the credit union.

Compare In your workbook or on a separate sheet of paper, list the banking services that are important to you. Then call or visit several banks in your area and compare services, costs, and interest rates that are available to you.

What services are most important to you? Which bank would you choose? Explain why.

or money order from a financial institution. You pay the amount of the check or money order plus a fee.

Traveler's checks allow you to obtain cash when you are away from home. You sign each check once when you purchase the checks and a second time when you cash one. Prepaid traveler's cards let travelers get local currency from ATMs throughout the world.

SECTION 5.2 ASSESSMENT

CHECK YOUR UNDERSTANDING

1. What are some of the costs and benefits of a certificate of deposit?
2. What factors can you use to evaluate a savings plan?
3. What are the costs and benefits of regular, activity, and interest-earning checking accounts?
4. What must you do to maintain your checking account?

THINK CRITICALLY

5. Why do you think a law was passed to standardize the ways in which financial institutions inform consumers of the terms and conditions of savings plans?

USING COMMUNICATION SKILLS

6. **The Business of Banking** Banks advertise to attract customers.
   Make a Poster Choose one or more features of savings or checking accounts and create an advertising poster that highlights those features in a way that will inform people and invite them to become customers.

SOLVING MONEY PROBLEMS

7. **Checking Account Choices** Matthew Dempsey has just moved to a new town and is about to open a checking account. He pays for all his monthly expenses—rent, phone, car payment, credit card bills, dry cleaning, and insurance—by check.
   Decide With a partner, examine the features of the different types of checking accounts and help Matthew decide which type would be best for him.

CHAPTER 5 ASSESSMENT

CHAPTER SUMMARY

- Financial services can be divided into three main categories: savings, payment services, and borrowing.

- Electronic banking services include direct deposit, automatic payments, automatic teller machines (ATMs), and plastic payments.

- You can choose from among deposit-type and nondeposit-type institutions.

- Among the types of savings plans are regular savings accounts, certificates of deposit, money market accounts, and U.S. Savings Bonds. Understanding the costs

and benefits of different savings plans will help you make sensible trade-offs.

- Evaluate savings plans on their rates of return, the effect of inflation on interest, tax considerations, liquidity, restrictions, and fees.

- Evaluate checking accounts for their restrictions, fees and charges, interest rates (if any), and special services.

- Using a checking account involves opening an account, writing checks, making deposits, and reconciling your checkbook to the bank's statements.

Internet zone

Understanding and Using Vocabulary

With a partner, practice using these key terms by writing a dialogue between a customer and a bank manager about the bank's services, interest rates, and costs. Use at least eight terms in your dialogue.

automatic teller machine (ATM)
debit card
point-of-sale transaction
commercial bank
savings and loan association (S&L)
credit union

certificate of deposit (CD)
money market account
rate of return
compounding
annual percentage yield (APY)
overdraft protection
stop-payment order
endorsement
bank reconciliation

Review Key Concepts

1. What are the features of an automatic payment service?
2. Name three trade-offs you may have to make when you select financial services.
3. How might you make the most of an investment in a certificate of deposit?
4. What are the main factors to consider when choosing a savings plan?
5. Describe the steps you should follow when writing a check.

Apply Key Concepts

1. Predict some possible drawbacks of using an automatic payment service.

CHAPTER 5 ASSESSMENT

2. Explain why people tend to place a greater value on their money than their time when making banking choices.
3. Prepare a profile of a person who would be a good candidate to invest money in certificates of deposit.
4. Using the formula for calculating interest, prepare a table showing how much $100 would grow in one year in a savings account if the interest rate is 10 percent, compounded quarterly.
5. Prepare a presentation on the benefits of paying with checks instead of cash.

 Problem Solving Today

GETTING THE BEST RATE OF RETURN

After you graduate from high school, you would like to work part-time and enroll in a nearby business school. Your parents have agreed to pay the $20,000 tuition, but they have asked you to pay it back in five years.

Analyze You have $10,000 in a regular savings account and would like to put it in a five-year certificate of deposit. The CD earns 8 percent interest, compounded annually. You also plan to give your parents $100 a month from your earnings. Between the certificate of deposit and your earnings, will you have enough money to pay your parents back at the end of five years?

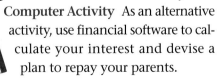 **Computer Activity** As an alternative activity, use financial software to calculate your interest and devise a plan to repay your parents.

Real-World Application

CONNECT WITH ECONOMICS

You are aware of the benefits of eating lots of fruits and vegetables. Because you want the produce you eat to be fresh, you go to the grocery store at least two times during any given week. Instead of having to remember to carry enough cash, you would like to have a debit card that lets you make online point-of-sale transactions.

Conduct Research Call several financial institutions in your area to find out what you would have to do to obtain the type of card that you want. Be sure to ask what type of savings or checking account is required and whether such a card carries any restrictions or fees.

 **FINANCE** *Online*

CYBERBANKING SERVICES

You want to learn how to protect yourself from fraud and invasion of privacy when you use financial services.

Connect Using different Internet search engines, look for information about avoiding fraud and maintaining your privacy when banking. Specifically, find answers to the following questions:
1. What are your rights regarding financial privacy?
2. What can you do to keep from becoming a victim of fraud?
3. What can you do if you are the victim of fraud?

CHAPTER 6

Consumer Credit

STANDARD &POOR'S

Q&A

Q: I just graduated from college and have four credit cards with balances totaling $5,000. I can barely make the minimum payments each month. What should I do?

A: You need to work out a plan to pay down these debts. It's important to keep in touch with the companies that have lent you money and let them know that you want to honor your obligation and maintain your good credit. They may be willing to accept payments of interest only for a few months while you look for ways to increase your income and cut your spending.

What Is Consumer Credit?

ricia is a college freshman who lives in Detroit. Even though she is a student and her annual income is small, she has received many credit card applications in the past year. Right now she has four cards; each one has an annual fee of $20 and an interest rate of 18 percent or higher. Tricia uses the cards to buy expensive clothes for herself and gifts for her friends and family. She even took a weeklong vacation in Florida. However, she is beginning to realize that something is very wrong. She has almost $9,000 in debts. Even if she stops using the cards right now, it will take years to pay back what she owes.

The Importance of Consumer Credit to the U.S. Economy

Like Tricia, almost everyone uses some form of *credit*, an arrangement to receive cash, goods, or services now and pay for them in the future. A *creditor*—an entity (a bank, finance company, credit union, business, or individual) to which money is owed—agrees to advance an individual the money, goods, or services. In turn, the individual agrees to repay the creditor, also called the lender, over a specified period of time.

In the United States, *consumer credit*, the use of credit for personal needs, dates back to colonial times. Although credit was originally a privilege of the rich, farmers came to use it extensively. At first, businesses added the cost of credit to the prices of the goods. When the automobile was introduced in the early 1900s, installment credit became an acceptable form of payment. Installment credit allows people to pay for expensive items with equal payments spread out over a period of time. Each installment payment includes part of the amount due on the purchase as well as part of the cost of credit.

Consumer credit is now a major force in the American economy, and the use of credit is a fact of life in personal and family financial

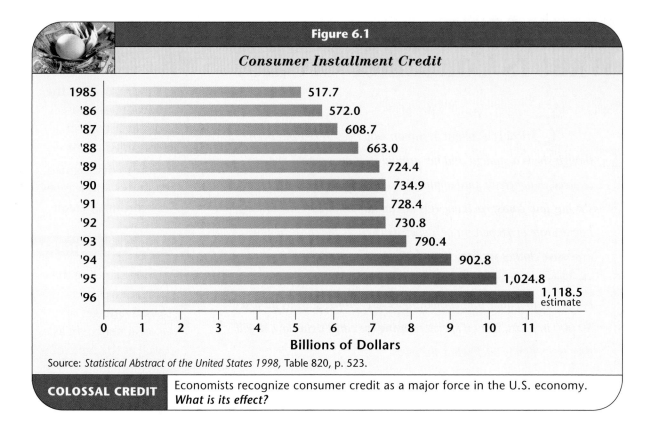

Figure 6.1

Consumer Installment Credit

Year	Billions of Dollars
1985	517.7
'86	572.0
'87	608.7
'88	663.0
'89	724.4
'90	734.9
'91	728.4
'92	730.8
'93	790.4
'94	902.8
'95	1,024.8
'96	1,118.5 estimate

Billions of Dollars

Source: *Statistical Abstract of the United States 1998,* Table 820, p. 523.

COLOSSAL CREDIT   Economists recognize consumer credit as a major force in the U.S. economy. *What is its effect?*

planning (see **Figure 6.1**). Sometimes using credit is necessary, and in some cases, it can even be to your advantage. However, paying for an item with credit also involves responsibility and certain risks.

Uses and Misuses of Credit

You can probably think of many valid reasons for using credit. Maybe you can buy something on credit now for less money than it will cost to pay in cash later. If you live in an area that lacks good public transportation, you may need a car to travel. However, if you can't afford a high monthly payment, it probably isn't a good idea to borrow money to buy a pricey sports car when all you really need is something simple and reliable. Although using credit increases the amount of money you can spend now, the trade-off is that it decreases the amount of money you'll be able to spend in the future. That's because you'll be paying back the money you borrowed as well as any charges for borrowing that money.

Factors to Consider Before Using Credit

Imagine that you have conducted research on the Internet regarding the possibility of financing—to give or get money for—a used car. Before you decide to finance a major purchase by using credit, you should consider the following points:

- Do you have the cash you need for the down payment?
- Do you want to use your savings instead of credit?
- Can you afford the item?
- Could you use the credit in some better way?
- Could you put off buying the item for a while?
- What are the costs of using credit?

Another important factor to consider is that when you buy something on credit, you agree to pay the fee that a creditor may add to the purchase price. If you don't pay your credit card bill in full every month, for example, you will be charged interest on the amount that has not been paid. *Interest* is a periodic charge in exchange for the use of credit. It's important, therefore, to think carefully before you decide to use credit. Make sure the benefits of making the purchase now outweigh the possible costs of credit. If you use credit intelligently, you can have more to enjoy. However, if you use it carelessly, you may eventually experience serious financial problems.

Advantages of Credit

The main advantage of using consumer credit is that it lets you enjoy goods and services now, perhaps when your funds are low, and pay for them later. You may discover other benefits of using credit. If you're a good customer and pay your bills on time, for example, a department store may send you special discount coupons and advance notice of sales. In general, credit cards also make shopping more convenient and allow you to combine several purchases, making just one monthly payment.

Credit may be the only acceptable method of paying for some services, such as electricity and the telephone. Every time you call a friend or switch on a light, you're using credit. The electric bill you receive in June is for the electricity you used in May.

If you're making hotel reservations, renting a car, or shopping by phone or online, you will probably need a credit card. Using credit gives you a record of your expenses. Because you can shop and travel without carrying a lot of cash, it's physically safer too.

Finally, if you use credit wisely, other lenders will view you as a responsible person. If you do not pay your bills on time, however, you will find that credit has a number of disadvantages.

QUESTION

Why is your good reputation as a borrower important to protect?

Disadvantages of Credit

Always remember that credit costs money. Perhaps the greatest disadvantage of using credit is the temptation to overspend. Using

What's Your Financial ID?

YOUR CREDIT IQ

Do you know how to use credit wisely? On a separate sheet of paper write the letter that best describes your answer to the following questions.

1. I pay any bills I have when they are due _____.
   a. always
   b. most of the time
   c. sometimes

2. If I need more money for my expenses, I borrow it _____.
   a. never
   b. sometimes
   c. often

3. If I want to see a copy of my credit report, I can contact _____.
   a. a credit reporting agency
   b. a bank
   c. the principal of my school

4. If I default (don't repay) on a loan, it will stay on my credit report for _____.
   a. 7 years
   b. 2 years
   c. 6 months

5. If I have serious credit problems, I should _____.
   a. contact my creditors to explain the problem
   b. contact only the most persistent creditors
   c. not contact my creditors and hope they will forget about me

6. I can begin building a good rating by _____.
   a. opening a savings account and making regular monthly deposits.
   b. paying most of my bills on time
   c. opening a checking account and bouncing checks

Scoring: Give yourself 3 points for each "a," 2 points for each "b," and 1 point for each "c." Add up the number of points.

If you scored 6–9 points, you might want to take a closer look at how credit works before you get over your head in debt.

If you scored 10–13 points, you're off to a good start, but be sure you know the pitfalls of opening a credit account.

If you scored 14–18 points, you know a lot about credit and how to use it responsibly.

Source: *How to Be Credit Smart* (Washington, DC, Consumer Education Foundation, 1994).

credit to buy goods or services you can't afford can lead to serious trouble. If you fail to repay a loan, you can lose your good credit reputation. You may also lose some of your income and property, which may be taken from you in order to repay your debts.

Using credit does not increase your total purchasing power, nor does it mean that you have more money. It just lets you buy things now that you must pay for later. If your income does not increase, you may have difficulty paying your bills. Therefore, you should always approach credit with caution and avoid using it for more than your budget allows.

Types of Credit

Two basic types of consumer credit exist: closed-end credit and open-end credit. You will probably use both types of credit during your lifetime.

Closed-End Credit

With *closed-end credit*, you receive a one-time loan that you will pay back over a specified period of time and in payments of equal amounts. Closed-end credit is used for a specific purpose and involves a definite amount of money. A mortgage—a long-term loan extended to someone who buys property—is a common use of closed-end credit. Automobile loans and installment loans for purchasing furniture or large appliances are also examples of closed-end credit. These types of loans usually carry lower interest rates than open-end credit does.

When the Petersons were ready to move out of their apartment, they decided to buy a three-bedroom house and apply for a mortgage from a local bank. The Petersons signed a written agreement that indicated how much their monthly payments would be, how many payments they would make, and the cost of the credit over the life of the loan. The bank will hold the title to the house until the Petersons have completed their payments.

Suppose that you want to buy a sofa and loveseat to furnish your living room. You might apply for an installment loan from a furniture company. You would usually sign a contract promising to repay the balance, plus interest, in equal installments over a specified period.

THINK FIRST Everyone likes to have nice things, but using credit unwisely can lead to problems. *What should you consider before using credit?*

Open-End Credit

With *open-end credit*, you borrow money for a variety of goods and services. The company issuing the credit gives you a certain limit on the amount of money you can borrow. A *line of credit* is the maximum amount of money the creditor has made available to you. Department store credit cards and bank credit cards, such as Visa or MasterCard, are examples of open-end credit. After a credit card company has approved your application for credit and you have received the card, you can use it to make as many purchases as you wish, as long as you don't exceed your line of credit. You are then billed periodically for at least partial payment of the total amount you owe.

Sources of Consumer Credit

Many sources of consumer credit are available, including commercial banks and credit unions. **Figure 6.2** summarizes the major sources of consumer credit. Study and compare the differences to determine which source might best meet your needs and requirements.

Loans

Loans involve borrowing money with an agreement to repay it, along with interest, within a certain amount of time. If you were considering taking out a loan, your immediate thought might be to go to your local bank. However, you might want to explore some other options first.

INEXPENSIVE LOANS   Parents or other family members are often the source of the least expensive loans—loans with low interest. They may charge only the interest they would have earned on the money if they had deposited it in a savings account. They may even give you a loan without interest. Be aware, however, that loans can complicate family relationships.

MEDIUM-PRICED LOANS   Often you can obtain medium-priced loans—loans with moderate interest—from commercial banks, savings and loan associations, and credit unions. Borrowing from credit unions has several advantages. They provide personalized-service, and usually they're willing to be patient with borrowers who can provide good reasons for late or missed payments. As you learned in Chapter 5, you must be a member of a credit union in order to get a loan from one.

EXPENSIVE LOANS   The easiest loans to obtain are also the most expensive. Finance companies and retail stores that lend to

Figure 6.2

Sources of Consumer Credit

Credit Source	Type of Loan	Lending Policies
Commercial Banks	Single-payment loan Personal installment loans Passbook loans Check-credit loans Credit card loans Second mortgages	• Seek customers with established credit history • Often require collateral or security • Prefer to deal in large loans, such as auto, home improvement, and home modernization, with the exception of credit card and check-credit plans • Determine repayment schedules according to the purpose of the loan • Vary credit rates according to the type of credit, time period, customer's credit history, and the security offered • May require several days to process a new credit application
Consumer Finance Companies	Personal installment loans Second mortgages	• Often lend to consumers without established credit history • Often make unsecured loans • Often vary rates according to the size of the loan balance • Offer a variety of repayment schedules • Make a higher percentage of small loans than other lenders • Maximum loan size limited by law • Process applications quickly, frequently on the same day the application is made
Credit Unions	Personal installment loans Share draft-credit plans Credit-card loans Second mortgages	• Lend to members only • Make unsecured loans • May require collateral or cosigner for loans over a specified amount • May require payroll deductions to pay off loan • May submit large loan applications to a committee of members for approval • Offer a variety of repayment schedules
Life Insurance Companies	Single-payment or partial-payment loans	• Lend on cash value of life insurance policy • No date or penalty on repayment • Deduct amount owed from the value of policy benefit if death or other maturity occurs before repayment
Federal Savings Banks (Savings and Loan Associations)	Personal installment loans (generally permitted by state-chartered savings associations) Home improvement loans Education loans Savings account loans Second mortgages	• Will lend to all creditworthy individuals • Often require collateral • Loan rates vary depending on size of loan, length of payment, and security involved Source: *Managing Your Credit* (Household International, 1988), pp. 18–19. © Household Financial Services, Prospect Heights, Illinois.

SEEKING CUSTOMERS Consumer credit is available from several types of sources. *Which sources seem to offer the widest variety of loans?*

consumers will frequently charge high interest rates, ranging from 12 to 25 percent. Banks also lend money to their credit card holders through cash advances—loans that are billed to the customer's credit card account. Most cards charge higher interest for a cash advance and charge interest from the day the cash advance is made. As a result, it is much more expensive to take out a cash advance than to charge a purchase to a credit card.

HOME EQUITY LOANS   A home equity loan is a loan based on your home equity—the difference between the current market value of your home and the amount you still owe on the mortgage. Unlike interest on most other types of credit, the interest you pay on a home equity loan is tax-deductible. You should use these loans only for major items such as education, home improvements, or medical bills, and you must use them with care. If you miss payments on a home equity loan, the lender can take your home. For more information about home equity loans, see Chapters 7 and 17.

Credit Cards

Credit cards are extremely popular. According to a recent *American Banker* survey, eight out of ten U.S. households carry one or more credit cards. One-third of all credit card users generally pay off their balances in full each month. These cardholders are often known as convenience users. Cardholders who do not pay off their balances every month are known as borrowers.

Most credit card companies offer a *grace period*, a time period during which no finance charges will be added to your account. A *finance charge* is the total dollar amount you pay to use credit. Usually, if you pay your entire balance before the due date stated on your monthly bill, you will not have to pay a finance charge. Borrowers carry balances beyond the grace period and pay finance charges.

The cost of a credit card depends on the type of credit card you have and the terms set forth by the lender. As a cardholder, you may have to pay interest or other finance charges. Some credit card companies charge cardholders an annual fee, usually about $20. However, many companies have eliminated annual fees in order to attract more customers. If you're looking for a credit card, be sure to shop around for one with no annual fee. **Figure 6.3** gives some other helpful hints for choosing a credit card.

QUICK CASH   Using a debit card can be a convenient way to get cash any time you need it. *How is a debit card different from a credit card?*

Figure 6.3

Choosing a Credit Card

When you choose a credit card, it pays to shop around. Follow these suggestions to find the card that best meets your needs and to use it wisely:

1) Department stores and gasoline companies are good places to obtain your first credit card.

2) Bank credit cards are offered through banks and savings and loan associations. Annual fees and finance charges vary widely, so shop around.

3) If you plan on paying off your balance every month, look for a card that has a grace period and carries no annual fee or a low annual fee. You might have a higher interest rate, but you plan to pay little or no interest anyway.

4) Watch out for creditors that offer low or no annual fees but instead charge a transaction fee every time you use the card.

5) If you plan to carry a balance, look for a card with a low monthly finance charge. Be sure that you understand how the finance charge is calculated.

6) Watch out for cards with variable interest rates. Your interest rate may rise and fall unpredictably.

7) Not all cards offer a grace period. When you use such a card, the bank begins charging you interest on the day you make the purchase or the day the purchase is recorded on your account.

8) If your card offers a grace period, take advantage of it by paying off your balance in full each month. With a grace period of 25 days, you actually get a free loan when you pay bills in full each month.

9) If you have a bad credit history and have trouble getting a credit card, look for a savings institution that will give you a secured credit card. With this type of card, your line of credit depends on how much money you keep in a savings account that you open at the same time.

10) Travel and entertainment cards often charge higher annual fees than most credit cards. Usually, you must make payment in full within 30 days of receiving your bill, or no further purchases will be approved on the account.

11) Many banks and credit card issuers may charge hidden fees, such as service charges. Make sure that you know what they are.

12) Think twice before you make a telephone call to a 900 number to request a credit card. You will pay from $2 to $50 for the 900 call and may never receive a credit card.

Sources: American Bankers Association, *Understanding Credit Card Costs* (San Francisco: Consumer Action), March 1994. *Choosing and Using Credit Cards* (Washington, DC: Federal Trade Commission), January 1999. American Institute of Certified Public Accountants. U.S. Office of Consumer Affairs. Federal Trade Commission.

CRITICAL THINKING

Before you enter the world of credit, you need to understand the various options that are available to you. *Which of these factors would be most important in your choice of a credit card?*

DEBIT CARDS   Don't confuse credit cards with debit cards. Although they may look alike, they're very different. A debit card electronically subtracts money from your savings or checking account to pay for a good or service. A credit card extends credit and delays your payment. Debit cards are most commonly used at automatic teller machines (ATMs). More and more, however, they are also used to purchase goods in stores and to make other types of payments. Review Chapter 5 for a detailed discussion of debit cards.

SMART CARDS   Some lenders are starting to offer a new kind of credit card called a smart card. A smart card is a plastic card equipped with a computer chip that can store 500 times as much data as a normal credit card. Smart cards can combine credit card balances, a driver's license, health care identification, medical history, and other information all in one place. In the future, they'll

Careers in Finance

CREDIT COUNSELOR

Though bad credit plagues hundreds of thousands of people, credit counselors can help consumers improve their credit profiles by reviewing credit reports and correcting wrong or outdated information. Credit counselors also help people budget for fixed expenses, such as car loans and mortgages, and variable expenses, such as utility bills and food. Credit counselors can consolidate the consumer's debt and arrange a repayment plan. The consumer pays the counseling agency, and the agency pays the creditors. Counselors may also teach classes on credit and budgeting.

Skills	Communication, computer, interpersonal, math, negotiation, organizational, problem solving
Personality	Able to see the big picture and work under stress, discreet, flexible, likes working with people, tactful
Education	Bachelor's degree or high school diploma with experience in a bank or consumer finance office; certification by organization such as National Foundation for Consumer Credit
Pay range	$20,000 to $50,000 a year, depending on experience and location

Determine People often get into debt by mistaking wants for needs. (You may want an expensive new sports car, but you only need a basic used car to get to work.) List your needs, such as a car, clothes, and food. Determine whether you have satisfied your needs with more expensive wants. How do you think a credit counselor would advise you if you needed to reduce your expenses?

 For more information on credit counselors visit finance.glencoe.com or your local library.

also provide a crucial link between the physical world and the Internet, causing major changes in business and finance practices.

TRAVEL AND ENTERTAINMENT (T&E) CARDS Travel and Entertainment (T&E) cards are really not credit cards because the balance is due in full each month. However, most people think of T&E cards—such as Diners Club or American Express cards—as credit cards because they don't pay for a good or service when they purchase it.

SECTION 6.1 ASSESSMENT

CHECK YOUR UNDERSTANDING

1. List two advantages and two disadvantages of using credit.
2. What is the difference between closed-end credit and open-end credit?
3. Give an example of an inexpensive loan, a medium-priced loan, and an expensive loan.

THINK CRITICALLY

4. Review **Figure 6.3**, which provides tips on choosing a credit card. How might you select the card that best meets your needs from among many offers?

USING COMMUNICATION SKILLS

5. **Cash or Charge?** The use of credit in the United States is widespread. Nevertheless, some people use credit cards and take out loans only in an emergency. Their philosophy is that if they don't have the cash to pay for something, they shouldn't take on a debt that they might not be able to repay. Other people believe that the use of credit is necessary for everyday living. These consumers are sure that they will eventually be able to pay off their debts.
Present a Point of View What is your view on the issue of using credit? Write a short essay that explains the role of credit cards and loans in your philosophy of money management.

SOLVING MONEY PROBLEMS

6. **Evaluating Credit** Garrett, a high school senior, wanted to get his girlfriend a special birthday gift. A local electronics store had one-day special discounts on stereos, with no payments required until after six months. With income from his part-time job, Garrett felt that he could incorporate the expense into his budget. His mother and sister tried to discourage him from buying the stereo.
Analyze How would you advise Garrett in this situation? Explain your reasoning.

Measuring the Cost of Credit and Obtaining Credit

Can You Afford a Loan?

What You'll Learn

- How to **determine** whether you can afford a loan
- How to **describe** what creditors look for in a credit applicant
- How to **develop** an effective strategy to build and maintain your credit rating

Why It's Important

Understanding the costs involved in obtaining credit will give you the tools to acquire the best source of credit. Knowing how to apply for credit and how to build your credit rating will increase your chances of getting the credit you want or need.

KEY TERMS

- net income
- annual percentage rate (APR)
- collateral
- simple interest
- principal
- minimum monthly payment
- credit rating

Taking out a loan can be a substantial financial burden. Before you take out a loan, you need to be sure that you can afford it. Will you be able to meet all your usual expenses plus the monthly loan payments you'll have to make? You can answer this question in several ways.

One way is to add up all your basic monthly expenses and then subtract the total from your take-home pay. If the difference is not enough to make a monthly loan payment and still have a little left over, you can't afford the loan.

LOOK BEFORE YOU LEAP   Before taking out a loan, you should sit down and figure out your finances. *What is perhaps the most important point you should consider?*

A second way is to consider what you might give up to make the monthly loan payment. For example, perhaps you're putting some of your monthly income into a savings account. Would you be willing to use that money to make loan payments instead? If not, would you consider cutting back on unnecessary but fun activities such as going to movies or eating out? Are you prepared to make this trade-off?

Although you can't measure your credit capacity exactly, you can use the debt payments-to-income ratio formula to decide whether you can safely take on the responsibility of credit.

Debt Payments-to-Income Ratio

The debt payments-to-income ratio is the percentage of debt you have in relation to your net income. *Net income* is the income you receive (your take-home pay, allowance, gifts, interest on bank accounts, and so on). Experts suggest that you spend no more than 20 percent of your net income on debt payments. For example, if your net income is $1,000 per month, your monthly debt payments should total no more than $200. Monthly debt payments include credit card and loan payments. You can calculate your debt payments-to-income ratio by dividing your total monthly debt payments (not including your rent or mortgage) by your monthly net income.

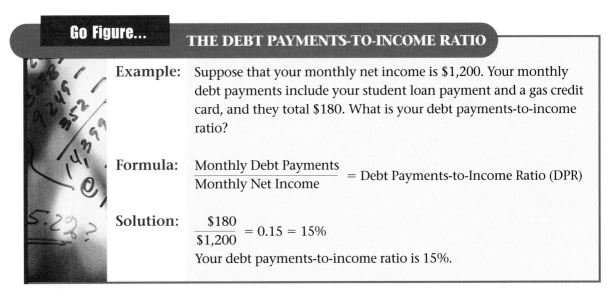

Go Figure...

THE DEBT PAYMENTS-TO-INCOME RATIO

Example: Suppose that your monthly net income is $1,200. Your monthly debt payments include your student loan payment and a gas credit card, and they total $180. What is your debt payments-to-income ratio?

Formula:
$$\frac{\text{Monthly Debt Payments}}{\text{Monthly Net Income}} = \text{Debt Payments-to-Income Ratio (DPR)}$$

Solution:
$$\frac{\$180}{\$1,200} = 0.15 = 15\%$$
Your debt payments-to-income ratio is 15%.

Twenty percent is the most you should spend on debt payments, but 15 percent is much better. The higher figure does not take into account emergency expenses, and it's based on an average family's average expenses. If you're a young adult who's just beginning to experiment with credit, play it safe and stay below the 20 percent limit.

The Cost of Credit

If you're thinking of taking out a loan or applying for a credit card, your first step should be to figure out how much it will cost you and whether you can afford it. Then you should shop for the best credit terms. Two key factors will be the finance charge and the annual percentage rate (APR).

The Finance Charge and the Annual Percentage Rate (APR)

The finance charge is the total dollar amount you pay to use credit. In most cases, you will have to pay finance charges to a creditor on any unpaid balance.

The finance charge is calculated using the annual percentage rate. The *annual percentage rate (APR)* shows how much credit costs you on a yearly basis, expressed as a percentage. For example, an APR of 18 percent means that you pay $18 per year on each $100 you owe. Every organization that extends credit of any kind must state the true APR that it charges its customers. This makes it easy to compare the cost of credit at several businesses or among several different credit cards.

To determine the total amount of finance charges that you will pay on $100 borrowed, look at **Figure 6.4.** Find the APR at the top of the chart and the number of payments at the left side of the chart. The point at which they meet is the total amount you will pay in finance charges for each $100 borrowed.

Figure 6.4				
Annual Percentage Rate Table for Monthly Payments				
Annual Percentage Rate—APR (Finance Charge per $100 Borrowed)				
Number of Monthly Payments	**7.0%**	**7.5%**	**8.0%**	**8.5%**	**9%**
6	$2.05	$2.20	$2.35	$2.49	$2.64
12	$3.83	$4.11	$4.39	$4.66	$4.94
18	$5.63	$6.04	$6.45	$6.86	$7.28
24	$7.45	$8.00	$8.55	$9.09	$9.64
30	$9.30	$9.98	$10.66	$11.35	$12.04

FINDING THE FINANCE CHARGE	If you borrow money and don't pay it back right away, you'll probably have to pay a finance charge. *What is the finance charge that you would pay if you borrowed $100 for 18 months at an APR of 9 percent?*

For example, find the column showing an APR of 8 percent. Follow it down until it meets the row showing 24 monthly payments. You'll see that if you borrow $100 at an APR of 8 percent for two years (24 months), you will pay $8.55 in finance charges. Under the Truth in Lending Act, the creditor must inform you, in writing and before you sign any agreement, of the finance charge and the APR.

Tackling the Trade-offs

When you select your financing, you will have to make trade-offs. You'll have to choose among various features, including the length of the loan, the size of monthly payments, and the interest rate. Here are some of the major trade-offs you should consider.

TERM VERSUS INTEREST COSTS   Many people choose longer-term financing because they want smaller monthly payments. However, the longer the term (the period of time) of a loan at a given interest rate, the greater the amount you will pay in interest charges. Compare the following credit arrangements on a $6,000 loan:

	APR	Term of Loan	Monthly Payment	Total Finance Charge	Total Cost
Creditor A	14%	3 years	$205.07	$1,382.52	$7,382.52
Creditor B	14%	4 years	163.96	1,870.08	7,870.08

How do these choices compare? The answer depends partly on what you need. The lower-cost loan is available from Creditor A. If you're looking for lower monthly payments, you could repay the loan over a longer period of time. However, you would have to pay more in total costs. A loan from Creditor B provides smaller monthly payments but adds about $488 to your total finance charge.

LENDER RISK VERSUS INTEREST RATE   You may prefer financing that requires a minimum down payment, a portion of the total cost of an item that is required at the time of purchase. Another option is to take out a loan that features low fixed payments with a large final payment. Keep in mind that the lender's goal is to minimize risk, or make sure that you pay back the loan in full. Consumers who want these types of features have to accept a trade-off—a more expensive loan.

To reduce lender risk and increase your chance of getting a loan at a lower interest rate, consider the following options:

- **Variable Interest Rate**   A variable interest rate is based on changing rates in the banking system. This means that the interest rate you pay on your loan will vary from time to time. If you have a loan with a variable interest rate and overall interest rates rise, the rate on your loan is adjusted accordingly. Therefore, the lender may offer you a lower beginning interest rate than you would have with a fixed-rate loan.

- **A Secured Loan**   You'll probably receive a lower interest rate on your loan if you pledge collateral. *Collateral* is a form of security to help guarantee that the creditor will be repaid. It indicates that if you lost your source of income, you could repay your loan with the collateral, such as your savings, or by selling some of your property. If you don't pay back the loan, the lender may have the legal right to take whatever you pledged as collateral.
- **Up-Front Cash**   Many lenders believe that you have a higher stake in repaying a loan if you make a large down payment. Thus, you may have a better chance of getting the other loan features you want.
- **A Shorter Term**   The shorter the period of time (or term) for which you borrow, the smaller the chance that something will prevent you from repaying your loan. This lowers the risk to the lender. Therefore, you may be able to borrow at a lower interest rate if you accept a shorter-term loan, but your monthly payments will be higher.

Calculating the Cost of Credit

The most common method of calculating interest is the simple interest formula. Other methods, such as simple interest on the declining balance and add-on interest, are variations of this formula.

SIMPLE INTEREST   *Simple interest* is the interest computed only on the *principal*, the amount that you borrow. It is based on three factors: the principal, the interest rate, and the amount of time for which the principal is borrowed. To calculate the simple interest on a loan, multiply the principal by the interest rate and by the amount of time (in years) for which the money is borrowed. (See the Go Figure box on the following page.)

SIMPLE INTEREST ON THE DECLINING BALANCE When a simple interest loan is paid back in more than one payment, the method of computing interest is known as the declining balance method. You pay interest only on the amount of principal that you have not yet repaid. The more often you make payments, the lower the interest you'll pay. Most credit unions use this method.

ADD-ON INTEREST   With the add-on interest method, interest is calculated on the full amount of the original principal, no matter how often you make payments. When you pay off the loan with one payment, this method produces the same annual

Go Figure... SIMPLE INTEREST ON A LOAN

Example: Damon convinced his aunt to lend him $1,000 to purchase a used laptop computer. She has agreed to charge only 5% simple interest, and he has agreed to repay the loan at the end of one year. How much interest will he pay for the year?

Formula: Principal × Interest Rate × Amount of Time = Simple Interest

Solution: $1,000 × 5% × 1 = $50
Damon will pay $50 in interest.

percentage rate (APR) as the simple interest method. However, if you pay in installments, your actual rate of interest will be higher than the stated rate. Interest payments on this type of loan do not decrease as the loan is repaid. The longer you take to repay the loan, the more interest you'll pay.

COST OF OPEN-END CREDIT The Truth in Lending Act requires that open-end creditors inform consumers as to how the finance charge and the APR will affect their costs. For example, they must explain how they calculate the finance charge. They must also inform you when finance charges on your credit account begin to accrue so that you know how much time you have to pay your bills before a finance charge is added.

COST OF CREDIT AND EXPECTED INFLATION Inflation reduces the buying power of money. Each percentage point increase in inflation means a decrease of about 1 percent in the quantity of goods and services you can buy with the same amount of money. Because of this, lenders incorporate the expected rate of inflation when deciding how much interest to charge.

Remember the earlier example in which Damon borrowed $1,000 from his aunt at the bargain rate of 5 percent for one year? If the inflation rate was 4 percent that year, his aunt's actual rate of return on the loan would have been only about 1 percent (5 percent stated interest minus 4 percent inflation rate). A professional lender that wanted to receive 5 percent interest on Damon's loan might have charged him 9 percent interest (5 percent interest plus 4 percent-anticipated inflation rate).

AVOID THE MINIMUM MONTHLY PAYMENT TRAP On credit card bills and with certain other forms of credit, the *minimum monthly payment* is the smallest amount you can pay and remain a borrower in good standing. Lenders often encourage you to make

PREDICT

Why is it unwise to pay only the monthly minimum balance on a credit card debt?

STANDARD &POOR'S

CASE STUDY

*E*stella Mendez recently graduated from technical school and has just been offered a position as a computer programmer. She and her best friend have decided to rent an apartment together and share expenses. Estella has always lived at home with her parents, but now she's ready for a new life on her own. She has no debt, but she has never really handled her own finances. In the next few months Estella would like to buy a car, so she decided to sign up for a personal finance seminar at the local community center. In addition to learning about budgeting, investing, and savings, Estella will learn the importance of establishing and maintaining good credit. At this point she has no credit at all and wonders what she should do to begin building a credit history. Estella turned to the experts at Standard & Poor's for advice.

STANDARD &POOR'S **Analysis:** Estella is well on her way to living a life free of financial worries. Her technical training is a valuable skill that has already landed her a promising job, and she is planning ahead to live within her income. Estella needs to consider how much she can afford to pay for a car, including maintenance and insurance costs, and whether it's better to save or borrow for this purchase.

STANDARD &POOR'S **Recommendation:** It won't be long before Estella begins receiving letters from companies offering her preapproved credit cards. Credit cards usually carry a high interest rate compared with other types of loans, so Estella should start building her credit history by opening a savings account and putting at least 10 percent of each paycheck into savings. After a few months she can take out a modest installment loan. With this type of loan Estella will pay a set amount each month. These payments should be no more than the amount Estella practiced saving each month from her paycheck. By agreeing to use the money she borrows to purchase a certificate of deposit or Treasury bill to secure the loan, Estella will qualify for a low rate. At the same time she'll earn interest at a slightly lower rate on her investment. When the loan is repaid, Estella may decide to use the savings she has accumulated to purchase an older used car or to make a down payment on a new car.

Critical Thinking Questions

1. What are some of the costs of establishing credit through a credit card company compared with a bank loan?
2. Why might Estella decide to use her savings to buy an older used car rather than finance a more expensive new one?
3. What types of purchases might it make sense to borrow for?

the minimum payment because it will then take you longer to pay off the loan. However, if you're paying only the minimum amount on your monthly statement, you need to plan your budget more carefully. The longer it takes for you to pay off a bill, the more interest you pay. The finance charges you pay on an item could end up being more than the item is worth.

For example, suppose that Natasha is buying new books for college. She spends $500 on textbooks, using a credit card that charges 19.8 percent interest, and she makes only the minimum monthly payment of $21.67. It will take Natasha approximately two and one-half years to pay off the loan, adding $150 in interest charges to the cost of her purchase.

Applying for Credit

When you're ready to apply for a loan or a credit card, you should understand the factors that determine whether a lender will extend credit to you.

The Five Cs of Credit

When a lender extends credit to consumers, it takes for granted that some people will be unable or unwilling to pay their debts. Therefore, lenders establish policies for determining who will receive credit. Most lenders build such policies around the "five Cs of credit": character, capacity, capital, collateral, and credit history.

CHARACTER: WILL YOU REPAY THE LOAN?   Creditors want to know what kind of person they will be lending money to. They want to know that you're trustworthy and stable. They may ask for personal or professional references, and they may check to see whether you have a history of trouble with the law. Some questions a lender might ask to determine your character are:

- Have you used credit before?
- How long have you lived at your present address?
- How long have you held your current job?

CAPACITY: CAN YOU REPAY THE LOAN?   Your income and the debts you already have will affect your ability to pay additional debts. If you already have a large amount of debt in proportion to your income, lenders probably won't extend more credit to you. Some questions a creditor may ask about your income and expenses are:

- What is your job, and how much is your salary?
- Do you have other sources of income?
- What are your current debts?

HISTORY

In 1950 Diners Club issued the first travel and entertainment card, which allowed members to charge meals in 27 restaurants in New York City. In 1958 the first bank credit card appeared. By 1965 about 5 million credit cards were in circulation. In 1997 U.S. consumers had more than 1.3 billion credit cards. Credit cards make it much easier for us to buy, but we have less incentive to save. Do you think credit cards have created a society of people who want instant gratification?

CAPITAL: WHAT ARE YOUR ASSETS AND NET WORTH?

You may recall from Chapter 3 that assets are any items of value that you own, including cash, property, personal possessions, and investments. Your capital is the amount of your assets that exceed your liabilities, or the debts you owe. Lenders want to be sure that you have enough capital to pay back a loan. That way, if you lost your source of income, you could repay your loan from your savings or by selling some of your assets. A lender might ask:

- What are your assets?
- What are your liabilities?

COLLATERAL: WHAT IF YOU DON'T REPAY THE LOAN?

Creditors look at what kinds of property or savings you already have, because these can be offered as collateral to secure the loan. If you fail to repay the loan, the creditor may take whatever you pledged as collateral. A creditor might ask:

- What assets do you have to secure the loan (such as a car, your home, or furniture)?
- Do you have any other valuable assets (such as bonds or savings)?

CREDIT HISTORY: WHAT IS YOUR CREDIT HISTORY?

Lenders will review your credit history to find out whether you've used credit responsibly in the past. They'll probably obtain a copy of your credit report from a credit bureau. Some questions a creditor might ask about your credit history are:

- Do you pay your bills on time?
- Have you ever filed for bankruptcy?

The information gathered from your application and the credit bureau establishes your credit rating.

A *credit rating* is a measure of a person's ability and willingness to make credit payments on time. The factors that determine a person's credit rating are income, curent debt, information about a character, and how debts have been repaid in the past. If you always make your payments on time, you will probably have an excellent credit rating. If not, your credit rating will be poor, and a lender probably won't extend credit to you. A good credit rating is a valuable asset that you should protect.

Creditors use different combinations of the five Cs to reach their decisions. Some creditors set unusually high standards, and others simply do not offer certain types of loans. Creditors also use various rating systems. Some rely strictly on their own instincts and experience. Others use a credit scoring or statistical system to predict whether an applicant is a good credit risk. When you apply for a

Figure 6.5

Sample Credit Application Questions

- Amount of loan requested
- Proposed use of the loan
- Your name and birth date
- Social Security and driver's license numbers
- Present and previous street addresses
- Present and previous employers and their addresses

- Present salary
- Number and ages of dependents
- Other income and sources of other income
- Have you ever received credit from us?
- If so, when and at which office?
- Checking account number, institution, and branch

- Savings account number, institution, and branch
- Name of nearest relative not living with you
- Relative's address and telephone number
- Your marital status

WHO ARE YOU? A potential lender will require you to answer a number of specific questions on a credit application. *Why do you think that a creditor would want to know the names and addresses of your present and previous employers?*

loan, the lender is likely to evaluate your application by asking questions such as those included in the checklist in **Figure 6.5.**

You should also know what factors a lender cannot consider, according to the law. The Equal Credit Opportunity Act (ECOA) gives all credit applicants the same basic rights. It states that race, nationality, age, sex, marital status, and certain other factors may not be used to discriminate against you in any part of a credit dealing.

Age

The Equal Credit Opportunity Act (ECOA) is very specific about how a person's age may be used as a factor in credit decisions. A creditor may request that you state your age on an application, but if you're old enough to sign a legal contract (usually 18 or 21 years old, depending on state law), a creditor may not turn you down or decrease your credit because of your age. Creditors may not close your credit account because you reach a certain age or retire.

Public Assistance

You may not be denied credit because you receive Social Security or public assistance. However, certain information related to this source of income can be considered in determining your creditworthiness.

Housing Loans

The ECOA also covers applications for mortgages or home improvement loans. In particular, it bans discrimination against you based on the race or nationality of the people in the neighborhood where you live or want to buy your home, a practice called redlining.

RESPOND

Which ECOA protection do you think is most important? Explain your reasoning.

EQUAL PLAYING FIELD Part of the American dream is to own a home. *What federal law ensures that all applicants for mortgages or home improvement loans will be treated equally?*

What If Your Application Is Denied?

If your credit application is denied, the ECOA gives you the right to know the reasons. If the denial is based on a credit report from a credit bureau, you're entitled to know what specific information in the report led to the denial. After you receive this information, you can contact the credit bureau and ask for a copy of your credit report. The bureau cannot charge a fee for this service as long as you ask to see your files within 60 days of notification that your credit application has been denied. You're entitled to ask the bureau to investigate any inaccurate or incomplete information and correct its records. (See **Figure 6.6**.)

Your Credit Report

When you apply for a loan, the lender will review your credit history very closely. The record of your complete credit history is called your credit report, or credit file. Your credit records are collected and maintained by credit bureaus. Most lenders rely heavily on credit reports when they consider loan applications. **Figure 6.7** on page 176, provides a checklist for building and protecting your credit history.

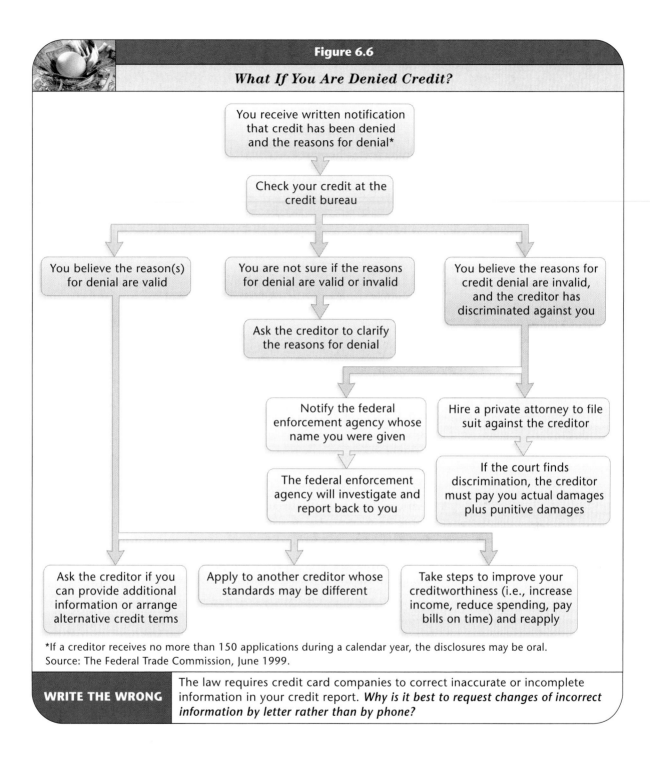

Figure 6.6

What If You Are Denied Credit?

You receive written notification that credit has been denied and the reasons for denial*

Check your credit at the credit bureau

You believe the reason(s) for denial are valid

You are not sure if the reasons for denial are valid or invalid

You believe the reasons for credit denial are invalid, and the creditor has discriminated against you

Ask the creditor to clarify the reasons for denial

Notify the federal enforcement agency whose name you were given

Hire a private attorney to file suit against the creditor

The federal enforcement agency will investigate and report back to you

If the court finds discrimination, the creditor must pay you actual damages plus punitive damages

Ask the creditor if you can provide additional information or arrange alternative credit terms

Apply to another creditor whose standards may be different

Take steps to improve your creditworthiness (i.e., increase income, reduce spending, pay bills on time) and reapply

*If a creditor receives no more than 150 applications during a calendar year, the disclosures may be oral.
Source: The Federal Trade Commission, June 1999.

WRITE THE WRONG The law requires credit card companies to correct inaccurate or incomplete information in your credit report. *Why is it best to request changes of incorrect information by letter rather than by phone?*

Credit Bureaus

A credit bureau is an agency that collects information on how promptly people and businesses pay their bills. The three major credit bureaus are Experian Information Solutions (formerly TRW, Inc.), Trans

Figure 6.7

Checklist for Building and Protecting Your Credit History

It is simple and sensible to build and protect your own credit history. Here are some steps to get you started:

- Open a checking or savings account, or both.
- Apply for a local department store credit card.
- Take out a small loan from your bank. Make payments on time.

A creditor must:

1. evaluate all applicants on the same basis
2. consider income from part-time employment
3. consider the payment history of all joint accounts, if this accurately reflects your credit history
4. disregard information on accounts if you can prove that it doesn't affect your ability or willingness to repay

Remember that a creditor cannot:

1. refuse you individual credit in your own name if you are creditworthy
2. require your spouse to cosign a loan. Any creditworthy person can be your cosigner if one is required
3. ask about your family plans or assume that your income will be interrupted to have children
4. consider whether you have a telephone listing in your name

Source: Reprinted by permission of the Federal Reserve Bank of Minneapolis.

FIRM FOUNDATION | If you want a good credit rating, you must use credit wisely. *Why is it a good idea to apply for a local department store credit card or a small loan from your bank?*

Union Credit Information Company, and Equifax Services, Inc. Each of these bureaus maintains more than 200 million credit files on individuals, based on information they receive from lenders. Several thousand smaller credit bureaus also collect credit information about consumers. These firms make money by selling the information they collect to creditors who are considering loan applications.

Credit bureaus get their information from banks, finance companies, stores, credit card companies, and other lenders. These sources regularly transmit information about the types of credit they extend to customers, the amounts and terms of the loans, and the customers' payment habits. Credit bureaus also collect some information from other sources, such as court records.

What's in Your Credit Files?

A typical credit bureau file contains your name, address, Social Security number, and birth date. It may also include the following information:

- Your employer, position, and income
- Your previous address

- Your previous employer
- Your spouse's name, Social Security number, employer, and income
- Whether you rent or own your home
- Checks returned for insufficient funds

In addition, your credit file contains detailed credit information. Each time you use credit to make a purchase or take out a loan of any kind, a credit bureau is informed of your account number and the date, amount, terms, and type of credit. Your file is updated regularly to show how many payments you've made, how many payments were late or missed, and how much you owe. Any lawsuits or

INTERNATIONAL FINANCE   Panama

$\mathcal{E}$veryone takes shortcuts between two places. One of the most famous shortcuts is the Panama Canal, which stretches across the Isthmus of Panama and connects the Atlantic and Pacific Oceans. Every year, about 13,500 ships make the 50-mile crossing in eight to ten hours. On average, each ship pays a $42,000 toll, bringing in more than $400 million a year for Panama. In 1997, the passenger ship *Rhapsody of the Seas* paid the highest toll: $156,662.66. In 1928, an American explorer paid the lowest, 36 cents, to swim the canal. Here's a snapshot of Panama.

Geographic area	29,762 sq. mi.
Population	2,809,000
Capital	Panama City (pop. 464,900)
Language	Spanish, English
Currency	balboa
Gross domestic product (GDP)	$18 billion
Per capita GDP	$6,700
Economy	Industry: construction, petroleum refining, brewing, cement and other construction materials. Agriculture: bananas, rice; livestock; fishing (shrimp). Exports: bananas, shrimp, sugar, clothing, coffee.

The Panama Canal connects the Atlantic and Pacific Oceans.

Thinking Critically

Calculate Before the Panama Canal opened in 1914, ships had to round the tip of South America when traveling ocean to ocean. Find a map of North and South America. Using a ruler and the map's scale, calculate how many miles a ship will save if it sails from New York to San Francisco by way of the Panama Canal. Then take the average toll of $42,000 and calculate how much a ship would pay per mile to travel through the canal.

For more information on Panama visit finance.glencoe.com **or your local library.**

judgments against you may appear as well. Federal law protects your rights if the information in your credit file is incorrect.

Fair Credit Reporting

Fair and accurate credit reporting is vital to both creditors and consumers. In 1971 the U.S. Congress enacted the Fair Credit Reporting Act, which regulates the use of credit reports. This law requires the deletion of out-of-date information and gives consumers access to their files as well as the right to correct any misinformation that the files may include. The act also places limits on who can obtain your credit report.

Who Can Obtain a Credit Report?

Your credit report may be issued only to properly identified persons for approved purposes. It may be supplied in response to a court order or by your own written request. A credit report may also be provided for use in connection with a credit transaction, underwriting of insurance, or some other legitimate business need. Friends, neighbors, and other individuals cannot be given access to credit information about you. In fact, if they even request such information, they may be subject to a fine, imprisonment, or both.

Time Limits on Unfavorable Data

Most of the information in your credit file may be reported for only seven years. However, if you've declared personal bankruptcy, that fact may be reported for ten years. A credit reporting agency can't disclose information in your credit file that's more than seven or ten years old unless you're being reviewed for a credit application of $75,000 or more, or unless you apply to purchase life insurance of $150,000 or more.

Incorrect Information in Your Credit File

Credit bureaus are required to follow reasonable procedures to make sure that the information in their files is correct. Mistakes can and do occur, however. If you think that a credit bureau may be reporting incorrect data from your file, contact the bureau to dispute the information. The credit bureau must check its records and change or remove the incorrect items. If you challenge the accuracy of an item on your credit report, the bureau must remove the item unless the lender can verify that the information is accurate.

If you're denied credit, insurance, employment, or rental housing based on the information in a credit report, you can get a free copy of your report. Remember to request it within 60 days of notification that your application has been denied.

What Are Your Legal Rights?

You have a legal right to sue a credit bureau or creditor that has caused you harm by not following the rules established by the Fair Credit Reporting Act.

SECTION 6.2   ASSESSMENT

CHECK YOUR UNDERSTANDING

1. Name several ways to determine whether you can afford a loan.
2. What are the 5 Cs of credit that lenders consider when reviewing your credit application?
3. Identify three steps you could take to maintain a good credit rating.

THINK CRITICALLY

4. Summarize ways in which you can reduce lender risk to increase your chance of getting a loan at a lower interest rate.

USING MATH SKILLS

5. **Debt Payments-to-Income Ratio** Kim Lee is trying to decide whether she can afford a loan she needs in order to go to chiropractic school. Right now Kim is living at home and works in a shoe store, earning a gross income of $820 per month. Her employer deducts a total of $145 for taxes from her monthly pay. Kim also pays $95 on several credit card debts each month. The loan she needs for chiropractic school will cost an additional $120 per month. **Calculate** Help Kim make her decision by calculating her debt payments-to-income ratio with and without the college loan. (Remember the 20 percent rule.)

SOLVING MONEY PROBLEMS

6. **Equal Credit Opportunity Act** Eleanor Davis is a single woman. Although she has a good income and uses credit wisely, she has been denied a loan to buy a house and does not know why. She believes that she may have been discriminated against or that there may be some incorrect information in her credit record. **Identify Alternatives** Using the information in the section on applying for credit, discuss Eleanor's rights and options in finding out why she was denied credit.

What You'll Learn

- How to **identify** ways to protect your credit

Why It's Important

Knowing your rights and the procedures to follow when problems arise in your credit dealings will allow you to protect your financial situation and your financial reputation.

KEY TERMS

- **co-signing**

Protecting Your Credit

Billing Errors and Disputes

Have you ever received a bill for something you didn't buy? Have you ever made a payment that wasn't credited to your account? If so, you're not alone. You may be a responsible consumer who pays bills promptly and manages personal finances carefully. Even so, mistakes can happen. If you want to protect your credit rating, your time, and your money, you need to know how to correct mistakes that may pop up in your credit dealings.

Follow these steps if you think that a bill is wrong or want more information about it. First, notify your creditor in writing, and include any information that might support your case. (A telephone call is not sufficient and will not protect your rights.) Then pay the portion of the bill that is not in question.

Your creditor must acknowledge your letter within 30 days. Then, within two billing periods (but not longer than 90 days), the creditor must either adjust your account or tell you why the bill is correct. If the creditor made a mistake, you don't have to pay any finance charges on the disputed amount. If no mistake is found, the creditor must promptly send you an explanation of the situation and a statement of what you owe, including any finance charges that may have accumulated and any minimum payments you missed while you were questioning the bill.

Protecting Your Credit Rating

According to law, a creditor may not threaten your credit rating or do anything to damage your credit reputation while you're negotiating a billing dispute. In addition, the creditor may not take any action to collect the amount in question until your complaint has been answered.

Defective Goods and Services

Theo used his credit card to buy a new mountain bike. When it arrived, he discovered that some of the gears didn't work properly. He tried to return it, but the store would not accept a return. He asked the store to repair or replace the bike—but still he had no luck.

According to the Fair Credit Billing Act, he may tell his credit card company to stop payment for the bicycle because he has made a sincere attempt to resolve the problem with the store.

Identity Crisis: What to Do If Your Identity Is Stolen

"I don't remember charging those items. I've never been in that store." Maybe you never charged those goods and services, but someone else did—someone who used your name and personal information to commit fraud. When impostors use your personal information for their own purposes, they are committing a crime.

The biggest problem? You may not know that your identity has been stolen until you notice that something is wrong: You may get bills for a credit card account you never opened, or you may see charges to your account for things that you didn't purchase.

If you think that your identity has been stolen and that someone is using it to charge purchases or obtain credit in some other way, you can take action. See **Figure 6.8** for information on what to do if your identity is stolen.

PLAYING FAIR Suppose that you buy something with your credit card, and it turns out to be defective. *If you try to get your money back and the store refuses your request, what might you do?*

Protecting Your Credit from Theft or Loss

Some thieves will pick through your trash in the hope of coming across your personal information. You can prevent this from happening by tearing or shredding any papers that contain personal information before you throw them out.

If you believe that an identity thief has accessed your bank accounts, close the accounts immediately. If your checks have been stolen or misused, stop payment on them. If your debit card has been lost or stolen, cancel it and get another with a new Personal Identification Number (PIN).

Lost credit cards are a key element in credit card fraud. To protect your card, you should take the following actions:

- Be sure that your card is returned to you after a purchase. Unreturned cards can find their way into the wrong hands.
- Keep a record of your credit card number. You should keep this

PREDICT

How can your "identity" be stolen?

- Keep a record of your credit card number. You should keep this record separate from your card.
- Notify the credit card company immediately if your card is lost or stolen. Under the Consumer Credit Protection Act, the maximum amount that you must pay if someone uses your card illegally is $50. However, if you manage to inform the company before the card is used illegally, you have no obligation to pay at all.

Protecting Your Credit Information on the Internet

CONNECT

Do you, your friends, or family members shop online? How do you or they make sure all transactions are secure?

The Internet is becoming almost as important to daily life as the telephone and television. Increasing numbers of consumers use the Internet for financial activities, such as investing, banking, and shopping.

When you make purchases online, make sure that your transactions are secure, that your personal information is protected, and that your "fraud sensors" are sharpened. Although you can't control

FIGURE 6.8

Dealing with a Stolen Identity

If someone has stolen your identity, the Federal Trade Commission recommends that you take three actions immediately:

1 **Contact the Credit Bureaus** *Tell them to flag your file with a fraud alert, including a statement that creditors should call you for permission before they open any new accounts in your name.*

fraud or deception on the Internet, you can take steps to recognize it, avoid it, and report it. Here's how:

- Use a secure browser.
- Keep records of your online transactions.
- Review your monthly bank and credit card statements.
- Read the privacy and security policies of Web sites you visit.
- Keep your personal information private.
- Never give your password to anyone online.
- Don't download files sent to you by strangers.

Co-signing a Loan

If a friend or relative ever asks you to co-sign a loan, think twice. *Co-signing* a loan means that you agree to be responsible for loan payments if the other party fails to make them. When you co-sign, you're taking a chance that a professional lender will not take. The lender would not require a cosigner if the borrower were considered a good risk.

If you co-sign a loan and the borrower does not pay the debt, you may have to pay up to the full amount of the debt as well as any late fees or collection costs. The creditor can even collect the debt from you without first trying to collect from the borrower. The

2 Contact the Creditors **Contact the creditors for any accounts that have been tampered with or opened fraudulently. Follow up in writing.**

3 File a Police Report **Keep a copy of the police report in case your creditors need proof of the crime. If you're still having identity problems, stay alert to new instances of identity theft. You can also contact the Privacy Rights Clearinghouse. Call (619) 298-3396.**

creditor can use the same collection methods against you that can be used against the borrower. If the debt is not repaid, that fact will appear on your credit record.

Complaining About Consumer Credit

If you believe that a lender is not following the consumer credit protection laws, first try to solve the problem directly with the lender. If that fails, then you should use more formal complaint procedures. This section describes how to file a complaint with the federal agencies that administer consumer credit protection laws.

Consumer Credit Protection Laws

If you have a particular problem with a bank in connection with any of the consumer credit protection laws, you can get advice and help from the Federal Reserve System. You don't need to have an account at the bank to file a complaint. You may also take legal action against a creditor. If you decide to file a lawsuit, you should be aware of the various consumer credit protection laws described below.

TRUTH IN LENDING AND CONSUMER LEASING ACTS If a creditor fails to disclose information as required under the Truth in Lending Act or the Consumer Leasing Act, or gives inaccurate information, you can sue for any money loss you suffer. You can also sue a creditor that does not follow rules regarding credit cards. In addition, the Truth in Lending Act and the Consumer Leasing Act permit class-action lawsuits. A class-action suit is a legal action on behalf of all of the people who have suffered the same injustice.

EQUAL CREDIT OPPORTUNITY ACT (ECOA) If you think that you can prove that a creditor has discriminated against you for any reason prohibited by the ECOA, you may sue for actual damages plus punitive damages—a payment used to punish the creditor who has violated the law—up to $10,000.

FAIR CREDIT BILLING ACT A creditor that fails to follow the rules that apply to correcting any billing errors will automatically give up the amount owed on the item in question and any finance charges on it, up to a combined total of $50. This is true even if the bill was correct. You may also sue for actual damages plus twice the amount of any finance charges.

FAIR CREDIT REPORTING ACT You may sue any credit bureau or creditor that violates the rules regarding access to your credit records or that fails to correct errors in your credit file. You're entitled to actual damages plus any punitive damages the court allows if the violation is proven to have been intentional.

CONSUMER CREDIT REPORTING REFORM ACT The Consumer Credit Reporting Reform Act of 1997 places the burden of proof for accurate credit information on the credit bureau rather than on you. Under this law, the creditor must prove that disputed information is accurate. If a creditor or the credit bureau verifies incorrect data, you can sue for damages.

Your Rights Under Consumer Credit Laws

If you believe that you've been refused credit because of discrimination, you can take one or more of the following steps:

- Complain to the creditor. Let the creditor know that you are aware of the law.

Figure 6.9

Federal Government Agencies that Enforce the Consumer Credit Laws

If you think you've been discriminated against by:	You may file a complaint with the following agency:
A retailer, nonbank credit card issuer, consumer finance company, state-chartered credit union or bank, noninsured savings and loan institution	Federal Trade Commission (FTC) Equal Credit Opportunity Washington, DC 20580
A national bank	Comptroller of the Currency Consumer Affairs Division Washington, DC 20219
A Federal Reserve member bank	Board of Governors of the Federal Reserve System Director, Division of Consumer Affairs Washington, DC 20551
Other insured banks	Federal Deposit Insurance Corporation Office of Bank Customer Affairs Washington, DC 20429
Insured savings and loan institutions	Federal Home Loan Bank Board Equal Credit Opportunity Washington, DC 20552
The FHA mortgage program	Housing and Urban Development (HUD) Department of Health, Education and Welfare Washington, DC 20410
A federal credit union	National Credit Union Administration 2025 M Street, N.W. Washington, DC 20455

PROTECTING YOUR RIGHTS The law gives you certain rights as a consumer of credit. *What types of complaints about a creditor might you report to these government agencies?*

- File a complaint with the government. You can report any violations to the appropriate government enforcement agency, as shown in **Figure 6.9**.
- If all else fails, sue the creditor. You have the right to bring a case in a federal district court. If you win, you can receive actual damages and punitive damages of up to $10,000. You can also recover reasonable attorneys' fees and court costs.

SECTION 6.3 ASSESSMENT

CHECK YOUR UNDERSTANDING

1. What should you do if you think that a bill is wrong or want more information about it? How should your creditor respond to your attempt to resolve the situation?
2. How can you protect yourself against credit card theft or loss?
3. How does the Fair Credit Reporting Act protect you?

THINK CRITICALLY

4. Recall the suggestions for protecting your credit information on the Internet. Predict the problems that could result from not following the guidelines.

USING COMMUNICATION SKILLS

5. **Co-signing a Loan** Suppose that a close friend has asked you to co-sign a loan she needs to start up a children's clothing store. You would like to help if you can. However, your friend is currently unemployed, and you're concerned that she won't be able to repay the loan. After much thought, you decide not to co-sign the loan.
   Write a Letter Write a letter to your friend explaining why you've decided not to co-sign her loan. In the letter, point out what the consequences to you will be if she is unable to repay the loan.

SOLVING MONEY PROBLEMS

6. **Putting a Stop to Fraud** Joel went to the ATM the other day to withdraw some cash. When he checked his receipt, he noticed that the balance on his savings account was $500 less than it should have been. After discussing the matter with a customer service representative at his bank, he realized that someone else had gained access to his account number and Personal Identification Number (PIN).
   Apply Using what you've learned about protecting yourself from fraud, what advice can you give Joel about the steps he should take to stop any further damage from being done?

Managing Your Debts

Warning Signs of Debt Problems

Carl Reynolds is in his early 20s. A recent college graduate, he has a steady job and earns an annual income of $40,000. With the latest model sports car parked in the driveway of his new home, it would appear that Carl has the ideal life.

However, Carl is deeply in debt. He is drowning in a sea of bills. Almost all of his income is tied up in debt payments. The bank has already begun foreclosure proceedings on his home, and several stores have court orders to repossess practically all of his new furniture and electronic gadgets. His current car payment is overdue, and he is behind in payments on all of his credit cards. If he doesn't come up with a plan of action, he'll lose everything.

Carl's situation is all too common. Some people who seem to be wealthy are just barely keeping their heads above water financially. Generally, the problem they share is financial immaturity. They lack

LIVING IT UP Some people use credit to finance a comfortable lifestyle. *How might this cause problems in the future?*

self-discipline and don't control their impulses. They use poor judgment or fail to accept responsibility for managing their money.

Carl and others like him aren't necessarily bad people. They simply haven't thought about their long-term financial goals. Someday you could find yourself in a situation similar to Carl's. Here are some warning signs that you may be in financial trouble:

RESPOND

What corrective steps would you take if you were experiencing the debt troubles listed here?

- You make only the minimum monthly payment on credit cards.
- You're having trouble making even the minimum monthly payment on your credit card bills.
- The total balance on your credit cards increases every month.
- You miss loan payments or often pay late.
- You use savings to pay for necessities such as food and utilities.
- You receive second or third payment due notices from creditors.
- You borrow money to pay off old debts.
- You exceed the credit limits on your credit cards.
- You've been denied credit because of a bad credit bureau report.

If you are experiencing two or more of these warning signs, it's time for you to rethink your priorities before it's too late.

Debt Collection Practices

The Federal Trade Commission enforces the Fair Debt Collection Practices Act (FDCPA). This act prohibits certain practices by *debt collectors*—businesses that collect debts for creditors. The act does not erase the legitimate debts that consumers owe, but it does control the ways in which debt collection agencies may do business.

Financial Counseling Services

If you're having trouble paying your bills and need help, you have several options. You can contact your creditors and try to work out an adjusted repayment plan, or you can contact a nonprofit financial counseling program.

Consumer Credit Counseling Service

The Consumer Credit Counseling Service (CCCS) is a nonprofit organization affiliated with the National Foundation for Consumer Credit (NFCC). Local branches of the CCCS provide debt counseling services for families and individuals with serious financial problems. The CCCS is not a charity, a lending institution, or a government agency. CCCS counseling is usually free. However, when the organization supervises a debt repayment plan, it sometimes charges a small fee to help pay administrative costs.

According to the NFCC, millions of consumers contact CCCS offices each year for help with their personal financial problems. To find an office near you, check the white pages of your local telephone directory under Consumer Credit Counseling Service, or call 1-800-388-CCCS. All information is kept confidential.

Credit counselors know that most individuals who are overwhelmed with debt are basically honest people who want to clear up their unmanageable *indebtedness*, the condition of being deeply in debt. Too often, such problems arise from a lack of planning or a miscalculation of earnings. The CCCS is concerned with preventing problems as much as it is with solving them. As a result, its activities are divided into two parts:

- Aiding families with serious debt problems by helping them to manage their money better and set up a realistic budget
- Helping people prevent indebtedness by teaching them the importance of budget planning, educating them about the pitfalls of unwise credit buying, and encouraging credit institutions to withhold credit from people who cannot afford it

Other Counseling Services

In addition to the CCCS, universities, credit unions, military bases, and state and federal housing authorities sometimes provide nonprofit credit counseling services. These organizations usually charge little or nothing for their assistance. You can also check with your bank or local consumer protection office to see whether it has a listing of reputable financial counseling services, such as the Debt Counselors of America.

Declaring Personal Bankruptcy

What if a debtor suffers from an extreme case of financial woes? Can there be any relief? The answer is bankruptcy proceedings. *Bankruptcy* is a legal process in which some or all of the assets of a debtor are distributed among the creditors because the debtor is unable to pay his or her debts. Bankruptcy may also include a plan for the debtor to repay creditors on an installment basis. Declaring bankruptcy is a last resort because it severely damages your credit rating.

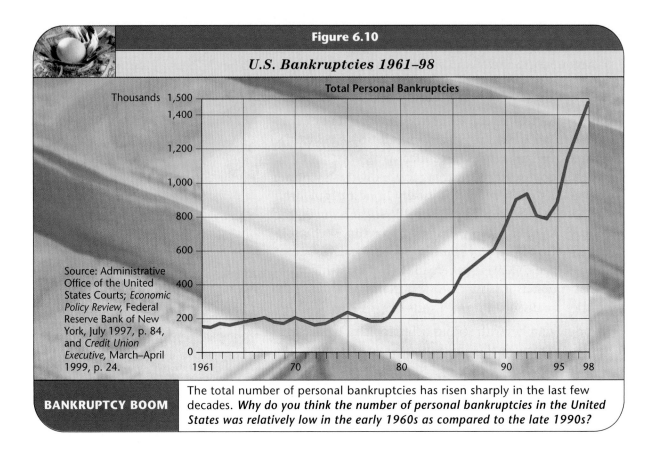

Figure 6.10

U.S. Bankruptcies 1961–98

Total Personal Bankruptcies

Source: Administrative Office of the United States Courts; *Economic Policy Review*, Federal Reserve Bank of New York, July 1997, p. 84, and *Credit Union Executive*, March–April 1999, p. 24.

BANKRUPTCY BOOM The total number of personal bankruptcies has risen sharply in the last few decades. *Why do you think the number of personal bankruptcies in the United States was relatively low in the early 1960s as compared to the late 1990s?*

Prakrit Singh illustrates the new face of bankruptcy. A 43-year-old freelance photographer from California, she was never in serious financial trouble until she began running up big medical costs. She reached for her credit cards to pay the bills. Because Prakrit didn't have health insurance, her debt quickly mounted and soon reached $17,000—too much to pay off with her $25,000-a-year income. Her solution was to declare personal bankruptcy and enjoy the immediate freedom it would bring from creditors' demands.

In 1994 the U.S. Senate passed a bill that reduced the time and cost of bankruptcy proceedings. The bill strengthened creditor rights and enabled more individuals to get through bankruptcy proceedings without selling their assets. Today, legislators continue to propose new bankruptcy law reforms that are intended to end perceived abuses of the current bankruptcy system.

The U.S. Bankruptcy Act of 1978

Figure 6.10 illustrates the rate of personal bankruptcy in the United States. The vast majority of bankruptcies in the United States, like Prakrit Singh's, are filed under a part of the U.S. bankruptcy code known as Chapter 7. You have two choices in declaring personal bankruptcy: Chapter 7 (a straight bankruptcy) and Chapter 13 (a wage earner plan bankruptcy). Both choices are undesirable, and neither should be considered an easy way to get out of debt.

CHAPTER 7 BANKRUPTCY   In a Chapter 7 bankruptcy, an individual is required to draw up a petition listing his or her assets and liabilities. A person who files for relief under the bankruptcy code is called a debtor. The debtor submits the petition to a U.S. district court and pays a filing fee.

Chapter 7 is a straight bankruptcy in which many, but not all, debts are forgiven. Most of the debtor's assets are sold to pay off creditors. Certain assets, however, receive some protection. Among the assets usually protected are Social Security payments, unemployment compensation, and the net value of your home, car or truck, household goods and appliances, tools used in your work, and books.

The release from debt does not affect alimony, child support, certain taxes, fines, certain debts arising from educational loans, or debts that you fail to disclose properly to the bankruptcy court. Furthermore, debts arising from fraud, driving while intoxicated, or certain other acts or crimes may also be excluded.

CHAPTER 13 BANKRUPTCY   In a Chapter 13 bankruptcy, a debtor with a regular income proposes a plan for using future earnings or assets to eliminate his or her debts over a period of time. In such a bankruptcy, the debtor normally keeps all or most of his or her property.

During the period when the plan is in effect, which can be as long as five years, the debtor makes regular payments to a Chapter 13 trustee, or representative, who then distributes the money to the creditors. Under certain circumstances, the bankruptcy court may approve a plan that permits the debtor to keep all property even though he or she repays less than the full amount of the debts.

Effects of Bankruptcy

People have varying experiences in obtaining credit after they file for bankruptcy. Some find the process more difficult, whereas others find it easier because they have removed the burden of prior debts or because creditors know that they cannot file another bankruptcy case for a certain period of time. Obtaining credit may be easier for people who file a Chapter 13 bankruptcy and repay some of their debts than for those who file a Chapter 7 bankruptcy and make no effort to repay any of their debts.

QUESTION

How will filing for bankruptcy negatively impact a person's future?

One Is Enough

When you turn 18, you may start receiving applications for credit cards. Be a smart consumer and compare interest rates, annual fees, and any other fees. Decide which credit card best suits your needs and apply for that one. Toss any other applications you get into the trash.

Your Financial Portfolio

Credit Cards: Getting the Best Deal

Melanie's parents want to give her a credit card she could use for emergencies. They made it clear that if she could eat it, wear it, or listen to it, it was *not* an emergency. They asked Melanie to do the homework to find the best deal. She called the bank where she has a savings account and another neighborhood bank and asked about the following credit card information.

Melanie's Mighty Credit Card Cost Comparison		
Credit card company	**Peabody Bank**	**Imperial Bank**
Phone number	800/555-1274	800/555-9201
Annual percentage rate (APR)	15.74%	10.9%
Introductory rate	2.9% on transferred balances	5% for first 6 months
Annual fee	$50	none
Grace period	18 days	25 days
Cash advance fee	19.8%	19.9%
Late payment fee	$25	$29
Credit limit for new customers	based on income	based on income
Premium offers and services:		
Travel accident insurance	$150,000	$1,000
Other travel-related services	airline miles; lost luggage insurance; emergency travel services	lost luggage insurance; emergency travel services
Protection if the cards are lost or stolen	yes	yes

Melanie chose the credit card with Imperial Bank because there was no annual fee and the percentage rate was lower. She didn't think she would spend enough to make Peabody Bank's offer of airline miles useful. Melanie was surprised at the high penalty for late payments, so she made a mental note to be sure to make her payment on time.

If you wanted a credit card, which company would you prefer? Explain why. Would you be influenced by the offer of airline miles?

Research In your workbook or on a separate sheet of paper, research two credit card companies. List their fees and any advantages they offer.

Bankruptcy reports are kept on file in credit bureaus for ten years, a fact that is likely to make getting credit more difficult during that time. Therefore, you should take the extreme step of declaring bankruptcy only when you have no other options for solving your financial problems.

SECTION 6.4   ASSESSMENT

CHECK YOUR UNDERSTANDING

1. What are some of the warning signs of debt problems?
2. Identify the consumer credit counseling services that are available, and describe their services.
3. Discuss the differences between declaring Chapter 7 and Chapter 13 bankruptcy.

THINK CRITICALLY

4. Consider your own financial situation and determine whether any of the warning signs of debt problems might apply to you or to someone you know. Analyze what you might do to correct them or how you might advise someone else.

USING MATH SKILLS

5. **Declaring Bankruptcy** Unfortunately for some people, bankruptcy has become an acceptable form of money management.
   Analyze Data Using the graph in **Figure 6.10**, determine the percent increase of total personal bankruptcies between 1990 and 1998. Do you think that this figure will continue to rise? Why?

SOLVING MONEY PROBLEMS

6. **Making Financial Decisions** Deanne is a customer service representative for a popular fitness club. Her income is modest, but that doesn't stop her from satisfying her most important desire—to travel. Deanne takes two vacations a year, and she has been all over the world. She has paid for most of her trips to faraway places with her credit card. However, when she received the bills for her last trip to India, reality hit hard. Her monthly debt payments are actually greater than her monthly net income.
   Problem Solving According to what you've learned in this section, what can Deanne do to solve her problem? Consider the options she might have, and draw a conclusion about the best way for her to get out of this situation.

CHAPTER 6 ASSESSMENT

CHAPTER SUMMARY

- By understanding the advantages and disadvantages of consumer credit, you will be able to use it in a way that provides personal satisfaction and allows you to meet your financial goals.

- The two basic types of consumer credit are closed-end credit and open-end credit.

- If you're thinking of taking out a loan or applying for a credit card, you should first determine how much it will cost you and whether you can afford it.

- Most lenders establish policies for determining who will receive credit based on the five Cs of credit.

- Building and maintaining a good credit rating is essential to your use of credit now and in the future.

- Knowing how to handle billing errors and fraud will prevent others from damaging your credit rating.

- Consumer credit laws are designed to protect your rights as a consumer.

- If you're having trouble paying your bills, you can try to work out an adjusted repayment plan with your creditors, or you can contact a nonprofit financial counseling program.

- Declaring bankruptcy is a last resort to manage your debts.

internet zone

Understanding and Using Vocabulary

With a partner, write an imaginary meeting between a lender and a credit applicant. Use as many terms as possible.

credit	open-end credit
creditor	line of credit
consumer credit	grace period
interest	finance charge
closed-end credit	net income
annual percentage rate (APR)	credit rating
	co-signing
collateral	debt collectors
simple interest	indebtedness

principal   bankruptcy
minimum monthly payment

Review Key Concepts

1. What are several issues that you might consider before you decide to use credit?
2. Discuss the financial services that come with a credit card, smart card, debit card, and travel and entertainment card.
3. Define the debt payments-to-income ratio.
4. What three things should you do if your identity is stolen?
5. What is the last resort in solving a serious debt problem?

CHAPTER 6 ASSESSMENT

Apply Key Concepts

1. "A young adult who is independent and has a steady income should buy a house if he or she wants one." Do you agree or disagree with this statement? Why?
2. What types of consumers would benefit from a travel and entertainment card?
3. Explain how calculating your debt payments-to-income ratio can help you analyze your ability to afford a loan.
4. Explain how each of the three approaches to dealing with a case of stolen identity can solve the problem or prevent it.
5. Identify the consequences of declaring bankruptcy for a young adult.

 ## Problem Solving Today

THE INSTALLMENT PLAN

For the next year, Victor, your friend from Germany, will be renting an apartment in New York. He will need to buy a television, a desk and chair, a used car, and a sofa. He wants to know what his monthly expenses will be for these items if he uses installment credit and agrees to pay off the debt in one year. Victor will earn a monthly net income of $2,000.

Calculate You found out that the price for these items (including interest) is as follows: television—$250, desk and chair—$270, used car—$5,000, and sofa—$600. Determine Victor's total monthly debt payment if he purchases these items with installment credit. Calculate his debt payments-to-income ratio.

 **Computer Activity** As an alternative activity, use financial software to calculate Victor's total monthly debt payment and his debt payments-to-income ratio.

Real-World Application

CONNECT WITH ECONOMICS Suppose that you are moving into your own apartment. Make a list of some of the items you will need—a couch, a table, a bed, cooking utensils, and so on.

Think Critically Choose three items from your list and indicate whether you would buy each with cash or credit. Discuss your reasons for using cash or credit. If you decide to use credit, determine whether you would use a credit card or a loan, and specify the type of loan.

FINANCE *Online*

GRADUATE SCHOOL OUTLOOK

You have a degree in English and would like to obtain a master's degree and a Ph.D. You have three potential sources for the funds you'll need: grants, scholarships, and student loans.

Connect Use various Internet search engines to find out about the grants, scholarships, and student loan opportunities available to students in your position. Investigate the possibility of applying for these items directly over the Internet. You might begin by checking the Web sites of several colleges or universities you're interested in attending.

CHAPTER 7

The Finances of Housing

STANDARD &POOR'S

Q&A

Q: I love my job as an X-ray technician and plan to work for this hospital for at least five years. How should I decide whether to buy a house or continue renting?

A: A home can be an excellent investment. You'll need to decide what you can afford for a down payment and monthly mortgage payments. Also consider whether you want to spend time maintaining a house; if not, a condominium may be a better choice. If you find a place that you can afford, but you would not want to live there for a long time, consider whether it will be easy to resell or rent your home at a later date.

FOR SALE OR RENT

Evaluating Housing Alternatives

What You'll Learn

- How to **evaluate** available housing alternatives

*S*ue and Don Oliver live in Boston, where they have been renting the same apartment ever since they were married five years ago. During that time, they've been able to put some money aside toward a down payment on a house. They've recently started talking about the type of house they would like to buy and what they can afford.

Sue dreams of having a small, fairly new house in the suburbs, with a backyard. She doesn't want to live in the city any longer. It's crowded, and many of the houses are old and need renovation. Sue wants a house that requires little maintenance. Although Don is skilled with tools, Sue doesn't think that he'll have time to make repairs.

Don thrives on the excitement and diversity of the city and thinks the suburbs are boring. Moreover, he fears that living in the suburbs will add too much time and aggravation to his commute to work. He is also concerned that Sue's dream house would be too small for their needs. Don wants to look at a **handyman's special**—a home that is priced lower because it needs repairs and improvements. He says that he can do the work himself, so that the Olivers can afford more house on their budget.

Why It's Important

The cost of renting or buying your residence will be one of your primary living expenses. The more you know about the housing options available to you, the more wisely you will be able to spend your money now and in the future.

KEY TERMS

- **handyman's special**
- **lifestyle**
- **mobility**

Your Lifestyle and Your Choice of Housing

The Olivers need to spend more time evaluating their wants and needs before they make any decision about moving. One factor they need to consider is their *lifestyle*, the way they choose to spend their time and money.

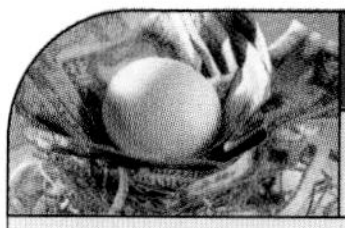

Figure 7.1

Possible Housing for Different Life Situations

Life Situation	Possible Housing Types
Young single	Rent an apartment or house because mobility is important and finances are low Buy a small home for tax advantages and possible increase in value
Single parent	Rent an apartment or house because time for maintenance is at a premium and playmates for children may be nearby Buy a home to build long-term financial security
Young couple, no children	Rent an apartment or house because mobility is important and finances are low Buy a home to build long-term financial security
Couple with children	Rent an apartment or house because time for maintenance is at a premium and playmates for children may be nearby Buy a house to build long-term financial security and to provide more space and privacy
Retired person	Rent an apartment or house to meet financial, social, and physical needs Buy a home that needs little maintenance, offers convenience, and provides different services

RENT OR BUY? Different life situations will require different housing choices. *What might be a wise housing choice for a single parent? Explain your reasoning.*

For example, do they like to host big family gatherings? If so, they'll probably want a large living room or family room. Perhaps Sue would enjoy a bathroom with a full-size tub so that she can relax after work. The Olivers' lifestyle will determine how close to their work they want to live, how long they plan to stay in one place, and how much privacy they would like to have. **Figure 7.1** lists types of housing for people in different life situations.

Finances also play an important role in housing decisions. Whether you're renting a small apartment in a city or buying a house in the country, you'll have to consider your financial situation. You can use your budget and the other personal financial statements discussed in Chapter 3 to determine how much you should spend for housing.

CONNECT

Do you plan to own a house? Explain why or why not.

Opportunity Costs of Housing Choices

As the story of Sue and Don Oliver suggests, a housing decision often requires many trade-offs, or opportunity costs. For example, a house or apartment that is close to your workplace may not be in an area where you want to live, or it may be too expensive. Renting an apartment may give you freedom to pick up and move on short notice, but you'll give up certain tax advantages that homeowners enjoy. Handyman's specials may be great bargains, but they may require large investments of time and money to make them livable. When you make choices about housing, you can't just look at the benefits of a possible decision. You also have to consider what you would be giving up in terms of time, effort, or money.

Renting Versus Buying

One of the most basic considerations as you decide where to live is whether to rent or buy. Your decision will depend on your lifestyle and on financial factors.

Renting is often a good choice for young adults who have recently begun working. It also appeals to people who want or need

What's Your Financial ID?

WHERE WOULD YOU LIKE TO LIVE?

Many factors will help you decide where to live, and these may change over the next few years. You'll need to consider your lifestyle, family situation, finances, and future plans. Here's a quick quiz to test your preferences. Write your answers on a separate sheet of paper.

1. I don't care about having a yard.
   True   False
2. My income varies right now.
   True   False
3. I never want to own a house or condominium.
   True   False
4. I need to be able to move at any time.
   True   False
5. I want to keep my expenses as low as possible.
   True   False
6. I don't want to be responsible for repairs and upkeep.
   True   False
7. I don't plan to have a family for a while.
   True   False

Scoring: The more "true" answers you have, the better it is for you to rent an apartment and postpone house hunting until you're ready.

Figure 7.2

Evaluating Housing Alternatives

	Advantages	Disadvantages
Renting an Apartment	easy to move; low maintenance responsibility; low financial commitment	no tax advantage; limitations on activities; less privacy
Renting a House	easy to move; low maintenance responsibility; low financial commitment; more space	higher utility expenses; some limitations on activities; no tax advantage
Owning a House	pride of ownership; plenty of space; tax benefits	financial commitment; high living expenses; limited mobility
Owning a Condominium	pride of ownership; fewer maintenance costs or responsibilities than a house; tax benefits; access to recreation and businesses	financial commitment; less privacy than in a house; need to get along with others; typically small and limited space; may be hard to sell
Owning a Mobile Home	less expensive than other ownership options	may be hard to sell; possible poor construction quality

ON THE OTHER HAND

Choosing a type of housing is a decision that involves many trade-offs. *Find the three advantages or disadvantages on this list that seem most important to you right now.*

mobility—the ability to move easily from place to place. Renting is also a good choice for people who don't want to devote time to maintenance. Because renting is often—though not always—cheaper than owning a home, it appeals to people whose funds are limited.

In contrast, owning property is often a wise choice for people who want a certain amount of stability in their lives and want more space than they can find or afford in an apartment. Buying a home also gives the owner privacy and some freedoms that may not be available to a renter. For instance, you may not be allowed to have pets or large parties in an apartment, but you can do so in a house that you own. While ownership can be costly—at least in the short run—it offers some financial benefits, too. Homeowners receive tax advantages, and the value of houses often increases, making the purchase of a home a good long-term investment. See **Figure 7.2** for more information about renting and buying.

QUESTION

What are some factors that might make the value of a house increase or decrease?

Housing Information Sources

Housing information is plentiful, and often it is free. The public library will probably have books and other basic resources on the subject. You can find articles on renting, buying, and other housing topics in the real estate section of a newspaper. Friends and family can share information about their own housing choices. You might seek the services of a real estate agent who knows the local housing

Careers in Finance

REAL ESTATE AGENT

When you're ready to buy a home, you'll probably seek the help of a real estate agent. Why? Because real estate agents know the real estate market in your community. They can help you find the neighborhood and home that will best suit your needs and budget. The real estate agent negotiates the sale between a buyer and seller, helps find financing for the buyer, and oversees the entire sale process. Real estate agents are independent salespeople who work for a licensed broker on contract. They work on commission, which means they receive a percentage of the value of the sale.

Skills	communication, computer knowledge, interpersonal, math, organizational skills, problem solving, sales ability
Personality	discreet, honest, likes working with people, mature, neat, tactful
Education	High school diploma, plus training through a real estate company or organization such as the National Association of Realtors
Pay range	$12,000 to $80,000 plus a year, but can vary greatly depending on the value of the property sold

Research   Invite a real estate agent to your class. Ask the agent to discuss the challenges of selling real estate, and what type of training he or she received.

For more information on real estate agents visit finance.glencoe.com **or your local library.**

market inside and out. You can also write to government agencies, such as the Department of Housing. Finally, the Internet can provide home buying tips, the latest mortgage rates, and data on the available housing in your area and in other parts of the United States. Any combination of these sources will provide the information you need to make wise housing decisions.

SECTION 7.1 ASSESSMENT

CHECK YOUR UNDERSTANDING

1. What should you consider when you evaluate available housing alternatives?
2. When might buying be a better choice than renting?
3. Name at least three sources of housing information.

THINK CRITICALLY

4. Write a short paragraph explaining the probable housing needs of a family that consists of two working adults and three school-age children. Decide whether this family should rent or buy, and explain why you think so.

USING COMMUNICATION SKILLS

5. **Housing Options** Your uncle's company has transferred him to your area, and he and his wife will be moving within the next two months. Because they're both so busy with their jobs, they have little time to research a place to live. You've offered to do some background work to get them started.
   Make a Chart Review the real estate section of your local newspaper. Choose several houses and apartments of about the same size, and prepare a chart that compares the prices, locations, and features of each option.

SOLVING MONEY PROBLEMS

6. **Housing and Lifestyle** Your cousin Leila, 25 years old and single, tells you that she's thinking of buying a house in a suburb of the city to which she moved last year. Leila has been in her job for eight months and loves it so far, but she hasn't made many friends yet. The house she's looking at is 10 miles from her workplace. Leila says that the house needs a new roof, and the basement sometimes floods, but otherwise it's in good shape. She thinks that she'll be able to afford it easily once she gets her first raise.
   Analyze Help Leila apply the discussion of lifestyle and opportunity costs to this potential purchase. Would buying the house be a good decision for Leila? Explain your answer.

Renting Your Residence

Are you interested in a "3-bdrm apt., a/c, w/w carpet, pvt back ent, $800 + utils, ref reqd"? This isn't a secret spy code. It's just a short way of describing an apartment for rent listed in the classified ads of a newspaper. Decoded, the message reads "Three-bedroom apartment for rent. It has air conditioning, wall-to-wall carpeting, and a private back entrance. The rent is $800, and the renter must also pay for heat and electricity. You must provide references from other people if you're interested in renting the apartment." Reading such ads is just one of the skills you'll need if you're thinking about living in some type of rental housing.

Selecting a Rental Unit

When you rent the place where you live, you become a *tenant*—a person who pays for the right to live in a residence owned by someone else. The person who owns the property that you rent is your *landlord*. Rental units vary considerably in size, location, and cost.

Most people who rent live in apartments. These units may be located in a two-story house, in a high-rise building in a city, or in an apartment complex. An apartment building contains a number of separate living units that can range in size from one room (known

Rentals

HAMILTON TWP—2 bdrm 1 bath, off str prkg. quiet nghborhd. Use of cellar. $800 mo. 602-989-7767.

PRINCETON—Close to campus. Pvt 1st flr, 1 bdrm. apt., wood flr., lndry. & prkg. No smkg/pets. $925/mo + utils. Avail 7/1 or 8/1. 1 yr lse. 616-433-8756.

TRENTON—Historic dist. Attractive apt. Refinished wood fire, 1 large bdrm, lg liv rm, lg kit, bsmnt storage & yard. $750/mo. 677-547-6400.

SIERRAS—2 bdrm 1 bath, beautiful view, quiet nghborhd. $700 mo. 612-999-7647.

AUSTIN—Close to stores. 1 bdrm. apt., wood flr., lndry. & prkg. No smkg/pets. $825/mo + 1st and last. Avail 10/2 or 11/2. 788-997-8211.

UPSTATE—Affordable rental. Spacious apt. Refinished wood floor, 2 large bdrm, lg kit, din rm, bsmnt storage. $950/mo. 565-989-5466.

MEET THE PRESS   Newspaper ads are one way to find out about available rental units. *What are some of the advantages and disadvantages of looking for an apartment in the classifieds?*

as an efficiency or studio) to three-bedroom or larger units. If a unit features a patio and a bit of lawn, it may be called a garden apartment. Some apartments are located in complexes with on-site swimming pools, tennis courts, and laundry facilities.

A family or individual who needs more space than an apartment provides may prefer to rent a house. The trade-off for the extra space is often higher rent. A single person with very few possessions might choose to rent a private room in a house. He or she will usually have to share common areas such as the kitchen and bathroom.

To find a rental unit, you can check the classified section of the local newspaper. Friends and coworkers are good sources of suggestions, too. You can also check with real estate offices and rental offices. **Figure 7.3** describes what to look for in selecting an apartment.

PREDICT

Where would you look to find information about rental units in your area?

Advantages of Renting

The three main advantages of renting are greater mobility, fewer responsibilities, and lower initial costs.

Mobility and Fewer Responsibilities

For many people, the appeal of renting is the mobility it offers. If you want to move, you can usually notify your landlord 30 days

Figure 7.3
What to Look for in Selecting an Apartment

Location

- Near school, work
- Near church, mosque, synagogue
- Near shopping
- Near public transportation
- Near recreation: parks, museums

Finances

- Amount of monthly rent
- Amount of security deposit
- Cost of utilities
- Length of lease

Building

- Condition of building and grounds
- Parking facilities
- Recreation on premises
- Security system
- Condition of hallways, stairs, and elevators
- Access to mailboxes

Layout and Facilities

- Size and condition of unit
- Type and controls of heating and cooling systems
- Plumbing and water pressure
- Type and condition of appliances
- Condition of doors, locks, windows, closets, and floors

ON YOUR OWN Many considerations go into renting an apartment. *Which of the four broad categories above would be most important to you right now?*

ON THE MOVE Many people like to rent because it allows them to move easily to a different place. *What types of individuals might find such mobility most attractive?*

before you plan to leave, and he or she can find a new tenant. If you're offered a job in another town, you can move quickly and simply. This is also an advantage for growing families who need more space. If your landlord increases your rent beyond the amount you have budgeted, or if you decide that you want to live in a different community, making a change will be fairly easy.

Tenants don't have many of the responsibilities that homeowners do. Making major repairs and maintaining the property are the landlord's concerns. Tenants don't have to worry about property taxes or property insurance. Of course, they must pay the rent and any utility bills on time and are expected to keep their homes clean.

Low Initial Costs

A third advantage to renting, at least initially, is cost. Buying a house typically requires thousands of dollars for the down payment and other costs. In contrast, you will usually pay the equivalent of one or two months' rent to move into a rental unit.

Disadvantages of Renting

Although renting is a good option for many people, it has disadvantages. It offers few financial benefits, may contribute to a more restricted lifestyle, and involves various legal concerns.

Finances and Lifestyle Restrictions

Although it carries lower initial costs, renting may actually be more expensive than owning property. Certain financial benefits are available to homeowners but not to tenants. Homeowners, for example, are eligible for various tax deductions. They also benefit as the value of their property increases. Over time, homeowners pay back any money they borrowed to buy their home, eventually eliminating their monthly housing payments. Tenants, on the other hand, must continue to pay housing costs each month for as long as they continue to rent. They're also subject to rent increases.

Tenants must accept certain limitations with regard to their activities in the places they rent. For instance, you might not be allowed to paint your walls without first getting permission from your landlord. Homeowners have more freedom to do what they want on their own property.

Legal Concerns

If you decide to rent, you will probably have to sign a *lease*, a legal document that defines the conditions of the rental agreement between the tenant and the landlord (see **Figure 7.4**).

Never sign a lease without making sure that you understand and agree with what it says. Pay special attention to the amount and due date of the monthly rent and the length of the rental period. Also, check to see whether you have the right to sublet the property if you want to move out before the lease expires. To *sublet* is to have a person other than the original tenant take over the rental unit and payments for the remaining term of the lease. If you disagree with any of the terms of the lease, discuss those issues with the landlord before you sign the lease—not afterward. Sometimes landlords are willing to negotiate changes to the document.

A lease is designed to protect the rights of both the landlord and the tenant. The tenant is usually protected from rent increases during the lease term. In most states, the tenant cannot be locked out or forced to move without a court hearing. However, the lease gives the landlord the right to take legal action against a tenant who does not pay his rent or who damages the property.

Costs of Renting

The amount of your monthly rent will usually depend on the area in which you choose to live (see **Figure 7.5 on page 208**). You may decide that you are willing to live near the freeway if it costs less than

Figure 7.4

A Typical Lease Agreement

Description of the property, including its address

RENTAL AGREEMENT OF PROPERTY
AT 4744 LEMONA STREET, EAST TROY, WISCONSIN 53120

Names of owners and tenants

Parties in agreement are Blanca Romero and April Shullman. Blanca Romero has rented the second floor apartment to be used as a private residence, for his or her (one person) use only and for no other purpose, for a term of six months.

Dates during which the lease is valid

The term of this agreement will be from June 1, 2002, to November 30, 2002, at which time another six month agreement will be drawn.

Amount of the security deposit

The rent will be $540 per month. There will be a security deposit of one and one-half months' rent, for a total of $810. The monies held as security will be held until such time that the tenant desires to move or until he/she is asked to vacate the premises. The security deposit along with any interest it accrues will be returned to the tenant, minus any monies held for repair of damages, rubbish removal, or cleaning to be done.

Amount and due date of monthly rent and penalties for late payment

Rent will be due from the tenant on the first of each month and not later than five days after the first of each month. A late penalty of 5% of the monthly rent will be assessed for any rent not paid by the end of the five-day grace period.

The tenant is personally responsible for paying the monthly expenses, including electric, telephone, and cable service. These expenses are not included in any monthly rent payment.

The tenant was advised that there is to be NO SMOKING in the apartment, while he/she is in residence at this address.

List of restrictions regarding pets, remodeling, activities, and so on

There will be no pets allowed at any time in the apartment while he/she resides here.

If the tenant or landlord decides that the tenant must vacate the apartment, a thirty (30) day notice must be given before the first of the month.

Tenant's right to sublet the rental unit

The tenant may not sublease (rent to another person) this property without the landlord's written permission.

The tenant must provide his/her own insurance on the contents of the apartment, such as furniture, jewelry, clothes, etc. The tenant will not hold the landlord or landlord's agent responsible in the event of a loss.

Conditions under which the landlord may enter the apartment

The tenant agrees to let landlord enter property at reasonable hours to inspect or repair the property. Landlord will notify the tenant 24 hours in advance and give the time and reason for the visit.

This place of residence shall be occupied by no more than one (1) person.

Charges to the tenant for damage or for moving out of the unit early or refusing to pay rent

At the expiration of tenancy, the tenant will surrender the premises to the landlord in as good condition as when received. The tenant will remove all rubbish from the premises. Failing to do so, the tenant will forfeit part of the security deposit in order for the landlord to pay for removal. If tenant breaks the lease for any reason, the landlord may keep the security deposit.

This agreement is between Blanca Romero and April Shullman. On this day, this agreement is signed by both parties.

Blanca Romero 6/1/02
Tenant   Date

signature 6/1/02
Landlord   Date

MAKING A DEAL
A lease is a legal document extending protection to both tenant and landlord.
Which components of a lease are likely to be most negotiable?

living elsewhere and is more convenient to shopping. You may be willing to pay more for an apartment that is close to a park or work.

The price of a rental unit will also depend on the amount of space that you require. The least expensive choice might be a private room in a house, but you have to be willing to share common areas. Apartments, which are more expensive, often feature one to four bedrooms. Your most costly option might be to rent a town house or single-family house. You might consider living with one or more roommates to share expenses.

As a tenant, you'll find that your biggest expense will be the monthly rent. You may also have to pay for utilities, such as electricity, gas, and telephone service. Ask your landlord what the rent payment includes.

When you sign a lease, you may have to pay the landlord a *security deposit*, an amount of money paid to the owner of the property by a tenant to guard against any financial loss that the tenant might cause. Security deposits usually amount to one or two months' rent.

When you move out, your landlord must return the security deposit, minus any charges for damage you may have caused to the

Figure 7.5

Finding and Living in Rental Housing

Step 1: The Search
- Choose a location and a price that fit your needs.
- Compare costs and features among possible rental units.
- Talk to people who live in the apartment complex or the neighborhood where the units are located.

Step 2: Before Signing a Lease
- Be sure that you understand and agree with all aspects of the lease.
- Note the condition of the rental unit in writing. Have the unit's owner sign it.

Step 4: At the End of the Lease
- Leave the unit in at least as good condition as it was when you moved in.
- Tell your landlord where to send your refunded security deposit.
- Ask that any deductions from your deposit be explained in writing.

Step 3: Living in Rental Property
- Keep the place in good, clean condition.
- Notify the owner of any necessary repairs.
- Respect the rights of neighbors.
- Obtain renter's insurance to protect personal belongings.

SEEING EYE TO EYE Renting involves more than just finding a desirable apartment. *In what ways do these steps protect the rights of both tenant and landlord?*

apartment or for any unpaid rent. Most states require landlords to return the security deposit within one month. In California, however, it must be returned within two weeks.

Another expense is *renters insurance*, a type of insurance that covers the loss of a tenant's personal property as a result of damage or theft. Many tenants neglect to buy renters insurance, wrongly assuming that their clothing, electronic equipment, jewelry, and other possessions are covered by their landlord's insurance. Renters insurance may cost a few hundred dollars a year, but most tenants who buy it find the cost well worth the peace of mind it brings.

SECTION 7.2 ASSESSMENT

CHECK YOUR UNDERSTANDING

1. What are the three main advantages of renting your residence?
2. Describe the disadvantages of renting your residence.
3. What are the costs of renting your residence?

THINK CRITICALLY

4. Which types of apartments would best suit two friends who plan to be roommates? Why?

USING MATH SKILLS

5. **Sharing Costs** Raji is currently paying $675 a month for a one-bedroom apartment, and the cost of all utilities is included in the rent. He is thinking about renting a house with his friend Jon. The monthly rent on the house is $900. Utilities, which aren't included, will amount to about $300 a month. Raji and Jon have agreed to split all costs evenly.
   Compare Costs Calculate how much the move would save or cost Raji each month and over the course of a year.

SOLVING MONEY PROBLEMS

6. **Lease Terms** Jaycee is a college student and has a small apartment for which she pays $450 a month in rent. The lease she signed in August specified that no pets were allowed. However, while visiting her parents over winter break, Jaycee found a stray cat, and she would very much like to keep it.
   Evaluate What options does Jaycee have? Consider all possibilities, and rank them from most to least desirable.

What You'll Learn

- How to **describe** the home buying process
- How to **calculate** the costs of home buying
- How to **develop** a plan for selling a home

Why It's Important

By understanding the home buying process, you'll be better able to decide whether to purchase a home

KEY TERMS

- equity
- zoning laws
- earnest money
- escrow account
- private mortgage insurance (PMI)
- mortgage
- points
- amortization
- conventional mortgage
- adjustable-rate mortgage (ARM)
- default
- home equity loan
- refinance
- closing
- closing costs
- title insurance
- deed
- appraisal

The Home Buying Process

Step 1: Determine Your Home Ownership Needs

Many people dream of owning a home. Buying a home, however, is a huge financial commitment. It will probably be the most costly purchase you'll ever make. To make an informed decision about whether to buy a home, you'll need to consider the benefits and drawbacks of ownership. You'll also need to evaluate the types of homes that are available and determine how much you can afford to spend.

Owning Your Residence: Possible Benefits

While renters may be attracted to the idea of mobility, homeowners enjoy a sense of stability and permanence. Home ownership also lets you express your individuality. You have much more freedom to decorate and change your own home and to have pets. Many people find this flexibility very appealing.

As a homeowner, you will also reap financial benefits. You can deduct the interest charges on your loan payments from your federal income taxes each year. Your property taxes are also deductible. Moreover, the value of many homes rises steadily, so homeowners often can sell their homes for a profit depending on their *equity*—the value of the home less the amount still owed on the money borrowed to purchase it. Finally, once the money they borrowed is paid off, homeowners have no further financial obligation other than property taxes, homeowner's insurance, and maintenance costs.

Owning Your Residence: Possible Drawbacks

Of course, buying a home doesn't guarantee happiness. Home ownership involves financial risk. Saving money for a down payment on a home is very difficult for many people. Moreover, the tax deductions may not make up for high loan payments. Property values don't always go up, either; in some cases, they may even decline.

A second drawback is limited mobility. A homeowner who wants to move must either sell his or her property or arrange to rent it. In both cases, the process can be slow and may result in a financial loss.

FREEDOM OF EXPRESSION For many people, one of the most appealing advantages of home ownership is the ability to decorate or remodel freely. *Can you think of any situations in which homeowners are not completely free to change the look of their homes?*

Finally, owning a home often involves high living expenses. Homeowners must pay for all maintenance and repairs, such as fixing a leaky roof, cleaning out a flooded basement, putting up new wallpaper, and replacing broken appliances. The costs of taking good care of a home can be quite high, even if the homeowners do most of the work themselves.

Types of Housing That Can Be Purchased

Just as people come in all shapes and sizes, housing alternatives are available for a range of budgets and lifestyles.

SINGLE-FAMILY DWELLINGS The most popular type of housing in the United States is the single-family house. A single-family house usually stands on a separate lot with a lawn and some outdoor living space. The home is not attached to any other buildings. Such houses range from old three-story Victorian houses to one-story ranches and split-level houses. Because a single-family dwelling provides the most privacy of any type of housing, it's often the most expensive.

MULTIUNIT DWELLINGS This category of housing includes duplexes and town houses. A duplex is a single building divided into living spaces for two families. The individual units can be arranged side by side or one above the other. Each unit has its own outside entrance. A town house is one of many single-family units attached to other units.

CONDOMINIUMS A condominium is one of a group of apartments or town houses that people own rather than rent. Condominium owners pay a monthly fee to cover the cost of maintenance, repairs, improvements, and insurance for the building and its common spaces. The owners of the units within the building come together to form a condominium association, which manages the housing complex. Common spaces, such as hallways, lawns, elevators, and recreational areas, belong to the association, not to individual owners.

COOPERATIVE HOUSING Cooperative housing is another apartment-style living arrangement in which a building that contains a number of units is owned by a nonprofit organization. Members of the organization pay monthly rent for their units.

MANUFACTURED HOMES A manufactured home is usually one of two types. Prefabricated houses are partly assembled at a factory. The pieces are then transported to a building site and put together there. Prefabricated homes are often cheaper than other single-family houses because the mass production of their pieces and partial assembly at the factory help keep costs down.

GOLDEN YEARS In some parts of the country, mobile home communities are very popular among retired people and senior citizens. *Why do you think those groups find such communities so appealing?*

The other type of manufactured home is known as a mobile home, although most are never moved from their original sites. Mobile homes are fully assembled in factories. Generally small, they nevertheless contain many of the features of larger houses, such as fully equipped kitchens, bathrooms, and fireplaces. Some mobile home owners purchase the land on which their houses are located. Spaces can also be rented in mobile home parks where access to community recreation facilities is often included.

Compared with other housing choices, mobile homes are relatively inexpensive. However, they're not as well constructed or as safe as many other types of housing, and they usually don't increase in value the way single-family houses do.

How Much Can You Afford?

Selecting a type of dwelling is only one part of determining your home ownership needs. You'll also need to consider the price of a home, its size, and its quality.

PRICE AND DOWN PAYMENT   To determine how much you can afford to spend on a home, you'll need to examine your income, your savings, and your current living expenses. Can you afford to make a large down payment when you buy a home? (Remember that a down payment is a portion of the total cost of an item that is required at the time of purchase.) You'll need to make monthly payments on a loan, pay property taxes, and buy homeowners insurance, too. The exact amounts will depend on interest rates and local economic conditions. Is your income enough to cover these costs as well as other current expenses? Before you look for the home of your dreams, it's smart to know just what you can afford to pay.

SIZE AND QUALITY   Ideally, the home you buy will be big enough for your needs and will be in good condition. If you're a first-time buyer, though, you may not be able to get everything you want. Most financial experts recommend buying what you can afford, even if you have to sacrifice some features you'd love to have. As you advance in your career and your income increases, you may be able to purchase a home with some extra comforts.

Eight years ago, Kanya bought a condominium that had only a tiny garden and one small bathroom. Last week she sold it and moved into a new house, where she'll be able to plant a vegetable and flower garden and enjoy the convenience of two full baths.

Step 2: Find and Evaluate a Property to Purchase

Once you know what type of residence you would prefer and what you can afford, you'll be able to start searching for a property to purchase.

Selecting a Location

The location of your home is of critical importance. Would you rather live in a city, in the suburbs, or in a small-town or country setting? Perhaps you want a neighborhood with parks and trails that accommodate cyclists and runners. If you commute to work by bus, you'll have to make sure that your house provides easy access to the bus lines. The distance between home and work, the quality of the local school system, your interests and lifestyle, and other factors help determine where you'll want to live.

Some communities have strict *zoning laws*, regulations that limit how property in a given area can be used. The existence of such laws may also affect your housing decisions. William wanted to live in an all-residential area, so he bought a duplex in a neighborhood where local zoning laws ban any commercial construction such as stores and business buildings. In contrast, Alicia bought a condominium in a much less restrictive community because she wanted to be able to walk to nearby restaurants and businesses.

Hiring a Real Estate Agent

Real estate agents are people who arrange the sale and purchase of homes as well as other buildings and land. As such, they're good sources of information about the availability, prices, and quality of homes in local areas. Potential home buyers often use real estate agents to help them find housing. The agents can also negotiate the purchase price between buyer and seller. They help buyers arrange financing for the purchase; and they can recommend lawyers, insurance agents, and home inspectors to serve the buyers' needs.

Real estate services are usually free to the buyer. The agents typically represent the sellers, who pay them when the property is sold. Some real estate agents, however, represent buyers rather than sellers. In this case, the agent may be paid by either the buyer or the seller.

STANDARD &POOR'S

CASE STUDY

ason Howard and Sarah Ballard are planning to get married in November. Jason graduated from college last year and is working as a computer support consultant for the Department of Transportation. Sarah works as a customer service specialist for an investment broker. After the wedding, Sarah plans to go back to school part-time and finish her college degree. When they marry, Jason will move into Sarah's apartment. Their rent will be $425 per month. Both Jason and Sarah are anxious to purchase a home. They plan to save $25,000, which they think they can accomplish in four years. They hope to purchase a home within the $120,000 to $150,000 price range. Jason and Sarah have lots of questions about buying a home. They turned to the experts at Standard & Poor's for advice.

STANDARD &POOR'S **Analysis:** Jason and Sarah are wise to discuss their financial goals and develop a plan to meet them. The more they learn now about how to choose and finance their first home, the better prepared Jason and Sarah will be to buy a home that they can enjoy for many years.

STANDARD &POOR'S **Recommendation:** Jason and Sarah will need to decide how best to manage their savings for a down payment on a house. Because their time frame is only four years, Jason and Sarah should invest most of their savings in money market funds and bonds. Money market funds invest in certificates of deposit, government securities, and other safe investments. Up to 25 percent of their savings might be invested in stock mutual funds to provide higher growth potential, but there is also the possibility that these higher risk investments will lose money. Jason and Sarah should also plan now to qualify for a mortgage. They can maintain a good credit rating by paying their bills on time. To meet basic mortgage lending requirements, their total monthly debt should be no more than 28 percent of their monthly income, and their total monthly expenses should not exceed 36 percent. When Jason and Sarah are ready to purchase a home, they'll want to consider interest rates, the amount of down payment required, the term of the loan, and closing costs.

Critical Thinking Questions

1. How much of their expected $25,000 in savings do you think Jason and Sarah should use toward a down payment on a home?
2. How might home ownership change the couple's financial situation?
3. Do you think buying a home is a good investment compared to other alternatives? Why?

Conducting a Home Inspection

Before you make a final decision to buy property, it's important to get an evaluation of the house and land by a qualified home inspector (see **Figure 7.6**). Josh Samuels called in a home inspector to check the house he wanted to buy, and he was glad that he had. The inspector found cracks in the foundation, an overloaded electrical system, and problems with the water quality. Josh still wanted the house, and was willing to do some of the repairs himself, but he was able to negotiate a lower selling price once he had the inspector's report. A home inspection costs money, but it can save you from problems and unplanned expenses in the future.

Step 3: Price the Property

After you've checked out the property as thoroughly as possible, it's time to consider making an offer to the current owner. This is usually done through a real estate agent, unless the owner is acting as his or her own agent.

Determining the Price of the Home

Every home that is for sale has a listing price, the price that the owner is asking for it. That price is not necessarily the price you'll pay, however. You're free to make a lower offer, and many people do so. What should you offer? Here are some factors to consider:

- How long has the home been on the market? The longer the current owner has been trying to sell, the more likely it is that you'll be able to buy it for a lower price.
- What have similar homes in the neighborhood sold for recently? Some listing prices are simply too high, so offer less.
- How tight is the housing market? If homes are in high demand, sellers are in a better position to get top dollar. This is called a "seller's market." In this case, you may have to consider offering full price or even more. If the market has an abundant supply of homes for sale, it's a "buyer's market," and you'll be in a better position to make a lower offer.
- Do the current owners need to sell in a hurry? If so, they may be willing to accept less than they feel the home is worth.
- How well does the condition of the home and its features meet your needs? The better the home fits your ideal, the more you may be willing to pay for it.

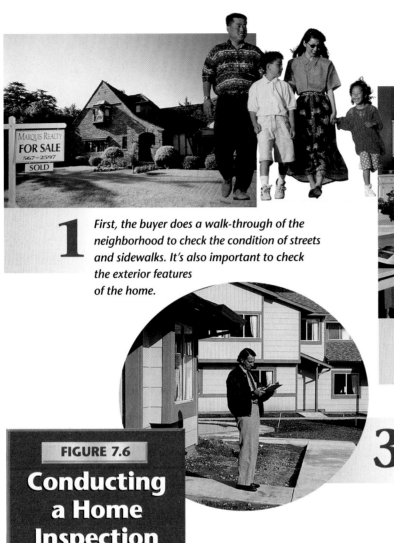

1 First, the buyer does a walk-through of the neighborhood to check the condition of streets and sidewalks. It's also important to check the exterior features of the home.

2 Next, the buyer looks at the interior design of the home to be sure that it will meet his or her needs.

3 In the next step, the buyer hires a home inspector who checks the exterior: windows, foundation, chimney, and roof. The home inspector will also look at the interior construction: electrical wiring, plumbing, heating system, walls, floors, and much more.

FIGURE 7.6

Conducting a Home Inspection

Carefully evaluating a home before you buy it may save you unplanned expenses and disappointments later.

```
        Apple Pie Home Inspection Service
              21044 Manitowoc Avenue
              Woodland Hills, CA 91364

Inspection No:        Inspector: Michelle Cabalu
099422909             Client: Peggie Howard
Inspection Date:      Address: 6301 Glade Rd.
09/29/02                       Reseda, CA 91335

The house is a single-family dwelling, one-
story structure built on a flat lot.
Estimated age is approximately 35 to 40 years
old. Weather at time of inspection was sunny.

100 EXTERIOR

101 Driveway: Concrete with cracks noted.
102 Walks: Concrete and brick
    with cracks noted. Missing bricks noted.
103 Fence/Gates: Wood and chain links.
    Detached wood fence noted.
104 Siding: Stucco and wood with cracks noted.
105 Trim: Wood.
106 Window Frames: Metal and wood.
107 Elec. Fixtures: S
108 Gutters/Downspouts: S
```

4 The potential buyers review the home inspector's report to decide whether this is the right home to buy.

- How easily can you arrange financing? If interest rates are high, you may not be able to afford a payment above a certain amount.

Negotiating the Purchase Price

Once you've decided on a reasonable offer, the real estate agent will relay it to the seller, who may either accept or reject it. If your offer is accepted, congratulations! You'll soon have a new home—and at a price you were willing to pay.

Sometimes the sellers won't accept your offer if it's below the listing price. In that case you'll have to make a second, higher offer, or start looking for a different home. A seller may also make a counteroffer in response to your bid. Making a counteroffer means dropping the asking price. Jian Wang, for example, offered $78,900 for a condominium that was listed at $86,000. The sellers rejected his offer but made a counteroffer of $84,500. Jian thought that the price was still too high, so he submitted a bid of $82,000. They eventually settled on a purchase price of $83,000.

Once the buyer and seller agree on a price, they must sign a purchase agreement, or purchase contract, that states their intention of completing the sale. Most purchase contracts are conditional; that is, they take effect only if certain other events occur. For example, the contract may be valid only if the buyers can obtain financing, or only if they can sell their current home. If these events don't happen within a specified period of time, the deal is off.

At this point in the process, the buyer also must pay the seller a portion of the purchase price, called *earnest money*. This money shows that the offer is serious. It is held in an escrow account until the sale is completed. An *escrow account* is an account in which money is held in trust until it can be delivered to the designated party. If all goes well, the earnest money is applied toward the down payment when the deal is finalized. If the sale cannot be completed for reasons beyond the buyer's control, the earnest money is usually returned to the buyer.

Step 4: Obtain Financing

After you've decided to purchase a specific home and have agreed on a price, you'll have to think about how you'll pay for your purchase. First, you'll have to come up with the money for the down payment. Next, you'll probably have to get a loan to help pay for

THE TEST Applying for a loan requires paperwork that will be examined by the lender to determine your eligibility for the loan. *Why is this process so important to the lender?*

the remainder of the purchase price. Finally, you'll be responsible for fees related to the settlement of the real estate transaction.

Determining Amount of Down Payment

As a general rule, the greater the portion of the purchase price you can pay up front, the easier it will be to obtain a loan. Many lenders suggest that you put down 20 percent or more of the purchase price as a down payment. The most common sources of funds for down payments are personal savings accounts, sales of investments and other assets, and gifts or loans from relatives.

Lower down payments are acceptable. However, if the down payment is less than 20 percent of the purchase price, many lenders will require you to obtain private mortgage insurance. *Private mortgage insurance (PMI)* is a special policy that protects the lender in case the buyer can't make payments, or can't make them on time. Sometimes buyers will pay the cost of PMI up front, and sometimes they will agree to spread the cost over the life of the loan. Once the borrower has paid between 20 and 25 percent of the purchase price, the insurance can be dropped.

Qualifying for a Mortgage

A long-term loan extended to someone who buys property is called a *mortgage*. A bank, credit union, savings and loan association, or mortgage company pays the full amount of the loan to the seller. In return, the buyer pays the lender a monthly fee. These monthly payments are usually made over a period of 15, 20, or 30 years. The home you buy serves as collateral, a type of guarantee that the loan will be repaid. If you fail to repay the loan or make regular payments, the lender can take possession of the property.

To take out a mortgage, you'll need to meet certain criteria, just as you would to qualify for any other type of loan. Lenders will look at your income, your debts, and your savings to decide whether you're a good risk. These figures are put into a formula to determine how much you can afford to pay.

The size of your mortgage will also depend on the current interest rate. The higher the rate, the more you'll need to pay in interest each month. That means that less of your money will be available to pay off the purchase price. As interest rates rise, fewer people are able to afford the cost of an average-priced home.

In contrast, low rates increase the size of the loan that you can receive. Bernadette qualifies for a monthly mortgage payment of $700. If interest rates are 7 percent, she'll be able to take out a 30-year loan of $105,215. However, if interest rates increase to 12 percent, she'll qualify for only a 30-year loan for $68,053. The difference can be quite surprising.

CONNECT

Right now, would you be a good candidate for a mortgage? If not, what things would you need to change in order to qualify?

Evaluating Points

Different lenders may offer slightly different interest rates for mortgages. When you compare the cost of doing business with various lenders, you'll also have to consider other factors. If you want a lower interest rate, you may have to provide a higher down payment and *points*—extra charges that must be paid by the buyer in order to get a lower interest rate. Each point equals 1 percent of the loan amount. For example, suppose that a bank offers you a $100,000 mortgage with two points. Since 2 percent of $100,000 is $2,000, you'll need to pay an extra $2,000 when you purchase your home.

How does a high interest rate with no points compare to a low interest rate with points? A lower interest rate results in a lower monthly payment, but you'll have to pay more money up front. If you keep your new home for only a short time, you'll probably lose money with the lower rate because the monthly savings won't add up to what you had to pay in points. If you keep the home for several years, however, your monthly savings with a low interest rate will eventually make up for what you paid in points. As a rule, the longer you plan to keep the home, the better off you are paying the points in exchange for a lower interest rate.

The Application Process

Most lenders charge home buyers a fee of between $100 and $300 to apply for a mortgage. To apply, the buyer must fill out forms, giving details of his or her income, employment, debts, and other information. The lender will verify this information by obtaining a credit report on the buyer. After a careful examination of the buyer's financial history and the size, location, and condition of the property, the lender will decide whether to approve or deny the

INTERNATIONAL FINANCE   **Egypt**

Egypt

Africa

Egypt's Aswan Dam, completed in 1970, made headlines around the world. The dam blocked the Nile River, providing year-round irrigation, increasing farmland, and generating much of the country's electricity. The pooled water earlier threatened to submerge an ancient temple called Abu Simbel. The solution? International rescue teams cut the temple and 1,200-ton statues of Ramses II into more than 1,000 giant blocks. Then, like puzzle pieces, the teams put them back together on higher ground. The late Egyptian President Anwar Sadat said of the four and one-half year effort: "When people work together for a good cause they can achieve miracles." Here's a snapshot of Egypt.

Geographic area	386,662 sq. mi.
Population	66,924,000
Capital	Cairo (pop. 6,800,000)
Language	Arabic, English, French
Currency	pound
Gross domestic product (GDP)	$267.1 billion
Per capita GDP	$4,400
Economy	Industry: textiles, food processing, tourism, chemicals, petroleum.
	Agriculture: cotton, rice, corn, wheat, beans, fruits, cattle, fish.
	Exports: crude oil, petroleum products, cotton yarn, raw cotton, textiles.

Abu Simbel

Thinking Critically

Assess Dams often bring about positive changes, but they can also be harmful. List some of the ways that the Aswan Dam helped Egypt's economy. What are some of the ways that damming the Nile River hurt Egypt?

For more information on Egypt visit finance.glencoe.com **or your local library.**

application. If it's approved, then the purchase contract between seller and buyer becomes legally binding. If not, then the deal is off unless the buyer can find some other way to finance the purchase.

Types of Mortgages

For most people, a mortgage is the greatest financial obligation of their life. Depending on the terms of the loan, a homeowner will have to make monthly payments for many years.

The monthly payments on a mortgage are set at a level that allows amortization of the loan. *Amortization* means that the balance of the loan is reduced every time you make a payment. The amount of your payment is applied first to the interest owed and then to the principal, the amount you borrowed. In the first years of the loan, only a small part of each monthly payment goes to reduce the principal; most goes toward paying off the interest. Near the end of the loan period, on the other hand, almost all of each payment goes toward reducing the principal. By the end of the loan period, both interest and principal will be completely paid off.

It's often possible to pay a mortgage off early. Paying a little extra each month and applying that amount to the principal will save interest charges over the long run. For example, paying $25 extra a month on a 30-year, 10 percent mortgage of $75,000 will save more than $34,000 in interest charges—and will repay the entire loan more than five years early. Some lenders charge an extra fee for the privilege of prepaying; others do not.

Fixed-Rate/Fixed-Payment Mortgages

The most common type of fixed-rate mortgage, also known as a fixed-payment mortgage, is a conventional mortgage. A *conventional mortgage* offers the buyer a fixed interest rate and a fixed schedule of payments. Conventional mortgages typically run for a period of 15, 20, or 30 years and come with a guaranteed interest rate. For example, if the interest rate is 8.75 percent when the loan is granted, then the homeowner will continue to pay 8.75 percent throughout the life of the loan, even if interest rates for new loans rise. Conventional mortgages offer homeowners peace of mind, because they know that their monthly payments will always remain the same.

Adjustable-Rate/Variable-Payment Mortgages

Fixed-rate loans guarantee a particular interest rate. An *adjustable-rate mortgage (ARM)*, also known as a variable-payment mortgage, has an interest rate that increases or decreases during the life of the loan. The rate changes according to an economic indicator, such as changes in the rates on U.S. Treasury securities, the Federal Home Loan Bank Board's mortgage rate index, or the lender's own cost-of-funds index. As a result, your loan payments will not always remain the same.

Specific details as to how and when the rate changes will depend on the terms of your agreement with the lender. Generally, if interest rates decline and stay low, an ARM will save you substantial amounts of money. However, if rates increase and stay high, an ARM may cost you a lot of money.

Most adjustable-rate mortgages have a rate cap, which limits the amount the interest rate on the loan can rise or fall. Rate caps generally limit increases (or decreases) to one or two percentage points in a year or no more than five points over the life of the loan.

Similarly, some ARMs carry payment caps, which limit the size of monthly payments. That may seem like good protection for the buyer, but it has drawbacks. When interest rates rise while monthly payments remain the same, the payments will not cover the interest. As a result, the loan balance increases, and payments may have to be extended over a longer time.

Some lenders offer convertible ARMs. Convertible ARMs permit borrowers to convert, or change, their adjustable-rate mortgage into a fixed-rate mortgage during a certain period of time. If you decide to make the change, your interest rate will be 0.25 to 0.50 percent higher than current rates for conventional 30-year mortgages. You'll also have to pay a conversion fee, which is usually no more than about $500.

Consider several factors when you evaluate adjustable-rate mortgages:

1. Determine the frequency of and restrictions on allowed changes in interest rates.
2. Consider the frequency of and restrictions on changes in the monthly payment.
3. Find out what index the lender will use to set the mortgage interest rate over the term of the loan.

GOVERNMENT-GUARANTEED FINANCING PROGRAMS

The Federal Housing Administration (FHA) and the Veterans Administration (VA) help home buyers obtain low-interest, low down-payment loans. These loans are available to people who meet certain qualifications. FHA loans are primarily offered to low- and moderate-income buyers, whereas VA loans are available to eligible veterans of the armed services.

Common Cents

On Your Own

Sharing an apartment or a house with a roommate is a great way to cut costs and can be fun to boot. It's a good idea to have a trial period to make sure you get along before making a long-term commitment.

These government agencies don't actually loan the money. Instead, they help qualified buyers arrange for loans from regular lenders. Typically, lenders are guaranteed repayment by the agency if the borrower *defaults*, or is unable to make payments. As a result, many government-guaranteed loans are offered at lower interest rates. Although extra insurance fees may be added onto these loans, government-backed mortgages are a good deal for those who qualify for them.

Home Equity Loans

A second mortgage, more commonly called a *home equity loan*, is a loan based on the difference between the current market value of your home and the amount you still owe on the mortgage. To determine the amount of this type of loan, the financial institution will find out the current market value of your home and how much equity you have in the property. Such loans can provide money for education, home improvement, or other purposes, although some states limit the ways in which the money may be used.

Second mortgages are an easy source of extra cash for homeowners. You must use them with care, however. Taking out additional loans can keep you continually in debt, and if you default on a second mortgage, the lender can take your home.

For more information on home equity loans, see Chapter 17.

Refinancing

Esther Aquino took out a fixed-rate mortgage at 11 percent interest and then watched in dismay as interest rates fell to 6 percent. Fortunately, she was able to *refinance* her home: that is, to take out a new mortgage at a lower interest rate. In Esther's case, her monthly payment dropped considerably.

Refinancing isn't always a good choice. To refinance, you usually need to pay extra fees, which may offset any savings from a small drop in interest rates. Moreover, refinancing may extend the life of your loan. In general, refinancing is to your advantage when the interest rate drops two or more points below your current rate, and when you plan to stay in your present home for at least two or more years.

Step 5: Close the Purchase Transaction

The final step in the home buying process is the *closing*, a meeting of the seller, the buyer, and the lender of funds, or representatives of each party to complete the transaction. At the closing, documents are signed, last-minute details are settled, and appropriate money is paid. The seller and buyer are also responsible for a number of fees and charges when a real estate transaction is completed. These are known generally as settlement costs, or *closing costs*.

Closing Costs

Most closing costs involve the legal details related to purchasing a home. For example, a title company researches the property to make sure that no disputes exist over its ownership or that there are no unpaid real estate taxes that could interfere with the sale. The title company also offers *title insurance*, a type of insurance that protects the buyer in case problems with the title are found later. The title company's fee for these services is one closing cost. See **Figure 7.7** for a list of other common closing costs.

Another typical closing cost is a fee for recording the *deed*, the official document transferring ownership from seller to buyer. Still another possible closing cost is the private mortgage insurance that protects the lender from any loss resulting from default on the loan.

Figure 7.7

Common Closing Costs

Item	Cost Range	
	Buyer	Seller
Title search fee	$ 50–$150	–
Title insurance	$100–$600	$100–$600
Attorney's fee	$ 50–$700	$ 50–$700
Property survey	–	$100–$400
Appraisal fee	$100–$300	–
Recording fees	$ 15–$ 30	$ 15–$ 30
Credit report	$ 25–$ 75	–
Termite inspection	$ 50–$150	–
Lender's origination fee	1–3% of loan	–
Real estate agent's commission	–	5–7% of purchase price
Insurance, taxes, and interest	varies	–

COSTS ADD UP Closing costs add to the expense of buying a home. *Assuming a loan amount of $100,000 with $3,500 due up front in insurance, taxes, and interest, about what could a buyer expect to pay in closing fees based on the figures in this chart?*

Escrow Account

Homeowners must pay property taxes and homeowners insurance in addition to their mortgage payments. Property taxes generally cover the cost of public services, such as police and fire protection, garbage removal, and street repair. They may also help pay to maintain neighborhood schools and playgrounds. Homeowners insurance protects the lender's investment in case of damage to your home from fire or other hazards.

At the closing and when you make your monthly payments, your lender may require that you deposit money into an escrow account. The money, usually held by the lender, is set aside for the payment of property taxes and insurance bills when they become due. That way, the lender doesn't have to worry whether the borrower is paying these obligations. This precaution keeps the property protected from tax claims and loss due to fire and other hazards. See **Figure 7.8** for a list of home buying issues.

Figure 7.8

The Elements of Buying a Home

It's important to consider the following when making a home purchase.

Location. Consider both the surrounding community and the geographic region. The same home may vary greatly in cost depending on where it's located: in Kansas or California, on a busy highway or a quiet street, in a leafy suburb or an urban neighborhood.

Down Payment. A large down payment reduces your mortgage costs, but how much can you afford to pay up front?

Mortgage Rates and Points. You'll have to choose between a lower mortgage rate with points and a higher mortgage rate without points. You'll also need to consider what type of mortgage to arrange. When you apply for the loan, be prepared to provide the lender with copies of your financial records and other relevant information.

Closing Costs. Settlement costs may range anywhere from 2 to 6 percent of the total amount you borrow. That's in addition to the down payment.

Monthly Payments. Your monthly payment for interest, principal, insurance, and taxes will be among your largest, most enduring expenses. Beware of buying a home that costs more than you can afford.

Maintenance Costs. Homes require a lot of repair and maintenance. Be sure to set aside funds for these necessities.

THINK IT OVER Buying a home is a complicated process. *What are some possible results of not thinking through all the elements listed above?*

Renting Versus Buying Your Place of Residence

Atul and Elena saved enough money to buy a house and they found one they like, but they need to consider how much it will actually cost to live there. The rent on their apartment is $700 a month ($8,400 a year) and the house costs $85,000. In making their decision, they will need to consider any additional costs for maintaining a house as well as their lifestyle choices.

Atul and Elena's Dilemma	
Rental Costs	
Annual rent payments	$8,400
Renter's insurance	170
Total annual cost of renting	**$8,570**
Buying Costs	
Down payment (at 10%)	8,500
Annual mortgage payments	8,060
Property taxes (annual costs)	1,275
Mortgage insurance (annual premium)	536
Homeowners insurance (annual premium)	400
Estimated maintenance costs	850
Financial benefits of home ownership	
Less: Tax savings for mortgage interest	–1,820
Less: Tax savings for property taxes	–357
Total cost of buying first year	**$17,444**
Less: one-time down payment	–8,500
Estimated annual appreciation (3%)*	–2,550
Total long-term annual cost of buying	**$6,394**

*Nationwide average; actual appreciation varies by geographic area and economic conditions.

Atul and Elena compared the annual costs of renting ($8,570) and buying ($6,394) and decided that it would be a good investment to buy the house.

Compare In your workbook or on a separate sheet of paper, compare renting versus buying your place of residence. Check a newspaper for a typical rental price for a two-bedroom apartment and a typical selling price for a two-bedroom house. Use those figures to complete your comparison.

Selling Your Home

As your needs change, someday you may decide to sell your home. You'll have to get it ready for the market, set a price, and decide whether to sell it on your own or with professional help.

Preparing Your Home for Selling

The nicer your home looks, the faster it will sell, and the better chance you have of getting a good price for it. Dora and Dennis Muldoon repainted several rooms, replaced some light fixtures, and changed the living room carpet before they put their house on the market. They took pains to keep the house as clean, neat, bright, and airy as possible while prospective buyers were visiting. They also made sure that the lawn was cut regularly and that their children didn't leave toys in the yard. Their work paid off: the Muldoons accepted an offer within several months of listing their home.

Determining the Selling Price

Setting a price on your home can be difficult. A price that's too high may scare off potential buyers. Setting the price too low, however, will cost money. Some sellers pay for an *appraisal*—an estimate of the current value of the property—and use that as a basis for a listing price. You'll also need to find out whether the current market and demand for housing favors buyers or sellers, decide how quickly you need to sell your home, and evaluate any improvements you've made to the property. Adding certain features—such as a deck, improvements to the kitchen, or an extra bathroom—can increase your home's value.

Listing with a Real Estate Agent

Most sellers choose to put the sale of their home into the hands of a licensed real estate agent. You have a wide choice of firms and agents, from small local real estate agencies to nationally known companies. The most important factor in choosing an agent is to pick someone who knows your area well and is eager to sell your home.

Real estate agents provide various services. They can help you determine a selling price, attract potential buyers and show them your home, and handle the financial aspects of the sale. In exchange, they're paid a commission, or fee, upon the sale of your home—usually 5 to 7 percent of the purchase price.

Sale by Owner

Each year about 10 percent of home sales are made directly by the owners of a home without the help of real estate agents. Selling your home yourself can save you thousands of dollars, but it will cost you time and energy. Advertising the home will be up to you; consider newspaper ads and flyers emphasizing your home's good points. Showing the home to prospective buyers will also be your responsibility. Be sure to use the services of a lawyer or a title company to help you with the contract, closing, and other legal matters.

QUESTION

What are the advantages and disadvantages of selling your house yourself?

SECTION 7.3   ASSESSMENT

CHECK YOUR UNDERSTANDING

1. Name five steps that make up the process of buying a home.
2. What costs are associated with buying a home?
3. Discuss the activities associated with selling a home.

THINK CRITICALLY

4. State three reasons you should carefully inspect the property you plan to purchase.

USING COMMUNICATION SKILLS

5. **Owner Obligations** Imagine that you are a condominium owner attending a meeting of the condominium association.
   Persuade Prepare a short speech that you as a homeowner might make to answer one of the following questions at the meeting: What should the association do about a homeowner who leaves garbage in the hallway? Should the association limit the use of the pool and tennis courts to owners or their family members? Who should be responsible for shoveling snow?

SOLVING MONEY PROBLEMS

6. **Making an Offer** After several weeks of searching for a new home, Renee has found a house that seems to be in good shape and is located in a nice neighborhood. The listing price is $125,000, about $15,000 more than she had hoped to pay. She would like to make a lower bid, but the housing market is tight, and she worries that someone else may buy the house at the listing price. Renee wonders what she should do.
   Analyze Working in a small group, formulate some ideas about what Renee should consider in making a decision.

CHAPTER 7 ASSESSMENT

CHAPTER SUMMARY

- Your lifestyle will affect the type of housing that you choose. You'll probably have to accept some trade-offs when you make housing decisions.

- One basic housing decision is whether to rent a residence or buy a home. Each option has financial benefits and drawbacks.

- The advantages of renting include mobility, few responsibilities, and low initial costs. The disadvantages are fewer financial benefits, a restricted lifestyle, and some legal concerns.

- Your rent payment will depend on the location and the amount of space that you want. In addition to rent, you can expect to pay for some utilities, the security deposit, and renters insurance.

- The home buying process has several steps: determining your needs, finding and evaluating a property, pricing the property, obtaining financing, and closing the transaction.

- The cost of buying a home will depend on its location, size, and quality. When you have selected a property, you will be responsible for the down payment, financing of the remaining portion of the purchase price, closing costs, property taxes, homeowners insurance, and maintenance costs.

- Selling a home involves preparing it for the market, setting a price, and deciding whether to sell it on your own or with professional help.

Internet zone

Understanding and Using Vocabulary

Write a conversation between a person who is looking for a home and a real estate agent who is eager to help. Use 8 to 12 of the following terms.

handyman's special	equity
lifestyle	zoning laws
mobility	earnest money
tenant	escrow account
landlord	private mortgage
lease	insurance
sublet	mortgage
security deposit	points
renters insurance	amortization

conventional mortgage	refinance
	closing
adjustable-rate mortgage	closing costs
	title insurance
default	deed
home equity loan	appraisal

Review Key Concepts

1. What are some of the drawbacks and benefits associated with renting a house?
2. Name at least one document often associated with renting. Name another associated with buying.

CHAPTER 7 ASSESSMENT

3. What are the most important aspects of the home buying process?
4. Name the types of homes that are available for purchase.
5. What are some of the factors that determine the selling price of a home?

Apply Key Concepts

1. Evaluate the drawbacks and benefits of renting as a single 25-year-old with a steady income and an active social life might see them.
2. Compare a lease with a mortgage. How are they alike? How do they differ?
3. Draw a flowchart or diagram showing the process of buying real estate.
4. Of the different types of homes available for purchase, rank the three you find most appealing and explain your choices. Then speculate on the ranking your parents would give them.
5. Explain how the laws of supply and demand affect the prices of homes.

 Problem Solving Today

PRICING A HOME

Working with a partner, create an imaginary home that would blend well into your neighborhood. Write a detailed description that includes the type of home it is, how many rooms it has, what sort of condition it's in, its location, and its features.

Compare Look at real estate ads in newspapers and compare your imagined home with real ones. 1) How do these homes compare to the one you designed? 2) Use the real homes and their

prices to come up with a reasonable listing price for your imagined home.

Computer Activity As an alternative activity, use online real estate listings to help you determine the value of this home.

Real-World Application

CONNECT WITH SOCIAL STUDIES

The period between 1890 and 1920 was a difficult one for many tenants in the United States. Some lived in company towns, in which all property belonged to a corporation whose workers rented homes from the company. Many other tenants lived in cities, in crowded buildings called tenements.

Conduct Research Find out more about these turn-of-the-century tenants and their lives. Compare conditions in tenements and company towns with the conditions in which renters typically live today.

FINANCE *Online*

FIRST RATE!

Your parents are thinking of buying a new home. Because you're a computer wizard, they ask you to help them find out what interest rates plus points are currently being offered for various types of mortgages.

Connect Using Internet search engines and real estate Web sites, find at least four different interest rate quotes from various lenders. Evaluate these rates to see which one seems like the best deal.

Get a Financial Life!

CASE STUDY

Home Ownership

Overview

Karla Cunningham finished her associate in science degree at the local community college and is now employed as a computer network engineer for Keller's Computers. Last year she married David Farnier, a high school math teacher and football coach. Karla and David have many decisions to make as a married couple. One of their goals is to purchase a home within the next two years. Recently, Karla and David met with a real estate agent and a banker. The real estate agent helped them think about the features and location they want for their future residence. The banker discussed mortgages and budgeting with the young couple. Both Karla and David realize that they have a lot of research and planning ahead of them.

Resources

- Crayons, markers, colored pencils
  - Internet (optional)
  - Newspapers and real estate magazines
  - Portfolio (ring binder or file folder)
  - Public or school library
  - Spreadsheet software (optional)
- Word processor

Procedures

Step A **THE PROCESS**

Karla and David's combined income is $68,000 a year. Their banker told them that the most they should spend for a home is 2.5 times their annual income.

1. Determine the maximum amount that Karla and David should spend on their future home.

2. Help Karla and David decide what features they should take into consideration when they buy a home. Create a list of the features. Then write a two-paragraph description of their future home and draw a picture of it.

3. Using the newspaper, real estate magazines, the Internet, or other resources, locate an ad for a home in Karla and David's price range. Clip or print the ad.

4. Request an amortization table from a local bank, or find one on the Internet. Determine Karla and David's monthly mortgage payment based on the price of the home you selected and today's current interest rate.

5. Contact an insurance company that sells homeowners insurance, and find out what it would cost to insure the home that you selected.

6. Contact companies that provide the following services: electricity, gas, water, cable television, telephone, and trash pickup. Where applicable, determine the installation fees, deposits, and approximate monthly cost of each service for the home you selected.

7. Karla and David have budgeted approximately $10,000 to furnish their home. Using newspapers, catalogs, garage sale ads, the Internet, or any other sources, "spend" their money to furnish their home. Provide a printed picture or a drawing to illustrate each expense.

8. Prepare a budget for Karla and David for their first year as homeowners. If possible, use a spreadsheet program to prepare the budget.

Step B CREATE YOUR PORTFOLIO

As you work through the process, save the results so that you can refer, review, and refine. Use a ring binder or a file folder to create a portfolio of your work.

1. The title of the binder or folder should be "Home Ownership." Decorate the front of the binder or folder—be creative.

2. Organize the results of Step A (2–8) in your binder or folder. If possible, use a word processor to ensure that your work is neat and easy to read.

3. Read a magazine article on one of the following topics: (1) buying your first home, (2) making home repairs, (3) decorating a home, or (4) landscaping a home. Present a summary of the article to the class.

Step C TECHNICAL WRITING AND READING

Many workplaces need employees who are skilled in technical writing and reading. Technical writing is the process of communicating technical information in writing, clearly and accurately. To practice technical writing, complete either activity 1 or activity 2 (below). Activity 3 will allow you to practice technical reading.

1. Karla and David will make many decisions as a couple. When they are ready to purchase their home, they'll have to decide which lender to use in order to obtain a mortgage. Write a technical paper (approximately one or two pages) outlining the steps Karla and David must take in order to choose the appropriate mortgage for their purchase.

2. Karla and David have decided to acquire a credit card. Write a technical paper (approximately one or two pages) outlining the steps Karla and David must take in order to choose the appropriate credit card.

3. Exchange your technical writing paper with another student. Read your classmate's paper and critique it for accuracy, completeness, punctuation, and grammar. Return each other's papers and edit them as necessary.

INVESTING YOUR FINANCIAL RESOURCES

*U*nit 3 helps you put your financial plans into action through investing. Increasing your resources is an important part of achieving your personal financial goals. The next few chapters will discuss the fundamental aspects of investing in stocks, bonds, mutual funds, real estate, and other items.

READING STRATEGIES

To get the most out of your reading

- ▨ **PREDICT** what the section will be about.
- ▨ **CONNECT** what you read with your own life.
- ▨ **QUESTION** as you read to make sure you understand the content.
- ▨ **RESPOND** to what you've read.

START TODAY

Wise Investing

Investing provides an opportunity to earn income for the future and to achieve your financial goals. What can you do today to get started as an investor?

The Fundamentals of Investing

STANDARD &POOR'S

Q&A

Q: I don't have much money. Any extra that I get I just put in the bank. It seems safe there. Why should I even consider investing?

A: As your savings account balance grows, you should consider other investments that can earn a potentially higher return. If inflation increases at a higher rate than your savings account return, you can lose purchasing power. Consider that a loaf of bread that cost 50 cents 20 years ago now costs about $2, an increase of 400 percent. Money you set aside for long-term goals, such as retirement, will need to earn more than the rates usually paid on savings accounts to stay ahead of inflation and taxes.

Preparing for an Investment Program

Charlene has been cutting and styling her friends' hair since she was about 12 years old. After she received her license in cosmetology several years ago, she began to work for a salon in Los Angeles. Although she likes her job, she dreams of opening her own salon and spa. Colleagues have told her that even if she plans to start small, she will need quite a bit of money to rent a place and buy equipment. Charlene is beginning to realize that she will have to start investing in order to obtain the money required to make her dream a reality.

What You'll Learn

- How to **explain** the way to prepare for and establish an investment program
- How to **assess** the factors that affect your investment choices

Why It's Important

Laying a good foundation for your investment program will help ensure that you meet your future financial goals.

KEY TERMS

- **emergency fund**
- **speculative investment**
- **retained earnings**
- **investment liquidity**

Establishing Your Investment Goals

When you think about the future, do you picture yourself owning your own home or being the president of your own company? Do you hope to retire at 50 and travel around the world? No matter how much you may want to do or have something, you won't achieve your goal if you can't pay for it.

To gather the funds you'll need, you'll have to plan carefully—and practice some discipline along the way. If you're investing to meet a goal that will make you happy and financially secure, any sacrifices you may have to make will be worth it.

An investment plan starts with a specific, measurable goal. For example, you may want to save $15,000 to make a down payment on a house within five years of graduating from school.

Your goal should correspond with your values. At one extreme, some people save or invest as much of each paycheck as possible. Their investment programs and the satisfaction they get from obtaining their long-term financial goals are more important to them than the immediate pleasure of spending a lot of money on something temporary, like a weekend getaway trip. At the other extreme are people who spend every cent that they earn and run out of money before they receive their next paycheck.

It's probably wisest to take a middle-of-the-road approach. You can spend money on things that you like to do or have and still save enough to fund an investment program. As you will see, even a small amount of money saved or invested on a regular basis can amount to a large sum over a period of time.

As you outline your financial goals, ask these questions:

- What will you use the money for?
- How much money do you need to satisfy your goals?
- How will you get the money?
- How long will it take you to get the money?
- How much risk are you willing to take when you invest?
- What conditions, either in the economy or in your own life, could change your investment goals?
- Considering your circumstances, or what you think they will be in the next few years, are your goals reasonable?
- Are you willing to make sacrifices to save?
- What will happen if you don't meet your goals?

FIGURE 8.1

Performing a Financial Checkup

Knowing that your personal finances are in order is an important step in meeting your long-term financial goals.

1 *Balance your budget: spend less money than you make, stay out of debt, and limit your credit card use. Eventually, the amount of cash remaining after your pay your bills will increase. You'll be able to use that money to start a savings program.*

2 *When you're on your own, you should have enough insurance to cover financial losses from events, such as a car accident, a medical emergency, or a theft.*

Performing a Financial Checkup

Before you can even think of investing for the future, you must take steps to be sure your personal finances are in good shape. Only then will you be ready to move ahead with your financial plan. See **Figure 8.1** for tips on how to perform a financial checkup.

Obtaining the Money You Need to Get Started

After you've set your goals and completed your financial checkup, you're almost ready to start investing. First, though, you have to obtain the money. Here are a few suggestions about how to do that.

Pay Yourself First

Too often people save or invest what is left over after they have paid for everything else, from monthly expenses to video games. As you might guess, in many cases nothing is left over, and

3 Start an *emergency fund* (money that you can access quickly for an immediate need) to help you pay for unexpected events, such as not being able to work. You should have enough saved to cover living expenses for three to nine months.

4 Have access to other sources of cash, such as a line of credit with a financial institution or cash advance capability from a credit card company. Use it only for serious emergencies, because paying off the loan will delay you in reaching your investment goals.

the investment program is put on hold for another month. Here is a much better approach: (1) Include the amount you want to save in your monthly expenses. Pay that amount first; consider it a bill you

What's Your Financial ID?

ARE YOU A RISK TAKER?

As a general rule, the greater the promised return on an investment, the greater the risk involved. Risk tolerance is your ability to ride out the ups and downs of the market without panicking when the value of your investment goes down. The amount of risk you're willing to take with your investments sometimes depends on your personality. This quiz will help you gauge your own risk tolerance. Using a separate sheet a paper, answer the following questions.

1. Which best describes your feelings about investing?
   a. Better safe than sorry
   b. Moderation in all things
   c. Nothing ventured, nothing gained.

2. Which is most important to you as an investor?
   a. You receive a steady income
   b. You receive a steady income and growth
   c. The price of your investments rises rapidly

3. You won! Which prize would you pick?
   a. $4,000 in cash
   b. A 50 percent chance to win $10,000
   c. A 20 percent chance to win $100,000

4. The stocks you own have dropped 20 percent since the last quarter. The market experts are optimistic. What would you do?
   a. Sell the stocks to avoid losing more
   b. Keep the stocks and wait for their value to rebound

   c. Buy more stocks because they are cheaper now

5. The stocks you own have gone up 20 percent since the last quarter. You have no further information. What would you do?
   a. Sell the stocks and take the gains
   b. Keep the stocks and hope the price goes up higher
   c. Buy more stocks because the price may go up higher

6. Would you borrow money to take advantage of a good investment opportunity?
   a. Never
   b. Maybe
   c. Yes

7. How would you characterize yourself?
   a. I don't like to take risks
   b. I'm a moderate risk taker
   c. I enjoy taking risks

Give yourself one point for each question that you answered with "a."
Give yourself two points for each question that you answered with "b."
Give yourself three points for each question that you answered with "c."

If you scored 7–11 points, you're a conservative investor who prefers to minimize financial risks.

If you scored 12–16 points, you're a moderate risk taker.

If you scored 17–21 points, you're comfortable taking risks in pursuit of greater returns.

Source: "Five-Minute Quiz" from Standard & Poor's *Your Financial Future* (© 1996 by The McGraw-Hill Companies)

owe to yourself. (2) Pay your monthly living expenses, such as rent and food. (3) Use any money that may be left over for personal pleasures, such as a new jacket or DVD.

Take Advantage of Employer-Sponsored Retirement Plans

If your employer offers a retirement plan and you're eligible to participate, you can take advantage of a ready-made investment program. Many employers match part or all of the money you put into the plan. For example, for every dollar you contribute, your employer may put in 25 cents, 50 cents, or even a dollar. In addition, money put into a retirement fund isn't taxed until you withdraw it—usually at retirement age. Retirement plans are discussed in detail in Chapter 15.

Participate in an Elective Savings Program

Some employers will give you the option of having money automatically withheld from your paycheck and deposited in a savings account. On your own, you can also arrange with a mutual fund or brokerage firm to take a fixed amount from your bank account every month and invest it. This is a painless way to save because you don't have to think about it. You will be less tempted to use the money if you never see it.

Make a Special Savings Effort One or Two Months Each Year

Another way to save is to set aside a specific time each year when you cut back sharply on what you spend and put the money you save in an investment fund.

Take Advantage of Gifts, Inheritances, and Windfalls

When Gabriel received his income tax refund, his friends suggested that this would be the perfect time to buy a big-screen television. Gabriel's friends were disappointed when he decided to put the money in a certificate of deposit earning 6 percent interest. For the chance to add to his investments, Gabriel didn't mind watching television on his parents' 19-inch screen.

During your lifetime, you will probably receive gifts of money; perhaps inherit some money; and get bonuses at work, tax refunds, and salary raises. What would you do with the money: follow Gabriel's plan or go along with his friends?

The Value of Long-Term Investment Programs

Many people don't start investing because they have only a small amount of money. Others think that they're too young to start. Don't let your bank account balance or your age stop you.

Even small amounts add up because of the time value of money. As you read in Chapter 1, the time value of money is the increase in an amount of money as a result of interest or dividends earned.

Figure 8.2 shows the growth of $2,000 for different time periods and at different rates of return (the percentage of increase in the value of your savings from earned interest). As you can see, the higher the rate of return and the longer the time period, the greater the balance. Keep in mind, too, that you have to continue to add money to your investments to see the kind of growth that is illustrated in the figure.

Factors That Affect Your Choice of Investments

Once you know how much money you'll need to meet your goals, you have to think about where to invest it. To make that decision,

Figure 8.2

Effect of Long-Term Investing on Growth

| Rate of Return | Balance at End of Year | | | | | |
	1	5	10	20	30	40
6%	$2,000	$11,274	$26,362	$73,572	$158,116	$309,520
7%	2,000	11,502	27,632	81,990	188,922	399,280
8%	2,000	11,734	28,974	91,524	226,560	518,120
9%	2,000	11,970	30,386	102,320	272,620	675,780
10%	2,000	12,210	31,874	114,550	328,980	885,180
11%	2,000	12,456	33,444	128,406	398,040	1,163,660
12%	2,000	12,706	35,098	144,104	482,660	1,534,180

GROWING WILD The growth shown in this table assumes that you will invest $2,000 at the end of every year and allow your earnings to accumulate. *Why might you be willing to invest $2,000 a year for this type of return?*

Liechtenstein
Switzerland
Italy

$\mathcal{A}$re you a collector? Shells, coins, books, Beanie Babies, CDs? If you're a stamp collector, or philatelist, you've probably heard of Liechtenstein. It's a tiny principality in the European Alps and bears the name of its royal family. Known as the postage stamp nation, Liechtenstein sells stamps worldwide. Every three months it issues a new stamp, which collectors quickly buy. Many of the beautiful stamps depict paintings that are in the royal house. Others depict common themes: nature, history, sports, folklore. Liechtenstein began its stamp trade in 1912. The first reference to stamp collecting, however, was found in the *Times* of London in 1841, when a young woman planning to decorate her dressing room walls advertised for canceled stamps. Here's a snapshot of Liechtenstein.

Geographic area	62 sq. mi.
Population	32,000
Capital	Vaduz (pop. 5,000)
Language	German, Alemannic dialect
Currency	franc
Gross domestic product (GDP)	$713 million
Per capita GDP	$23,000
Economy	Industry: electronics, metal manufacturing, textiles, ceramics. Agriculture: wheat, barley, livestock. Exports: small specialty machinery, dental products, stamps, hardware.

Liechtenstein issues a wide variety of stamps.

Thinking Critically

Apply Name some of the characteristics that you think add to a stamp's value. If you collected stamps for a hobby, what characteristics would you find most interesting?

For more information on Liechtenstein visit finance.glencoe.com or your local library.

you'll have to look at risk factors. You'll also have to review each investment's potential for income and growth as well as its liquidity.

Safety and Risk

In the financial world, the words "safety" and "risk" have specific meanings. "Safety" means that the chance of losing your money in an investment is fairly small. "Risk" indicates that you cannot be certain about the outcome of your investment. You can select investments that are very safe or very risky or anywhere in between these extremes.

Generally, if you choose a safe investment, your rate of return will be low. A *speculative investment*, on the other hand, is a high-risk investment made in the hope of earning a relatively large profit in a short time. The downside of speculative investments is the possibility that at any time, you could lose most or all of the money you invested. **Figure 8.3** categorizes various types of investments according to their safety record.

One basic rule sums up the relationship between the factors of safety and risk: The potential return on any investment should be directly related to the risk you, the investor, take. Your attitude toward risk will vary according to your circumstances. For example, when you're young, you may be more willing to take risks because your investment goals may be longer-term. When you're nearing retirement, you may decide to shift your investments from speculative to conservative ones to be sure that you won't lose your lifetime savings. If you're injured on the job and can no longer work, you may invest your settlement money conservatively so that you can live off the money for many years.

Often, beginning investors are afraid of the risk associated with many investments. However, it helps to remember that without the risk, it is impossible to obtain the larger returns that really make an investment program grow. The key is to determine how much risk you're willing to assume. Then choose quality investments that offer higher returns without an unacceptably high risk.

Five Components of the Risk Factor

The level of risk of an investment can change over time. You can evaluate the overall risk factor by examining five different

PREDICT

What are some risks associated with investing?

Figure 8.3

Risks Involved in Typical Investments

Safe	Can Vary	High Risk

• Government bonds and debt securities
  Treasury bills
  Treasury notes
  Treasury bonds
  Municipal bonds
  U.S. Savings Bonds
• Savings accounts
• Certificates of deposit
	• Stocks
	• Corporate bonds
	• Mutual funds
	• Real estate
		• Commodities
		• Options
		• Precious metals and gems
		• Collectibles, such as coins, stamps, and comic books

INVESTMENT SPECTRUM   Only you can decide how much risk you're willing to take. *Why do you think savings accounts and certificates of deposit are considered safe investments?*

TAKING A CHANCE Some investments, like some sports, carry a higher risk than others. *Can you lose money by taking a chance on a speculative investment?*

components of risk—inflation, the interest rate, business failure, the financial market, and global investment.

INFLATION RISK When Harry Majors opened his deli in 1981, he framed the first dollar he earned and hung it on the wall. Twenty years later, one of his customers reminded him that his dollar could now buy less than 50 cents' worth of salami. Harry just laughed. For him, the sentiment was worth it.

The loss of value to Harry's dollar was a result of inflation, which is a general rise in prices that affects everybody. Investing your money can help you stay ahead of inflation. However, during periods of rapid inflation, you take the risk that the return from your investments won't keep up with the inflation rate. When that happens, you lose buying power. When you go to spend the money, you'll be able to buy less with it than you could have when you made the investment.

You can determine the effect of inflation on investments. First, subtract the rate of interest you're earning from the inflation rate. This is your loss of buying power in percent. Then multiply this number by the original price of your investment. The result is your loss of buying power in dollars.

In addition, you can find out the current price of your investment, based on the rate of inflation during the period that you held the investment. Multiply the original price of the investment by the rate of inflation. Add that figure to the original price of the investment. The result is how much it would cost you to purchase the same investment today.

Example: Nina put $500 in a certificate of deposit for one year at 3% interest. The inflation rate during that year was 5%. How much of her buying power did she lose? How much money would she need at the end of the year to buy what she bought a year ago with $500?

A. Calculate the loss of buying power in percent.

Formula: Inflation Rate − Interest Rate = Loss of Buying Power in Percent

Solution: 5% − 3% = 2%

B. Find the loss of buying power in dollars.

Formula: Original Price of Investment × Loss of Buying Power in Percent = Loss of Buying Power in Dollars

Solution: $500 × 2% = $10
Nina lost 2% of her buying power, or $10.

C. Calculate how much it would cost to buy the same investment today.

Formula: (Original Price of Investment × Inflation Rate) + Original Price of Investment = Current Price of Investment

Solution: ($500 × 5%) + $500 = $525

Nina would need $525 at the end of the year to buy what she bought a year ago with $500.

Some investments will protect you from inflation better than others. For example, when the compounded rate of return on common stocks was adjusted for inflation, it was 7.4 percent over the period from 1926 to 1996. During that same time, U.S. Treasury bills had an inflation-adjusted compounded rate of return of only 0.6 percent.

INTEREST RATE RISK   If you put money in an investment that gives you a fixed rate of return, such as government or corporate bonds, the value of your investment will go down if interest rates go up. If you have to sell your bonds at that time, you'll get less than you originally paid.

To figure out the market price of a bond you have purchased if interest rates go up, divide the annual interest earned by the new interest rate. (See the **Go Figure** box on the top of the following page.)

If you held onto the bond until maturity, you could get your full $1,000 back, but you would have received 8 percent annual interest while everyone else was getting 10 percent on their new bonds.

Go Figure...   A BOND'S MARKET PRICE WHEN INTEREST RATES GO UP

Example: You buy a $1,000 corporate bond that pays a fixed rate of 8% interest. You earn $80 a year ($1,000 × 8% = $80) until maturity. What price would you get if you sold it before the maturity date at a time when bond rates were 10%?

Formula:
$$\frac{\text{Annual Interest Earned}}{\text{New Interest Rate}} = \text{Market Price}$$

Solution:
$$\frac{\$80}{10\%} = \$800$$

You would get $800, which equals a loss of $200 ($1,000 − $800 = $200).

Of course, if interest rates go down, your bonds will go up in value. You can figure out how much you would get for a bond if interest rates went down by dividing the annual interest earned by the new interest rate.

Go Figure...   A BOND'S MARKET PRICE WHEN INTEREST RATES GO DOWN

Example: Your $1,000 corporate bond pays a fixed rate of 8% interest, or $80 a year ($1,000 × 8% = $80). What price would you get if you sold it before maturity when bond rates were 6%?

Formula:
$$\frac{\text{Annual Interest Earned}}{\text{New Interest Rate}} = \text{Market Price}$$

Solution:
$$\frac{\$80}{6\%} = \$1,333.33$$

You would receive $1,333.33, which equals a profit of $333.33 ($1,333.33 − $1,000 = $333.33).

BUSINESS FAILURE RISK   This risk applies to common stock, preferred stock, and corporate bonds. With each of these investments, you face the possibility that the company in which you invest will be less profitable than you had hoped—for example, if the company is poorly managed. Even if the company offers a valuable product or service, positive response from consumers is not guaranteed. Lower profits usually mean lower dividends or perhaps none at all. If the company declares bankruptcy, your investment may become worthless. Your best protection is to do careful research on companies in which you might invest. Another good idea is not to invest all your money in one company.

FINANCIAL MARKET RISK   Sometimes the prices of stocks, bonds, mutual funds, and other investments go up or down just because of the overall state of financial markets. Thus, the value of a stock may decrease even though the company is financially healthy. Factors that affect financial markets include social and political conditions. For instance, the price of oil stocks may be affected by the political situation in the Middle East, where much of the world's oil supply is produced.

GLOBAL INVESTMENT RISK   Today more investors are investing their money in stocks and bonds issued by companies in other countries. Because these types of investments may be risky, financial analysts advise small investors to limit their international dealings to global mutual funds. Global mutual funds are offered by U.S. firms but specialize in companies that operate in another nation or region of the world. Mutual funds spread the risk among many stocks or bonds and thus may offer more safety than stocks or bonds issued by one company. If you plan to invest outside the United States, consider two factors:

1. You have to evaluate the investments just as you would U.S. investments. However, because of different accounting standards in other countries, it may be hard to find out the true financial condition of companies there.

2. Keep in mind that the currency exchange rate may affect the return on your investment. If you buy stock in a French company, for example, dividends will be paid to you in francs and then converted to dollars. Your return is determined not only by how well your investment performs but also by whether the currency exchange rate is more or less favorable during the time you hold the investment.

Remember that it is risky to invest in stocks and bonds issued by individual companies in other countries. Only experienced investors with large amounts of money to invest should consider this option. Also, keep in mind that the economic and political stability of a country can affect the value of your investment.

Investment Income

If you want a source of income you can count on, you have several choices of investments. The safest investments—savings accounts, certificates of deposit (CDs), U.S. Savings Bonds, and U.S.

Treasury bills—are the most predictable sources of income. You know what the interest rate is and how much income you will be paid on a specific date.

For income, you may also select government bonds, corporate bonds, preferred stocks, utility stocks, or certain common stocks. Before investing in stocks or corporate bonds, you should obtain information about the company's overall profits, its history of dividend payments, and its outlook for the future.

Mutual funds and real estate rental property may also offer income, but it isn't guaranteed. For example, your profits from a rental property may be lower than you had expected if you have vacancies or expensive repairs. Speculative investments, such as commodities, options, precious metals and gems, and collectibles, offer very little, if any, potential for regular income.

WHAT YOU DON'T KNOW When investing in global mutual funds, you have to evaluate your options carefully. *What risks are associated with global investments?*

Investment Growth

To investors, "growth" means that their investments will increase in value. The best opportunities for growth usually come from investments in common stocks. During the 1990s, investors found that stocks issued by corporations in the electronics, technology, energy, and health care industries provided the greatest potential growth.

Growth companies typically reinvest their profits rather than pay dividends. The profits that are reinvested are called *retained earnings*. Companies use these earnings to expand or to conduct research and development. Growth that is financed by retained earnings usually contributes to increases in the stock's dollar value. Therefore, if you buy stock in a growth company, you will probably have to give up immediate cash dividends, but you will benefit from the greater dollar value of your shares of stock in the future.

Government and corporate bonds, mutual funds, and real estate may also offer opportunities for growth. More speculative investments, such as precious metals and gems and collectibles, have less potential for growth. Commodities and options usually focus on immediate returns.

QUESTION

When would it be advantageous to invest for growth rather than for income?

Investment Liquidity

A final factor that will affect your choice of investments is investment liquidity. *Investment liquidity* is the ability to buy or sell an investment quickly without substantially affecting its value. You may be able to sell some investments quickly, but market conditions or other factors may prevent you from regaining the amount of money you originally invested. For example, depending on the demand for your real estate, you might have trouble selling it and have to accept a lower price in order to sell immediately.

SECTION 8.1 ASSESSMENT

CHECK YOUR UNDERSTANDING

1. What steps should you take when preparing to establish an investment program?
2. How can you obtain the money you need to start investing?
3. What factors might affect your investment choices?

THINK CRITICALLY

4. How might you advise a friend about what to do with a $500 bonus she just received for accepting a job at a software design firm?

USING COMMUNICATION SKILLS

5. **Risk Tolerance** Everyone has a different tolerance for risk. Some people will try anything once, including skydiving and white-water rafting. Others take every precaution to avoid danger.
   Roundtable Discussion With a group of classmates, discuss the five components of the risk factor. Decide which components have the greatest chance of affecting every investor.

SOLVING MONEY PROBLEMS

6. **Preparing for Emergencies** Roya and Sashi are performing a financial checkup before they develop their investment plan. They are trying to decide how much money to put into an emergency fund and what type of account to set up. The couple has $3,000 in take-home pay a month and monthly living expenses of $2,600. Roya and Sashi have a young child and a very limited health insurance plan. They are worried about unexpected expenses.
   Compute Decide how much money Roya and Sashi should have in their emergency fund and what type of account they should put it in. Explain how you reached your answer.

An Overview of Investment Alternatives

Types of Investments

Once you have your personal finances in order—an emergency fund set up, some money put aside to invest, and an idea of how much risk you want to take—you need to learn about where you can invest your money. Here is a brief overview of the following investment alternatives: stocks, bonds, mutual funds, and real estate.

Stock or Equity Financing

Equity capital is money that a business gets from its owners in order to operate. A business that is owned by one person gets its money from that person, who is called the sole proprietor. In a partnership, the partners provide the equity capital. A corporation gets its money from its stockholders, who become owners when they buy shares of stock in the company. Stock can be an attractive investment because as owners, stockholders share in the success of the company.

However, you should consider two facts before you invest in stock:

1. A corporation does not have to repay you what you paid for the stock. If you want to sell your stock, you have to find another investor who will buy your shares. Along with other factors, the current value of your stock is determined by how much another investor is willing to pay you for your shares.
2. The corporation does not have to pay you *dividends*, which are distributions of money, stock, or other property that a corporation sometimes pays to stockholders. If the company has a bad year, or if it decides to reinvest the earnings for the purpose of expansion or other activities, then the board of directors can vote to eliminate dividend payments.

The two basic types of stock are common and preferred. *Common stock* is stock that provides the most basic form of corporate ownership, and it entitles you to voting privileges. Common stock can provide you with a source of income if the company pays dividends. You also gain growth potential if the dollar value of the stock increases, or if the company splits its stock (divides shares that are

RESPOND

Given the risks of the stock market, why do you think people choose to invest in it?

already owned into a larger number of shares, giving you more shares). Most large corporations generate much of the money they need by selling common stock.

A corporation may also issue preferred stock. *Preferred stock* is stock that gives the owner the advantage of receiving cash dividends before common stockholders receive any. This is important if a company is having financial problems; preferred stockholders will receive their dividends before common stockholders. If a company fails, preferred stockholders also have the right to receive any assets that are left before common stockholders receive anything. Chapter 9 discusses other factors you should consider when buying common or preferred stock.

Corporate and Government Bonds

You may also consider investing in bonds. A *corporate bond* is a corporation's written pledge to repay a specified amount of money, along with interest. A *government bond* is the written pledge of a government or a municipality to repay a specified sum of money with interest. When you buy a bond, you are lending money to a corporation or government agency for a certain period of time.

PAYING UP   Government bonds offer a fixed rate of interest. *What are two key considerations when you're buying a government bond?*

Two key factors affect the value of a bond: (1) whether the bond will be repaid at maturity and (2) whether the corporation or government agency will be able to pay interest until maturity. Maturity dates range from 1 to 30 years, and interest is usually paid every 6 months. You can keep a bond until maturity and then redeem it, or you can sell it to another investor. Chapter 10 contains more information on bonds.

Mutual Funds

A *mutual fund* is an investment alternative in which investors pool their money to buy stocks, bonds, and other securities based on the selections of professional managers who work for an investment company. If one of the stocks or other securities does poorly, the loss can be made up by the gains in another stock or security in the fund. Professionals manage the investments, and their knowledge is an advantage for investors who have little financial experience. In the end, though, you are responsible for evaluating your own mutual fund investment.

Mutual funds are available to suit the investment goals and interests of almost every type of investor. Some are very conservative and some highly speculative, with many in between. Chapter 10 provides information on the different types of funds, their costs, and ways to evaluate these types of investments.

Real Estate

The goal in real estate investing may be to have the property increase in value so you can sell it at a profit or to receive rental income. When you invest in real estate, you need to find out if the property is priced competitively with similar properties. You also need to know what kind of financing is available and how much the taxes will be.

Before making a decision to purchase any property, ask the following questions: Why are the present owners selling? Is the property in good condition? What is the condition of other properties in the area? Is there a chance that the property will decrease in value and that you will lose your money?

When you sell real estate, consider these issues: Can you find an interested buyer? Can the buyer get the necessary financing to buy the property? Chapter 11 provides more information on how to evaluate a real estate investment.

$AVVY SAVER

Giving Is Fun Too

1. Give whatever you can afford to a charity or cause you believe in.
2. Donate old clothes, toys, books, or eyeglasses instead of money.
3. Take bottles and cans to a recycling center and give the money to a favorite cause.
4. Volunteer your time to a hospital, nursing home, animal shelter, or favorite charity.
5. Remember that giving your money and your time can be as much fun as spending money on yourself and often more satisfying.

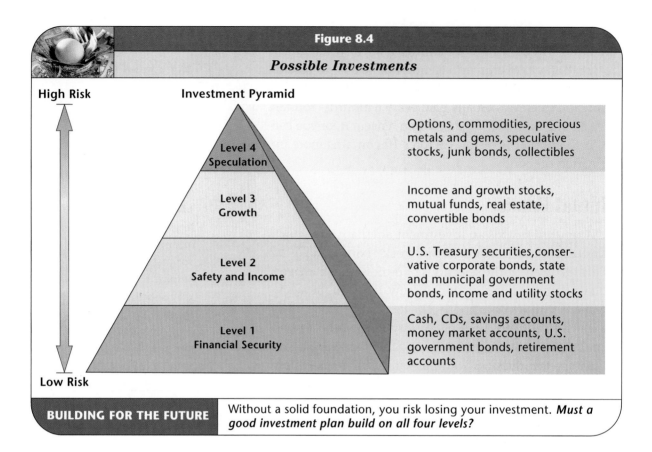

Figure 8.4

Possible Investments

High Risk   Investment Pyramid

Level 4 Speculation — Options, commodities, precious metals and gems, speculative stocks, junk bonds, collectibles

Level 3 Growth — Income and growth stocks, mutual funds, real estate, convertible bonds

Level 2 Safety and Income — U.S. Treasury securities, conservative corporate bonds, state and municipal government bonds, income and utility stocks

Level 1 Financial Security — Cash, CDs, savings accounts, money market accounts, U.S. government bonds, retirement accounts

Low Risk

BUILDING FOR THE FUTURE   Without a solid foundation, you risk losing your investment. *Must a good investment plan build on all four levels?*

Evaluating Investment Alternatives

You have looked at how safety, risk, income, growth, and liquidity affect investment choices, and you have surveyed various investment possibilities. Which ones would you select?

As you make your choices, remember that it's wise to diversify. *Diversification* is the process of spreading your assets among several different types of investments to lessen risk. You want to avoid "putting all your eggs into one basket." Many financial advisers suggest that you think of your investment program as a pyramid, as illustrated in **Figure 8.4**. This approach provides you with both financial growth and protection no matter what your age, circumstances, or level of financial knowledge. Level 1 provides a solid foundation with safe investments. Once that foundation is built, you may choose from the alternatives listed in Levels 2 and 3, which carry moderate risk. Because the investments in Level 4 are so highly speculative, you may want to skip that level entirely.

Developing a Personal Investment Plan

To be a successful investor, you must develop a plan and put it into action. You may find these steps helpful as you get under way.

1. Establish investment goals.
2. Decide how much money you will need in order to reach those goals by a particular date.
3. Determine the amount of money you have to invest.
4. List all the investments you want to evaluate.
5. Evaluate the risks and potential return for each investment on your list. You can do this on your own, but it is also a good idea to get some advice from a financial expert.
6. Reduce the list of possible investments to a reasonable number.
7. Choose at least two investments to give you some diversity. You may want to add to this number as the value of your

CONNECT

What are some of your investing goals?

Careers in Finance

PERSONAL PROPERTY APPRAISER

Not long ago a piece of virtual art—an electronic image on the Internet—was auctioned for the first time for a stunning $11,600. Personal property appraisers all over the world paid attention. Appraisers determine the value of all different kinds of art, jewelry, furniture, and other items for their clients. Their appraisals, or estimates, of value are used to insure property for the right amount of money or to determine how an estate should be divided. Appraisers evaluate the quality and authenticity of an item and compare it with similar items on the market, then write up their findings. Their expert appraisals may also be required for court cases. Appraisers often specialize in one kind of personal property, such as jewelry or classic cars.

Skills	Analytical, communication, interpersonal, math, research, speaking, writing
Personality	Discreet; honest; likes working with things, people, and numbers; tactful
Education	Suggested bachelor's degree, continuing education; experience in specialty; certification from ISA (International Society of Appraisers), ASA (American Society of Appraisers), AAA (Appraisers Association of America), or NAJA (National Association of Jewelry Appraisers)
Pay range	$30,000 to $80,000 plus a year

Critical Thinking How would personal property appraisers stay up-to-date in their field?

For more information on personal property appraisers visit finance.glencoe.com or your local library.

STANDARD &POOR'S

CASE STUDY

Rebecca Weinberg has been teaching middle school math for four years. She's single, lives at home, and her biggest expense is her car payment. Rebecca pays all her own bills including rent to her parents. Recently, Rebecca began thinking about her financial future. Her short-term goals include moving out on her own, saving for a Roth IRA, and going back to school for a master's degree. Rebecca's long-term goal is to retire in 35 years. Every two weeks, Rebecca puts $50 into a savings account and has another $50 invested in a tax-sheltered annuity consisting of mutual funds. She figured since she was so young, high-risk mutual funds were the best choice for her investment dollars. However, the more she reads and learns about investing, the more questions she has. Rebecca turned to the experts at Standard & Poor's for advice.

STANDARD &POOR'S **Analysis:** Deciding on short- and long-term goals is the first step toward creating an investment plan. Rebecca is wise to save for retirement in a tax-deferred account. By starting now, even with small amounts, Rebecca can take advantage of tax-deferred compounding to build a sizable retirement nest egg.

STANDARD &POOR'S **Recommendation:** Rebecca should choose a mix of investments to match her short- and long-term goals. Stocks offer the highest potential for gain but are also more likely to drop in value over the short term. Bonds also fluctuate in value on a daily basis, but typically carry less risk of loss than stocks. Some investments, such as savings accounts, certificates of deposit, and Treasury bills, offer low returns over time but pose very little risk. Because her retirement is many years away, Rebecca should invest 90 percent of her retirement savings in a variety of stock mutual funds and the rest in bonds. This allocation will give Rebecca a higher potential return over time at a lower level of risk than if she invested 100 percent of her retirement savings in stocks. Money Rebecca will use for goals that are one or two years away should be invested in low-risk investments. For goals that are three to five years away, Rebecca can invest in bonds or bond mutual funds.

Critical Thinking Questions

1. Why is it not a good idea to invest money earmarked for short-term goals in stocks?
2. What might the results be if Rebecca invests most of her retirement money in low-risk investments like savings accounts and Treasury bills?
3. Why does allocating 90 percent of a portfolio to stocks and 10 percent to bonds result in a higher return over time than a 100 percent allocation to stocks?

investments grows. That way you can spread your risk among different investments.

8. Because your investment goals may change as you go through life, recheck your investment program periodically. Remember that changes in the economy could cause you to reevaluate where to invest your money. For example, if rates on certificates of deposit are high, you may want to put some of your money there.

Consider this case: Ginny is single and has recently started her first full-time job after graduation. Her monthly take-home pay (after deductions for taxes and other

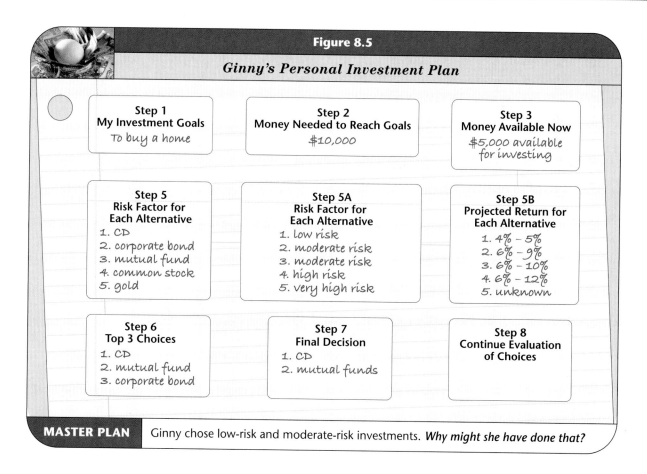

Figure 8.5

Ginny's Personal Investment Plan

Step 1
My Investment Goals
To buy a home

Step 2
Money Needed to Reach Goals
$10,000

Step 3
Money Available Now
$5,000 available for investing

Step 5
Risk Factor for Each Alternative
1. CD
2. corporate bond
3. mutual fund
4. common stock
5. gold

Step 5A
Risk Factor for Each Alternative
1. low risk
2. moderate risk
3. moderate risk
4. high risk
5. very high risk

Step 5B
Projected Return for Each Alternative
1. 4% – 5%
2. 6% – 9%
3. 6% – 10%
4. 6% – 12%
5. unknown

Step 6
Top 3 Choices
1. CD
2. mutual fund
3. corporate bond

Step 7
Final Decision
1. CD
2. mutual funds

Step 8
Continue Evaluation of Choices

MASTER PLAN   Ginny chose low-risk and moderate-risk investments. *Why might she have done that?*

items) is $1,600. Her monthly expenses are $1,200. She has a surplus of $400 a month. She is using her surplus to set up an emergency fund. She recently received an inheritance of $5,000 when her grandfather died. She plans to use this money to fund her investments. **Figure 8.5** on page 257 illustrates how Ginny developed her individual investment plan.

Your plan may be quite different, but the steps will be the same. Just establish your goals and then follow through. If your goals are important to you, you'll be willing to work to attain them.

SECTION 8.2   ASSESSMENT

CHECK YOUR UNDERSTANDING

1. What are the main types of investment alternatives?
2. When choosing investment alternatives, why is it wise to diversify?
3. What are the steps in developing a personal investment plan?

THINK CRITICALLY

4. Why do financial advisers suggest that your investment program be set up like a pyramid?

USING COMMUNICATION SKILLS

5. **Hidden Treasures?** Today many people purchase collectible items. They buy baseball cards, commemorative coins, stuffed animals, and art by unknown artists in the hope that these items will increase in value.
   Weigh Arguments With a partner, develop two arguments: one that explains why these high-risk investments are not wise and one that discusses why this type of investment is attractive to some people. Draw conclusions about what type of person might be best suited to this type of investment.

SOLVING MONEY PROBLEMS

6. **Developing an Investment Plan** Every day after school, Trent volunteers at his neighborhood community center. He helps the younger children with their homework and organizes sports activities to keep them occupied until their parents pick them up after work. Trent really believes in the work that the center is doing and would like to contribute a significant amount of money to its programs. He knows that by investing his money, he'll be able to increase the size of his gift. He just doesn't know how to get started.
   Analyze Help Trent develop a personal investment plan so that he can reach his goal.

Reducing Investment Risk and Obtaining Investment Information

The Role of the Financial Planner

When making your investment decisions, you may want to consult a *financial planner*, a specialist who is trained to offer specific financial help and advice.

Types of Financial Planners

Financial planners may work for insurance companies, investment companies, real estate agencies, or law firms. Some are self-employed. These are the four main types:

1. Fee-only planners may charge an hourly rate from $75 to $200 or a flat fee ranging from about $500 to several thousand dollars. They may also charge an annual fee ranging from 0.04 percent to 1 percent of the value of the investments they manage.
2. Fee-offset planners charge an hourly or annual fee, but they reduce, or offset, it with the commissions, or earnings, they make by buying or selling investments.
3. Fee-and-commission planners charge a fixed fee for a financial plan and earn commissions from the financial products they sell.
4. Commission-only planners earn all their money through the commissions they make on sales of insurance, mutual funds, and other investments.

You must be very careful to understand clearly what the fees are and how and when they will be collected from you. Be especially careful of hidden commission charges when the financial planner has said that the service is fee only.

Do You Need a Financial Planner?

Two main factors to consider when deciding whether you need a financial planner are your income and how willing you are to make financial decisions on your own. If you are making less than $40,000 a year, you probably don't need a planner's services. Also, if you are willing to take the time and effort to keep up-to-date on financial developments, you may be able to manage your own plan.

Selecting a Financial Planner

A financial planner should provide these basic services:

- Help you assess your current financial situation
- Offer a clearly written plan, including investment recommendations, and discuss the features of the plan with you
- Help you keep track of your progress
- Guide you to other financial experts and services as needed

You can find a financial planner in the yellow pages of the phone book, by contacting financial institutions, and by getting names from friends, coworkers, or professional contacts. It is very important that you feel comfortable with the planner and that he or she communicates clearly with you. You are, after all, putting your money and your financial future in this person's hands. **Figure 8.6** suggests questions that you might ask a financial planner.

Certification of Financial Planners

The requirements for becoming a financial planner vary from state to state. Some states require that financial planners pass an exam. Other states issue licenses to either individual planners or planning companies. Some states have no regulations at all. The federal government requires that the Securities and Exchange Commission (SEC) monitor the largest financial advisers.

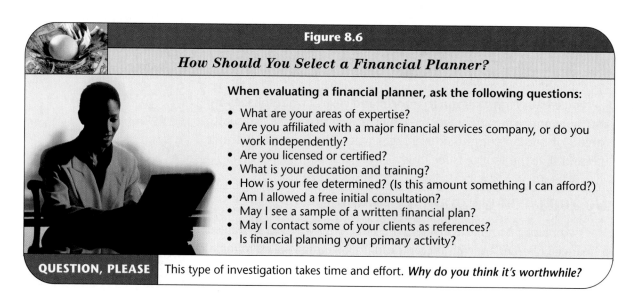

Figure 8.6

How Should You Select a Financial Planner?

When evaluating a financial planner, ask the following questions:

- What are your areas of expertise?
- Are you affiliated with a major financial services company, or do you work independently?
- Are you licensed or certified?
- What is your education and training?
- How is your fee determined? (Is this amount something I can afford?)
- Am I allowed a free initial consultation?
- May I see a sample of a written financial plan?
- May I contact some of your clients as references?
- Is financial planning your primary activity?

QUESTION, PLEASE This type of investigation takes time and effort. *Why do you think it's worthwhile?*

A financial planner may have credentials such as Certified Financial Planner (CFP) or Chartered Financial Consultant (ChFC). Not all planners are licensed, however. It is up to you to be cautious and investigate thoroughly any financial planner you're thinking of hiring.

Your Role in the Investment Process

Reviewing your investments is a continual process. Even if you have a financial planner, you shouldn't ignore your money.

Evaluate Potential Investments

Suppose that you invest $2,000. With a 10 percent return the first year, you will earn $200. Your money is working for you, and you have to be willing to work for it. Conduct research before you invest so that you can make an informed decision and continue to evaluate investment opportunities. Sources for information are discussed later in this section.

Monitor the Value of Your Investments

Marie never bothers to find out what her investments are worth. She doesn't know whether she has made money or lost money. She has no idea whether she should sell her investments or continue to hold on to them. A much better approach is to monitor the value of your investments. Keep track of the value of your stocks, bonds, or mutual funds by checking price quotations that are reported on the Internet, in newspapers, and on financial news programs on television. You may want to keep a chart of the value of your investments to check their progress over time.

Keep Accurate and Current Records

Accurate recordkeeping helps you spot opportunities to increase your profits or reduce losses when you sell your investments. It can

PREDICT

How will taxes influence your investments?

also help you decide whether to put more money in a stock, bond, or other investment. At the very least, you should keep purchase records that list the cost of the investment and commissions or fees you paid. It's also a good idea to keep the sources of information you used to evaluate an investment. Then you'll know where to begin your research when it's time to reevaluate the investments you own.

Tax Considerations

In general, investment income falls into three categories: tax-exempt, tax-deferred, and taxable. *Tax-exempt income* is income that is not taxed. For example, the interest you receive on most state and municipal bonds is exempt from federal income tax. *Tax-deferred income* is income that will be taxed at a later date. The most common type of tax-deferred income is that which is earned on a traditional individual retirement account (IRA). When you start to withdraw the earnings from your IRA, you must pay federal income tax. The 401(k) and 403(b) retirement plans provided by many employers are also tax-deferred. The income from all other investments is taxable income. It is your responsibility to determine how taxes affect your investments.

DIVIDENDS, INTEREST INCOME, AND RENTAL INCOME You must report cash dividends on your tax return as ordinary income. You also have to pay tax on the interest from banks, credit unions, and savings and loan associations. In addition, any interest you receive from bonds (unless tax-exempt), promissory notes, loans, and U.S. securities must be reported as ordinary income. Income from rental property is also taxable.

CAPITAL GAINS AND CAPITAL LOSSES A *capital gain* is the profit from the sale of an asset such as stocks, bonds, or real estate. Capital gains are taxed according to whether they are short-term or long-term. Under current law, a short-term capital gain is one made when you sell stocks, mutual funds, bonds, land, or certain types of personal property that you have owned for 12 months or less. It is taxed as ordinary income. If you're in the 15 percent tax bracket, for example, you'll pay 15 percent tax on your short-term capital gains.

The gain on the sale of investments held for more than 12 months is considered a long-term capital gain. Long-term capital gains are taxed at the rate of 20 percent for most people, but only 10 percent for those in the 15 percent tax bracket. Long-term capital gains on investments sold after December 31, 2000, that were held for more than five years will be taxed at 18 percent for most people and 8 percent for those in the 15 percent tax bracket.

A *capital loss* is the sale of an investment for less than its purchase price. You can subtract up to $3,000 a year in capital losses from your ordinary income. If your losses are greater than $3,000, you can subtract the rest in later tax years.

Sources of Investment Information

Because the available information on most investments is more than you can read and understand, you have to be selective. The important thing is to be sure that the source is accurate and reliable.

The Internet and Online Computer Services

The Internet offers a wealth of information on investments with the press of a key. One of the best ways to wade through it is to use a search engine. Search engines are available through many Internet service providers, including commercial online companies. Just type the key words for the topic in which you're interested and you'll get a list of Web sites that provide information on that topic. Most large investment firms also have Web sites. You can find interest rates for certificates of deposit; current status of stocks, bonds, and other securities; and help in starting an investment program. You can even trade securities online.

Newspapers and News Programs

The financial pages of your metropolitan newspaper or the *Wall Street Journal* are readily available sources of investment information. Many radio and television stations broadcast investment market summaries and economic information as part of their regular news programs. In addition, several television channels, such as CNN Financial, are dedicated to financial news.

Business Periodicals and Government Publications

Barron's, Business Week, Forbes, Fortune, Harvard Business Review, and similar publications provide general news about the economy as

A Dollar a Day

Do you know that if you save a dollar a day, less than what you would spend on a soda and a candy bar, and invest it at 5 percent interest, in 5 years you'll have more than $2,000? In 10 years you'll have $4,600, and in 40 years you'll have almost $45,000! Why not start saving today!

RESPOND

What steps would you take to evaluate the reliability of online financial information?

IN THE KNOW Keeping up with financial news helps you track your investments and may help you reach your goals. *Name at least three publications that could help you become a smarter investor.*

well as information about individual companies. Other publications cover specific industries. In addition, magazines such as *Money, Consumer Reports, Smart Money,* and *Kiplinger's Personal Finance Magazine* provide information and advice designed to improve your investment skills. Newsmagazines often feature stories on the economy and finance.

Don't overlook the federal government, the world's largest provider of information, much of it free. The *Federal Reserve Bulletin,* published by the Federal Reserve System, and the *Survey of Current Business*, published by the Department of Commerce, are two sources of useful financial information. You can read articles from both of these publications on the Internet.

Corporate Reports

As required by the federal government, any corporation selling new issues of securities must provide investors with a *prospectus*, a document that discloses information about a company's earnings, assets and liabilities, its products or services, and the qualifications of its management. All publicly owned corporations also send investors quarterly reports and an annual report that contains detailed financial data.

Statistical Averages

You can gauge the value of your investments by following one or more recognized statistical averages, such as the Dow Jones Industrial Average or the Standard & Poor's 500 Stock Index. The average indicates whether the category it measures is increasing or decreasing in value. It won't pinpoint the value of any specific investment, but it will show the general direction of stocks, bonds, mutual funds, and so forth. **Figure 8.7** lists some of the most widely used averages.

Figure 8.7

Statistical Averages Used to Evaluate Investments

Statistical Average	Type of Investment
Dow Jones Industrial Average	Stocks
Standard & Poor's 500 Stock Index	Stocks
Value Line Stock Index	Stocks
New York Stock Exchange Index	Stocks on New York Stock Exchange
American Stock Exchange Index	Stocks on American Stock Exchange
NASDAQ Composite Stock Index	Over-the-counter stocks
Lipper Mutual Funds Index	Mutual funds
Dow Jones Bond Average	Corporate bonds
Barron's Money Rates	Interest rates
New One-Family House Price Index	Real estate
Dow Jones Spot Market Index	Commodities
Sotheby's Fine Art Index	Art/paintings
Linn's Trends of Stamp Values	Stamps

TRENDSETTER You can locate these averages in the newspaper and on the Internet. *How much importance should you give to them?*

Avoiding Future Shock

Mackenzie is already showing signs of being a great scholar even at three years old. At least that's what her dad, Jasper, thinks. He wants Mackenzie to be able to continue her education so he has decided to start a college fund for her now. Jasper has $2,000 to start and has decided to invest $175 a month. He has developed an investment plan to reach his goal.

Goal Tending	
Established goal:	College
Amount of money needed:	$50,000
Initial amount to invest:	$2,000
Possible investment alternatives:	(1) savings account (2) CD (3) money market account (4) mutual fund (5) stock
Risk factor for each alternative:	(1) low risk (2) low risk (3) low risk (4) moderate risk (5) high risk
Expected return on each alternative:	(1) 1%–3% (2) 4%–5% (3) 4%–6% (4) 6%–10% (5) 6%–12%
Top 3 choices:	(1) mutual fund (2) stock (3) CD
Final choice:	mutual fund

Jasper figures he has 15 years to invest and will invest in an aggressive stock mutual fund. He feels that the diversity of a mutual fund will be safer and give greater returns. Jasper has plenty of time to take a fair amount of risk and is comfortable that he will have Mackenzie's college money when she needs it.

Prepare Choose a short-term or long-term financial goal you would like to reach. In your workbook or on a separate sheet of paper, and using the same guidelines as shown above, prepare an investment plan for yourself. Research some of the available investments and come up with your own investment alternatives. Explain the reasons for your final choice.

Investor Services

Many stockbrokers and financial planners periodically mail a free newsletter to their clients. In addition, investor services, such as Moody's Investors Service, sell subscription newsletters, available in print and on the Internet. Five widely used and useful publications are *Standard & Poor's Stock and Bond Guide, Value Line Investment Survey, Handbook of Common Stocks,* which provide information on companies; and *Morningstar Mutual Funds* and *Wiesenberger Investment Companies Yearbook,* which cover mutual funds.

SECTION 8.3 ASSESSMENT

CHECK YOUR UNDERSTANDING

1. What is a financial planner's role in a personal financial program?
2. What is your role in a personal investment program?
3. Where can you find sources of financial information?

THINK CRITICALLY

4. Why do you think some people don't keep track of their investments? Give reasons why they should.

USING MATH SKILLS

5. **Tax Considerations** Elliott is going to receive capital gains on some stock he just sold. He owned the stock for less than a year and made a profit of $200. He is in the 15 percent tax bracket.
   Calculate How much will Elliott pay in capital gains tax on the profits from his stock sale?

SOLVING MONEY PROBLEMS

6. **Finding a Financial Planner** Helene has decided to hire a financial planner. She has to rely on ads and the yellow pages for names because she is new in town. She wants to meet with several people before choosing one.
   Develop Compile a list of specific questions that Helene should ask candidates when she interviews them.

CHAPTER 8 ASSESSMENT

CHAPTER SUMMARY

- To establish an investment plan, start by setting specific goals that are in line with your values and by making sure that your personal finances are in good shape.

- Consider how to obtain the money you need to start investing.

- To decide where to invest your money, consider the safety and/or risk of each investment, its potential for providing income or growth, and its liquidity.

- As you choose from among the main types of investments—stock or equity financing, corporate and government bonds, mutual funds, and real estate—remember that it is wise to diversify.

- To be a successful investor, you must develop a plan and put it into action.

- Financial planners are professionals who help investors with financial decisions.

- Whether you have a financial planner or invest on your own, you should evaluate each investment before buying, monitor it while you own it, keep accurate records, and be aware of tax considerations.

- Valuable sources of financial information are the Internet, newspapers and news programs, business magazines and government publications, corporate reports, statistical averages, and investor services and newsletters.

Internet zone

Understanding and Using Vocabulary

Prepare a motivational speech that you might give to someone who has just begun investing. Use as many key terms as possible in the speech.

emergency fund
speculative
   investment
retained earnings
investment liquidity
equity capital
dividends

common stock
preferred stock
corporate bond
government bond
mutual fund
diversification
financial planner

tax-exempt income   capital loss
tax-deferred income   prospectus
capital gain

Review Key Concepts

1. What four steps should you take to get in good financial shape to invest?
2. Name five sources of money that you can use for investment.
3. Explain the relationship between safety and risk.
4. What are two points to consider before investing in stock?

CHAPTER 8 ASSESSMENT

5. What is one of the best ways to find information about financial investments on the Internet?

Apply Key Concepts

1. Why should you reduce your credit card balances before starting to invest?
2. Explain how the time value of money makes investing even small amounts worthwhile.
3. What types of investments would you suggest for a friend who is afraid to take chances with his money?
4. When you are considering whether to invest in government bonds or in stock, which would be a better choice if you wanted to minimize inflation risk and interest rate risk?
5. What steps might you take to be sure that a Web site that you visit for financial information is reliable?

 ### Problem Solving Today

BUYING A CAR

You've found a car you like for $13,000. You plan to make a down payment of $2,000. However, you need to sell some bonds to obtain the cash. You have two $1,000 bonds. Neither one matures for another year. One pays a fixed rate of 9 percent interest and the other pays 6 percent. Current bond interest rates are 8 percent.

Analyze How much money will you have if you sell both bonds now? Will you have enough to make the down payment you had planned? If not, what will you do?

Computer Activity As an alternative activity, use financial software to calculate the market price of the two bonds and devise a plan for financing your new car.

Real-World Application

CONNECT WITH ECONOMICS

Frederick is thinking about putting his money into an international mutual fund that invests heavily in Asian stocks. He would like to know more about the economic situation in Asia to decide whether he should invest in that fund.

Think Critically Help Frederick find the information he needs. Use library and Internet resources to find out more about current economic conditions in Japan and other Asian nations. Then decide whether Frederick should put his money into the fund.

FINANCE Online

MAKING A PERSONAL FINANCIAL PLAN

You want to prepare your individual investment plan and would like to get general financial planning information and look at suggested plans.

Connect Using different Internet search engines, look for information on investment planning. Go to the sites that offer to prepare a personalized plan for you. Then answer the following:
1. Which plan did you feel best suited your needs and values?
2. What general investment information was most helpful to you as a beginner?

Stocks

Q&A

Q: My parents gave me stock certificates for a graduation present. I plan to put them in a safe-deposit box and save them for retirement. Is that a smart thing to do?

A: A safe-deposit box is a good way to store important documents. A better option is to open a brokerage account with a bank or brokerage firm. They will hold your certificates in custody for you. An advantage of this strategy is that you'll receive a quarterly or annual statement showing the value of your shares and dividends paid. If you want to buy or sell shares of this or other stocks, you'll find it easy to do.

Common Stock and Preferred Stock

*S*uzette was watching the basketball playoffs. It seemed that every 10 minutes she saw a commercial for a company that allowed people to buy and sell stocks on the Internet. The actors in the ads were young, which seemed odd, because Suzette always thought that buying stocks was something that older people, like her parents, did. Suzette has been putting most of her wages from her part-time job as a lifeguard into a savings account. Now several of her friends are urging her to buy stocks because they've heard that money will grow faster that way. Suzette likes the idea, but she doesn't know how to find out about stocks. She also doesn't think that she would even understand the information if she found it.

Many beginning investors express similar fears, which underscores the importance of learning about all types of securities. *Securities* are all of the investments, including stocks, bonds, mutual funds, options, and commodities, that are traded—bought and sold—on securities exchanges or the over-the-counter market. These securities exchanges and the over-the-counter market are generally referred to as the stock market. This chapter examines stocks, shares of ownership of a corporation. There are two types of stock: common and preferred.

Common Stock

When investors buy shares of stock in a company, the company uses that money to make and sell its products, fund its operations, and expand. If the company earns a profit, the stockholders (owners of shares of stock in the company) earn a return, or gain, on their investment. People buy and sell stocks for one reason: They want larger returns than they can get from more conservative investments such as savings accounts or government bonds.

Before you invest your money in stock, it might help you to understand why corporations issue common stock. As you may recall from Chapter 8, common stock is stock that provides the most basic form of corporate ownership.

Why Corporations Issue Common Stock

Companies issue common stock to raise money to start up their business and then to help pay for its ongoing activities. A *private*

What's Your Financial ID?

THE TRUTH ABOUT STOCKS

Just for fun, test your knowledge of stocks before you read the chapter and again after reading it. Write your answers on a separate sheet of paper. The first time you take this quiz, you probably won't know all the answers. If you had the money, would you be ready to invest in stocks?

1. All stocks pay dividends.

   True   False

2. Blue-chip stocks are generally a safe investment that attracts conservative investors.

   True   False

3. A bull market occurs when ranchers take their cattle to the stockyards.

   True   False

4. An initial public offering (IPO) occurs when a company first sells its products or services to the public.

   True   False

5. The price-earnings (PE) ratio is the price of one share of stock divided by the stock's earnings per share.

   True   False

6. A good way to learn about the financial health of a company is by reading its annual report.

   True   False

7. An income statement shows a company's profits and losses.

   True   False

8. The appeal of investing in high-risk stocks is the possibility of large returns.

   True   False

---

corporation, also called a closely held corporation, is one whose shares are owned by a relatively small group of people and are not traded openly in stock markets. On the other hand, a *public corporation*, or publicly held corporation, is one that sells its shares openly in stock markets where anyone can buy them. Some large corporations, such as AT&T, General Electric, Procter & Gamble, and General Motors, have thousands or even millions of stockholders. Financial managers of public corporations prefer to sell common stock as a method of funding their business activities for several reasons.

A FORM OF EQUITY Corporations don't have to repay the money a stockholder pays for stock. Generally a stockholder can sell his or her stock to another investor. The price is set according to how much the buyer is willing to pay. If demand for a certain company's stock increases, the price goes up. If demand decreases, the price goes down. Demand for a stock changes when information about the company is released to the public. News on expected sales revenues, earnings, company expansions, or mergers with other companies can make demand for the stock go up or down. As a result, the market value of the stock—the price that buyers are willing to pay—will go up or down as well.

UNDERSTANDING STOCKS Investors buy stocks in the hopes of earning a large return on their investments. *What causes the demand for stock to change?*

DIVIDENDS NOT MANDATORY It is up to the corporate board of directors, a group of individuals elected to make the major decisions for the corporation, to decide whether any profits will be paid to stockholders as dividends. Companies that are growing quickly may pay low or no dividends. Instead, they may decide to use the profits to expand the company even further. Of course, any company's board of directors can reduce or even stop dividend payments when a corporation has had a bad year.

VOTING RIGHTS AND CONTROL OF THE COMPANY In return for your money, management gives you certain rights as a stockholder. For example, the corporation is required by law to hold a meeting every year where stockholders can vote on company business. Stockholders usually get one vote for each share they own. They can vote in person or by proxy. A *proxy* is a document that transfers a stockholder's voting rights to someone else. Stockholders may be asked to vote for major changes in company policy or to elect new members to the board of directors.

RESPOND

Imagine that you own stock in a small Web design firm. Describe a situation where preemptive rights would be beneficial to you.

Some states require that corporations offer existing stockholders a preemptive right. A *preemptive right* gives current stockholders the right to buy any new stock the corporation issues before the stock is offered to the general public. By buying more shares, a stockholder can keep the same proportion of ownership in the company. This can be very important when a corporation is small and management control of the company is critical.

Finally, corporations must send annual and quarterly reports to stockholders. These reports include details about sales, earnings, and other financial matters.

Why Investors Purchase Common Stock

Investors who purchase common stock can make money in three ways. They profit when they receive dividends, when the dollar value of their stock appreciates (increases), and when the stock splits and increases in value.

Figure 9.1

Tracking Your Stock Investments

1. Monitor
Graph the dollar value of your stock on a daily or weekly basis.

2. Watch the financials
Continually evaluate the company's current sales and profits and those projected for the future. Compare its progress to the performance of other companies in the same industry. If it can't compete, sell.

3. Track the products
Poor-quality products, or a lack of new or up-to-date products, can make the value of a company's stock drop.

4. Watch the economy
The inflation rate, the state of the overall economy, and other economic factors can have an effect on your company's stock price.

5. Be patient
If you think that you have bought into a good company, hang on. Over time, your investment will usually increase in value.

EVALUATING STOCKS By keeping up with information about the companies in which you have stock, you are more likely to increase the return on your investment. *Why is patience important in investing?*

INCOME FROM DIVIDENDS   Although a corporation's board members do not have to pay dividends, they do want to keep stockholders happy because these same stockholders are funding their business. As a result, most board members vote to pay dividends as long as the company is able to.

With a cash dividend, each common stockholder receives an equal amount per share. Most dividends are paid quarterly, or every three months. Some companies that have large increases in earnings might declare a special cash dividend at the end of the year. You might also receive a dividend of company stock, or even of company products, although this is very unusual.

DOLLAR APPRECIATION OF STOCK VALUE   You usually hold on to a stock for a while after you buy it. If the market value of the stock increases, you must decide whether to sell the stock at the higher price or continue to hold on to it. If you sell, the difference between the price that you paid for it and the price at which you sell it is your profit. Of course, if the value of the stock falls, then your return will be less than your original investment. **Figure 9.1** provides tips for tracking your stock investment.

POSSIBILITY OF INCREASED VALUE FROM STOCK SPLITS   Your profits can also increase through a stock split. A *stock split* is a process in which the shares of stock owned by existing stockholders are divided into a larger number of shares. For example, in a 2-for-1 stock split, the corporation doubles the number of outstanding shares. Suppose that a corporation has 10,000 shares of stock valued at $50 a share. If the corporation splits its stock, the value of each share decreases to $25. The number of outstanding shares increases to 20,000. If you owned 200 shares before the split, you would own 400 shares after it.

	Before	After
Value	$50	$25
Shares issued	10,000	20,000
Your shares	200	400

Why do corporations split their stock? Often the management believes that the stock should be trading at an ideal price range. If the market value is a lot higher than this range, a stock split brings the market value back into line. Stock splits often make shares of stock more attractive to investors, so the price starts to rise. The public wants to buy because of the general belief that most corporations split their stock only when the company's financial future looks very good. Be warned: A stock's market value is not guaranteed to go up after a split.

Preferred Stock

You could buy preferred stock in addition to, or instead of, common stock. Remember from Chapter 8 that preferred stock gives the owner the advantage of receiving cash dividends before common stockholders receive any cash dividends. If the company were having a hard time financially, then the preferred stockholder might get dividends when the common stockholder would not.

When you buy preferred stock, you know the actual dollar amount of the dividend you will receive before you buy. It is either a specific amount of money or a percentage of the par value of the stock. The *par value* is an assigned (and often random) dollar value that is printed on a stock certificate. If the par value of a stock is $30 and the dividend rate is 5 percent, then the dollar amount of the dividend is $1.50 per share ($30 $\times$ 5% = $1.50).

Why Corporations Issue Preferred Stock

Preferred stock is used less often than common stock as a way of raising money, and only by a few corporations. However, for some companies, it is another method of financing that may attract more conservative investors who do not want to buy common stock. Preferred stockholders also receive limited voting rights, usually voting only if the corporation is in financial trouble.

Why Investors Purchase Preferred Stock

Preferred stock is considered a "middle investment." It is placed between common stock and corporate bonds. The yield on preferred stock is generally lower than the yield on bonds but higher than the yield on common stock. Preferred stock is usually considered a safer investment than common stock, but not as safe as bonds. People who want a steady source of income often buy preferred stock. However, preferred stocks lack the potential for growth that common stocks offer. As a result, preferred stocks are not considered a good investment for most people.

To make preferred stocks more attractive to investors, some corporations may offer cumulative preferred stock, convertible preferred stock, or a participation feature.

CUMULATIVE PREFERRED STOCK Corporations may sell cumulative preferred stock, which is stock whose unpaid dividends build up and must be paid before any cash dividend is paid to the common stockholders. This means that if a corporation decides to omit one or more dividend payments to preferred stockholders, people who hold cumulative preferred stock will still receive those dividend payments during a later payment period.

CONVERTIBLE PREFERRED STOCK Convertible preferred stock is stock that can be exchanged for a specified number of shares of common stock. This provides an investor with the added safety of preferred stock and the possibility of greater returns through conversion to common stock.

PARTICIPATION FEATURE Some corporations offer a participation feature, which allows preferred stockholders to share in the corporation's earnings with the common stockholders. After a required dividend is paid to preferred stockholders and a stated dividend is paid to common stockholders, the remainder of the available earnings is shared by preferred and common stockholders. This feature is rare.

SECTION 9.1 ASSESSMENT

CHECK YOUR UNDERSTANDING

1. Explain why corporations issue common stock.
2. Why do investors purchase common stock?
3. Why do investors purchase preferred stock?

THINK CRITICALLY

4. Justify a corporation's decision to split its stock when the stock price has risen significantly.

USING COMMUNICATION SKILLS

5. **Part Owners** Investors purchase common stock as a way to increase their income. As stockholders, they earn the right to vote on company business.
   Explain Write a paragraph that tells why a stockholder might wish to exercise his or her voting rights.

SOLVING MONEY PROBLEMS

6. **Perks of Preferred Stock** Kwame's grandmother recently gave him 25 shares of preferred stock. Kwame would like to figure out the actual dollar amount of the dividend, which is a percentage of the par value of the stock.
   Calculate According to the stock certificates that Kwame's grandmother gave to him, the par value of each share is $45 and the dividend rate is 6 percent. What is the total dollar amount that Kwame should receive each year?

Evaluation of a Stock Issue

Types of Stock Investments

What You'll Learn

- How to **evaluate** stock investments

Why It's Important

Understanding how to evaluate stocks and learning how they are bought and sold will help you invest in stocks wisely and increase the value of your investments.

KEY TERMS

- blue-chip stock
- income stock
- growth stock
- cyclical stock
- defensive stock
- large cap stock
- capitalization
- small cap stock
- penny stock
- bull market
- bear market
- current yield
- total return
- earnings per share
- price-earnings (PE) ratio

Financial professionals classify most stocks into the following categories: blue-chip stocks, income stocks, growth stocks, cyclical stocks, defensive stocks, large cap stocks, small cap stocks, and penny stocks.

Blue-Chip Stocks

A *blue-chip stock* is considered a safe investment that generally attracts conservative investors. These stocks are issued by the strongest and most respected companies, such as AT&T, General Electric, and Kellogg. If you're interested in a blue-chip stock, look for leadership in an industry, a history of stable earnings, and consistency in the payment of dividends.

Income Stock

An *income stock* pays higher-than-average dividends compared to other stock issues. Many times the buyers of preferred stock are also attracted to this type of common stock because the dividends are predictable. Stocks issued by Bristol-Myers Squibb and Dow

CLASSIFYING STOCKS This corporation issues blue-chip stocks. *Why do conservative investors like blue-chip stocks?*

Chemical are classified as income stocks. This is also the type of stock issued by gas and electric companies.

Growth Stock

A *growth stock* is issued by a corporation whose potential earnings may be higher than the average earnings predicted for all the firms in the country. Stocks issued by these corporations generally do not pay dividends. Look for signs that the company is engaged in activities that produce higher earnings and sales revenues: building new facilities; introducing new, high-quality products; or conducting recognized research and development. Growth companies in the late 1990s included Home Depot, Adobe Systems, and Southwest Airlines.

Cyclical Stock

A *cyclical stock* has a market value that tends to reflect the state of the economy. When the economy is improving, the market value of a cyclical stock usually goes up. During an economic decline, the market value of a cyclical stock generally decreases. This is because the products and services of these companies are linked directly to activities of a strong economy. Investors try to buy these stocks when they are still inexpensive, just before the economy starts to improve. Then they seek to sell them just before the economy declines. Stocks issued by Ford and Centex (a construction firm) are considered cyclical stocks.

Defensive Stock

A *defensive stock* is a stock that remains stable during declines in the economy. The companies that issue such stocks have steady earnings and can continue dividend payments even in periods of economic decline. Many blue-chip stocks and income stocks may also be considered defensive stocks, such as those issued by Procter & Gamble and Kellogg.

Large Cap and Small Cap Stocks

A *large cap stock* is the stock of a corporation that has issued a large number of shares of stock and has a large amount of capitalization. *Capitalization* is usually defined as the total amount of stocks and bonds issued by a corporation. The stocks listed in the Dow Jones averages are typically large cap stocks. These stocks appeal to conservative investors because they are considered secure.

QUESTION

What type of investor would prefer growth stock over blue-chip stock?

ECONOMY DEPENDENT
When the economy is doing well, people have more money to spend, which allows the economy to grow even more. *What kind of stock is most closely linked with the state of the economy?*

A *small cap stock* is a stock issued by a company with a capitalization of $150 million or less. Because small companies issue these stocks, they are considered to be a higher investment risk.

Penny Stock

A *penny stock* typically sells for less than $1 a share, although it can sell for as much as $10 a share. These stocks are issued by new companies or companies whose sales are very unsteady. The prices of these stocks can go up and down wildly. It is often hard to keep track of a penny stock's performance because information about

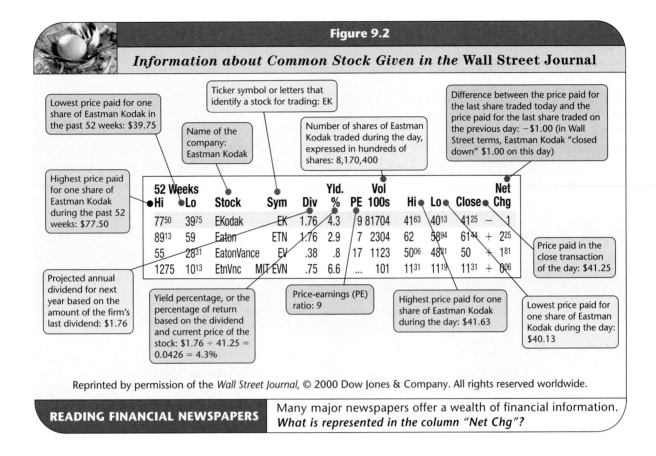

Figure 9.2

Information about Common Stock Given in the Wall Street Journal

Lowest price paid for one share of Eastman Kodak in the past 52 weeks: $39.75

Ticker symbol or letters that identify a stock for trading: EK

Name of the company: Eastman Kodak

Number of shares of Eastman Kodak traded during the day, expressed in hundreds of shares: 8,170,400

Difference between the price paid for the last share traded today and the price paid for the last share traded on the previous day: −$1.00 (in Wall Street terms, Eastman Kodak "closed down" $1.00 on this day)

Highest price paid for one share of Eastman Kodak during the past 52 weeks: $77.50

| 52 Weeks | | | | | Yld. | | Vol | | | | Net |
Hi	Lo	Stock	Sym	Div	%	PE	100s	Hi	Lo	Close	Chg
77⁵⁰	39⁷⁵	EKodak	EK	1.76	4.3	9	81704	41⁶³	40¹³	41²⁵	− 1
89¹³	59	Eaton	ETN	1.76	2.9	7	2304	62	58⁹⁴	61¹⁴	+ 2²⁵
55	28³¹	EatonVance	EV	.38	.8	17	1123	50⁰⁶	48³¹	50	+ 1⁸¹
1275	10¹³	EtnVnc MIT	EVN	.75	6.6	...	101	11³¹	11¹⁹	11³¹	+ 0⁰⁶

Price paid in the close transaction of the day: $41.25

Projected annual dividend for next year based on the amount of the firm's last dividend: $1.76

Yield percentage, or the percentage of return based on the dividend and current price of the stock: $1.76 ÷ 41.25 = 0.0426 = 4.3%

Price-earnings (PE) ratio: 9

Highest price paid for one share of Eastman Kodak during the day: $41.63

Lowest price paid for one share of Eastman Kodak during the day: $40.13

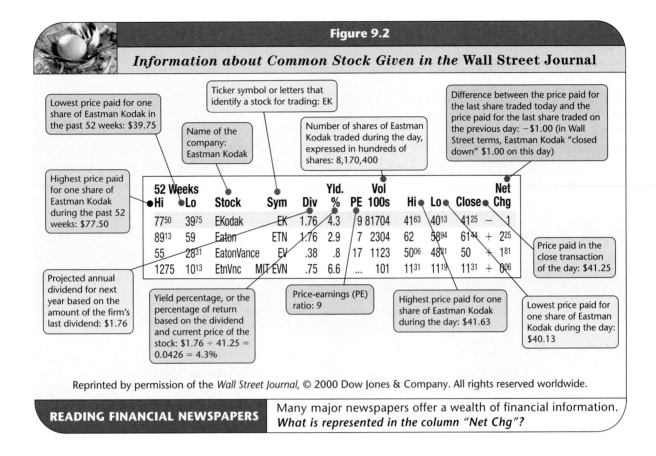

Reprinted by permission of the *Wall Street Journal*, © 2000 Dow Jones & Company. All rights reserved worldwide.

READING FINANCIAL NEWSPAPERS | Many major newspapers offer a wealth of financial information. *What is represented in the column "Net Chg"?*

them is hard to find. Penny stocks are very risky and should be purchased only by investors who understand all the risks.

Sources for Evaluating Stock Investments

There are many sources where you can find information about stocks before making investment decisions.

The Financial Section of the Newspaper

Most major newspapers contain information about stocks that are listed on the New York Stock Exchange (NYSE), the American Stock Exchange (AMEX), other major stock exchanges, and the over-the-counter market. Newspapers may also cover stocks of local interest. Although all newspapers don't print exactly the same information, they always provide the basic financial data. **Figure 9.2** contains detailed information about Eastman Kodak.

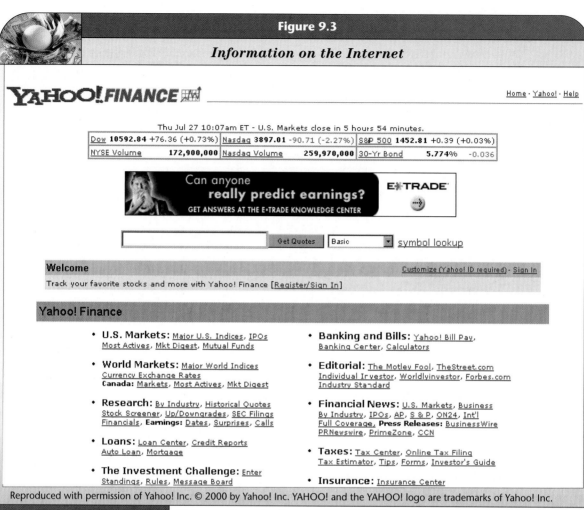

Figure 9.3

Information on the Internet

YAHOO! FINANCE

Home · Yahoo! · Help

Thu Jul 27 10:07am ET - U.S. Markets close in 5 hours 54 minutes.

| Dow 10592.84 +76.36 (+0.73%) | Nasdaq 3897.01 -90.71 (-2.27%) | S&P 500 1452.81 +0.39 (+0.03%) |
| NYSE Volume 172,900,000 | Nasdaq Volume 259,970,000 | 30-Yr Bond 5.774% -0.036 |

Can anyone **really predict earnings?** GET ANSWERS AT THE E·TRADE KNOWLEDGE CENTER

E·TRADE

Get Quotes | Basic | symbol lookup

Welcome
Customize (Yahoo! ID required) · Sign In
Track your favorite stocks and more with Yahoo! Finance [Register/Sign In]

Yahoo! Finance

- **U.S. Markets:** Major U.S. Indices, IPOs, Most Actives, Mkt Digest, Mutual Funds

- **World Markets:** Major World Indices Currency Exchange Rates **Canada:** Markets, Most Actives, Mkt Digest

- **Research:** By Industry, Historical Quotes Stock Screener, Up/Downgrades, SEC Filings Financials, **Earnings:** Dates, Surprises, Calls

- **Loans:** Loan Center, Credit Reports Auto Loan, Mortgage

- **The Investment Challenge:** Enter Standings, Rules, Message Board

- **Banking and Bills:** Yahoo! Bill Pay, Banking Center, Calculators

- **Editorial:** The Motley Fool, TheStreet.com Individual Investor, Worldlyinvestor, Forbes.com Industry Standard

- **Financial News:** U.S. Markets, Business By Industry, IPOs, AP, S & P, ON24, Int'l Full Coverage, **Press Releases:** BusinessWire PRNewswire, PrimeZone, CCN

- **Taxes:** Tax Center, Online Tax Filing Tax Estimator, Tips, Forms, Investor's Guide

- **Insurance:** Insurance Center

UTILIZING THE INTERNET

This search engine is one example of the many Web sites that can be used to find financial information. *What Web sites would help you find up-to-date information about a corporation's financial status?*

The Internet

The number of Web sites that deal with personal finance and investments is enormous. Today most corporations have their own home pages. All you have to do is make an Internet connection and search by the company's name. The information may be more up-to-date and detailed than material from the corporation's printed publications.

You can also use search engines to find information about investing in stocks. **Figure 9.3** shows the opening page for the Yahoo! Finance Web site. Search engines can help you find sites that provide everything from general financial news to specific information about a company and its stock's performance.

STANDARD &POOR'S

CASE STUDY

Angela Bizzari is a senior in high school. Recently she played a stock market simulation game in her personal finance class. The class was divided into six teams. Each team started with an investment of $50,000 and had two months to research, buy, and sell stocks. The team with the highest dollar value in their portfolio at the end of the two months would be declared the winner. The local winners then competed at the state level, and Angela's team ended up with a $256,000 portfolio and came in second place. Through this game, Angela became interested in the stock market. She has been reading the *Wall Street Journal* and listening to financial shows on the radio. Last month, she even attended a personal finance workshop conducted by a local stockbroker. She regularly uses the Internet to continue tracking the stocks she "purchased" during the school simulation. Angela works part-time and has saved about $1,500 that she could invest. However, she is not quite sure where to begin. She turned to the experts at Standard & Poor's for advice.

STANDARD &POOR'S **Analysis:** Managing an imaginary stock portfolio is an excellent way to learn about stock investing. Before Angela invests her hard-earned money, she should consider whether she could comfortably set aside her $1,500 for at least three to five years. Angela should also set realistic expectations. Since 1926 the stock market overall has earned an average annual return of 10 to 12 percent. In some years the market fell by more than 20 percent! Individual stocks often have even bigger price drops than the overall market.

STANDARD &POOR'S **Recommendation:** A stock mutual fund offers Angela instant diversification and is an inexpensive way to invest small amounts. If Angela invests in individual stocks, she should plan to eventually build a portfolio of 10 to 15 stocks. Angela can make a list of companies whose products and services she knows, and the industries that these companies represent. Angela can then research each company using *Standard & Poor's Stock and Bond Guide* and *Value Line Investment Survey*, which she can find at her local library. If she chooses to work with a broker, Angela can ask for the full-service brokerage firm's research reports on the stocks she is interested in. To start, Angela may be able to afford to buy only a few shares each of companies in different industries. She will pay a higher commission than if she simply bought shares of one company, but her risk of losing money is potentially less if she invests in several different stocks.

Critical Thinking Questions

1. Should Angela try to find a broker with a full-service brokerage firm to make recommendations?
2. Why might Angela choose to invest in individual stocks rather than in a mutual fund?
3. What might you learn about stock investing from managing an imaginary stock portfolio?

Figure 9.4

A Basic Financial Report

REEBOK INTERNATIONAL, LTD.

EXCH.	SYM.	REC. PRICE	P/E RATIO	YLD.	MKT. CAP.	RANGE (52-WK.)	'99 Y/E PR.
NYSE	RBK	15¹⁵/₁₆ (6/30/00)	36.2	...	$0.90 bill.	18¾ - 6¹⁵/₁₆	8³/₁₆

LOWER MEDIUM GRADE. THE COMPANY AND FOOT LOCKER LAUNCHED BLACKTOP, A COLLECTION OF OUTDOOR BASKETBALL FOOTWEAR AND APPAREL DESIGNED AND ENGINEERED BY RBK.

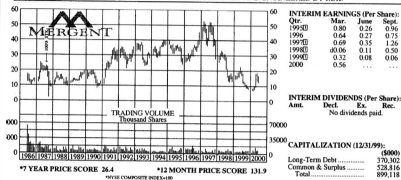

INTERIM EARNINGS (Per Share):

Qtr.	Mar.	June	Sept.	Dec.
1995①	0.80	0.26	0.96	0.02
1996	0.64	0.27	0.75	0.35
1997①	0.69	0.35	1.26	0.01
1998①	d0.06	0.11	0.50	d0.13
1999①	0.32	0.08	0.06	d0.26
2000	0.56	...	...	...

INTERIM DIVIDENDS (Per Share):

Amt.	Decl.	Ex.	Rec.	Pay.
		No dividends paid.		

TRADING VOLUME
Thousand Shares

1986 1987 1988 1989 1990 1991 1992 1993 1994 1995 1996 1997 1998 1999 2000

*7 YEAR PRICE SCORE 26.4   *12 MONTH PRICE SCORE 131.9
*NYSE COMPOSITE INDEX=100

CAPITALIZATION (12/31/99):

	($000)	(%)
Long-Term Debt	370,302	41.2
Common & Surplus	528,816	58.8
Total	899,118	100.0

BUSINESS:

Reebok International, Ltd. is a worldwide company engaged primarily in the design and marketing of sports and fitness products, including footwear and apparel, as well as the design and marketing of footwear and apparel for casual use. The Company has four major brand groups. The Reebok Division designs, produces and markets sports, fitness and casual footwear, apparel and accessories under the REEBOK® brand. The Rockport Company designs, produces and distributes specially-engineered comfort footwear for men and women worldwide under the ROCKPORT® brand. Ralph Lauren Footwear Co., Inc., a subsidiary of the Company, is responsible for footwear and certain apparel sold under the RALPH LAUREN® and POLO SPORT® brands. The Greg Norman Division produces a range of men's apparel and accessories marketed under the GREG NORMAN name and logo. Avia Group International was sold in June 1996.

RECENT DEVELOPMENTS:

For the quarter ended 3/31/00, net income jumped 77.1% to $31.7 million compared with $17.9 million a year ago. Total revenues declined 1.6% to $744.7 million. Reebok footwear sales in the United States declined 3.0% to $258.2 million and apparel sales, including sales of the Greg Norman Collection, dropped 15.4% to $57.7 million. Sales of the Reebok brand outside the U.S. increased 2.7% to $325.6 million.

PROSPECTS:

On 5/26/00, the Company and Foot Locker launched Blacktop, a collection of outdoor basketball footwear and apparel designed and engineered by RBK. Going forward, the Company will continue to focus on improving the performance of the Reebok brand in the U.S. As a result, the Company plans to expand the sales and distribution of its DMX technology, improve the overall fashionability of its products and increase product sell throughs at retail. RBK expects an improvement in Rockport's business later this year mainly due to new product offerings. Results for the Ralph Lauren footwear division should benefit from an expanded product line, new collections and improved product quality and style.

ANNUAL FINANCIAL DATA:

FISCAL YEAR	TOT. REVS. ($mil.)	NET INC. ($mil.)	TOT. ASSETS ($mil.)	OPER. PROFIT %	NET PROFIT %	RET. ON EQUITY %	RET. ON ASSETS %	CURR. RATIO	EARN. PER SH. $	CASH FL. PER SH. $	TANG. BK. VAL. $	DIV. PER SH. $	PRICE RANGE	AVG. P/E RATIO	AVG. YIELD %
12/31/99	2,891.2	① 11.0	1,564.1	4.5	0.4	2.1	0.7	2.0	① 0.20	1.06	8.17	...	22¾ - 7¹³/₁₆	76.4	...
12/31/98	3,205.4	① 23.9	1,739.6	3.8	0.7	4.6	1.4	2.2	① 0.42	1.26	8.05	...	33³/₁₆ - 12⁹/₁₆	54.5	...
12/31/97	3,637.4	① 135.1	1,756.1	7.4	3.7	26.6	7.7	2.5	① 2.32	3.13	8.27	...	52⁷/₈ - 27⅝	17.3	...
12/31/96	3,482.9	139.0	1,786.2	7.7	4.0	36.4	7.8	2.8	2.00	2.65	5.58	0.30	45¼ - 25⅜	17.7	0.8
12/31/95	3,484.6	① 164.8	1,656.2	10.5	4.7	18.4	10.0	3.1	① 2.07	2.57	11.11	0.30	39⅝ - 24⅛	15.4	0.9
12/31/94	3,287.6	254.5	1,649.5	13.0	7.7	25.7	15.4	2.6	3.02	3.46	11.05	0.30	40¼ - 28⅜	11.4	0.9
12/31/93	2,893.9	① 223.4	1,391.7	13.6	7.7	26.4	16.1	2.8	① 2.53	2.93	8.99	0.30	38⅝ - 23	12.2	1.0
12/31/92	3,060.6	① 114.8	1,345.3	14.0	3.8	13.7	8.5	2.7	① 1.24	1.72	8.23	0.30	35⅝ - 21⅜	23.0	1.1
12/31/91	2,736.1	234.7	1,430.8	14.9	8.6	28.5	16.4	2.4	2.37	2.76	6.36	0.30	35⅛ - 10¾	9.7	1.3
12/31/90	2,158.4	176.6	1,403.2	13.8	8.2	17.7	12.6	3.5	1.54	1.86	6.48	0.30	20 - 8⅛	9.1	2.1

Statistics are as originally reported. ① Incl. non-recurr. chrg. 1999, $61.6 mill.; 1998, $35.0 mill.; 1997, $58.2 mill.; 1995, $72.1 mill.; 1993, $8.4 mill.; 1992, $155.0 mill.

OFFICERS:
P. B. Fireman, Chmn., Pres., C.E.O.
K. I. Watchmaker, Exec. V.P., C.F.O., Treas.
D. A. Pace, V.P., Gen. Couns.

PRINCIPAL OFFICE: 100 Technology Center Drive, Stoughton, MA 02072

TELEPHONE NUMBER: (781) 401-5000
WEB: www.reebok.com

NO. OF EMPLOYEES: 6,500 (avg.)

SHAREHOLDERS: 6,630

ANNUAL MEETING: In May

INCORPORATED: MA, July, 1979

INSTITUTIONAL HOLDINGS:
No. of Institutions: 124
Shares Held: 33,883,774
% Held: 60.2

INDUSTRY: Rubber and plastics footwear (SIC: 3021)

TRANSFER AGENT(S): BankBoston, N.A., Boston, MA.

Report for Reebok International, Ltd. (Source: *Handbook of Common Stocks*, © 1999 by Mergent FIS. Reprinted by permission.)

UP AND DOWN

This financial report from the *Handbook of Common Stocks* provides information about Reebok International, Ltd. **What does the line graph show you about this company?**

Stock Advisory Services

In addition to newspapers and the Internet, you can use stock advisory services to evaluate potential stock investments. Many stock advisory services charge fees for their information, which can vary from simple alphabetic listings to detailed financial reports. As mentioned in Chapter 8, four widely used services for information on companies are Standard & Poor's, Value Line, Moody's Investors Service, and Mergent's Financial Investors Service.

As shown in **Figure 9.4**, a basic financial report from Mergent's *Handbook of Common Stocks* consists of six sections. One section contains information about stock prices and capitalization, earnings, and dividends. A background section, "Business," provides a detailed description of the company's major operations, such as the products they produce. A third section, "Recent Developments," offers current information about net income and sales revenue. A "Prospects" section describes the company's outlook, or prospects for the future. The "Annual Financial Data" section provides important statistics on the company for a specific length of time in the past. A final section lists information such as important officers in the corporation and the location of its headquarters.

ONCE A YEAR An annual report can provide a great deal of information for investors. *How can you get a copy of an annual report?*

BULL AND BEAR MARKETS Knowing what kind of market an economy is in is important when you make decisions as an investor. *How does a bull market affect stocks?*

Corporate News

Annual and quarterly reports offer a summary of a corporation's activities and detailed financial information. You do not have to be a stockholder to get an annual report. Simply call, write, or e-mail to request a copy from the company's headquarters. Financial publications such as *Barron's, Business Week, Fortune, Kiplinger's Personal Finance Magazine, Money,* and *Smart Money* also provide information about specific companies.

Factors That Influence the Price of Stock

PREDICT

What factors should you consider when deciding whether a stock is worth buying or selling?

Many factors influence the price of a stock. A *bull market* occurs when investors are optimistic about the economy and buy stocks. Because of the greater demand for stock, the value of many stocks and the value of the stock market as a whole increases. A *bear market* occurs when investors are pessimistic about the economy and sell stocks. As a result of this decline in demand, the value of individual stocks and the stock market as a whole decreases.

When you're deciding whether it's the right time to buy or sell a particular stock, you must also consider a company's profits or losses and other numerical measures of its financial situation.

Numerical Measures for a Corporation

One of the most common calculations investors use to track the value of their investments is the current yield. *Current yield* is the annual dividend divided by the investment's current market value. The current yield is expressed as a percentage.

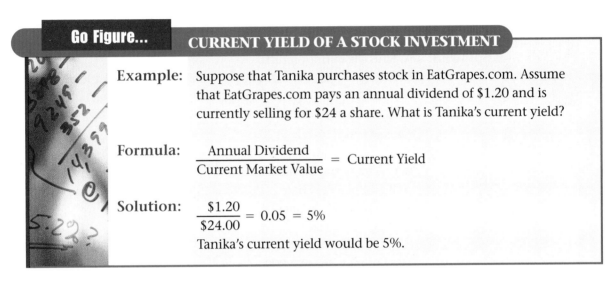

Go Figure...   **CURRENT YIELD OF A STOCK INVESTMENT**

Example: Suppose that Tanika purchases stock in EatGrapes.com. Assume that EatGrapes.com pays an annual dividend of $1.20 and is currently selling for $24 a share. What is Tanika's current yield?

Formula: $\dfrac{\text{Annual Dividend}}{\text{Current Market Value}} = \text{Current Yield}$

Solution: $\dfrac{\$1.20}{\$24.00} = 0.05 = 5\%$

Tanika's current yield would be 5%.

As a general rule, an increase in current yield is a healthy sign for any investment. The current yield calculation is useful, but you also need to know whether your investment is increasing or decreasing in dollar value. *Total return* is a calculation that includes the annual dividend as well as any increase or decrease in the original purchase price of the investment.

To calculate total return, you would add the current return on your investment to its capital gain. The current return is the total amount of dividends paid to you, based on the number of shares and how long you held them. To figure out your current return, you would multiply your dividend amount per share by the number of shares and the length of time that you held the shares.

Next you would determine your capital gain. As you learned in Chapter 8, capital gain is the profit you make from the sale of an asset, or the difference between the selling price and the purchase price. To compute your capital gain, subtract the purchase price per share from the selling price per share. Then multiply that number by the number of shares held.

Once you have determined your current return and your capital gain, add those two figures to arrive at your total return.

Go Figure... TOTAL RETURN

Example: Two years ago Mark bought 40 shares of Ferguson's Motor Company for $70 a share. The stock pays an annual dividend of $1.50. Mark is going to sell his stock at the current price of $120 a share. What would be the total return on his investment?

Formula: Current Return + Capital Gain = Total Return

Solution: **A.** Find the current return.
Dividend × Number of Shares × Years Held = Current Return

$1.50 × 40 × 2 = $120
The current return is $120.

B. Calculate the capital gain.
(Selling Price Per Share − Purchase Price Per Share) × Number of Shares Held = Capital Gain

($120 − $70) × 40 = $2,000
The capital gain is $2,000.

C. Find the total return.
Current Return + Capital Gain = Total Return

$120 + $2,000 = $2,120
The total return on Mark's investment would be $2,120.

In this example Mark's investment in Ferguson's Motor Company increased in value so the total return was greater than the current return. For an investment that decreases in value, the total return will be less than the current return. Although it may seem obvious, the larger the dollar amount of the total return, the better.

Another measurement of a company's performance is earnings per share. *Earnings per share* are a corporation's net, or after-tax, earnings divided by the number of outstanding shares of common stock. This calculation measures the amount of corporate profit that can be assigned to each share of common stock.

Go Figure...   EARNINGS PER SHARE

Example: EFG Corporation had net earnings of $800,000 in 2001. EFG has 100,000 outstanding shares of common stock. What are EFG's earnings per share?

Formula: $$\frac{\text{Net Earnings}}{\text{Common Stock Outstanding}} = \text{Earnings Per Share}$$

Solution: $$\frac{\$800,000}{100,000} = \$8$$

EFG's earnings per share are $8.

This figure gives a stockholder an idea of how profitable the company is. In general, an increase in earnings per share is a good sign for any corporation and its stockholders.

The ***price-earnings (PE) ratio*** is the price of one share of stock divided by the corporation's earnings per share of stock outstanding over the last 12 months. This measurement is commonly used to compare the corporate earnings to the market price of a corporation's stock.

Go Figure...   PRICE-EARNINGS RATIO

Example: EFG's stock is selling for $96 a share. EFG's earnings per share are $8. What is EFG's price-earnings ratio?

Formula: $$\frac{\text{Market Price Per Share}}{\text{Earnings Per Share}} = \text{Price-Earnings Ratio}$$

Solution: $$\frac{\$96}{\$8} = 12$$

EFG's price-earnings ratio is 12.

The PE ratio is a key factor that serious investors as well as beginners can use to decide whether to invest in a stock. A low PE ratio indicates that a stock may be a good investment. The company has a lot of earnings when compared to the price of the stock. A high PE ratio tells you that it might be a poor investment. The company has little earnings when compared to the price of the stock. Generally, you should study the PE ratio for a corporation over a period of time so that you can see a range. Although PE ratios vary by industry, they range between 5 and 35 for most corporations.

Investment Theories

Over the years theories have developed about ways to evaluate possible investments. Three investment theories dominate. The fundamental theory assumes that a stock's real value is determined by looking at the company's future earnings. If earnings are expected to increase in the future, then the stock's price should go up too. People who believe in the fundamental theory also look at the financial strength of the company, the type of industry the company is in, its new products, and the state of the economy.

The technical theory is based on the idea that a stock's value is really determined by forces in the stock market itself. Technical theorists look at factors such as the number of stocks bought or sold over a certain period or the total number of shares traded.

Careers in Finance

ACCOUNT EXECUTIVE (STOCKBROKER)

Some of you may dream of making millions in the stock market, but would you know how? Some people like to learn about and choose their own investments, while others prefer to depend on the advice of their account executives. More often known as stockbrokers, account executives buy and sell financial securities, such as stocks, bonds, and mutual funds, for their customers. Although stockbrokers must be affiliated with a brokerage firm, they usually have to find their own clients through leads and by calling people on the phone. Stockbrokers are paid a commission, which is a percentage of the value of their sales.

Skills	Communication, computer, interpersonal, math, sales ability
Personality	Desire to succeed, ethical, honest, independent, likes sales
Education	Bachelor's degree; must pass the General Securities Registered Representative Examination
Pay range	$24,000 to $100,000 plus a year, depending on commissions

Assess Why do you think a stockbroker must be honest and ethical?

 For more information on account executives visit finance.glencoe.com or your local library.

In the efficient market theory, sometimes called the random walk theory, the argument is that stock price movements are purely random. This theory declares that investors have considered all of the available information as they make their decisions. According to the efficient market theory, it is impossible for an investor to outperform the stock market average over a long period of time.

SECTION 9.2 ASSESSMENT

CHECK YOUR UNDERSTANDING

1. Briefly describe each of the different types of stock investments.
2. List the sources that you might use to evaluate stock investments.
3. What numerical measures of corporations can be used to evaluate stock investments?

THINK CRITICALLY

4. Explain how the calculations that involve a company's earnings might help you to make a decision about buying or selling a particular stock.

USING MATH SKILLS

5. **Total Return** Andrei bought 100 shares of Snowland, a ski apparel company, two years ago. The price of the stock is up $10 from the $20-a-share purchase price, and the stock even paid a dividend of $0.50 per share each year. Andrei wants to determine his total return on the stock to see whether he should hold on to the stock or sell it.
   Calculate Use the formula from this section to determine the total return on Andrei's shares in Snowland.

SOLVING MONEY PROBLEMS

6. **Finding Stock Information** Sandy's mother works for Arf, a nationwide chain of dog kennels. She is receiving company stock as part of her employee retirement plan. She wants to track the stock's performance to see how her retirement nest egg is doing.
   Identify Suggest two items in the stock reports in the newspaper for her mother to look at every week to get an idea of how the company's stock is doing. Explain to Sandy why this information is useful.

Buying and Selling Stocks

Primary Markets for Stocks

To buy common or preferred stock, you usually have to go through a brokerage firm. In turn, the brokerage firm must buy the stock in the primary or secondary market.

The *primary market* is a market in which an investor purchases securities from a corporation through an investment bank or some other representative of the corporation. An investment bank is a financial firm that helps corporations to raise funds, usually by helping to sell new securities. The investors are commercial banks, insurance companies, pension funds, mutual funds, and the general public.

An *initial public offering (IPO)* occurs when a company sells stock to the general public for the first time. Companies use IPOs to fund new business start-ups or to finance new corporate growth and expansion. If these companies use the money they raise from the IPOs wisely, they can grow and prosper. In turn, those investors who take part in an IPO will earn profits. Nevertheless, IPOs are considered a high-risk investment.

A corporation can also get financing through the primary market by selling directly to its current stockholders. In bypassing the investment bank and avoiding any fees it might have had to pay to the investment bank, a corporation can obtain financing at a lower cost.

Secondary Markets for Stocks

After stocks are sold on the primary market, they are sold in the secondary market. The *secondary market* is a market for existing financial securities that are currently traded among investors. They may be sold time and again to many different investors on securities exchanges or through the over-the-counter market.

Securities Exchanges

A *securities exchange* is a marketplace where brokers who represent investors meet to buy and sell securities. Many securities issued by national corporations are traded at either the New York Stock Exchange (NYSE) or the American Stock Exchange (AMEX). They must first be registered with the exchange on which they will be traded. Exchanges in San Francisco, Boston, Chicago, and other cities trade the stocks of companies in their respective regions. American firms that do business abroad may also be traded in other countries—on the Tokyo, London, or Paris exchanges, for example.

The New York Stock Exchange is one of the largest securities exchanges in the world, listing more than 3,000 corporations with a total market value of about $16 trillion. Most of its 1,366 members, or seats, represent brokerage firms.

In order to be traded on the NYSE, a corporation must have a very large capitalization and trade many shares, in addition to meeting other requirements. Companies that cannot meet the NYSE requirements can use AMEX or regional exchanges as a place for their stock to be bought and sold.

THE BIG BOARD The New York Stock Exchange (NYSE) is one of the largest securities exchanges in the world. *What qualifications must a corporation meet to be traded on the NYSE?*

Over-the-Counter Market

Not all stocks are traded on organized exchanges. Several thousand companies trade their stock in the over-the-counter market. The *over-the-counter (OTC) market* is a network of dealers who buy and sell the stocks of corporations that are not listed on a securities exchange.

Most over-the-counter stocks are traded through Nasdaq (pronounced NAZZ-dack), an electronic marketplace for more than 4,000 different stocks. When you want to buy or sell a stock that trades on Nasdaq—Microsoft, for example—your brokerage firm sends your order in to the Nasdaq computer system. It shows up on a screen with all the other orders from people who want to buy or sell Microsoft. Then a Nasdaq dealer matches the orders of those who want to buy and those who want to sell Microsoft. Once a match is found, your order is completed.

Typically, Nasdaq handles trades for many forward-looking companies, many of whom are fairly small. However, some very large companies such as Microsoft, Intel, and MCI are also traded on Nasdaq.

Account Executives

An *account executive*, or stockbroker, is a licensed individual who buys or sells securities for clients. Whether he or she is called an account executive or stockbroker, this person deals with all types of securities, not just stocks, and can handle your entire portfolio. A

ANOTHER WAY More than 4,000 different stocks are traded on Nasdaq. *What market does Nasdaq serve?*

portfolio consists of all the securities held by an investor. Some account executives will take risks, while others are more conservative. Before you choose an account executive, make sure that you can clearly describe your short-term and long-term financial goals.

Remember that account executives can make errors, so be sure to stay actively involved in decisions concerning your investments. Never let the stockbroker take action on your account without your permission. Brokerage firms are usually not responsible for financial losses that are caused by a recommendation by your account executive.

Be aware of a practice known as "churning." Churning occurs when an account executive does a lot of buying and selling of stocks within your portfolio to generate more commissions. A *commission* is a fee charged by a brokerage firm for the buying and/or selling of a security. Although churning is illegal, it is difficult to prove. Note that the value of your portfolio doesn't increase through churning; rather, it stays about the same.

Brokerage Firms

Today you can choose a full-service or discount brokerage firm or trade stocks online. The biggest difference is the amount of the commissions you will be charged when you buy or sell securities. Generally, full-service and discount brokerage firms charge higher commissions than online brokerage firms. Full-service firms usually charge the highest commissions in exchange for personalized service and free research information. However, there may be other differences among the types of firms.

First, consider the amount of research information that will be available to you and how much it costs. All of these firms offer excellent research materials, but you are more likely to pay extra for information if you choose a discount brokerage or online firm. Although most discount brokerage firms don't charge a lot of money for research reports, the fees can add up. Second, consider how much help you will need in order to make an investment decision. The full-service account executive doesn't have much time to spend with every client, but you can expect him or her to answer questions and make recommendations.

Discount and online firms generally believe that you alone are in charge of your investment plan and that the most successful investors are totally involved in their programs. They usually have printed material or information on their Web sites to help you become a better investor.

A Sample Stock Transaction

When you're ready to trade a stock, it's time to execute an order to buy or sell. Most investors do this either over the telephone or on the Internet. You can also go to a brokerage firm and place your order in person. The types of orders used to trade stocks are known as market orders, limit orders, stop orders, and discretionary orders.

A *market order* is a request to buy or sell a stock at the current market value. Because the stock market is essentially an auction, the account executive's representative will try to get the best price possible and make the transaction as soon as possible. **Figure 9.5** demonstrates how a typical market order on the New York Stock Exchange would be executed. Note that every stock listed on the NYSE is traded at a computer-equipped trading post on the floor of the exchange. A computer monitor above the trading post indicates current price information for all stocks traded at each post.

Then each transaction is recorded, and the necessary information, the ticker symbol (the letters that identify a stock for trading), number of shares, and price, is transmitted through a communications network called the ticker system. The NYSE has also installed the Super Dot System, which transmits orders electronically, making it possible for the exchange to handle daily trading volumes of more than 2 billion shares.

Payment for stocks is generally required within three business days. Then, in about four to six weeks, a stock certificate (proof of

YOUR BROKER One of the biggest advantages of a full-service brokerage firm is personal attention from your account executive. *How can you protect your portfolio from a dishonest or incompetent account executive?*

RESPOND

If you had $5,000 to invest in the stock market right now, what type of brokerage firm would you choose? Explain your reasoning.

1 *Your account executive receives your order to sell stock and relays the order electronically to the brokerage firm's representative at the stock exchange.*

2 *A clerk for the firm signals the transaction to a floor broker on the stock exchange floor.*

FIGURE 9.5

Trading Stock

The Steps Involved in a Typical Transaction for Stock Traded on the New York Stock Exchange

3 *The floor broker goes to the trading post at which this specific stock is traded and trades with a floor broker (employed by another firm) who has an order to buy.*

4 *The floor broker signals the transaction back to the clerk. Then a floor reporter—an employee of the NYSE—collects the information about the transaction and inputs it into the ticker system.*

5 *The sale appears on the price board, and a confirmation is relayed back to your account executive, who then notifies you of the completed transaction.*

ownership) is sent to the purchaser. **Figure 9.6** shows a sample of a common stock certificate. Often the certificate is sent to the brokerage firm, which is more convenient when it comes time to sell the stock. The phrase "left in the street name" is used to describe investor-owned securities held by a brokerage firm.

A *limit order* is a request to buy or sell a stock at a specified price. You agree to buy the stock at the best price up to a certain dollar amount. When you are selling, the limit order ensures that you will sell at the best price but not below a certain price. For example, if you place a limit order to buy Kellogg common stock for $34 a share, the stock will not be purchased until the price drops to $34 or lower. If you place a limit order to sell a stock, it works the same way: the Kellogg stock will not be sold until the price rises to $34 or higher.

However, limit orders present problems. A limit order does not guarantee that the purchase or sale will be made when the desired price is reached. Limit orders are filled in the order in which they are received, so other investors may get their orders filled before yours. If the price of

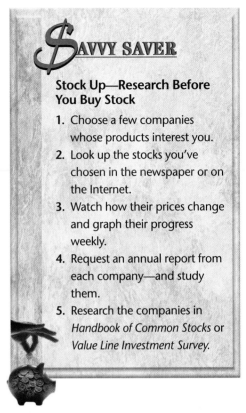

Figure 9.6

A Common Stock Certificate

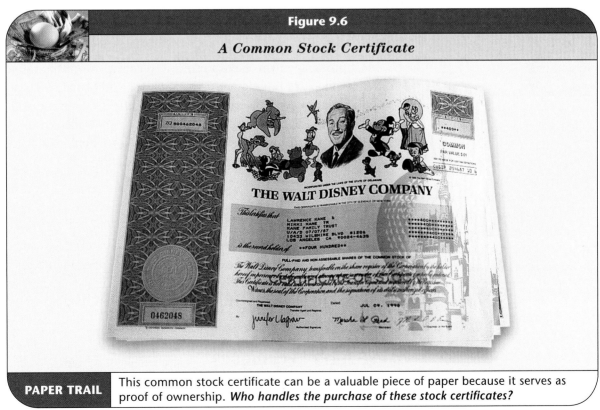

PAPER TRAIL This common stock certificate can be a valuable piece of paper because it serves as proof of ownership. *Who handles the purchase of these stock certificates?*

Kellogg, for example, continues to rise while the purchase orders ahead of yours are being filled, then when your turn comes, the price may have reached $36, and you will have missed the chance to buy the stock at $34.

You can also place a stop order, which is used for selling stock. A *stop order* is a type of limit order to sell a particular stock at the next available opportunity after its market price reaches a specified amount. While a stop order does not guarantee that your stock will be sold at the price you specified, it does guarantee that it will be sold at the next available opportunity. Both stop and limit orders can be good for a day, a week, a month, or until they're canceled.

Computerized Transactions

More and more people are using their computers to make securities transactions. To meet the demand for this service, discount brokerage firms and some full-service firms allow investors to trade online. You can use a software package or the brokerage's Web site to help you evaluate stocks, track your portfolio and monitor its value, and buy and sell securities online. Of course, you are still responsible for doing research and analyzing the information you get. The computer is just a tool, but it can help you complete transactions more quickly at less cost.

Commission Charges

Most brokerage firms have a minimum commission that ranges from $25 to $55 for buying and selling stocks. Additional fees based on the number of shares and the value of the stock can also be charged. On the floors of the exchanges, stocks are traded in *round lots*—100 shares or multiples of 100 shares of a particular stock. An *odd lot* contains fewer than 100 shares of a stock.

Investment Strategies

Once you purchase stock, the investment may be categorized as long-term or short-term. Generally, if you hold investments for at least a year, you are called an investor. If you routinely buy and sell investments within short periods of time, you are called a speculator or a trader.

Long-Term Techniques

BUY-AND-HOLD TECHNIQUE   A typical long-term investing method is to buy stock and hold on to it for a number of years. You

academic
Connection

may get dividends, and the price of the stock may go up. The stock may be split. Generally, after a stock splits, its value increases over time.

DOLLAR COST AVERAGING   With this method, you buy an equal dollar amount of the same stock at equal intervals. Suppose that you invested $2,000 in Johnson & Johnson common stock each year for a period of three years. When the price of the stock went up, your $2,000 purchased fewer shares, and when it went down, your $2,000 purchased more shares. This system protects investors from buying at high prices and selling at low prices. The price you pay for the stock averages out over time.

DIRECT INVESTMENT AND DIVIDEND RE-INVESTMENT PLANS   A large number of companies sell their stock directly to investors. This lets you buy stock without going through your account executive and paying commissions. You have the same advantage with a dividend reinvestment plan, which automatically reinvests any dividends you earn by buying more shares of that stock.

Short-Term Techniques

Investors sometimes use more speculative, short-term techniques. Beware: The methods presented in this section are quite risky; do not use them unless you fully understand the risks.

BUYING STOCK ON MARGIN   When buying stock on margin, an investor borrows through a brokerage firm part of the money needed to purchase a stock. The Federal Reserve Board currently limits the margin requirement to 50 percent and $2,000, which means that you can borrow up to half of the purchase price as long as you have at least $2,000 in your brokerage account. Although the Federal Reserve regulates margin rules, brokers and dealers may have different margin requirements and charge different interest rates on the loans. Investors buy stock on margin in order to purchase more shares. If the shares go up in value, the investor makes more money. However, if the shares go down in value, the investor loses more money.

SELLING SHORT   Your ability to make money buying and selling securities is related to how well you can predict what the stock is going to do—whether it will rise or fall in value. Normally you want to buy a stock that will go up in value, and this is called buying long. Of course, the value of stocks can decrease, too.

You can actually make money by selling short when the value of a stock looks as if it may go down. *Selling short* is selling a stock that has been borrowed from a brokerage firm and that must be replaced

QUESTION

Why would some investors be attracted to a dividend reinvestment plan? Describe the type of investor who might choose this option.

Investing in Stock

Rick would like to invest in the stock market. Before he invests any money, Rick is researching a company he thinks has potential. He picked Pop-Up Cafés, a chain of Internet coffeehouses. Along with the price of stock, he watches for any announcements or industry changes that may affect the stock.

Taking Stock of the Future

Pop-Up Cafés	
Specialty coffees and focaccia-style sandwiches; Internet-access computer stations.	
Highest price paid per share during the past 52 weeks	$41.80
Lowest price paid per share in the past 52 weeks	$19.89
Current price paid per share	$35.35
Price-earnings (PE) ratio	23
Earnings per share	$1.78

Rick has studied Pop-Up's financial reports and also keeps tabs on its financial news reports. He believes Pop-Up Cafés will continue to be successful, but he plans to keep on watching the stock a little longer before he makes his decision to invest.

Research In your workbook or on a separate sheet of paper, choose a stock you would like to invest in and research it. You can get information about a company in the financial section of major newspapers, the Internet, and from the companies themselves. You can also find information from *Standard & Poor's Stock and Bond Guide*, Mergent's *Handbook of Common Stocks*, or *Value Line Investment Survey*. What type of stock would you be interested in purchasing? Explain why. Do you think the company you chose to research would be a wise investment choice? Explain your answer.

at a later date. You sell the stock you have borrowed today, knowing that you'll have to buy the stock at a later date. Here is how it is done:

1. Arrange to borrow a stock certificate for a certain number of shares of a particular stock from a brokerage firm.
2. Sell the borrowed stock, assuming that it will drop in value in a reasonably short period of time.
3. Buy the stock at a lower price than the price it sold for in Step 2.
4. Use the stock you purchased in Step 3 to replace the stock that you borrowed from the brokerage firm in Step 1.

Remember that when you borrow the stock, it really belongs to someone else, so if a dividend is due, you must pay it. Eventually these dividends may absorb all the profits you make on the short transaction. To make money, you have to predict correctly that the value of the stock will go down. If the value increases, you lose money.

SECTION 9.3 ASSESSMENT

CHECK YOUR UNDERSTANDING

1. What is the difference between the primary and secondary markets for stocks?
2. Compare full-service, discount, and online brokerage firms in terms of service and cost.
3. Name the trading techniques that are used by investors and speculators.

THINK CRITICALLY

4. Design a handout for students, explaining the various long-term investment strategies.

USING COMMUNICATION SKILLS

5. **Short-term Trading** Some of your classmates are boasting that they can make a killing by trading stocks over a short period of time.
   Write a Song Create song lyrics that warn of the dangers of short-term trading methods. Be as specific about the methods as you can, noting why beginning investors could get "burned."

SOLVING MONEY PROBLEMS

6. **Using a Broker** Bruce is a high school senior, and his fall schedule is very busy. He saved enough money from his part-time job to start investing, but he has no time to monitor his investments or make decisions. He wants to let his account executive buy or sell stocks without bothering him.
   Analyze List and explain the dangers of Bruce's plan to let his account executive act without consulting him.

CHAPTER 9 ASSESSMENT

CHAPTER SUMMARY

- Investors who purchase common stock can make money from dividends, the dollar appreciation of stock value, and increases in stock value as a result of a stock split.

- Investors who want a steady source of income often buy preferred stock.

- You can use the newspaper, the Internet, information from stock advisory services, and corporate news to evaluate stocks.

- When deciding whether to buy or sell a particular stock, you should consider a company's profits or losses and other numerical measures.

- To buy common or preferred stock, you generally have to go through a brokerage firm. In turn, the brokerage firm must buy the stock in the primary or secondary market.

- The types of orders used to trade stocks are known as market orders, limit orders, stop orders.

- Long-term investment strategies include the buy-and-hold technique, dollar cost averaging, and direct investment and dividend reinvestment plans.

- Investors sometimes use more speculative, short-term techniques, but these are quite risky.

Internet zone

Understanding and Using Vocabulary

Practice using these terms. With a partner, role-play an imaginary conversation between a client and an account executive. Use as many key terms in your discussion as you can.

securities
private corporation
public corporation
proxy
preemptive right
stock split
par value
blue-chip stock
income stock

growth stock
cyclical stock
defensive stock
large cap stock
capitalization
small cap stock
penny stock
bull market
bear market

current yield
total return
earnings per share
price-earnings (PE) ratio
primary market
initial public offering
   (IPO)
secondary market
securities exchange
over-the-counter
   (OTC) market

account executive
portfolio
commission
market order
limit order
stop order
round lot
odd lot
selling short

Review Key Concepts

1. Why do corporations issue common stock as a form of equity?

CHAPTER 9 ASSESSMENT

2. Contrast cyclical and defensive stocks.
3. What is the difference between a securities exchange and the over-the-counter market?
4. How might an investor buy stock?
5. How is the ability to predict an increase or decrease in a stock's value related to short-term investing strategies?

Apply Key Concepts

1. Prepare a brief presentation for the board of directors of an imaginary new corporation, explaining the advantages of issuing common stock.
2. Discuss the ways that the economy affects different types of stock.
3. Why might a large corporation trade its stock on Nasdaq instead of trading on the New York Stock Exchange?
4. Explain the advantages of a stop order over a limit order.
5. Show how a wrong prediction in selling short could end up costing you money.

? Problem Solving Today

COMPARING STOCKS

You bought 100 shares of a penny stock for $10 a share during its initial public offering three years ago. The company began operations one year before the IPO. The stock does not pay any dividends. Six months ago the stock was selling at $98 a share. Currently it's selling for $28. You also purchased 100 shares of a blue-chip stock at $20 per share three years ago. Quarterly dividends have been $0.52 per share. The current market value of the stock is $45 a share.

Calculate Figure the total return on each investment, and create a bar graph to illustrate

each stock's performance. Which one is more likely to produce long-term stability? Why?

Computer Activity As an alternative activity, use presentation software to illustrate the returns on your investment.

Real-World Application

CONNECT WITH SOCIAL STUDIES

Rhonda recently discovered several trading sites on the Internet and bought two stocks online last month.

Research Using the Internet and your library, find articles and discussions of how the Internet has changed the investing behavior of Americans. Do you think that the Internet has been a positive or negative addition? What techniques can investors use to invest online?

FINANCE Online

INVESTMENT BANKING

You are considering investment banking as a college major. You want to find out whether this industry is expected to grow and what the job outlook is like.

Connect Using different search engines, look for information on the latest trends in investment banking as a business and as a career. Then find out the following:

1. What do investment banks really do?
2. How is the industry developing? What changes, if any, is it undergoing?
3. How competitive is the industry?

Bonds and Mutual Funds

STANDARD &POOR'S

Q&A

Q: I only have about $50 a month to invest. Any ideas?

A: Many mutual fund companies offer systematic investment programs in which you invest small amounts each month. This strategy is known as dollar cost averaging. Minimum investment requirements are typically waived with this type of program. You invest the same amount each month regardless of changes in the share price. As a result, your dollars buy more shares when prices are low and fewer shares when prices are high. Over time, this strategy can result in a lower average cost per share than the average price; however, it does not guarantee a profit or protect against a loss.

Corporate Bonds

What You'll Learn

- How to **identify** the characteristics of corporate bonds
- How to **explain** the reasons corporate bonds are bought and sold

Why It's Important

Understanding corporate bonds and why they are bought and sold will give you more choices to consider when investing your money.

KEY TERMS

- maturity date
- face value
- debenture
- mortgage bond
- subordinated debenture
- convertible bond
- call feature
- bond indenture
- sinking fund
- serial bond
- registered bond
- registered coupon bond
- bearer bond
- zero-coupon bond

While in college Claire didn't have a lot of money to save, but she put some of the money she earned from her part-time job into a savings account. After she had a thousand dollars saved, Claire opened a certificate of deposit (CD).

Claire recently landed a job as an assistant to a financial advisor. Brianna, her boss, was explaining to her that savings accounts and CDs are the most predictable sources of income. However, because they are among the safest investments, the profit that they earn is low. She said that the potential return on an investment is directly related to the risk that a person is willing to take. Brianna said that corporate bonds would provide higher income because the risk associated with such investments varies. Brianna encouraged Claire to consider buying corporate bonds. Claire decided that she would learn more about the basic aspects of bonds.

Characteristics of Corporate Bonds

When you buy a corporate bond, you're really loaning money to a corporation. A corporate bond is a corporation's written pledge to repay a specified amount of money, with interest. **Figure 10.1** on page 307 shows how a typical corporate bond might look. It states the interest rate, the maturity date, and the face value of the bond. The *maturity date* is the date when a bond will be repaid. The *face value* is the dollar amount that the bondholder (the person who owns the bond) will receive at the bond's maturity. Typically, the face value of a corporate bond is $1,000. However, corporate bonds can have face values as low as $25 or as high as $50,000.

Between the date when you buy a bond and the maturity date, the corporation pays you annual interest at the rate stated on the bond. Interest is usually paid twice a year, or semiannually. By multiplying the face value by the interest rate, you can calculate how much interest you would earn each year.

Go Figure...

A BOND'S ANNUAL INTEREST

Example: Suppose that you purchase the $1,000 Mobil Corporation bond shown in **Figure 10.1**. The interest rate for this bond is $8\frac{1}{2}\%$ (8.5%). How much annual interest would you earn on this bond?

Formula: Face Value $\times$ Interest Rate $=$ Annual Interest

Solution: $1,000 $\times$ 8.5% $=$ $85
You would receive interest of $85 a year from Mobil, paid in two installments of $42.50.

At the maturity date, you would cash the bond in to Mobil and receive a check in the amount of the bond's face value. Maturity dates for bonds generally range from 1 to 30 years. Maturities for corporate bonds are classified as short term (less than 5 years), intermediate term (5 to 15 years), and long term (more than 15 years).

Why Corporations Sell Corporate Bonds

Just like individuals, corporations borrow money when they don't have enough funds to pay for major purchases. Corporations also sell bonds to raise money when it is difficult or impossible to sell stock. Often companies use bonds simply to finance regular business activities. Selling bonds can also reduce the amount of tax a corporation must pay because the interest paid to bondholders is tax-deductible. When a company makes available a quantity of bonds at one time, it is called a bond issue.

A corporation may sell both bonds and stocks to help pay for its activities. However, the corporation's responsibility to investors is different for bonds and for stocks. Bondholders must be repaid at a future date. Stockholders do not have to be repaid. Companies are required to pay interest on bonds. They can choose whether to pay dividends to their stockholders. Finally, if a corporation files for bankruptcy, bondholders' claims to assets are paid before the claims of stockholders.

Figure 10.1

A Typical Corporate Bond

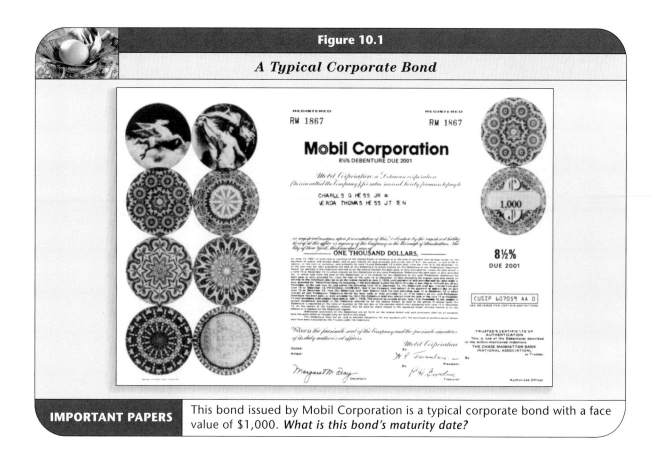

IMPORTANT PAPERS This bond issued by Mobil Corporation is a typical corporate bond with a face value of $1,000. *What is this bond's maturity date?*

Types of Corporate Bonds

Most corporate bonds are debentures. A *debenture* is a bond that is backed only by the reputation of the issuing corporation rather than by its specific assets. Investors buy these bonds because they believe that the issuing company is on solid financial ground and will be able to repay the face value of the bond and make interest payments until maturity.

To make a bond issue more appealing to conservative investors, a corporation may issue a mortgage bond. A *mortgage bond*, sometimes referred to as a secured bond, is a bond that is backed by assets of the corporation. A mortgage bond is safer than a debenture because corporate assets, such as real estate or equipment, may be sold to repay the mortgage bondholders if the corporation fails to make good on its bonds. Because risk to the investor is lower, mortgage bonds usually earn less interest than debentures.

A third type of corporate bond is called a subordinated debenture. A *subordinated debenture* is an unsecured bond that gives bondholders a claim to interest payments and assets of the corporation only after all other bondholders have been paid. Because subordinated

debentures are more speculative than other bonds, investors who buy them usually receive higher interest rates than other bondholders.

Another type of bond is a convertible bond. A *convertible bond* is a bond that an investor can trade for shares of the corporation's common stock. Because of the unique flexibility that it offers investors, the interest rate on a convertible bond is often 1 to 2 percent lower than that on other types of corporate bonds.

Many bondholders choose not to convert their bonds into stock even when stock values are high. The reason for this is simple: As the market value of a company's common stock increases, the market value of the company's convertible bonds also increases. Bondholders can enjoy this increase in value while keeping the relative safety of the bond and its interest income.

Methods Corporations Use to Repay Bonds

Today most corporate bonds are "callable." A *call feature* allows a corporation to buy back bonds from bondholders before the maturity date. Corporations may get the money to call a bond by selling stock, by using profits, or by selling new bonds at a lower interest rate. Suppose that interest rates dropped to 4.5 percent on comparable bonds. Mobil Corporation might decide to call the bonds it had issued at 8.5 percent. By buying back these bonds early, Mobil would not have to pay bondholders interest at that high rate. Instead, Mobil could sell new bonds with a much lower interest rate, perhaps 4.5 percent.

Usually, companies agree not to call their bonds for the first five to ten years. When they do call their bonds, they may have to pay bondholders a premium. A premium is an additional amount above the face value of the bond. The amount of the premium is stated in the *bond indenture*—a legal document that details all of the conditions pertaining to a particular bond issue.

A corporation may use one of two methods to make sure that it has enough funds to pay off a bond issue. First, the corporation may set up a sinking fund. A *sinking fund* is a fund to which a corporation makes deposits for the purpose of paying back a bond issue. If the bond indenture states that the corporation will deposit money in a sinking fund, investors can be confident that the company will be able to repay its bonds.

Second, a corporation may issue serial bonds. *Serial bonds* are bonds issued at the same time that mature on different dates. For example, Seaside Productions issued $100 million of serial bonds for a 20-year period. None of the bonds matured during the first ten years. Therefore, the company didn't have to pay any bondholders during that time. Instead, Seaside Productions used the funds raised by selling the bonds to grow its business. After that, only 10 percent of the bonds matured each year until all the bonds were retired at the end of 20 years. That allowed Seaside Productions to repay its bonds a few at a time instead of having to repay all $100 million at once.

What's Your Financial ID?

WHAT'S YOUR INVESTING IQ?

The more you know about investing, the greater your chance for higher returns. Before you read this chapter, answer the questions below on a separate sheet of paper. After you've studied the chapter in class, take the quiz again to see how much you've learned.

1. Liquidity is the ability to _____.
   a. easily convert your financial resources into cash without a loss in value
   b. invest in any liquid substance
   c. transfer funds electronically

2. The least speculative investment listed below is _____.
   a. municipal bonds
   b. Treasury bonds
   c. zero-coupon bonds

3. A mutual fund prospectus is _____.
   a. a possible date for Saturday night
   b. a report that provides potential investors with information about the fund
   c. a statement of your earnings

4. Federally tax-exempt interest can be earned on _____.
   a. an annuity

   b. a convertible bond
   c. a municipal bond

5. Investors buy junk bond funds because _____.
   a. of the possibility of a high yield
   b. municipalities always need to remove junk
   c. they usually resist fluctuations in the stock market

6. Mutual funds are popular because _____.
   a. they generally receive the highest (AAA) rating
   b. investors can choose which stocks are in their portfolio
   c. investors can acquire a diversified portfolio

QUESTION

What does diversify mean, and why is diversification a good idea for investors?

Why Investors Buy Corporate Bonds

Historically, stocks have resulted in greater profits for investors than bonds or U.S. Treasury bills. Why, then, should you consider investing in bonds? Many corporate and government bonds are safe investments. Some investors use corporate and government bonds to diversify their investment portfolios (all the securities held by an investor). Bonds offer you three other benefits as well. First, most bonds provide interest income. Second, bonds may increase in value depending on the bond market, overall interest rates in the economy, and the reputation and assets of the issuer. Finally, the face value of a bond is repaid when it reaches maturity.

Interest Income

Bondholders usually receive interest payments every six months. The dollar amount of annual interest is determined by multiplying the interest rate by the face value of the bond. The method used by a company to pay you that interest depends on the type of corporate bond you purchase.

A *registered bond* is a bond registered in the owner's name by the company that issues the bond. This ensures that only the owner can collect money from the bond. Interest checks for registered bonds are mailed directly to the bondholder.

A *registered coupon bond* is a bond that is registered in the owner's name for the face value only and not for interest. This type of bond comes with detachable coupons. Because the face value of the bond is registered, only the bond's owner can collect the face value. However, anyone who holds the coupons can collect the interest. To collect an interest payment on a registered coupon bond, you simply present one of the detachable coupons to the issuing corporation or the appropriate bank or broker.

A third type of bond is called a bearer bond. A *bearer bond* is a bond that is not registered in the investor's name. As with registered coupon bonds, the owner of a bearer bond must present coupons in order to collect interest payments. If you own bearer bonds, you could be out of luck if they are lost or stolen. Anyone who has physical possession of the bonds or their coupons can collect on them. Although some bearer bonds are still in circulation, they are no longer issued by corporations.

Savings Mind-Set

It's exciting when you get a raise or finally pay off a loan. You know you'll now have more money to spend. Be a smart saver—stick to your current budget and stash that newfound money into your savings or investment account.

CLIPPING COUPONS Registered coupon bonds come with detachable coupons. *How are the coupons used?*

A *zero-coupon bond* is a bond that provides no interest payments and is redeemed for its face value at maturity. It is sold at a price far below its face value. Because you bought it for less than its face value, you automatically make a profit when your zero-coupon bond is repaid.

A Bond's Market Value

Most beginning investors think that a $1,000 bond is always worth $1,000. Actually, the market value of a corporate bond may change many times before its maturity date. Usually, shifts in bond prices result from changes in overall interest rates in the economy. Suppose that Vanessa has a bond with a 7.5 percent interest rate. If overall interest rates fall below 7.5 percent, Vanessa's bond will go up in market value because it earns more interest than bonds issued at the new lower rate. If overall interest rates rise above 7.5 percent, the market value of Vanessa's bond will fall because it earns less interest than bonds issued at the new higher rate.

When a bond is selling for less than its face value, it is said to be selling at a discount. When a bond is selling for more than its face value, it is said to be selling at a premium. It is also possible to calculate a bond's approximate market value by using a formula that compares the bond's interest rate to that of similar new corporate bonds. First,

PREDICT

What factors determine a bond's market value?

find the dollar amount of the bond's annual interest by multiplying the face value by the annual interest rate. Then compute the bond's approximate market value by dividing the dollar amount of annual interest by the interest rate of comparable new corporate bonds.

Go Figure... APPROXIMATE MARKET VALUE OF A BOND

Example: Shawn purchased a New York Telephone bond that pays 4.5% interest based on a face value of $1,000. Comparable new corporate bond issues are paying 7%. How much is Shawn's bond worth?

Formula:

$$\frac{\text{Dollar Amount of Annual Interest}}{\text{Interest Rate of Comparable New Corporate Bonds}} = \text{Approximate Market Value}$$

Solution: A. Find the dollar amount of annual interest.

$$\text{Face Value of Bond} \times \text{Annual Interest Rate} = \text{Dollar Amount of Annual Interest}$$

$$\$1,000 \times 4.5\% = \$45$$

The dollar amount of annual interest is $45.

B. Solve for approximate market value.

$$\frac{\text{Dollar Amount of Annual Interest}}{\text{Interest Rate of Comparable New Corporate Bonds}} = \text{Approximate Market Value}$$

$$\frac{\$45}{7\%} = \$642.86$$

The approximate market value of Shawn's New York Telephone bond is $642.86.

The market value of a bond may also be affected by the financial condition of the company that issues it. In addition, the law of supply and demand as well as changes in the overall economy can affect a bond's market value.

Bond Repayment at Maturity

Corporate bonds are repaid at maturity. After you purchase a bond, you have two choices. You can keep the bond until its maturity date and then cash it in. You can also sell the bond at any time to another investor. In either case the value of the bond is closely tied to the corporation's ability to repay it. Other investors will pay more money to get a quality bond that has solid prospects of repayment.

RESPOND

Explain some of the pros and cons of buying a corporate bond.

A Typical Bond Transaction

Most bonds are sold through full-service brokerage firms, discount brokerage firms, or online. If you use a full-service brokerage firm, your account executive should provide information and advice about bond investments. If you use a discount brokerage firm or buy bonds online, you must do your own research and make your own decisions. However, you'll probably pay a lower commission.

Bonds are purchased in much the same way as stocks. Corporate bonds may be purchased in the primary market or the secondary market. In the primary market, you purchase financial securities from an investment banker representing the corporation or government agency that issued them. In the secondary market you trade financial securities with other investors. In the secondary market, corporate bonds issued by large companies are traded on either the New York Bond Exchange or the American Bond Exchange.

You can also buy corporate bonds directly from account executives or brokerage firms. As with stocks, if you buy or sell a $1,000 bond through an account executive or brokerage firm, you should expect to pay a commission.

On October 8, 1992, Ms. Mansfield purchased an 8.375 percent corporate bond issued by Borden, Inc. She paid $680 for the bond plus a $10 commission. On October 8, 2003, she sold it at its current market value of $1,030 minus a $10 commission.

After paying commissions for buying and selling her Borden bond, Ms. Mansfield had a capital gain of $330 ($1,020 − $690 = $330).

Figure 10.2

Ms. Mansfield's Borden, Inc., Bond Transaction

Interest, 8.375 percent; maturity date, 2016; purchased October 8, 1992; sold October 8, 2003

Costs when purchased

1 bond @ $680	$680
Plus commission	+ 10
Total investment	$690

Return when sold

1 bond @ $1,030	$1,030
Minus commission	− 10
Dollar return	$1,020

Transaction summary

Dollar return	$1,020.00
Minus total investment	− 690.00
Profit from bond sale	$ 330.00
Plus interest ($83.75 for 11 years)	+ 921.25
Total return on the transaction	$1,251.25

COMMISSION COSTS Ms. Mansfield paid a commission fee both when she bought her bond and when she sold it. *How did these fees affect the cost of her investment and the profit she made from selling the bond?*

The market value of the bond increased because overall interest rates in the economy declined during the time she owned the bond. Borden also established a good business reputation during this period, making the bond more secure and, therefore, more valuable.

Ms. Mansfield also made money on her Borden bond by collecting interest payments. For each of the 11 years she owned the bond, Borden paid her $83.75 ($1,000 × 8.375% = $83.75) interest. By the time she sold the bond, she had received interest payments totaling $921.25. These earnings, together with her $330 capital gain, added up to a total return of $1,251.25. **Figure 10.2** on page 313 shows Ms. Mansfield's entire Borden bond transaction.

SECTION 10.1 ASSESSMENT

CHECK YOUR UNDERSTANDING

1. What are three important characteristics of corporate bonds?
2. Why might a company decide to issue corporate bonds?
3. Identify three reasons why investors buy corporate bonds.

THINK CRITICALLY

4. What advantages do bonds offer investors that common stocks do not offer?

USING COMMUNICATION SKILLS

5. **Convertible Bonds** Choose a well-known company and imagine that the company is issuing convertible bonds.
   Present a Point of View Write one or two paragraphs making your case for investing in the company's convertible bonds. Discuss the company's stability and reputation, the types of income investors can receive from corporate bonds, and the special characteristics of convertible bonds.

SOLVING MONEY PROBLEMS

6. **Choosing the Best Bonds** Mr. Blackhorse is preparing to invest in corporate bonds. He does not want to risk losing a lot of money, but he would like to receive the highest possible return on his investment.
   Analyze Information Help Mr. Blackhorse choose the type of bond that best meets his needs by comparing and analyzing the various types of bonds. Try to find the one that will protect his money and also provide him with interest income.

Government Bonds and Securities

Treasury Bills, Notes, and Bonds

Like private corporations, the federal government and state and local governments issue bonds to help raise the money they need to operate. The federal government issues Treasury bills, Treasury notes, Treasury bonds, and a few other types of securities. State and local governments offer municipal bonds.

The federal government sells bonds and other securities to help fund its regular activities and to help reduce the national debt. U.S. government securities are thought to be almost risk-free, making them appealing to investors. After all, they're backed by the full faith and credit of the U.S. government. However, because they have a low risk of default, or failure to pay their debts, they offer lower interest rates than corporate bonds.

The U.S. Treasury Department issues four basic types of securities: Treasury bills, Treasury notes, Treasury bonds, and U.S. Savings Bonds. You can buy Treasury bills, notes, and bonds directly from a Federal Reserve bank or one of its branches. When you buy through the Federal Reserve System, you don't have to pay a commission. You can also buy Treasury bills, notes, and bonds through banks or brokers, which charge a commission for their services.

U.S. Savings Bonds can be purchased through the Federal Reserve banks and branches, commercial banks, savings and loan associations, or other financial institutions.

U.S. government securities can be held until maturity or cashed in before the maturity date. You must pay federal income tax on interest you receive from these investments. State and local governments, however, do not tax this income.

TREASURY BILLS   Treasury bills, also known as T-bills, are sold in units of $1,000. They may reach maturity in 13 weeks, 26 weeks, or 52 weeks. T-bills are discounted securities. That means that the actual purchase price you pay is less than the face value of the T-bill. On the maturity date you receive the full face value of the T-bill.

To figure out the dollar amount of return on a T-bill, just subtract the purchase price of the T-bill from the face value. For example, suppose that you buy a 52-week T-bill for $950 and that

What You'll Learn

- How to **discuss** the reasons governments issue bonds
- How to **describe** the reasons investors purchase government bonds

Why It's Important

Understanding the various types of government bonds and securities will enable you to decide which ones are best for your investment needs. It will also help you evaluate the differences between government and corporate securities.

KEY TERMS

- **municipal bond**
- **general obligation bond**
- **revenue bond**

on the maturity date you receive the face value of $1,000. The dollar amount of your return is $50 ($1,000 − $950 = $50). To find the rate of return on your investment, divide the dollar amount of return by the purchase price ($50 ÷ $950 = .0526 = 5.26%). The rate of return on your T-bill is 5.26 percent.

TREASURY NOTES   Treasury notes are issued in $1,000 units with a maturity of between one and ten years. Interest rates for Treasury notes are slightly higher than those for Treasury bills because investors must wait longer to get their money back.

TREASURY BONDS   Treasury bonds are issued in minimum units of $1,000 and have maturities that range from 10 to 30 years. The most common maturity is 30 years. Because of the length of time to maturity, interest rates for Treasury bonds are usually higher than those for Treasury bills or Treasury notes.

U.S. SAVINGS BONDS (SERIES EE BONDS)   As you learned in Chapter 5, the federal government also offers savings bonds called Series EE Bonds. The purchase price for a Series EE Savings Bond is one-half of its face value. For example, a $100 bond costs $50. You can redeem a savings bond anytime from 6 months to 30 years after you purchase it. When you cash it in, you receive the amount that you paid for it plus interest. Series EE Savings Bonds can accumulate interest for up to 30 years.

The interest on Series EE Savings Bonds is not taxed by state or local governments. You don't pay federal taxes on the interest until you cash in the bond. For more information on Series EE Savings Bonds, see Chapter 5.

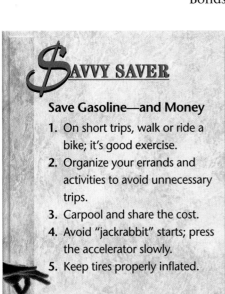

$AVVY SAVER

Save Gasoline—and Money

1. On short trips, walk or ride a bike; it's good exercise.
2. Organize your errands and activities to avoid unnecessary trips.
3. Carpool and share the cost.
4. Avoid "jackrabbit" starts; press the accelerator slowly.
5. Keep tires properly inflated.

Bonds Issued by Federal Agencies

In addition to the securities issued by the U.S. Treasury Department, bonds are issued by other federal agencies. Agency bonds, such as the participation certificates issued by the Federal National Mortgage Association (sometimes referred to as Fannie Mae), are almost completely risk-free. However, they offer a slightly higher interest rate than securities issued by the Treasury Department and have an average maturity of about 15 years. You will learn more about these types of investments in Chapter 11.

TEAM EFFORT State and local governments often finance major projects such as schools, airports, and highways by selling municipal bonds. *Where can you buy municipal bonds?*

Bonds Issued by State and Local Governments

A *municipal bond*, sometimes called a "muni," is a security issued by a state or local (town, city, county) government to pay for its ongoing activities. These bonds may also pay for major projects such as airports, schools, and highways. You can buy them directly from the government that issues them or through an account executive (a licensed individual who buys or sells securities for his or her clients).

State and local government securities are classified as either general obligation bonds or revenue bonds. A *general obligation bond* is a bond that is backed by the full faith and credit of the government that issued it. A *revenue bond* is a bond that is repaid from the income generated by the project it is designed to finance.

Although these bonds are relatively safe, on rare occasions governments have defaulted, or failed to repay their bonds. When a government defaults, it costs investors millions of dollars.

If the risk of default worries you, you might consider buying insured municipal bonds. Some states offer to guarantee payments on selected securities. Also, three large private insurers guarantee

CONNECT

Do you know of any major improvements planned for your community (a new library, for example) that might be paid for with municipal bonds?

such bonds: MBIA, Inc.; the Financial Security Assurance Corporation; and the Financial Guaranty Insurance Corporation. Because of the reduced risk of default, guaranteed municipal securities usually carry a slightly lower interest rate than uninsured bonds.

The interest on municipal bonds may be exempt from federal taxes. Whether or not the interest on municipal bonds is tax-exempt often depends on how the money from their sale is used. Before you invest in a particular municipal bond, find out whether the interest that you'll receive from it is taxable.

Like a corporate bond, a municipal bond may be callable by the government that issued it. If interest rates fall, it's quite possible that your municipal bond may be called. Then the government that issued it can sell new bonds with lower rates. In most cases the municipality

INTERNATIONAL FINANCE   Nepal

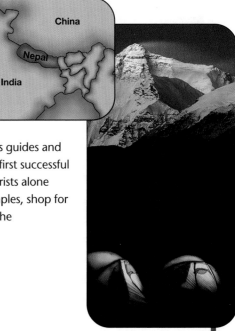

Mount Everest

ount Everest, the world's highest mountain, is part of the Himalaya, the mountain range, that forms Nepal's northern border. More than five miles high, Mount Everest is the ultimate pilgrimage for mountain climbers, who hire local people as guides and porters. Hundreds of climbers have reached Everest's summit since the first successful ascent in 1953. There's more to Nepal than scaling its heights. U.S. tourists alone bring in more than $50 million annually. Tourists can visit Buddhist temples, shop for Nepal's world-famous handmade carpets, or go on safaris in search of the endangered Bengal tiger. Here's a snapshot of Nepal.

Geographic area	54,362 sq. mi.
Population	24,303,000
Capital	Kathmandu (pop. 421,000)
Language	Nepali, 20 other languages
Currency	rupee
Gross domestic product (GDP)	$31.1 billion
Per capita GDP	$1,370
Economy	Industry: tourism, carpets, textiles, small mills, cigarettes. Agriculture: rice, corn, wheat, sugarcane, milk, water buffalo. Exports: carpets, clothing, leather goods, jute goods, grain.

Thinking Critically

Determine Tourists bring money to Nepal by hiring local guides, buying handmade carpets, and going on safaris. What are some other ways tourists can contribute to Nepal's economy?

For more information on Nepal visit finance.glencoe.com **or your local library.**

that issues the bond agrees not to call it for the first ten years. If your municipal bond is not called, you have the same two choices as with corporate bonds. You can hold the bond until the maturity date or sell it to another investor.

CHECK YOUR UNDERSTANDING

1. Why does the federal government issue bonds and other securities?
2. Why do state and local governments issue bonds?
3. Identify three reasons why an investor might purchase a government bond.

THINK CRITICALLY

4. Analyze ways in which securities issued by state and local governments are similar to corporate bonds.

USING MATH SKILLS

5. **T-bill Prices** Joshua and his sister Sharon are considering investing in Treasury bills. Joshua has $1,000 to invest, and he is considering a T-bill that matures in 52 weeks and costs $940. Sharon also has $1,000 to invest, but she wants a T-bill that matures before she goes to college next fall. Sharon has decided to buy a 26-week T-bill that costs $970.
   Calculate Figure the returns for Joshua's T-bill and for Sharon's T-bill. How much money (dollar amount of return) will Joshua earn from his T-bill? What is the annual rate of return on his investment? How much money will Sharon earn from her T-bill? What is the annual rate of return on her investment?

SOLVING MONEY PROBLEMS

6. **Personal and Financial Goals** The municipality in which Marie Kilbane lives is selling bonds to finance a new storm sewer system. Marie knows that the storm sewers need replacing—her street was flooded just last week! At the same time, she knows that her municipality is not very stable financially. She is not sure that the bonds are a good investment.
   Draw Conclusions Use what you've learned about personal satisfaction and financial goals in previous chapters to help Marie decide what to do. Should she buy the bonds to help improve her community and her own personal living conditions, or should she invest her money in another way that has a better chance of helping her meet her financial goals? Explain your reasoning.

The Investor's Decision to Buy or Sell Bonds

Bond Price Quotations

Before you buy or sell bonds you should become familiar with bond price quotations. Not all local newspapers contain bond price quotations, but many metropolitan newspapers publish complete information on the subject. Two other sources for bond information are the *Wall Street Journal* and *Barron's*.

In a bond price quotation, the price of a particular bond is given as a percentage of its face value. Remember that a bond's face value is usually $1,000. To find the current market value, or price, for a bond, you must multiply the face value ($1,000) by the price quotation given in the newspaper. For example, a price quoted as 84 means that the current market value is 84 percent of the face value. Therefore, the selling price is $840 ($1,000 × 84% = $840). Purchases and sales of bonds are reported in tables like the one at the top of **Figure 10.3**.

For government bonds, most financial publications include two price quotations. The first price quotation, or the bid price, is the amount a seller could receive for the bond. The second price quotation, or the asked price, represents the amount for which a buyer could purchase the bond. Newspaper bond sections also provide information about interest rates, maturity dates, and yields.

Annual Reports

As a bondholder you should always be aware of the financial stability of the issuer of your bonds. The most important questions are whether the bond will be repaid at maturity and whether you will receive interest payments until maturity.

It may be difficult to answer these questions with complete accuracy. However, the information contained in a firm's annual report is a good place to start investigating. This report provides detailed financial information about the company and describes its products, services, activities, goals, and future plans. You'll also find news about the company's position in its industry and the major trends in that industry.

Figure 10.3

Financial Information about Corporate Bonds

NEW YORK EXCHANGE BONDS

Quotations as of 4 p.m. Eastern Time
Friday, January 28, 2000

Volume $9,685,000

SALES SINCE JANUARY 1
(000 omitted)

2000	1999	1998
$197,143	$267,622	$367,124

	Domestic Fri.	Domestic Thu.	All Issues Fri.	All Issues Thu.
Issues Traded	176	170	184	178
Advances	63	88	64	92
Declines	84	56	88	59
Unchanged	29	26	32	27
New highs	1	1	1	1
New lows	24	17	24	17

Dow Jones Bond Averages

–1999– High	–1999– Low	–2000– High	–2000– Low		---2000--- Close	---2000--- Chg.	---2000--- %Yld	--1999-- Close	--1999-- Chg.
106.88	96.80	97.17	94.90	20 Bonds	95.70	–0.01	7.97	106.45	–0.23
104.72	94.96	95.09	93.20	10 Utilities	93.88	+0.15	7.83	104.41	–0.31
109.44	98.31	99.36	96.47	10 Industrials	97.51	–0.18	8.12	108.49	–0.15

CORPORATION BONDS
Volume, $9,628,000

Bonds	Cur Yld.	Vol.	Close		Net Chg.
AES Cp 4½05	cv	3	148		...
AES Cp 8s8	8.6	74	92½		...
AMF 10⅞06	24.7	12	44	–	20½
AMF zr06	...	13	33	–	17
AMR 9s16	8.6	50	104½	–	⅜
ATT 5⅛01	5.2	28	98⅛	+	⅛
ATT 7⅛02	7.1	51	100⅛	–	⅝
ATT 6¾04	6.9	93	97⅞	+	⅛
ATT 5⅝04	6.0	305	94⅛		...
Honywll zr03	...	40	75¾	+	⅝
Honywll zr07	...	5	56	+	1⅝
HuntPly 11¾04	11.6	35	101½	+	⅝
IRT Pr 7.3s03	cv	5	93	+	½
IllPwr 6¾05	7.2	10	94¼	+	⅛
IBM 6⅜00	6.4	50	99¾		...
IBM 7¼02	7.2	440	100½	–	⅛
IBM 6.45s07	6.8	72	94½	–	⅛
IBM 7½13	7.4	102	101⅛	+	2⅛
IBM 8⅜19	7.8	45	107¾	–	⅜
IBM 7s25	7.6	79	92⅝	+	⅛
ReynTob 8s01	8.2	11	98	+	⅝
ReynTob 7⅝03	8.2	11	93½	+	¾
ReynTob 8¾04	9.4	15	93	–	1⅝
ReynTob 9¼13	10.2	5	90⅝	–	⅝
RobMyr 63	cv	15	94	+	¼
Safwy 10s01	9.7	25	103¼	–	⅜
Safwy 9.65s04	9.0	187	106⅝		...
Safwy 9.3s07	8.7	5	106⅞	–	⅝
SouBell 4⅜01	4.5	20	96⅞		...
StdCmcl 07	cv	50	48	–	¾
StdPac 8½07	9.1	31	93¾	–	¼
StoneC 9⅞01	9.9	90	100⅛	–	⅛
StoneC 10¾02A	10.8	76	99⅞	–	⅜
StoneC 11½04	11.1	5	103⅝	+	¼
StoneCn 6¾07	cv	10	85¼	+	⅜
TVA 6s00	6.0	10	100⅝	+	1/32
TVA 6⅛03	6.3	11	96¾	–	¼
TVA 8¼34	8.3	50	99⅜	–	¼
TVA 7¼43	7.7	10	94⅝	–	⅝
TVA 6⅞43	7.6	60	90½		...
Tenet 8s05	8.3	24	96	–	¾
Tenet 8⅝07	9.0	55	95½	–	⅜
TerR 4s19	5.8	20	68⅞	–	4½
TmeWar 8.11s06	7.9	5	102⅞	+	1⅜
TmeWar 8.18s07	8.0	23	102	+	¾
TmeWar 9⅛13	8.6	3	106⅝	–	¾
TolEd 8s03	8.0	5	99½	–	¼
Tosco 9⅝02	9.3	10	103⅝	–	1
WsteM 4s02	cv	5	89½	+	½
Webb 9¾03	10.4	142	93⅜	+	½
Webb 9s06	10.5	58	85½	–	⅝
Webb 9¾08	11.3	181	86½	–	¾
Webb 10¼10	11.5	20	89⅜	+	⅜
WebbDel 9⅜09	11.1	130	84⅜		...
Weirton 10¾05	10.8	91	99⅝	–	⅜
WhlPit 9⅜03	9.0	10	104	+	⅛
viKCS En 8⅞08f	...	10	36	–	1

Look at the bond quotation highlighted above. Each column includes specific information about this bond. Reading from left to right:

Column 1: Bonds. The name (often abbreviated) of the issuing firm is ATT. This bond pays annual interest at the rate of 6¾ percent of the face value. This bond matures in the year 2004.

Column 2: Current Yield. This bond's current yield, or return, is 6.9 percent of the market price on January 28, 2000.

Column 3: Volume. Ninety-three of these bonds were traded on January 28.

Column 4: Close. The current market price of this bond at the close of trading on January 28 was 97⅞ percent of the bond's face value.

Column 5: Net Change. The price of this bond at the close of trading on January 28 was ⅛ percent of the face value higher than the price at the close of trading on the previous day.

CALCULATE IT

Newspaper bond quotations like this one indicate each bond's interest, yield, and price as a percentage of its face value. ***What was the current market price in dollars of the ATT bond highlighted here?***

RESPOND

Explain, in your own words, the difference between bid price and asked price.

To receive an annual report, just call, e-mail, or write to the corporation's headquarters. Many companies have toll-free telephone numbers for your use. You may also find annual reports for major corporations on the Internet or in the reference section of some large libraries.

As you read an annual report, look for signs of financial strength or weakness. Is the firm profitable? Are sales increasing? Are long-term liabilities increasing? How might the company's current activities and future plans affect its ability to repay bonds?

Other Sources of Information

You can access a wealth of information about bond investments on the Internet. You'll find answers to many of your questions on corporate Web sites, which typically offer information about a company's financial performance. Some sites even include financial information from past years, which allows you to compare one year's performance with another's. Other sites are devoted to general information about bonds. However, many of the better bond Web sites charge a fee for their research and recommendations.

Once your research is completed, you can even use the Internet to purchase bonds, to monitor the value of your bonds, and to manage your investments. If you trade bonds online, it's possible that you will pay lower commissions than you would if you used a full-service or discount brokerage firm.

Another way to research possible bond investments is by reading business magazines. They provide information about the overall economy and give detailed financial data about companies that issue bonds.

You also can consult reports and research published by the government to track the nation's economy. If you want to buy U.S. Treasury bills, notes, or bonds, or U.S. Savings Bonds, check Web sites run by the Federal Reserve System. You can also review information from the Securities and Exchange Commission by accessing its Web site. Finally, state and local governments will give you information about specific municipal bond issues upon request.

Bond Ratings

Before you invest in a particular corporate or municipal bond, you should check its rating. This rating will give you a good idea of the quality and risk associated with that bond. Bond issues are rated or evaluated by independent rating companies. These companies assign to each bond a rating based on the financial stability of its issuer. Two

Figure 10.4

Bond Ratings

Quality	Moody's	Standard & Poor's	Description
High-grade	Aaa	AAA	Bonds that are judged to be of the best quality. They have the lowest risk and the most secure interest and principal payments.
	Aa	AA	Bonds that are judged to be of high quality by all standards. Protection of principal and interest payments is only slightly less than the best.
Medium-grade	A	A	Bonds that have many favorable investment attributes and adequate security.
	Baa	BBB	Bonds that are neither highly protected nor poorly secured.
Speculative	Ba	BB	Bonds that have some risky elements. Often their protection of principal and interest payment is very moderate.
	B	B	Bonds that lack the characteristics of a desirable investment. Investors can't be sure that interest and principal will be paid in the future.
Default	Caa	CCC	Bonds that are of poor standing. They are currently unlikely to be repaid.
	Ca	CC	Bonds that are highly risky.
	C		Moody's lowest-rated class of bonds, considered the poorest investments.
		C	Standard & Poor's rating given to bonds whose issuers have filed for bankruptcy.
		D	Bond issues that are in default, or are failing to make payments.

SOURCES: From *Standard & Poor's Stock and Bond Guide,* © 1999 The McGraw-Hill Companies. Reprinted by permission. From *Bond Survey* © 1999 by Mergent FIS. Reprinted by permission.

KNOW YOUR AAABC'S Most investors check a bond's rating before they buy. *Why are these ratings important to investors?*

of the best-known sources of bond ratings are *Moody's Bond Survey*, published by Moody's Investors Service, Inc., and *Standard & Poor's Stock and Bond Guide*, published by Standard & Poor's. Investors rely heavily on this information when making investment decisions. You can find bond ratings on the Internet and at your public library.

As you can see in **Figure 10.4**, bond ratings are generally categorized from AAA (the highest—the best) to D (the lowest—the worst). The top four categories (Moody's Aaa, Aa, A, and Baa and Standard & Poor's AAA, AA, A, and BBB) include investment-grade bonds. *Investment-grade bonds* are bonds that are issued by financially stable companies

STANDARD &POOR'S

CASE STUDY

Rafael Masino's grandfather drives an old Rambler from the 1950s and collects World War II medals. Now that Rafael is in high school, his grandfather has started talking to him about his future. Recently, Rafael found out that his grandfather is a very smart investor. Although he is not a fan of the stock market or mutual funds, Rafael's grandfather has quite a large portfolio of corporate and government bonds. His favorites are those issued by large corporations. Last week, Rafael's grandfather offered Rafael $10,000 with one condition—he had to invest the money in bonds. Rafael is very excited about this opportunity but is not sure which bonds to purchase or how to conduct a bond transaction. He turned to the experts at Standard & Poor's for advice.

Analysis: Rafael is fortunate to have this opportunity to learn firsthand about investing. Bonds are an excellent investment for Rafael's grandfather because they provide regular income. Rafael can start building a portfolio for college savings by investing in bonds. If he has earnings from a part-time job later on, he might add some stocks to the mix to provide potentially greater growth opportunities.

Recommendation: There are many different types of bonds, each with different risks and returns. Bonds can be purchased through banks and brokerage firms. Rafael might consider buying a Treasury bond or note with a maturity date of five to ten years. Because the government guarantees the face value and interest, these bonds carry virtually no risk. Bonds issued by corporations generally offer higher rates of interest but also carry more risks. Corporate bonds that are rated AAA by independent rating companies, such as Moody's Investors Service and Standard & Poor's, are considered to have little risk of default. Rafael will also want to evaluate interest rate risk. As interest rates rise, bond prices typically fall. By choosing bonds that he can hold until maturity, Rafael will not have to worry about day-to-day changes in their values. Bond mutual funds offer a convenient and inexpensive way to invest in a pool of bonds, however, there is greater risk of loss with bond mutual funds than with bonds that can be held to maturity.

Critical Thinking Questions

1. Why do you think Rafael's grandfather prefers investing in individual bonds rather than bond mutual funds or stocks?
2. Are bonds an appropriate investment for Rafael?
3. What might happen if Rafael invests in bonds that have 20 to 30 years left until they mature?

or municipalities. They are considered safe investments that will provide a predictable source of income. Bonds in the next two categories (Moody's Ba and B and Standard & Poor's BB and B) are considered riskier, or speculative. Bonds in the C and D categories may be in default or cannot continue interest payments to bondholders.

U.S. government securities are usually not rated because they are basically risk-free. Long-term municipal bonds are rated in much the same way as corporate bonds. However, short-term municipal bonds are rated differently. Standard & Poor's rates municipal bonds that have maturity dates of three years or less with the following system:

- SP-1: Strong ability to pay face value and interest. Bonds with very safe characteristics get a plus (+) sign.
- SP-2: Satisfactory ability to pay face value and interest.
- SP-3: Doubtful ability to pay face value and interest.

QUESTION

Why would an investor even consider purchasing Ba, B, or BB bonds?

Calculating the Yield of a Bond Investment

To determine how much profit a particular bond may produce, investors calculate and track its yield. The *yield* is the rate of return, usually stated as a percentage, earned by an investor who holds a bond for a certain period of time.

The simplest way to measure a bond's yield is to calculate its current yield. To find the current yield of a bond, divide the dollar amount of annual interest income by its current market value.

Go Figure...   **CURRENT YIELD OF A BOND INVESTMENT**

Example: Suppose that you own a $1,000 AT&T corporate bond that pays 7.5% interest per year. This means that each year you will receive $75 ($1,000 × 7.5% = $75) in interest. Assume that the current market value of the AT&T bond is $960. What is the current yield of your bond investment?

Formula: $\dfrac{\text{Dollar Amount of Annual Interest Income}}{\text{Current Market Value}} = \text{Current Yield of a Bond}$

Solution: $\dfrac{\$75}{\$960} = 0.078 = 7.8\%$

The current yield of your bond investment is 7.8%.

This calculation lets you compare the yield on a bond investment with the yields of other investment alternatives. If the current market value is higher than the bond's face value, the current yield decreases. If the current market value is less than the bond's face value, the current yield increases. Obviously, the higher the current yield, the better.

ASSESSMENT

CHECK YOUR UNDERSTANDING

1. Name three pieces of information about specific corporate bonds that you could find in the bond section of a newspaper.
2. What information in a company's annual report would be important to an investor who is interested in its corporate bonds?
3. How could you use the Internet to help you invest in bonds?

THINK CRITICALLY

4. Identify two sources of bond ratings, and explain what a bond rating tells you about a bond.

USING MATH SKILLS

5. **Bond Quotations** Every day Elise looks at the bond section of the *Wall Street Journal* to see if she can get a good deal on a bond and add it to her portfolio. This morning a price quotation of 98 for TechnoWiz, a telecommunications firm, caught her interest.
   Calculate Help Elise figure out the current market value of the bond.

SOLVING MONEY PROBLEMS

6. **Calculating Bond Yields** Tom and Rika Nagata plan to retire in ten years. In 2001 they purchased several bonds:
   - Two 20-year AT&T corporate bonds, each with a face value of $1,000 and 7 percent annual interest. The purchase price was $830 each. The current market value is $910 each.
   - A 30-year Coca-Cola corporate bond, with a face value of $1,000 and 8.5 percent annual interest. The purchase price was $1,050. The current market value is $1,020.

   As part of the planning process, they need to know the yield on the bonds they own right now.
   Calculate Use the formula in this section to help Tom and Rika calculate the current yield on their bond investments.

Mutual Funds

Mutual funds are an excellent choice for many investors. A mutual fund is an investment alternative in which investors pool their money to buy stocks, bonds, and other securities based on the selections of professional managers who work for an investment company. By buying shares in a mutual fund, even an investor with limited resources can own part of an entire portfolio of diverse securities. Often these funds can also be used for retirement accounts, such as 401(k) and 403(b) plans, individual retirement accounts (IRAs), and Roth IRAs, which you will learn more about in Chapter 15.

Why Investors Buy Mutual Funds

One major reason for purchasing a mutual fund is professional management. Investment companies employ professional fund managers who try to pick the best securities for their funds' portfolios. However, this can lead some investors to become careless. Many mutual fund investors simply assume that their investments will increase in value. They don't research and evaluate funds carefully before they buy, and they often neglect to track the performance of the funds they own. Even the best portfolio managers make mistakes. Therefore, wise investors review their mutual funds regularly.

Another key reason for buying a mutual fund is diversification. Mutual funds include a variety of securities, which lessens the shareholders' risk. An occasional loss from one investment in a mutual fund is usually offset by gains from other investments in the fund. Researching and tracking the right mutual fund can provide great results with less effort than it would take to maintain such a diverse portfolio on your own.

Because of these advantages, mutual funds have become extremely popular investments. In 1970 there were 361 mutual funds. By 2000 there were more than 7,500 mutual funds, and the combined assets owned by mutual funds in the United States were worth more than $6 trillion. In the month of July 1999 alone, investors poured more than $12.3 billion into mutual fund investments. Read the material in this section to see if mutual funds are right for you.

What You'll Learn

- How to **recognize** the characteristics of mutual fund investments
- How to **distinguish** among the types of mutual funds

Why It's Important

Understanding the many kinds of mutual funds will help you decide which funds might be a smart investment for you.

KEY TERMS

- **closed-end fund**
- **open-end fund**
- **net asset value (NAV)**
- **load fund**
- **no-load fund**
- **12b-1 fee**
- **prospectus**
- **family of funds**

GREAT TIP Mutual funds can be wise investments for people who have little time and a limited amount of money to invest. **Why might mutual funds be a good choice for such investors?**

Characteristics of Mutual Funds

An investment company is a firm that, for a management fee, invests the pooled funds of many investors in various securities. Mutual funds managed by investment companies may be classified as either closed-end funds or open-end funds.

CLOSED-END FUNDS   About 10 percent of all mutual funds are closed-end funds offered by investment companies. A *closed-end fund* is a mutual fund with a fixed number of shares that are issued by an investment company when the fund is first organized. After all the original shares have been sold, an investor can buy shares only from another investor. Shares of closed-end funds are traded (bought and sold) on the floors of stock exchanges or in the over-the-counter market. A special section of the *Wall Street Journal* provides information about closed-end funds.

OPEN-END FUNDS   Nearly 90 percent of all mutual funds are open-end funds. An *open-end fund* is a mutual fund with an unlimited number of shares that are issued and redeemed by an investment company at the investors' request. Shares of open-end funds are bought and sold on any business day by contacting the investment company that manages the mutual fund.

Investors are free to buy and sell shares at the net asset value. The *net asset value (NAV)* is the amount one share of a mutual fund is worth. To calculate the net asset value of a mutual fund, subtract

PREDICT

What are the advantages of investing in a mutual fund?

the fund's liabilities from the value of the fund's portfolio, and divide the result by the number of shares outstanding. Shares outstanding are the number of shares held by all the investors.

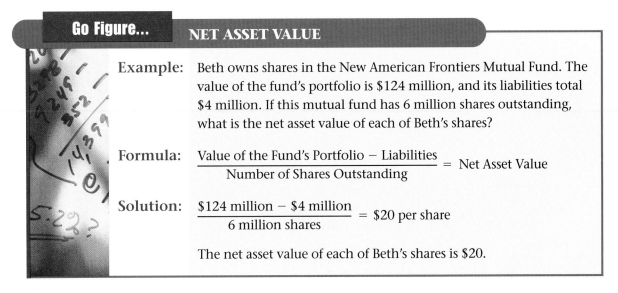

Go Figure... **NET ASSET VALUE**

Example: Beth owns shares in the New American Frontiers Mutual Fund. The value of the fund's portfolio is $124 million, and its liabilities total $4 million. If this mutual fund has 6 million shares outstanding, what is the net asset value of each of Beth's shares?

Formula:
$$\frac{\text{Value of the Fund's Portfolio} - \text{Liabilities}}{\text{Number of Shares Outstanding}} = \text{Net Asset Value}$$

Solution:
$$\frac{\$124 \text{ million} - \$4 \text{ million}}{6 \text{ million shares}} = \$20 \text{ per share}$$

The net asset value of each of Beth's shares is $20.

If you buy shares of an open-end fund from an investment company, you gain access to a wide variety of services. These services include payroll deduction programs, automatic reinvestment programs, and automatic withdrawal programs.

LOAD FUNDS   Before investing in mutual funds, you should compare the cost of this type of investment with the cost of other types of investments. Mutual funds are classified as either load funds or no-load funds. A *load fund* (sometimes referred to as an "A" fund) is a mutual fund in which you pay a commission every time you purchase shares. The commission can be as high as 8.5 percent. The supposed advantage of a load fund is that the fund's salespeople will offer advice and guidance as to when shares of the fund should be bought or sold.

NO-LOAD FUNDS   A *no-load fund* is a mutual fund in which the individual investor pays no commission. No-load funds don't charge commissions when you buy shares because they have no salespeople. No-load funds offer the same investment opportunities as load funds. If you have a choice between a load fund and a no-load fund, and both offer the same investment opportunities, choose the no-load fund.

MANAGEMENT FEES AND OTHER CHARGES   Once you've determined whether a particular fund is a load or no-load fund, you'll need to find out what other fees you might incur. The investment companies that sponsor mutual funds charge management fees. This fee is a fixed percentage of the fund's asset value. Most management fees are between 0.25 and 1 percent.

Instead of charging investors a fee when they purchase shares, some mutual funds charge a contingent deferred sales load, also known as a back-end load. This is a fee that is charged for withdrawing money from the fund. Such funds are sometimes called "B" funds. Their fees range from 1 to 6 percent and are based on how long you own shares of the mutual fund before making a withdrawal. The longer you own shares of the fund, the lower your fee will be. If you own the shares in the fund for more than five to seven years, often you will not be charged any withdrawal fee. Obviously, a back-end load (contingent deferred sales load) is designed to discourage early withdrawals. If all other factors are equal, a fund that doesn't charge a back-end load is preferable to a fund that does.

Some mutual funds have a 12b-1 fee, sometimes referred to as a distribution fee. A *12b-1 fee* is a fee that an investment company charges to help pay for marketing and advertising a mutual fund. The 12b-1 fee is calculated on the value of a fund's assets. It is approximately 1 percent of a fund's assets per year. Unlike the one-time fees charged for buying or selling shares, the 12b-1 fee is an ongoing fee that is charged on an annual basis. A 12b-1 fee can cost you a lot of money over a period of years.

Careers in Finance

CERTIFIED FINANCIAL PLANNER

Some people acquire a few assets and think that their financial future is secure. Without a clear financial plan, however, their fortune could change for the worse. For this reason, many people turn to certified financial planners to help them manage their money. Extra training in tax and estate planning enables these stockbrokers to prepare their clients for the future with insurance, pension plans, and investment strategies. Financial planners also give advice on tax strategies and real estate investments. After interviewing new clients about their assets, liabilities, and financial goals, they tailor a financial plan to fit individual needs.

Skills	Communication, computer, interpersonal, math, reading, research, writing
Personality	Ability to see the big picture, ethical, honest, likes working with people
Education	Bachelor's or master's degree in accounting, business administration, economics, or finance; Certified Financial Planner license
Pay range	$40,000 to $100,000 plus a year, depending on experience, location, and clientele

Analyze Why would someone hire a certified financial planner?

 For more information on certified financial planners visit finance.glencoe.com or your local library.

Categories of Mutual Funds

The managers of mutual funds tailor their investment portfolios to the investment objectives of their customers. Usually a fund's objectives are clearly explained in its *prospectus*—a report that provides potential investors with detailed information about a particular mutual fund. It can be helpful to sort mutual funds into three main groups: stock mutual funds, bond mutual funds, and mixed mutual funds. Within each group, mutual funds may fall into one of many categories. Note that different sources of investment information may use different categories for the same mutual fund. The major fund groups and categories are described below.

Stock Mutual Funds

Most mutual funds are part of the stock mutual funds group. Stock mutual funds invest in stocks. These funds typically fall into 12 categories that describe the objectives of the funds and the types of stock they buy.

AGGRESSIVE GROWTH FUNDS   Aggressive growth funds (sometimes called capital appreciation funds) seek to grow money rapidly by purchasing stocks whose prices will increase greatly in a short period of time. Because the stocks in an aggressive growth fund's portfolio are often risky, or highly speculative, the market value of shares in this type of fund frequently swings between low and high.

EQUITY INCOME FUNDS   Equity income funds buy stocks issued by companies with a long history of paying dividends. The major objective of these funds is to provide steady income to shareholders. These funds are attractive investment choices for conservative or retired investors.

GLOBAL STOCK FUNDS   Global stock funds invest in stocks of companies throughout the world, including the United States. The managers of global funds are not restricted by national boundaries.

GROWTH FUNDS   Growth funds buy shares of companies expecting higher-than-average revenue and earnings growth. While similar to aggressive growth funds, growth funds tend to invest in larger, less risky companies that may pay some dividends. As a result the market value of shares in a growth fund are more stable when compared to aggressive growth funds.

GROWTH AND INCOME FUNDS   Growth and income funds purchase stocks that provide both a steady source of dividend income and the potential for growth. These funds are considered conservative because they invest in large, established companies.

CONNECT

Name two or more mutual funds that you've seen advertised on television, the Internet, or in your local newspaper.

INDEX FUNDS   Index funds invest in the same companies that are included in an index like the Standard & Poor's 500 Stock Index. Fund managers select stocks issued by the companies that are included in the index. Thus, an index fund should provide about the same performance as the index. Index funds often have lower management fees.

INTERNATIONAL FUNDS   International funds purchase foreign stocks that are sold in securities markets throughout the world. That way, if the economy in one region or nation is in a decline, profits can still be earned in others. A true international fund invests only outside the United States.

MID CAP FUNDS   Mid cap funds buy shares of companies with total assets of at least $500 million. Mid cap funds offer more security than small cap funds and more growth potential than funds that invest in large corporations.

REGIONAL FUNDS   Regional funds seek to purchase stocks that are traded within one region of the world. Examples include the European region, the Latin American region, and the Pacific region.

SECTOR FUNDS   Sector funds invest in companies within the same industry. Examples of sectors include health and biotechnology, science and technology, computers, and natural resources.

MUCHO DINERO Regional funds invest in stocks from a particular region in the world. *Why might an investor choose a Latin American regional fund?*

SMALL CAP FUNDS   Small cap funds buy shares of companies with total assets of less than $500 million. Because these companies are small and innovative, they offer high growth potential. These funds are riskier, or more speculative, than funds that invest in larger, more established companies.

UTILITY FUNDS   Utility funds invest in companies that provide utility services to their customers. Because these funds are generally safe and stable investments, they are often chosen by conservative investors, such as retired people.

Bond Mutual Funds

Mutual funds in the bond mutual funds group invest only in bonds. The bond fund categories are based on the type of bond the mutual funds purchase.

HIGH-YIELD (JUNK) BOND FUNDS   High-yield (junk) bond funds purchase high-yield, high-risk corporate bonds.

INSURED MUNICIPAL BOND FUNDS   Insured municipal bond funds buy municipal bonds that provide tax-exempt income. An outside company insures them against the risk of default, or nonpayment.

INTERMEDIATE CORPORATE BOND FUNDS   Intermediate corporate bond funds invest in investment-grade corporate bonds with maturities between five and ten years.

INTERMEDIATE U.S. BOND FUNDS   Intermediate U.S. bond funds purchase U.S. Treasury notes with maturities between five and ten years.

LONG-TERM CORPORATE BOND FUNDS   Long-term corporate bond funds buy investment-grade corporate bonds with maturities of longer than ten years.

LONG-TERM U.S. BOND FUNDS   Long-term U.S. bond funds purchase U.S. Treasury bonds and zero-coupon bonds with maturities of longer than ten years.

MUNICIPAL BOND FUNDS   Municipal bond funds invest in municipal bonds that provide investors with tax-exempt interest income.

SHORT-TERM CORPORATE BOND FUNDS   Short-term corporate bond funds buy investment-grade bond issues with maturities of between one and five years.

SHORT-TERM U.S. BOND FUNDS   Short-term U.S. bond funds invest in U.S. Treasury bills and some Treasury notes with maturities of between one and five years.

PATRIOTIC INVESTMENTS Bond mutual funds can be sorted into categories by the type of bonds they buy. *Which bond mutual funds invest in U.S. Treasury securities?*

Mixed Mutual Funds

The remaining mutual funds are part of the third group—mixed mutual funds. These funds invest in a mix of stocks and bonds or in various other types of securities. The funds fall into three categories: balanced funds, money-market funds, and stock/bond blend funds.

BALANCED FUNDS Balanced funds invest in both stocks and bonds with the primary objective of protecting the shareholder's investment. Often the percentage of stocks and bonds is stated in the fund's prospectus.

MONEY-MARKET FUNDS Money-market funds invest in certificates of deposit, government securities, and other safe investments. It is relatively easy to withdraw money from a money-market fund.

STOCK/BOND BLEND FUNDS Stock/bond blend funds invest in both stocks and bonds to achieve a variety of objectives.

A variety of mutual funds managed by one investment company is called a *family of funds*. Each mutual fund within the family has a different financial objective. For instance, one fund may be a short-term U.S. bond fund and another a growth stock fund. Most investment companies make it easy for shareholders to switch among the mutual funds within a family. This allows investors to adjust their investments conveniently to suit their changing needs or to maximize their profits over time.

SECTION 10.4 ASSESSMENT

CHECK YOUR UNDERSTANDING

1. What are the characteristics of closed-end mutual funds?
2. What is an open-end mutual fund?
3. Name the three main groups into which mutual funds can be sorted.

THINK CRITICALLY

4. Choose three categories of stock or bond funds in which you think you might like to invest. Explain why you think that they are a good investment.

USING MATH SKILLS

5. **Load Fund** Noah is thinking about investing $1,000 in a global mutual fund. However, the fund is a load fund, which charges a commission of 8.5 percent. The investment company would deduct this fee from Noah's $1,000 before his money is invested in the fund. **Calculate and Advise** What is the dollar amount of the commission that Noah must pay the investment company in order to invest in this fund? Would you advise him to look for a no-load fund? Why?

SOLVING MONEY PROBLEMS

6. **Fund Objectives** Hilda wants to invest her savings in a mutual fund. However, she is concerned about the risk of investing and wants to find a mutual fund that will be stable and safe. Her friend Ana recommends that she consider utility funds and money-market funds. Her friend Jack says that she should explore aggressive growth funds and high-yield (junk) bond funds.
Analyze Review the characteristics of utility funds, money-market funds, aggressive growth funds, and high-yield (junk) bond funds. Analyze the objectives of these funds. Whose advice best addresses Hilda's concerns? Why?

The Investor's Decision to Buy or Sell Mutual Funds

What You'll Learn

- How to **evaluate** mutual funds to determine which funds might be right for you
- How to **describe** the reasons investors buy and sell mutual funds and the methods that they use

Why It's Important

Knowing how to evaluate mutual funds will enable you to invest wisely. Understanding why and how investors buy and sell mutual funds will help you make investment decisions that suit your personal financial goals.

KEY TERMS

- **income dividends**
- **capital gain distributions**
- **capital gain**

How to Make a Decision to Buy or Sell Mutual Funds

Which mutual funds are best for you? When should you buy or sell your shares? You'll have to decide for yourself. Fortunately, you'll find a great deal of information that you can use to evaluate a specific mutual fund. Use that information to guide you through the decision-making process of buying or selling shares in a mutual fund.

How to Read the Mutual Funds Section of a Newspaper

Most large metropolitan newspapers and financial newspapers, such as the *Wall Street Journal* and *Barron's*, provide a wealth of information about mutual funds. Much of this same information is also available on the Internet.

As shown in **Figure 10.5**, mutual fund quotations contain information about a fund's net asset value, objective, performance, and cost. When you read mutual fund quotations, remember to note any letters beside the name of a specific fund. Then look up their meanings in the footnotes that accompany the quotations.

Reading mutual fund quotations is a simple way to start your search for a mutual fund. It's also a smart way of monitoring the value of your mutual fund investments. However, other sources of information provide a more complete basis for evaluating mutual fund investments.

Considering Your Financial Objectives

You have a lot to consider when you're thinking about your investment goals. How old are you? What is your family situation? How much risk do you want to take? How much money do you make now? How much money are you likely to make in the future? Only after you've considered these factors can you set your investment goals.

Once you know your goals, it's time to find a mutual fund with investment objectives that match your own. Start by reading a financial newspaper or magazine. Look for articles that spotlight a

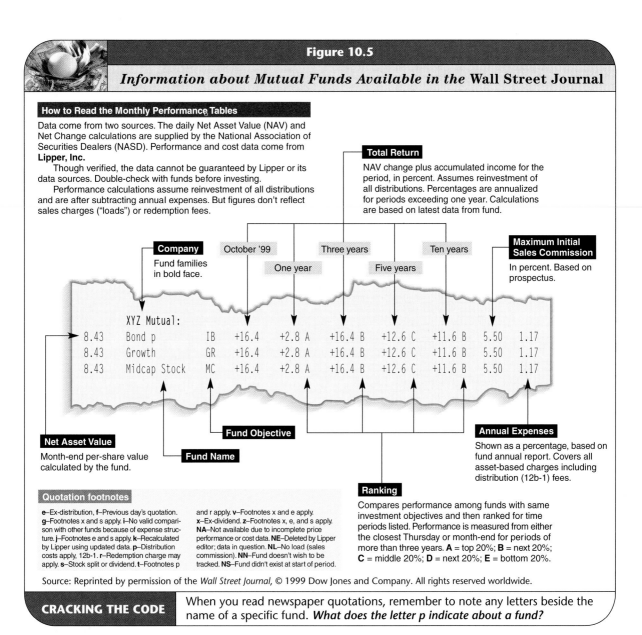

Figure 10.5

Information about Mutual Funds Available in the Wall Street Journal

How to Read the Monthly Performance Tables

Data come from two sources. The daily Net Asset Value (NAV) and Net Change calculations are supplied by the National Association of Securities Dealers (NASD). Performance and cost data come from **Lipper, Inc.**

Though verified, the data cannot be guaranteed by Lipper or its data sources. Double-check with funds before investing.

Performance calculations assume reinvestment of all distributions and are after subtracting annual expenses. But figures don't reflect sales charges ("loads") or redemption fees.

Total Return

NAV change plus accumulated income for the period, in percent. Assumes reinvestment of all distributions. Percentages are annualized for periods exceeding one year. Calculations are based on latest data from fund.

Company

Fund families in bold face.

October '99

One year

Three years

Five years

Ten years

Maximum Initial Sales Commission

In percent. Based on prospectus.

```
        XYZ Mutual:
 8.43   Bond p         IB   +16.4   +2.8 A   +16.4 B   +12.6 C   +11.6 B   5.50   1.17
 8.43   Growth         GR   +16.4   +2.8 A   +16.4 B   +12.6 C   +11.6 B   5.50   1.17
 8.43   Midcap Stock   MC   +16.4   +2.8 A   +16.4 B   +12.6 C   +11.6 B   5.50   1.17
```

Fund Objective

Net Asset Value

Month-end per-share value calculated by the fund.

Fund Name

Annual Expenses

Shown as a percentage, based on fund annual report. Covers all asset-based charges including distribution (12b-1) fees.

Ranking

Compares performance among funds with same investment objectives and then ranked for time periods listed. Performance is measured from either the closest Thursday or month-end for periods of more than three years. **A** = top 20%; **B** = next 20%; **C** = middle 20%; **D** = next 20%; **E** = bottom 20%.

Quotation footnotes

e–Ex-distribution. **f**–Previous day's quotation. **g**–Footnotes x and s apply. **i**–No valid comparison with other funds because of expense structure. **j**–Footnotes e and s apply. **k**–Recalculated by Lipper using updated data. **p**–Distribution costs apply, 12b-1. **r**–Redemption charge may apply. **s**–Stock split or dividend. **t**–Footnotes p and r apply. **v**–Footnotes x and e apply. **x**–Ex-dividend. **z**–Footnotes x, e, and s apply. **NA**–Not available due to incomplete price performance or cost data. **NE**–Deleted by Lipper editor; data in question. **NL**–No load (sales commission). **NN**–Fund doesn't wish to be tracked. **NS**–Fund didn't exist at start of period.

Source: Reprinted by permission of the *Wall Street Journal*, © 1999 Dow Jones and Company. All rights reserved worldwide.

CRACKING THE CODE When you read newspaper quotations, remember to note any letters beside the name of a specific fund. *What does the letter p indicate about a fund?*

particular fund, review a specific investment category, or discuss the top performers in each category. You can also search personal finance Web sites for information about mutual funds and their objectives.

Mutual Fund Prospectus

After you've narrowed your search, check out the prospectuses of several mutual funds that most interest you. To get a copy of a mutual fund prospectus, call, write, or e-mail the investment company that manages the mutual fund. Many investment companies have toll-free telephone numbers that you can find by calling the toll-free information number (1-800-555-1212). An investment company sponsoring a mutual fund must give potential investors, like you, a prospectus.

Read the prospectus completely before you invest. In addition to summarizing the fund's objective, a prospectus includes a fee table that lists any fees you will have to pay. The prospectus usually provides the following information as well:

- A description of the fund's objective and the risk factor associated with the fund
- A description of the fund's past performance
- A description of the type of investments contained in the fund's portfolio
- Information about dividends, distributions, and taxes
- Information about the fund's management
- Information on limitations or requirements the fund must honor when choosing investments
- The process by which investors can buy or sell shares in the fund
- A description of services provided to investors—and any related fees
- Information about how often the fund's investment portfolio changes (sometimes referred to as its turnover ratio)

Mutual Fund Annual Report

If you're a potential investor, you may request an annual report by mail, telephone, or the Internet. Once you are a shareholder, the investment company will automatically send you an annual report. A fund's annual report contains a letter from the president of the investment company, the fund manager, or both. Don't forget the role of the fund manager in determining a fund's success. If a fund's present manager has been doing a good job for five years or longer, chances are that he or she will continue to perform well in the future.

The annual report also contains detailed information about the fund's assets and liabilities. It includes a statement of operations that describes expenses and day-to-day operating costs of the fund, a statement of changes in net assets, and a schedule of investments. Finally, most annual reports include a letter from the fund's independent auditors. This letter backs up the information contained in the report.

Financial Publications

Financial magazines such as *Business Week, Forbes, Kiplinger's Personal Finance Magazine,* and *Money* are another source of information about mutual funds. These publications provide annual surveys

Figure 10.6

A Portion of the Mutual Fund Scoreboard by Business Week

MUTUAL FUND SCOREBOARD

Closed-End Equity Funds

FUND	RATING	CATEGORY	RISK	SIZE ASSETS $MIL.	FEES EXPENSE RATIO (%)	NAV. RET. (%) 1 YR.	3 YRS.	SHARES RET. (%) 1 YR.	3 YRS.	YIELD (%)	HISTORY RESULTS VS. ALL FUNDS	1999 HIGH	LOW	1/21/00
ADAMS EXPRESS	A	Large-cap Blend	Low	1757.2	0.22	25.3	26.4	27.6	26.4	1.2		−14.9	−19.6	−15.5
ALLIANCE ALL-MARKET ADVANTAGE	A	Large-cap Growth	Average	156.0	2.52	36.7	44.6	15.0	43.4	10.1		6.6	−14.8	−13.4
ARGENTINA	C−	Latin America	Average	140.8	1.48	40.1	11.5	37.7	4.0	2.5		−17.5	−30.0	−26.6
ASA LIMITED	D	Precious Metals	High	191.1	1.15	53.5	−7.5	25.8	−15.1	3.2		9.3	−19.0	−24.3
ASIA PACIFIC	C−	Pacific ex-Japan	High	216.8	1.56	77.0	0.8	68.8	−1.4	1.2		−3.3	−25.2	−24.8
ASIA TIGERS	C−	Pacific ex-Japan	High	203.5	1.74	72.1	0.9	57.4	−1.7	0.7		−10.7	−26.3	−25.9
AUSTRIA	C	Europe	Average	90.0	1.68	38.0	20.1	40.9	26.0	7.9		−6.6	−24.3	−23.2
AVALON CAPITAL	B	Large-cap Growth	Average	11.4	NA	4.0	16.8	1.7	20.6	2.8		7.6	−21.3	−1.3
BAKER FENTRESS	B	Large-cap Value	Very low	830.3	0.76	−2.2	8.2	21.4	16.3	6.9		−3.4	−27.5	−1.7*
BERGSTROM CAPITAL	A	Large-cap Growth	Low	218.4	0.74	48.5	35.6	47.9	34.5	0.1		−6.8	−17.2	−12.5
BLUE CHIP VALUE	B	Large-cap Value	Low	161.1	0.94	5.9	17.6	6.4	14.8	5.3		1.5	−8.2	0.8
BRAZIL	C−	Latin America	High	278.9	1.56	64.0	13.5	74.4	9.5	2.4		−9.9	−25.1	−23.5
BRAZILIAN EQUITY	D	Latin America	High	33.9	2.07	51.9	−5.4	57.6	−7.4	0.0		−4.6	−23.9	−23.6
CENTRAL EUROPEAN EQUITY	C−	Europe	Average	160.2	1.17	13.5	1.4	8.5	0.3	0.0		−16.8	−26.5	−21.9
CENTRAL EUROPEAN VALUE	C−	Europe	Average	5.9	2.09	5.5	−0.9	15.1	−0.2	0.0		−9.3	−22.8	−18.3
CENTRAL FUND OF CANADA	C−	Precious Metals	Average	71.9	NA	2.6	−4.0	22.1	−1.7	0.2		12.2	−8.9	−5.8
CENTRAL SECURITIES	B+	Mid-cap Value	Low	509.1	0.51	30.8	23.4	23.9	13.9	1.3		−13.5	−22.4	−20.7
CHARTWELL DIVIDEND & INCOME		Large-cap Value		NA	NA	1.2	NA	−17.8	NA	12.1		5.3	−21.7	−19.0
CHILE	C−	Latin America	High	215.1	1.62	26.4	3.8	29.8	−3.7	0.6		−18.7	−28.3	−25.8
CHINA	D	Pacific ex-Japan	High	96.4	2.22	38.1	−2.3	30.1	−4.6	1.0		−13.7	−27.7	−24.1
CLEMENTE GLOBAL GROWTH	B+	World	Low	78.8	1.91	32.2	27.7	42.5	38.8	0.0		−4.0	−16.7	−13.1
COHEN & STEERS REALTY INCOME	C	Real Estate	Low	20.2	NA	−7.0	−2.1	−8.7	−5.3	9.9		23.8	1.4	6.7
COHEN & STEERS TOTAL RETURN REALTY	C	Real Estate	Low	81.5	NA	−6.6	−0.8	−10.1	−0.1	9.3		13.4	−1.7	3.2
DELAWARE DIVIDEND & INCOME	B	Dom. Hybrid	Low	212.2	0.80	−7.0	4.9	−27.9	0.6	12.2		15.0	−19.0	−11.0
DELAWARE GLOBAL DIVIDEND & INCOME	B	Dom. Hybrid	Low	101.1	1.03	2.2	7.0	−18.3	−0.5	12.3		−0.5	−20.9	−16.4
DUFF & PHELPS UTILITIES INCOME	B	Utilities	Low	2015.9	1.46	−8.5	9.5	−20.1	6.8	9.5		17.1	−5.2	−2.8
EMERGING MARKETS INFRASTRUCTURE	C−	Div. Emg. Mkts.	Average	159.1	2.07	59.0	6.5	57.3	3.7	1.4		−14.8	−25.9	−22.3
EMERGING MARKETS TELECOM.	C	Div. Emg. Mkts.	Average	95.2	2.09	85.9	21.3	83.2	18.1	0.0		−10.6	−24.3	−22.7
ENGEX	D	Small-cap Growth	High	10.3	5.78	116.8	10.0	145.5	17.1	0.0		4.9	−24.7	6.2
EQUUS II	C−	Dom. Hybrid	Average	110.0	4.57	−13.8	−3.8	−18.9	−5.0	0.0		−24.3	−35.2	−34.6
EUROPE	B+	Europe	Low	200.1	1.27	20.5	19.3	15.9	20.6	0.6		−0.8	−14.4	−14.3
EUROPEAN WARRANT	B+	Europe	Average	232.2	1.77	45.2	46.7	27.5	49.0	0.0		0.1	−25.1	−26.1
FIDELITY ADVISOR KOREA	D	Pacific ex-Japan	Very high	51.8	2.30	134.5	24.2	95.7	6.6	0.0		−5.7	−28.3	−25.9

NA = Not available.
* Last NAV reported Jan. 7, 2000.

DATA: MORNINGSTAR, INC., CHICAGO, IL.

How to Use the Tables

Closed-end funds are publicly traded investment companies. Their results are measured two ways: one, by the change in net asset value (NAV), which is generated by the fund's manager; the other, by the change in the shares' market price. Total returns, which include dividends and capital gains, are shown for one- and three-year periods. The three-year figure is an average annual return. All returns are pretax.

BUSINESS WEEK RATING
Ratings are based on three-year risk-adjusted performance of the fund's portfolio. A rating is calculated by subtracting a fund's risk-of-loss factor from total return. Equity funds are rated against each other, and to earn an above-average rating, must beat the S&P 500 on a risk-adjusted basis. For ratings, municipal bond funds are separated from other bond funds.

A	SUPERIOR
B+	VERY GOOD
B	ABOVE AVERAGE
C	AVERAGE
C−	BELOW AVERAGE
D	POOR
F	VERY POOR

RISK
For each fund, the monthly Treasury bill return is subtracted from the monthly NAV return in each month of the rating period. When a fund has underperformed Treasury bills, this monthly result is negative. The sum of these negative numbers is then divided by the number of months. The result is a negative number, and the greater its magnitude, the higher the risk of loss.

EXPENSE RATIO
Fund expenses for 1999 as a percent of average net assets. Ratio may include interest expense.

YIELD
Income earned during 1999, as a percentage of yearend NAV per share, adjusted for capital gains.

MATURITY
The average maturity of the securities in a bond fund, weighted according to their market value.

HISTORY
A fund's relative performance during 1997, 1998, and 1999. From left to right, the numbers designate which quartile the fund was in for each period: ■ for the top quartile; ■ for the second quartile; ■ for the third quartile; and ■ for the bottom quartile.

PREMIUM/DISCOUNT
The market price of closed-end funds is either less than the value of their securities, a discount, or more, a premium, to their NAVs.

WHAT'S THE SCORE? This annual mutual fund survey by *Business Week,* rates various mutual funds based on performance and risk. *What other information does it provide about each mutual fund?*

of mutual funds, such as the one shown in **Figure 10.6** on page 339, and rank them in several different ways.

A fund's past long-term performance is no guarantee of future success. However, it is a valid predictor. For this reason, most annual surveys include information about a fund's total return over time.

In addition to annual surveys, a number of mutual fund guidebooks are published. You'll find them at a bookstore or your local public library.

Professional Advice

Professional advisory services provide detailed information on mutual funds (see **Figure 10.7**). Standard & Poor's; Lipper Analytical Services; Morningstar, Inc.; Value Line; and Wiesenberger Investment Companies are five popular sources. In addition, various mutual fund newsletters provide financial information to subscribers for a fee. These publications are expensive, but you may be able to obtain copies of them from brokerage firms or public libraries.

Professional advisory services, such as Morningstar, also offer on-line research reports for mutual funds. Many investors find that the research reports provided by such companies are well worth the $5 or $10 fee they charge. The information is basically the same as that in the printed reports. However, the ability to obtain the information quickly can be a real advantage.

The Internet

Many investors research mutual fund investments on the Internet. You may access this information online by one of several methods. If you know the name or the four- or five-letter symbol for a fund, you may obtain current market values by using an Internet source like Yahoo! Finance. You can also get a price history and a profile for the fund.

Most investment companies that sponsor mutual funds have Web sites. These sites are another source of useful information. However, don't forget that investment companies want you to become a shareholder, and therefore any of their Web sites may read like a sales pitch. Look at the facts before you invest your money.

Return on Investment

Whether you choose a closed-end fund or an open-end fund, the purpose of investing in a mutual fund is to receive income. As a mutual fund shareholder, you may gain income in one of three ways.

Figure 10.7

Mutual Fund Research Information Provided by Morningstar, Inc.

Published February 24, 2000. Reprinted by permission of Morningstar.

Source: From *Morningstar Mutual Funds*, February 24, 2000. © 2000 by Morningstar, Inc. Reprinted by permission.

WATCH THE STARS This report shows the type of information that Morningstar, Inc., provides to an investor who is interested in the Davis NY Venture Fund. *What can you learn by reading the small box entitled "Historical Profile" at the top of the report?*

First, you may receive income dividends. *Income dividends* are the earnings a fund pays to shareholders. Second, you may earn capital gain distributions. *Capital gain distributions* are payments made to shareholders that result from the sale of securities in the fund's portfolio. Third, you may make a profit by buying shares at a low price and then selling them after the price increases.

When you sell shares in a mutual fund, the profit that results from an increase in value is referred to as a capital gain. Note the difference between a capital gain distribution and a capital gain. A capital gain distribution occurs when the fund sells securities within the fund's portfolio and distributes profits to shareholders. A *capital gain* is the profit you make from selling your shares in a mutual fund for a higher price than you paid for them. Of course, if the price of a fund's shares goes down between the time of purchase and the time of sale, you will lose money.

QUESTION

What factors will influence the price of a fund's shares?

Taxes and Mutual Funds

Income dividends, capital gain distributions, and capital gains are all taxable earnings. At the end of every year, investment companies and brokerage firms send each shareholder a statement detailing the income dividends and capital gain distributions he or she received. Usually, this information is provided on the IRS Form 1099 DIV. When an investor sells shares, most investment companies and brokerage firms will send a statement identifying his or her capital gains or losses. However, the investor is responsible for maintaining clear and accurate records of the purchase and sale prices. The following are some general guidelines on how mutual fund transactions are taxed:

- Income dividends are reported along with all other dividend amounts you have received. They are taxed as regular income.
- Capital gain distributions are reported on your federal income tax return.
- Capital gains or losses that result from your selling shares in a mutual fund are reported on your federal income tax return.

You should be aware of two factors when you pay taxes on your mutual funds. First, almost all investment companies allow you to reinvest the capital gains distributions and income dividends you earn instead of receiving cash. Even though you didn't receive cash, these distributions are taxable and must be reported on your income tax return. Second, when you purchase shares of stock or corporate bonds or make other investments, you can decide when to sell them.

Thus, you can pick the tax year when you pay tax or deduct losses on these investments. Mutual funds, on the other hand, buy and sell securities on a regular basis during any 12-month period. Unlike investments that you manage, you have no control over when the mutual fund sells securities. Therefore, you have no control over when you are taxed on capital gain distributions.

Buying and Selling Mutual Funds

The main reason for investing is the opportunity to make money on your investment. Mutual funds can provide investors with income dividends, capital gain distributions, and profits that result from their decision to sell their shares. Various purchase options and withdrawal options allow you to manage your mutual fund investments and profits in a way that meets your financial goals.

Purchase Options

Before you can buy shares in a fund, you'll need to consider several different purchase options. Different types of funds are sold by different means. Closed-end funds are traded through stock exchanges, such as the New York Stock Exchange, or in the over-the-counter market. You can purchase shares of an open-end fund from a brokerage firm or by contacting the investment company that sponsors the fund.

A wide variety of both no-load and load funds can also be bought from mutual fund supermarkets that are available through brokerage firms such as Charles Schwab and E*Trade. Mutual fund supermarkets offer at least two advantages to you as an investor. First, instead of dealing with several investment companies, you can make one toll-free phone call to buy or sell a large number of mutual funds. Second, you receive one statement from the brokerage firm instead of receiving a statement from each investment company that you deal with. This statement provides the information that you need to monitor all of your investments in one place and in the same format.

When you buy shares in an open-end mutual fund from an investment company, you have several options. You can choose a regular account transaction, a voluntary savings plan, a contractual savings plan, or a reinvestment plan. The most popular and least complicated way to buy such shares is through a regular account transaction. With this method you decide how much money to invest and when to invest it. Then you simply buy as many shares as possible.

VOLUNTARY SAVINGS PLAN   A voluntary savings plan lets you make smaller purchases than the minimum required by the regular account transaction. However, when you make your first purchase, you also must commit to making regular minimum purchases of the fund's shares. Such small monthly investments can be a great way to save for long-term objectives. For most voluntary savings plans, the minimum purchase ranges from $25 to $100. Most voluntary savings plans also offer payroll deduction plans. This means that with your approval, the investment company will deduct a certain amount from your paycheck each month and invest it in your mutual fund. Mutual fund savings plans can also be used to invest money that is contributed to tax-deferred 401(k) and 403(b) retirement plans or individual retirement accounts (IRAs).

CONTRACTUAL SAVINGS PLAN   Contractual savings plans require you to make regular purchases of shares over a specific period of time, usually 10 to 15 years. You will pay penalty fees if you do not make the required purchases. Financial experts and government agencies disapprove of contractual savings plans because many investors lose money with these plans.

REINVESTMENT PLAN   You can also buy shares in an open-end fund by using the fund's reinvestment plan. With a reinvestment plan, your income dividends and capital gain distributions are automatically reinvested to buy additional shares of the fund. Most reinvestment plans let shareholders reinvest without having to pay additional sales charges or commissions. Reinvestment is a great way to add to your portfolio.

Withdrawal Options

If you choose to invest in mutual funds, you'll also need to know how you can take your money out of a fund. You can sell shares of closed-end funds to another investor anytime you want on the stock exchange or in the over-the-counter market. Shares in an open-end fund can be sold to the investment company that sponsors the fund.

THE GOLDEN YEARS Many people use mutual funds to save for their retirement. *How might you use mutual funds to build a retirement nest egg?*

Your Financial Portfolio

Evaluating Mutual Funds

Eric is looking at a mutual fund because it might earn a greater return than a CD. He used the following checklist as a way to evaluate the Pacific Sun Growth Fund, a stock mutual fund.

Pacific Sun Growth Fund	
1. Name of mutual fund	1. Pacific Sun Growth Fund
2. Mutual fund group and category	2. Stock mutual fund/aggressive growth
3. Mutual fund's objective (Aggressive growth, moderate growth, income and safety, and income)	3. Aggressive growth of capital
4. Yield in the last twelve months	4. 40.25%
5. Average return or yield for the last five years	5. 33.04%
6. Average return or yield for the last ten years	6. 27.54%
7. Load fees or redemption fees	7. no fees
8. What is the minimum investment?	8. $1,000
9. Is the fund closed to new investors?	9. No
10. Morningstar rating (in stars and risk)	10. Five-star rating and below-average risk

After evaluating Pacific Sun Growth Fund, Eric has decided that he likes the high return and the below-average risk. He may go with the fund, even though he needs $1,000 to make his initial investment.

Research Call an investment company for a prospectus of a mutual fund. You can also visit your local library and look in *Morningstar Mutual Funds* or *Weisenberger Investment Companies Yearbook*. In your workbook or on a separate sheet of paper, fill in the information on the checklist to evaluate the fund.

RESPOND

Which purchasing plan do you think would be best for a beginning investor?

In this case all you have to do is give proper notification, and the fund will send you a check for the net asset value of your shares. With some funds you can even write checks to withdraw money.

If you have at least $5,000 worth of shares in a mutual fund, most funds will offer you four additional ways of withdrawing money. First, you may withdraw a certain amount each investment period until your fund has been exhausted. Typically, an investment period is three months, and most funds require investors to withdraw a minimum amount, usually $50.

A second option is to liquidate or "sell off" a certain number of shares each investment period. Of course, the net asset value of shares in a fund varies from one period to the next. Therefore, the amount of money you receive will also vary. When shares are sold, a check is mailed directly to you.

A third choice lets you withdraw a prearranged percentage of your investment's asset growth, or the amount by which your portfolio has increased in value. For example, suppose that you arrange to receive 60 percent of the asset growth of your portfolio. The asset growth of your portfolio was $800 in a particular investment period. For that period you will receive a check for $480 ($800 × 60% = $480). If the value of your portfolio does not increase, you receive no payment. Under this option, your principal (the amount of your original investment) remains untouched.

A final option allows you to withdraw all income that results from income dividends and capital gains distributions earned during an investment period. Under this option, too, your principal remains untouched.

ASSESSMENT

CHECK YOUR UNDERSTANDING

1. What type of information does a newspaper mutual fund quotation provide to help you evaluate a fund?
2. Identify three ways in which you can receive income from your mutual fund investments.
3. Describe the withdrawal options that are available to you when selling shares in a mutual fund.

THINK CRITICALLY

4. Newspaper mutual fund quotations, financial magazines, and the Internet are three sources you might use to start to search for a mutual fund that matches your financial objectives. Decide which source you would use first, and explain why.

USING COMMUNICATION SKILLS

5. **Sales Pitch** Imagine that you are the professional manager of a large mutual fund. You are looking for investors to buy shares in your fund.
   Prepare a Flyer Prepare a flyer that will convince people to invest in your fund. Name your fund, and give as many reasons as possible why it would be a solid investment. Make your flyer inviting by using exciting language and by including pictures, charts, and graphs. What questions would investors ask when evaluating your fund?

SOLVING MONEY PROBLEMS

6. **Purchase Options** Malia has invested in a mutual fund. She wants to add to her investment on a regular basis and is trying to decide which purchase option to use. Her mutual fund offers a voluntary savings plan, a contractual savings plan, and a reinvestment plan.
   Analyze and Advise Analyze the advantages and disadvantages of the three purchase options available to Malia. What advice would you offer her? Why?

CHAPTER 10 ASSESSMENT

CHAPTER SUMMARY

- Characteristics of corporate bonds include interest rate, maturity date, and face value.

- Among the reasons corporations sell corporate bonds are to finance business activities and to make major purchases.

- Investors buy corporate bonds because they provide interest income and because they will be repaid at the maturity date.

- Federal, state, and local governments issue bonds to help raise the money they need to operate.

- Investors buy government bonds because they are considered almost risk-free.

- To research bonds, analyze bond price quotations, annual reports, other sources

of information, and check bond ratings.

- Mutual funds may be closed-end or open-end funds and load or no-load funds.

- The main groups of mutual funds are stock funds, bond funds, and mixed funds.

- To research a mutual fund, review mutual fund information in newspapers, in financial and advisory service publications, and on the Internet; study the fund prospectus and its annual report.

- Mutual funds provide income to investors through income dividends, capital gain distributions, and capital gains; they offer various purchase and withdrawal options.

Internet zone

Understanding and Using Vocabulary

Write a dialogue between a person who wants to make an investment in bonds and mutual funds and a financial planner. Use 8 to 12 of the following terms in creating this conversation.

maturity date
face value
debenture
mortgage bond
subordinated
    debenture
convertible bond
call feature

bond indenture
sinking fund
serial bond
registered bond
registered coupon
    bond
bearer bond
zero-coupon bond

municipal bond
general obligation
    bond
revenue bond
investment-grade
    bonds
yield
closed-end fund
open-end fund
net asset value (NAV)

load fund
no-load fund
12b-1 fee
prospectus
family of funds
income dividends
capital gain
    distributions
capital gain

Review Key Concepts

1. Explain the call feature of most corporate bonds.

CHAPTER 10 ASSESSMENT

2. What are the four basic types of securities issued by the U.S. Treasury Department?
3. What is the purpose of calculating the yield on a bond investment?
4. Identify the primary characteristics of two different stock mutual funds.
5. Describe four pieces of information that are included in a mutual fund's prospectus.

Apply Key Concepts

1. How do corporations protect bondholders from the possible negative effects of a bond's call feature?
2. Describe the similarities and differences among Treasury bills, notes, and bonds.
3. Explain how to measure a bond's yield.
4. Which stock funds would appeal to conservative or retired investors? Why?
5. Considering your own financial objectives, identify the elements in a mutual fund's prospectus that would be of the greatest importance to you.

 Problem Solving Today

THINKING AHEAD

You have 150 shares in a mutual fund and would like to find out how much money you would make if you sold them. The total value of your mutual fund's portfolio is $500 million. The fund also has liabilities totaling $24 million and 17 million shares outstanding.

Calculate Use the formula for calculating net asset value to determine how much one share in your mutual fund is worth. Then determine how much money you will make by selling all of your shares.

Computer Activity As an alternative activity, use financial software to calculate how much money you will make.

Real-World Application

CONNECT WITH ECONOMICS

You have $3,000 to invest and plan to buy a bond and shares of a mutual fund. Using a newspaper or the Internet, choose a bond and a mutual fund that you believe will perform well. Note today's actual market price for both on a sheet of paper. Every day for two weeks, check the prices.

Analyze At the end of the two weeks, analyze the performance of your investments. Which one performed better? How much did the bond and mutual fund gain or lose in value from the beginning of the two weeks?

FINANCE *Online*

THE MAZE OF MUTUAL FUNDS

Suppose you are ready to invest in mutual funds. Before you take the next step, conduct research on the topic.

Connect Use a variety of search engines to answer the following questions:
1. What risks must you accept if you invest in mutual funds?
2. How many mutual funds should you invest in?
3. Choose a fund group, such as stock mutual funds or bond mutual funds. Find out more about the differences among funds in that group.

CHAPTER 11

Real Estate and Other Investment Alternatives

STANDARD &POOR'S

Q&A

Q: I collect Beanie Babies and have more than a hundred different ones. Some are very valuable. Do you think I've made a smart investment for my retirement?

A: Collectibles are not a mainstay of retirement planning. The Beanie Babies fad has already peaked, and in 20 years you may find that your collection is worth about what it is now or even less. You should focus your retirement planning efforts on building a diversified portfolio that may include stock and bond investments. The values of these investments are easy to track, and they are readily bought and sold. Collectibles may play a small part in that portfolio, but their returns are very unpredictable.

Investing in Real Estate

*B*uried in the back of Roberto's closet is a big box full of childhood memories. Beanie Babies and Star Wars action figures sit tumbled together with NBA trading cards and a baseball signed by Sammy Sosa. As Roberto grew older, his interests changed. Now he's 17 years old and his bedroom is littered with CDs, inline skates, hockey sticks, and posters from his favorite movies. Roberto hasn't thought about that box in the closet for years. Maybe he should.

Beanie Babies, trading cards, Star Wars action figures, and sports memorabilia are all collectibles. Collectibles can be any objects that people find interesting and desirable, such as dolls, postage stamps, pottery, or Civil War battlefield souvenirs. The rarest or most important of these collectibles can be worth quite a bit of money. In 2000 an online exchange that bought and sold Beanie Babies offered to buy a certain one for nearly $4,000! Roberto's box of childhood playthings just might contain a treasure or two.

Of course, investing in collectibles can be risky, and it's not a wise way to prepare for your financial future. What you want is a sensible investment plan—one that is diversified. That means that the plan includes solid, sound investments along with some riskier ones. Traditionally, one of the most reliable investments has been real estate.

Real Estate Investments

Real estate has always been a favorite investment for Americans. Unlike stocks and bonds, a piece of property is something you can see and touch and take pride in. However, if you are new to the real estate market, you may be confused by all the different choices you have.

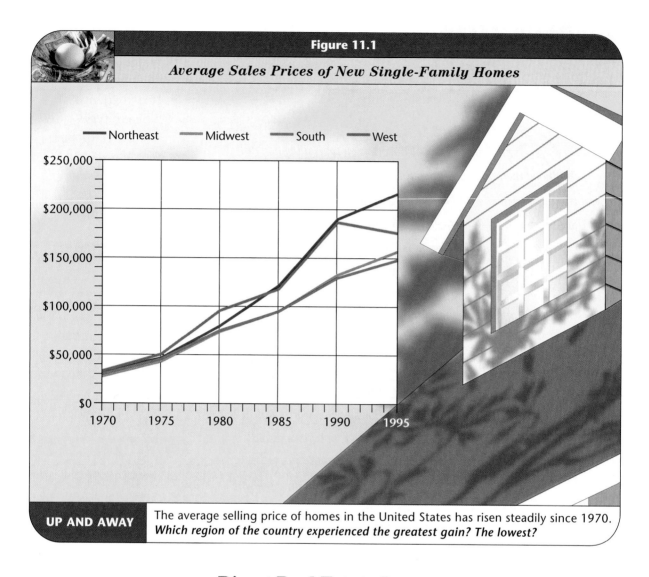

Figure 11.1

Average Sales Prices of New Single-Family Homes

— Northeast — Midwest — South — West

UP AND AWAY The average selling price of homes in the United States has risen steadily since 1970. *Which region of the country experienced the greatest gain? The lowest?*

Direct Real Estate Investments

Real estate investments can be direct or indirect. The owner of a *direct investment* holds legal title to the property he or she has purchased. Direct investments include single-family houses, duplexes, apartments, land, and commercial property.

YOUR HOME AS AN INVESTMENT What is your home? Most obviously, it's the place where you and your family live. However, owning a home can also be a good investment.

According to the Federal National Mortgage Association, at the end of the 1900s Americans had about $9.4 trillion invested in single-family houses. Homeowners' equity, the value of a home less the amount still owed on the money borrowed to purchase it, totaled about $6.5 trillion. That's about $650 billion more than Americans owned in stocks, bonds, and mutual funds combined.

PREDICT

Why is investing in real estate so popular with Americans?

As discussed in Chapter 8, during periods of inflation, the purchasing power of your money declines. Investing your money can help you stay ahead of inflation. Owning a home is a good investment because, generally, home prices have risen steadily over the years, as shown in **Figure 11.1**. In fact, during the past 150 years, owning a home produced an average rate of return after inflation of about 2.5 percent. That's about the same rate of return you would expect from a bond.

If you own your home, you probably have a mortgage. This gives you tax benefits. You can report the interest charges on your mortgage payments as well as your property taxes as a deduction on your income tax return.

YOUR VACATION HOME　Kevin's family owns a vacation home on Fox Lake. It's a good investment because the family uses it year-round and never rents it out to others. According to the federal government, that qualifies it as a second home. Therefore, Kevin's parents can take advantage of tax deductions. If the family rented the home for more than 14 days each year, the government would consider it a rental property. Any tax deductions would depend on whether Kevin's family actively managed the property and on the size of his parents' income.

INVESTMENT IN LEISURE　A vacation home like this can be part of a sensible investment strategy. *Why are vacation homes smart investments?*

COMMERCIAL PROPERTY   In addition to the vacation home on the lake, Kevin's parents also own commercial property. *Commercial property* is land and buildings that produce lease, or rental, income. Kevin's parents own an apartment building that adds to their income. Other examples of commercial property include duplexes, hotels, office buildings, and stores. Besides a home, the real estate investment that most small investors favor is a duplex, fourplex, or small apartment building. Many investors start by purchasing a small commercial property. Then they buy larger properties as the equity in their original investment increases.

LAND   In 1986 Kevin's parents received quite a shock. The U.S. tax laws were rewritten so that many popular real estate investments,

What's Your Financial ID?

ALL THAT GLITTERS

Whether you buy precious stones and metals as an investment, a gift, or for yourself, you have the edge when you know what you're buying. Here's a chance to test your knowledge. Write your answers on a separate sheet of paper.

1. Precious stones generally have more commercial value than semiprecious stones. Some precious stones are (choose all that apply)

_____ garnet

_____ diamond

_____ turquoise

_____ pearl

_____ ruby

_____ sapphire

_____ black onyx

_____ amethyst

_____ opal

_____ topaz

_____ emerald

2. Rank these precious metals from 1 (most valuable per ounce) to 4 (least valuable).

_____ silver

_____ gold

_____ platinum

_____ copper

3. The word "brilliant" describes a diamond's _____.

a. color

b. cut

c. clarity

4. When it comes to diamonds, the word "flawless" refers to _____.

a. cut

b. color

c. clarity

5. All diamonds have a cubic crystal structure and are made primarily of _____.

a. boron

b. carbon

c. nitrogen

such as apartment buildings, lost some of their tax advantages. Owning commercial property became less appeal-ing to some real estate investors. Many of these investors, like Kevin's parents, turned to land that was ready to be developed.

Kevin's parents talked to an investment banker before they purchased any land. She told them that while land investments often promise tremendous gains, they also pose enormous risks. If construction in general slowed or business activity declined, Kevin's parents might not be able to sell their property at a profit. Even worse, they might not be able to get the price that they had paid for it. Furthermore, the banker reminded them that unlike an apartment building, land usually does not produce any income.

The banker also cautioned Kevin's parents about buying land and then dividing it into smaller lots to build single-family houses. They must be certain, she told them, that water, sewers, and other utilities would be available. Otherwise, they as the property owners would have to supply these services. The most common and least expensive way to obtain water and sewer service is to connect with existing services in a nearby city or town.

$AVVY SAVER

Wedding Bells with Smaller Bills

1. Use a friend or relative's home or garden for your ceremony and reception.
2. Design your own invitations and print them on prepackaged stationery.
3. Offer a simple buffet instead of a sit-down dinner.
4. Limit the number of guests to what you can afford.
5. Enlist your friends to arrange flowers, take photographs, and so on.

Indirect Real Estate Investments

Suppose that you want to invest in real estate, but you just don't have enough money to purchase property on your own. The answer may be an indirect real estate investment. An *indirect investment* is one in which a person known as a trustee is appointed to hold legal title to the property on behalf of an investor or group of investors. Indirect investments include real estate syndicates, real estate investment trusts, high-risk mortgages, and participation certificates.

REAL ESTATE SYNDICATES OR LIMITED PARTNER-SHIPS A *syndicate* is a temporary association of individuals or business firms organized to perform a task that requires a large amount of funds. A real estate syndicate invests in real estate. A syndicate may be organized as a corporation or as a trust. Most commonly, however, a syndicate is organized as a limited partnership.

Here's how a limited partnership works: A general partner, who takes complete responsibility for all of the partnership's liabilities, forms the partnership. The general partner then sells participation units, or shares, to a number of limited partners, or investors. Suppose that you decide to join the syndicate. As a limited partner, you're

CASE STUDY

*R*ita and Tom Jordan have been married for three years. They enjoy researching stocks and other investments and have put together quite an impressive portfolio. Rita's Uncle Vic got them interested in the stock market by giving them ten shares of stock. Currently, they own seven different stocks, two mutual funds, and several corporate bonds. Uncle Vic is trying to convince Rita and Tom that real estate should be their next investment. Rita and Tom thought Uncle Vic was suggesting they purchase their first home. However, he was actually recommending real estate investment trusts (REITs). All Rita knows about REITs is that they are now considered a mainstream investment that would diversify their portfolio. Rita and Tom are not sure if REITs should be their next investment. They turned to the experts at Standard & Poor's for advice.

Analysis: A REIT invests in a group of managed properties, such as office buildings, apartments, and warehouses. Shares of stock issued by a REIT are traded on stock exchanges. Over the long term REITs have posted average returns compared to other types of stocks. Because real estate prices often rise with inflation, REITs can increase in price when prices of other stocks are falling. REITs also can provide tax advantages, as some of their dividends are considered a return of money invested and are not taxed. REITs can help make a stock portfolio less risky.

Recommendation: REITs often hold a single type of real estate or buy properties in one region of the country. Tom and Rita should consider a REIT mutual fund that invests in many different real estate stocks. If they want to choose their own investments, they should invest in at least three to five REITs, to avoid having too narrow a focus. Rita and Tom might consider investing 5 to 10 percent of their total portfolio in REITs. For more information about REITs, Rita and Tom can contact the National Association of Real Estate Investment Trusts, which tracks performances of REITs and provides information on the industry. Things to consider in purchasing REITs include yield, the amount of debt, and management expertise. Unusually high yields and debt may mean there's not enough money being invested for future growth.

Critical Thinking Questions

1. How is an investment in a REIT different from buying a house?
2. What factors might affect the performance of a REIT?
3. What other types of investments might Tom and Rita consider to diversify their portfolio?

liable for only the amount of money you have invested, perhaps $5,000 or $10,000. This limited liability is an important condition of a real estate syndicate because the syndicate's mortgage debt may be more than your personal net worth or that of the other limited partners.

A real estate syndicate offers you and the other partners a variety of benefits. For example, if the syndicate purchases several types of property, your investment will be diversified. That is, you will be part owner of different types of property. In addition, the property owned by the syndicate is professionally managed. You don't need to care for it yourself.

At one time, people joined real estate syndicates to create a tax shelter, a legal way to take advantage of income tax deductions. However, the Tax Reform Act of 1986 limits the tax advantages available to syndicate investors. For example, you can no longer use losses from your syndicate investments to offset, or reduce, your income from other sources. The 1986 law limits deductions for interest and for depreciation, or the loss of property value. It also raised the tax on capital gains.

REAL ESTATE INVESTMENT TRUSTS (REITs) Another real estate investment choice is a real estate investment trust (REIT). A REIT works much like a mutual fund. Like mutual funds, REITs combine money from many investors. However, while mutual funds invest in stocks, bonds, and other securities, REITs invest the participants' money in real estate or in construction or mortgage loans. Shares in REITs are traded on stock exchanges or the over-the-counter market.

If a REIT seems like your kind of investment, you should know that there are three types. If you choose an equity REIT, your money will be invested in properties. Choosing a mortgage REIT will put your money to work financing construction loans and mortgages on developed properties. If you want to combine the investment goals of equity and mortgage REITs, you can choose a hybrid REIT.

PART OF SOMETHING BIG Giant corporate complexes can cost millions of dollars to build and maintain. *Do you need to be extremely wealthy to invest in enormous commercial properties like the one shown here? Why?*

According to federal government regulations, REITs are required to:

- distribute at least 95 percent of their net annual earnings to shareholders;
- avoid investing in risky, short-term real estate holdings in the hope of selling them for quick profits;
- hire independent real estate professionals to carry out certain management activities;
- have at least 100 shareholders, with no more than half the shares owned by five or fewer people.

If you're interested in finding out more about REITs, you can write to the National Association of Real Estate Investment Trusts, 1129 20th Street NW, Washington, DC 20036.

HIGH-RISK MORTGAGES   Mr. Moy is a wealthy investor who purchases mortgages and other debt contracts. Because of his wealth, Mr. Moy is willing to take risks that financial institutions, such as banks and savings and loan associations, will not. For example, Mr. Moy might purchase the mortgage on a property that is not in demand. Perhaps the title to the property is not legally clear or insurable. Because of these risks, Mr. Moy and other investors like him might receive a high rate of return on their investments.

PARTICIPATION CERTIFICATES   Unlike Mr. Moy, not all investors can afford to take such risks with their money. If you're looking for a risk-free real estate investment, then participation certificates (PCs) might be your choice. A *participation certificate* is an investment in a group of mortgages that have been purchased by a government agency. You can buy participation certificates from any of these federal agencies:

- Government National Mortgage Association (Ginnie Mae)
- Federal Home Loan Mortgage Corporation (Freddie Mac)
- Federal National Mortgage Association (Fannie Mae)
- Student Loan Marketing Association (Sallie Mae)

A few states also issue participation certificates. You can purchase PCs from the State of New York Mortgage Agency (Sonny Mae) and the New England Education Loan Marketing Corporation (Nellie Mae).

Maes and Macs are guaranteed by agencies with close ties to the federal government, making these PCs as secure as U.S. Treasury bonds and notes. At one time an investor needed a minimum of $25,000 to invest in PCs. However, with the introduction of Maes and Macs mutual funds, you now need as little as $1,000 to buy shares in these securities. Each month, as payments are made on the mortgages, you receive a check for the principal and interest. If you wish, the mutual fund will reinvest these profits for you.

Advantages of Real Estate Investments

Before you invest in real estate, you'll want to weigh the advantages and disadvantages. Following are some of the advantages enjoyed by certain types of real estate investments.

HEDGE AGAINST INFLATION When inflation rises, your purchasing power decreases. That's why it's wise to make investments that provide some protection against inflation, such as real estate. Historically, real estate often continues to increase in value or at least hold its value, thus protecting investors from declining purchasing power.

EASY ENTRY Real estate syndicates make it easy to become a part owner of an apartment building or a shopping center. By combining your money with that of other investors, you can purchase property that you might never be able to afford on your own.

LIMITED FINANCIAL LIABILITY As a limited partner in a real estate syndicate, you are not liable for losses beyond your original investment. This advantage is important if the syndicate is investing in a risky venture, from which returns are not guaranteed.

Careers in Finance

COMMERCIAL PROPERTY MANAGER

Your local mall, downtown high-rises, and the office building where your parents might work all experience plumbing problems, burglaries, broken windows, and complaints from tenants. Usually the owners of these large commercial properties don't have time to manage them, so they hire commercial property managers to troubleshoot and look after the property. Property managers hire employees, such as janitors and gardeners, and arrange for services like security and trash removal. They're also responsible for paying the mortgages, taxes, insurance premiums, and payroll on time. When a basement floods or a heating system fails, they make sure the repairs are done quickly. Different problems may arise every day, which makes this job challenging.

Skills	Accounting, communication, decision making, management, math, organizational, problem solving, time management
Personality	Discreet, good judgment, likes working with people and numbers, tactful
Education	Suggested bachelor's or master's degree in business administration, finance, administration, or related fields
Pay range	$25,000 to $60,000 a year, depending on experience and size of property managed

Write a classified ad Pretend that you own a high-rise apartment building and need to find someone to manage your property. Write a classified ad describing the ideal person for the job.

 For more information on commercial property managers visit finance.glencoe.com **or your local library.**

FINANCIAL LEVERAGE *Financial leverage* is the use of borrowed funds for investment purposes. By using borrowed money, you can purchase more expensive property than you could on your own. If property values and incomes are rising, investing with borrowed money can be a real advantage.

Suppose that Deborah buys a building for $100,000 with no borrowed funds. She then sells the building for $120,000. Deborah's $20,000 profit represents a 20 percent return on her $100,000 investment ($20,000 ÷ $100,000 = 0.20 = 20%). On the other hand, suppose that Deborah invested just $10,000 of her own money and had a $90,000 mortgage with an interest rate of 8.5 percent. If after three years she sold the property for $120,000, her profit would be $7,721 ($20,000 profit − $12,279 in interest = $7,721). Her profit would represent a 77 percent return on her $10,000 investment ($7,721 ÷ $10,000 = 0.7721 = 77.21%).

Disadvantages of Real Estate Investments

Unfortunately, Deborah can't be certain that her real estate investment will pay off. Some real estate investments come with several disadvantages.

ILLIQUIDITY Real estate is an illiquid investment, which means that it cannot be easily converted into cash without a loss in value. It may take months or even years to sell commercial property or shares in a limited partnership.

DECLINING PROPERTY VALUES As discussed earlier, real estate investments usually offer some protection against inflation. However, when interest rates fall, or if the economy is in a decline, the value of your real estate investments may decrease. You may have to make the difficult decision to sell your property for less than you paid for it and accept a loss.

LACK OF DIVERSIFICATION Because real estate is expensive, you may be able to afford only one or two properties. That's going to make it difficult for you to build a diversified real estate investment portfolio. Keep in mind, however, that REITs, Ginnie Maes, Freddie Macs, and syndicates do offer various levels of diversification.

LACK OF A TAX SHELTER Real estate syndicates were once tax shelters for investors. However, the Tax Reform Act of 1986 eliminated that advantage. As a syndicate investor, you can no longer deduct your real estate losses from the income you generate through wages, dividends, and interest.

MANAGEMENT PROBLEMS When you invest in REITs, syndicates, or participation certificates, property management is provided as a part of your investment. When you invest in mortgages, property management isn't even an issue. However, when you buy your own properties, you have the responsibility to manage them. That means that you have to find reliable tenants, replace worn carpeting, and fix the furnace when it breaks down in the middle of the night. Property management can be a full-time job, and many investors are not willing to take on that much responsibility.

SECTION 11.1 ASSESSMENT

CHECK YOUR UNDERSTANDING

1. Name several examples of direct and indirect real estate investments.
2. What are the advantages of indirect real estate investments?
3. What are the disadvantages of direct and indirect real estate investments?

THINK CRITICALLY

4. Identify the similarities and differences among REITs, limited partnerships, and participation certificates.

USING COMMUNICATION SKILLS

5. **Selling Participation Certificates** Participation certificates are considered risk-free investments. How would you interest potential investors in these certificates?
   Create an Advertisement Write a persuasive ad that points out the types and advantages of participation certificates. Be sure to include information that highlights the risk-free nature of these investments.

SOLVING MONEY PROBLEMS

6. **Diversification** Teresa has been working as an advertising copywriter for five years. For the first time in her life, she feels that she is earning enough money to begin investing some of it. She has saved $10,000 and is interested in real estate. Teresa wants to make sure that her real estate investments will be diversified, not too risky, and easy for her to manage.
   Explain Give Teresa some advice about the types of real estate that would best meet her investment goals.

Investing in Precious Metals, Gems, and Collectibles

Gold

Precious metals include such valuable ores as gold, platinum, and silver. Many people invest their money in precious metals as a hedge against inflation.

When Mark graduated from high school, his grandfather gave him a gold pocket watch. Ever since, Mark has been fascinated by gold and has wanted to own more of it. If you are interested in purchasing gold, you have several choices, as shown in **Figure 11.2**.

The price of gold rises when people believe that war, political unrest, or inflation may be just around the corner. As international tensions ease or the political situation stabilizes, the price of gold falls. In August 2000 the price of gold was about $277 an ounce. **Figure 11.3** on page 364 shows how the price of gold rose and fell from 1976 to 2000.

Silver, Platinum, Palladium, and Rhodium

Other precious metals that rise in value during times of political or economic trouble are silver, platinum, palladium, and rhodium. Silver prices have ranged from an historic low of 24.25 cents an ounce in 1932 to more than $50 an ounce in early 1980. In August 2000 the price of silver was about $5 an ounce.

Platinum, palladium, and rhodium, three lesser-known precious metals, are also popular investments. All have industrial uses, particularly in automobile production. In August 2000 platinum sold for about $560 an ounce, palladium for about $880 an ounce, and rhodium for about $2,350 an ounce.

Storing precious metals can be tricky. Twenty thousand dollars' worth of gold, for example, is about the size of a thick paperback

1 BULLION You can purchase gold bullion, offered in bars and wafers, from dealers of precious metals and from banks. The seller's commission can range from 1 to 8 percent. If you do not store the gold with the dealer, you must have it reassayed (tested for quality) before you can resell it.

FIGURE 11.2

Investing in Gold

When the economy weakens or political unrest plagues the globe, some people believe that gold is the safest investment they can make. Investments in gold can take many forms.

2 COINS Gold coins represent a simple way to invest in this precious metal. Most coin dealers require a minimum order of ten coins and will charge you a seller's commission of at least 2 percent.

3 STOCKS You can diversify your investment portfolio by purchasing common stock in gold mining companies. When the economy is healthy, the price of gold stocks tends to fall while the value of other investments rises. When the economy falters so that traditional investments lose value, gold stocks tend to rise in value.

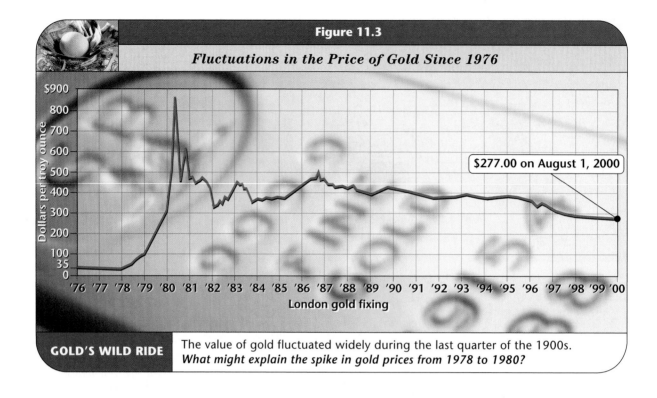

Figure 11.3

Fluctuations in the Price of Gold Since 1976

$277.00 on August 1, 2000

London gold fixing

GOLD'S WILD RIDE The value of gold fluctuated widely during the last quarter of the 1900s. *What might explain the spike in gold prices from 1978 to 1980?*

book. That same amount in silver weighs more than 200 pounds and could require several safe-deposit boxes for storage space.

Finally, remember that while stocks, bonds, and other interest-bearing investments are earning money for you, precious metals sit in vaults, earning nothing. In order to make a profit when you sell your precious metals, you must correctly predict the behavior of the market and sell the metals when their value is higher than you paid for them.

Precious Gems

RESPOND

Explain why you might want to purchase precious metals, even though they don't earn money like stocks and bonds.

When Queen Elizabeth opens the British Parliament, she wears a crown and carries a scepter; both are covered with diamonds, rubies, sapphires, and other glittering gems. As soon as the ceremony is over, those royal ornaments are quickly locked up again in the Jewel House at the Tower of London.

Throughout history people have prized the precious gems that lie embedded in rock below the earth's surface. *Precious gems* are rough mineral deposits (usually crystals) that are dug from the earth by miners and then cut and shaped into brilliant jewels. These gems include diamonds, sapphires, rubies, and emeralds. They appeal to investors because of their small size, ease of storage, great durability,

CROWN JEWELS   Throughout history, precious gems have been associated with royalty. *Why do you think diamonds, rubies, and other precious stones fascinate people?*

academic Connection

SCIENCE

For centuries, precious metals and stones have fascinated people around the world. Billions of dollars change hands every year as valuable metals and stones are bought and sold. Gold, silver, diamonds, rubies, and emeralds are just some that appeal to investors. Choose a precious metal or stone and find out:

- where it is found,
- how it is formed,
- its physical characteristics,
- what makes it valuable.

and their potential as protection against inflation. The inflation that occurred in the United States during the 1970s prompted investors to put more of their money into tangible assets such as gemstones. The result was a 40-fold increase in the price of diamonds. A few lucky investors made fortunes.

Whether you are buying precious gems to store in a safe-deposit box or to wear as jewelry, you'll want to keep in mind the risks associated with this type of investment. First, you cannot easily convert diamonds and other precious gems into cash. Also, as a beginning investor, you may have difficulty determining whether the gems you are purchasing are of high quality. Political unrest in gem-producing countries can affect supply and prices. Finally, you will likely have to buy your gems at higher retail prices and sell them at lower wholesale prices. The difference is usually 10 to 15 percent and sometimes as high as 50 percent.

The best way to know exactly what you are getting in an expensive precious gem is to have the stone certified by an independent geological laboratory, such as the Gemological Institute of America. The certificate should list the stone's characteristics, including its weight, color, clarity, and quality of cut. The grading of gems, however, is not an exact science. Experiments have shown that the same stone submitted twice to the same laboratory may get two different ratings.

Despite the attraction of precious metals and gems, the investment risks are sizable, and metals and gems can fluctuate greatly in value. In 1980 some investors bought gold for as much as $850 an ounce, platinum for $1,040 an ounce, silver at $48 an ounce, and a one-carat diamond for $62,000!

Collectibles

When you read about that box in Roberto's closet at the beginning of this chapter, you learned that collectibles are another type of investment. *Collectibles* include rare coins, works of art, antiques,

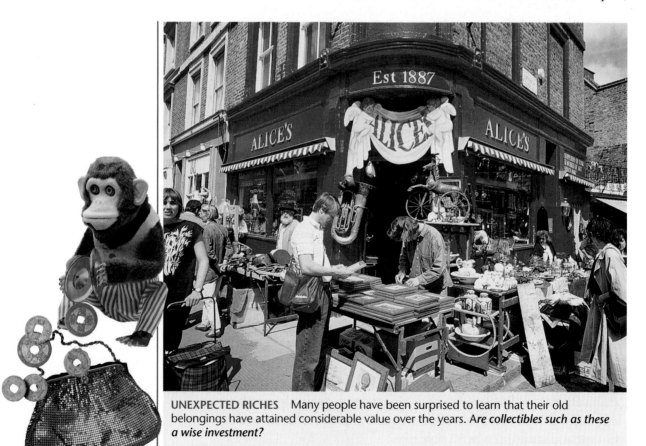

UNEXPECTED RICHES   Many people have been surprised to learn that their old belongings have attained considerable value over the years. *Are collectibles such as these a wise investment?*

stamps, rare books, comic books, sports memorabilia, rugs, ceramics, paintings, and other items that appeal to collectors and investors. Each of these items offers the knowledgeable collector or investor both pleasure and an opportunity for profit. Many collectors have been surprised to discover that items they bought for their own enjoyment had increased greatly in value while they owned them.

CONNECT

Take a mental inventory of your keepsakes and favorite possessions. Do you own any items that might be considered collectibles in the future?

Collectibles on the Internet

Before the era of the World Wide Web, finding items to add to your collections could be quite time consuming. You would have to

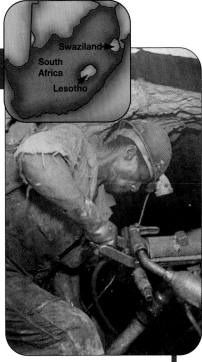

INTERNATIONAL FINANCE   South Africa

*W*e wear it around our necks, wrists, and fingers. It never tarnishes. Its chemical symbol Au comes from *aurum,* the Latin word for "shining dawn." What is it? Gold. South Africa produces 80 percent of the world's supply. South Africans, famous for their deep-mining skills, sometimes labor more than two and a half miles beneath the earth's surface. In an underground described as a cross between *Star Wars* and *Mad Max,* they excavate gold by the ton in nuggets, sheets, and microscopic particles. Here's a snapshot of South Africa.

Geographic area	471,445 sq. mi.
Population	42,579,000
Capital	Pretoria, administrative (pop. 525,000); Cape Town, legislative (2,350,000); Bloemfontein, judicial (126,900)
Language	Afrikaans, English, Ndebele, Pedi, Sotho, Swazi, Tsonga, Tswana, Venda, Xhosa, Zulu (all official)
Currency	rand
Gross domestic product (GDP)	$270 billion
Per capita GDP	$6,200
Economy	Industry: mining (platinum, gold, chromium), automobile assembly, metalworking. Agriculture: corn, wheat, sugarcane, fruits, vegetables, beef. Exports: gold, other minerals and metals, food, chemicals.

A miner in a South African gold mine

Thinking Critically

Compare In 1980 gold reached an all-time high of $850 per ounce. Check your newspaper's financial section under "Commodities" to see what an ounce of gold costs today. By what percentage has the price increased or decreased?

For more information on South Africa visit finance.glencoe.com or your local library.

pore over collectors' trade magazines to research the value of items you wished to buy. Then you would have to head out to shows, sometimes far away, where collectors met to buy and sell their merchandise.

Today that process has changed dramatically. The Internet has made buying and selling collectibles efficient and convenient, and the number of Web sites for collectors has exploded. In 1998, when Guernsey's Auction House offered Mark McGwire's 70th home run baseball to bidders, they opened the bidding process to online buyers as well. Although the baseball went to an anonymous telephone bidder for $3 million, the use of the Internet as an auction site was firmly established.

It's easy to see why the Internet has such appeal. As a buyer, you can search for items to add to your collection with a few keystrokes,

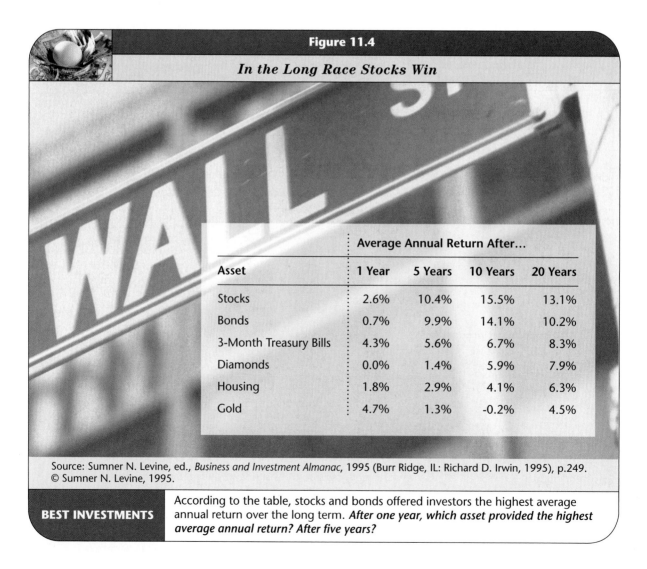

Figure 11.4

In the Long Race Stocks Win

Asset	Average Annual Return After...			
	1 Year	5 Years	10 Years	20 Years
Stocks	2.6%	10.4%	15.5%	13.1%
Bonds	0.7%	9.9%	14.1%	10.2%
3-Month Treasury Bills	4.3%	5.6%	6.7%	8.3%
Diamonds	0.0%	1.4%	5.9%	7.9%
Housing	1.8%	2.9%	4.1%	6.3%
Gold	4.7%	1.3%	-0.2%	4.5%

Source: Sumner N. Levine, ed., *Business and Investment Almanac*, 1995 (Burr Ridge, IL: Richard D. Irwin, 1995), p.249. © Sumner N. Levine, 1995.

BEST INVESTMENTS According to the table, stocks and bonds offered investors the highest average annual return over the long term. *After one year, which asset provided the highest average annual return? After five years?*

and sellers can reach people all around the world. Prices aren't necessarily low on the Internet. Still, comparison shopping is easier, and most sites don't charge a buyer's commission.

Of course, collecting on the Internet has its drawbacks. As an online buyer, you can't size up a dealer face-to-face or easily examine objects for flaws or trademarks. Furthermore, fraud is an ever-present danger.

Let the Collector Beware

Collecting—on or off the Internet—can be a satisfying hobby and a good investment. Nevertheless, a wise collector must always be alert for schemes and scams.

For example, how do you know that the fielder's glove you bought was actually signed by Mickey Mantle? Could your Civil War–era postage stamps be counterfeit? Is that Barbie doll, Lionel locomotive, or Darth Vader action figure really as rare and valuable as you've been told?

How about online auction and exchange sites? According to figures from Internet Fraud Watch, sponsored by the National Consumers League, 87 percent of the fraud complaints it received during the first five months of 1999 were related to online auctions. In the same year, Cyveillance, an online monitoring company, estimated that 10 to 20 percent of all items for sale online could be fakes.

The safest way to steer clear of collectibles-related fraud is to learn everything you can about the items you collect and to buy and sell only with reputable dealers and Web sites. Remember that as the popularity of collecting has increased, so has the number of cheats and con artists.

You should also remember that collectibles do not offer interest or dividends. What's more, you may have a hard time selling items in your collection at a good price on short notice. If your collection grows significantly in value, you will have to purchase insurance against damage and theft. As you can see in **Figure 11.4**, the in-

Collecting Treasures

Russell inherited three diamonds from his grandmother and needs to decide whether to keep them or sell them. He already had them evaluated for the "4 Cs"—clarity, color, cut, and carat weight—but not their actual dollar value. He took the diamonds and the evaluation papers to the Downtown Diamond Mart.

A sales representative at Diamond Exchange appraised them. The four-carat diamond was the most valuable because it was beautifully cut in a marquise shape, and it also had good clarity, meaning it had few microscopic bits of other elements embedded in it. Color also added to its value. It was close to the whitest end of the scale. The other two diamonds, a matched set of one-carat gems cut as round brilliants, were of a higher quality in clarity but more yellow. The appraiser told Russell that the three diamonds could be worth $5,000, but gem dealers would probably offer him about half that. He also told him the Diamond Exchange would not be interested in buying them.

Russell went to another store that had a sign, "We Buy Diamonds," but the most the store could offer was $2,350. He decided to keep the diamonds in a safe-deposit box. They had value to him because they had belonged to his grandmother. By keeping them he had the option of turning them into cash in the future, possibly selling them for more money. He also liked the idea of making them into jewelry someday. After researching his grandmother's diamonds, Russell is now interested in finding out more about other gems. One day he would like to start a gem collection.

Apply In your workbook or on a separate sheet of paper, list five things you might enjoy collecting that will keep their value or possibly be worth more in the future. Choose one and describe why it appeals to you. Describe how the experts could appraise its value, such as age, quality, rarity, and popular demand. Why would this collectible be interesting for you to keep? Do you think it would be a good or bad long-term investment? Explain why?

vestments that provide the best return, such as stocks and bonds, may not be the most interesting or exciting, but they have proven to be the most stable in the long run.

The best advice is to plan your investment portfolio wisely. Research the available investments so you can make an informed decision. Weigh the advantages and disadvantages of each type of investment. Ask yourself how much risk and responsibility you're willing to assume.

SECTION 11.2 ASSESSMENT

CHECK YOUR UNDERSTANDING

1. What are the risks of investing in precious metals?
2. Why do precious gems appeal to investors?
3. How has the Internet increased the risks of investing in collectibles?

THINK CRITICALLY

4. Describe two different scenarios: one that causes the price of diamonds to rise and one that causes the price to fall.

USING MATH SKILLS

5. **All That Glitters** In 1978 Raul bought 50 troy ounces of gold for $1,750 as protection against rising inflation. He sold half the gold in 1980 at a price of $300 an ounce. Raul sold the other half in 1982 when the price was $400 an ounce.
    Compute Calculate Raul's profit in 1980 and his profit in 1982. What would Raul's profit have been if he had sold all of his gold in 1980?

SOLVING MONEY PROBLEMS

6. **Evaluating an Inheritance** Samantha inherited a diamond-and-ruby necklace from her grandmother's estate. Unfortunately, the settings for the stones are damaged beyond repair. Samantha is trying to decide what to do with her inheritance.
    Recommend Create an evaluation strategy that will help Samantha determine the value of her inheritance and how she might increase that value.

CHAPTER 11 ASSESSMENT

CHAPTER SUMMARY

- You can invest directly in real estate by purchasing and holding legal title to houses, duplexes, apartments, land, or commercial property.

- Indirect real estate investments enable you to join with other investors in purchasing property and mortgage debt.

- The advantages of investing directly and indirectly in real estate include protection against inflation, easy entry into the market, limited financial liability, and financial leverage.

- The disadvantages of investing directly and indirectly in real estate include illiquidity, possible decline in property values, lack of diversification and tax shelters, and management problems.

- Precious metals, precious gems, and collectibles provide investors with opportunities for profit, but the investment risks are sizable.

Understanding and Using Vocabulary

The following key terms will help you remember important information about investing in real estate, precious metals and gems, and collectibles. Write a summary of Chapter 11 in which you use and explain the meaning of each of these terms.

direct investment
commercial property
indirect investment
syndicate
participation certificate

financial leverage
precious metals
precious gems
collectibles

Review Key Concepts

1. What are the differences between direct and indirect real estate investments?

2. How do real estate investments protect you from inflation?

3. What is the least risky real estate investment and why?

4. What are the disadvantages of investing in precious metals and gems?

5. What impact has the Internet had on the business of investing in collectibles?

Apply Key Concepts

1. Identify the advantages of investing in a limited partnership. Explain why limited partnerships might appeal to beginning investors.

2. Predict what would happen to $10,000 placed in a savings account and a $10,000 investment in a home during a period of rapidly rising inflation. Select the wiser investment, and explain your choice.

CHAPTER 11 ASSESSMENT

3. Explain why investors with limited funds are drawn to participation certificates.
4. Predict what would happen to investments in precious metals and gems if the economy were strong. How would the results differ if the economy suffered a decline?
5. Explain how one could use the Internet to enhance the size and value of a collection.

 ## Problem Solving Today

INVESTMENT ALTERNATIVES

Suppose that you have $5,000 to invest. You want to create a portfolio that includes real estate, precious metals or gems, and collectibles. From a newspaper, get current prices for these different investments. Then create an investment plan that uses your $5,000. Keep in mind the amount of risk you're willing to take for the financial gains you expect. Using the Internet or a newspaper, track your gains and losses over a period of two weeks.

 **Computer Activity** As an alternative activity, use a spreadsheet program to set up your investment plan and to track your gains and losses.

▌ Real-World Application

CONNECT WITH LANGUAGE ARTS

Real estate brokers, coin dealers, jewelers, and collectors in your community have the experience to offer advice about the investment potential of their specialties. You can take advantage of these resources to become a wiser investor.

Conduct Interviews Talk to the experts of your choice in your community. What can the experts at the trading card outlet tell you about the history of trading card prices? Can a local realtor provide examples of real estate investments that have returned healthy profits? Once you've selected an expert to interview, plan your questions carefully. After the interview, write a brief report summarizing what you have learned, and share it with the class.

FINANCE Online

SURFING FOR REAL ESTATE

If you type the words "real estate investments" into any popular Internet search engine, you'll probably receive a list of hundreds of sites. You may find opportunities to buy a timber plantation in New Zealand, a trailer park in Idaho, or a black-pearl farm in Tahiti. If you're looking for something a bit more conservative, you may want to research REITs.

Connect Using different Internet search engines, look for information on REITs. Answer the following:

1. How do different REITs distinguish themselves from their competitors?
2. What types of specialties do you see among the REITs?
3. In your search, did you encounter an offer for a REIT or other real estate investment that seemed very risky? What made it seem risky? How could you research the offer to better assess its value?

Get a Financial Life!

CASE STUDY

Investment Strategies

Overview

Karla and David are about to celebrate their 35th birthdays. Karla recently accepted a new position as the vice president of an Internet company. David is now an assistant principal. Through the years, Karla and David have saved money in traditional savings accounts and certificates of deposit. In addition, Karla has invested money in a 401(k). Because David has been working for the public school system, he has been investing in a 403(b). Besides saving for retirement, Karla and David realize that they will have to accumulate enough money to put their children, Eva and Jack, through college. Therefore, they would like to expand their investment strategies.

Resources

- Career development book
- Crayons, markers, colored pencils
- Internet (optional)
- Multimedia tools (videos, music, and so on)
- Portfolio (ring binder or file folder)
- Poster board
- Presentation software (optional)
- Public or school library
- Word processor

Procedures

Step A THE PROCESS

Imagine that you are a financial planner. Karla and David have hired you to help them make investment decisions for their future. They have $25,000 in savings that they want to invest in stocks, bonds, mutual funds, and/or real estate.

1. Prepare a mock résumé for yourself as a financial planner. Showcase your experiences and qualifications so that Karla and David will feel confident that they have hired an expert.

2. Recommend appropriate investment options for Karla and David. To ensure a diverse portfolio, you must make at least three different recommendations.

3. Using the various sources of investment information (the financial section of a newspaper, business magazines, the Internet, investor services, and corporate reports), collect articles and other relevant information about the investment options that you will recommend. Your research should demonstrate to Karla and David that your recommendations are sensible.

4. Contact a financial planner, investment counselor, banker, or accountant. Arrange for a time when you can discuss the investment decisions you have made for Karla and David. Prepare a report of your conversation.

Step B **CREATE YOUR PORTFOLIO**

As you work through the process, save the results so that you can refer, review, and refine. Create a professional-looking portfolio of investment recommendations that you will present to Karla and David.

1. The first page should be a title page, with the following information centered:
   Investment Options
   Presented to Karla and David Farnier
   By (Your Name)
2. Next, include the résumé that you prepared.
3. Prepare a section in the portfolio for each investment option that you recommend. Include the recommendation and the research that supports your suggestion.
4. In the last section, include the report of the conversation you had with the financial expert you interviewed in Step A (4) on the previous page.

Step C **TEAMWORK**

Teamwork is a major focus of today's workplace. Many companies are replacing the traditional management structure with self-managed work teams. Team members must be able to accept more responsibility, communicate effectively, and get along well with others. Teamwork is not always easy. A group of people with different backgrounds, personalities, expertise, and abilities must work together for a common goal. Teamwork takes time and practice in order to achieve success.

Create a team of at least four classmates. As a team, you'll prepare a 15-minute seminar and present it to other members of your class or to other classes in the school. Organize your team in order to accomplish the following tasks in the best and most efficient way possible.

1. Choose one topic from Chapters 8–11 for your seminar.
2. Prepare an oral presentation, using presentation software, multimedia tools, posters, or other visuals.
3. Draft a written outline of the presentation.
4. Create handouts for the audience.
5. Prepare a pretest and posttest for the audience. After you have administered the tests, compile the results in graph form.
6. Present the seminar to other members of your class or to other classes in the school.

$\mathscr{P}$ROTECTING YOUR FINANCES

Unit 4 provides basic information about ways to protect your financial resources. The next four chapters will discuss the importance of taxes for personal financial planning; home and automobile insurance; health, disability, and life insurance; and retirement and estate planning.

READING STRATEGIES

To get the most out of your reading

- ▨ **PREDICT** what the section will be about.
- ▨ **CONNECT** what you read with your own life.
- ▨ **QUESTION** as you read to make sure you understand the content.
- ▨ **RESPOND** to what you've read.

START TODAY

Planning for the Future

During the next 50 years or so you will be earning, spending, and hopefully saving money. It's crucial that you have enough resources to live on after you retire. What can you start doing today that will protect your finances in the future?

Planning Your Tax Strategy

STANDARD &POOR'S

Q&A

Q: Isn't it a little risky to file my tax return electronically?

A: The Internal Revenue Service offers several options for electronic filers, including filing by telephone and over the Internet. If you are concerned about potential penalties that may apply if your tax return is not received by the IRS, you can protect yourself by using filing services that offer a receipt, such as a confirmation number or e-mail confirmation.

The Fundamentals of Income Taxes

*A*aron has been thinking about taxes lately, and not because he wants to. The fact is, Aaron feels bombarded by talk of taxes. His U.S. senator supports a reduction in federal income taxes. The legislature in Aaron's state recently voted to raise taxes on cigarettes and alcohol to support drug education programs. Property taxes in the school district where Aaron lives have been increased to pay for a new high school and to hire more teachers. The state has proposed a new gasoline tax to help finance the resurfacing of a major highway. As if all this talk about taxes weren't enough, Aaron just received his first paycheck from the bank where he works; to his surprise, more than 25 percent of his salary has been eaten up by taxes!

Taxes and Financial Planning

Like Aaron, you may be hearing more about taxes than you ever imagined. Actually, that's not a bad thing. Taxes are an important part of financial planning. The more you know, the better off you'll be.

Taxes and You

Taxes, as Aaron has discovered, are an everyday part of life. You probably pay taxes every time you get a paycheck, order a pizza, buy a new CD, or fill up your car with gas. In fact, the U.S. Bureau of the Census reports that about two out of three American households have no money left after paying taxes and normal living expenses. Each year the Tax Foundation, an independent public policy research group, determines how much of the year the average person works to pay taxes. In recent years, "Tax Freedom Day" came in early May. This means that from January 1 until early May, all the money you earn goes toward taxes!

What You'll Learn

- How to **describe** the importance of taxes in financial planning
- How to **identify** your taxable income
- How to **complete** a W-4 form

Why It's Important

The more you know about taxes, the better prepared you will be to create a financial plan that reduces the amount of taxes you'll owe.

KEY TERMS

- tax liability
- excise tax
- estate tax
- inheritance tax
- gift tax
- withhold
- income tax return
- earned income
- interest income
- dividend income
- exclusion
- adjusted gross income
- taxable income
- tax deduction
- standard deduction
- itemized deduction
- exemption
- tax credit
- allowance

As a citizen, you expect your local, state, and federal governments to provide important services. You want police and fire protection, public schools, road maintenance, parks, libraries, and safety inspection of foods, drugs, and other products. Such services are expensive, and taxes pay the bills.

What's Your Financial ID?

TEST YOUR TAX FACTS

The more you know about the way tax laws relate to your personal finances, the easier it is to file your taxes. To test your knowledge of tax strategy, write the answer to these questions on a separate sheet of paper.

1. The tax-reporting requirement for cash tips is _____.
   a. you need to report tips and pay taxes on them
   b. you don't need to report cash tips on your tax return
   c. your employer takes care of it

2. Besides saving your tax returns you need to keep all necessary paperwork and receipts for at least _____.
   a. 1 year
   b. 6 years
   c. 20 years

3. Tax-deferred income is _____.
   a. income that's not subject to tax
   b. income that has had all its fur removed
   c. income that will be taxed at a later date

4. Tax-exempt income is _____.
   a. income that's not subject to tax
   b. income that you invest
   c. income that will be taxed at a later date

5. You would use the standard deduction instead of itemizing your deductions when _____.
   a. itemized deductions are more than the standard deduction
   b. itemized deductions are less than the standard deduction
   c. line 32 on Schedule C exceeds the allowable limit of line 12 on Schedule E on Form 1040A

6. Estate tax is a _____.
   a. tax on capital gains from selling a house
   b. tax on money withdrawn from a retirement account
   c. tax on the value of a person's property at the time of death

7. The person responsible for the contents of your tax return is _____.
   a. your tax preparer
   b. your mom and dad
   c. you

8. If you itemize your deductions, you can deduct interest on _____.
   a. credit cards
   b. mortgages, home equity, and student loans
   c. car loans

If you would like to avoid becoming one of those people who has no money left after paying for taxes and living expenses, the key is effective tax planning. First, find out how the current tax laws and regulations affect you. Second, make an effort to maintain complete and accurate tax records. Finally, learn how to make decisions that can reduce your *tax liability*, or the total amount of taxes you owe. If you follow these strategies, you'll pay your fair share of taxes while taking advantage of various tax benefits.

YOUR TAX DOLLARS Highways are built and maintained with your taxes. *What else do your tax dollars pay for?*

Types of Taxes

Throughout your life, you're probably going to pay taxes in four major categories: purchases, property, wealth, and earnings.

TAXES ON PURCHASES   You probably pay sales tax on many of your purchases. These taxes are collected by state and local governments and are added to the prices of most products you buy. In order to reduce the economic burden of this tax on people with low incomes, many states don't charge sales tax on food and medicines.

A special type of sales tax, known as an *excise tax*, is a tax collected by federal and state governments on specific goods and services, such as gasoline, air travel, and telephone service.

TAXES ON PROPERTY   Real estate property taxes are major sources of income for local governments. These taxes are based on the value of land and buildings. As the value of any real estate you own goes up, the amount of property tax you must pay often rises as well. This can be especially burdensome for anyone living on a fixed income.

In some areas of the country, you will have to pay personal property taxes. State and local governments may assess taxes on the value of such property as automobiles, boats, furniture, and farm equipment.

TAXES ON WEALTH   You may not know it, but even the deceased pay taxes. When Mr. Mendoza died, the federal government taxed his property. An *estate tax* is tax collected on the value of a person's property at the time of his or her death.

Unfortunately, that was not the end of Mr. Mendoza's tax liability. He left all of his money and property to his wife and children, and the state in which the Mendoza family lives collects an inheritance tax. An *inheritance tax* is a tax collected on the property left by a person in his or her will. Before Mrs. Mendoza and her children can claim their inheritance, they'll have to pay the tax.

CONNECT

If you were to purchase a CD player for $100 from an electronics store near your home, how much sales tax would you pay?

Another federal tax on wealth is the gift tax. A *gift tax* is a tax collected on money or property valued at more than $10,000, given by one person to another in a single year. Gifts of any amount that are given to help a person pay educational or medical expenses are not subject to gift taxes. Some states also collect a gift tax on money that a person, shortly before his or her death, transfers to another person in order to avoid estate and inheritance taxes.

TAXES ON EARNINGS   The two main taxes on wages (payments received for each hour of work) and salaries (payments received weekly or monthly regardless of the number of hours worked) are Social Security and income taxes. Social Security taxes are collected to finance the retirement, disability, and life insurance benefits of the federal government's Social Security program. The personal income tax, which is the tax you pay on the income you receive, is the federal government's leading source of revenue (money). Some states and cities also collect personal income taxes. The Internal Revenue Service (IRS) is the federal agency that collects these taxes, or tax revenues.

Headquartered in Washington, D.C., the IRS is an agency of the Department of the Treasury. The two primary missions of the IRS are to collect federal income taxes and to enforce the nation's tax laws.

Taxes on earnings are collected on a pay-as-you-earn basis. Throughout the year, your employer must *withhold*, or take out, Social Security and income tax payments from your paycheck and send the money to the IRS. If you own your own business or have retired, you may be required to make estimated tax payments several times each year. However, both types of payments are only estimates. You will determine if you have paid too much or too little when you complete your federal income tax return.

The Terminology of Income Taxes

Every year millions of taxpayers prepare income tax returns and file their completed returns with the IRS. These taxpayers determine the amount of tax that they owe. Then they compare that amount to the estimated income tax payments their employers withheld from their paychecks during the year.

If the income tax they paid through their employers was greater than their tax liability (the total taxes that they owe), they will receive a refund (because they had more tax withheld than they needed to). However, if their tax liability is greater than the tax they paid, they will need to pay the difference to the U.S. Treasury (because they owe more taxes than they had withheld). An *income tax return* is a form on which you report how much money you received from working and other sources and the exact taxes, if any, that you owe. Calculating your income tax will be much easier if you are familiar with the terminology of taxation.

Determining Your Adjusted Gross Income

Most, but not all income, is subject to taxation. Your gross, or total income, will probably consist of three main components:

1. *Earned income* is the money you receive for working. It may include wages, salary, commissions, fees, tips, or bonuses.
2. *Interest income* is the interest that you receive from banks, credit unions, and savings and loan associations.

INTERNATIONAL FINANCE   France

Competitors in the Tour de France

*M*ost of us bicycle just for fun, but in France bicycling is serious business, at least each summer. Sponsored by giant industries and small businesses alike, more than a hundred cyclists from many nations gather for one of the world's most famous races: the Tour de France, a 2,500-mile race mostly through the French countryside. For 21 days competitors pedal at breakneck speeds from city to city—up mountains, down steep slopes, around sharp curves, through wind and rain. Remarkably, only four cyclists have died from falls since the race began in 1903. Crowds cheer along the route, and at the traditional finish line in Paris everyone celebrates. Here's a snapshot of France.

Geographic area	210,026 sq. mi.
Population	59,067,000
Capital	Paris (pop. 2,152,300)
Language	French
Currency	franc
Gross domestic product (GDP)	$1.32 trillion
Per capita GDP	$22,700
Economy	Industry: steel, machinery, chemicals, automobiles, metals. Agriculture: wheat, cereals, sugar beets, potatoes, wine grapes, beef, fish. Exports: machinery, transportation equipment, chemicals, foodstuffs.

Thinking Critically

Analyze The Tour de France, like the Olympics, attracts world attention. In what ways can this kind of recognition help boost the French economy?

 For more information on France visit finance.glencoe.com or your local library.

3. *Dividend income* includes the cash dividends that you receive from investments.

Your gross income can also be affected by exclusions. An *exclusion* is an amount of income that is not included in your gross income. Exclusions are also called tax-exempt income, or income that is not subject to taxes. For example, interest earned on most municipal bonds is exempt from federal income tax.

In contrast, tax-deferred income is income that will be taxed at a later date. The earnings on an individual retirement account (IRA) are tax-deferred income. Although these earnings are credited to your account now, you don't have to pay tax on this money until you withdraw it from the account.

Your *adjusted gross income* is your gross income after certain reductions have been made. These reductions, called adjustments to income, can include contributions to an IRA or student loan interest, for example. Calculating your adjusted gross income accurately is important because it is used as the basis for other tax calculations. (Note: If you have any adjustments to income, you cannot use Form 1040EZ.)

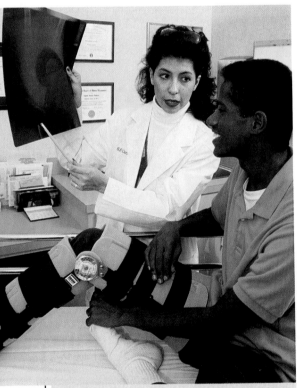

MEDICAL DEDUCTIONS Medical expenses are among the most common itemized deductions. **When would a medical expense qualify as an itemized deduction?**

Identifying Your Taxable Income

Once you've determined your adjusted gross income, you can figure out your taxable income. Your *taxable income* is your adjusted gross income less any allowable tax deductions and exemptions. Your taxable income is the amount on which your income tax is computed.

TAX DEDUCTIONS A *tax deduction* is an expense that you are allowed to subtract from your adjusted gross income to arrive at your taxable income. Every taxpayer receives at least the *standard deduction*, an amount set by the IRS on which no taxes are paid. In 1999 a single person's standard deduction was $4,300. A married couple filing a joint tax return could deduct $7,200. People over age 65 or people who are blind are entitled to higher standard deductions.

You may qualify for more than the standard deduction. An *itemized deduction* is a specific expense, such as mortgage interest, that you deduct from your adjusted gross income. You can either take the standard deduction or itemize your deductions, but you can't do both. You'll take the standard deduction if it's greater than your allowable itemized deductions.

The following are a few of the most common itemized deductions:

- Medical and dental expenses. These include doctors' fees, prescription medications, hospital expenses, medical insurance premiums, eyeglasses, hearing aids, and medical travel that has not been reimbursed or paid by others, such as a health insurance provider. The amount of this deduction is the medical and dental expenses that exceed 7.5 percent (as of 1999) of your adjusted gross income. Therefore, if your adjusted gross income is $10,000, you can deduct only the amount of nonreimbursed medical and dental expenses that exceeds $750.
- Taxes. You can deduct state and local income tax, real estate property tax, and state and local personal property tax from your adjusted gross income.
- Interest. You can deduct home mortgage interest and home equity loan interest.
- Contributions. You can deduct contributions of cash or property to qualified charities. If your contribution is more than 20 percent of your adjusted gross income, it will be subject to certain limitations.

You are required to keep records to document tax deductions. For more information about storing and organizing your personal financial records, review Chapter 3.

EXEMPTIONS   An *exemption* is a deduction from your adjusted gross income for yourself, your spouse, and qualified dependents. A dependent is someone you support financially, such as a child. To qualify as a dependent, a person must meet all of the following conditions:

- He or she must be under age 19 or a full-time student under age 24.
- He or she must live in his or her parent's house or be a relative of the adult or adults with whom he or she lives.
- More than half of his or her support must be provided by the individual or individuals who claim him or her on their tax return.
- He or she must meet certain citizenship requirements.

Calculating How Much You Owe

Once you know your taxable income, you can calculate how much income tax you owe.

TAX RATES   In 1999 the IRS recognized five tax rates: 15, 28, 31, 36, and 39.6 percent. The more income you have, the higher your tax rate, as shown in **Figure 12.1** on page 386.

TAX CREDITS   Your income tax may be reduced by a *tax credit*, an amount subtracted directly from the amount of taxes you

Figure 12.1

The Five-Rate System for Federal Income Tax

Rate on Taxable Income	Single Taxpayers	Married Taxpayers	Heads of Household
15%	Up to $25,750	Up to $43,050	Up to $34,550
28%	$25,750–$62,450	$43,050–$104,050	$34,550–$89,150
31%	$62,450–$130,250	$104,050–$158,550	$89,150–$144,400
36%	$130,250–$283,150	$158,550–$283,150	$144,400–$283,150
39.6%	Over $283,150	Over $283,150	Over $283,150

RATES AND INCOME The tax rate you pay is based on the amount of your taxable income. *As a single person, what is the maximum amount of taxable income you can have and still be included in the 15 percent tax bracket?*

owe. A tax credit is different from a deduction. A tax credit, such as eligible child-care costs or other dependent expenses, results in a dollar-for-dollar reduction in the amount of taxes owed. Suppose that you owe $300 in taxes. If you have a $100 tax credit, you owe only $200 ($300 − $100 = $200). In contrast, a tax deduction is an expense that you are allowed to subtract from your adjusted gross income to arrive at your taxable income.

Low-income workers can benefit from the earned income credit (EIC). This federal tax credit is for certain people who work and whose taxable income is less than a certain amount. People who don't earn enough to owe federal income tax are also eligible for the EIC. When they file a return and attach a special form called Schedule EIC, they receive a check from the IRS in the amount of their tax credit.

Making Tax Payments

You can pay your income taxes to the federal government in two ways: through payroll withholding or estimated payments.

PAYROLL WITHHOLDING When James Irving began his job as an assistant to the manager of human resources, his employer asked him to complete a W-4 form, or the Employee's Withholding Allowance Certificate. This form tells your employer how much federal income tax to withhold from your paycheck. The amount your employer withholds depends on the number of allowances you claim. An *allowance* is an adjustment to the tax withheld from your paycheck, based on your marital status and whether you are supporting other people with your money.

To complete the W-4 form, follow these simple instructions:

1. Fill in your name and address.
2. Fill in your Social Security number.

RESPOND

Why is it important for you to keep accurate and organized tax records?

3. Indicate whether you are single or married by checking the appropriate box.
4. Check the box if your last name is different from the name shown on your Social Security card.
5. Write the number of allowances you are claiming. To figure out how many allowances you can claim, complete the Personal

---

Personal Allowances Worksheet (Keep for your records.)

A Enter "1" for **yourself** if no one else can claim you as a dependent . . . . **A** _1_

B Enter "1" if: { • You are single and have only one job; or
• You are married, have only one job, and your spouse does not work; or
• Your wages from a second job or your spouse s wages (or the total of both) are $1,000 or less. } . . **B** _1_

C Enter "1" for your **spouse**. But, you may choose to enter -0- if you are married and have either a working spouse or more than one job. (Entering -0- may help you avoid having too little tax withheld.) . . . . **C** _____

D Enter number of **dependents** (other than your spouse or yourself) you will claim on your tax return . . . . **D** _____

E Enter "1" if you will file as **head of household** on your tax return (see conditions under **Head of household** above) . . **E** _____

F Enter "1" if you have at least $1,500 of **child or dependent care expenses** for which you plan to claim a credit . . **F** _____

G **Child Tax Credit:**
• If your total income will be between $18,000 and $50,000 ($23,000 and $63,000 if married), enter "1" for each eligible child.
• If your total income will be between $50,000 and $80,000 ($63,000 and $115,000 if married), enter "1" if you have two eligible children, enter "2" if you have three or four eligible children, or enter "3" if you have five or more eligible children **G** _____

H Add lines A through G and enter total here. **Note:** This may be different from the number of exemptions you claim on your tax return. ▶ **H** _2_

For accuracy, complete all worksheets that apply. {
• If you plan to **itemize or claim adjustments to income** and want to reduce your withholding, see the **Deductions and Adjustments Worksheet** on page 2.
• If you are **single**, have **more than one job** and your combined earnings from all jobs exceed $34,000, OR if you are **married** and have a **working spouse or more than one job** and the combined earnings from all jobs exceed $60,000, see the **Two-Earner/Two-Job Worksheet** on page 2 to avoid having too little tax withheld.
• If **neither** of the above situations applies, **stop here** and enter the number from line H on line 5 of Form W-4 below.
}

- - - - - - - - - - - - - - - - - **Cut here and give Form W-4 to your employer. Keep the top part for your records.** - - - - - - - - - - - - - - -

Form **W-4**
Department of the Treasury
Internal Revenue Service

Employee's Withholding Allowance Certificate

▶ **For Privacy Act and Paperwork Reduction Act Notice, see page 2.**

OMB No. 1545-0010

19**99**

1 Type or print your first name and middle initial
JAMES A.
Last name
IRVING
2 Your social security number
123 456 789

Home address (number and street or rural route)
25 CEDAR GLENN LANE
3 ☒ Single ☐ Married ☐ Married, but withhold at higher Single rate.
Note: If married, but legally separated, or spouse is a nonresident alien, check the Single box.

City or town, state, and ZIP code
ARLINGTON, IL 61312
4 If your last name differs from that on your social security card, check here. **You must call 1-800-772-1213 for a new card** . . ▶ ☐

5 Total number of allowances you are claiming (from line **H** above **OR** from the applicable worksheet on page 2) **5** _2_

6 Additional amount, if any, you want withheld from each paycheck . . . . **6** $ _____

7 I claim exemption from withholding for 2000, and I certify that I meet **BOTH** of the following conditions for exemption:
• Last year I had a right to a refund of **ALL** Federal income tax withheld because I had **NO** tax liability **AND**
• This year I expect a refund of **ALL** Federal income tax withheld because I expect to have **NO** tax liability.
If you meet both conditions, write "EXEMPT" here . . . . ▶ **7**

Under penalties of perjury, I certify that I am entitled to the number of withholding allowances claimed on this certificate, or I am entitled to claim exempt status.

Employee's signature
(Form is not valid
unless you sign it) ▶ _James a. Irving_
Date ▶ 1/3/99

8 Employer s name and address (Employer: Complete lines 8 and 10 only if sending to the IRS.)
9 Office code (optional)
10 Employer identification number

Cat. No. 10220Q

TAX WITHHOLDING The W-4 form allows employers to withhold federal income tax from their employees' paychecks. *How many allowances might you claim on your W-4 if you are married, you have only one job, and your spouse does not work?*

Allowances Worksheet at the top of the W-4 form. The more allowances you can claim, the less tax your employer will withhold.

6. Indicate how much additional money, if any, you wish to have withheld from each paycheck.

7. If you meet the conditions listed on the form and indicate that you are exempt, or excused, from paying income tax, no income tax will be withheld. However, Social Security payments will still be deducted.

8. Sign and date the form.

Some employees claim fewer allowances than they are entitled to. In fact, some employees don't claim any allowances. This means that their employers will withhold more money from each paycheck.

Some people look forward to receiving a large refund from the government when they file their tax returns, and claiming few or no allowances on their W-4 forms is one way to get that refund. What these taxpayers don't realize is that the extra money deducted every time they get paid is actually an interest-free loan to the government. The government doesn't have to return the extra money for over a year! Wise taxpayers claim all the allowances to which they are entitled. That puts the money into their bank accounts, not the government's.

Careers in Finance

TAX PREPARER

Because U.S. tax laws are complex and constantly changing and more people are self-employed, professional tax preparers will continue to be in demand. Tax preparers fill out tax returns and answer questions about taxes. In order to give their clients accurate information, they must keep up with the changing tax laws. Although the work is demanding during tax season, it's exciting to help people solve problems, answer questions, and get it all done by April 15, the annual deadline for filing tax returns.

Skills	Accounting, analytical, communication, computer, decision making, interpersonal, problem solving, and time management
Personality	Flexible, honest, likes working with numbers and people
Education	High school diploma for tax preparer; bachelor's degree in accounting for CPA tax preparer
Pay range	$35,000 to $50,000, depending on education, experience, and location

Critical Thinking What are some ways that a tax preparer could become more marketable?

 For more information on tax preparers visit finance.glencoe.com **or your local library.**

ESTIMATED PAYMENTS Every summer John earns money by running his own landscaping business. How does he pay his taxes?

Like other self-employed workers, John makes estimated payments to the government. These payments are due April 15, June 15, September 15, and January 15 (the last payment is for the previous year). John's payments are based on his estimate of taxes due at the end of the year. John's estimated payments must be at least equal to what he owed last year in taxes or be at least 90 percent of the current year's taxes to avoid penalties for underpayment.

SECTION 12.1 ASSESSMENT

CHECK YOUR UNDERSTANDING

1. What is the relationship between taxes and personal financial planning?
2. Explain how you would figure out your taxable income.
3. What steps should you follow to complete a W-4 form?

THINK CRITICALLY

4. Explain how deductions and tax credits affect the amount of income tax you pay.

USING COMMUNICATION SKILLS

5. **Raising Funds** As budget director for a small state, you must raise $350 million for emergency repairs to the state's bridges. You have several ways to fund the project. Your options include: place a sales tax of 5 percent on all purchases except food and prescription drugs; place a personal property tax on cars based on the purchase price and age of the vehicle, with a minimum tax of $25; place tolls on each bridge being repaired; the tolls would total about $4 per round-trip.
   Drawing Conclusions Weigh the pros and cons of each alternative and make a recommendation.

SOLVING MONEY PROBLEMS

6. **Withholding** Eric is single, he has no children or other dependents, and he is not claimed as a dependent on anyone else's tax return. He has only one job, as a manager at the local supermarket, and earns $35,000 a year. Leland, on the other hand, is married and has twin daughters, whom he will claim as dependents on his income tax return. He works full-time at an architecture firm, his only job, and also earns $35,000 a year.
   Evaluate Using the Personal Allowances Worksheet on the W-4 form, determine who will have more money withheld from his paycheck: Eric or Leland. Explain your answer.

What You'll Learn

• How to **prepare** a federal income tax return

Why It's Important

By completing your income tax return correctly, you can avoid costly mistakes and possible penalties and take full advantage of tax deductions, exemptions, and credits.

Preparing Your Income Tax Return

The W-2 Form

When it comes time for James to file his yearly income tax return, his employer will send him a W-2 form, or the Wage and Tax Statement. This form will report his annual earnings and the amount withheld from his paychecks for federal income taxes, Social Security, and any applicable state and local income taxes. By law, your employer must send you this form by January 31.

The Federal Income Tax Return

Now that you know how to compute your taxable income, you are ready to begin the annual ritual of filling out your income tax return and sending it to the IRS. It's a good idea to make a rough draft of your return before completing your final copy.

Who Must File?

Kerry is a single woman under the age of 65, and her gross income is more than $7,050. She is required to file an income tax return. Kerry would also be required to file an income tax return if she were a single person over age 65 and had a gross income of more than $8,100. Even if Kerry didn't meet the filing requirements, she should still file a tax return to obtain a refund of the income tax withheld from her paycheck.

Are you a citizen or resident of the United States? Are you a U.S. citizen who resides in Puerto Rico? If so, then you are required to file a federal income tax return if your income is above a certain amount. That amount is based on your filing status and other factors, such as your age. These are the five filing status categories:

• Single—never-married, divorced, or legally separated individuals with no dependents
• Married, filing a joint return—combines the income of a husband and wife

a Control number	22222	Void ☐	For Official Use Only ▶ OMB No. 1545-0008	

b Employer identification number 37-19876541		**1** Wages, tips, other compensation 10,250.00	**2** Federal income tax withheld 1,375.00
c Employer's name, address, and ZIP code ADVANTAGE ADVERTISING 400 N. MICHIGAN AVE. CHICAGO, IL 60613		**3** Social security wages 10,250.00	**4** Social security tax withheld 837.00
		5 Medicare wages and tips	**6** Medicare tax withheld
		7 Social security tips	**8** Allocated tips
d Employee's social security number 123-45-6789		**9** Advance EIC payment	**10** Dependent care benefits
e Employee's name (first, middle initial, last) JAMES A. IRVING 25 CEDAR GLENN LANE ARLINGTON, IL 61312		**11** Nonqualified plans	**12** Benefits included in box 1
		13 See instrs. for box 13	**14** Other
		15 Statutory employee ☐ Deceased ☐ Pension plan ☐ Legal rep. ☐ Deferred compensation ☐	
f Employee's address and ZIP code			

16 State Employer's state I.D. no. 37-19876541	**17** State wages, tips, etc.	**18** State income tax	**19** Locality name	**20** Local wages, tips, etc.	**21** Local income tax

Form W-2 Wage and Tax Statement 1999

Copy A For Social Security Administration—Send this entire page with Form W-3 to the Social Security Administration; photocopies are **not** acceptable.

Cat. No. 10134D

Department of the Treasury—Internal Revenue Service

For Privacy Act and Paperwork Reduction Act Notice, see separate instructions.

Do NOT Cut, Staple, or Separate Forms on This Page — Do NOT Cut, Staple, or Separate Forms on This Page

W-2 FORM Every January, employers send each of their employees a W-2 form. *Why does James need his W-2 form to complete his income tax return?*

- Married, filing separate returns—each spouse responsible for his or her own tax
- Head of household—an unmarried individual or a surviving spouse who maintains a household, paying more than one-half of the costs for a child or other dependent relative
- Qualifying widow or widower—an individual whose spouse died within the last two years and who has a dependent

In some situations, you may have a choice of filing status. In such cases, compute your taxes for both, and then choose the one that provides greater advantages for you.

Deadlines and Penalties

You are required to file an income tax return each year by April 15, unless that date falls on a Saturday or Sunday. In that case, you must file by the following Monday. If you have a refund due, it is wise to file your return as early as possible. The longer you wait, the longer it will

CASE STUDY

*M*ira Wilkowski has been working at Pete's Pizza Palace for almost a year. She works as a server from 4 to 9 p.m. five nights a week. This is her first job, and in addition to the tips she earns, her boss pays her $100 in cash each Monday. Last week an IRS representative came to her economics class and presented a seminar on how to file an income tax return using Form 1040EZ. When the presentation was over, Mira had a sinking feeling in her stomach. No one had ever told her to keep track of her tips and although each week Mira put half of her tips in the bank, she usually spent the other half. When she spoke to her boss about getting her W-2 form, he said, "Since you are only 17, you don't need to be bothered with all that paperwork." Mira is not sure what to do now, so she turned to the experts at Standard & Poor's for advice.

Analysis: Mira is in a difficult situation. Employers usually deduct income and Social Security taxes (including supplemental Medicare) from an employee's paycheck. They also pay one-half of the Social Security tax. Mira will now have to pay the uncollected Social Security taxes along with any federal and state income taxes that she owes. Unfortunately, Mira may also end up paying interest and penalties for late payment of these taxes.

Recommendation: Mira should notify her employer in writing that she is required to file a tax return and request that a W-2 form be sent to her. She should then attach a copy of this letter to her income tax return, and report her estimated wages and tips on her tax return form. Since she saved half of her tips each week, she can use her savings record to estimate the total amount of her tips. Mira may need to use Form 1040 to properly report taxes due on her tips. If possible, Mira should include a check with her return for the tax she owes. If Mira does not have enough money to pay her taxes, she should still file her tax return and pay as much as she can. The IRS will then send Mira a bill for any additional amounts including penalties. Mira may also need to file estimated tax withholding forms for each quarter she has worked since the end of the tax year. Finally, Mira should consider looking for a new job with a company that will respect her legal rights and responsibilities.

Critical Thinking Questions

1. Why might Mira's boss think that because Mira is only 17, she doesn't have to file a tax return?
2. What advantages does Mira's employer gain by not reporting her wages and tips?
3. If Mira doesn't have the money to pay the taxes she owes, what should she do?

take for you to receive your refund. Failure to file on time, even if you're just one day late, can result in financial penalties. If for some reason you can't meet the deadline, you can file Form 4868 by April 15 to obtain a four-month extension. However, this extension is only for the filing of your tax return. It doesn't delay your tax liability. When you submit Form 4868, you must also submit a check for the estimated amount of the tax you owe.

If you make quarterly estimated tax payments, they must be on time. Also, if you underestimate the amount owed, you have to pay interest plus the amount you should have paid. Underpayment due to negligence or fraud can result in large penalties. Failing to file a tax return at all is a serious violation of the tax code and can result in a substantial penalty.

The good news is that if you claim a refund several months or years late, perhaps because you discovered a computation error or had failed to take an allowable deduction, the IRS will pay you interest. You must claim your refund and interest within three years of filing the return or within two years of paying the tax.

Which Tax Form Should You Use?

Believe it or not, the IRS offers about 400 tax forms and schedules. Don't panic! You have a choice of three basic forms: the short forms known as Forms 1040EZ and 1040A, and the long form known as Form 1040.

FORM 1040EZ   Form 1040EZ is the simplest tax form to complete. You may use this form if you meet the following qualifications:

- You are single or married (filing a joint tax return), under age 65, and claim no dependents.
- Your income consisted of only wages, salaries, tips, and not more than $400 of taxable interest.
- Your taxable income is less than $50,000.
- You don't itemize deductions, claim any adjustments to income, or claim any tax credits.

Yasmeen Nazari, a high school senior, works part-time at a health clinic. Because she is single, earned less than the amount needed to file, and had only $11 in interest income last year, Yasmeen was able to use Form 1040EZ to obtain a refund of the income tax withheld from her paychecks during the previous year.

FORM 1040A   You may use this form if:

- you have less than $50,000 in taxable income from wages, salaries, tips, unemployment compensation, interest, or dividends;
- you claim the standard deduction;
- you can claim deductions for IRA contributions;
- you can claim a tax credit for child-care and dependent care expenses.

If you qualify to use either Form 1040EZ or Form 1040A, you will be able to simplify the process of filing your tax return. However, be aware that by using Form 1040, you may be able to pay less tax.

FORM 1040   Form 1040 is an expanded version of Form 1040A; it includes sections covering all types of income. You are required to use this form if your taxable income exceeds $50,000 or you can be claimed as a dependent on someone else's income tax return and you had interest or dividends over a set limit.

Form 1040 also allows you to itemize your deductions using Schedule A. You can deduct allowable expenses, such as medical and dental expenses, home mortgage interest, and real estate property tax. These deductions will reduce your taxable income and thus reduce the amount of tax you must pay.

QUESTION

In what situations would it be advantageous to file Form 1040, even if it weren't required?

Completing the Federal Income Tax Return

Filling out a federal income tax return doesn't have to be difficult as long as you are prepared and understand the form you are completing.

Gathering Information

Being prepared at tax time means having all the necessary documents on hand and in good order. The following checklist will contribute to a successful tax return:

- Be sure that you have the most current tax forms and instruction booklets that contain the latest tax information. Once you've filed your first tax return, the IRS will send these to you each year in January. If you need different or additional forms, you can find them at many post offices, libraries, and banks, and at your local IRS office. You can also download forms and instructions from the Internal Revenue Service's Web site.

PAYER'S name, street address, city, state, ZIP code, and telephone no.	Payer's RTN (optional)	OMB No. 1545-0112	
BAILEY'S BANK 1155 DARNESTOWN ROAD ARLINGTON, IL 61312		**19 99** Form **1099-INT**	**Interest Income**

PAYER'S Federal identification number	RECIPIENT'S identification number	**1** Interest income not included in box 3		**Copy A**
521283179	123456789	$ 45.00		**For**
RECIPIENT'S name JAMES A. IRVING		**2** Early withdrawal penalty $ .00	**3** Interest on U.S. Savings Bonds and Treas. obligations $ .00	**Internal Revenue Service Center** File with Form 1096.
Street address (including apt. no.) 25 CEDAR GLENN LANE		**4** Federal income tax withheld $ .00	**5** Investment expenses $ .00	For Privacy Act and Paperwork Reduction Act Notice and instructions for completing this
City, state, and ZIP code ARLINGTON, IL 61312		**6** Foreign tax paid	**7** Foreign country or U.S. possession	form, see the **1999 Instructions for Forms 1099, 1098,**
Account number (optional) 894-6210	2nd TIN Not. ☐	$ .00		**5498, and W-2G.**

Form **1099-INT**   Cat. No. 14410K   Department of the Treasury - Internal Revenue Service

Do NOT Cut or Separate Forms on This Page — Do NOT Cut or Separate Forms on This Page

INTEREST EARNED You'll receive a 1099-INT from any institution that paid you interest over the year. *What box on the form would indicate your interest income on a savings account?*

- It's also a good idea to have copies of your tax returns from previous years—unless, of course, you are filing for the first time.
- Your W-2 form is essential. You must attach a copy of it to your tax return if you are filing by mail. If you worked for more than one employer during the tax year, you will have more than one W-2.
- You may also have Form 1099-INT, which reports your interest income, and Form 1099-DIV, which reports your dividend income.
- Be sure to save copies of your tax returns and all supporting documents in a safe place for at least six years.

Completing the Form 1040EZ

After you've assembled all the necessary tax documents, it's time to begin filling out your tax return. Take a look at **Figure 12.2**. Here's how James Irving completes Form 1040EZ:

1. After printing his name, address, and Social Security number, James enters the total wages from his W-2 form on line 1 in the income section.
2. James earned $45 in interest on his savings account. (This was reported on Form 1099-INT.) He enters this amount on line 2.
3. James has nothing to report on line 3, so he leaves it blank.
4. James adds lines 1, 2, and 3 to get his adjusted gross income. He records it on line 4.

Figure 12.2

Form 1040 EZ

Department of the Treasury—Internal Revenue Service

Income Tax Return for Single and Joint Filers With No Dependents (P) **1999**   OMB No. 1545-0675

Form **1040EZ**

Use the IRS label here	Your first name and initial JAMES A. Last name IRVING	Your social security number 1 2 3 4 5 6 7 8 9
	If a joint return, spouse's first name and initial Last name	Spouse's social security number
	Home address (number and street). If you have a P.O. box, see page 12. Apt. no. 25 CEDAR GLENN	
	City, town or post office, state, and ZIP code. If you have a foreign address, see page 12. ARLINGTON, IL 61312	▲ IMPORTANT! ▲ You must enter your SSN(s) above.

Presidential Election Campaign
(See page 12.)

Note. *Checking "Yes" will not change your tax or reduce your refund.*

Do you want $3 to go to this fund? ▶   Yes ☐ No ☐

If a joint return, does your spouse want $3 to go to this fund? ▶ Yes ☐ No ☐

			Dollars	Cents
Income Attach Copy B of Form(s) W-2 here. Enclose, but do not staple, any payment.	**1** Total wages, salaries, and tips. This should be shown in box 1 of your W-2 form(s). Attach your W-2 form(s).	**1**	10 250	00
	2 Taxable interest. If the total is over $400, you cannot use Form 1040EZ.	**2**	45	00
	3 Unemployment compensation, qualified state tuition program earnings, and Alaska Permanent Fund dividends (see page 14).	**3**		
	4 Add lines 1, 2, and 3. This is your **adjusted gross income.**	**4**	10 295	00
Note. You **must** check Yes or No.	**5** Can your parents (or someone else) claim you on their return? **Yes.** Enter amount ✕ from worksheet on back. **No.** If **single**, enter 7,050.00. If **married**, enter 12,700.00. See back for explanation.	**5**	4 300	00
	6 Subtract line 5 from line 4. If line 5 is larger than line 4, enter 0. This is your **taxable income.** ▶	**6**	5 995	00
Payments and tax	**7** Enter your Federal income tax withheld from box 2 of your W-2 form(s).	**7**	1 375	00
	8a Earned income credit (see page 15). **b** Nontaxable earned income: enter type and amount below. Type ____ $ ____	**8a**		
	9 Add lines 7 and 8a. These are your **total payments.**	**9**	1 375	00
	10 Tax. Use the amount on **line 6 above** to find your tax in the tax table on pages 24–28 of the booklet. Then, enter the tax from the table on this line.	**10**	896	00
Refund Have it directly deposited! See page 20 and fill in 11b, 11c, and 11d.	**11a** If line 9 is larger than line 10, subtract line 10 from line 9. This is your **refund.**	**11a**	479	00
	b Routing number ____			
	c Type: ☐ Checking ☐ Savings **d** Account number			
Amount you owe	**12** If line 10 is larger than line 9, subtract line 9 from line 10. This is the **amount you owe.** See page 21 for details on how to pay.	**12**		

I have read this return. Under penalties of perjury, I declare that to the best of my knowledge and belief, the return is true, correct, and accurately lists all amounts and sources of income I received during the tax year.

Sign here ▶
Keep copy for your records.

Your signature *James A. Irving*	Spouse's signature if joint return. See page 11.	For Official Use Only
Date 2/2/00 Your occupation ASSISTANT	Date Spouse's occupation	

Figure 12.2

(continued)

Form 1040EZ (1999)   Page **2**

Use this form if

- Your filing status is single or married filing jointly.
- You do not claim any dependents.
- You do not claim a student loan interest deduction (see page 8) or an education credit.
- You had **only** wages, salaries, tips, taxable scholarship or fellowship grants, unemployment compensation, qualified state tuition program earnings, or Alaska Permanent Fund dividends, and your taxable interest was not over $400. **But** if you earned tips, including allocated tips, that are not included in box 5 and box 7 of your W-2, you may not be able to use Form 1040EZ. See page 13. If you are planning to use Form 1040EZ for a child who received Alaska Permanent Fund dividends, see page 14.
- You did not receive any advance earned income credit payments.

- You (and your spouse if married) were under 65 on January 1, 2000, and not blind at the end of 1999.
- Your taxable income (line 6) is less than $50,000.

If you are not sure about your filing status, see page 11. If you have questions about dependents, use TeleTax topic 354 (see page 6). If you **cannot use this form,** use TeleTax topic 352 (see page 6).

Filling in your return

For tips on how to avoid common mistakes, see page 29.

Enter your (and your spouse's if married) social security number on the front. Because this form is read by a machine, please print your numbers inside the boxes like this:

| 9 | 8 | 7 | 6 | 5 | 4 | 3 | 2 | 1 | 0 |

Do not type your numbers. Do not use dollar signs.

If you received a scholarship or fellowship grant or tax-exempt interest income, such as on municipal bonds, see the booklet before filling in the form. Also, see the booklet if you received a Form 1099-INT showing Federal income tax withheld or if Federal income tax was withheld from your unemployment compensation or Alaska Permanent Fund dividends.

Remember, you must report all wages, salaries, and tips even if you do not get a W-2 form from your employer. You must also report all your taxable interest, including interest from banks, savings and loans, credit unions, etc., even if you do not get a Form 1099-INT.

Worksheet for dependents who checked "Yes" on line 5

(keep a copy for your records)

Use this worksheet to figure the amount to enter on line 5 if someone can claim you (or your spouse if married) as a dependent, even if that person chooses not to do so. To find out if someone can claim you as a dependent, use TeleTax topic 354 (see page 6).

A. Amount, if any, from line 1 on front 10,250.00

      +   250.00 Enter total ▶   **A.**   10,500.00

B. Minimum standard deduction . . . . **B.**   700.00

C. Enter the LARGER of line A or line B here . . . . **C.**   10,500.00

D. Maximum standard deduction. If **single,** enter 4,300.00; if **married,** enter 7,200.00 . . . . **D.**   4,300.00

E. Enter the SMALLER of line C or line D here. This is your standard deduction . . . . **E.**   4,300.00

F. Exemption amount.
- If single, enter 0.
- If married and—
 —both you and your spouse can be claimed as dependents, enter 0.
 —only one of you can be claimed as a dependent, enter 2,750.00.   **F.**   0

G. Add lines E and F. Enter the total here and on line 5 on the front . . **G.**   4,300.00

If you checked "No" on line 5 because no one can claim you (or your spouse if married) as a dependent, enter on line 5 the amount shown below that applies to you.

- Single, enter 7,050.00. This is the total of your standard deduction (4,300.00) and your exemption (2,750.00).
- Married, enter 12,700.00. This is the total of your standard deduction (7,200.00), your exemption (2,750.00), and your spouse's exemption (2,750.00).

Mailing return

Mail your return by **April 17, 2000.** Use the envelope that came with your booklet. If you do not have that envelope, see page 32 for the address to use.

Paid preparer's use only

See page 21.

Under penalties of perjury, I declare that I have examined this return, and to the best of my knowledge and belief, it is true, correct, and accurately lists all amounts and sources of income received during the tax year. This declaration is based on all information of which I have any knowledge.

| Preparer's signature ▶ | | Date | Check if self-employed ☐ | Preparer's SSN or PTIN |

| Firm's name (or yours if self-employed) and address ▶ | | | EIN | |
| | | | ZIP code | |

✪ *Printed on recycled paper*

Form **1040EZ** (1999)

☆ U.S. GOVERNMENT PRINTING OFFICE: 1999–456-540

A REFUND OPTION   James has a choice about how to receive his refund. *What are the purposes of lines 11b, c, and d?*

PREDICT

List the different methods a person can use to file an income tax return.

5. James's parents claim him as a dependent on their income tax return, so James uses the worksheet on the back of Form 1040EZ to calculate his maximum standard deduction. (See **Figure 12.2.**) He enters $4,300 on line 5.

6. By subtracting his deduction from his adjusted gross income, James computes his taxable income: $5,995. He writes it on line 6.

7. On line 7, in the payments and tax section, James enters the amount of income tax that was withheld from his paychecks ($1,375) as reported on his W-2 form.

8. James cannot claim any earned income credit, so he leaves line 8a blank.

9. He adds lines 7 and 8a to find his total payments ($1,375). He enters this amount on line 9.

10. Now it's time for James to find out how much tax he owes. He knows from line 6 that his taxable income is $5,995. He checks the

Figure 12.3

Tax Table

1999 Tax Table

For persons with taxable income of less than $50,000

Example. Mr. Brown is single. His taxable income on line 6 of Form 1040EZ is $26,250. First, he finds the $26,250–26,300 income line. Next, he finds the "Single" column and reads down the column. The amount shown where the income line and filing status column meet ➤ is $4,010. This is the tax amount he should enter on line 10 of Form 1040EZ.

At least	But less than	Single	Married filing jointly
			Your tax is—
26,200	26,250	3,996	3,934
26,250	26,300	(4,010)	3,941
26,300	26,350	4,024	3,949
26,350	26,400	4,038	3,956

If Form 1040EZ, line 6, is—		And you are—		If Form 1040EZ, line 6, is—		And you are—		If Form 1040EZ, line 6, is—		And you are—	
At least	But less than	Single	Married filing jointly	At least	But less than	Single	Married filing jointly	At least	But less than	Single	Married filing jointly
		Your tax is—				**Your tax is—**				**Your tax is—**	
4,000				**5,000**				**6,000**			
4,000	4,050	604	604	5,000	5,050	754	754	6,000	6,050	904	904
4,050	4,100	611	611	5,050	5,100	761	761	6,050	6,100	911	911
4,100	4,150	619	619	5,100	5,150	769	769	6,100	6,150	919	919
4,150	4,200	626	626	5,150	5,200	776	776	6,150	6,200	926	926
4,200	4,250	634	634	5,200	5,250	784	784	6,200	6,250	934	934
4,250	4,300	641	641	5,250	5,300	791	791	6,250	6,300	941	941
4,300	4,350	649	649	5,300	5,350	799	799	6,300	6,350	949	949
4,350	4,400	656	656	5,350	5,400	806	806	6,350	6,400	956	956
4,400	4,450	664	664	5,400	5,450	814	814	6,400	6,450	964	964
4,450	4,500	671	671	5,450	5,500	821	821	6,450	6,500	971	971
4,500	4,550	679	679	5,500	5,550	829	829	6,500	6,550	979	979
4,550	4,600	686	686	5,550	5,600	836	836	6,550	6,600	986	986
4,600	4,650	694	694	5,600	5,650	844	844	6,600	6,650	994	994
4,650	4,700	701	701	5,650	5,700	851	851	6,650	6,700	1,001	1,001
4,700	4,750	709	709	5,700	5,750	859	859	6,700	6,750	1,009	1,009
4,750	4,800	716	716	5,750	5,800	866	866	6,750	6,800	1,016	1,016
4,800	4,850	724	724	5,800	5,850	874	874	6,800	6,850	1,024	1,024
4,850	4,900	731	731	5,850	5,900	881	881	6,850	6,900	1,031	1,031
4,900	4,950	739	739	5,900	5,950	889	889	6,900	6,950	1,039	1,039
4,950	5,000	746	746	5,950	6,000	896	896	6,950	7,000	1,046	1,046

WHAT IF? The tax table in the Form 1040EZ instruction booklet tells you how much tax you owe, and thus it allows you to determine the refund you should receive, if any. *If James's Form 1040EZ, line 6, was at least $5,000 but less than $5,050, how much tax would he owe?*

tax table in the Form 1040EZ instruction booklet (see **Figure 12.3**) and finds the column that says "If Form 1040EZ, line 6, is" and the row that corresponds with "At least" $5,950 "But less than" $6,000. Because he is single, he owes $896. He enters this amount on line 10.

11. James's employer withheld more tax than James owed. By subtracting his tax owed (line 10) from his tax withheld (line 9), James finds that the IRS owes him a refund of $479, which he enters on line 11a. If he fills in lines 11b, 11c, and 11d, he can have his refund deposited directly into his bank account. He leaves the lines blank so that he will receive a refund check.

12. Pleased that he will receive a refund, he signs and dates his income tax return and enters his occupation. James then makes a photocopy of his tax return for his records, attaches his W-2 to the original tax return, and mails the completed return to the IRS.

Completing the Form 1040A

James used Form 1040EZ because his tax situation was uncomplicated. Some taxpayers, however, will benefit from using Form 1040A, shown in **Figure 12.4**. Form 1040A enables taxpayers to claim deductions that will reduce the amount of tax they must pay.

Filing Your Federal Income Tax Return

Keep in mind that you may be able to file using one of several options. You can file the traditional paper return by filling out the forms and mailing them to the IRS. If you file electronically, your return is transmitted over telephone lines directly to an IRS computer.

The IRS provides three ways for individuals to file electronically. First, you can use an authorized IRS e-file provider. With this method, either you or a tax professional would prepare your tax return. The tax professional would transmit it to the IRS. Second, you can file using your personal computer and tax software. Depending on which software program you use to file your taxes, you will need a modem and/or Internet access. Finally, many people who use Form 1040EZ have the option of filing their taxes electronically using only their touch-tone telephones. With this

Figure 12.4

Form 1040A

Form **1040A** — Department of the Treasury—Internal Revenue Service
U.S. Individual Income Tax Return (99) **1999**   IRS Use Only—Do not write or staple in this space.

OMB No. 1545-0085

Label (See page 19.)

Use the IRS label.
Otherwise, please print or type.

Your first name and initial: ROBERT S.   Last name: PARK
Your social security number: 129 61 1523

If a joint return, spouse's first name and initial: JI SUN   Last name: PARK
Spouse's social security number: 156 41 9129

Home address (number and street). If you have a P.O. box, see page 20.: 140 OAK LANE   Apt. no.

City, town or post office, state, and ZIP code. If you have a foreign address, see page 20.: CHARLOTTESVILLE, VA 22901

▲ **IMPORTANT!** ▲
You **must** enter your SSN(s) above.

Presidential Election Campaign Fund (See page 20.)
Do you want $3 to go to this fund? — Yes ☐ No ☐
If a joint return, does your spouse want $3 to go to this fund? — Yes ☐ No ☐

Note. Checking "Yes" will not change your tax or reduce your refund.

Filing status

Check only one box.

1 ☐ Single
2 ☒ Married filing joint return (even if only one had income)
3 ☐ Married filing separate return. Enter spouse's social security number above and full name here. ▶
4 ☐ Head of household (with qualifying person). (See page 21.) If the qualifying person is a child but not your dependent, enter this child's name here. ▶
5 ☐ Qualifying widow(er) with dependent child (year spouse died ▶ 19   ). (See page 22.)

Exemptions

6a ☒ **Yourself.** If your parent (or someone else) can claim you as a dependent on his or her tax return, **do not** check box 6a.
b ☒ **Spouse**

No. of boxes checked on 6a and 6b: **2**

c **Dependents:**

(1) First name Last name	(2) Dependent's social security number	(3) Dependent's relationship to you	(4) ✓ If qualifying child for child tax credit (see page 23)
LILY SUN PARK	201 92 4211	DAUGHTER	☐
MICHAEL JOON PARK	901 42 1611	SON	☐
			☐
			☐
			☐
			☐
			☐

If more than seven dependents, see page 22.

No. of your children on 6c who:
• lived with you: **2**
• did not live with you due to divorce or separation (see page 24)
Dependents on 6c not entered above

d Total number of exemptions claimed.

Add numbers entered on lines above: **4**

Income

Attach Copy B of your Form(s) W-2 here. Also attach Form(s) 1099-R if tax was withheld.

If you did not get a W-2, see page 25.

Enclose, but do not staple, any payment.

7 Wages, salaries, tips, etc. Attach Form(s) W-2.   7   47,500 00

8a **Taxable** interest. Attach Schedule 1 if required.   8a   325 00
b **Tax-exempt** interest. DO NOT include on line 8a.   8b

9 Ordinary dividends. Attach Schedule 1 if required.   9

10a Total IRA distributions.   10a   10b Taxable amount (see page 25).   10b

11a Total pensions and annuities.   11a   11b Taxable amount (see page 26).   11b

12 Unemployment compensation, qualified state tuition program earnings, and Alaska Permanent Fund dividends.   12

13a Social security benefits.   13a   13b Taxable amount (see page 28).   13b

14 Add lines 7 through 13b (far right column). This is your **total income.** ▶   14   47,825 00

Adjusted gross income

15 IRA deduction (see page 30).   15   4,000 00

16 Student loan interest deduction (see page 30).   16

17 Add lines 15 and 16. These are your **total adjustments.**   17   4,000 00

18 Subtract line 17 from line 14. This is your **adjusted gross income.** ▶   18   43,825 00

For Disclosure, Privacy Act, and Paperwork Reduction Act Notice, see page 53.   Cat. No. 11327A   Form **1040A** (1999)

Figure 12.4

(continued)

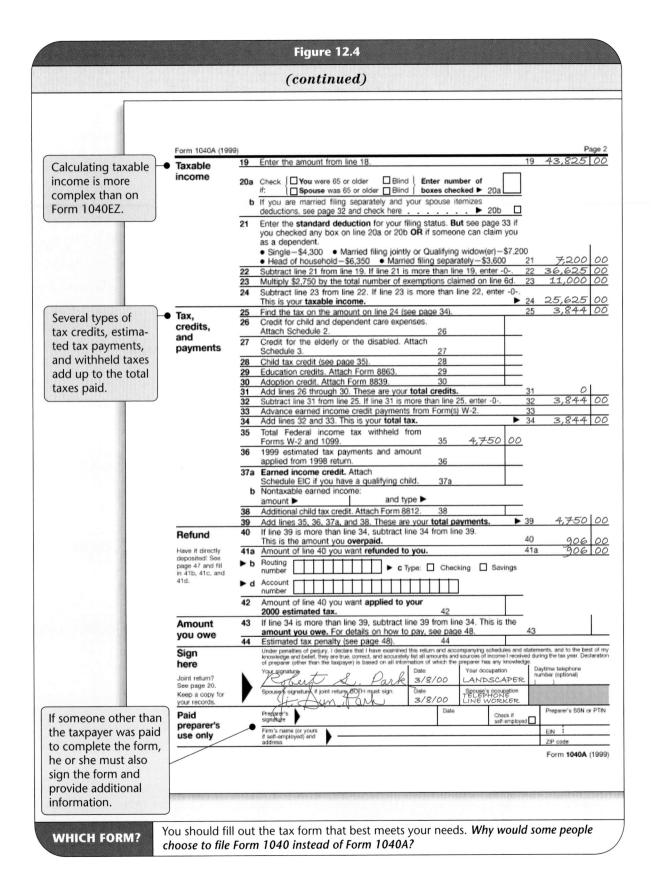

Calculating taxable income is more complex than on Form 1040EZ.

Several types of tax credits, estimated tax payments, and withheld taxes add up to the total taxes paid.

If someone other than the taxpayer was paid to complete the form, he or she must also sign the form and provide additional information.

Form 1040A (1999)   Page 2

Taxable income

19   Enter the amount from line 18.   19   43,825 00

20a   Check if: ☐ **You** were 65 or older   ☐ Blind   **Enter number of boxes checked ▶** 20a ☐ Spouse was 65 or older ☐ Blind

b   If you are married filing separately and your spouse itemizes deductions, see page 32 and check here . . . . ▶ 20b ☐

21   Enter the **standard deduction** for your filing status. **But** see page 33 if you checked any box on line 20a or 20b **OR** if someone can claim you as a dependent.
- Single—$4,300 • Married filing jointly or Qualifying widow(er)—$7,200
- Head of household—$6,350 • Married filing separately—$3,600   21   7,200 00

22   Subtract line 21 from line 19. If line 21 is more than line 19, enter -0-.   22   36,625 00

23   Multiply $2,750 by the total number of exemptions claimed on line 6d.   23   11,000 00

24   Subtract line 23 from line 22. If line 23 is more than line 22, enter -0-. This is your **taxable income.**   ▶ 24   25,625 00

Tax, credits, and payments

25   Find the tax on the amount on line 24 (see page 34).   25   3,844 00

26   Credit for child and dependent care expenses. Attach Schedule 2.   26

27   Credit for the elderly or the disabled. Attach Schedule 3.   27

28   Child tax credit (see page 35).   28

29   Education credits. Attach Form 8863.   29

30   Adoption credit. Attach Form 8839.   30

31   Add lines 26 through 30. These are your **total credits.**   31   0

32   Subtract line 31 from line 25. If line 31 is more than line 25, enter -0-.   32   3,844 00

33   Advance earned income credit payments from Form(s) W-2.   33

34   Add lines 32 and 33. This is your **total tax.**   ▶ 34   3,844 00

35   Total Federal income tax withheld from Forms W-2 and 1099.   35   4,750 00

36   1999 estimated tax payments and amount applied from 1998 return.   36

37a   **Earned income credit.** Attach Schedule EIC if you have a qualifying child.   37a

b   Nontaxable earned income: amount ▶   and type ▶

38   Additional child tax credit. Attach Form 8812.   38

39   Add lines 35, 36, 37a, and 38. These are your **total payments.**   ▶ 39   4,750 00

Refund

Have it directly deposited! See page 47 and fill in 41b, 41c, and 41d.

40   If line 39 is more than line 34, subtract line 34 from line 39. This is the amount you **overpaid.**   40   906 00

41a   Amount of line 40 you want **refunded to you.**   41a   906 00

▶ b   Routing number   ▶ c Type: ☐ Checking ☐ Savings

▶ d   Account number

42   Amount of line 40 you want **applied to your 2000 estimated tax.**   42

Amount you owe

43   If line 34 is more than line 39, subtract line 39 from line 34. This is the **amount you owe.** For details on how to pay, see page 48.   43

44   Estimated tax penalty (see page 48).   44

Sign here

Joint return? See page 20. Keep a copy for your records.

Under penalties of perjury, I declare that I have examined this return and accompanying schedules and statements, and to the best of my knowledge and belief, they are true, correct, and accurately list all amounts and sources of income I received during the tax year. Declaration of preparer (other than the taxpayer) is based on all information of which the preparer has any knowledge.

Your signature: *Robert S. Park*   Date 3/8/00   Your occupation LANDSCAPER   Daytime telephone number (optional)

Spouse's signature. If joint return, BOTH must sign. *Ji Sun Park*   Date 3/8/00   Spouse's occupation TELEPHONE LINE WORKER

Paid preparer's use only

Preparer's signature ▶   Date   Check if self-employed ☐   Preparer's SSN or PTIN

Firm's name (or yours if self-employed) and address ▶   EIN   ZIP code

Form **1040A** (1999)

WHICH FORM?   You should fill out the tax form that best meets your needs. *Why would some people choose to file Form 1040 instead of Form 1040A?*

method, called TeleFile, you don't have to send any paperwork to the IRS.

Completing State Income Tax Returns

If you live in a state that has its own income tax, you will have to complete a state income tax return. States usually require their income tax returns to be filed at the same time as federal income tax returns. To find out more about state income tax forms and preparation, contact your state's department of revenue or tax board.

SECTION 12.2 ASSESSMENT

CHECK YOUR UNDERSTANDING

1. Who must file a federal income tax return?
2. Describe the three basic tax forms.
3. What documents do you need to begin to prepare your tax return?

THINK CRITICALLY

4. Describe situations in which it would be advantageous to use Form 1040A instead of Form 1040EZ.

USING MATH SKILLS

5. **A Taxing Question** Last year, Shirley, a single college student, made $12,500 in total wages, salaries, and tips. She had $1,200 of federal income tax withheld. Her taxable interest was $59. No one was able to claim Shirley as a dependent on his or her tax return. **Calculate** Given the information above, use Form 1040EZ in **Figure 12.2** and the corresponding tax table in **Figure 12.3** to determine whether Shirley will owe the government money or whether she will obtain a refund. How much money will she owe, or how much will her refund be?

SOLVING MONEY PROBLEMS

6. **Planning for Tax Time** Poor Fred. Tax time is drawing near, and he doesn't know how to begin to prepare his income tax return. He has piles of forms and other paperwork, but he just can't figure out what to do with them. Fred needs help, and fast!
Give Advice Advise Fred on the best way to prepare to file an income tax return. Tell him which forms are important and why, where he can go to get any forms he might be missing, and so on.

Tax Assistance and Tax Strategies

Tax Assistance

As your personal finances become more complex, so do your taxes. All the rules and regulations can be confusing. Don't worry. You'll find plenty of people and agencies willing to answer your questions and offer sound advice. Furthermore, you can choose from a variety of software programs that aid in tax preparation. **Figure 12.5** shows you some of the available options.

What If Your Return Is Audited?

The IRS reviews all tax returns for completeness and accuracy. If your math is incorrect, the IRS refigures your tax return for you and sends you either a bill or a refund. However, in special cases, the IRS may audit your tax return and request additional information. A *tax audit* is a detailed examination of your tax return by the IRS. The IRS does periodic audits to determine whether taxpayers are paying all of their required taxes. While the IRS does not reveal its basis for auditing returns, the agency may look for unusually large deductions or for deductions that you cannot claim with your filing status.

If you receive an audit notice, you have the right to request time to prepare. You may also ask the IRS for clarification of items they are questioning. When the day of the audit arrives, you should be on time for the appointment and bring only documents that are both relevant and consistent with the tax law. Be sure to answer the auditor's questions clearly, completely, and briefly. You should also maintain a positive attitude during the audit. If you choose, your tax preparer, accountant, or lawyer may be present. As long as you have

What You'll Learn

- How to **identify** sources of tax assistance
- How to **select** the best tax strategies for your financial and personal needs

Why It's Important

As your income and investments increase and your personal life changes, preparing your taxes will become more complex. Many taxpayers seek professional assistance to meet these challenges successfully.

KEY TERM

- tax audit

THE DIGITAL DAILY

1 *Like all government agencies, the IRS is online. You can download forms and obtain important tax information and advice. You will find the same services at your local IRS office.*

2 *A visit to a bookstore will uncover shelves of how-to books about tax planning and completing tax forms. Personal finance magazines offer tax information as well.*

FIGURE 12.5

Tax Assistance Is Close at Hand

When it's time to file your income tax returns, take advantage of these tax assistance products and services.

3 *Tax preparation software is updated yearly to reflect changes in the tax laws.*

4 *Tax professionals can help you with your tax preparation, answer questions, and determine whether you are eligible for deductions and credits.*

maintained complete and accurate financial records, the audit should go smoothly.

Tax Planning Strategies

Smart taxpayers know how to minimize the amount of tax they have to pay, and they do so legally. You must pay your fair share, but you don't have to pay more. The following strategies will be helpful for reducing the amount of tax you owe.

Consumer Purchasing

The buying decisions you make can affect the amount of taxes you pay. For example, if you purchase a house, both the interest you pay on your mortgage and your real estate property taxes are deductible. You can also deduct the interest on a home equity loan. The IRS allows you to deduct the interest on home equity loans up to $100,000.

Some job-related expenses may also be deducted. Union dues, some travel and education expenses, business tools, and certain job search expenses qualify. Only the portion of these job-related expenses that exceeds 2 percent of your adjusted gross income is deductible. Expenses related to finding your first job or obtaining work in a different field are not deductible.

Investment Decisions

Some investment decisions can increase your income while lowering your taxes. For example, the interest on municipal bonds is not usually taxed. Other investments may be tax-deferred. That is, the income is taxed at a later date.

Retirement Plans

It may sound strange to someone your age, but now is the time to start planning for your retirement. To encourage such early planning, the government allows you to defer paying taxes on money that you invest in retirement plans. If you open an Individual Retirement Account, or an IRA, this year, the money you invest, up to a certain amount and under certain conditions, may qualify as a tax deduction. You won't have to pay any income tax on this money until you withdraw it—perhaps 50 years from now!

Layaway Works

If you must have that special dress, pair of pants, or coat, ask the store about its layaway plan. You pay in installments and get the item when the last payment is made. This is a no-interest way of paying for something over time.

CONNECT

Do you know family, friends, or relatives who have been audited? If so, how do they describe the experience?

QUESTION

Why would the government want to encourage early savings for retirement?

Take it EZ

Jasmine Owen earned $11,288 working at the Crestview Hotel. She also earned $67 in interest on her savings account. Her employer withheld $837.26 in federal income taxes. Jasmine filed the Form 1040EZ. After calculating her taxable income, she checked the tax table and found that she owed $649 in taxes and would be receiving a refund check for $188.26.

Using the sample Form 1040EZ in your workbook or a blank Form 1040EZ, complete your income tax return. Assume that your wages for the year were $13,220 and you earned $137 in interest. Your W-2 form shows that you had $1,003 in federal income tax withheld. Your parents cannot claim you on their income tax return. Find your tax in a current tax table or use the one on page 398; then calculate your refund or amount you owe.

Department of the Treasury—Internal Revenue Service

Form 1040EZ | **Income Tax Return for Single and Joint Filers With No Dependents** (P) **1999** | OMB No. 1545-0675

Use the IRS label here

Your first name and initial: JASMINE W.   Last name: OWEN
If a joint return, spouse's first name and initial   Last name

Home address (number and street). If you have a P.O. box, see page 12.   Apt. no.
195 S. BARRINGTON STREET   111
City, town or post office, state, and ZIP code. If you have a foreign address, see page 12.
SPRINGFIELD, IL 62704

Your social security number: 1 4 2 3 4 3 4 2 4

Spouse's social security number

▲ IMPORTANT! ▲ You must enter your SSN(s) above.

Presidential Election Campaign (See page 12.)

Note. *Checking "Yes" will not change your tax or reduce your refund.*
Do you want $3 to go to this fund? ▶ Yes [X] No [ ]
If a joint return, does your spouse want $3 to go to this fund? ▶ Yes [ ] No [ ]

		Dollars	Cents
Income Attach Copy B of Form(s) W-2 here. Enclose, but do not staple, any payment.	**1** Total wages, salaries, and tips. This should be shown in box 1 of your W-2 form(s). Attach your W-2 form(s). **1**	11 288	00
	2 Taxable interest. If the total is over $400, you cannot use Form 1040EZ. **2**	67	00
	3 Unemployment compensation, qualified state tuition program earnings, and Alaska Permanent Fund dividends (see page 14). **3**		
	4 Add lines 1, 2, and 3. This is your **adjusted gross income.** **4**	11 355	00
Note. You **must** check Yes or No.	**5** Can your parents (or someone else) claim you on their return? **Yes.** Enter amount from worksheet on back. **No.** If **single,** enter 7,050.00. If **married,** enter 12,700.00. See back for explanation. **5**	7 050	00
	6 Subtract line 5 from line 4. If line 5 is larger than line 4, enter 0. This is your **taxable income.** ▶ **6**	4 305	00
Payments and tax	**7** Enter your Federal income tax withheld from box 2 of your W-2 form(s). **7**	837	26
	8a Earned income credit (see page 15). **b** Nontaxable earned income: enter type and amount below. Type $ **8a**		
	9 Add lines 7 and 8a. These are your **total payments.** **9**	837	26
	10 Tax. Use the amount on **line 6 above** to find your tax in the tax table on pages 24–28 of the booklet. Then, enter the tax from the table on this line. **10**	649	00
Refund Have it directly deposited! See page 20 and fill in 11b, 11c, and 11d.	**11a** If line 9 is larger than line 10, subtract line 10 from line 9. This is your **refund.** **11a**	188	26
	b Routing number		
	c Type: Checking [ ] Savings [ ] **d** Account number		
Amount you owe	**12** If line 10 is larger than line 9, subtract line 9 from line 10. This is the **amount you owe.** See page 21 for details on how to pay. **12**		

I have read this return. Under penalties of perjury, I declare that to the best of my knowledge and belief, the return is true, correct, and accurately lists all amounts and sources of income I received during the tax year.

Sign here
Keep copy for your records.
Your signature: Jasmine W. Owen   Spouse's signature if joint return. See page 11.
Date: 3/14/00   Your occupation: CLERK   Date   Spouse's occupation

For Official Use Only

For Disclosure, Privacy Act, and Paperwork Reduction Act Notice, see page 23.   Cat. No. 12616G   1999 Form 1040EZ

Changing Your Tax Strategy

People pay taxes because they have to, not because they want to. The government tries to find ways to minimize the taxes you owe without jeopardizing the important services it provides. This is one reason why the tax laws are always changing. Your tax strategies should change, too. As new deductions are allowed or deductible amounts change, you'll want to review your financial plans to take full advantage of new tax laws.

SECTION 12.3   ASSESSMENT

CHECK YOUR UNDERSTANDING

1. Name several sources of tax assistance.
2. How can your buying decisions affect the amount of taxes you pay?
3. What types of investments might you make for tax purposes?

THINK CRITICALLY

4. Using what you've learned in this chapter, recommend several precautions that you might take to avoid a tax audit.

USING COMMUNICATION SKILLS

5. **Personalized Tax Assistance** Tax professionals can provide you with advice about how to minimize the amount of tax you have to pay and still pay your fair share of taxes.
   Role-Play In pairs, role-play the parts of tax professional and client. The client should ask the tax professional for tax planning strategies. The tax professional should provide accurate and helpful answers to the client's questions.

SOLVING MONEY PROBLEMS

6. **Tax Audits** Felicia can't believe it. She has just heard from the IRS that they'll be auditing her tax return from two years ago. She has no idea why. Felicia doesn't know where to begin to prepare for what she's sure will be the worst day of her life.
   Formulate Help Felicia put together a plan of action. What does she need? Whom should she consult? How should she act?

CHAPTER 12 ASSESSMENT

CHAPTER SUMMARY

- Effective tax planning involves finding out how current tax laws affect you, making an effort to maintain complete and accurate tax records, and learning how to make decisions that reduce the amount of taxes you owe.

- Throughout your life, you will pay taxes on purchases, property, wealth, and earnings.

- Calculating your adjusted gross income will enable you to compute your taxable income, the amount that determines the rate at which you will be taxed.

- Preparing a W-4 form correctly can help

you have the correct amount withheld from your paycheck throughout the year.

- Knowing the appropriate tax form to use and how to complete it correctly will enable you to file your taxes efficiently.

- You can gain assistance in preparing your taxes from the IRS, books, personal finance magazines, tax preparation software, online resources, and tax professionals.

- Choosing appropriate tax strategies for your financial and personal situation can maximize your earnings and reduce your tax liability.

Internet zone

Understanding and Using Vocabulary

The following key terms will help you to remember important information about taxes and tax strategies. Choose ten of these terms, and write a sentence for each one. Each sentence should explain the term in your own words.

tax liability
excise tax
estate tax
inheritance tax
gift tax
withhold

earned income
interest income
dividend income
exclusion
adjusted gross
   income

income tax return
tax deduction
standard deduction
itemized deduction
exemption

taxable income
tax credit
allowance
tax audit

Review Key Concepts

1. What are the four main categories of taxes?
2. What are the differences among gross income, adjusted gross income, and taxable income?

CHAPTER 12 ASSESSMENT

3. What is the difference between the W-4 form and the W-2 form?
4. Name the three basic income tax forms people can use.
5. Why does the IRS audit some people's income tax returns?

Apply Key Concepts

1. Explain how the tax laws might affect you if you inherited money or property.
2. How should you calculate taxable income?
3. Explain how the number of allowances you claim on the W-4 form affects your taxes.
4. Describe the similarities and differences between Form 1040EZ and Form 1040A.
5. Identify some actions that might cause the IRS to audit your tax return.

? Problem Solving Today

FINDING YOUR ADJUSTED GROSS INCOME

You are preparing your tax return. Your annual wages, tips, and other compensation totaled $22,500. Your taxable interest was $21, and you did not receive any other income. Last year you paid $640 in interest on your student loan. Choose the form you should use to prepare your federal income tax return.

Calculate Once you have selected a form, find your adjusted gross income based on the information above.

Computer Activity As an alternative activity, use financial planning software to find your adjusted gross income.

Real-World Application

CONNECT WITH SOCIAL STUDIES

From the founding of the nation, the people of the United States have valued their freedom and independence. This philosophy has led some citizens to avoid paying taxes as a form of social protest.

Conduct Research Examine the history of tax protest in the United States. Focus on one or two examples, and write a report explaining the nature of the protest and the reasons for it. Share your report with the class, and discuss the positive and negative aspects of such protests.

FINANCE Online

TAKING THE MYSTERY OUT OF TAXES

The Internet offers a wide variety of personal tax guides that provide free advice.

Connect Using different search engines, look for information about tax planning and how to make the most of your money. Then find out the following:

1. Which specific types of financial documents and related paperwork do you have to keep in order to complete your tax return? What can you safely throw away?
2. Besides wages, salary, commissions, fees, tips, bonuses, interest, and dividends from investments, what other forms of income are taxable?
3. What types of income are not taxable?

CHAPTER 13

Home and Automobile Insurance

Q&A

Q: I'm a male teenager with an excellent driving record. Why are my automobile insurance rates higher than rates for females in my same age group?

A: Insurance rates are based on an analysis of accident statistics for all types of drivers. Historically, young men have had a higher incidence of being involved in accidents than have young women. Some insurance companies offer special programs for young adults who buy coverage in conjunction with a parent's policy. If you live with your parents, ask to speak with their insurance agent about possible discounts that may be available to you.

CALIFORNIA EARTHQUAKE AUTHORITY
Dwelling
BASIC EARTHQUAKE POLICY
BEQ - 3

FLOODED

California
Earthquake
Authority

Insurance and Risk Management

*I*n today's world of the "strange but true," you can get insurance for just about anything. You might purchase a policy to protect yourself in the event that you're abducted by aliens. Some insurance companies will offer you protection if you think that you have a risk of turning into a werewolf. If you're a fast runner, you might be able to get a discount on a life insurance policy. Some people buy wedding disaster insurance just in case something goes wrong on the big day. You may never need these types of insurance, but you'll certainly need insurance on your home, your car, and your personal property. The more you know about insurance, the better able you will be to make decisions about buying it.

What Is Insurance?

Insurance is protection against possible financial loss. You can't predict the future. However, insurance allows you to be prepared for the worst. It provides protection against many risks, such as unexpected property loss, illness, and injury. Although many kinds of insurance exist, they all have several characteristics in common. They give you peace of mind, and they protect you from financial loss when trouble strikes.

An *insurance company*, or *insurer*, is a risk-sharing business that agrees to pay for losses that may happen to someone it insures. A person joins the risk-sharing group by purchasing a contract known as a *policy*. The purchaser of the policy is called a *policyholder*. Under the policy, the insurance company agrees to take on the risk. In return the policyholder pays the company a *premium*, or fee. The protection provided by the terms of an insurance policy is known as *coverage*, and the people protected by the policy are known as the *insured*.

What You'll Learn

- How to **identify** types of risks and risk management methods
- How to **develop** an insurance program as a way to manage risks
- How to **recognize** the importance of property and liability insurance

Why It's Important

Recognizing the importance of insurance and knowing how to develop an insurance program can protect you from financial loss.

KEY TERMS

- insurance
- insurance company
- insurer
- policy
- policyholder
- premium
- coverage
- insured
- risk
- peril
- hazard
- negligence
- deductible
- claim
- liability

Types of Risks

You face risks every day. You can't cross the street without some danger that a motor vehicle might hit you. You can't own property without running the risk that it will be lost, stolen, damaged, or destroyed.

What's Your Financial ID?

AUTO INSURANCE QUIZ

When you insure your car, you'll need to make decisions about the insurance you carry. Test your knowledge about auto insurance by writing the answers to the following questions on a separate sheet of paper.

1. Liability coverage pays for _____.
   a. theft, fire, vandalism, or other damages not related to an accident
   b. the accident-related cost of repairing or replacing your car
   c. damage or injury for which you're responsible

2. Collision coverage pays for _____.
   a. theft, fire, vandalism, or other damages not related to an accident
   b. the accident-related cost of repairing or replacing your car
   c. damage or injury for which you're responsible

3. Comprehensive coverage pays for _____.
   a. theft, fire, vandalism, or other damages not related to an accident
   b. the accident-related cost of repairing or replacing your car
   c. all the items that passengers lose behind the backseat of your car

4. If you're in an accident, your auto insurance medical coverage handles _____.
   a. only people injured in your car
   b. anyone injured
   c. only people injured who were not in your car

5. A higher deductible results in _____.
   a. a higher premium
   b. a lower premium
   c. tax savings

6. Speeding tickets or accidents may result in _____.
   a. a higher premium
   b. a lower premium
   c. migraine headaches

7. Safety features such as antitheft devices and automatic seat belts may result in a _____.
   a. higher premium
   b. lower premium
   c. higher resale value

8. Taking driver education classes may result in a _____.
   a. higher premium
   b. lower premium
   c. later curfew

"Risk," "peril," and "hazard" are important terms in insurance. In everyday use, these terms have almost the same meanings. In the insurance business, however, each has a distinct and special meaning.

Risk is the chance of loss or injury. In insurance it refers to the fact that no one can predict trouble. This means that an insurance company is taking a chance every time it issues a policy. Insurance companies frequently refer to the insured person or property as the risk.

Peril is anything that may possibly cause a loss. It's the reason why someone takes out insurance. People buy policies for protection against a wide range of perils, including fire, windstorms, explosions, robbery, and accidents.

Hazard is anything that increases the likelihood of loss through some peril. For example, defective house wiring is a hazard that increases the chance that a fire will start.

The most common risks are personal risks, property risks, and liability risks. Personal risks involve loss of income or life due to illness, disability, old age, or unemployment. Property risks include losses to property caused by perils, such as fire or theft, and hazards. Liability risks involve losses caused by negligence that leads to injury or property damage. *Negligence* is the failure to take ordinary or reasonable care to prevent accidents from happening. If a homeowner doesn't clear the ice from the front steps of her house, for example, she creates a liability risk because visitors could fall on the ice.

Personal risks, property risks, and liability risks are types of pure, or insurable, risk. The insurance company will have to pay only if some event that the insurance covers actually happens. Pure risks are accidental and unintentional. Although no one can predict whether a pure risk will occur, it's possible to predict how much it will cost if it does.

A speculative risk is a risk that carries a chance of either loss or gain. Starting a small business that may or may not succeed is an example of speculative risk. Speculative risks are not insurable.

QUESTION

Why do most people want to have their cars, home, and personal property insured?

Risk Management Methods

Risk management is an organized plan for protecting yourself, your family, and your property. It helps reduce financial losses caused by destructive events. Risk management is a long-range planning process. Your risk management needs will change at various points in your life. If you understand how to manage risks, you can provide better protection for yourself and your family. Most people think of risk management as buying insurance. However, insurance is not the only way of dealing with risk.

Risk Avoidance

You can avoid the risk of an automobile accident by not driving to work. A car manufacturer can avoid the risk of product failure by not introducing new cars. These are both examples of risk avoidance. They are ways to avoid risks, but they involve serious trade-offs. You might have to give up your job if you can't get there. The car manufacturer might lose business to competitors who take the risk of producing exciting new cars.

In some cases, though, risk avoidance is practical. By taking precautions in high-crime areas, you might avoid the risk that you will be robbed.

Risk Reduction

You can't avoid risks completely. However, you can decrease the likelihood that they will cause you harm. For example, you can reduce the risk of injury in an automobile accident by wearing a seat belt. You can reduce the risk of developing lung cancer by not smoking. By installing fire extinguishers in your home, you reduce the potential damage that could be caused by a fire. Your risk of illness might be lower if you eat properly and exercise regularly.

Risk Assumption

Risk assumption means taking on responsibility for the negative results of a risk. It makes sense to assume a risk if you know that the possible loss will be small. It also makes sense when you've taken all the precautions you can to avoid or reduce the risk.

When insurance coverage for a particular item is expensive, it may not be worth insuring. For instance, you might decide not to purchase collision insurance on an older car. If an accident happens, the car may be wrecked, but it wasn't worth much anyway.

Self-insurance is setting up a special fund, perhaps from savings, to cover the cost of a loss. Self-insurance does not eliminate risks, but it does provide a way of covering losses as an alternative to an insurance policy. Some people self-insure because they can't obtain insurance from an insurance company.

Risk Shifting

The most common method of dealing with risk is to shift it. That simply means to transfer it to an insurance company. In exchange for the fee you pay, the insurance company agrees to pay for your losses.

REDUCING RISKS Taking steps to protect yourself and your property from harm can reduce your risk of financial loss. *Besides wearing your seat belt, what are some other ways of reducing risks?*

Figure 13.1

Examples of Risks and Risk Management Strategies

| Risks | | Strategies for Reducing Financial Impact |
Personal Events	Financial Impact	
Disability	• Loss of income • Increased expenses	• Savings and investments • Disability insurance
Death	• Loss of income	• Life insurance • Estate planning
Property Loss	• Catastrophic storm damage to property • Repair or replacement • Cost of theft	• Property repair and upkeep • Auto insurance • Homeowners insurance • Flood or earthquake insurance
Liability	• Claims and settlement costs • Lawsuits and legal expenses • Loss of personal assets and income	• Maintaining property • Homeowners insurance • Auto insurance

RISKY BUSINESS Risk management strategies help reduce the financial impact of various risks. *Can you think of any other strategies that would apply to the risks mentioned in the chart?*

Most types of insurance policies include deductibles. Deductibles are a combination of risk assumption and risk shifting. A *deductible* is the set amount that the policyholder must pay per loss on an insurance policy. For example, if a falling tree damages your car, you may have to pay $200 toward the repairs. Your insurance company will pay the rest.

Figure 13.1 summarizes various risks and effective ways of managing them.

Planning an Insurance Program

Your personal insurance program should change along with your needs and goals. Kirk and Luanne are a young married couple. How will they plan their insurance program to meet their needs and goals?

Step 1   Set Insurance Goals

Kirk and Luanne's main goal should be to minimize personal, property, and liability risks. They also need to decide how they will cover costs resulting from a potential loss. Income, age, family size, lifestyle, experience, and responsibilities will be important factors in the goals they set. The insurance they buy must reflect those goals.

Kirk and Luanne should try to come up with a basic risk management plan that achieves the following:

- Reduces possible loss of income caused by premature death, illness, accident, or unemployment
- Reduces possible loss of property caused by perils, such as fire or theft, or hazards
- Reduces possible loss of income, savings, and property because of personal negligence

Step 2 Develop a Plan to Reach Your Goals

Planning is a way of taking control of life instead of just letting life happen to you. Kirk and Luanne need to determine what risks they face and what risks they can afford to take. They also have to determine what resources can help them reduce the damage that could be caused by serious risks.

Furthermore, they need to know what kind of insurance is available. The cost of different kinds of insurance and the way the costs vary among companies will be key factors in their plan. Finally, this couple needs to research the record of reliability of different insurance companies.

Kirk and Luanne must ask four questions as they develop their risk management plan:

- What do they need to insure?
- How much should they insure it for?
- What kind of insurance should they buy?
- Who should they buy insurance from?

Step 3 Put Your Plan into Action

Once they've developed their plan, Kirk and Luanne need to follow through by putting it into action. During this process they might discover that they don't have enough insurance protection. If that's the case, they could purchase additional coverage or change the kind of coverage they have. Another alternative would be to adjust their budget to cover the cost of additional insurance. Finally, Kirk and Luanne might expand their savings or investment programs and use those funds in the case of an emergency.

The best risk management plans will be flexible enough to allow Kirk and Luanne to respond to changing life situations. Their goal should be to create an insurance program that can grow or shrink as their protection needs change.

Review Your Results

Kirk and Luanne should take the time to review their plan every two or three years, or whenever their family circumstances change.

Until recently Kirk and Luanne were satisfied with the coverage provided by their insurance policies. However, when the couple bought a house six months ago, it was time for them to review their insurance plan. With the new house the risks became much greater. After all, what would happen if a fire destroyed part of their home?

The needs of a couple who rent an apartment differ from those of a couple who own a house. Both couples face similar risks, but their financial responsibility differs greatly. When you're developing or reviewing a risk management plan, ask yourself if you're providing the financial resources you'll need to protect yourself, your family, and your property.

$AVVY SAVER

Auto Insurance Tips

1. Shop around. Different insurance companies offer different rates.
2. Increase your deductible and save.
3. Consider dropping collision and comprehensive physical damage coverage as your car gets older.
4. Maintain a good driving record; it could reduce your rates.
5. Ask your insurance company which cars cost less to insure.

Property and Liability Insurance in Your Financial Plan

Major natural disasters have caused catastrophic amounts of property loss in the United States and other parts of the world. In 1989 Hurricane Hugo caused $4.2 billion in damages. In 1992 Hurricane Andrew resulted in $15 billion worth of insurance *claims*, or requests for payment to cover financial losses. In the Midwest in 1993, floods caused more than $2 billion worth of damage.

Most people invest large amounts of money in their homes and motor vehicles. Therefore, protecting these items from loss is extremely important. Each year homeowners and renters in the United States lose billions of dollars from more than 3 million burglaries, 500,000 fires, and 200,000 cases of damage from other perils. The cost of injuries and property damage caused by automobiles is also enormous.

Think of the price you pay for home and automobile insurance as an investment in protecting your most valuable possessions. The cost of such insurance may seem high. However, the financial losses from which it protects you are much higher.

Two main types of risks are related to your home and your car or other vehicle. One is the risk of damage to or loss of your property. The second type involves your responsibility for injuries to other people or damage to their property.

RESPOND

Describe how Kirk and Luanne's insurance needs might change over the course of their lives.

DISASTROUS RESULTS Events such as hurricanes can cause widespread devastation. *What can you do to protect against natural disasters?*

Potential Property Losses

People spend a great deal of money on their houses, automobiles, furniture, clothing, and other personal property. Property owners face two basic types of risks. The first is physical damage caused by perils, such as fire, wind, water, and smoke. These perils can damage or destroy your property. For example, a windstorm might cause a large tree branch to smash the windshield of your car. You would have to find another way to get around while it was being repaired. The second type of risk is loss or damage caused by criminal behavior, such as robbery, burglary, vandalism, and arson.

Liability Protection

You also need to protect yourself from liability. *Liability* is legal responsibility for the financial cost of another person's losses or injuries. You can be judged legally responsible even if the injury or damage was not your fault. For example, suppose that Terry falls and gets hurt while playing in her friend Lisa's yard. Terry's family may be able to sue Lisa's parents even though Lisa's parents did nothing wrong. Similarly, suppose that Sanjay accidentally damages a valuable painting while helping Ed move some furniture. Ed may take legal action against Sanjay to pay for the cost of the painting.

Usually, if you're found liable, or legally responsible, in a situation, it's because negligence on your part caused the mishap. Examples of such negligence include letting young children swim in a pool without supervision or cluttering a staircase with things that could cause someone to slip and fall.

SECTION 13.1 · ASSESSMENT

CHECK YOUR UNDERSTANDING

1. Name the three main types of insurable risks.
2. Explain how developing an insurance program can help you manage risk.
3. Describe how property and liability insurance can protect a homeowner from financial loss.

THINK CRITICALLY

4. Do you agree or disagree with this statement? "Insurance is a waste of money. If and when you suffer a financial loss because of an accident or some other event, you can pay for it from your savings account." Explain your position.

USING COMMUNICATION SKILLS

5. **My Favorite Things** Make a list of your most valuable possessions.
   Explain the Consequences Discuss the personal and financial consequences of having the items on your list lost, stolen, damaged, or destroyed. Then explain how having the items insured would affect the consequences that you've mentioned.

SOLVING MONEY PROBLEMS

6. **Paying for Insurance Protection** Hans has recently purchased a car. It's a fully restored 1957 Chevy, something he has always dreamed of having. The car cost $35,000, but for Hans the price was worth it. After shopping around for insurance, Hans realizes that the cost of insuring such a vehicle is quite significant. The best price he can find on the coverage he needs is $2,500 per year. He is thinking about cutting corners on his insurance coverage to save money. However, he knows he would be taking a risk by doing so.
   Compare Costs Help Hans solve his problem by comparing the cost of his insurance with the cost of his vehicle. Is it worth the insurance expense to protect his prized vehicle, or is it too much to spend to insure what is, after all, just a car?

What You'll Learn

- How to **describe** the insurance coverages and policy types available to home-owners and renters
- How to **analyze** the factors that influence the amount of coverage and cost of home insurance

Why It's Important

You will need to develop an effective risk management plan for your home or apartment and your personal belongings. When purchasing insurance, your goal is to get the best protection at the lowest cost.

KEY TERMS

- **homeowners insurance**
- **household inventory**
- **personal property floater**
- **umbrella policy**
- **medical payments coverage**
- **endorsement**
- **actual cash value**
- **replacement value**

Principles of Home and Property Insurance

Homeowners Insurance Coverages

Insuring your residence and its contents is absolutely necessary to protect your investment. *Homeowners insurance* is coverage that provides protection for your residence and its associated financial risks, such as damage to personal property and injuries to others.

A homeowners policy provides coverage for the following:

- The building in which you live and any other structures on the property
- Additional living expenses
- Personal property
- Personal liability and related coverages
- Specialized coverages

Buildings and Other Structures

The main purpose of homeowners insurance is to protect you against financial loss in case your home is damaged or destroyed. Detached structures on your property, such as a garage or toolshed, are also covered. Homeowners coverage even includes trees, shrubs, and plants.

Additional Living Expenses

If a fire or other event damages your home, additional living expense coverage pays for you to stay somewhere else. For example, you may need to stay in a motel or rent an apartment while your home is being repaired. These extra living expenses will be paid for by your insurance. Some policies limit additional living expense coverage to 10 to 20 percent of the home's coverage amount. They may also limit payments to a maximum of six to nine months. Other policies may pay additional living expenses for up to a year.

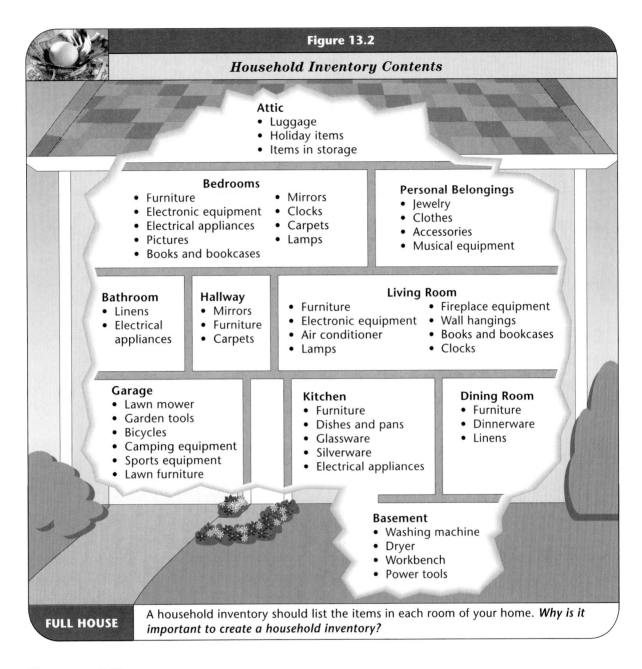

Figure 13.2

Household Inventory Contents

Attic
- Luggage
- Holiday items
- Items in storage

Bedrooms
- Furniture
- Electronic equipment
- Electrical appliances
- Pictures
- Books and bookcases
- Mirrors
- Clocks
- Carpets
- Lamps

Personal Belongings
- Jewelry
- Clothes
- Accessories
- Musical equipment

Bathroom
- Linens
- Electrical appliances

Hallway
- Mirrors
- Furniture
- Carpets

Living Room
- Furniture
- Electronic equipment
- Air conditioner
- Lamps
- Fireplace equipment
- Wall hangings
- Books and bookcases
- Clocks

Garage
- Lawn mower
- Garden tools
- Bicycles
- Camping equipment
- Sports equipment
- Lawn furniture

Kitchen
- Furniture
- Dishes and pans
- Glassware
- Silverware
- Electrical appliances

Dining Room
- Furniture
- Dinnerware
- Linens

Basement
- Washing machine
- Dryer
- Workbench
- Power tools

FULL HOUSE A household inventory should list the items in each room of your home. *Why is it important to create a household inventory?*

Personal Property

Homeowners insurance covers your household belongings, such as furniture, appliances, and clothing, up to a portion of the insured value of the home. That portion is usually 55, 70, or 75 percent. For example, a home insured for $80,000 might have $56,000 (70 percent) worth of coverage for household belongings.

Personal property coverage typically includes limits for the theft of certain items, such as $1,000 for jewelry. It provides protection against the loss or damage of articles that you take with you when you are away from home. For example, items you take on vacation or use at school are usually covered up to the policy limit. Personal property coverage even extends to property that you rent, such as a rug cleaner, while it's in your possession.

Most homeowners policies cover personal computers up to a certain limit, usually about $2,500. Contact your insurance agent to determine whether the equipment is covered against data loss and damage from spilled drinks or power surges.

If something does happen to your personal property, you must prove how much it was worth and that it belonged to you. To make the process easier, you can create a household inventory. A *household inventory* is a list or other documentation of personal belongings, with purchase dates and cost information. You can get a form for such an inventory from an insurance agent. **Figure 13.2** on page 421 provides a list of items you might include if you decide to compile your own inventory. For items of special value, you should have receipts, serial numbers, brand names, model names, and proof of value.

Your household inventory can include a video recording or photographs of your home and its contents. Make sure that the closet and storage area doors are photographed open. On the backs of the photographs, indicate the date and the value of the objects. Update your inventory, photos, and related documents on a regular basis. Keep a copy of each document in a secure location, such as a safe-deposit box.

If you own valuable items, such as expensive musical instruments, or need added protection for computers and related equipment, you can purchase a personal property floater. A *personal property floater* is additional property insurance that covers the damage or loss of a specific item of high value. The insurance company will require a detailed description of the item and its worth. You'll also need to have the item appraised, or evaluated by an expert, from time to time to make sure that its value hasn't changed.

PREDICT

What risks are covered by personal liability coverage?

Personal Liability and Related Coverages

Every day people face the risk of financial loss due to injuries to other people or their property. The following are examples of this risk:

- A guest falls on a patch of ice on the steps to your home and breaks his arm.
- A spark from the barbecue in your backyard starts a fire that damages a neighbor's roof.
- Your son or daughter accidentally breaks an antique lamp while playing at a neighbor's house.

In each of these situations, you could be held responsible for paying for the damage. The personal liability portion of a homeowners policy protects you and members of your family if others sue you for injuries they suffer or damage to their property. This coverage includes the cost of legal defense.

Not all individuals who come to your property are covered by your liability insurance. Friends, guests, and baby-sitters are probably covered. However, if you have regular employees, such as a housekeeper, a cook, or a gardener, you may need to obtain worker's compensation coverage for them.

Most homeowners policies provide basic personal liability coverage of $100,000, but often that's not enough. An *umbrella policy*, also called a personal catastrophe policy, supplements your basic personal liability coverage. This added protection covers you for all kinds of personal injury claims. For instance, an umbrella policy will cover you if someone sues you for saying or writing something negative or untrue or for damaging his or her reputation. Extended liability policies are sold in amounts of $1 million or more and are useful for wealthy people. If you are a business owner, you may need other types of liability coverage as well.

ADDITIONAL PROTECTION The purchase of a valuable item such as a high-quality musical instrument is a major investment. *Why would a person who buys an expensive piano decide to get a personal property floater on it?*

Medical payments coverage pays the costs of minor accidental injuries to visitors on your property. It also covers minor injuries caused by you, members of your family, or even your pets, away from home. Settlements under medical payments coverage are made without determining who was at fault. This makes it fast and easy for the insurance company to process small claims, generally up to $5,000. If the injury is more serious, the personal liability portion of the homeowners policy covers it. Medical payments coverage does not cover injury to you or the other people who live in your home.

If you or a family member should accidentally damage another person's property, the supplementary coverage of homeowners insurance will pay for it. This protection is usually limited to $500 or $1,000. Again, payments are made regardless of fault. If the damage is more expensive, however, it's handled under the personal liability coverage.

Specialized Coverages

Homeowners insurance usually doesn't cover losses from floods and earthquakes. If you live in an area that has frequent floods or earthquakes, you need to purchase special coverage. In some places the National Flood Insurance Program makes flood insurance available. This protection is separate from a homeowners policy. An insurance agent or the Federal Emergency Management Agency (FEMA) of the Federal Insurance Administration can give you additional information about this coverage.

You may be able to get earthquake insurance as an *endorsement*—addition of coverage—to a homeowners policy or through a state-run insurance program. The most serious earthquakes occur in the Pacific Coast region. However, earthquakes can happen in other

INTERNATIONAL FINANCE Vietnam

ittle more than a quarter century after the Vietnam War, Vietnam's youth enjoy freedoms their parents couldn't have imagined. They wear trendy fashions, listen to the hottest hits, and buy cell phones and pagers. With more than 40 million inhabitants under the age of 25, the consumer clout of this "youthquake" has helped widen the door to free trade. New businesses are springing up everywhere. In 1998 Vietnam's largest and most modern mall, or hypermarket, opened outside Ho Chi Minh City, formerly known as Saigon. The market carries more than 20,000 products, from French bread to stylish shoes.

Geographic area	127,242 sq. mi.
Population	79,490,000
Capital	Hanoi (pop. 1,089,800)
Language	Vietnamese, Chinese, English, French, Khmer, tribal languages
Currency	dong
Gross domestic product (GDP)	$128 billion
Per capita GDP	$1,700
Economy	Industry: food processing, garments, shoes. Agriculture: paddy rice, corn, poultry, fish. Exports: crude oil, marine products, rice, coffee.

Shoppers in Vietnam

Thinking Critically

Apply Many U.S. businesses are moving into Vietnam. Since most Vietnamese teenagers like anything American, list the types of businesses you think would be successful in Vietnam.

For more information on Vietnam visit finance.glencoe.com **or your local library.**

regions, too. If you plan to purchase a home in an area that has a high risk of floods or earthquakes, you may have to buy the necessary insurance in order to be approved for a mortgage loan.

Renters Insurance

For people who rent, home insurance coverages include personal property protection, additional living expenses coverage, and personal liability and related coverages. Renters insurance does not provide coverage on the building or other structures.

The most important part of renters insurance is the protection it provides for your personal property. Many renters believe that they are covered under their landlords' insurance. In fact, that's only the case when the landlord is proved liable for some damage. For example, if bad wiring causes a fire and damages a tenant's property, the tenant may be able to collect money from the landlord. Renters insurance is relatively inexpensive and provides many of the same kinds of protection as a homeowners policy.

Home Insurance Policy Forms

Home insurance policies are available in several forms. The forms provide different combinations of coverage. Some forms are not available in all areas.

The basic form (HO-1) protects against perils such as fire, lightning, windstorms, hail, volcanic eruptions, explosions, smoke, theft, vandalism, glass breakage, and riots. The broad form (HO-2) covers an even wider range of perils, including falling objects and damage from ice, snow, or sleet.

The special form (HO-3) covers all basic- and broad-form risks, plus any other risks except those specifically excluded from the policy. Common exclusions are flood, earthquake, war, and nuclear accidents. Personal property is covered for the risks listed in the policy.

The tenants' form (HO-4) protects the personal property of renters against the risks listed in the policy. It does not include coverage on the building or other structures.

The comprehensive form (HO-5) expands the coverage of the HO-3. The HO-5 includes endorsements for items such as replacement cost coverage on contents and guaranteed replacement cost coverage on buildings.

Condominium owners insurance (HO-6) protects personal property and any additions or improvements made to the living unit. These might include bookshelves, electrical fixtures, wallpaper, or carpeting. The condominium association purchases insurance on the building and other structures.

Manufactured housing units and mobile homes usually qualify for insurance coverage with conventional policies. However, some mobile homes may need special policies with higher rates because the way they are built increases their risk of fire and wind damage. The cost of mobile home insurance coverage depends on the home's location and the way it's attached to the ground. Mobile home insurance is quite expensive: a $20,000 mobile home can cost as much to insure as a $60,000 house.

In addition to the risks previously discussed, home insurance policies include coverage for:

- credit card fraud, check forgery, and counterfeit money;
- the cost of removing damaged property;
- emergency removal of property to protect it from damage;
- temporary repairs after a loss to prevent further damage;
- fire department charges in areas with such fees.

Not everything is covered by home insurance. (see **Figure 13.3**)

How Much Coverage Do You Need?

You can get the best insurance value by choosing the right coverage amount and knowing the factors that affect insurance costs.

Figure 13.3
Not Everything Is Covered

Certain personal property is not covered by homeowners insurance:

- Items insured separately, such as jewelry, furs, boats, or expensive electronic equipment
- Animals, birds, or fish
- Motorized vehicles not licensed for road use, except those used for home maintenance
- Sound devices, such as radios, tape players, and tapes used in motor vehicles

- Aircraft and parts
- Property belonging to tenants
- Property contained in a rental apartment
- Property rented by the homeowner to other people
- Business property

COVERAGE EXCLUSIONS Separate coverage may be available for personal property that is not covered by a homeowners insurance policy. *Give an example of another type of policy that would cover one of the items listed here.*

CLAIM SETTLEMENTS Insurance companies use two different methods for settling insurance claims. *If your family's television is damaged in a fire, how will your family be reimbursed for the television under the actual cash value method? Under the replacement value method?*

Your insurance should be based on the amount of money you would need to rebuild or repair your house, not the amount you paid for it. As construction costs rise, you should increase the amount of coverage. In fact, today most insurance policies automatically increase coverage as construction costs rise.

In the past, many homeowners' policies insured the building for only 80 percent of the replacement value. If the building were destroyed, the homeowner would have to pay for part of the cost of replacing it, which could be expensive. Today most companies recommend full coverage.

If you are borrowing money to buy a home, the lender will require that you have property insurance. Remember, too, that the amount of insurance on your home determines the coverage on your personal belongings. Coverage for personal belongings is usually from 55 to 75 percent of the insurance amount on your home.

Insurance companies base claim settlements on one of two methods. Under the *actual cash value* (ACV) method, the payment you receive is based on the replacement cost of an item minus depreciation. Depreciation is the loss of value of an item as it gets older. This means you would receive less for a five-year-old bicycle than you originally paid for it.

Under the *replacement value* method for settling claims, you receive the full cost of repairing or replacing an item. Depreciation

QUESTION

Which policy would be most likely to pay you more if your home burned down: actual cash value coverage or replacement value coverage?

is not considered. Many companies limit the replacement cost to 400 percent of the item's actual cash value. Replacement value coverage is more expensive than actual cash value coverage.

Factors That Affect Home Insurance Costs

The cost of your home insurance will depend on several factors, such as the location of the building and the type of building and construction materials. The amount of coverage and type of policy you choose will also affect the cost of home insurance. Furthermore, different insurance companies offer different rates.

Location of Home

The location of your home affects your insurance rates. Insurance companies offer lower rates to people whose homes are close to a water supply or fire hydrant or located in an area that has a good fire department. On the other hand, rates are higher in areas where crime is common. People living in regions that experience severe weather, such as tornadoes and hurricanes, may also pay more for insurance.

Type of Structure

The type of home and its construction influence the price of insurance coverage. A brick house, for example, will usually cost less to insure than a similar structure made of wood. However, earthquake coverage is more expensive for a brick house than for a wood dwelling because a wooden house is more likely to survive an earthquake. Also, an older house may be more difficult to restore to its original condition. That means that it will cost more to insure.

Coverage Amount and Policy Type

The policy and the amount of coverage you select affect the premium you pay. Obviously, it costs more to insure a $300,000 home than a $100,000 home.

The deductible amount in your policy also affects the cost of your insurance. If you increase the amount of your deductible, your premium will be lower because the company will pay out less in claims. The most common deductible amount is $250. Raising the deductible from $250 to $500 or $1,000 can reduce the premium you pay by 15 percent or more.

LOWER YOUR PREMIUM
Fires can cause costly damage to property and personal possessions. *Why do insurance companies often offer discounts to people who install smoke detectors and fire extinguishers in their homes?*

Home Insurance Discounts

Most companies offer discounts if you take action to reduce risks to your home. Your premium may be lower if you have smoke detectors or a fire extinguisher. If your home has dead-bolt locks and alarm systems, which make it harder for thieves to get in, insurance costs may be lower. Some companies offer discounts to people who don't file any claims for a certain number of years.

Company Differences

You can save up to 25 percent on homeowners insurance by comparing rates from several companies. Some insurance agents work for only one company. Others are independent agents who represent several different companies. Talk to both types of agents. You'll get the information you need to compare rates.

Don't select a company on the basis of price alone. Also consider service and coverage. Not all companies settle claims in the same way. Suppose that all of the homes on Evergreen Terrace are dented

Careers in Finance

INSURANCE CLAIMS ADJUSTER

When disasters strike, insurance claims adjusters are on the scene. To help bring quick relief to victims who are insured, adjusters inspect the damage from devastating fires, earthquakes, or floods right away. People also contact an adjuster when their cars or homes are damaged or when they're injured in an accident. Adjusters work for insurance companies. Minor claims are often handled on the phone. For more complex claims, adjusters interview clients, witnesses, and police, check hospital records, or inspect property damage. They take photographs, record information, and prepare reports. They sometimes work evenings and weekends or travel to the sites of disasters, such as hurricanes. After researching a claim, adjusters decide to pay or deny the claim. If a claim is contested, they may have to testify in court.

Skills	Analytical, communication, computer, math, writing
Personality	Able to work under stress, detail oriented, likes working with people, observant
Education	High school diploma or bachelor's degree; training by an industry organization
Pay range	$18,000 to $58,000, depending on experience, location, and company

Analyze What are some difficulties or challenges that insurance adjusters might experience in their daily work?

 For more information on insurance claims adjusters visit finance.glencoe.com **or your local library.**

on one side by large hail. They all have the same kind of siding. Unfortunately, the homeowners discover that this type of siding is no longer available, so all the siding on all of the houses will need to be replaced. Some insurance companies will pay to replace all the siding. Others will pay only to replace the damaged parts.

State insurance commissions and consumer organizations can give you information about different insurance companies. *Consumer Reports* rates insurance companies on a regular basis.

SECTION 13.2 ASSESSMENT

CHECK YOUR UNDERSTANDING

1. Name the six home insurance policy forms.
2. Describe the type of coverage provided by a personal property floater.
3. Explain how the location of a home can affect insurance costs.

THINK CRITICALLY

4. Create at least two situations for which personal liability coverage might be required.

USING MATH SKILLS

5. **Insurance Coverage** Homeowners insurance covers your personal possessions up to a percentage of the insured value of your home. When Carolina's house burned down, she lost household items worth a total of $25,000. Her house was insured for $80,000, and her homeowners policy provided coverage for personal belongings up to 55 percent of the insured value of the house.
   Calculate Determine how much insurance coverage Carolina's policy provides for her personal possessions and whether she will receive payment for all of the items destroyed in the fire.

SOLVING MONEY PROBLEMS

6. **Analyzing Insurance Costs** Kara and Adam Gottlieb are in the process of buying their first home. After months of shopping, they've narrowed their choices down to two. One is an older house near a river, where flooding occasionally occurs. The other is a newer house that is located farther from the river. They need to know how much homeowners insurance will cost for each house before making a final decision.
   Compare and Contrast Given this information, make your best educated guess about which house would be the more economical to insure.

Automobile Insurance

Motor vehicle crashes cost more than $150 billion in lost wages and medical bills every year. Traffic accidents can destroy people's lives physically, financially, and emotionally. Buying insurance can't eliminate the pain and suffering that automobile accidents cause. It can, however, reduce the financial impact.

Every state in the United States has a *financial responsibility law*, a law that requires drivers to prove that they can pay for damage or injury caused by an automobile accident. As of 2000, more than 40 states had laws requiring people to carry automobile insurance. In the remaining states, most people buy automobile insurance by choice. Very few people have the money they would need to meet financial responsibility requirements on their own.

The coverage provided by automobile insurance falls into two categories. One is protection for bodily injury. The other is protection for property damage. (see **Figure 13.4**)

Motor Vehicle Bodily Injury Coverages

Most of the money that automobile insurance companies pay out in claims goes for legal expenses, medical expenses, and other costs that arise when someone is injured. The main types of bodily injury coverages are bodily injury liability, medical payments, and uninsured motorist's protection.

Bodily Injury Liability

Bodily injury liability is insurance that covers physical injuries caused by an automobile accident for which you were responsible. If pedestrians, people in other cars, or passengers in your car are injured or killed, bodily injury liability coverage pays for expenses related to the crash.

Bodily injury liability coverage is usually expressed by three numbers, such as 100/300/50. These amounts represent thousands of dollars of coverage. The first two numbers refer to bodily injury coverage. In the example above, $100,000 is the maximum amount that the

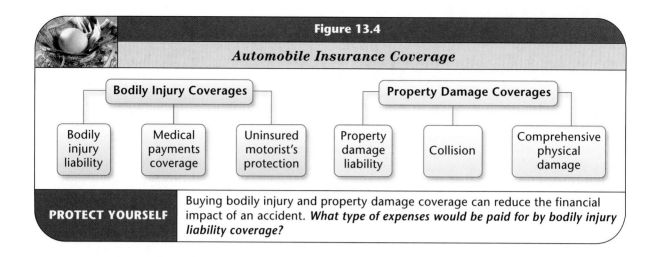

Figure 13.4

Automobile Insurance Coverage

Bodily Injury Coverages
- Bodily injury liability
- Medical payments coverage
- Uninsured motorist's protection

Property Damage Coverages
- Property damage liability
- Collision
- Comprehensive physical damage

PROTECT YOURSELF Buying bodily injury and property damage coverage can reduce the financial impact of an accident. *What type of expenses would be paid for by bodily injury liability coverage?*

insurance company will pay for the injuries of any one person in any one accident. The second number, $300,000, is the maximum amount the company will pay for all injured parties (two or more) in any one accident. The third number, $50,000, indicates the limit for payment for damage to the property of others. (see **Figure 13.5**)

Medical Payments Coverage

Medical payments coverage is insurance that applies to the medical expenses of anyone who is injured in your automobile, including you. This type of coverage also provides additional medical benefits for you and members of your family; it pays medical expenses if you or your family members are injured while riding in another person's car or if any of you are hit by a car.

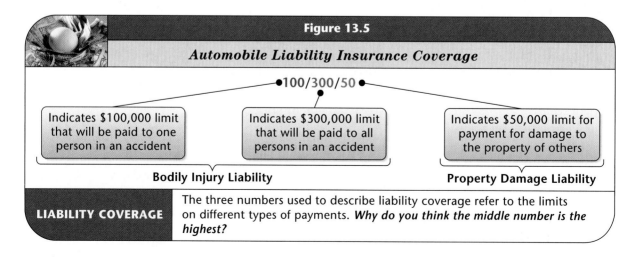

Figure 13.5

Automobile Liability Insurance Coverage

●100/300/50●

| Indicates $100,000 limit that will be paid to one person in an accident | Indicates $300,000 limit that will be paid to all persons in an accident | Indicates $50,000 limit for payment for damage to the property of others |

Bodily Injury Liability　　　　**Property Damage Liability**

LIABILITY COVERAGE The three numbers used to describe liability coverage refer to the limits on different types of payments. *Why do you think the middle number is the highest?*

Uninsured Motorist's Protection

Unfortunately, you cannot assume that everyone who is behind the wheel is carrying insurance. How can you guard yourself and your passengers against the risk of getting into an accident with someone who has no insurance? The answer is uninsured motorist's protection.

Uninsured motorist's protection is insurance that covers you and your family members if you are involved in an accident with an uninsured or hit-and-run driver. In most states it does not cover damage to the vehicle itself. Penalties for driving uninsured vary by state, but they generally include stiff fines and suspension of driving privileges.

Underinsured motorist's coverage protects you when another driver has some insurance, but not enough to pay for the injuries he or she has caused.

Motor Vehicle Property Damage Coverages

One afternoon, during a summer storm, Carrie was driving home from her job as a hostess at a pancake house. The rain was coming down in buckets, and she couldn't see very well. As a result, she didn't realize that the car in front of her had stopped to make a left turn, and she hit the car. The crash totaled Carrie's new car. Fortunately, she had purchased property damage coverage. Property damage coverage protects you from financial loss if you damage someone else's property or if your car is damaged. It includes property damage liability, collision, and comprehensive physical damage.

Property Damage Liability

Property damage liability is automobile insurance that applies when you damage the property of others. In addition, it protects you when you're driving another person's car with the owner's permission. Although the damaged property is usually another car, the coverage also extends to buildings and to equipment such as street signs and telephone poles.

Collision

Collision insurance covers damage to your car when it is involved in an accident. It allows you to collect money no matter who was at fault. However, the amount you can collect is limited to the actual

CONNECT

If you own a car, does your state require you to carry automobile insurance? If so, what coverage is required? What are the penalties for not carrying insurance?

cash value of your car at the time of the accident. If your car has many extra features, make sure that you have a record of its condition and value.

Comprehensive Physical Damage

Comprehensive physical damage coverage protects you if your car is damaged in a nonaccident situation. It covers your car against risks such as fire, theft, falling objects, vandalism, hail, floods, tornadoes, earthquakes, and avalanches.

No-Fault Insurance

To reduce the time and cost of settling automobile injury cases, various states are trying a number of alternatives. Under the *no-fault system*, drivers who are involved in accidents collect money from their own insurance companies. It doesn't matter who caused the accident. Each company pays the insured up to the limits of his or her coverage. Because no-fault systems vary by state, you should investigate the coverages of no-fault insurance in your state.

Other Coverages

Several other kinds of automobile insurance are available to you. Wage loss insurance pays for any salary or income you might have lost because of being injured in an automobile accident. Wage loss insurance is usually required in states with a no-fault insurance system. In other states it's available by choice.

Emergency road service coverage pays for mechanical assistance in the event that your car breaks down. This can be helpful on long trips or during bad weather. If necessary, you can get your car towed to a service station. However, once your car arrives at the repair shop, you're responsible for paying the bill. If you belong to an automobile club, your membership may include towing coverage. If that's the case, paying for emergency road service coverage could be a waste of money. Rental reimbursement coverage pays for a rental car if your vehicle is stolen or being repaired.

Automobile Insurance Costs

Automobile insurance is not cheap. The average household spends more than $1,200 for automobile insurance yearly. The premiums are related to the amount of claims insurance companies pay out each year.

Frank, a high school junior, recently got his license. At his part-time job, he earns minimum wage. As a result he needs to get the best insurance value for his money.

PREDICT

What factors will influence the cost of your automobile insurance?

Amount of Coverage

The amount Frank will pay for insurance depends on the amount of coverage he requires. He needs enough coverage to protect himself legally and financially.

LEGAL CONCERNS As discussed earlier, most people who are involved in auto accidents cannot afford to pay an expensive court settlement with their own money. For this reason, most drivers buy liability insurance.

In the past, bodily injury liability coverage of 10/20 was usually enough. However, some people have been awarded millions of dollars in recent cases, so coverage of 100/300 is usually recommended.

PROPERTY VALUES Just as medical expenses and legal settlements have increased, so has the cost of cars. Therefore, Frank should consider a policy with a limit of $50,000 or even $100,000 for property damage liability.

Automobile Insurance Premium Factors

Vehicle type, rating territory, and driver classification are three other factors that influence automobile insurance costs.

VEHICLE TYPE The year, make, and model of a vehicle will affect insurance costs. Cars that have expensive replacement parts and require complicated repairs will cost more to insure. Also, premiums will probably be higher for car makes and models that are frequently stolen.

RATING TERRITORY In most states your rating territory is the place of residence used to determine your automobile insurance premium. Different locations have different costs. For example, rural areas usually have fewer accidents and less frequent occurrences of theft. Your insurance would probably cost less there than if you lived in a large city.

OPTIONAL COVERAGE If a car breaks down on the road, the driver may need to get help. *What type of assistance is usually paid for by emergency road service coverage?*

Susan Witmer and Nora Brannan are excited about their vacation to Florida. They've decided to rent a car because Nora drives an unreliable clunker and Susan doesn't want to put the mileage on her car. When they go to pick up the rental car, the sales agent asks them if they want insurance, which costs $10 per day. They don't want to spend the extra money, but neither one knows if her personal insurance covers rental cars. Nora says she carries the minimum insurance on her car because it isn't worth enough to need the additional coverage. Susan has never really paid much attention to the insurance coverage she carries. Nora says she's heard that if you use certain credit cards to pay for a rental car, then you are protected against damage. Unfortunately, Nora doesn't know whether her credit card will protect her or not. Nora and Susan turned to the experts at Standard & Poor's for advice.

STANDARD &POOR'S

Analysis: Many people are not sure whether their automobile insurance covers rental cars. Nora and Susan will need to make sure that they have enough insurance. If their rental car is damaged or stolen, the rental company will hold them fully responsible. Nora is correct in thinking that some credit cards include rental car insurance automatically. Insurance may also be a benefit of auto clubs, such as AAA.

STANDARD &POOR'S

Recommendation: A few phone calls can clarify what coverage Nora and Susan already have. Nora probably does not have collision, and Susan's policy may apply only to her own car and other cars involved in an accident. Even if Susan's insurance already provides collision insurance on a car rental, they may want to buy additional insurance from the rental company. Otherwise, if Susan has to file a claim on her insurance, her rates may increase. Also, Nora should not drive the car unless she either buys the additional insurance or is covered by a credit card she uses to rent the car. Nora and Susan should check with their credit card companies to find out whether their rental is covered. At a minimum, Nora and Susan need to make sure that they have bodily injury liability.

Critical Thinking Questions

1. Why would Nora choose to carry only the minimum amount of insurance on her car?
2. Why might it be worth it to buy additional insurance for a rental car than you would carry on your own car?
3. What factors do you think are important in deciding on how much bodily injury liability to carry?

DRIVER CLASSIFICATION Driver classification is based on age, sex, marital status, driving record, and driving habits. In general, young drivers (under 25) and elderly drivers (over 70) have more frequent and more serious accidents. As a result these groups pay higher premiums. Your driving record will also influence your insurance premiums. If you have accidents or receive tickets for traffic violations, your rates will increase.

The cost and number of claims that you file with your insurance company will also affect your premium. If you file expensive claims, your rates will increase. If you have too many claims, your insurance company may cancel your policy. That will make it harder for you to get coverage from another company. To deal with this problem, every state has an assigned risk pool. An *assigned risk pool* includes all the people who can't get automobile insurance. Some of these people are assigned to each insurance company operating in the state. These policyholders pay several times the normal rates, but they do get coverage. Once they establish a good driving record, they can reapply for insurance at regular rates.

Reducing Automobile Insurance Premiums

Two ways in which Frank can reduce his automobile insurance costs are by comparing companies and taking advantage of discounts.

COMPARING COMPANIES Rates and services vary among automobile insurance companies. Even among companies in the same area, premiums can vary by as much as 100 percent. Frank should compare the service and rates of local insurance agents. Most states publish this type of information. Furthermore, Frank can check a company's reputation with sources such as *Consumer Reports* or his state insurance department.

PREMIUM DISCOUNTS The best way for Frank to keep his rates down is to maintain a good driving record by avoiding accidents and traffic tickets. In addition, most insurance companies offer various discounts. Because Frank is under 25, he can qualify for reduced rates by taking a driver training program or maintaining good grades in school.

Furthermore, installing security devices will decrease the chance of theft and lower Frank's insurance costs. Being a nonsmoker can qualify him for lower automobile insurance premiums as well. Discounts are also offered for insuring two or more vehicles with the same company.

Increasing the amounts of deductibles will also lead to a lower premium. If Frank has an old car that's not worth much, he may

DRIVER CLASSIFICATION A driver's age affects the price of insurance premiums. *Who is likely to pay more for insurance: this teen or her parents? Why?*

Auto Insurance—How Much Will It Cost?

Before Mario bought the car he wanted, he needed to be sure he could afford the insurance for it. In this example he chose low liability, uninsured motorist coverage, and high deductibles to keep his insurance payments as low as possible. Clearly insurer B offered a lower price for the same coverage.

Investigating Insurance Companies		
	Insurer A	**Insurer B**
Bodily Injury Coverage:		
• Bodily injury liability $50,000 each person; $100,000 each accident	$472	$358
• Uninsured motorist's protection	208	84
• Medical payments coverage: $2,000 each person	48	46
Property Damage Coverage:		
• Property damage liability $50,000 each accident	182	178
• Collision with $500 deductible	562	372
• Comprehensive physical damage with $500 deductible	263	202
Car rental:	40	32
Discounts: good driver, air bags, garage parking	(165)	
Annual total	$1,610	$1,272

Research   Identify a make, model, and year of a car you might like to own. Research two insurance companies and get prices using this example. You can get their rates by telephone. Many also have Web sites. Using your workbook or on a separate sheet of paper, record your findings. How do they compare? Which company would you choose and why?

decide not to pay for collision and comprehensive coverages. However, before he makes this move, he should compare the value of his car for getting to school or work with the cost of these coverages.

ASSESSMENT

CHECK YOUR UNDERSTANDING

1. Describe the three main types of automobile insurance that cover bodily injuries.
2. Explain the difference between collision and comprehensive physical damage coverages.
3. Why do some insurance companies offer discounts to drivers who install security devices in their cars?

THINK CRITICALLY

4. Draw conclusions about which ways of reducing automobile insurance premiums might be best for you.

USING COMMUNICATION SKILLS

5. **Drinking and Driving** Alcohol use is a factor in more than 60 percent of all traffic accidents. Interview classmates, parents, and others to get their views on this subject. Consider contacting an organization such as MADD (Mothers Against Drunk Driving) for more information.
   Prepare a Public Service Announcement You've probably seen or heard public service announcements urging people not to drink and drive. Use what you've learned to create your own public service announcement. It may be in the form of a radio or television script. If possible, get some friends to help you produce your spot, using audio or video recording equipment.

SOLVING MONEY PROBLEMS

6. **Cost of Automobile Insurance** Malcolm thinks that it's about time to buy a brand-new car. He has been eyeing an expensive sport-utility vehicle. However, his mechanic has warned him that the replacement parts for the car that he wants are costly. His friend Ishiro is on a tight budget and doesn't have a car. He is considering buying a car that is reported to have low maintenance costs. Malcolm and Ishiro live in the same neighborhood. Malcolm has never had a car accident, but he received one traffic ticket last year. Ishiro's driving record is perfect.
   Compare Costs Using what you've learned, compare the insurance premiums Malcolm and Ishiro will probably have to pay on their cars. Explain how you reached your answer.

Chapter 13 *Home and Automobile Insurance* 439

CHAPTER 13 ASSESSMENT

CHAPTER SUMMARY

- The main types of risk are personal risk, property risk, and liability risk. Risk management methods include avoidance, reduction, assumption, and shifting.

- Planning an insurance program is a way to manage risks.

- Property and liability insurance protect your homes and motor vehicles against financial loss.

- A homeowners policy provides coverage for buildings and other structures, additional living expenses, personal property, personal liability and related coverages, and specialized coverages.

- Renters insurance provides many of the same kinds of protection as homeowners policies.

- The factors that affect home insurance coverage and costs include the location, the type of structure, the coverage amount and policy type, discounts, and the choice of insurance company.

- Motor vehicle bodily injury coverages include bodily injury liability, medical payments coverage, and uninsured motorist's protection.

- Motor vehicle property damage coverages include property damage liability, collision, and comprehensive physical damage.

- Automobile insurance costs depend on the amount of coverage you need as well as automobile type, rating territory, and driver classification.

Understanding and Using Vocabulary

Practice using these terms. With a partner, role-play an imaginary meeting with an insurance agent. Discuss your options for buying homeowners insurance and automobile insurance. Take turns being the insurance agent and the potential customer. Use as many key terms in your discussion as you can.

insurance
insurance company
insurer
policy
policyholder
premium
coverage
insured

risk
peril
hazard
negligence
deductible
claim
liability
homeowners insurance
household inventory
personal property floater
umbrella policy
medical payments coverage

endorsement
actual cash value
replacement value
financial responsibility law
bodily injury liability
medical payments coverage
uninsured motorist's protection
property damage liability
collision
no-fault system
assigned risk pool

CHAPTER 13 ASSESSMENT

Review Key Concepts

1. List methods of managing risk.
2. Describe the four steps in developing an insurance program.
3. What is the main difference between homeowners insurance and renters insurance?
4. What factors affect home insurance costs?
5. What factors affect auto insurance costs?

Apply Key Concepts

1. Prepare a speech on how best to manage risks.
2. Summarize how the four steps in developing an insurance plan can help people meet their financial needs and goals.
3. Compare and contrast the insurance needs of a homeowner and a person who rents.
4. Write a description of a homeowners or renters insurance policy for your family. What types of coverage would they need?
5. Analyze the ways in which the factors that affect automobile insurance costs may lead to lower premiums.

 Problem Solving Today

ALL WET

You've invested thousands of dollars in computer equipment and set it up in your apartment. When you got home, you found that the roof was leaking. Your equipment was ruined beyond repair. Although you do have renters insurance, you didn't buy extra coverage for these expensive items. Besides, you think that the landlord should pay you for the damages.

Gather Data Conduct library research to find out the legal and financial aspects of your situation. Can you collect money from your landlord's insurance? Is there anything your insurance company can do to help?

 **Computer Activity** As an alternative activity, use Internet Web sites to find the information you need.

Real-World Application

CONNECT WITH TECHNOLOGY

Many cars have safety features such as air bags. Buying a car with such features could reduce the cost of your automobile insurance.

Conduct Interviews Talk with a science teacher or auto mechanic to find out why certain automobile features make driving safer. Contact an insurance agent to determine the difference between the cost of insurance for a car with these features and for one that doesn't have them.

FINANCE *Online*

BEATING THE ODDS

Insurance companies compile statistics about various risks and analyze them to see which risks are more or less likely to happen. They use this information to determine how much to charge for insurance coverages.

Connect Using different Internet search engines, find insurance company Web sites or other sites that might provide some of these statistics. Look for information on topics such as traffic accidents, fires, floods, and theft. How might this information help you develop an insurance plan.

CHAPTER 14

Health, Disability, and Life Insurance

STANDARD
&POOR'S

Q&A

Q: I'm a high school student. Why should I be concerned about health care costs now?

A: Your health care costs, now and in the future, can be affected by your personal health habits. Many health problems result from poor habits, such as lack of exercise or inadequate diet, and may take years to develop. By establishing good habits now, you can reduce the likelihood of future health problems and related expenses.

Health Insurance and Financial Planning

*W*arren was riding his bike on a country road when he skidded on some loose gravel and crashed into a tree. The accident meant a trip to the hospital. A few days later, he received a bill for the visit to the emergency room, an additional bill from the doctor who had treated him, and an X-ray technician's bill.

Warren has no health insurance, which might have paid some or all of these costs. He called the doctors and the hospital. He explained the situation to them, and they agreed to let him make monthly payments on the debt. When Warren finished making these calls, he decided to make a few more—to companies that provided health insurance policies.

What Is Health Insurance?

Health insurance is a form of protection that eases the financial burden people may experience as a result of illness or injury. You pay a premium, or fee, to the insurer. In return the company pays most of your medical costs. Although plans vary in what they cover, they may reimburse you for hospital stays, doctors' visits, medications, and sometimes vision and dental care.

Health insurance includes both medical expense insurance, as discussed above, and disability income insurance. Medical expense insurance typically pays only the actual medical costs. Disability income insurance provides payments to make up for some of the income of a person who cannot work as a result of injury or illness. In this chapter the term "health insurance" generally refers to medical expense insurance.

Health insurance plans can be purchased in several different ways: group health insurance, individual health insurance, and COBRA.

What You'll Learn

- How to **explain** the importance of health insurance in financial planning
- How to **analyze** the costs and benefits of various types of health insurance coverage
- How to **assess** the trade-offs of different health insurance policies

Why It's Important

Knowing how to determine the type of health insurance plan that you need can help you meet your financial goals even when dealing with unexpected medical costs.

KEY TERMS

- health insurance
- coinsurance
- stop-loss
- copayment

Group Health Insurance

Most people who have health insurance are covered under group plans. Typically, these plans are employer sponsored. This means that the employer offers the plans and usually pays some or all of the premiums. Other organizations, such as labor unions and professional associations, also offer group plans. Group insurance plans cover you and your immediate family. The Health Insurance Portability and Accountability Act of 1996 set new federal standards that ensure that workers would not lose their health insurance if they

What's Your Financial ID?

INSURANCE FACTS AND FICTION

Insurance may not be a big issue for you now, but once you're no longer covered under your parents' or guardian's policies or you start full-time employment, you'll need to know your options. Here's an opportunity to test your knowledge. Write your answers to the following questions on a separate sheet of paper.

1. Health insurance is only available as a benefit from an employer.
   True   False

2. You can continue your health insurance even if you leave a job.
   True   False

3. A copayment is the small amount you pay for a doctor's visit or prescription.
   True   False

4. In general the younger you are, the less expensive life insurance is.
   True   False

5. Life insurance can also be used as an investment for retirement.
   True   False

6. Life insurance companies can cancel policies if you develop a serious illness after you're insured.
   True   False

7. You can collect life insurance benefits before you die.
   True   False

8. The amount of disability insurance you can buy is based on a percentage of your total income.
   True   False

changed jobs. As a result, a parent with a sick child, for example, can move from one group health plan to another without a lapse in coverage. Moreover, the parent will not have to pay more for coverage than other employees do.

The cost of group insurance is fairly low because many people are insured under the same policy—a contract with a risk-sharing group, or insurance company. However, group insurance plans vary in the amount of protection that they provide. For example, some plans limit the amount that they will pay for hospital stays and surgical procedures. If your plan does not cover all of your health insurance needs, you have several choices.

If you are married, you may be able to take advantage of a coordination of benefits (COB) provision, which is included in most group insurance plans. This provision allows you to combine the benefits from more than one insurance plan. The benefits received from all plans are limited to 100 percent of all allowable medical expenses. For example, a couple could use benefits from the wife's group plan and from the husband's group plan up to 100 percent.

If this type of provision is not available to you, or if you are single, you can get added protection by buying individual health insurance.

Individual Health Insurance

Some people do not have access to an employer-sponsored group insurance plan because they are self-employed. Others are simply dissatisfied with the coverage that their group plan provides. In these cases individual health insurance may be the answer. You can buy individual health insurance directly from the company of your choice. Plans usually cover you as an individual or cover you and your family. Individual plans can be adapted to meet your own needs. You should comparison shop, however, because rates can vary.

COBRA

Hakeem had a group insurance plan through his employer, but he was recently laid off. He wondered how he would be able to get medical coverage until he found a new job. Fortunately for Hakeem, the Consolidated Omnibus Budget Reconciliation Act of 1986, known as COBRA, allowed him to keep his former employer's group coverage for a set period of time. He had to pay the premiums himself, but at least the coverage wasn't canceled. When he found a new job, he was then able to switch to that employer's group plan with no break in coverage.

RESPOND

Imagine and describe at least two scenarios where a young, healthy person would need health insurance.

Not everyone qualifies for COBRA. You have to work for a private company or a state or local government to benefit.

Types of Health Insurance Coverage

PREDICT

What does major medical expense insurance cover and why is it beneficial?

Several types of health insurance coverage are available, either through a group plan or through individual purchase. Some benefits are included in nearly every health insurance plan; other benefits are much less common.

Basic Health Insurance Coverage

Basic health insurance coverage includes hospital expense coverage, surgical expense coverage, and physician expense coverage.

HOSPITAL EXPENSE Hospital expense coverage pays for some or all of the daily costs of room and board during a hospital stay. Routine nursing care, minor medical supplies, and the use of other hospital facilities are covered as well. For example, covered expenses would include anesthesia, laboratory fees, dressings, X rays, local ambulance service, and the use of an operating room.

Be aware, though, that most policies set a maximum amount they will pay for each day you are in the hospital. They may also limit the number of days they will cover. As you may remember from Chapter 13, many policies may also require a deductible. A deductible is a set amount that the policyholder must pay toward medical expenses before the insurance company pays benefits.

SURGICAL EXPENSE Surgical expense coverage pays all or part of the surgeon's fees for an operation, whether it is done in the hospital or in the doctor's office. Policies often have a list of the services that they cover, which specifies the maximum payment for each type of operation. For example, a policy might allow $500 for an appendectomy. If the entire surgeon's bill is not covered, the policyholder has to pay the difference. People often buy surgical expense coverage in combination with hospital expense coverage.

PHYSICIAN EXPENSE Physician expense coverage meets some or all of the costs of physician care that do not involve surgery. This form of health insurance covers treatment in a hospital, a doctor's office, or even the patient's home. Plans may cover routine doctor visits, X rays, and lab tests. Like surgical expense, physician expense includes maximum benefits for specific services. Physician expense coverage is usually combined with surgical and hospital coverage in a package called basic health insurance.

Major Medical Expense Insurance

Most people find that basic health insurance meets their usual needs. The cost of a serious illness or accident, however, can quickly go beyond the amounts that basic health insurance will pay. Chen had emergency surgery, which meant an operation, a two-week hospital stay, a number of lab tests, and several follow-up visits. He was shocked to discover that his basic health insurance paid less than half of the total bill, leaving him with debts of more than $10,000.

Chen would have been better protected if he had had major medical expense insurance. This coverage pays the large costs involved in long hospital stays and multiple surgeries. In other words, it takes up where basic health insurance coverage leaves off. Almost every type of care and treatment prescribed by a physician, in or out of a hospital, is covered. Maximum benefits can range from $10,000 up to $1 million per illness per year.

Of course, this type of coverage isn't cheap. To keep premiums low, most major medical plans require a deductible. Some plans also include a coinsurance provision. *Coinsurance* is the percentage of the medical expenses the policyholder must pay in addition to the deductible amount. Many policies require policyholders to pay 20 or 25 percent of expenses after they have paid the deductible.

Ariana's policy includes an $800 deductible and a coinsurance provision requiring her to pay 20 percent of all bills. If her bills total $3,800, for instance, the company will first exclude $800 from coverage, which is Ariana's deductible. It will then pay 80 percent of the remaining $3,000, or $2,400. Therefore, Ariana's total costs are $1,400 ($800 for the deductible and $600 for the coinsurance).

Some major medical policies contain a stop-loss provision. *Stop-loss* is a provision that requires the policyholder to pay all costs up to a certain amount, after which the insurance company pays 100 percent of the remaining expenses, as long as they are covered in the policy. Typically, the policyholder will pay between $3,000 and $5,000 in out-of-pocket expenses before the coverage begins.

Major medical expense insurance may be offered as a single policy with basic health insurance coverage, or it can be bought

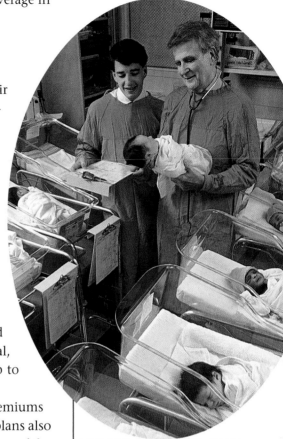

MATERNITY WARD The medical costs of giving birth can be high. *What costs of a delivery would be paid for by hospital expense coverage?*

separately. Comprehensive major medical insurance is a type of complete health insurance that helps pay hospital, surgical, medical, and other bills. It has a very low deductible, usually $200 to $300. Many major medical policies set limits on the benefits they will pay for certain expenses, such as surgery and hospital room and board.

Hospital Indemnity Policies

A hospital indemnity policy pays benefits when you're hospitalized. Unlike most of the other plans mentioned, however, these

---

INTERNATIONAL FINANCE   Pitcairn Island

Pacific Ocean

Pitcairn Island

*H*ave you read *Mutiny on the Bounty*? It's a true story. In 1790 the *Bounty*, a British cargo ship, set sail for the West Indies from Tahiti. During the long voyage a number of sea-weary sailors mutinied. Their captain, William Bligh, and 18 loyal crewmen were set adrift in the South Pacific. The mutineers and their Tahitian companions sailed on, eventually landing on deserted Pitcairn Island. The small community lived there secretly until it was discovered by American whalers in 1808. Pitcairn has been a stopover for passenger ships ever since. Tourists come to see living history. They're also the island's major source of cash, buying colorful postage stamps and hand-carved crafts from the descendants of the *Bounty* mutineers.

Pitcairn Islanders
selling crafts

Geographic area	2 sq. mi.
Population	49 (July 1999 est.)
Capital	Adamstown
Language	English (official), Pitcairnese, Tahitian, 18th-century English dialect
Currency	New Zealand dollar
Gross domestic product (GDP)	Not available
Per capita GDP	Not available
Economy	Industry: tourism, postage stamps, and hand-carved curios. Agriculture: wide variety of fruits and vegetables. Exports: fruits, vegetables, and curios.

Thinking Critically

Apply Pitcairn Islanders use the barter system—paying for goods and services with other goods and services instead of with money. What types of bartering could you do with your friends and family?

For more information on Pitcairn Island visit finance.glencoe.com or your local library.

---

policies don't directly cover medical costs. Instead you are paid in cash, which you can spend on medical or nonmedical expenses as you choose. Hospital indemnity policies are used as a supplement to—and not a replacement for—basic health or major medical policies. The average person who buys such a policy, however, usually pays much more in premiums than he or she receives in payments.

Dental Expense Insurance

Dental expense insurance provides reimbursement for the expenses of dental services and supplies. It encourages preventive dental care. The coverage normally provides for oral examinations (including X rays and cleanings), fillings, extractions, oral surgery, dentures, and braces. As with other insurance plans, dental insurance may have a deductible and a coinsurance provision, stating that the policyholder pays from 20 to 50 percent after the deductible.

Vision Care Insurance

An increasing number of insurance companies are including vision care insurance as part of group plans. Vision care insurance may cover eye examinations, glasses, contact lenses, eye surgery, and the treatment of eye diseases.

Dread Disease Policies

Dread disease, trip accident, death insurance, and cancer policies are usually sold through the mail, in newspapers and magazines, or by door-to-door salespeople. These kinds of policies play upon unrealistic fears, and they are illegal in many states. They only cover very specific conditions, which are already fully covered if you are insured under a major medical plan.

Long-Term Care Insurance

Long-term care insurance provides coverage for the expense of daily help that you may need if you become seriously ill or disabled and are unable to care for yourself. It is useful whether you require a lengthy stay in a nursing home or just need help at home with daily activities such as dressing, bathing, and household chores. Annual premiums range from less than $900 up to $15,000, depending on your age and the extent of the coverage.

Fitness Fun

Don't get carried away buying expensive exercise clothes; they may look good, but they don't improve your workout. Instead of paying to join a health club, you can get your exercise by walking or jogging in your neighborhood or at your school's track. All you need is a good pair of athletic shoes.

Major Provisions in a Health Insurance Policy

All health insurance policies have certain provisions in common. You have to be sure that you understand what your policy covers. What are the benefits? What are the limits? The following are details of provisions that are commonly found in health insurance policies:

- **Eligibility** defines the people covered by the policy. That usually includes you, your spouse, and your children up to a certain age.
- **Assigned Benefits** You are reimbursed for payments when you turn in your bills and claim forms. When you assign benefits, you let your insurer make direct payments to your doctor or hospital.
- **Internal Limits** A policy with internal limits sets specific levels of repayment for certain services. Even if your hospital room costs $400 a day, you won't be able to get more than $250 with an internal limit specifying that maximum.
- **Copayment** A *copayment* is a flat fee that you pay every time you receive a covered service. The fee is usually between $5 and $15, and the insurer pays the balance of the cost of the service. This is different from coinsurance, which is the percentage of your medical costs for which you are responsible after paying your deductible.
- **Service Benefits** Policies with this provision list coverage in terms of services, not dollar amounts: You're entitled to X rays, for instance, not $40 worth of X rays per visit. Service benefits provisions are always preferable to dollar amount coverage because the insurer will pay all of the costs.
- **Benefit Limits** This provision defines a maximum benefit, either in terms of a dollar amount or in terms of number of days spent in the hospital.
- **Exclusions and Limitations** This provision specifies services that the policy does not cover. That may include preexisting conditions (a condition you were diagnosed with before your insurance plan took effect), cosmetic surgery, or more.
- **Guaranteed Renewable** This provision means that the insurer can't cancel the policy unless you fail to pay the premiums. It also forbids insurers to raise your premiums unless they raise all premiums for all members of your group.
- **Cancellation and Termination** This provision explains the circumstances under which the insurer can cancel your coverage. It also explains how you can convert your group contract into an individual contract.

academic Connection

SPEECH

In the United States, most health insurance is privately owned. In many European countries, however, the government provides insurance for the sick and disabled. Germany was the first country to offer national health insurance. Great Britain has one of the most comprehensive systems. In the United States, national health insurance continues to be hotly debated. In groups of three or four, research this topic. Then write a debate on the pros and cons of national health insurance. Present the debates orally to another group in your class.

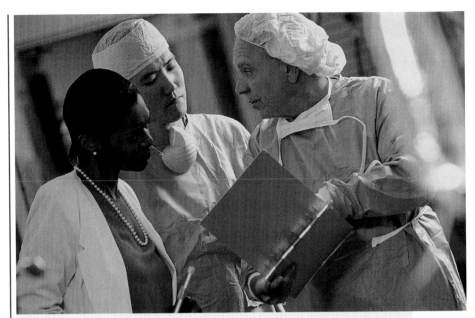

SHARING THE COST All health insurance policies have certain provisions in common. *What is a copayment?*

Which Coverage Should You Choose?

Now that you are familiar with the available types of health insurance and some of their major provisions, how do you choose one? The type of coverage you choose will be affected by the amount you can afford to spend on the premiums and the level of benefits that you feel you want and need. It may also be affected by the kind of coverage your employer offers, if you are covered through your employer.

You can buy basic health coverage, major medical coverage, or both basic and major medical coverage. Any of these three choices will take care of at least some of your medical expenses. Ideally, you should get a basic plan and a major medical supplement. Another option is to purchase a comprehensive major medical policy that combines the value of both plans in a single policy. **Figure 14.1** on page 452 describes the most basic features you should look for.

Health Insurance Trade-Offs

Different health insurance policies may offer very different benefits. As you decide which insurance plan to buy, consider the following trade-offs.

Figure 14.1

Health Insurance Must-Haves

A health insurance plan should:

- Offer basic coverage for hospital and doctor bills
- Provide at least 120 days' hospital room and board in full
- Provide at least a $1 million lifetime maximum for each family member
- Pay at least 80 percent for out-of-hospital expenses after a yearly deductible of $500 per person or $1,000 per family
- Impose no unreasonable exclusions
- Limit your out-of-pocket expenses to no more than $3,000 to $5,000 a year, excluding dental, vision care, and prescription costs

HEALTH INSURANCE ESSENTIALS Although health insurance plans vary greatly, all plans should have the same basic features. *Would you add anything to this list of must-haves?*

REIMBURSEMENT VERSUS INDEMNITY A reimbursement policy pays you back for actual expenses. An indemnity policy provides you with specified amounts, regardless of how much the actual expenses may be.

Katie and Seth are both charged $200 for an office visit to the same specialist. Katie's reimbursement policy has a deductible of $300. Once she has met the deductible, the policy will cover the full cost of such a visit. Seth's indemnity policy will pay him only $125, which is what his plan provides for a visit to any specialist.

INTERNAL LIMITS VERSUS AGGREGATE LIMITS A policy with internal limits will cover only a fixed amount for an expense, such as the daily cost of room and board during a hospital stay. A policy with aggregate limits will limit only the total amount of coverage (the maximum dollar amount paid for all benefits in a year), such as $1 million in major expense benefits, or it may have no limits.

DEDUCTIBLES AND COINSURANCE The cost of a health insurance policy can be greatly affected by the size of the deductible (the set amount that the policyholder must pay toward medical expenses before the insurance company pays benefits). It can also be affected by the terms of the coinsurance provision (which states what percentage of the medical expenses the policyholder must pay in addition to the deductible amount).

OUT-OF-POCKET LIMITS Some policies limit the amount of money you must pay for the deductible and coinsurance. After you have reached that limit, the insurance company covers 100 percent of any additional costs. Out-of-pocket limits help you lower your financial risk, but they also increase your premiums.

BENEFITS BASED ON REASONABLE AND CUSTOMARY CHARGES Some policies consider the average fee for a service in a particular geographical area. They then use that amount to set a limit on payments to policyholders. If the standard cost of a certain procedure is $1,500 in your part of the country, then your policy won't pay more than that amount.

SECTION 14.1 ASSESSMENT

CHECK YOUR UNDERSTANDING

1. Why is it important to include health insurance in your financial planning?
2. Describe the benefits that are provided by hospital expense coverage, surgical expense coverage, and physician expense coverage.
3. What are some of the trade-offs of different health insurance policies?

THINK CRITICALLY

4. Explain why you think it is necessary for insurance companies to place limits on the amount of costs they will cover.

USING COMMUNICATION SKILLS

5. **Benefits of Insurance** Your 25-year-old sister says that she never gets sick and that she leads an active life. She sees no reason to buy health insurance and calls the premiums a waste of money.
   Role-Play With a partner, role-play a response to your sister's argument. Explain why she might benefit from health insurance regardless of her current situation.

SOLVING MONEY PROBLEMS

6. **Choosing an Insurance Plan** Richard is 35, single, and in reasonably good health. He has the choice of three health insurance plans offered by his employer. The first has a lifetime benefit of $1 million for all covered expenses, an annual deductible of $500, and a 15 percent coinsurance provision up to the first $2,000 in covered charges. The second requires a monthly premium of $50, and sets a $500,000 lifetime limit on benefits, no annual deductible, and a $15 copayment per office visit. The third has an annual deductible of $250 and a 25 percent coinsurance provision up to the first $1,500 in covered charges, with a lifetime limit on benefits of $700,000.
   Analyze Help Richard determine which of these three plans makes the most sense for his particular situation. Be prepared to defend your reasoning.

Private Health Care Plans and Government Health Care Programs

Private Health Care Plans

Most health insurance in the United States is provided by private organizations rather than by the government. Private health care plans may be offered by a number of sources: private insurance companies; hospital and medical service plans; health maintenance organizations; preferred provider organizations; home health care agencies; and employer self-funded health plans.

Private Insurance Companies

More than 800 private insurance companies are in the health insurance business. They provide mostly group health plans to employers, which in turn offer them to their employees as a benefit. Premiums may be fully or partially paid by the employer, with the employee paying any remainder. These policies typically pay you for medical costs you incur, or they send the payment directly to the doctor, hospital, or lab that provides the services.

Hospital and Medical Service Plans

Blue Cross and Blue Shield are statewide organizations similar to private health insurance companies. Each state has its own Blue Cross and Blue Shield. The "Blues" provide private health insurance to millions of Americans. *Blue Cross* provides hospital care benefits. *Blue Shield* provides benefits for surgical and medical services performed by physicians.

Health Maintenance Organizations

Rising health care costs have led to an increase in managed care plans. According to a recent industry survey, 85 percent of employed Americans are enrolled in some form of managed care. *Managed care* refers to prepaid health plans that provide comprehensive health care

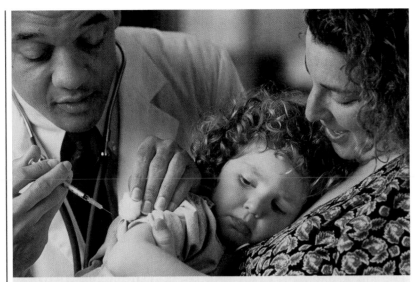

HEALTH MAINTENANCE HMOs are based in the idea that preventive services will minimize future medical problems. *What kinds of preventive services do HMOs cover?*

to their members. Managed care is designed to control the cost of health care services by controlling how they are used. Managed care is offered by health maintenance organizations (HMOs), preferred provider organizations (PPOs), and point-of-service plans (POSs).

Health maintenance organizations are an alternative to basic health insurance and major medical expense insurance. A *health maintenance organization (HMO)* is a health insurance plan that directly employs or contracts with selected physicians and other medical professionals to provide health care services in exchange for a fixed, prepaid monthly premium.

HMOs are based on the idea that preventive services will minimize future medical problems. Therefore, these plans typically cover routine immunizations and checkups, screening programs, and diagnostic tests. They also provide customers with coverage for surgery, hospitalization, and emergency care. If you have an HMO, you will usually pay a small copayment for each covered service. Supplemental services may include vision care and prescription services, which are typically available for an additional fee.

When you first enroll in an HMO, you must choose a plan physician from a list of doctors provided by the HMO. This physician provides or arranges for all of your health care services. You must receive care through your plan physician; if you don't, you are responsible for the cost of the service. The only exception to this rule is in the case of a medical emergency. If you experience a sudden illness or injury that would threaten your life or health if not treated immediately, you may go to the emergency room of the nearest hospital. All other care must be provided by hospitals and doctors under contract with the HMO.

HMOs are not for everyone. Many HMO customers complain that their HMO denies them necessary care. Others feel restricted by the limited choice of doctors.

Here are some tips on using and choosing an HMO: Because HMOs require you to use only certain doctors, you should make sure that these doctors are near your home or office. You should also be able to change doctors easily if you don't like your first choice. Similarly, second opinions should always be available at the HMO's expense, and you should be able to appeal any case in which the HMO denies care. Finally, look at the costs and benefits—whether you will incur out-of-pocket expenses or copayments and what services the plan will provide.

QUESTION

Why would a point-of-service plan be attractive to someone buying insurance?

Preferred Provider Organizations

A variation on the HMO is a *preferred provider organization (PPO)*, a group of doctors and hospitals that agree to provide specified medical services to members at prearranged fees. PPOs offer these discounted services to employers either directly or indirectly through an insurance company. The premiums for PPOs are slightly higher than the premiums for HMOs.

PPO plan members often pay no deductibles and may make minimal copayments. While HMOs require members to receive care from HMO providers only, PPOs allow members greater flexibility. Members can either visit a preferred provider (a physician whom you select from a list, as in an HMO) or go to their own physicians. Patients who decide to use their own doctors do not lose coverage as they would with an HMO. Instead they must pay deductibles and larger copayments.

Increasingly, the difference between PPOs and HMOs is becoming less clear. A *point-of-service plan (POS)* combines features of both HMOs and PPOs. POSs use a network of participating physicians and medical professionals who have contracted to provide services for certain fees. As with an HMO, you choose a plan physician who manages your care and controls referrals to specialists. As long as you receive care from a plan provider, you pay little or nothing, just as you would with an HMO. However, you're allowed to seek care outside the network at a higher charge, as with a PPO.

$AVVY SAVER

Kick the Smoking Habit— and Save

1. Buying a pack of cigarettes a day for 15 years will cost you about $20,000.
2. Smokers miss more work than nonsmokers do.
3. Smokers spend more on medical treatment.
4. Smokers pay more for health insurance.
5. Smokers pay almost twice as much for life insurance.

Home Health Care Agencies

Rising hospital costs, new medical technology, and the increasing number of elderly people have helped make home care one of the fastest growing areas of the health care industry. Home health care consists of home health agencies; home care aide organizations; and hospices, facilities that care for the terminally ill. These providers offer medical care in a home setting in agreement with a medical order, often at a fraction of the cost hospitals would charge for a similar service.

Employer Self-Funded Health Plans

Some companies choose to self-insure. The company runs its own insurance plan, collecting premiums from employees and paying medical benefits as needed. However, these companies must cover any costs that exceed the income from premiums. Unfortunately, not all corporations have the financial assets necessary to cover these situations, which can mean a financial disaster for the company and its employees.

Government Health Care Programs

The health insurance coverages discussed so far are normally purchased through private companies. Some consumers, however, are eligible for health insurance coverage under programs offered by federal and state governments.

Medicare

Perhaps the best-known government program is Medicare. *Medicare* is a federally funded health insurance program available mainly to people over 65 and to people with certain disabilities. Medicare has two parts: hospital insurance (Part A) and medical insurance (Part B). Medicare hospital insurance is funded by part of the Social Security payroll tax. Part A helps pay for inpatient hospital care, inpatient care in a skilled nursing facility, home health care, and hospice care. Program participants pay a single annual deductible.

Part B helps pay for doctors' services and a variety of other medical services and supplies not covered or not fully covered by Part A. Part B has a deductible and a 20 percent coinsurance provision.

CONNECT

How do you plan to prepare for this projected shortfall in Medicare funds?

Medicare medical insurance is a supplemental program paid for by individuals who feel that they need it. A regular monthly premium is charged. The federal government matches this amount.

Medicare is constantly in financial trouble. Health care costs continue to grow, and the proportion of senior citizens in society is rising. This situation puts Medicare in danger of running out of funds. According to projections in 1999, the program will be bankrupt by the year 2008 if no changes are made.

The Balanced Budget Act of 1997 created the new Medicare + Choice program. This program allows many Medicare members to choose a managed care plan in addition to their Medicare coverage. For some additional costs, members can receive greater benefits.

WHAT IS NOT COVERED BY MEDICARE? Although Medicare is very helpful for meeting medical costs, it does not cover everything. In addition to the deductibles and coinsurance payments, Medicare will not cover some medical expenses at all. These are certain types of skilled or long-term nursing care, out-of-hospital

Careers in Finance

INSURANCE AGENT

Insurance agents sell protection against financial loss due to death, illness, car accidents, and loss of or damage to personal property. As salespeople for insurance companies, they help customers find the coverage that's right for them. Agents sell insurance, keep customers' coverage current, maintain their records, and help settle claims. They may work for one company or as an independent agent representing different insurance companies. Agents sell many types of insurance—life, health, disability, long-term care, auto, and homeowners. They usually work on commission, which means they receive a percentage of every sale they make.

Skills	Communication, computer, interpersonal, math, sales ability, time management
Personality	Desire to help customers, good judgment, likes working with people, mature, outgoing, tactful
Education	High school diploma or a bachelor's degree in business or economics; must take courses in insurance, pass an exam, and be licensed
Pay range	$17,000 to $80,000 plus a year, depending on experience, location, type and amount of insurance sold

Critical Thinking If you were an insurance agent, what reasons would you give to prospective customers for purchasing health and life insurance?

 For more information on insurance agents visit finance.glencoe.com **or your local library.**

prescription drugs, routine checkups, dental care, and most immunizations. Medicare also severely limits the types of services it will cover and the amount it will pay for those services. If your doctor does not accept Medicare's approved amount as payment in full, you're responsible for the difference.

MEDIGAP Those eligible for Medicare who would like more coverage may buy Medigap insurance. Medigap insurance supplements Medicare by filling the gap between Medicare payments and medical costs not covered by Medicare. It is offered by private companies.

Medicaid

The other well-known government health program is *Medicaid*, a medical assistance program offered to certain low-income individuals and families. Medicaid is administered by states, but it is financed by a combination of state and federal funds. Unlike Medicare, Medicaid coverage is so comprehensive that people with Medicaid do not need supplemental insurance. Typical Medicaid benefits include physicians' services, inpatient and outpatient hospital services, lab services, skilled nursing and home health services, prescription drugs, eyeglasses, and preventive care for people under 21.

Government Consumer Health Information Web Sites

The Department of Health and Human Services operates more than 60 Web sites with a wealth of reliable information related to health and medicine.

HEALTHFINDER Healthfinder includes links to over a thousand Web pages operated by government and nonprofit organizations. It lists topics according to subject.

MEDLINE Medline is the world's largest collection of published medical information. It was originally designed for health professionals

GROWING PAINS Medicare now covers more people because of the increasing number of senior citizens. *What services do Parts A and B of this program cover?*

and researchers, but it's also valuable for students and others who are interested in health care and medical issues.

NIH HEALTH INFORMATION PAGE The National Institutes of Health (NIH) operates a Web site called the NIH Health Information Page, which can direct you to the consumer health information in NIH publications and on the Internet.

FDA The Food and Drug Administration (FDA) also runs a Web site. This consumer protection agency's site provides information about the safety of various foods, drugs, cosmetics, and medical devices.

SECTION 14.2 — ASSESSMENT

CHECK YOUR UNDERSTANDING

1. What types of coverage do Blue Cross and Blue Shield provide?
2. Explain the differences between an HMO and a PPO.
3. What is the difference between Medicare and Medicaid?

THINK CRITICALLY

4. Identify the benefits and drawbacks to membership in an HMO.

USING MATH SKILLS

5. **PPOs** Last month Rose was involved in a car accident and was rushed to the emergency room. After receiving stitches for a facial wound and treatment for a broken finger, she was released from the hospital.

   Calculate Under Rose's preferred provider organization (PPO) emergency room care at a network hospital is 80 percent covered after the member has met a $300 annual deductible. Assume that Rose went to a hospital within the PPO network. Her total emergency room bill was $850. What amount did Rose have to pay? What amount did the PPO cover?

SOLVING MONEY PROBLEMS

6. **HMOs** Your Aunt Alice will soon be 65. She pays $100 a month in premiums for an HMO with which she is unhappy. She'll soon be eligible for Medicare and is wondering if she should drop the HMO coverage at that time.

   Analyze With a partner, discuss whether Aunt Alice should drop her HMO coverage and whether she has any alternatives.

Disability Income Insurance

The Need for Disability Income

Before disability insurance existed, people who were ill often lost more money from missed paychecks than from medical bills. Disability income insurance was set up to protect against such loss of income. This kind of coverage is very common today, and several hundred insurance companies offer it.

Disability income insurance provides regular cash income when you're unable to work because of a pregnancy, a nonwork-related accident, or an illness. It protects your earning power, your most valuable resource.

The exact definition of a disability varies from insurer to insurer. Some insurers will pay you when you are unable to work at your regular job. Others will pay only if you are so ill or badly hurt that you basically can't work at any job. A violinist with a hand injury, for instance, might have trouble doing his or her regular work but might be able to perform a range of other jobs. A good disability insurance

ACCIDENTS HAPPEN Disability income insurance can be very important. *How would disability income insurance help a dancer who broke a leg in a bicycling accident?*

What You'll Learn

- How to **explain** the importance of disability insurance in financial planning
- How to **identify** sources of disability income
- How to **determine** the trade-offs of different private disability income insurance policies

Why It's Important

Because you're young, you may overlook the need for disability income insurance. Nevertheless, it will become important in the event that you are unable to work.

KEY TERM

- disability income insurance

PREDICT

What does disability income insurance cover?

plan pays you if you can't work at your regular job. A good plan will also pay partial benefits if you are only able to work part-time.

Many people make the mistake of ignoring disability insurance, not realizing that it's very important insurance to have. Disability can cause even greater financial problems than death. Disabled persons lose their earning power but still have to meet their living expenses. In addition, they often face huge costs for the medical treatment and special care that their disabilities require.

Sources of Disability Income

Before you buy disability income insurance from a private insurance company, remember that you may already have some form of insurance of this kind. This coverage may be available through worker's compensation if you're injured on the job. Disability benefits may also be available through your employer or through Social Security in case of a long-term disability.

WORKER'S COMPENSATION If your disability is a result of an accident or illness that occurred on the job, you may be eligible to receive worker's compensation benefits in your state. Benefits will depend on your salary and your work history.

EMPLOYER Many employers provide disability income insurance through group insurance plans. In most cases your employer will pay part or all of the cost of such insurance. Some policies may only provide continued wages for several months, while others will give you long-term protection.

SOCIAL SECURITY Social Security may be best known as a source of retirement income, but it also provides disability benefits. If you're a worker who pays into the Social Security system, you're eligible for Social Security funds if you become disabled. How much you get depends on your salary and the number of years you've been paying into Social Security. Your dependents also qualify for certain benefits. However, Social Security has very strict rules. Workers are considered disabled if they have a physical or mental condition that prevents them from working and that is expected to last for at least 12 months or to result in death. Benefits start at the sixth full month the person is disabled. They stay in effect as long as the disability lasts.

PRIVATE INCOME INSURANCE PROGRAMS Privately owned insurance companies offer many policies to protect people from loss of income resulting from illness or disability. Disability

YOU NEVER KNOW Your chances of becoming disabled are greater in professions that involve physical risk. *What program would provide disability income for a construction worker who is injured on the job?*

RESPOND

Does Social Security disability benefits provide enough coverage for you to feel comfortable about your financial future? Explain your answer.

income insurance gives weekly or monthly cash payments to people who cannot work because of illness or accident. The amount paid is usually 40 to 60 percent of a person's normal income. Some plans, however, pay as much as 75 percent.

Disability Insurance Trade-Offs

As with the purchase of health insurance, you must make certain trade-offs when you decide among different private disability insurance policies. Keep the following in mind as you look for a plan that is right for you.

WAITING OR ELIMINATION PERIOD Benefits won't begin the day you become disabled. You'll have to wait anywhere between one and six months before you can begin collecting. This span of time is called an elimination period. Usually a policy with a longer elimination period charges lower premiums.

DURATION OF BENEFITS Every policy names a specified period during which benefits will be paid. Some policies are valid for only a few years. Others are automatically canceled when you turn 65. Still others continue to make payments for life. You should look for a policy that pays benefits for life. If your policy stops payments when you turn 65, then permanent disability could be a major financial as well as physical loss.

AMOUNT OF BENEFITS You should aim for a benefit amount that, when added to other sources of income, will equal 70 to 80 percent of your take-home pay. Of course, the greater the benefit, the greater the cost, or premium.

ACCIDENT AND SICKNESS COVERAGE Some disability policies pay only for accidents. Coverage for sickness is important, though. Accidents are not the only cause of disability.

GUARANTEED RENEWABILITY If your health becomes poor, your disability insurer may try to cancel your coverage. Look for a plan that guarantees coverage as long as you continue to pay your premiums. The cost may be higher, but it's worth the extra security and peace of mind. You may even be able to find a plan that will stop charging the premiums if you become disabled, which is an added benefit.

Your Disability Income Needs

Once you have found out what your benefits from the numerous public and private sources would be, you should determine whether those benefits would meet your disability income needs. Ideally, you'll want to replace all the income you otherwise would have earned. This should enable you to pay your day-to-day expenses while you're recovering. You won't have work-related expenses and your taxes will be lower during the time that you are disabled. In some cases you may not have to pay certain taxes at all.

SECTION 14.3 ASSESSMENT

CHECK YOUR UNDERSTANDING

1. Why is disability income insurance important in financial planning?
2. Describe the four main sources of disability income.
3. Discuss two trade-offs that you might have to make when choosing among different private disability insurance policies.

THINK CRITICALLY

4. Create and discuss at least two situations for which a person might need disability income insurance.

USING COMMUNICATION SKILLS

5. **Earning Power** Many people who insure their houses, cars, and other property fail to insure their most valuable resource: their earning power.
   Write a Column Imagine that you are a health columnist for a newsletter aimed at people in the entertainment industry, such as dancers, actors, writers, and musicians. Explain why these artists should make sure that they are adequately covered. Point out the potential outcome for someone who becomes disabled without complete disability income coverage.

SOLVING MONEY PROBLEMS

6. **About Disability Income Insurance** Your next-door neighbor has about nine months' salary saved up. He is 58, has no dependents, and plans to retire in seven years. He has just changed jobs—he now works in the office of a road-building company—and has a choice of disability insurance plans. Of course, he also has Social Security benefits if he needs them.
   Discuss What features should your neighbor be looking for in a disability income insurance plan?

Life Insurance

What Is Life Insurance?

When you buy life insurance, you're making a contract with the company issuing the policy. You agree to pay a certain amount of money—the premium—periodically. In return the company agrees to pay a death benefit, or a stated sum of money upon your death, to your beneficiary. A *beneficiary* is a person named to receive the benefits from an insurance policy.

The Purpose of Life Insurance

Most people buy life insurance to protect the people who depend upon them from financial losses caused by their death. Those people could include a spouse, children, an aging parent, or a business partner or corporation. Life insurance benefits may be used to:

- pay off a home mortgage or other debts at the time of death,
- provide lump-sum payments through an endowment for children when they reach a certain age,
- provide an education or income for children,
- make charitable donations after death,
- provide a retirement income,
- accumulate savings,
- establish a regular income for survivors,
- set up an estate plan, or
- pay estate and death taxes.

The Principle of Life Insurance

No one can say with any certainty how long a particular person will live. Still, insurance companies are able to make some educated guesses. Over the years they've compiled tables that show about how long people live. Using these tables, the companies will make a rough guess about a person's life span and charge him or her accordingly. The sooner a person is likely to die, the higher the premiums he or she will pay.

What You'll Learn

- How to **describe** the purpose of life insurance
- How to **analyze** various types of life insurance coverage
- How to **identify** the key provisions in a life insurance policy

Why It's Important

Life insurance helps protect the people who depend on you. Deciding whether you need it and choosing the right policy takes time, research, and careful thought.

KEY TERMS

- beneficiary
- term insurance
- whole life insurance
- cash value
- endowment
- rider
- double indemnity

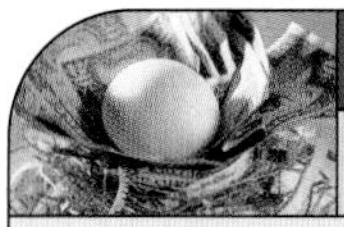

Figure 14.2

Life Expectancy Tables, All Races, 1996

Age	Both Sexes	Male	Female	Age	Both Sexes	Male	Female
0	76.1	73.0	79.0	45	33.9	31.5	36.0
1	75.6	72.6	78.6	50	29.4	27.1	31.5
5	71.7	68.7	74.7	55	25.2	23.0	27.1
10	66.8	63.8	69.7	60	21.2	19.2	22.9
15	61.9	58.9	64.8	65	17.5	15.7	18.9
20	57.1	54.2	59.9	70	14.1	12.5	15.3
25	52.4	49.6	55.1	75	11.1	9.8	11.9
30	47.7	44.9	50.2	80	8.3	7.3	8.9
35	43.0	40.4	45.4	85	6.1	5.4	6.4
40	38.4	35.9	40.7				

THE AVERAGE LIFE This table helps insurance companies determine insurance premiums. *Use the table to find the average number of additional years a 15-year-old male and female are expected to live.*

How Long Will You Live?

If history is any guide, you'll live longer than your ancestors did. In 1900 an American male could be expected to live 46.3 years; an American female could be expected to live 48.3 years. By 1996, in contrast, life expectancy had risen to 73.0 years for men and 79.0 for women. **Figure 14.2** shows about how many years a person can be expected to live today. For instance, a 30-year-old woman can be expected to live another 50.2 years. That doesn't mean that she has a high probability of dying at age 80.2. This just means that 50.2 is the average number of additional years a 30-year-old woman may expect to live.

Do You Need Life Insurance?

Before you buy life insurance, you'll have to decide whether you need it at all. Generally, if your death would cause financial hardship for somebody, then life insurance is a wise purchase. Households with children usually have the greatest need for life insurance. Single people who live alone or with their parents, however, usually have little or no need for life insurance.

Types of Life Insurance Policies

You can purchase life insurance from two types of life insurance companies: stock life insurance companies, owned by shareholders, and mutual life insurance companies, owned by their policyholders. About 95 percent of U.S. life insurance companies are stock companies. Insurance policies can be divided into two types: term insurance and whole life insurance.

CONNECT

Imagine your life 5, 10, and 15 years from now. At what point would you want a good life insurance policy?

Term Insurance

Term insurance, sometimes called temporary life insurance, provides protection against loss of life for only a specified term, or period of time. A term insurance policy pays a benefit only if you die during the period it covers, which may be 1, 5, 10, or 20 years, or up to age 70. If you stop paying the premiums, your coverage stops. Term insurance is often the best value for customers. You need insurance coverage most while you are raising children. As your children become independent and your assets increase, you can reduce your coverage. Term insurance comes in many different forms. Here are some examples.

RENEWABLE TERM The coverage of term insurance ends at the conclusion of the term, but you can continue it for another term—five years, for example—if you have a renewable option. However, the premium will increase because you will be older. It also usually has an age limit; you cannot renew after you reach a certain age.

MULTIYEAR LEVEL TERM A multiyear level term, or straight term, policy guarantees that you will pay the same premium for the duration of your policy.

CONVERSION TERM This type of policy allows you to change from term to permanent coverage. This will cost a higher premium.

DECREASING TERM Term insurance is also available in a form that pays less to the beneficiary as time passes. The insurance period you select might depend on your age or on how long you decide that the coverage will be needed. For example, if you have a mortgage on a house, you might buy a 25-year decreasing term policy as a way to make sure that the debt could be paid if you died. The coverage would decrease as the balance on the loan decreased.

Whole Life Insurance

The other major type of life insurance is known as whole life insurance (also called a straight life policy, a cash value policy, or an ordinary life policy). *Whole life insurance* is a permanent policy for which you pay a specified premium each year for the rest of your life. In return the insurance company pays your beneficiary a stated sum when you die. The amount of your premium depends mostly on the age at which you purchase the insurance.

Whole life insurance can also serve as an investment. Part of each premium you pay is set aside in a savings account. When and if you cancel the policy, you are entitled to the accumulated savings, which is known as the *cash value*. Whole life policies are popular because they provide both a death benefit and a savings component. You can also borrow from your cash value if necessary, although you must pay interest on the loan. Cash value policies may make sense for people who intend to keep the policies for the long term or for people who want a more structured way to save. However, the Consumer Federation of America Insurance Group suggests that you explore other savings and investment strategies before investing your money in a permanent policy.

The premium on a term insurance policy will increase each time you renew your insurance. In contrast, whole life policies have higher annual premiums at first, but the rate remains the same for the rest of your life. Several types of whole life policies have been developed to meet the needs of different customers. These include the limited payment policy, the variable life policy, the adjustable life policy, and universal life insurance.

LIMITED PAYMENT POLICY Limited payment policies charge premiums for only a certain length of time, usually 20 or 30 years or until the insured reaches a certain age. At the end of this time, the policy is "paid up," and the policyholder remains insured for life. When the policyholder dies, the beneficiary receives the full death benefit. The annual premiums are higher for limited payment policies because the premiums have to be paid within a shorter period of time.

VARIABLE LIFE POLICY With a variable life policy, your premium payments are fixed. As with a cash value policy, part of your premium is placed into a separate account; this money is invested in a stock, bond, or money market fund. The death benefit is guaranteed, but the cash value of the benefit can vary considerably according to the ups and downs of the stock market. Your death benefit can also increase, depending on the earnings of that separate fund.

ADJUSTABLE LIFE POLICY An adjustable life policy allows you to change your coverage as your needs change. For example, if you want to increase or decrease your death benefit, you can change either the premium payments or the period of coverage.

UNIVERSAL LIFE Universal life insurance is essentially a term policy with a cash value. Part of your premium goes into an investment account that grows and earns interest. You are able to borrow or withdraw your cash value. Unlike a traditional whole life policy, a universal life policy allows you to change your premium without changing your coverage.

QUESTION

What are the risks and benefits associated with variable life insurance?

COMING TO TERMS Many experts say that term insurance is the best choice for most people. *Name the types of term insurance policies that might be available to you.*

Other Types of Life Insurance Policies

Other types of life insurance policies include group life insurance, credit life insurance, and endowment life insurance.

GROUP LIFE INSURANCE Group life insurance is basically a variation of term insurance. It covers a large number of people under a single policy. The people included in the group do not need medical examinations to get the coverage. Group insurance is usually offered through employers, who pay part or all of the costs for their employees, or through professional organizations, which allow members to sign up for the coverage. Although group plans make it easy to enroll, they can be much more expensive than similar term policies.

CREDIT LIFE INSURANCE Credit life insurance is used to pay off certain debts, such as auto loans or mortgages, in the event that you die before they are paid in full. These types of policies are not the best buy for the protection that they offer. Decreasing term insurance is a better option.

ENDOWMENT LIFE INSURANCE *Endowment* is life insurance that provides coverage for a specific period of time and pays an agreed-upon sum of money to the policyholder if he or she is still living at the end of the endowment period. If the policyholder dies before that time, the beneficiary receives the money.

CASE STUDY

Marian and Clifford Kline recently had their first baby, Abigail. Their combined income is $70,000, and they recently purchased a home and have a mortgage of $100,000. They have not started to save for retirement or college for Abigail. Now that they have a child who is financially dependent on them, they have decided to buy life insurance. Term life, decreasing term, whole life, variable life—the Klines don't know where to begin. They turned to the experts at Standard & Poor's for advice.

Analysis: Many young people may not realize how important insurance can be to their financial security. Young adults, even if they are single, are wise to make sure that they at least have disability and health insurance. In addition to these, Marian and Clifford should have enough life insurance to provide for the care of their child should something happen to either of them. There are many different types of insurance available, and the choices can seem overwhelming. To find the one that is right for them, Marian and Clifford should think carefully about their current and future needs.

Recommendation: Because their child is so young, the Klines should lean toward more rather than less insurance. They'll want a policy that when invested, will replace their required income each year and provide for future needs such as college tuition. Assuming they need $50,000 a year, this works out to about $600,000 in insurance. The next step is to decide what type of insurance the couple can afford. Term insurance is the least expensive because it provides coverage for only a specified period of time and is a good choice for the Klines' situation. They can buy a 10- or 20-year term policy to cover the years that Abigail is in school. A decreasing term policy can be purchased to match their mortgage and is another inexpensive option. Other types of life insurance combine permanent insurance with an investment component. These policies, such as whole life and universal life, charge higher premiums and fees in the early years but accumulate value over time. Variable life policies offer opportunities to invest in higher risk securities including stocks. The Klines might consider gradually replacing their term policy with whole life insurance when they have more spending money.

Critical Thinking Questions

1. Why is term insurance less expensive than whole life or universal life insurance?
2. In what types of situations might it make sense to buy whole life insurance?
3. What risk is involved in buying a variable life policy?

Key Provisions in a Life Insurance Policy

Study the provisions in your policy carefully. The following are some of the most common features.

Naming Your Beneficiary

You decide who receives the benefits of your life insurance policy: your spouse, your child, or your business partner, for example. You can also name contingent beneficiaries, those who will receive the money if your primary beneficiary dies before or at the same time as you do. Update your list of beneficiaries as your needs change.

Incontestability Clause

The incontestability clause says that the insurer can't cancel the policy if it's been in force for two years or more. After that time the policy is considered valid during the lifetime of the insured. This is true even if the policy was gained through fraud. The incontestability clause protects the beneficiaries from financial loss in the event that the insurance company refuses to meet the terms of the policy.

Suicide Clause

Within the first two years of coverage, the beneficiaries of someone who dies by suicide will receive only the amount of the premiums paid. After two years the beneficiaries receive the full value of the death benefits.

Riders to Life Insurance Policies

An insurance company can change the conditions of a policy by adding a rider to it. A *rider* is a document attached to a policy that changes its terms by adding or excluding specified conditions or altering its benefits.

WAIVER OF PREMIUM DISABILITY BENEFIT One common rider is a waiver of premium disability benefit. This clause allows you to stop paying premiums if you're totally and permanently disabled before you reach a certain age, usually 60. The company continues to pay the premiums at its own expense.

ACCIDENTAL DEATH BENEFIT Another common rider to life insurance policies is an accidental death benefit, sometimes called *double indemnity*. Double indemnity pays twice the value of the

Comparing Life Insurance

Sean Richards is investigating the cost of life insurance. He contacted two reputable insurance companies and based his comparison on $100,000 worth of insurance. He's 28 years old, married, and has two children.

Type of Policy	Company A	Company B
20-year decreasing term insurance $100,000		
Monthly premium	$14.00	$8.25
Total premiums, 20 years	$3,360.00	$1,980.00
Cash value in 20 years	none	none
Whole life insurance (limited payment) $100,000		
Monthly premium	$82.00	$62.60
Total premiums, 20 years	$19,280.00	$15,024.00
Cash value in 20 years	$25,000.00	$21,243.00

Sean chose the 20-year decreasing term insurance because of the low cost, even though it cannot be converted into cash at a future date. He purchased his policy with Company B.

Compare In the workbook or on a separate sheet of paper, follow Sean's chart to compare life insurance rates. Use the Internet, or visit, telephone, or write to two different insurance companies. Base the quote on (1) a 20-year decreasing term insurance policy for $100,000 and (2) a whole life (limited payment) insurance policy for $100,000. Use your own age.

policy if you are killed in an accident. Again, the accident must occur before a certain age, generally 60 or 65. Experts counsel against adding this rider to your coverage. The benefit is expensive, and your chances of dying in an accident are slim.

GUARANTEED INSURABILITY OPTION A third important rider is known as a guaranteed insurability option. This rider allows you to buy a specified additional amount of life insurance at certain intervals without undergoing medical exams. This is a good option for people who anticipate needing more life insurance in the future.

SECTION 14.4 ASSESSMENT

CHECK YOUR UNDERSTANDING

1. What is the purpose of life insurance?
2. Compare term insurance and whole life insurance.
3. What are the key provisions in a life insurance policy?

THINK CRITICALLY

4. "Term life insurance is a wise choice for consumers." Do you agree or disagree with this statement? Support your argument.

USING MATH SKILLS

5. **Life Expectancy** Review the life expectancy tables in **Figure 14.2.**
   Create a Line Graph Show life expectancy at various ages for both genders in the form of a line graph. Remember to add the number of years already lived to the number of years expected to remain. For example, at age 50, total life expectancy is 79.4 years (50 + 29.4 = 79.4). What trends do you notice?

SOLVING MONEY PROBLEMS

6. **Life Insurance Comparisons** Lawrence is a 27-year-old single man with no children. He has a developmentally disabled younger sister. Both his parents are still living, though neither is in good health. Lawrence has an auto loan and a $50,000 mortgage on his condominium.
   Analyze Is Lawrence a good candidate for life insurance? If so, what kind, and how much life insurance should he buy? In a small group, discuss Lawrence's situation and his needs.

CHAPTER 14 ASSESSMENT

CHAPTER SUMMARY

- Health insurance eases the financial burden people might experience as a result of illness or injury.

- Types of health insurance coverage include basic health insurance coverage, major medical expense insurance, hospital indemnity policies, dental expense insurance, vision care insurance, dread disease policies, and long-term care insurance.

- All insurance policies have certain provisions in common. It's important to be familiar with the benefits and limitations of your policy.

- As you decide which health insurance plan to purchase, you will have to make trade-offs.

- Private health care plans are offered by a number of different sources.

- Some individuals receive health insurance coverage under Medicare and Medicaid,

programs financed by the federal and state governments.

- Disability income insurance protects your earning power.

- Disability income may be available through worker's compensation benefits, an employer, Social Security, or private income insurance programs.

- You must make certain trade-offs when you decide among different private disability income insurance policies.

- Life insurance protects the people who depend on you from financial losses caused by your death.

- Life insurance policies are usually one of two main types: term and whole.

- Most life insurance policies have standard features. An insurance company can change the conditions of a policy by adding a rider to it.

Internet zone

Understanding and Using Vocabulary

Write a conversation with another student. One of you should write the part of a young person asking questions about insurance. The other should write the part of an adult who acts as a guide through the process of searching for a good policy. Use at least ten of the key terms below in your conversation.

health insurance

coinsurance

stop-loss
copayment
Blue Cross
Blue Shield
managed care
health maintenance
  organization (HMO)
preferred provider
  organization (PPO)
point-of-service plan
  (POS)

Medicare
Medicaid
disability income
  insurance
beneficiary
term insurance
whole life insurance
cash value
endowment
rider
double indemnity

CHAPTER 14 ASSESSMENT

Review Key Concepts

1. What is major medical expense insurance?
2. Describe the characteristics of a point-of-service plan.
3. What are some questions you should ask yourself before buying disability income insurance?
4. Under what circumstances might you choose not to buy life insurance?
5. Discuss specific ways in which a rider might change the conditions of a life insurance policy.

Apply Key Concepts

1. In what types of life situations might you have to consider purchasing major medical insurance?
2. Would you prefer to be covered under an HMO, a PPO, or a POS? Justify your answer.
3. List three considerations that might be important in choosing a disability policy at age 30.
4. Write two brief scenarios describing people you know. For each, explain whether life insurance is a good buy.
5. Under what types of circumstances might you decide to add a guaranteed insurability option to your life insurance policy?

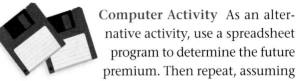 **Computer Activity** As an alternative activity, use a spreadsheet program to determine the future premium. Then repeat, assuming an annual rise in premiums of 4 percent.

Real-World Application

CONNECT WITH SOCIAL STUDIES

The insurance industry has always relied heavily on statistical information to determine risks. The primary workers responsible for providing this information are called actuaries.

Conduct Research Find out exactly how actuaries work and what they do. Determine the level of education and type of training they need.

FINANCE *Online*

FINDING LIFE INSURANCE ONLINE

Although you probably don't need to buy a life insurance policy now, as you get older, the need for this type of insurance will be greater.

Connect Using different search engines, find Web sites that offer basic information about various life insurance policies. Get a quote on at least three different policies, based on your current circumstances. Then answer the following:

1. What information did each company require before giving you a quote?
2. Which policy do you feel would be best for you, considering the costs and benefits?

? *Problem Solving Today*

HOW MUCH WILL YOU PAY?

Assume that your health insurance premiums are currently $1,200 a year. If they rise at a rate of 5 percent a year every year, what would be the annual premium ten years from now?

CHAPTER 15

Retirement and Estate Planning

Q&A

Q: How old should I be when I write a will?

A: The laws of the state in which you live will govern at what age you are legally considered to own property and able to enter into certain types of legal agreements.

The Basics of Retirement Planning

$\mathcal{R}$owena's grandmother lives in a special housing complex for the elderly that provides personal and medical services. She moved there a few years ago because she was having problems getting around after her hip replacement operation.

Rowena recently learned that her grandparents had planned carefully for retirement during their working years. They watched as some of their friends spent money with little concern for the future. Rowena's grandparents, on the other hand, made sure that they saved enough money to have a comfortable retirement. Even though it seemed far in the future, Rowena decided to start planning early for her own retirement, just as her grandparents had done.

Planning for Retirement

Your retirement years may seem a long way off right now. After all, you are still in high school, and after you graduate you will probably work for many years to come. The fact is, it's never too early to start planning for retirement. Planning can help you cope with sudden changes that may occur in your life and give you a sense of control over your future.

If you haven't done any research on the subject of retirement, you may hold some outdated beliefs about your "golden years." Some common mistaken beliefs include:

- You have plenty of time to start saving for retirement.
- Saving just a little bit won't help.
- You'll spend less money when you retire.
- Your retirement will only last about 15 years.
- You can depend on Social Security and a company pension plan to pay your basic living expenses.
- Your pension benefits will increase to keep pace with inflation.

What You'll Learn

- How to **recognize** the importance of retirement planning
- How to **estimate** your retirement living costs
- How to **identify** your retirement housing needs

Why It's Important

Retirement planning is important because you'll probably spend many years in retirement. Properly estimating your retirement living costs and housing needs will enable you to save or invest enough money to live comfortably during retirement.

KEY TERM

- **assisted-living facility (ALF)**

• Your employer's health insurance plan and Medicare will cover all your medical expenses when you retire.

Some of these statements were once true but are no longer true today. You may live for many years after you retire. If you want your retirement to be a happy and comfortable time of your life, you'll need enough money to suit your lifestyle. You can't count on others to provide for you. That's why you need to start planning and saving as early as possible. It's never too late to start saving for retirement, but the sooner you start, the better off you'll be.

Suppose that you want to have at least $1 million when you retire at age 65. If you start saving for retirement at age 25, you can

RESPOND

Explain why these myths about retirement are not necessarily true.

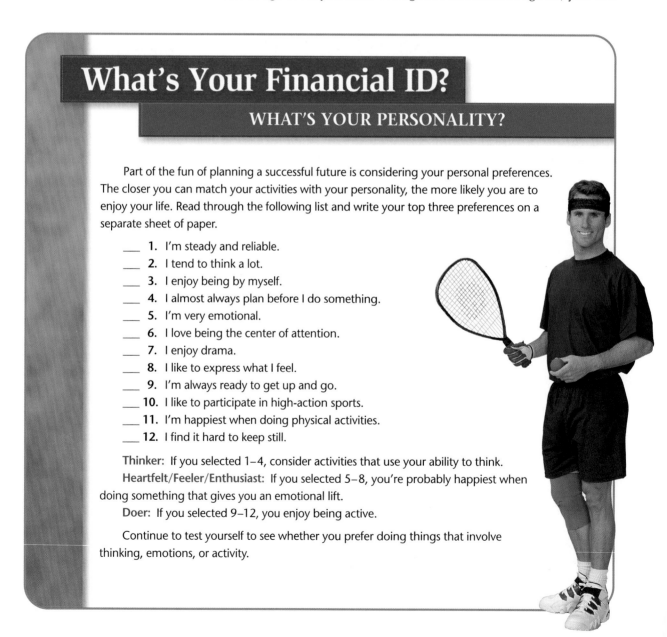

What's Your Financial ID?

WHAT'S YOUR PERSONALITY?

Part of the fun of planning a successful future is considering your personal preferences. The closer you can match your activities with your personality, the more likely you are to enjoy your life. Read through the following list and write your top three preferences on a separate sheet of paper.

___ 1. I'm steady and reliable.
___ 2. I tend to think a lot.
___ 3. I enjoy being by myself.
___ 4. I almost always plan before I do something.
___ 5. I'm very emotional.
___ 6. I love being the center of attention.
___ 7. I enjoy drama.
___ 8. I like to express what I feel.
___ 9. I'm always ready to get up and go.
___ 10. I like to participate in high-action sports.
___ 11. I'm happiest when doing physical activities.
___ 12. I find it hard to keep still.

Thinker: If you selected 1–4, consider activities that use your ability to think.
Heartfelt/Feeler/Enthusiast: If you selected 5–8, you're probably happiest when doing something that gives you an emotional lift.
Doer: If you selected 9–12, you enjoy being active.

Continue to test yourself to see whether you prefer doing things that involve thinking, emotions, or activity.

LIVING THE GOOD LIFE Not everyone can afford to take lavish vacations or buy lots of expensive items. *What are some of the decisions you'll have to make now to ensure a comfortable retirement?*

meet that goal by putting about $127 per month into investment funds that grow at a rate of about 11 percent each year. If you wait until you're 50, the monthly amount skyrockets to $2,244.

As you think about your retirement years, consider your long-range goals. What does retirement mean to you? Maybe it will simply be a time to stop working, sit back, and relax. Perhaps you imagine traveling the world, developing a hobby, or starting a second career. Where do you want to live after you retire? What type of lifestyle would you like to have? Once you've pondered these questions, you have to determine your current financial situation. That requires you to analyze your current assets and liabilities.

Conducting a Financial Analysis

As you learned in Chapter 3, an asset is any item of value that you own, including cash, property, personal possessions, and investments. This includes cash in checking and savings accounts, a house, a car, a television, and so on. It also includes the current value of any stocks, bonds, and other investments that you may have as well as the current value of any life insurance and pension funds.

Your liabilities, on the other hand, are the debts you owe. That includes the remaining balance on a mortgage or automobile loan, credit card balances, unpaid taxes, and so on. If you subtract your liabilities from your assets, you get your net worth. Ideally, your net worth should increase each year as you move closer to retirement. The checklist in **Figure 15.1** is an example of how you might analyze your assets and liabilities.

Figure 15.1

Assets, Liabilities, and Net Worth

Assets:

Cash:		
Checking account	$	800
Savings account		4,500
Investments:		
U.S. savings bonds		
(current cash-in value)		5,000
Stocks, mutual funds		4,500
Life insurance:		
Cash value, accumulated dividends		10,000
Company pension rights:		
Accrued pension benefit		20,000
Property:		
House (resale value)		50,000
Furniture and appliances		8,000
Collections and jewelry		2,000
Automobile		3,000
Other:		
Loan to brother		1,000
Gross assets		**$108,800**

Liabilities:

Current unpaid bills	$	600
Home mortgage		
(remaining balance)		9,700
Auto loan		1,200
Property taxes		1,100
Home improvement loan		3,700
Total liabilities		**$16,300**

Net worth:

Assets − Liabilities = Net Worth
$108,800 − $16,300 = $92,500

CALCULATING NET WORTH Assets are everything that you own, while liabilities are everything you owe. *How can you determine your net worth?*

It's a good idea to review your assets on a regular basis. You may need to make adjustments in your saving, spending, and investments in order to stay on track. As you review your assets, consider the following factors: housing, life insurance, and other investments. Each will have an important effect on your retirement income.

HOUSING A house will probably be your most valuable asset. However, if you buy a home with a large mortgage that prevents you from saving, you risk not being able to meet your retirement goals. In that case you might consider buying a smaller, less expensive place to live. Remember that a smaller house is usually easier and cheaper to maintain. You can use the money you save to increase your retirement fund.

LIFE INSURANCE At some point in the future, you may buy life insurance to provide financial support for your children in case you die while they are still young. As you near retirement, though, your children will probably be self-sufficient. When that time comes, you might reduce your premium payments by decreasing your life insurance coverage. This would give you extra money to spend on living expenses or to invest for additional income.

OTHER INVESTMENTS When you review your assets, you'll also want to evaluate any other investments you have. When you originally chose these investments, you may have been more interested in making your money grow than in getting an early return from them. When you are ready to retire, however, you may want to use the income from those investments to help cover living expenses instead of reinvesting it.

QUESTION

How might your investing strategies change as you approach retirement?

Retirement Living Expenses

Next you should estimate how much money you'll need to live comfortably during your retirement years. You can't predict exactly how much money you'll need when you retire. You can, however, estimate what your basic needs will be. To do this, you'll have to think about how your spending patterns and living situation will change when you retire.

For instance, you'll probably spend more money on recreation, health insurance, and medical care in retirement than you do now. At the same time, you may spend less on transportation and clothing. Your federal income taxes may be lower. Also, some income from various retirement plans may be taxed at a lower rate or not at all. As you consider your retirement living expenses, remember to plan for emergencies. Look at **Figure 15.2** for an example of retirement spending patterns.

Don't forget to take inflation into account. Estimate high when calculating how much the prices of goods and services will rise by the time you retire (see **Figure 15.3**). Even a 3 percent rate of inflation will cause prices to double every 24 years.

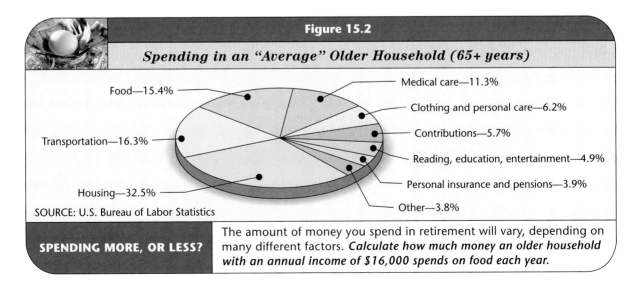

Figure 15.2

Spending in an "Average" Older Household (65+ years)

Food—15.4%
Medical care—11.3%
Clothing and personal care—6.2%
Contributions—5.7%
Transportation—16.3%
Reading, education, entertainment—4.9%
Personal insurance and pensions—3.9%
Housing—32.5%
Other—3.8%

SOURCE: U.S. Bureau of Labor Statistics

SPENDING MORE, OR LESS? The amount of money you spend in retirement will vary, depending on many different factors. *Calculate how much money an older household with an annual income of $16,000 spends on food each year.*

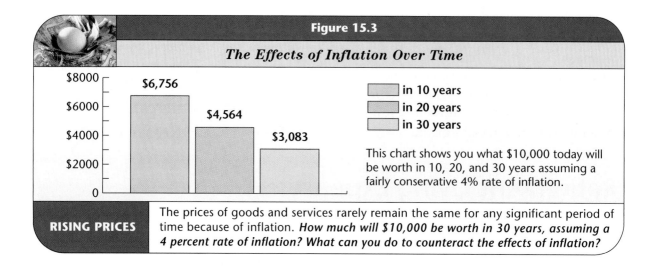

Figure 15.3

The Effects of Inflation Over Time

- in 10 years
- in 20 years
- in 30 years

This chart shows you what $10,000 today will be worth in 10, 20, and 30 years assuming a fairly conservative 4% rate of inflation.

RISING PRICES The prices of goods and services rarely remain the same for any significant period of time because of inflation. *How much will $10,000 be worth in 30 years, assuming a 4 percent rate of inflation? What can you do to counteract the effects of inflation?*

Your Retirement Housing

The place where you choose to live during retirement can have a significant impact on your financial needs. Use vacations in the years before you retire to explore areas you think you might enjoy. If you find a place you really like, go there at different times of the year. That way you'll know what the climate is like. Meet people who live in the area and learn about activities, transportation, and taxes.

Consider the downside of moving to a new location. You may find yourself stuck in a place you really don't like after all. Moving can also be expensive and emotionally draining. You may miss your children, your grandchildren, and the friends and relatives you leave behind. Be realistic about what you'll have to give up as well as what you'll gain if you move after you retire.

Avoiding Retirement Relocation Pitfalls

Some retired people move to the location of their dreams and then discover that they've made a big mistake financially. Here are some tips from retirement specialists on how to uncover hidden taxes and other costs before you move to a new area:

- Contact the local chamber of commerce to get details on area property taxes and the local economy.
- Contact the state tax department to find out about income, sales, and inheritance taxes as well as special exemptions for retirees.
- Read the Sunday edition of the local newspaper of the city where you're thinking of moving.

- Check with local utility companies to get estimates on energy costs.
- Visit the area in different seasons, and talk to local residents about the various costs of living.
- Rent for a while instead of buying a home immediately.

Types of Housing

Even if you decide not to move to a new location, your housing needs may change after you retire. You'll probably want a home that's easy and inexpensive to maintain. It may also be important for you to be near public transportation, stores, and recreation areas. You may decide to move into a smaller house, a condominium, or an apartment. In addition, you may want to make arrangements to move into an assisted-living facility later in your retirement. Look at the housing options described in **Figure 15.4**.

An *assisted-living facility (ALF)* is a residence complex that provides personal and medical services for the elderly. Assisted-living

ESTATE PLANNING ATTORNEY

Suppose your uncle passed away and left his successful business to his family, but they had to sell most of it to pay taxes. If your uncle had consulted an attorney who specializes in estate planning, his family might have avoided this unfortunate outcome. Estate planning attorneys advise clients about the different types of retirement savings plans (such as Roth IRAs), tax liabilities, and the effect that estate taxes have on investments. Estate planning attorneys can also make arrangements so that, in case of death, businesses can be transferred or sold in an orderly way. They help clients write wills and decide how to divide their estates after death.

Skills	Ability to see the big picture, analytical, communication, decision making, long-range planning, math
Personality	Discreet, good judgment, likes working with people and numbers, tactful
Education	Bachelor's degree and law degree
Pay range	$25,000 to $125,000 plus a year, depending on legal experience and location

Research List five questions you might ask an estate planning attorney. After you research estate planning at the library or on the Internet, write down the answers to your questions.

For more information on estate planning attorneys visit finance.glencoe.com **or your local library.**

1 Most retired people decide to remain where they are and continue living in their own home.

2 Living with grown children and young grandchildren can be a choice for some elderly retired people and their families.

FIGURE 15.4

Retirement Housing Options

Housing options for retirement are based on various personal, financial, and medical factors. The goal of most retirees is to have comfortable and affordable housing that meets their own particular needs.

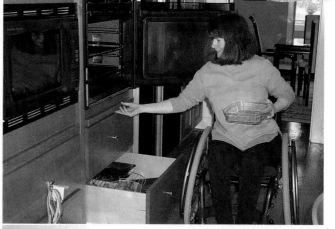

3 For retired people with disabilities, a universal design home built with special features, such as extra-wide doors, lower appliances, and automatic faucets, can be both appealing and practical. These homes help the elderly and disabled to maintain their independence.

facilities offer everything from minimal services to full, continuous nursing care. Although they vary greatly in quality, ALFs are becoming increasingly popular with elderly retirees, some of whom are no longer able to live alone and care for themselves.

SECTION 15.1 ASSESSMENT

CHECK YOUR UNDERSTANDING

1. Name several reasons for the importance of early retirement planning.
2. What factors should you consider when estimating your retirement living expenses?
3. Identify different housing options for retirees. Summarize the features and benefits of an assisted-living facility.

THINK CRITICALLY

4. Discuss the advantages and disadvantages of spending a large portion of your income to purchase an expensive home about 20 years before retirement.

USING COMMUNICATION SKILLS

5. **Free at Last!** Jeff and Maureen McBride have both been working at the same company for almost 35 years and are nearing retirement. They've been looking forward to the time when they'll be free to do almost anything they want. They already have a long list of places they would like to visit, things they would like to do, and ways they would like to spend their time after they retire.
   Create a Collage Imagine the type of life you would like to have when you retire. Combine pictures and words to create a collage that expresses your thoughts and feelings about your retirement dreams.

SOLVING MONEY PROBLEMS

6. **Changing Lifestyles** Enrique and his wife, Maribel, have been retired for a couple of years. Although their income is lower than when they were working, they've continued to live their lives as they did before retirement. They have a three-bedroom house in New Jersey. Twice a year they travel to California to visit their children and grandchildren. Unfortunately, now they find themselves in a bit of a financial pinch. They've concluded that they need to cut back on their expenses. However, they're having trouble agreeing on ways to live more economically without giving up the lifestyle they enjoy.
   Resolve Help Enrique and Maribel solve their problem by discussing various options they might have for saving money.

Planning Your Retirement Income

Public Pension Plans

What You'll Learn

- How to **describe** the role of Social Security in planning for retirement
- How to **discuss** the retirement benefits offered under employer pension plans
- How to **distinguish** among various personal retirement plans
- How to **plan** the best use of retirement income

Why It's Important

Assessing various types of retirement plans will help you predict what your financial situation and needs will be in retirement.

KEY TERMS

- defined-contribution plan
- 401(k) plan
- vesting
- defined-benefit plan
- individual retirement account (IRA)
- Keogh plan
- annuity
- heirs

One source of retirement income is Social Security, a public pension plan established by the U.S. government in 1935. The government agency that manages the program is called the Social Security Administration. As you may recall from Chapter 2, a pension plan is a retirement plan that is funded, at least in part, by an employer.

Social Security

Social Security is an important source of retirement income for most Americans. The program covers 97 percent of all workers, and almost one out of every six Americans currently collects some form of Social Security benefit. Social Security is actually a package of protection that provides benefits to retirees, survivors, and disabled persons. The package protects you and your family while you work and after you retire. Nevertheless, you should not rely on Social Security to cover all of your retirement expenses. Social Security was never intended to provide 100 percent of your retirement income.

Who Is Eligible for Social Security Benefits?

The amount of retirement benefits you receive from Social Security is based on your earnings over the years. The more you work and the higher your earnings, the greater your benefits, up to a certain maximum amount. The Social Security Administration automatically provides you with a statement that reports the history of your earnings. The statement also includes an estimate, in today's dollars, of how much you'll get each month from Social Security when you retire.

To qualify for retirement benefits you must earn a certain number of credits. These credits are based on the length of time you work and pay into the system through the Social Security tax, or contribution, on your earnings. You and your employer pay equal amounts of the Social Security tax. Your credits are calculated on a quarterly basis. The number of quarters you need depends on your year of birth. People born after 1928 need 40 quarters to qualify for benefits.

Certain dependents may receive benefits under this part of the Social Security program. They include a wife or dependent husband age 62 or older, unmarried children under 18 (or under 19 if they are full-time students), and unmarried, disabled children aged 18 or older.

Receiving Social Security

Today most people can begin collecting full Social Security benefits at age 65. Widows or widowers can receive Social Security benefits earlier. Generally, you can qualify for reduced benefits at age 62. If you postpone applying for benefits beyond age 65, your monthly payments will increase slightly for each year you wait, but only up to age 70.

People are living longer today than when Social Security was first established in 1935. As a result the Social Security Administration has begun to increase the retirement age at which individuals can receive full benefits. Beginning in 2003, the retirement age for full benefits will be gradually increased until it reaches age 67. Those who retire before reaching 67 will receive reduced benefits.

CONNECT

If you currently hold a job, look at a recent paycheck stub. Are you paying into Social Security?

SOCIAL SECURITY BENEFITS Social Security is an important source of income for many retired people. *How are Social Security benefits calculated?*

Social Security Information

For more information about Social Security, you can visit the Social Security Web site. It provides access to forms and publications and gives links to other valuable information. To learn more about the taxability of Social Security benefits, contact the Internal Revenue Service at 1-800-829-3676 and ask for Publication 554, *Older Americans' Tax Guide*, and Publication 915, *Social Security and Equivalent Railroad Retirement Benefits*.

Other Public Pension Plans

PREDICT

Besides Social Security, what other retirement plans are available to you?

Besides Social Security, the federal government provides several other special retirement plans for federal government workers and railroad employees. Employees covered under these plans are not covered by Social Security. The Veterans Administration provides pensions for survivors of people who died while in the armed forces. It also offers disability pensions for eligible veterans. Many state and local governments provide retirement plans for their employees as well.

Employer Pension Plans

Another possible source of retirement income is an employer pension plan offered by the company for which you work. With this type of plan, your employer contributes to your retirement benefits, and sometimes you contribute too. These contributions and their earnings remain tax-deferred until you start to withdraw them in retirement.

Private employer pension plans vary. If the company you work for offers one, you should know when you become eligible to receive pension benefits. You'll also need to know what benefits you'll receive. Most employer plans are one of two basic types: defined-contribution plans or defined-benefit plans.

Defined-Contribution Plan

A *defined-contribution plan*, sometimes called an individual account plan, consists of an individual account for each employee to which the employer contributes a specific amount annually. This type of retirement plan does not guarantee any particular benefit. When you retire and become eligible for benefits, you simply receive the total amount of funds (including investment earnings) that have been placed in your account.

Several types of defined-contribution plans exist. With a money-purchase plan, your employer promises to set aside a certain amount of money for you each year. That amount is generally a percentage of your earnings. Under a stock bonus plan, your employer's contribution is used to buy stock in the company for you. The stock is usually held in trust until you retire. Then you can either keep your shares or sell them. Under a profit-sharing plan, your employer's contribution depends on the company's profits.

In a *401(k) plan*, also known as a salary-reduction plan, you set aside a portion of your salary from each paycheck to be deducted from your gross pay and placed in a special account. Your employer will often match your contribution up to a specific dollar amount or percentage of your salary. The funds in 401(k) plans are invested in stocks, bonds, and mutual funds. As a result you can accumulate a significant amount of money in this type of account if you begin contributing to it early in your career. In addition, the money that accumulates in your 401(k) plan is tax-deferred, meaning that you don't have to pay taxes on it until you withdraw it.

If you're employed by a tax-exempt institution, such as a hospital or a nonprofit organization, the salary-reduction plan is called a Section 403(b) plan. As in a 401(k) plan, the funds in a 403(b) plan are tax-deferred. The 401(k) and 403(b) plans are often referred to as tax-sheltered annuity (TSA) plans. The amount that can be contributed annually to 401(k) and 403(b) plans is limited by law, as is the amount of annual contributions to money-purchase plans, stock bonus plans, and profit-sharing plans.

Employee contributions to a pension plan belong to you, the employee, regardless of the amount of time that you are with a particular employer. What happens to the contributions that the employer has made to your account if you change jobs and move to another company before you retire? One of the most important aspects of such plans is vesting. *Vesting* is the point at which you become eligible to receive the employer's pension plan contributions that you've gained, even if you leave the company before retiring. After a certain number of years with the company, you will become fully vested, or entitled to receive 100 percent of the company's contributions to the plan on your behalf. Under some plans, vesting may occur in stages. For example, you might become eligible to receive 20 percent of your benefits after three years and gain another 20 percent each year until you are fully vested.

Defined-Benefit Plan

A *defined-benefit plan* specifies the benefits you'll receive at retirement age, based on your total earnings and years on the job. The plan does not specify how much the employer must contribute

academic Connection

TECHNOLOGY

As you begin to develop career plans, retirement seems a long way off. Although the future is hard to predict, technology will undoubtedly play a major role. Imagine what your life will be like in 50 years. How will technology affect your life? What impact will it have on housing, transportation, health issues, and leisure activities? Create a poster or other visual showcasing your vision of what technology will be like during your retirement.

each year. Instead your employer's contributions are based on how much money will be needed in the fund as each participant in the plan retires. If the fund is inadequate, the employer will have to make additional contributions.

Carrying Benefits from One Plan to Another

Some pension plans allow portability, which means that you can carry earned benefits from one pension plan to another when you change jobs. Workers are also protected by the Employee Retirement Income Security Act of 1974 (ERISA), which sets minimum standards for pension plans. Under this act the federal government insures part of the payments promised by defined-benefit plans.

Personal Retirement Plans

In addition to public and employer retirement plans, many people choose to set up personal retirement plans. Such plans are especially important to self-employed people and other workers who are not covered by employer pension plans. Among the most popular personal retirement plans are individual retirement accounts (IRAs) and Keogh accounts.

Individual Retirement Accounts

An *individual retirement account (IRA)* is a special account in which the employee sets aside a portion of his or her income for retirement; taxes are not paid on the principal or interest until money is withdrawn from the account.

REGULAR IRA A regular (traditional or classic) IRA lets you contribute up to $2,000 annually until age 70½. Depending on your tax filing status and income, the contribution may be fully or partially tax-deductible. The tax deductibility of a traditional IRA also depends on whether you belong to an employer-provided retirement plan.

ROTH IRA Annual contributions to a Roth IRA are not tax-deductible, but the earnings accumulate tax-free. You may contribute up to $2,000 per year if you're a single taxpayer with an adjusted gross income (AGI) of less than $95,000. For married couples the combined AGI must be less than $150,000. You can continue to make annual contributions to a Roth IRA even after age 70½. If you have a Roth IRA, you can withdraw money from the account tax-free and penalty-free after five years if you are at least 59½ years old or plan to use the money to help buy your first home. You may convert a regular IRA to a Roth IRA. Depending on your situation, one type of account may be better for you than the other.

SIMPLIFIED EMPLOYEE PENSION (SEP) PLAN A Simplified Employee Pension (SEP) plan, also known as a SEP-IRA, is an individual retirement account funded by an employer. Each employee sets up his or her own IRA account at a bank or other financial institution. Then the employer makes an annual contribution of up to 15 percent of the employee's salary, or $30,000, whichever amount is lower. The employees' contributions, which can vary from year to year, are fully tax-deductible, and earnings are tax-deferred.

INTERNATIONAL FINANCE Brazil

Brazil
South America

ould you like to take a trip on the wild side? If your answer is yes, then you'd enjoy a visit to Brazil's Amazon region. Each year ecotourism, an industry promoting travel that aims to preserve the natural world and to sustain the human cultures that inhabit it, encourages adventurers to explore the world's largest river, the Amazon, and its rain forest. In this tropical realm that covers one-twentieth of the earth's land surface, you can search for the elusive jaguar while hiking jungle trails, or hunt alligators with a camera, not a gun. You might even catch sight of a macaw or two. The largest members of the parrot family, these birds sport rainbow-colored plumage, a hooked bill, and a bare face that blushes when excited. Here's a snapshot of Brazil.

The Amazon rain forest teems with birdlife, including colorful macaws.

Geographic area	3,286,488 sq. mi.
Population	167,988,000
Capital	Brasília (pop. 1,737,800)
Language	Portuguese, Spanish, English
Currency	real
Gross domestic product (GDP)	$1.04 trillion
Per capita GDP	$6,300
Economy	Industry: textiles, shoes, chemicals, cement, lumber. Agriculture: coffee, soybeans, wheat, rice, corn, sugarcane, cocoa, citrus, beef. Exports: iron ore, soybean, orange juice, footwear, coffee

Thinking Critically

Assess Ecotourism is a growing industry. What are some of the ways that ecotourism can help protect the natural areas of the world and sustain the people who live there?

 For more information on Brazil visit finance.glencoe.com or your local library.

Figure 15.5

Various Types of IRAs

Type of IRA	IRA Features
Regular IRA	• Tax-deferred interest and earnings • $2,000 annual limit on individual contributions • Limited eligibility for tax-deductible contributions • Contributions do not reduce current taxes
Roth IRA	• Tax-deferred interest and earnings • $2,000 annual limit on individual contributions • Withdrawals are tax-free in specific cases • Contributions do not reduce current taxes
Simplified Employee Pension Plan (SEP-IRA)	• "Pay yourself first" payroll reduction contributions • Pre-tax contributions • Tax-deferred interest and earnings
Spousal IRA	• Tax-deferred interest and earnings • Both working spouse and nonworking spouse can contribute up to $2,000 each year • Limited eligibility for tax-deductible contributions • Contributions do not reduce current taxes
Rollover IRA	• Traditional IRA that accepts rollovers of all or a portion of your taxable distribution from a retirement plan • You can roll over to a Roth IRA
Education IRA	• Tax-deferred interest and earnings • 10% early withdrawal penalty is waived when money is used for higher-education expenses • $500 annual limit on individual contributions • Contributions do not reduce current taxes

PLANNING AHEAD IRAs can be a good way to save money for retirement. *What are the features of the Education IRA?*

SPOUSAL IRA A Spousal IRA lets you contribute up to $2,000 on behalf of your nonworking spouse if you file a joint tax return. As with a traditional IRA, this contribution may be fully or partially tax-deductible, depending on your income. This also depends on whether you belong to an employer-provided retirement plan.

ROLLOVER IRA A rollover IRA is a traditional IRA that lets you roll over, or transfer, all or a portion of your taxable distribution from a retirement plan or other IRA. This arrangement allows you to move your money from plan to plan without paying taxes on it. In order to avoid taxes, however, you must follow certain rules about transferring the money from one plan to another. If you change jobs or retire before age $59^{1}/_{2}$, a rollover IRA may be just what you need. It will let you avoid the penalty you would otherwise have to pay on early withdrawals.

EDUCATION IRA An Education IRA is a special IRA with certain restrictions. It allows individuals to contribute up to $500 per year toward the education of any child under age 18. The contributions are not tax-deductible. However, they do provide tax-free distributions for education expenses.

Figure 15.5 summarizes the various types of IRAs.

Whether or not you're covered by another type of pension plan, you can still make IRA contributions even though they are not tax-deductible. All of the income your IRA earns will compound, tax-deferred, until you begin making withdrawals. Remember, the biggest benefit of an IRA lies in its tax-deferred earnings growth. The longer the money accumulates tax-deferred, the bigger the benefit, as shown in **Figure 15.6**.

IRA WITHDRAWALS When you retire, you can withdraw the money from your IRA by one of several methods. You can take out all of the money at one time, but the entire amount will be taxed as income. If you decide to withdraw the money from your IRA in installments, you will have to pay tax only on the amount that you withdraw. A final alternative would be to place the money that you withdraw in an annuity that guarantees payments over your lifetime. See the discussion of annuities later in this section for further information about this option.

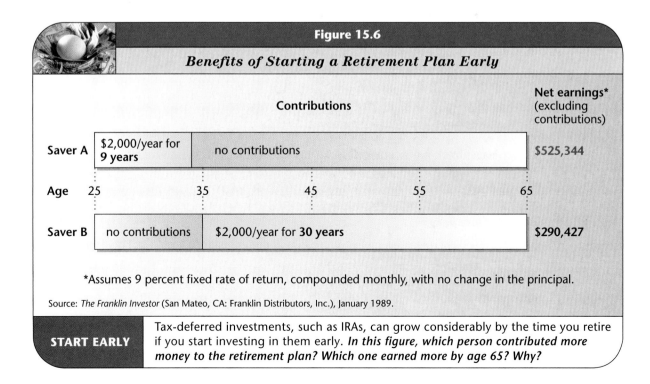

Figure 15.6

Benefits of Starting a Retirement Plan Early

	Contributions				Net earnings* (excluding contributions)
Saver A	$2,000/year for 9 years	no contributions			$525,344
Age	25	35	45	55	65
Saver B	no contributions	$2,000/year for **30 years**			$290,427

*Assumes 9 percent fixed rate of return, compounded monthly, with no change in the principal.

Source: *The Franklin Investor* (San Mateo, CA: Franklin Distributors, Inc.), January 1989.

START EARLY Tax-deferred investments, such as IRAs, can grow considerably by the time you retire if you start investing in them early. *In this figure, which person contributed more money to the retirement plan? Which one earned more by age 65? Why?*

*J*osephine Dale has just been offered her dream job—as budget analyst for a recording studio. She majored in music industry in college and was hoping she would find a job that would combine her love of music with her aptitude for finance. Now, as a single career woman, Josephine has many decisions to make. Josephine will have to move to New York City; her new company will pay a lump sum of $10,000 to cover her moving expenses. Josephine also has a variety of investment decisions to make. Although this is her first job, she knows she should start investing for retirement now. Her new company offers a 401(k) plan as well as stock options. Josephine has read about IRAs and thinks she should consider them. Because she has no experience with the various retirement options, she turns to the experts at Standard & Poor's for advice.

Analysis: The sooner Josephine starts saving for retirement, the easier it will be for her to build a sizable nest egg with small investments. Starting early means she may have to make contributions to her retirement savings only for 10 years or so. After that, compound earnings could provide all the additional growth in her investment account that she will need for a comfortable retirement. If Josephine waits until her 30s to start investing, she may find she has to contribute additional amounts toward her retirement until the day she actually retires!

Recommendation: By signing up for her company's 401(k) plan Josephine can defer taxes on part of her income and all of her investment earnings. If her company matches part of her contributions, investing in her 401(k) should be her first priority. When Josephine is settled in New York, she should consider investing additional amounts, up to $2,000 a year, in a traditional IRA or a Roth IRA. The amount she invests in a Roth IRA will not be tax deductible. However, unlike 401(k) plans and traditional IRAs, investment earnings in a Roth IRA can be withdrawn tax-free rather than tax-deferred. To qualify for this tax treatment, the account must be held for at least five years and the withdrawals must be made after reaching age 59½.

Critical Thinking Questions

1. How might the $10,000 in relocation money affect Josephine's decision to open a traditional IRA or a Roth IRA this year?

2. If her company does not match her contributions to her 401(k), which type of account should be Josephine's first priority to fund?

3. How should Josephine invest the money she contributes to her retirement plans?

Keogh Plans

A *Keogh plan*, also known as an H.R.10 plan or a self-employed retirement plan, is a retirement plan specially designed for self-employed people and their employees. Keogh plans have limits on the amount of annual tax-deductible contributions as well as various other restrictions. Keogh plans can be complicated to administer, so you should get professional tax advice before using this type of personal retirement plan.

Limits on Retirement Plans

With the exception of Roth IRAs, you cannot keep money in most tax-deferred retirement plans forever. When you retire, or by age 70½ at the latest, you must begin to receive "minimum lifetime distributions," withdrawals from the funds you have accumulated in the plan. The amount of the distributions is based on your life expectancy at the time the distributions begin. If you don't withdraw the minimum distributions from a retirement account, the IRS will charge you a penalty.

Annuities

What do you do if you have funded your 401(k), 403(b), Keogh, and profit-sharing plans up to the allowable limits and you want to put away more money for retirement? The answer may be an annuity. An *annuity* is a contract purchased from an insurance company that provides for a sum of money to be paid to a person at regular intervals for a certain number of years or for life.

You might purchase an annuity with the money you receive from an IRA or company pension. You can simply buy an annuity to supplement the income you'll receive from either of these types of plans.

You can choose to purchase an annuity that has a single payment or installment payments. You will also need to decide whether you want the insurance company to send the income from your annuity to you immediately or begin sending it to you at a later date. The payments you receive from an annuity are taxed as ordinary income. However, the interest you earn from the annuity accumulates tax-free until payments begin.

$AVVY SAVER

Making the Most of Your Company's 401(k) Plan

1. Begin contributing as soon as your company allows.
2. Contribute the maximum amount.
3. Learn as much as you can about the investment options offered.
4. Review your investments periodically.
5. Make adjustments to your investments as needed.

Types of Annuities

Annuities may be fixed, providing a certain amount of income for life, or variable, with payments guaranteed above a minimum amount depending on the return on your investment. Either way, the rate of return on an annuity is often tied to overall interest rates.

People approaching retirement age often purchase immediate annuities. These annuities provide income payments at once. They're usually purchased with a lump-sum payment. Once you're over age 65, your children will probably be out on their own. In that case, you may no longer need all of your life insurance coverage. You may decide to convert the cash value of your insurance policy into a lump-sum payment for an immediate annuity.

With deferred annuities, income payments start at some future date. Meanwhile, interest accumulates on the money you deposit. Younger people often buy such annuities to save money toward retirement. A deferred annuity purchased with a lump-sum payment is known as a single-premium deferred annuity. These annuities are popular because of the greater potential for tax-free growth. If you're buying a deferred annuity on an installment basis, you may want one that allows flexible premiums. That means that, your contributions can vary from year to year.

You have various choices regarding the form that an annuity and annuity income will take. Discuss all of the possible options with your insurance agent. The costs, fees, and other features of annuities differ from policy to policy. Ask about charges, fees, and interest rate guarantees. Also, be sure to check the financial health of the insurance company that offers the annuity.

RETIREMENT INCOME The income needed to live during retirement can come from various sources. *What are some possible sources of the income you'll need to meet your retirement goals?*

Living on Your Retirement Income

As you plan for retirement, you'll estimate a budget or spending plan. When the time to retire arrives, however, you may find that your expenses are higher than you expected. If that's the case, you'll have some work to do.

First, you'll have to make sure that you're getting all the income to which you're entitled. Are there other programs or benefits for which you might qualify? You'll also need to think about any assets or valuables you might be able to convert to cash or sources of income.

You may have to confront the trade-off between spending and saving again. For example, perhaps you can use your skills and time instead of your money. Instead of spending money on an expensive vacation, take advantage of free and low-cost recreation opportunities, such as public parks, museums, libraries, and fairs. Retirees often receive special discounts on movie tickets, meals, and more.

Working During Retirement

Some people decide to work part-time after they retire. Some even take new full-time jobs. Work can provide a person with a greater sense of usefulness, involvement, and self-worth. It may also be a good way to add to your retirement income.

Dipping into Your Nest Egg

When should you take money out of your savings during retirement? The answer depends on your financial circumstances, your age, and how much you want to leave to your heirs. (Your *heirs* are the people who will have the legal right to your assets when you die.) Your savings may be large enough to allow you to live comfortably on the interest alone. On the other hand, you may need to make regular withdrawals to help finance your retirement. Dipping into savings isn't wrong. However, you must do so with caution.

If you dip into your retirement nest egg, you should consider one important question: How long will your savings last

FOR LOVE OR MONEY Many people decide to work full- or part-time after they retire, sometimes pursuing hobbies that they enjoy. *What are some of the advantages of working after retirement?*

if you make regular withdrawals? For example, if you have $10,000 in savings that earns 5.5 percent interest, compounded quarterly, you could take out $68 every month for 20 years before reducing those savings to zero. If you have $40,000, you could withdraw $224 every month for 30 years. Whatever your situation, once your nest egg is gone, it's gone.

ASSESSMENT

CHECK YOUR UNDERSTANDING

1. How does a person become eligible for Social Security retirement benefits?
2. Compare and contrast defined-contribution plans and defined-benefit plans.
3. Explain the differences between regular IRAs and Roth IRAs.
4. If you were retired, what would you have to consider before you began to draw on your savings?

THINK CRITICALLY

5. Describe the trade-offs that you would consider if you reached retirement age and realized that your expenses were higher than you could afford.

USING MATH SKILLS

6. **Growing a Nest Egg** When Jamal Robinson graduated from college recently, his parents gave him $1,000 and told him to use it wisely. Jamal decided to use the money to start a retirement account. After doing some research about different options, he put the entire amount into a tax-deferred IRA that pays 11 percent interest, compounded annually. **Calculate** How much money will Jamal have in his IRA at the end of ten years, assuming that the interest rate remains the same and that he does not deposit any additional money? Show your calculations in the form of a chart.

SOLVING MONEY PROBLEMS

7. **Making Decisions** Mike Johnson has worked for the same company for 45 years. Now, at age 67, he is about to retire. When he does, he'll be entitled to receive the money that has been accumulating in his 401(k) plan. It's a lot of money—about $600,000—and Mike has to decide what to do with it. If he manages it wisely, it can help make his retirement years comfortable and rewarding. **Analyze** Use what you've learned in this section to help Mike decide what to do with his pension funds. Consider the options available to him, such as rollover IRAs and annuities. Explain why the option you recommend would make the best use of Mike's money.

Estate Planning

The Importance of Estate Planning

Many people think of estates as belonging only to the rich or elderly. The fact is, however, everyone has an estate. Simply defined, your *estate* consists of everything you own. During your working years your financial goal is to acquire and accumulate money for both your current and future needs. Many years from now, as you grow older, your point of view will change. Instead of working to acquire assets, you'll start to think about what will happen to your hard-earned wealth after you die. In most cases you'll want to pass that wealth along to your loved ones. That is where estate planning becomes important.

What Is Estate Planning?

Estate planning is the process of creating a detailed plan for managing your assets so that you can make the most of them while you're alive and ensure that they're distributed wisely after your

ASSETS AND POSSESSIONS Most people have various assets and many possessions that make up their estate. *What does your estate consist of at this point in your life?*

What You'll Learn

- How to **distinguish** among various types and formats of wills
- How to **discuss** several types of trusts
- How to **describe** common characteristics of estates

Why It's Important

Identifying various kinds of wills and trusts will help you devise an estate plan that protects your interests as well as those of your family. Creating an effective estate plan will allow you to prosper during retirement and provide for your loved ones when you die.

KEY TERMS

- estate
- estate planning
- beneficiary
- will
- intestate
- trust
- probate
- executor
- guardian
- codicil
- living will
- power of attorney

death. It's not pleasant to think about your own death. However, it's a part of estate planning. Without a good estate plan, the assets you accumulate during your lifetime might be greatly reduced by various taxes when you die.

Estate planning is an essential part of both retirement planning and financial planning. It has two stages. The first involves building your estate through savings, investments, and insurance. The second consists of making sure that your estate will be distributed as you wish at the time of your death. If you're married, your estate planning should take into account the needs of your spouse and children. If you're single, you still need to make sure that your financial affairs are in order for your beneficiaries. Your *beneficiary* is a person you've named to receive a portion of your estate after your death.

When you die, your surviving spouse, children, relatives, and friends will face a period of grief and loneliness. At the same time, one or more of these people will probably be responsible for settling your affairs. This will be a difficult time for them. In order for matters to go ahead smoothly, your estate plan must be clear and orderly. Otherwise, the people you've left behind may encounter problems settling your estate, and your intentions may not be carried out according to your wishes. One way to avoid such problems is to make sure that important documents are accessible, understandable, and legally proper.

Legal Documents

An estate plan typically involves various legal documents, one of which is usually a will. When you die, the person who is responsible for handling your affairs will need access to these and other important documents. The documents must be reviewed and verified before your survivors can receive the money and other assets to which they're entitled. If no one can find the necessary documents, your heirs may experience emotionally painful delays. They may even lose parts of their inheritance. The important papers you need to collect and organize include:

- Birth certificates for you, your spouse, and your children
- Marriage certificates and divorce papers
- Legal name changes (especially important to protect adopted children)
- Military service records
- Social Security documents
- Veteran's documents
- Insurance policies

- Transfer records of joint bank accounts
- Safe-deposit box records
- Automobile registrations
- Titles to stock and bond certificates

You should have several copies of certain documents that will be needed to process insurance claims and settle your estate. In some cases, children whose parents have died may need to provide documents proving their parents' births, marriage, or divorce.

Wills

One of the most important documents that every adult should have is a written will. A *will* is the legal document that specifies how you want your property to be distributed after your death. If you die *intestate*—without a valid will—your legal state of residence will step in and control the distribution of your estate without regard for any wishes you may have had.

You should avoid the possibility of dying intestate. The simplest way to do that is to make sure that you have a written will. Having an attorney help you draft a will can help your heirs avoid many difficulties. Legal fees for drafting a will vary with the size of your estate and your family situation. A standard will costs between $200 and $350. Make sure that you find an attorney who has experience with drafting wills and planning estates.

PEACE OF MIND Preparing a will can make things easier for your family after your death and ensure that your estate is distributed according to your wishes. *What would happen if you were to die without preparing a will?*

Types of Wills

You have several options in preparing a will. The four basic types of wills are the simple will, the traditional marital share will, the exemption trust will, and the stated dollar amount will. The differences among them can affect how your estate will be taxed.

Simple Will

A simple will leaves everything to your spouse. Such a will is generally sufficient for people with small estates. However, if you have

a large or complex estate, a simple will may not meet your objectives. It may also result in higher overall taxation, since everything you leave to your spouse will be taxed as part of his or her estate.

Traditional Marital Share Will

The traditional marital share will leaves one-half of the adjusted gross estate (the total value of the estate minus debts and costs) to the spouse. The other half of the estate may go to children or other heirs. It can also be held in trust for the family. A *trust* is an arrangement in which a designated person known as a trustee manages assets for the benefit of someone else. A trust can provide a spouse with a lifelong income and would not be taxed at his or her death.

Exemption Trust Will

With an exemption trust will, all of your assets go to your spouse except for a certain amount, which goes into a trust. This amount, plus any interest it earns, can provide your spouse with lifelong income that will not be taxed. As of 2001 the exemption amount was $675,000. It will increase to $1 million by 2006. The tax-free aspect of this type of will may become important if your property value increases considerably after you die.

Stated Dollar Amount Will

The stated dollar amount will allows you to pass on to your spouse any amount that satisfies your family's financial goals. For tax purposes you could pass the exempted amount of $675,000 (in 2001). However, you might decide to pass on a stated amount related to your family's future income needs or to the value of personal items.

State law may dictate how much you must leave to your spouse. Most states require that the spouse receive a certain amount, usually one-half or one-third of the value of the estate. States also have laws regarding when and how portions of the estate must pass to beneficiaries.

The stated dollar amount will has one major drawback. Suppose that you leave specific dollar amounts to your listed heirs and the balance to your spouse. Although these amounts may be fair and reasonable when the will is drafted, they can soon become outdated. What if the value of the estate decreases because of a business problem or a drop in the stock market? That decrease will not affect those who are left specific dollar amounts, but it will affect the value of your spouse's inheritance. For this reason most experts recommend using percentages rather than specific designated amounts.

Wills and Probate

The type of will that is best for your particular needs depends on many factors, including the size of your estate, inflation, your age, and your objectives. No matter what type of will you choose, it's best to avoid probate. *Probate* is the legal procedure of proving a will to be valid or invalid. It's the process by which your estate is managed and distributed after your death, according to the provisions of your will. A special probate court generally validates wills and makes sure that your debts are paid. You should avoid probate because it's expensive, lengthy, and public. As you'll read later, a living trust avoids probate and is also less expensive, quicker, and private.

Formats of Wills

Wills may be either holographic or formal. A holographic will is a handwritten will that you prepare yourself. It should be written, dated, and signed entirely in your own handwriting. No printed or typed information should appear on its pages. Some states do not recognize holographic wills as legal.

A formal will is usually prepared with the help of an attorney. It may be typed, or it may be a preprinted form that you fill out. You must sign the will in front of two witnesses; neither person can be a beneficiary named in the will. The witnesses must then sign the will in front of you.

A statutory will is prepared on a preprinted form, available from lawyers or stationery stores. There are serious risks in using preprinted forms to prepare your will. The form may include provisions that are not in the best interests of your heirs. If you change the preprinted wording, part or all of the will may be declared invalid. Furthermore, the form may not remain up-to-date with current laws regarding wills. For these reasons it is best to seek a lawyer's advice when you prepare your will.

Writing Your Will

Writing a will allows you to express exactly how you want your property to be distributed to your heirs. If you're married, you may think that all the property owned jointly by you and your spouse will automatically go to your spouse after your death. This is true of some assets, such as your house. Even so, writing a will is the only way to make sure that all of your property will end up where you want it.

Selecting an Executor

An *executor* is someone who is willing and able to perform the tasks involved in carrying out your will. These tasks include preparing an inventory of your assets, collecting any money due, and paying off your debts. Your executor must also prepare and file all income and estate tax returns. In addition, he or she will be responsible for making decisions about selling or reinvesting assets to pay off debts and provide income for your family while the estate is being settled. Finally, your executor must distribute the estate and make a final accounting to your beneficiaries and to the probate court.

An executor can be a family member, a friend, an attorney, an accountant, or the trust department of a bank. You may name one of your beneficiaries as your executor. State law sets fees for executors. If you do not name an executor in your will, the court will appoint one. Naming your own executor eliminates that possibility and helps prevent unnecessary delay in the distribution of your property. It will also minimize estate taxes and settlement costs.

Selecting a Guardian

If you have children, your will should also name a guardian to care for them in the event that you and your spouse die at the same time and the children cannot care for themselves. A *guardian* is a person who accepts the responsibility of providing children with personal care after their parents' death and managing the parents' estate for the children until they reach a certain age.

When you name a guardian for your children, choose someone who loves them and shares your beliefs about raising children. Of course, the person must also be willing to accept the responsibilities associated with that role.

PREDICT

What situations might motivate you to change your will?

Altering or Rewriting Your Will

Sometimes you'll need to change the provisions of your will because of changes in your life or in the law. Once you've made a will, review it frequently so that it remains current. Here are some reasons to review your will:

- You've moved to a new state that has different laws.
- You've sold property that is mentioned in the will.

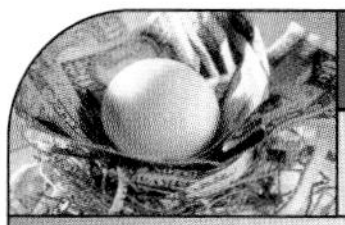

Figure 15.7

A Living Will

Living Will Declaration

Declaration made this _____ day of _____ (month, year)

I, _____, being of sound mind, willfully and voluntarily make known my desire that my dying shall not be artificially prolonged under the circumstances set forth below, do hereby declare

    If at any time I should have an incurable injury, disease, or illness regarded as a terminal condition by my physician and if my physician has determined that the application of life-sustaining procedures would serve only to artificially prolong the dying process and that my death will occur whether or not life-sustaining procedures are utilized, I direct that such procedures be withheld or withdrawn and that I be permitted to die with only the administration of medication or the performance of any medical procedure deemed necessary to provide me with comfort care.

    In the absence of my ability to give directions regarding the use of such life-sustaining procedures, it is my intention that this declaration shall be honored by my family and physician as the final expression of my legal right to refuse medical or surgical treatment and accept the consequences from such refusal. I understand the full import of this declaration, and I am emotionally and mentally competent to make this declaration.

Signed _____

City, County, and State of Residence _____

The declarant has been personally known to me, and I believe him or her to be of sound mind.

Witness _____

Witness _____

DYING WITH DIGNITY Some people who become terminally ill cannot make decisions on their own behalf. *What is the basic purpose of a living will?*

- The size and composition of your estate have changed.
- You've married, divorced, or remarried.
- Potential heirs have died, or new ones have been born.

Don't make any written changes on the pages of an existing will. Additions, deletions, or erasures on a will that has been signed and witnessed can invalidate the will. If you want to make only a few minor changes, adding a codicil may be the best choice. A *codicil* is a document that explains, adds, or deletes provisions in your existing will. To be valid, it must meet the legal requirements for a will. If you want to make major changes in your will, or if you've already added a codicil, it is best to prepare a new will. In the new will, be sure to include a clause that revokes, or cancels, all earlier wills and codicils.

A Living Will

At some point in your life you may become physically or mentally disabled and unable to act on your own behalf. If that happens, you'll need a living will. A *living will* is a document in which you state whether you want to be kept alive by artificial means if you become terminally ill and unable to make such a decision. Many states recognize living wills. **Figure 15.7** is an example of a typical living will.

To ensure the effectiveness of a living will, discuss your intention of preparing such a will with your family or other loved ones and your doctor. Sign and date the document before two witnesses. Witnessing shows that you signed the document by choice. Review your living will from time to time to make sure that your feelings haven't changed.

You may consider writing a living will when you draw up a traditional will. Most lawyers will produce a living will at no cost if they're already preparing a traditional will or your estate plan. You can also get the necessary forms for a living will from nonprofit groups such as Aging With Dignity and Choice in Dying.

Power of Attorney

Related to the idea of a living will is power of attorney. A *power of attorney* is a legal document that authorizes someone to act on your behalf. If you become seriously ill or injured, you'll probably need someone to take care of your needs and personal affairs. This can be done through a power of attorney.

You can assign a power of attorney to anyone you choose. You can give that person power to carry out only certain actions or transactions. Alternatively, you may allow the person to act on your behalf in all matters, including your living will.

Letter of Last Instruction

In addition to a traditional will and a living will, it's a good idea to prepare a letter of last instruction. This document is not legally binding, but it can provide your heirs with important information. It should contain your wishes for your funeral arrangements as well as the names of the people who are to be informed of your death. With a letter of last instruction you can also let people know the locations of your bank accounts, safe-deposit box, and other important items.

Trusts

Basically, a trust is a legal arrangement that helps manage the assets of your estate for your benefit or that of your beneficiaries. The creator of the trust is called the trustor, or grantor. The trustee might be a person or institution, such as a bank, that administers the trust. A bank charges a small fee for its services in administering a trust. The fee is usually based on the value of the assets in the trust.

Individual circumstances determine whether it makes sense to establish a trust. Some of the common reasons for setting up a trust are to:

- reduce or otherwise provide for payment of estate taxes;
- avoid probate and transfer your assets immediately to your beneficiaries;
- free yourself from managing your assets while you receive a regular income from the trust;
- provide income for a surviving spouse or other beneficiary;
- ensure that your property serves a desired purpose after your death.

Be a Volunteer

Are you interested in a certain career? Why not volunteer in that field? It's a great way for you to find out firsthand if you want to invest the time and money preparing for that profession.

Types of Trusts

There are many types of trusts, some of which are described in detail below. You'll need to choose the type of trust that's most appropriate for your particular situation. An estate attorney can advise you about the right type of trust for your personal and family needs.

All trusts are either revocable or irrevocable. A revocable trust is one in which you have the right to end the trust or change its terms during your lifetime. An irrevocable trust is one that cannot be changed or ended. Revocable trusts avoid the lengthy process of probate, but they do not protect assets from federal or state estate taxes. Irrevocable trusts avoid probate and help reduce estate taxes. However, by law you cannot remove any assets from an irrevocable trust, even if you need them at some later point in your life.

Credit-Shelter Trust

A credit-shelter trust is one that enables the spouse of a deceased person to avoid paying federal taxes on a certain amount of assets left to him or her as part of an estate. As of 2001 the exemption amount was $675,000. It will increase to $1 million by 2006. Perhaps the most common estate planning trust, the credit-shelter trust has many other names: bypass trust, "residuary" trust, A/B trust, exemption equivalent trust, or family trust.

Disclaimer Trust

A disclaimer trust is appropriate for couples who do not yet have enough assets to need a credit-shelter trust but may have in the future. With a disclaimer trust, the surviving spouse is left everything, but he or she has the right to disclaim, or deny, some portion of the estate. Anything that is disclaimed goes into a credit-shelter trust. This approach allows the surviving spouse to protect wealth from estate taxes.

Living Trust

A living trust, also known as an inter vivos trust, is a property management arrangement that you establish while you're alive. It allows you, as trustor, to receive benefits during your lifetime. To set up a living trust, you simply transfer some of your assets to a trustee. Then you give the trustee instructions for managing the trust while you're alive and after your death. A living trust has several advantages:

- It ensures privacy. A will is a public record; a trust is not.
- The assets held in trust avoid probate at your death. This eliminates probate costs and delays.
- It enables you to review your trustee's performance and make changes if necessary.
- It can relieve you of management responsibilities.

IN WHOM WE TRUST For some people, setting up a trust is an effective way to organize and manage an estate. *What are some of the main reasons to establish a trust?*

- It's less likely than a will to create arguments between heirs upon your death.
- It can guide your family and doctors if you become terminally ill or unable to make your own decisions.

Setting up a living trust costs more than creating a will. However, depending on your particular circumstances, a living trust can be a good estate planning option.

Testamentary Trust

A testamentary trust is one established by your will that becomes effective upon your death. Such a trust can be valuable if your beneficiaries are inexperienced in financial matters. It may also be your best option if your estate taxes will be high. A testamentary trust provides many of the same advantages as a living trust.

RESPOND

Summarize the advantages of creating a trust.

Estates

As you learned earlier in this chapter, your estate consists of everything you own. Therefore, an important step in estate planning is taking inventory of your assets. Don't forget to include jointly owned property, life insurance, employee retirement benefits, money owed to you by others, and all personal possessions in your inventory.

Some states are known as community-property states. Community property is any money earned by either spouse during the marriage and any property or possessions purchased with that money. It does not include assets received as gifts or through inheritances. In community-property states, each spouse owns 50 percent of the property. Thus, half of the couple's assets are included in each spouse's estate. In noncommunity-property states, property is included in the estate of the spouse who owns it. The way you own property can make a significant tax difference.

Joint Ownership

Joint ownership of property between spouses is very common. Joint ownership may also exist between parents and children or other relatives. Joint ownership may help avoid probate and inheritance taxes in some states. However, it does not avoid federal estate taxes. It may, in fact, increase the amount of federal estate taxes.

Three types of joint ownership exist, and each one has different tax and estate planning consequences. First, you and your spouse may own property as "joint tenants with the right of survivorship."

In this case, the property is considered to be owned 50–50 for estate tax purposes and will automatically pass to one spouse at the other's death. No estate tax is paid at the first death. However, when the surviving spouse dies, more estate taxes may be due than with a traditional marital share will.

In the second type of joint ownership, you and your spouse may own property as "tenants in common." Each individual is considered to own a certain share of property for tax purposes, and only your share is included in your estate. That share does not go to the other tenant in common at your death. Instead, it's included in your probate estate, and you decide who gets it. Gift and estate taxes do not apply to property that belongs to spouses.

The third type of joint ownership, "tenancy by the entirety," is limited to married couples. Under this type of joint ownership, both spouses own the property. When one spouse dies, the other gets the property automatically. Neither spouse may sell the property without the consent of the other.

Joint ownership is a poor substitute for a will because it gives you less control over the distribution and taxation of your property after death. State laws govern the types and effects of joint ownership. You should consult an attorney on these matters.

Life Insurance and Employee Benefits

If you have life insurance, the benefits of that insurance will be counted among the assets in your estate. Life insurance benefits are free of income tax, and they do not go through probate. They are also at least partially exempt from most state inheritance taxes. However, they are subject to federal estate taxes under certain circumstances, such as if you have the right to change beneficiaries, surrender the policy for cash, or make loans on the policy.

Death benefits from qualified employer pension plans or Keogh plans are usually excluded from your estate. One exception is if the benefits are payable to the estate. Another exception is if the beneficiary chooses a special provision for averaging income tax in lump-sum distributions.

Lifetime Gifts and Trusts

You may give part of your estate as a gift or set up a trust for your spouse or a child. Under certain conditions, such gifts and trusts are not included as part of your estate upon your death. However, if you keep any control or use of the gift or trust, it remains part of your estate and is subject to taxes. For example, if you transfer title of your home to a child but continue to live in it, the value of the home is taxed as part of your estate. Similarly, if you put property in trust but keep some control over the income or principal, the property is included in your estate even though you may not be able to obtain it yourself.

SECTION 15.3 ASSESSMENT

CHECK YOUR UNDERSTANDING

1. Name the four basic types of wills.
2. What are the differences among a credit-shelter trust, a disclaimer trust, and a living trust?
3. What does it mean to own property as joint tenants with the right of survivorship and to own property as tenants in common?

THINK CRITICALLY

4. Which format of a will—holographic or formal—is the best from a legal point of view? Why?

USING COMMUNICATION SKILLS

5. **Estate Plan** Review the information you read about wills, trusts, and estates. Think about how these three things work together to create an estate plan that protects the interests of people, provides for their survivors, and minimizes taxes.
   Prepare an Oral Report Arrange your conclusions about wills, trusts, and estates in the form of an oral report. Present your report to the class.

SOLVING MONEY PROBLEMS

6. **Cost versus Satisfaction** Irving and Irma Lansing are making plans for the distribution of their assets after they die. They have wills, but they want to make sure that they're using the right type of will to maximize the benefits for the surviving spouse and their four grown children. The estimated value of their estate is currently about $1.4 million. However, most of their assets are in high-risk stocks, which can vary greatly in value depending on economic conditions and the stock market.
   Compare Costs Help Irving and Irma by summarizing the benefits and drawbacks of the four main types of wills. Identify which type would be best for them.

Taxes and Estate Planning

What You'll Learn

- How to **identify** the types of taxes that affect estates
- How to **assess** strategies for paying taxes

Why It's Important

Identifying the various types of estate taxes can help you minimize your tax liability. Assessing strategies for paying estate taxes can help limit financial hardship for your heirs.

Federal and state governments impose various types of taxes that you must consider in planning your estate. The four major types of taxes are estate taxes, estate and trust income taxes, inheritance taxes, and gift taxes.

Estate Taxes

As you may remember from Chapter 12, an estate tax is a tax collected on the value of a person's property at the time of his or her death. The tax is based on the fair market value of the deceased person's investments, property, and bank accounts, less allowable deductions and other taxes. With careful estate planning, you may leave all of your property to your surviving spouse, free of federal estate taxes. As of 2001, if the value of the surviving spouse's estate were more than $675,000, any funds over this amount would incur estate taxes of 37 to 55 percent.

Estate and Trust Federal Income Taxes

Estates and certain trusts must also file federal income tax returns with the Internal Revenue Service. Taxable income for estates and trusts is handled similarly to taxable income for individuals. Trusts and estates must pay quarterly estimated taxes.

Inheritance Taxes

Your heirs will have to pay a tax for the right to acquire the property that they have inherited. An inheritance tax is a tax collected on the property left by a person in his or her will. The amount of the tax due depends on the value of the property and insurance received. It also depends on the relationship of the heir to the deceased.

Only state governments impose inheritance taxes. Most states collect an inheritance tax, but state laws differ widely as to exemptions and rates of taxation. A reasonable average for state inheritance taxes would be 4 to 10 percent of whatever the heir receives.

Gift Taxes

Both the federal and state governments impose a gift tax, a tax collected on money or property valued at more than $10,000 given by one person to another in a single year. One way to reduce the tax liability of your estate is to reduce the size of the estate while you're alive by giving away portions of it as gifts. You're free to make such gifts to your spouse, children, or anyone else at any time. (Don't give away assets if you may need them in your retirement!)

According to federal law, you may give up to $10,000 per person per year free of any gift tax. A married couple, acting together, may give up to $20,000 per person per year without paying the tax. Gifts that exceed those amounts are subject to the tax. Gift tax rates are currently the same as estate tax rates, and they are called unified transfer tax rates. However, gifts may be included in your estate for tax purposes if they were given within three years of your death. Many states have other gift tax laws as well.

Paying the Tax

After doing everything possible to reduce your estate taxes, you may still find that taxes will be due. In that case you'll have to think about the best way to help your heirs pay the taxes. The federal estate tax is due nine months after a death. State taxes, probate costs, debts, and other expenses also are usually due within that same period. These costs might result in a real financial problem for your survivors. Finding enough cash to pay taxes, debts, and other costs without causing financial hardship can be very difficult.

One way to handle this problem is through life insurance. A life insurance policy may be the best way to provide your family with the tax-free cash that they'll need to settle your estate.

Another solution is to set aside enough cash ahead of time to pay taxes and expenses when they're due. However, the cash may be subject to income tax during your lifetime and to estate tax at your death.

A third option is for your family to sell assets to pay taxes. However, this could result in the loss of important sources of income.

A fourth option is to consider borrowing money. However, it's unusual to find a commercial lender that will lend money to pay

QUESTION

Where would you look to find the current inheritance tax rates for your state?

DEATH AND TAXES Dealing with the financial aspects of a person's death can be a difficult burden. *How will your survivors pay your debts after you die?*

Saving for Retirement

Heinrich has become eligible to participate in his company's 401(k) program. He can invest from 2 to 15 percent of his salary, which is $20,000 a year. The company matches the first 5 percent at a rate of 50 percent, or 50 cents for every dollar he invests. He decided to save 5 percent of his salary. Based on the current investment return of 10 percent compounded annually, Heinrich calculated how much he would be able to save, with company-matching contributions factored in.

	Contributions	Interest	Total
Heinrich's contribution of 5 percent of his $20,000 salary	$1,000.00/year	10%	
Company contribution matching 50 percent of 5 percent of his salary	$500.00/year		
1st Year	$ 1,500	$ 150.00	$ 1,650.00
2nd Year	1,500	315.00	3,465.00
3rd Year	1,500	496.50	5,461.50
4th Year	1,500	696.15	7,657.65
5th Year	1,500	915.77	10,073.42
6th Year	1,500	1,157.34	12,730.76
7th Year	1,500	1,423.08	15,653.84
8th Year	1,500	1,715.38	18,869.22
9th Year	1,500	2,036.92	22,406.14
10th Year	1,500	2,390.61	26,296.75
Total	**$15,000**	**$11,296.75**	**$26,296.75**

Calculate In your workbook or on a separate sheet of paper, calculate how much you would have in ten years if you saved $2,000 a year at an annual interest rate of 10 percent, with the company contributing $500 a year.

Source: *The Franklin Investors* (San Mateo, CA: Franklin Distributors, Inc.) January 1989.

taxes. Besides, borrowing money only prolongs the problem and adds interest costs in the process.

Finally, if your family or beneficiaries can show that they have a reasonable cause, the IRS may allow them to make deferred or installment payments on the taxes that are due. That can be helpful. However, like borrowing, it really just prolongs the problem.

CONNECT

If you were the executor of an estate of a relative, how would you feel about paying off debts and taxes?

ASSESSMENT

CHECK YOUR UNDERSTANDING

1. Compare estate taxes and inheritance taxes.
2. How might you use gifts to reduce the size of your estate?
3. What are several strategies that you might use to arrange for paying taxes? Which strategy might be best?

THINK CRITICALLY

4. Some states are phasing out or eliminating the inheritance tax as a way to keep older, wealthy citizens as residents. How do you think this would benefit the state?

USING MATH SKILLS

5. **Too Much Money** Joel and Rachel Simon are both retired. Married for 50 years, they've amassed an estate worth $1.2 million. If either of them dies before 2006, the surviving spouse can receive $675,000 tax-free. The amount over that exemption will be subject to federal estate tax. The couple has no trusts or other types of tax-sheltered assets.
   Analyze Data If Joel or Rachel dies before 2006, how much federal estate tax would the surviving spouse have to pay, assuming that the estate is taxed at the 37 percent rate?

SOLVING MONEY PROBLEMS

6. **Analyzing Costs** Roland Nageotte, a widower, has learned that he is terminally ill. He has no way of knowing how much longer he will live. He does know that he may require expensive medical care, and he has minimal health insurance coverage. At present Roland's estate is worth about $500,000. In order to reduce the estate taxes that will need to be paid after his death, he is considering making gifts of assets to his four children. He would like to give each child $10,000 per year until he dies.
   Problem Solving Use what you know to make your best judgment about whether Roland should proceed with his plan. Explain the reasons for your recommendation.

CHAPTER 15 ASSESSMENT

CHAPTER SUMMARY

- If you want your retirement to be a happy and comfortable time in your life, you should start planning and saving early.

- To estimate your retirement living expenses, think about how your spending patterns and living situation will change when you retire.

- The type of housing and location you choose for retirement can affect your financial needs.

- Social Security is one of the important sources of retirement income for most Americans.

- The benefits you receive from an employer pension plan will vary depending on the type of plan.

- Among the most popular personal retirement plans are individual retirement accounts (IRAs) and Keogh accounts.

- Careful planning can help you make the best use of your retirement income.

- The four basic types of wills are the simple will, the traditional marital share will, the exemption trust will, and the stated dollar amount will.

- Types of trusts include the credit-shelter trust, the disclaimer trust, the living trust, and the testamentary trust.

- Your estate consists of everything you own.

- Federal and state governments impose various types of estate taxes; you can prepare a plan for paying these taxes.

Understanding and Using Vocabulary

Practice using the terms related to retirement and estate planning. With a partner, role-play an imaginary conversation with your spouse. Assume that you're both nearing retirement. Discuss your options for retirement and estate planning. Use as many key terms in your discussion as possible.

assisted-living facility (ALF)
defined-contribution plan
401(k) plan
vesting
defined-benefit plan
individual retirement account (IRA)
Keogh plan
annuity
heirs

estate
estate planning
beneficiary
will
intestate
trust
probate
executor
guardian
codicil
living will
power of attorney

Review Key Concepts

1. In what ways might a person's spending patterns change when he or she retires?
2. How long can a person keep money in a tax-deferred retirement plan?
3. Why might a person alter or rewrite a will?
4. Name two ways in which people can protect their wishes for their estates in case

CHAPTER 15 ASSESSMENT

they become seriously ill or otherwise unable to make decisions.

5. What is the difference between community-property states and noncommunity-property states?

Apply Key Concepts

1. Name several trade-offs that you personally might make to keep your spending at a reasonable level when you retire.
2. Describe two ways to maximize the benefits of an IRA when you retire.
3. If you move to another state when you retire, how might your will be affected?
4. Do you think that a living will would have been important to someone retiring 100 years ago? Explain your reasoning.
5. Suppose that a married woman purchases a car with money she earned. Explain how ownership of the car would be considered in a community-property state.

? Problem Solving Today

RETIREMENT HEAVEN

Imagine that you've been thinking about retirement recently. Although you enjoy living in the small Ohio town that has been your home for many years, you dream of spending your retirement in Florida. The problem is that you don't really know much about Florida, except for the images you've seen on television and in some magazines.

Gather Data Using the resources mentioned in this chapter, find out about the climate, housing, recreation, taxes, and cost of living in one region or city of Florida. Prepare a brief report of your findings.

Computer Activity As an alternative activity, use Internet search engines to find information about good places to retire.

Real-World Application

CONNECT WITH LANGUAGE ARTS

Suppose that you have a good job with a pension plan as well as a house, a car, and other assets. Although you are still quite young, you've made a will to ensure that your estate will go to your parents and two younger sisters in case anything happens to you. You've also decided to write a letter of last instruction.

Present a Plan Compose a letter that includes the following information: what type of funeral you would want, the names of the people that you would want notified of your death, and how your finances are arranged.

FINANCE Online

TAXATION WISDOM

Without good estate planning, the IRS is likely to get a large share of your estate. You've already learned about some of the ways to minimize your tax liability. However, you want to investigate other options.

Connect Using various search engines, find out more about the taxes that can affect your estate planning. Explore government agency Web sites as well as those offered by banks, brokerage firms, and tax advisers. Look for tips that will be useful to you in your attempts to reduce the taxes on your estate.

Get a Financial Life!

CASE STUDY

Planning for Retirement

Overview

Karla and David have been saving for their retirement for many years, and the time is nearing when it will become a reality. Spending time with their grandchildren, developing hobbies, traveling, volunteering, and maybe even working part-time are all options Karla and David are considering. Their goal is to retire within the next five years.

Resources

- Classroom notebook
- Internet (optional)
- Math textbook (for reference)
- Portfolio (ring binder or file folder)
- Public or school library
- Word processor

Procedures

Step A THE PROCESS

If you were Karla or David, how would you spend your retirement years?

1. Write a short story (one or two pages) describing how Karla and David will spend their retirement years. Where will they live? Will they travel? Will they work? Do they have hobbies? Use your creativity and imagination.

2. Research long-term care insurance. Then help Karla and David decide whether they should purchase it or invest their money in another way.

3. Watch a movie or TV show about people who are retired or nearing retirement age. Your choices could include *Grumpy Old Men, Space Cowboys, The Golden Girls,* or something similar. Make a list of the hobbies and activities of the characters. Write one or two paragraphs comparing the characters' hobbies and activities to those of people you know who are in their teens and twenties.

4. In 1998 about one in eight Americans was aged 65 or older. By 2030 that number will increase to one in five. Many of these Americans are or will be living in retirement communities, assisted-living facilities, or nursing homes. As a service project, plan an activity for a group of senior citizens in your community. You might develop a craft project, a songfest, or a game day. Use your imagination. Then contact a center and ask if you can implement your activity there.

Step B CREATE YOUR PORTFOLIO

As you work through the process, save the results so that you can refer, review, and refine. Create a portfolio to showcase the information you collected in Step A.

1. Include your short story about Karla and David's retirement years.
2. Present your recommendations and reasoning on whether or not Karla and David should purchase long-term care insurance.
3. Write a summary of the movie or TV show you watched. Include the list of hobbies and activities you created and the comparison paragraph you wrote.
4. Present your plan for the senior citizens' activity that you developed. If you are able to implement it, survey the participants to find out if they enjoyed the activity. Ask how you might improve it for another time.

Step C MATHEMATICS

Along with strong communication skills, employers often look for employees who have excellent math skills. Adding, subtracting, multiplying, dividing, working with fractions and decimals, and applying algebraic equations are the basic skills employers expect from their workers. These skills also are essential in order to plan and manage your own finances.

1. Create ten word problems using the basic mathematical skills described above to solve financial problems from this unit. For example: Tony's employer pays 85 percent of his health insurance premiums. If the total premium for his policy is $335 per month, how much will Tony have to pay? ($335 × 15% = $50.25)
2. Divide into groups of three, and as a team, solve the word problems.
3. Edit the problems if necessary, making sure that they are easy to understand.
4. Compile all the problems and their answers into a classroom notebook. Label the notebook "Mathematical Problems in Personal Finance." If possible, categorize the problems according to the skill (adding, subtracting, fractions, and so on).
5. During the rest of the course, practice your own skills by selecting problems from the notebook to solve.

INTRODUCTION TO BUSINESS FINANCE

Unit 5 explains the relationship between wise financial management and successful business operations. In the next four chapters, you'll learn how businesses manage their finances, obtain funding, perform accounting procedures, and manage payroll and inventory.

READING STRATEGIES

To get the most out of your reading

- **PREDICT** what the section will be about.
- **CONNECT** what you read with your own life.
- **QUESTION** as you read to make sure you understand the content.
- **RESPOND** to what you've read.

START TODAY

Business Know-How

Chances are that sometime in your life, you'll either become a business owner or will work for one. What can you start doing today that will help you prepare to be part of and succeed in the world of work?

Introduction to Financial Management for Business

STANDARD
&POOR'S

Q&A

Q: I'm running a very successful business making children's birthday cakes. Why do I need a business plan?

A: The process of creating a business plan can help you define clear goals for your business, including sales and profitability. Your plan can also establish a benchmark against which you can assess how higher costs may affect your business over time. If you are happy with your current sales, a business plan can help you identify what factors are critical to your continued success.

A Plan for Business

ike Bartram and Erin Waskom recently graduated from high school and want to start a landscaping business. They've worked with other landscapers and have experience taking care of a wide variety of flowers, plants, and trees. Both Mike and Erin feel that there is a growing need for this type of business, based on the number of homes being built and the fact that there is only one other, similar business in the area. Mike has been working part-time for the past two years with an uncle who has a small landscaping business. Erin worked this past summer for Sunny Gardens, a local nursery. Although Mike and Erin have experience, they realize that an understanding of landscape design isn't the only knowledge they'll need to start a successful business. They must also know how to run a business.

The Environment of Business

When you hear the word "business," what do you think of? Do you think of large businesses, like Microsoft, Ford, Coca-Cola, Disney, or IBM? Maybe you think of smaller businesses, like your neighborhood convenience store, flower shop, or hardware store. Despite their differences, all of these businesses are part of the free enterprise system. In a *free enterprise system*, people are free to choose what they buy, what they produce and sell, and where they work. Businesses in such a system must compete to attract the customers they need to continue to operate.

One of the main measurements of success for a business is the amount of profit it earns. *Profit* is the amount of money earned over and above the amount spent to keep the business operating. Profit motivates most people to take the risk of starting a business. It is the reward for taking that risk and for satisfying the needs and wants of consumers. Large or small, businesses must do two things to survive: They must operate at a profit, and they must attract and keep individuals who are willing to take the risk of running the business.

Creating a Business Plan

Whether you're starting a business of your own, as Mike and Erin want to do; purchasing an existing business; or taking over a family business, you must first develop a business plan. A *business plan* is a written outline of a new business venture that describes all aspects of the business. It helps you focus on exactly what you want to do, how you will do it, and what you expect to accomplish. It sets goals for the business just as you set goals for yourself.

A business plan has three basic parts. The first part is a *strategic plan*, which outlines your business goals and the steps you'll take to

What's Your Financial ID?

WHAT'S YOUR BUSINESS PERSONALITY?

Businesses need all types of personalities. Which four of the following statements best describe your personality? Write your answers on a separate sheet of paper, then add up the number of points.

___ I prefer activities where I can tell other people what to do. (5 points)

___ I can delegate responsibility. (3 points)

___ I prefer a clear definition of my responsibilities. (1 point)

___ I'm very good at brainstorming ideas. (5 points)

___ I'm good with details. (1 point)

___ I like to do things exactly right. (1 point)

___ I enjoy persuading others. (5 points)

___ I'm good at planning. (3 points)

___ I like to be in charge. (5 points)

___ I'm good at organizing. (3 points)

___ I prefer to follow others' instructions. (1 point)

___ I know how to give clear directions. (3 points)

Support staff: If you scored 4–8 points, you're a real team player and can provide essential support to any business enterprise.

Manager: If you scored 10–14 points, you may be on track for a management career.

Entrepreneur: If you scored 16–20 points, consider starting your own business when you're ready.

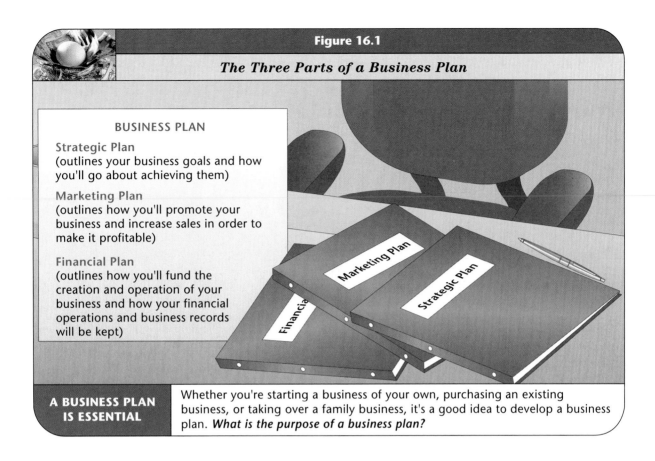

Figure 16.1

The Three Parts of a Business Plan

BUSINESS PLAN

Strategic Plan
(outlines your business goals and how you'll go about achieving them)

Marketing Plan
(outlines how you'll promote your business and increase sales in order to make it profitable)

Financial Plan
(outlines how you'll fund the creation and operation of your business and how your financial operations and business records will be kept)

A BUSINESS PLAN IS ESSENTIAL Whether you're starting a business of your own, purchasing an existing business, or taking over a family business, it's a good idea to develop a business plan. *What is the purpose of a business plan?*

achieve them. The second part is a *marketing plan*, which outlines how you'll promote your business to increase customers and sales in order to make a profit. The third part, often considered the most important, is a financial plan. A *financial plan* outlines not only how you'll get money to create and operate your business but also how you will maintain your financial operations and business records. Basically, it determines how you'll keep track of your money. **Figure 16.1** illustrates the three parts of a business plan. Following is a look at these three plans in more detail.

A Strategic Plan for Your Business

Both new and ongoing businesses must have sound strategic plans to be successful. You have to know where you want to go and choose a direction to follow. In the classic story *Alice in Wonderland*, Alice asks the Cheshire Cat which way she should walk. The Cheshire Cat replies, "That depends a good deal on where you want to get to." This is an appropriate observation about decision making. Every person and every business needs goals and a specific course of action to achieve those goals.

WORKING SIDE BY SIDE Both large and small businesses can prosper and grow as neighbors. *Can you name some large and small business operations that are on the same block in your city or town?*

Your ultimate goal is to have a successful and profitable business. In order to realize that objective, you must first determine the plan you will follow to keep the business growing and moving in the right direction.

A strategic plan is similar to a game plan you might have on your sports team. Simply saying "We want to win!" will not bring a victory. The coach must devise a plan that outlines how you'll achieve the big win. The team must work together to apply the strategies that the coach has developed. Similarly, a business owner or operator may say that he wants the business to succeed, but without a sound business plan, it probably won't happen. The first step in writing a strategic plan is setting goals.

SETTING GOALS Businesses set both short-term and long-term goals. In the business world, short-term goals are goals you expect to reach within one or two years. Long-term goals are those that may take three or more years to reach. Because long-term goals require a considerable amount of time, they are often less specific than short-term goals. You will probably revise them as you go.

Goals for businesses have the same guidelines as the goals you'll establish for your personal finances:

- They should be realistic.
- They should be specific.
- They should have a clear time frame.
- They should help you decide what type of action to take.

Whether you own a small convenience store in the city or run a multinational corporation like Kodak, the goals will be similar. Common objectives might include increasing sales, adding new customers, or updating equipment.

However, goals can also differ, depending on the size of the business. For example, the goals of a small business might include buying a computer system, introducing a new line of merchandise, or moving to a better location. Medium-sized businesses may want to open more stores or begin operating online to increase sales. Larger corporations often have more complex goals. They may want to expand their international markets, change distribution systems, or acquire other smaller corporations.

Goals should be designed according to the guidelines given above, regardless of the size of the business. Goals should be well thought out and in agreement with the philosophy of the business. In all cases, the business needs to determine whether the goals are financially possible.

IDENTIFY STEPS TO ACHIEVE YOUR GOALS When you studied personal finance, you learned that people set financial goals and then decide on ways to achieve those goals. For example, suppose that you have a short-term personal goal of making the honor

CONNECT

What are your financial goals for the future? List at least two short-term goals that will help you reach your long-term goals.

AIMING FOR GOALS Businesses of all sizes need short-term and long-term goals. *Can you name three short-term goals that this business might have?*

MARKETING SELLS With so many brands of athletic shoes on the market, a good marketing plan will give one company an edge over the others. *Can you name some of the ways athletic shoe companies market their product?*

roll. This is an admirable goal, but how do you accomplish it? You analyze the situation and plan your course of action. You identify specific actions you can take, such as writing better notes, doing your homework more carefully, and asking more questions in class.

Long-term goals involve more steps over a longer period of time. Suppose that your long-term goal is to become a successful fashion designer. What must you do to become a designer? You'll need a career plan. Then you will have to identify short-term steps, such as taking related courses in high school, selecting schools or colleges you want to attend, and completing the application process. Later you will probably focus your attention on long-term steps, such as graduating, getting a job, and acquiring professional experience. Hopefully, by taking these short-term and long-term steps, you'll achieve your goal of becoming a fashion designer.

When developing a strategic plan for your business, you should use the same technique. First, identify your short-term and long-term goals. Then create a plan that consists of specific steps toward each goal.

A STRATEGIC PLAN IN ACTION Because their business is new, Mike and Erin realize the importance of setting realistic, achievable goals. Their short-term goals include getting a new business loan with a low interest rate, purchasing basic equipment, locating suppliers for plants and flowers, and purchasing a low-cost phone system. Long-term goals include acquiring a storage facility, purchasing a heavy-duty truck to transport equipment, and increasing the number of customers by 20 percent a year.

In their strategic plan, Mike and Erin identify the steps they will take to achieve each of their goals. For example, suppose that one of Mike and Erin's short-term goals is for the business to show a profit after two years of operation. To reach that goal they plan to increase the number of customers, keep expenses as low as possible, and get the lowest available prices on supplies.

A Marketing Plan for Your Business

A marketing plan outlines the ways in which you will promote your business. You will show a profit or expand your operations only by adding customers. Therefore, you will want to communicate with

INTERNATIONAL FINANCE   Greece

*W*hat's the oldest building in your hometown? In most U.S. cities you probably won't find buildings more than 100 or 200 years old, but in Greece ruins dating back 2,500 years or more are common. Each year these ancient ruins attract more than 8 million visitors and take them back to the days of Socrates, the first Olympics, and the beginnings of democracy. Tourism has become Greece's leading industry and a major source of foreign currency. Athens attracts the majority of travelers. Few could leave the Greek capital without seeing its greatest ancient treasure: the Parthenon, the white marble temple atop the rocky hill called the Acropolis. Here's a snapshot of Greece.

The Acropolis, Athens

Geographic area	50,962 sq. mi.
Population	10,539,000
Capital	Athens (pop. 772,100)
Language	Greek, English, French
Currency	drachma
Gross domestic product (GDP)	$137.4 billion
Per capita GDP	$13,000
Economy	Industry: tourism, food processing, textiles, chemicals. Agriculture: wheat, corn, barley, sugar beets, olives, tomatoes, wine, tobacco, meat. Exports: manufactured goods, foodstuffs, fuels.

Thinking Critically

Convert An American tourist might typically pay $20 for a Greek meal. Check the Internet or the newspaper for the current exchange rate between the U.S. dollar and Greek drachma. Convert the cost of the meal to drachmas.

 For more information on Greece visit finance.glencoe.com **or your local library.**

Competition

Services offered

FIGURE 16.2

Preparing a Marketing Plan

To prepare a marketing plan, you first need to research the existing market. By seeing what's out there, you can better develop an effective marketing plan. This plan will become your road map for reaching new customers and expanding your business. Suppose that you want to open a hardware store. Areas you should identify and analyze include:

3 Current area pricing and advertising

4 Potential customers

as many potential customers as possible to tell them about your goods or services.

As with the creation of a strategic plan, you have to address some specific questions. If you have something to sell, how do you sell it? How do you reach people in an efficient manner? What promotions or advertising can you afford? To begin to answer these questions, you should research the existing market for your goods or services. See **Figure 16.2** for an illustration of this process.

Larger corporations may hire private marketing firms to assist them in developing marketing plans. Some corporations, such as Levi-Strauss, McDonald's, and Ford, have been very successful over the years. Effective marketing plans have allowed these corporations to introduce new products, maintain sales of existing products, and keep their name in the public eye.

A Financial Plan for Your Business

You've probably noticed that the elements in the strategic plan and the marketing plan involve the need for the efficient management of money. In order to make intelligent financial decisions regarding the direction and future of your business, you must record and report your finances in an orderly, consistent manner. Many people consider a financial plan to be the most important document for a successful business venture.

Sound financial decisions provide the opportunity for:

- sales to rise,
- expenses to fall,
- profits to increase,
- assets to be acquired,
- liabilities to be paid,
- credit to expand,
- customers to increase, and
- new products to be developed.

ASPECTS OF A FINANCIAL PLAN A financial plan outlines the essential financial elements for starting and running a business. An effective plan addresses three aspects of operating your business. First, it identifies the assets you'll need to purchase in order to begin or continue operating the business. Assets are property or items of value owned by a business. These might include the products to sell or the machines, supplies, office equipment, and transportation necessary for operations.

Second, your financial plan will address the method that you'll use to acquire or purchase these items. How will your business pay for the things it needs? Do you have sufficient cash available? Would borrowing the money from a bank or credit union be a better choice?

The third and most important aspect of the financial plan involves the daily financial operations of the business. This feature addresses the recording, summarizing, reporting, and analyzing of your business's finances.

IDENTIFYING NEEDED ASSETS The first aspect of creating a financial plan is to identify the assets that are necessary to start the business and then to make it grow and increase its profits. Suppose that Mike and Erin want to buy a new computer system. The system should be able to handle their present business operations as well as increased business activity in the future. They should consider features such as processing speed, memory capacity, upgradability, and the software that is included with the new system.

After Mike and Erin have determined the computer components that their business needs, they should analyze the prices of different systems. They will need to purchase the best system for the best price. When their analysis is complete, Mike and Erin will need to decide what computer system to buy. This research process should be a part of buying any major asset.

PRODUCT RESEARCH Good research leads to appropriate purchases for your company. *Can you name at least five items people might purchase that require a considerable amount of product research?*

PURCHASING ASSETS The next step is to determine by what method they will purchase the items. This is the second aspect of a financial plan.

Mike and Erin will need to address some specific questions. Can they purchase the computer system with available cash? Will they borrow money—either through a loan or by using credit—for part or all of the purchase? Will they be able to get loans or credit at reasonable interest rates? Can they take advantage of alternatives to purchasing, such as leasing? Can they get a better deal if they wait?

In answering these questions, Mike and Erin will have to perform a careful analysis of their existing finances. What is the current financial condition of their business? How much cash is available? Will they need cash for future expenses? What are their debts?

They must also investigate all sources of credit. Will the company that is selling them the computer extend credit to them? Should they apply for a short-term loan from a bank? By examining these and other questions, Mike and Erin are practicing effective financial management.

As a high school student, you make similar decisions about your personal finances. If you want to buy an inexpensive item, such as a CD, you'll probably pay cash. You'll give the purchase little financial consideration. However, if it's a more expensive item, such as a stereo or a used car, you must examine your situation more carefully. You should consider some of the following questions: Do you really need it? What is the most you can spend? How much money do you have now? Is there anything else you might need to spend that money on? You may not realize it, but you're performing a financial analysis of your purchase. You're practicing effective financial management.

As a business owner or operator, you might find that some items you want to purchase are beyond your means. You may not have enough cash. Especially when you're starting a business, you'll have to accept the fact that you won't be able to obtain everything that you want immediately. You'll have to work within your financial resources until your business begins to make a profit and you can afford to expand your assets. If you're working with limited resources, you must make decisions based on your need for the items and your ability to pay for them, whether with cash or credit.

RECORDING AND REPORTING BUSINESS FINANCES The third aspect of a financial plan involves the financial operation of a business. How will Mike and Erin keep daily financial records? Will the profit from sales cover their expenses? How will they ensure that cash will be available for unexpected costs? Will they be able to pay their bills on time?

academic Connection

LANGUAGE ARTS

In a student poll taken at the annual Intern Leadership Conference in 1999, 40 percent of today's college students expect to start their own business one day. Imagine yourself as an entrepreneur. Write a scenario describing your business and the type of product(s) or service(s) you'll sell. Include two short-term and two long-term goals. Then write a paragraph outlining your marketing plan and another paragraph describing your financial plan. Share your paper with a classmate. Evaluate each other's paper for grammar and sentence structure.

RESPOND

Explain how opportunity cost would figure into Mike and Erin's decision to purchase (or not purchase) the computer system.

Mike and Erin must know where their business stands financially at all times. The recording and handling of financial information, in an accurate and efficient manner, is essential. It includes using accepted accounting procedures, analyzing financial statements, controlling cash, and paying debts.

Without accurate, up-to-date financial information, sound decision making is impossible. If data isn't recorded in a timely manner or if the information isn't analyzed correctly, inappropriate financial decisions can result. For a new business or a small existing business, this could be disastrous. Thousands of small businesses close each year due to poor financial decisions.

SECTION 16.1 ASSESSMENT

CHECK YOUR UNDERSTANDING

1. Describe the three main parts of a business plan.
2. Why is financial management the most important aspect of a successful business?
3. What are the aspects of a financial plan?

THINK CRITICALLY

4. What might happen to a business that analyzes its finances only twice a year?

USING COMMUNICATION SKILLS

5. **Marketing Your Product** Carol and Blanca have been operating their own jewelry-making business for the past three months. During that time they have sold their creations to friends and relatives. However, they now want to market their products to a larger customer base.
   Design a Flyer Help Carol and Blanca market their jewelry by creating an advertising flyer. The flyer should be informative and persuasive.

SOLVING MONEY PROBLEMS

6. **Financial Plan Development** Santiago and his classmates want to raise money for Habitat for Humanity. Santiago has decided to sell doughnuts and hot chocolate three mornings a week at school to raise this money. His homeroom teacher has suggested that he identify the assets he will need to run his doughnut stand.
   Develop Help Santiago make a list of all the assets he will need to run his doughnut stand. Indicate which assets he may be able to borrow and which ones he will have to purchase.

Financial Management in Business

Aspects of Financial Management

As you learned in the first section, sound financial management is critical to the survival of any business. Financial management includes all aspects of operating your business. It's the glue that holds a business together. At the same time, it's the oil that helps it run smoothly. Many business functions and procedures are based on economic theories and practices. Supply and demand, pricing, market segments, and competition are just a few of the economic principles you need to know about. An understanding of accounting principles and procedures is also important. You should have the financial knowledge and skills to be able to collect, summarize, and analyze financial data.

Accounting: The Backbone of Financial Management

Accounting is a systematic process of recording and reporting the financial position of a business. The financial position depends on the transactions that occur in the daily operation of the business. A *transaction* is any activity that has an effect on the financial situation of a business. Every time you buy supplies, sell merchandise, buy a photocopier, or pay utility bills, your business is making a transaction. Accounting records and reports help a business operate efficiently—and profitably—by keeping track of how much the business earns and spends.

Accounting is often referred to as the "language of business." How can business have its own language? Well, it does! Accounting plays a vital role in the day-to-day activities of every business. The influence of accounting is demonstrated by the fact that much of its terminology has become commonplace. You've probably heard terms such as "assets," "liabilities," "expenses," "revenue," and "inventory." These are all accounting terms. Businesses use this language to communicate with other owners of the business, their creditors, and customers. They do this by issuing financial statements.

What You'll Learn

- How to **recognize** the importance of accounting in financial management
- How to **discuss** the primary functions of accounting

Why It's Important

To ensure effective financial management, knowledge and skills in accounting are essential.

KEY TERMS

- accounting
- transaction
- generally accepted accounting principles (GAAP)
- budget
- merchandise
- inventory
- cash flow
- negative cash flow

Chapter 16 *Introduction to Financial Management for Business* 535

STANDARD &POOR'S

CASE STUDY

Three years ago, Phil Keleman and his twin brother, Chris, started building custom kitchen cabinets for homebuilders in the area. Business is booming for the two brothers, and they are thinking about taking on individual homeowners as clients. Phil figures they will have to add employees, and he has some friends he would like to hire. Chris would prefer that he and Phil work round the clock to get all the work done instead of hiring additional staff. Although they wrote a business plan three years ago when they first began, Phil and Chris really haven't looked at it since. They don't have any idea how to market their business to homeowners. Phil takes care of the financial records, but when Chris took a look at them last week, he was shocked to see a disorganized mess. Phil says that as long as they are making money, it shouldn't bother Chris so much. Phil and Chris are excellent cabinetmakers, but they have very little business training. In need of some help, they turned to the experts at Standard & Poor's for advice.

STANDARD &POOR'S **Analysis:** A business plan needs to be revised each year and should project two to three years ahead. Chris is right to want financial information with which to manage the business. In thinking about hiring additional help, Phil is recognizing the practical limits of what he and Chris can do on their own. Phil and Chris will need to think carefully about the costs and potential sales resulting from expanding their business. Many businesses have been hurt by too rapid growth.

STANDARD &POOR'S **Recommendation:** Phil and Chris need to sort out their bills and receipts and set up a simple accounting system for their business. Then they can see how much money they are earning and have to work with. They also need a new business plan. The partners should talk to their customers and to other business people who know about the demand for new homes and home renovations in their area. Phil and Chris should assess how they will meet the needs of their current clients. They may need to hire and train other people to work for them as their orders grow. With these new employees, however, they may also need additional workspace and equipment. If Phil and Chris market their services to individual homeowners, they should plan to invest money in professional advertising.

Critical Thinking Questions

1. What types of financial information do Phil and Chris need to have?
2. How might their business be affected by a rise in interest rates?
3. Do you think that Phil and Chris should risk borrowing money to grow their business?

In recording and reporting financial changes in a business, owners, bookkeepers, and accountants must use a standard set of guidelines, which are referred to as *generally accepted accounting principles (GAAP)* (pronounced *GAP*). If General Motors, Ford, and Daimler Chrysler all prepared their financial reports in different ways, no one could compare the three corporations financially. Which one is more stable financially? Which had the highest percentage of profit? Which one is growing the fastest?

Using the GAAP guidelines allows investors, banks, suppliers, and government agencies to make comparisons of the financial condition of various companies. They can determine which businesses are financially stable, which ones have the highest percentage of profit, and which ones are growing the fastest.

Every business must have an accurate accounting system, either manual or computerized, to inform owners and managers of the business's financial position. Today computer software programs are used to handle much of the basic accounting work for most businesses. By using this modern technology, the owners and managers can spend more time analyzing their finances and planning for the future, and less time doing monotonous paperwork.

The accounting system has many functions and procedures. Some of the most essential functions of accounting include budgeting, inventory, payroll, cash flow, and investments.

Budgeting

One important function of accounting is budgeting. A *budget* for a business is a formal, written statement of expected income and expenses for a future period of time. For example, Mike and Erin project, or predict, the amount of money they think they'll earn through sales or other income in their landscaping business. They also project their production or operating costs (expenses) for the same period. The difference between these two amounts will be their projected profit or loss for the period. This gives them a financial glimpse into the future of their business. It provides the information they'll need to make decisions.

To be of value, a budget should be compared periodically with actual income and expenses. If you're working with a yearly budget, you should make monthly comparisons of the budgeted amounts to the actual amounts. If the actual amounts are not reasonably close to the budgeted figures, you'll need to make adjustments. If the

PREDICT

Explain why businesses need to make and follow well-planned budgets.

actual amounts are far greater than the projected figures, you'll need to take immediate action to avoid further financial problems. An important aspect of financial management is to recognize a problem and take action.

Accurate, current accounting statements and reports allow you to recognize a problem when it first develops so that you can make financial decisions and take corrective measures. When you do this, you're practicing effective financial management. Remember, if you don't examine and analyze your financial information, you might not recognize that a problem exists until it's too late to save your business.

Inventory

The largest asset of many businesses is the merchandise they have on hand to sell. *Merchandise* is the goods you buy with the intent to resell to customers. The merchandise you have on hand is referred to as your *inventory*. Most of your cash transactions involve the purchase, control, and sale of merchandise. Therefore, it's essential that inventory be carefully maintained and examined. By tracking their inventory, businesses know:

- how much merchandise is sold,
- what merchandise is selling well,
- when to reorder merchandise, and
- which merchandise should not be reordered.

The wrong level, or amount, of inventory can be costly for a business. Too little inventory means that the business may not be able to satisfy its customers' wants. For example, when you go a store to buy new CDs and they have very few on the shelves, you probably won't bother to look around the store. Instead, it's likely that you'll go to another store to make your purchase. Lost sales means lower profits.

If inventory is too high, it means that too much money has been spent on inventory and isn't available for other things. You might not be able to buy the new computer system you need for the business because cash isn't available. Inappropriate inventory levels, either too high or too low, are signs of poor management.

Most stores now use some form of computer program to monitor their inventory. These programs provide daily reports that detail what items have been sold, what is still available, and what has to be reordered.

Payroll

While merchandise is usually the largest asset of a business, payroll is usually the largest expense of a business. Large companies such as AT&T, Coca-Cola, and American Airlines employ thousands of people. Weekly payrolls are in the millions of dollars. Some smaller businesses employ fewer than a hundred people, and some very small businesses might have less than ten. Whether your business is large or small, payroll is usually your greatest expense.

Because payroll involves so much cash, it is regulated by state and federal laws and must be prepared according to generally accepted accounting principles (GAAP). Most businesses use computer programs to process payroll checks, complete payroll reports, and examine payroll information.

Efficient payroll management involves two important activities. First, you must determine whether you have the proper number of employees working at the proper times. Too many employees, or employees working at the wrong times, means that you're paying more in wages and salaries than you should. Your payroll expense must be reduced. If you don't have enough employees or are understaffed at certain times, your business risks losing sales. Both are examples of poor management.

QUESTION

Why is it vital for businesses to keep accurate and up-to-date payroll records?

CONTROLLING INVENTORY Proper levels of inventory are essential for a profitable business operation. *As a business owner, what might you do if you had too many of one model of television in stock?*

The second activity to ensure efficient payroll management is to make sure that generally accepted accounting principles (GAAP) are used in preparing payrolls. Paychecks must be issued on time, and all payroll taxes and voluntary deductions must be paid. All payroll records should also be available for managers and owners to evaluate immediately. Accurate, complete, and readily available payroll information is essential.

You'll learn more about payroll procedures and regulations in Chapter 19.

Cash Flow

Every person needs cash. Every business needs cash. Available cash often determines what a business can or can't do. An adequate amount of available cash allows your business to pay its debts, take advantage of discounts, and fund expansion.

In personal finance, "cash flow" refers to the amount of money that actually goes into and out of a person's wallet or bank accounts. For a business, *cash flow* is the amount of cash that is available at any given time. Money comes in; money goes out. This is cash flow. A goal of effective financial management is to assure a constant flow of cash through the business. This is easy to say, but it's not always easy to do. Economic and financial conditions constantly change. Sometimes sales are high and then suddenly drop off. Sometimes expenses are under control and then suddenly skyrocket. When a business spends more money than it receives, it experiences a condition known as a *negative cash flow*, also called a cash crunch. When your cash flow is negative, your business suffers.

As students you have probably experienced similar cash crunches. For example, suppose that you want to go to the movies on Friday night with your friends, but on Wednesday you bought the wool sweater you wanted. On Friday night you discover that you don't have enough money to go out. For you, this is a short-term disappointment. For a business, however, a shortage of money could mean serious problems. Without a sufficient flow of cash, merchandise can't be replaced, bills can't be paid, and funds for future

CONTROLLING HOURS
Identifying the shifts when employees are most needed helps businesses avoid unnecessary payment of wages. *What times of day would a restaurant have the greatest number of people working?*

growth and expansion can't be invested. Maintaining a positive cash flow is a primary goal of financial management.

Investments

Successful businesses invest for the future. As profits increase, money should be set aside or invested for future business needs. This reserve cash may be needed to purchase new equipment, relocate the business operation, or sell a new line of merchandise. For example, suppose that Mike and Erin's goal is to purchase a building for their landscaping business within the next five years. They should set aside money each year to ensure that sufficient funds will be available to finance the purchase.

Reserve cash may also be needed for emergencies or unexpected costs. If equipment breaks and needs repair, sales take an unexpected

Careers in Finance

ACCOUNTING TEACHER

If you're good with numbers and enjoy helping people, you might make an excellent accounting teacher. High school and college accounting teachers often find great satisfaction as they watch their students master a powerful and practical skill used in all businesses—accounting. They create daily lesson plans to give students experience working with new concepts. They also prepare exams to test the students' knowledge of accounting. Teachers advise their students and meet with parents, administrators, and other teachers to discuss ways to help students do well in class.

Skills	Accounting, communication, computer, math, organizational, time management
Personality	Likes working with people and numbers, patient, sense of humor
Education	Bachelor's degree in education or business education to teach high school; master's degree in accounting, finance, or business to teach community college; experience in the field
Pay range	$20,000 to $60,000 a year for high school; $30,000 to $70,000 a year for community college, depending on experience and location

Analyze List five types of businesses where you could find part-time work while you're going to school. How might those businesses use accounting skills?

For more information on accounting teachers visit finance.glencoe.com **or your local library.**

Your Financial Portfolio

Planning for Success

For several years Tom has been going with his father to yard sales. His father buys old clocks and radios. He fixes them if they need it and sells them at the Millerton Flea Market. Tom has an idea to start his own business and decided to organize his plans.

Oldies but Goodies

Type of business: Selling used CDs, movie videos, and video games

Location: Millertown Flea Market

Target customers: All ages, but mainly ages 10 to 25 for the CDs and movie videos, and ages 10 to 22 for the video games

Potential number of customers: About 300 to 800 people visit the flea market each day, which is open Friday through Sunday.

Competition: No one has been selling these products at the flea market since the Albertsons moved away.

Other competition: The nearest place to buy used CDs is about 10 miles away; all three local video stores sell used movie videos and video games.

Challenges: Getting enough products to sell. Jaimie McKerry buys surplus stock for Franklin's Discounts, and he will sell me used CDs for about $2.50 if I buy at least 100 at a time.

Costs: Purchasing the products, sharing expenses with Dad for renting the table ($50 for the weekend), and gas for when we go look at garage sales.

Potential profit: I used to look at all the CDs and videos when Vinnie Albertson had his table, and he seemed to move a lot of merchandise. I think I can make a profit of $3 a unit and sell 30–50 units a weekend.

Background and special skills: I've been going to garage sales with Dad for several years. There are always old CDs, movie videos, and video games that I can pick up cheap. I like negotiating when I buy and sell, and I like helping Dad at his table. I also know popular titles.

Prepare a Plan Select a merchandising business that you think you would like to own. In your workbook or on a separate sheet of paper, describe the type of business, the product(s) involved, and factors you think would make it successful. Describe why you think you could make this business a success.

drop, or a natural disaster hits your area, you'll need cash. Cash reserves, also called reserve funds, could save your business.

Cash should be carefully invested and closely monitored. Investments by businesses are similar to personal savings. You should save money for unexpected bills or events, such as a broken water heater or a medical bill. You also need to save for a new car, summer vacation, or computer.

Businesses must make a profit and invest part of that profit for future use. Making and monitoring investments is an important aspect of financial management. You'll learn more about these accounting functions and their role in managing your business's finances in the chapters that follow.

SECTION 16.2 ASSESSMENT

CHECK YOUR UNDERSTANDING

1. Define accounting and explain how it plays a role in the daily activities of every business.
2. What are five of the most essential functions of accounting?
3. Why is it important for a business to maintain and examine its inventory carefully?

THINK CRITICALLY

4. What can happen if a business doesn't have enough cash reserves?

USING MATH SKILLS

5. **Accounting Basics** You are the bookkeeper at a toy store. Last month, the following transactions occurred:

Sales:	$62,500
Payroll, rent, utilities:	$16,000
Merchandise Purchased:	$25,000

   Analyze Did the toy store have a positive or negative cash flow?

SOLVING MONEY PROBLEMS

6. **Analyze Accounting Statements** Vince and his sister, Kim, own a pool cleaning service. Kim analyzes the financial statements and reports each month. Recently she has noticed that sales are slipping and that expenses seem to be out of control. They need to take corrective measures as soon as possible.

   Group Investigation In small groups, work together to help Vince and Kim determine what might be happening to their business. Offer suggestions for correcting the situation.

CHAPTER 16 ASSESSMENT

CHAPTER SUMMARY

- When you start a business, you should create a business plan that includes a strategic plan, a marketing plan, and a financial plan.

- A strategic plan incorporates short-term and long-term goals and identifies the necessary steps to achieve those goals.

- A marketing plan describes how you will promote your business and increase sales in order to make a profit.

- A financial plan outlines the essential financial elements for starting and running your business.

- Accounting is a system of recording and reporting the financial position of a business.

- Some important functions of the accounting system include budgeting, inventory, payroll, cash flow, and investments.

Internet zone

Understanding and Using Vocabulary

Think about a small business that you would like to open when you graduare from high school or college. Write an imaginary letter to your local chamber of commerce requesting an opportunity to present your idea. Use at least ten of the key terms listed below in your letter. Exchange your letter with a classmate.

free enterprise
   system
profit
business plan
strategic plan
marketing plan
financial plan
accounting
transaction

generally accepted
   accounting
   principles (GAAP)
budget
merchandise
inventory
cash flow
negative cash flow

Review Key Concepts

1. What is profit, and why is it important to a business?
2. Describe the differences between a marketing plan and a financial plan.
3. How can you determine what method you will use to purchase assets for your business?
4. Why is it important for businesses to follow the generally accepted accounting principles?
5. What two activities help maintain efficient payroll management?

Apply Key Concepts

1. Explain how setting both short-term and long-term goals can help ensure that a business will make a profit.

CHAPTER 16 ASSESSMENT

2. Predict what might occur to a business that does not have a financial plan.
3. Create a scenario in which a new business owner wants to purchase items that are beyond his means. Specify the types of items that he might want to buy as well as what he might do to meet the business's short-term needs.
4. Explain the possible consequences of not keeping accurate accounting records.
5. Think about two businesses that you have visited recently. What would happen if these businesses were either understaffed or overstaffed?

 Problem Solving Today

MOUSING AROUND

You've decided to start a business selling custom-made mouse pads. After doing some research, you spend $900 for a vendor cart in the local mall. You make $7 in profit on each mouse pad and set a goal of selling enough mouse pads to pay for your cart within two months.

Analyze How many mouse pads will you need to sell to achieve your goal? Set a long-term goal for your business. Then suggest ways you might market your product.

Computer Activity As an alternative activity, use financial software to calculate the number of mouse pads you will need to sell to achieve your goal.

Using presentation software, create a plan for marketing your product.

Real-World Application

CONNECT WITH ECONOMICS

Charlotte owns one of several computer repair businesses in town. During the last several months, she has noticed that she has not been attracting many customers, and her sales have been declining. Charlotte has never done any advertising; she has relied only on word of mouth to get additional business.

Think Critically Charlotte wants to investigate the possibility of advertising to improve her business. She knows that she has a limited amount of money. Charlotte has come to you for advice. What should she do?

FLOWERSHOP.COM

You are ready to advertise your flower shop on the Internet.

Connect Using a variety of search engines, locate two other businesses that might compete with your company, and answer these questions:

1. What do they do to make you want to visit their Web site?
2. Is it easy to find the critical information—how to order, how much the flowers cost, and how to pay?
3. How could you make your site more unique and attractive than your competitors' sites?

Sources of Funding

Q&A

Q: My business needs $4,000 in a hurry, and I have no cash in reserves. How should I obtain the money?

A: If you have customers whom you have billed for your products, you can take those invoices to a bank and borrow against those receivables. If you have orders to fill but need money for supplies, you can speak to a lender about a short-term commercial loan.

Analyzing Your Financial Needs

What You'll Learn

- How to **distinguish** among start-up costs, operating costs, and reserve funds
- How to **identify** sources of personal and private financing
- How to **discuss** the options available through bank funding
- How to **explain** the criteria used in approving commercial loans

*A*pple Computer, Wendy's, Starbucks Coffee, Ben & Jerry's, and Microsoft are large corporations. You are probably familiar with their names and the products they sell. They have many employees, provide needed goods and services, and play a part in the American economy. How did these businesses become so successful? How did they get started?

These companies did not begin as major corporations. They all started as small businesses. Through vision, hard work, and sound management, they expanded their operations and became major forces in American business.

In 1978 Ben Cohen and Jerry Greenfield bought an old-fashioned rock salt ice cream machine and rented a renovated gas station in Burlington, Vermont. There they began making Ben & Jerry's Ice Cream. Today Ben & Jerry's is a multimillion-dollar business. In early 2000 Ben & Jerry's was sold for $326 million.

In 1969 Dave Thomas opened his first restaurant, Wendy's Old Fashioned Hamburgers, in Columbus, Ohio. Today Wendy's has more than 5,000 restaurants. Thomas, like the founders of Ben & Jerry's, created a business with a great success story.

Could you accomplish what these people have done? It's very possible. In fact, you may have already ventured into the world of small business without realizing it.

Why It's Important

To start or expand a business, you must review your financial position and accurately estimate the amount of funding you'll need.

KEY TERMS

- entrepreneur
- capital
- start-up costs
- operating costs
- reserve fund
- private financing
- commercial debt financing
- commercial loan
- line of credit
- secured loan
- unsecured loan

The Birth of a Lemonade Stand

Jenny, age 8, and Matt, age 7, are going into business. They're going to set up a lemonade stand—called J & M Lemonade—in front of Matt's house. A lot of people walk down that street, which is close to a school and a park. Jenny and Matt figure that their location will provide plenty of customers. It's a warm, sunny day, and people will be hot and thirsty. Cold lemonade will be in demand, so the market seems right to make money.

Before they begin selling lemonade, however, Jenny and Matt must decide what things they'll need to get their business started. In addition to lemonade, Jenny says that they also need a large pitcher, a stand or table, and some cups. Matt adds a large sign, a box for their money, and some ice cubes to the list. They agree that they also need some coins to make change.

As with all business operations, Jenny and Matt need cash, equipment, supplies, and goods or services to sell. How do you think they'll get these items? They'll probably do what you did when you were their age: They'll go home and see what they can find! Their families will help them find a pitcher, a table, and some cardboard to make a sign. They may give them some coins to use for change and possibly buy the lemonade and cups.

Soon Jenny and Matt have all the items they need, and they set up their stand. J & M Lemonade is now an active player in the free enterprise system.

THE AMERICAN DREAM Anyone can start at least a small business. *What do you think you would need to start your own business?*

Business Entrepreneurs

When you were younger, you may have had a small business similar to Jenny and Matt's lemonade stand. You just wanted to have fun and hopefully make a little money. You, Jenny, and Matt were all entrepreneurs. An *entrepreneur* is an individual who follows his or her dreams by assuming the risk of starting a new business. Entrepreneurs are highly motivated people who transform ideas for products or services into real-world businesses. About 75 percent of the 21 million business operations in the United States are run by one owner. Entrepreneurs are the backbone of the American economy.

Fred DeLuca is one successful entrepreneur. In 1965, after graduating from high school, DeLuca borrowed $1,000 from a friend and opened a sandwich shop in Bridgeport, Connecticut, called Pete's Super Submarines. Today you may know DeLuca's business as Subway. With more than 14,000 restaurants, it is the largest franchise business in the world.

CONNECT

Do you or your friends ever dream of owning your own business? What steps will it take to make those dreams come true?

What's Your Financial ID?

ARE YOU A GO-GETTER?

Finding the money to start a business and keep it going can seem like a huge obstacle. Just for fun, take the following quiz to see if you're a go-getter who can find funding. Write your answers on a separate sheet of paper.

1. I'm willing to defer getting paid in order to see my vision succeed.
   ____ Yes   ____ No

2. I'm willing to ask everyone I know if they want to invest in my enterprise.
   ____ Yes   ____ No

3. I'm investigating every possibility for financing I can think of.
   ____ Yes   ____ No

4. I have spoken to at least one person who's a successful entrepreneur.
   ____ Yes   ____ No

5. I have the perseverance to reach my goals.
   ____ Yes   ____ No

6. My ideas are so clear that I can convince others to help me make them a reality.
   ____ Yes   ____ No

7. I'm flexible and can readily adapt to change.
   ____ Yes   ____ No

Scoring: The more "yes" answers you have, the more likely that you'll find funding.

DeLuca started his business after finishing high school. Would you like to be an entrepreneur? Most high school students would. In a recent Gallup poll, seven out of every ten high school students said that they would like to start a business. However, before you start a business, you'll need money.

Funding a Business

When you decide to start a business, one of your major concerns is how you'll finance it. People who take on new business ventures usually need far more money than they realize they will.

Jenny and Matt started their lemonade stand with nothing. They had no lemonade, supplies, or cash. They funded their business with cash and other assets that their families provided. Hopefully, they'll sell several cups of lemonade and take in some money. Do you think that they'll make a profit? Chances are that the money they'll take in will not cover the cost of the lemonade and other supplies.

Careers in Finance

COMMERCIAL LOAN OFFICER

When businesses and corporations need to borrow money for new equipment or property, they may take out a commercial loan. Commercial loan officers act as the salespeople for the lending institution. Companies will often call a loan officer with whom they have a friendly relationship. The loan officer meets with the customer to explain the different types of loans that are available. After receiving a loan application, the loan officer requests a credit report from a credit bureau in order to check the borrower's ability to repay the loan. After consulting with a manager, the loan officer decides whether or not to grant the loan. Loan officers also look for customers by attending meetings of local community organizations. In addition, they call different businesses to ask if they're planning any projects that may require a loan. Some loan officers earn a salary, while others work on commission and receive a percentage of the value of the loan.

Skills	Communication, computer, decision making, math, problem solving, sales ability
Personality	Desire to help customers, detail oriented, likes working with people
Education	Bachelor's degree in finance, economics, business, or accounting
Pay range	$40,000 to $100,000 plus a year, depending on experience and location

Evaluate Why do you think lending institutions prefer to hire commercial loan officers who have sales experience?

For more information on commercial loan officers visit finance.glencoe.com or your local library.

Family members supported J & M Lemonade financially, but they did not expect to make a profit on their investment. They just wanted to provide an educational and fun experience for Jenny and Matt. If it were not for their financial support, Jenny and Matt would not have been able to start their business because other sources of funds were not available.

As a young adult you would require funding if you decided to start your own business. Unfortunately, it's not easy to get funding for a new business from an outside source. Banks are very selective about who receives a loan. They also expect to get a good return on their investment.

Determining Needed Capital

When you're starting a business, the first thing you must do is make a realistic estimate of how much capital you'll need. *Capital* is the money you'll need to establish a business, operate for the first few months, and expand the business. As you learned in Chapter 16, determining needed capital is one of the steps in developing a financial plan.

FUNDING CONCERNS Even franchises like this one needed money to start their operations. *Where do you think you might be able to obtain money for a new business venture?*

Start-up Costs

The first goal is to identify the costs of setting up your business, which are called *start-up costs*. Start-up costs usually require a large amount of cash. If you attempt to estimate the costs without careful analysis, your estimate will probably be too low.

To analyze your costs you should list everything you will require to begin to operate. Some common start-up costs are:

- the inventory you'll need to open the business;
- equipment, fixtures, and display cases;
- security deposit for rented space;
- advertising and promotions prior to opening;
- insurance;
- professional fees (such as lawyers' fees);
- remodeling costs (such as creating office space);
- legal permits and licenses; and
- supplies.

Your next task is to assign an estimated cost to each item. Unless you list every anticipated cost, your total estimate will not be realistic.

Landscaping firms and convenience stores are different types of businesses, and each one has different requirements for operating. Start-up costs vary among businesses and industries. Make sure that you research and explore the industry you are entering.

Operating Costs

Once you have determined your start-up costs, you must also estimate your operating costs. *Operating costs* are the ongoing expenses you expect to have for the first 90 to 120 days of operating a business.

Start-up costs and operating costs are separate cost categories. It is critical that you estimate both types of costs as accurately as possible. If you use all of your money for start-up, then you won't have any money available to pay your operating costs. When you start a new business, the amount you earn from sales usually will not be enough to cover your expenses. If you cannot pay your suppliers, rent, or utility bills, your business will be in serious trouble.

When you prepare your budget for the first 90 to 120 days, you'll include your expected income from sales as well as your estimated monthly costs. Following is a list of common operating costs:

- Payroll
- Rent
- Insurance premiums
- Utility bills
- Office expenses
- Advertising
- Delivery charges
- Bank charges and other fees

STANDARD & POOR'S

CASE STUDY

For ten years, Gina Billaris and her husband, Nicholas, have been running a catering business from their home. They specialize in Greek food, from moussaka to baklava and everything in between. Now they are ready to open a restaurant where they will serve lunch and dinner. They plan to continue the catering side of their business as well. When Gina and Nicholas began catering, they used their own personal savings to fund the business. At first, all their profits were invested back into the business to help it grow. During the last two years, Gina and Nicholas have been able to save $25,000. Gina has been researching the competition. She has also been looking for good restaurant sites, pricing equipment, and projecting possible expenses. Based on her best guess, Gina and Nicholas will need an additional $65,000 to open their restaurant. They need help identifying sources of funding, so they turned to the experts at Standard & Poor's for advice.

STANDARD &POOR'S **Analysis:** Gina and Nicholas have built a successful catering business that is showing a profit. Now they are thinking about expanding into another type of business. Restaurants are considered a high-risk business because it is difficult to predict the number of customers and to manage costs. Gina and Nicholas may find it easier to borrow to expand their catering business than to launch a restaurant.

STANDARD &POOR'S **Recommendation:** Gina and Nicholas can point to their past success in building their catering business. This may give them an advantage when talking to lenders. Business loans that are supported by assets such as equipment or property are good sources of funding. Gina and Nicholas can use this type of financing to buy the equipment they will need. Businesses also borrow "working capital," or money with which to buy supplies and inventory needed to fill orders. Until their restaurant shows signs of success, Gina and Nicholas may have difficulty obtaining this kind of financing. A smart strategy for the couple may be to focus first on growing their catering business by leasing a kitchen and equipment, with space for a small restaurant that they can later expand. They will likely have little trouble obtaining a loan with this approach. Gina and Nicholas should look into Small Business Administration loan programs.

Critical Thinking Questions

1. How is a restaurant different from a catering business?
2. What do you think lenders look for in making a loan to a start-up business?
3. If Gina and Nicholas cannot borrow the money they need to start a restaurant, what should they do?

Reserve Fund

Before starting a business, you will also have to estimate the amount of money you may need at a later date for growth. A *reserve fund* is money that can be made available for future expansion of your business. If your business operates according to your financial projections for the first few months, you may need additional money to purchase merchandise or equipment, or perhaps to lease a truck. This money will allow for growth and help you avoid having to borrow additional capital.

Jenny and Matt's lemonade stand lasted only about two hours. They did not plan to operate an ongoing business. You, of course, hope that your business will have a much longer life. Therefore, careful financial planning for the future is critical. Some points that you should consider when looking ahead and estimating your reserve fund are:

- getting and keeping the right amount of inventory,
- additional equipment you'll need for increased business,
- advertising and other promotional costs,
- capital for any unexpected costs or decreased sales,
- the need to maintain a positive cash flow, and
- expansion of facilities.

LOCATION, LOCATION In addition to having a great idea for a business, you must also find somewhere to operate it. *What features would you look for in choosing a location for a local business?*

Once you have estimated the amounts of your start-up and operating costs and reserve fund, you'll have a good idea of your financial needs. You'll see what your cash flow will look like during the first months of operation. You can then estimate the total amount of capital you'll need to establish your business and begin to operate.

After you've determined the amount of money you require, you have to figure out how you'll get it. Businesses have many sources of funding available.

Personal Financing and Private Financing

Getting affordable and sufficient financing is often a major problem when starting or expanding a business. Initially, you'll probably explore the possibility of personal financing.

Personal Financing

Many people who want to begin small businesses must use funds from their own personal assets. It is estimated that about 75 percent of new business ventures are funded this way.

The primary reason for using this method is that new, small businesses often have a hard time getting affordable funding. Banks and other financial institutions are not interested in risky or unproven business ventures. You can't just walk into a bank and tell them that you have a great idea and expect the loan officer to hand you money.

Banks are far more interested in funding existing businesses that have reported profit over a period of time. These businesses are safer investments and provide banks and other financial institutions with assurance of a good return on their money.

When starting a small business, you may have to rely on your own assets to finance the start-up and operating costs. You might use your personal savings or investments such as stocks or bonds. However, you might find that you don't have enough cash to get the business going.

CONSUMER LOANS In order to get the funds you need, you might consider applying for a consumer, or personal, loan. Most financial institutions require that consumer loans be secured with collateral. Collateral is a form of security (usually an asset such as your car or home) that helps guarantee that a creditor will be repaid.

PREDICT

What are the advantages and disadvantages of financing a business with a home equity loan?

When you pledge collateral for a loan, the risk to the bank is reduced. As a result you have a much better chance of getting funding and often receive better interest rates. If you cannot pay back the loan, the financial institution can take the property that you have pledged as collateral.

HOME EQUITY LOANS A home equity loan is a loan based on the difference between the current market value of your home and the amount you still owe on the mortgage. A home equity loan may also be called a second mortgage. Home equity loans are fairly safe for financial institutions because they are secured by property. As a result these loans are usually easier to get than consumer loans.

INTERNATIONAL FINANCE   Japan

_I_n Japan "fast track" means just that—one of the best transportation systems in the world. Recently Japan outdid its record-breaking bullet trains, which travel at almost 180 miles per hour. For a population that commutes long distances by rail, the future looks even faster. Although not quite ready for the public, the newest high-speed locomotion is called a maglev, short for "magnetic levitation." It works like this: Magnets have north and south poles. Opposite poles attract; like poles repel. The train's underside and the top of the tracks act as like poles. They repel each other, keeping the train four inches above the tracks. The magnetic effect pulls the wheelless train along, reaching a breathtaking speed of 343 miles per hour. Here's a snapshot of Japan.

Geographic area	145,875 sq. mi.
Population	126,745,000
Capital	Tokyo (pop. 11,573,000)
Language	Japanese
Currency	yen
Gross domestic product (GDP)	$3.08 trillion
Per capita GDP	$24,500
Economy	Industry: steel, nonferrous metallurgy, electrical equipment. Agriculture: rice, sugar beets, pork, fish. Exports: manufactured goods (machinery, motor vehicles, consumer electronics).

Train passing snowcapped Mount Fuji, Japan

Thinking Critically

Calculate The distance between Tokyo and Osaka is 250 miles. Approximately how long would it take a commuter who lives in Tokyo to get to work in Osaka riding nonstop on the maglev?

 For more information on Japan visit finance.glencoe.com or your local library.

To determine the amount of this type of loan, the financial institution will find out the current market value of your home and how much equity you have in the property. Your equity is the value of your home less the current balance on your mortgage. A bank will want you to maintain about 20 percent equity.

Suppose your house has a present market value of $175,000, and you have a mortgage with a balance of $65,000. Your equity in the house is $110,000 ($175,000 − $65,000 = $110,000).

Banks will usually allow you to borrow no more than 80 percent of the current market value of your home. In this example the maximum amount the bank would allow you to borrow on a home worth $175,000 would be $140,000 ($175,000 × 80% = $140,000). However, you already have an existing mortgage with a current balance of $65,000. Therefore, to figure out the amount that the bank would lend to you, you would have to subtract the mortgage balance from $140,000. In this example, your loan cannot exceed $75,000 ($140,000 − $65,000 = $75,000).

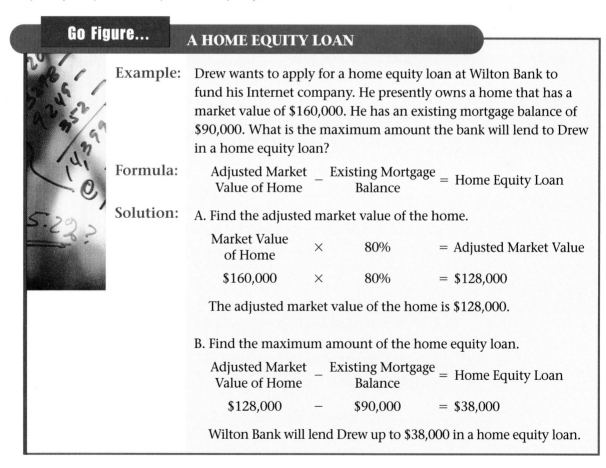

Go Figure...   **A HOME EQUITY LOAN**

Example: Drew wants to apply for a home equity loan at Wilton Bank to fund his Internet company. He presently owns a home that has a market value of $160,000. He has an existing mortgage balance of $90,000. What is the maximum amount the bank will lend to Drew in a home equity loan?

Formula: $$\text{Adjusted Market Value of Home} - \text{Existing Mortgage Balance} = \text{Home Equity Loan}$$

Solution: A. Find the adjusted market value of the home.

Market Value of Home	×	80%	= Adjusted Market Value
$160,000	×	80%	= $128,000

The adjusted market value of the home is $128,000.

B. Find the maximum amount of the home equity loan.

$$\text{Adjusted Market Value of Home} - \text{Existing Mortgage Balance} = \text{Home Equity Loan}$$

$128,000	−	$90,000	= $38,000

Wilton Bank will lend Drew up to $38,000 in a home equity loan.

This type of loan is available only if you have a substantial amount of equity in your property. In other words, your home must be worth a lot more than the amount you presently owe on your mortgage.

The negative aspect of a home equity loan is that if your business fails, you could lose your home. This is a tremendous personal financial risk. A recent study showed that more than one-half of new businesses fail during the first five years. Considering this high failure rate, you should think seriously about your level of risk before you finance your business with a home equity loan.

Private Financing

If you can't get enough capital through personal financing, you must look to other sources. The next option might be private financing. *Private financing* is borrowing money from your family or friends. This type of funding is attractive because it is done privately. It involves little paperwork and often requires no collateral and low, or no, interest payments. The disadvantage of this type of funding is that it can lead to personal conflicts if the business is unsuccessful. If you are unable to pay back your friends and family, they may not be very happy.

HOME SWEET HOME A home equity loan can be an easy source of financing for an entrepreneur. *What potential risk is involved in using a home equity loan to finance a business?*

Bank Funding

If personal and private financing are insufficient, you may have to apply for a business loan to get additional money. One of your first sources for such financing is your local bank.

When you borrow money from a bank or other financial institution to fund a business, it's called *commercial debt financing*. The loan that you take out to finance a new or ongoing business is called a *commercial loan*.

Larger banks give out commercial loans, but they are often interested in larger, more established business operations with revenues in the millions of dollars. When small businesses need money, local banks are a logical source. A small bank can better relate to a small business. It understands your needs, offers advice, and assists you with other services.

You should note that getting funding from local banks has both advantages and disadvantages. Advantages might include:

- They are highly experienced in dealing with small businesses.
- They offer a wide variety of loan plans.
- They offer advice and other business services.

- They are community-oriented and are interested in seeing local businesses succeed.

Disadvantages might include:

- They are closely regulated by the government. As a result, they require extensive paperwork, investigation, and documentation.
- They are conservative by nature and may reject your loan if your business appears too risky.

If you and your local bank are interested in establishing a working relationship, you should know what loan options are available to you. All banks offer a wide variety of loans, and a good banker will recommend the loan that is best for you and your business.

Short-Term Commercial Loans

A short-term commercial loan is a business loan that is usually made for a term of one year or less. Most are written for 30-, 60-, or 90-day periods. These loans are typical for small businesses. They're designed to help the business meet short-term financial obligations. You could use the money for purchasing merchandise before a peak sales period, acquiring equipment, or paying unexpected bills.

For example, during the summer months Durango's Ski Shop begins to prepare its inventory for the upcoming winter season. The owner, Sabrina, decides that she needs a large quantity of new skis. Because the ski shop's sales are typically low in the summer, she has to apply for temporary financing. With a short-term commercial loan Sabrina can purchase the inventory she needs now and repay the loan with the profits from winter ski sales.

BANK ON IT A local bank may be just the source of funding your business needs. *Why might a small, local bank be better prepared to help a new business than a larger bank?*

Long-Term Commercial Loans

A long-term commercial loan is a business loan that is made for a term of one to five years. These loans are normally used by larger, established businesses that require great amounts of funding. Because these are large loans, the businesses will need more time to pay them back. They may use the funds for expensive equipment, relocation of facilities, expansion of storage areas, or other major expenses.

New or smaller businesses might have trouble getting these loans. Banks consider such businesses to be less stable; therefore, they don't want to take the risk that the loan won't be repaid.

Lines Of Credit

A *line of credit* is an arrangement in which bank customers can borrow a certain amount of money from the bank immediately. Funds are available for unexpected costs or routine expenses. A store owner can borrow all or part of that money at any time and for any purpose. If the plumbing breaks and costs $8,000 to repair, money is available. The store can also use the money to purchase merchandise at a discounted price.

The main advantage of this type of funding is that you don't pay any interest unless you access the funds. Of course, the bank charges interest on any amount you borrow.

The bank will review your available credit every so often. Based on your history of accessing the account and on your repayment pattern, the bank may increase or decrease the amount of credit. This type of funding is intended for short-term costs that your business may not be able to handle. For this reason, the bank also expects you to repay the money in a short period of time.

Secured and Unsecured Loans

Secured loans are loans that are backed by collateral. Most short-term and long-term loans must be backed by collateral. Banks will hold the title to the equipment, facility, or merchandise until the loan is repaid. Because banks must be conservative in their loan policies, most business loans are secured. Only well-established, profitable businesses that have a good relationship with a bank can obtain unsecured loans. An *unsecured loan* is a loan that does not require collateral from the borrower. If an unsecured loan is approved, it is usually short term. Because of the increased risk to the creditor, the interest rate on an unsecured loan is usually higher than on a secured loan.

Commercial Loan Applications

New and expanding small businesses often have difficulty getting necessary funding. Banks use certain standards to judge a company's financial position and determine how much risk to accept. Banks are conservative and often very selective as to which businesses they approve for financing.

You've already learned about the criteria banks and credit card companies use to determine your creditworthiness. When you fill out an application for credit, you must answer questions regarding your credit history, your annual income, and your valuable assets. These institutions want a complete financial picture of you.

FULL INVENTORY A business that depends on seasonal sales will prepare its inventory in advance of the busy season. *What type of loan might such a business require?*

In evaluating commercial loan applications, banks will examine these same factors as well as other information. They want a financial picture of both you and your business.

The Five Cs of Credit

If you apply for a commercial loan, the bank will first examine the five Cs of credit.

CHARACTER Banks want to make sure that you're capable of paying off the loan on time. They'll consider your business experience and your dealings with other local businesses. Your prior history with the bank, your reputation in the local business community, and comments from your creditors will also be important. In addition, proof of your skills as a manager will be essential.

CAPACITY The bank will determine whether your business has or will have enough cash to repay the loan on time. It will also examine your sales history, statements of cash flow, and profits reported by your business.

CAPITAL The bank looks to see whether you've invested a considerable amount of your personal assets in the business. Financial institutions often require that you use your personal assets for at least 30 percent of the needed capital to start your business.

COLLATERAL The bank makes sure that you have enough business assets to secure the loan. Does your business own office equipment, machinery, delivery equipment, or real estate? Good collateral is also an important element for approval.

THE FIVE Cs A loan officer will look carefully at the information you provide before deciding whether the bank will grant you a commercial loan. *What criteria does a bank use to evaluate this?*

CREDIT HISTORY The bank will review both your credit history and that of your business. It will consider your payment history for consumer loans and commercial loans.

Business Plan

The bank will also examine your business plan to make sure that your business is financially sound. It looks to see whether you have a clear vision of where you want your business to go and whether you have identified the necessary steps to achieve your goals. This way the bank can better measure your financial need.

SECTION 17.1 **ASSESSMENT**

CHECK YOUR UNDERSTANDING

1. What is the difference between start-up costs and operating costs?
2. Describe several sources of personal financing.
3. Identify two ways in which a small business might use a line of credit.
4. What criteria do banks use to determine whether to grant a commercial loan?

THINK CRITICALLY

5. Which of the following do you think would be the best source of funding for a new business owner: a consumer loan, a home equity loan, or private financing? Explain your reasoning.

USING MATH SKILLS

6. **Cost of Borrowing** Mario has estimated start-up costs for a cappuccino stand to be $8,900. He projects that his operating costs for the first six months will be $6,300. He also wants to have $10,000 in his reserve fund. Mario has saved $20,000 to put toward the new business. **Calculate** How much money will he need to borrow? What percentage of his total costs will he borrow?

SOLVING MONEY PROBLEMS

7. **Sources of Funding** Christa has operated a résumé writing service out of her home for the past two years. Because she has added many new customers, her equipment and supplies will no longer fit in her extra bedroom. Christa is looking for a new location for the business, but she realizes that the change will bring additional costs.
Identify sources of funding that she may be able to access. Which sources of funding do you think she should avoid? Which sources do you think would be best?

Additional Sources of Funding

No matter how good your business may look on paper, banks are often not willing to extend the necessary financing. This is especially true for newer or start-up businesses. Many of these do not have enough collateral, experienced management, profit from operations, or a sound credit history. In order to get your loan, you will need some help. To whom do you turn? Your best alternative may be the federal government.

Small Business Administration

The federal government recognizes the importance of small businesses in the American economy and therefore provides assistance to them. The ***Small Business Administration (SBA)*** is an independent agency of the federal government that offers assistance to people who are starting small businesses and to those who want to expand existing businesses. Its services include management training, organizational guidance, and most important, assistance in getting funding.

It is estimated that almost 99 percent of American business operations are considered "small businesses" under the SBA guidelines. Thousands of businesses take advantage of services offered by the SBA every year. If the Small Business Administration did not exist, many small businesses would never get the money they need.

The SBA offers many loan programs to small businesses that have a hard time getting the funding they need through other methods. If you can't convince the bank that you're a good loan candidate and that your business will be successful, you might try one of the SBA loan programs.

SBA Guaranteed Loans

The most common type of SBA loan is obtained through the Guaranteed Loan Program. To get an SBA guaranteed loan for your small business, you apply to a bank or other financial institution for a commercial loan. If the bank denies your request, you can then

What You'll Learn
- How to **describe** the function of the Small Business Administration
- How to **identify** alternative sources of funding for a business

Why It's Important
Entrepreneurs can get funding through the help of the Small Business Administration and other sources.

KEY TERMS
- **Small Business Administration (SBA)**
- **LowDoc Program**
- **business credit card**
- **private investor**
- **commercial finance company**
- **venture capital firm**
- **Small Business Investment Companies (SBICs)**

FEDERAL ASSISTANCE The federal government provides help for entrepreneurs through the Small Business Administration (SBA). *How does the SBA's Guaranteed Loan Program work?*

complete an application for an SBA loan. Your bank submits your application to the SBA under the Guaranteed Loan Program.

The SBA examines your application. If it approves the loan, it authorizes the bank to give you the funding. The SBA then guarantees a major portion of the loan. At present the SBA will guarantee 80 percent of a bank loan for $100,000 or less and 75 percent of a loan for more than $100,000. The repayment period usually cannot exceed seven years.

With this guarantee by the federal government, banks are more willing to grant funding to a small business. The bank knows that if you default on the loan, the SBA will repay the majority of the money you owe. Remember, you don't borrow money from the SBA. You get your loan from a bank or some other financial institution, but the SBA guarantees a large portion of the loan.

In the past, many people trying to start small businesses were frustrated by the amount of paperwork and time it took to process an application through the SBA. In 1993 the SBA introduced the LowDoc (Low Documentation) Program. The *LowDoc Program* is a program that allows businesses applying for loans of less than $150,000 to submit a one-page application with a small amount of documentation. They receive a reply within 36 hours. This program also features electronic loan processing. The average LowDoc loan is about $58,000.

The SBA also offers a variety of other loans for specific groups or business endeavors. It has special guaranteed loan programs for international trade, pollution control, exporters, and businesses entering markets in economically depressed areas. Today the SBA is still the primary source of assistance in getting small business funding. Every year banks and other financial institutions loan billions of dollars to small business operations with SBA guarantees.

RESPOND

Why do you think the government is interested in supporting small businesses through the Small Business Administration?

Other Sources of Funding for Existing Businesses

Some business owners use personal resources or funds from family members or friends to expand their businesses. Many others use short-term commercial loans, which are often guaranteed by the SBA. However, you can also get funding through a business credit card, private investors, commercial finance companies, venture capital firms, and state and local governments.

Business Credit Card

In recent years financial institutions have developed alternative funding options to try to meet the needs of a wide variety of businesses. One of these options is to offer a line of credit through a business credit card. A *business credit card* is a credit card that is issued to a business rather than to an individual. The use of business credit cards has become the second most common form of short-term financing for small businesses. (Commercial loans from financial institutions are still the primary source.)

UNEXPECTED COSTS Having to purchase a new cash register or other business supplies unexpectedly can be a financial problem for business owners. *What kind of funding can be used to prepare for these types of emergencies?*

Business credit cards require the business to have a good credit history. They are suitable for businesses that want to expand or cover unexpected costs, but they are generally not issued for start-up financing.

A credit limit on a business credit card is usually under $15,000. The disadvantage of this quick source of funding is high interest rates, similar to those on personal credit cards. Business credit cards are good for emergencies but should be paid back as quickly as possible.

Visa, MasterCard, and American Express all offer small business credit cards. These cards often provide discounts on travel, car rentals, and insurance. Credit card issuers also provide advice and assistance through small business publications.

Private Investors

A *private investor* is a person outside an entrepreneur's circle of friends and relatives who provides funding because he or she is interested in helping your business to succeed. Typically called "angels," private investors will usually leave the management of the business to the owner.

Private investors are often financially successful people in your local community. They invest in your business because they believe that your business is good for the neighborhood or town. However, they're also interested in getting a good return on their money. Some private investors may require some equity in your business. This means that you may have to give them a share of ownership.

QUESTION

Why might it be preferable to finance your business with a bank loan rather than through a venture capital firm?

If you cannot locate private investors in your area, you can turn to the SBA. The SBA has set up a Web site called the Angel Capital Electronic Network (ACE-NET), which lists small businesses that are looking for investors. The SBA screens both entrepreneurs and investors to assure reliability. Once investors are approved, they can access thousands of businesses. You and the investor then negotiate your own deal.

Commercial Finance Companies

A *commercial finance company* is a firm that loans money only to businesses. Commercial finance companies insist that all loans be secured with collateral. Small businesses often pledge equipment or inventory. These companies are often helpful to existing businesses that need short-term financing.

A commercial finance company can assume more risk in granting loans because the government does not regulate these companies as closely as banks. However, because the finance company is granting you a riskier loan, they'll charge you higher interest rates. It is easier to get this kind of loan, but you'll pay more for it.

Venture Capital Firms

A *venture capital firm* is a company that provides private funding for small businesses that need a substantial amount of immediate cash. Because these businesses are high-risk, they cannot get adequate funding from primary lenders such as banks and commercial finance companies. Venture capital firms are willing to take the risk, but in turn they demand a large return on their investments. They often expect a 20 to 40 percent return each year.

Venture capital firms usually seek to make investments of at least $250,000. Small businesses with solid management and a unique product or service are good prospects. The venture capital firm is not merely loaning you some money; it is investing in your business. Therefore, venture capital firms expect to have a voice in major decisions and will examine your financial position carefully throughout the year.

Most venture capital firms are private. However, the SBA has created a public venture capital program called the Small Business Investment Companies Program. *Small Business Investment Companies (SBICs)* are private investment firms that work with the SBA to provide longer-term funding for small businesses. The advantage in dealing with the SBIC program is that the SBA regulates lenders, and financing terms must meet SBA guidelines. If small businesses need venture capital, they usually go to SBIC firms first.

State and Local Funding

Many states provide opportunities for small businesses to get funding through a variety of programs. These funding programs are often available in cities where local and state governments are encouraging individuals to open businesses in economically depressed neighborhoods. Local chambers of commerce or regional offices of the SBA can assist you.

Funding Your Dreams

The American economy has been built by entrepreneurs who were willing to take risks and explore new ventures. Ray Kroc was 52 years old when he purchased the rights to a hamburger stand owned by the McDonald brothers in San Bernardino, California. His venture

WHO WOULD HAVE THOUGHT! Business ideas do not always appear to be potential successes. Venture capital firms take great risks. *Can you name some recent new products that have been successful?*

Tanya's Toys

Tanya's mother brings home rejects and remnants of toweling from the mill where she works. Tanya's grandmother taught her how to sew the cloth into animal shapes and stuff them. They give these little stuffed animals as presents, and Tanya has also sold 25 of them at $8 each to raise money for the high school football team. Tanya and her friend, Lisa, decided to start a business making and selling "Tanya's Toys." Tanya has listed the expenses of making 100 stuffed animals and the sources of funding.

Item	Cost	Source of Funding
Toweling	$25	She spoke directly to the manager at the mill, who offered a special deal of $25 payable after the animals were sold.
Sewing machines	$430	Tanya was already using the sewing machine she had at home and located another used industrial machine. She and Lisa decided they would buy the second machine after they sold 500 toys.
Other sewing equipment: Sewing shears, tape measure, patterns	$45	Tanya's grandmother offered to loan them the money to buy good sewing shears.
Supplies: Thread, eyes, buttons, ribbon, and felt to decorate the animals	$25	Tanya and Lisa decided to fund the purchase of supplies from their savings.
Wages		Tanya and Lisa chose to reinvest the profits until they bought all the equipment and supplies.

Research What kind of business could you launch that would require minimal start-up costs? In your workbook or on a separate sheet of paper using the guidelines shown above, describe and name your business and list what equipment and supplies you would need. Also indicate how you would fund your enterprise. How much would your equipment and supplies cost? How could you persuade members of your family or friends to participate in your business?

would revolutionize the food industry. Robert Pittman was only 26 years old when he combined video and music and created MTV.

Entrepreneurs often fail, but many try again. In 1923 a young man went bankrupt with the Laugh-O-Gram Corporation, which delivered funny telegrams. That young entrepreneur, Walt Disney, did not give up. He went on to greater accomplishments.

Funding of small businesses is essential to the American economy. Almost all of the Fortune 500 companies started as small businesses. They began with little capital and obtained additional funds by using creativity. Today you can get funds through a variety of sources. Through private and public funding, you can pursue your dreams and own your own business.

SECTION 17.2 ASSESSMENT

CHECK YOUR UNDERSTANDING

1. What is the primary function of the Small Business Administration?
2. What are some alternative sources of funding for business owners?
3. How might you find venture capital for your business?

THINK CRITICALLY

4. For what types of expenses do you think a business should use a business credit card? For what expenses should a business not use a credit card? Explain.

USING COMMUNICATION SKILLS

5. **Loan Questions** Your friend Ashley is having trouble getting a loan to finance the start-up costs of her collectibles shop. Her local bank turned her down because the idea seems too risky. **Propose an Alternative** Tell Ashley about alternative means of getting approval for a commercial loan. Explain how the federal government might be able to help her.

SOLVING MONEY PROBLEMS

6. **Financing Options** Kimo owns a print shop. He offers a variety of services, including printing brochures and letterhead. He has been in business five years and is doing very well. Now Kimo wants to expand his business by offering multimedia services. To do this he needs about $50,000 to $60,000. Kimo has decided to investigate a bank loan guaranteed by the SBA, private investors, and venture capital firms as sources of money for his expansion. **Debate** In a small group, help Kimo decide which source to explore further. Justify your decision.

CHAPTER 17 ASSESSMENT

CHAPTER SUMMARY

- When starting a business, you must consider start-up costs, operating costs, and a reserve fund to determine the amount of money you need.

- Using personal assets and obtaining money from family members or friends are two common ways of financing a business.

- Banks may offer businesses funding through a commercial loan or a line of credit.

- Before a bank will grant a commercial loan, it will examine the company's five Cs of credit and its business plan.

- The Small Business Administration (SBA) offers management, organizational, and financial assistance to small businesses.

- Alternative sources of business funding include business credit cards, private investors, commercial finance companies, venture capital firms, and state and local governments.

Understanding and Using Vocabulary

Using ten of the following key terms, create a series of questions and answers for someone who is preparing to start a small business. Then, exchange your questions with a partner and answer each other's questions.

entrepreneur
capital
start-up costs
operating costs
reserve fund
private financing
commercial debt
   financing
commercial loan
line of credit

Small Business
   Investment
   Companies (SBICs)
secured loan
unsecured loan
Small Business
   Administration (SBA)
LowDoc Program
business credit card
private investor

commercial finance
   company

venture capital firm

Review Key Concepts

1. What must you do to determine how much capital you will need to start a business?
2. What are several disadvantages of using personal financing and private financing?
3. Why are local banks a logical source of funding for small businesses?
4. What types of services does the Small Business Administration offer?
5. How are private investors different from venture capital firms?

Apply Key Concepts

1. Select a business in your community. List the start-up and operating costs that you

CHAPTER 17 ASSESSMENT

think the business might have had. Then describe situations in which this business might have to use its reserve fund.

2. Write a letter to your favorite relative explaining your idea for a new business and requesting financial aid.

3. Explain the disadvantages of seeking funding for a start-up business from a local bank.

4. Why do you think the SBA loan programs were created?

5. Judge the effects of a venture capital firm's investing $1 million in a new Internet company. What might they expect in return?

 ## Problem Solving Today

CALCULATING BUSINESS COSTS

Although you are still in high school, you are ready to launch a business. After you made and gave custom gift baskets to several members of your family and to friends, people began asking you to make special baskets as gifts for them to give to loved ones. Your next logical step is to begin selling gift baskets for profit.

Create a Plan Draw up a plan that includes any possible start-up and operating costs for a gift basket business. Be sure to include money for a reserve fund.

Computer Activity As an alternative activity, use financial software to calculate the total costs for your new business.

Real-World Application

CONNECT WITH MATHEMATICS

Reed runs a vintage vinyl record store in a small town. He wants to install three listening booths so that his customers can listen to an album before they purchase it. However, the cost of the equipment and the installation—a total of about $10,000—is much more than Reed has in his reserve fund.

Calculate Reed has decided to take out a loan. Which of the following choices would be the least costly alternative? The choices are: (1) a short-term commercial loan with a 10 percent annual interest rate for 90 days; (2) a long-term commercial loan with a 7 percent annual interest rate for two years; or (3) a line of credit with an annual interest rate of 9.5 percent for six months. (Assume simple interest rates.)

EXPANSION IDEAS

Your best friend owns a bakery. After he closes the shop each day, he allows you to use the kitchen to make pizza, which you sell. Your pizza business is booming, and you are ready to expand. You need to find funding sources for the expansion.

Connect Using a variety of search engines, locate information on the Internet about funding a small business expansion. Then answer the following questions:

1. What sources of funding are available online?

2. How might you go about finding the best interest rates for commercial loans online?

Financial Accounting

STANDARD &POOR'S

Q&A

Q: Why do I need to understand the accounting cycle? When I start my business, I am going to hire an accountant to keep my records.

A: Accounting is said to be the language of business. It is always a good idea to enlist the services of a professional to help you maintain financial records. However, you will still need to understand what information is represented in your financial statements and its relevance to the many different decisions you will need to make as you manage your business. Many otherwise successful businesses have ended in failure because their founders paid too little attention to financial issues.

The First Five Steps of the Accounting Cycle

ave you ever wondered how a rap group or a rock band determines what cities their tours will play? What determines the price of tickets, and how much does a national tour cost? These questions are all examined by professional teams made up of accountants and financial advisers.

Accounting plays a vital role in the day-to-day activities of your business—and of every business. Accounting records and reports help your business operate efficiently—and profitably—by keeping track of how much is earned and how much is spent. Accounting is so much a part of the business world that it's often called "the language of business."

The Accounting System

Whether you're keeping financial records for a rock band, a neighborhood bike shop, or a major corporation, accounting principles and procedures are universal. All businesses use the same system, which follows established accounting guidelines called "generally accepted accounting principles," or GAAP. With all businesses using the same system, anyone who is interested in examining the records of a business will be able to understand its financial reports.

The accounting system is designed to collect, record, and report on financial transactions that affect your business. *Financial reports* summarize the results of financial transactions affecting a business and report its current financial position. They indicate how well your business is doing. Many groups or individuals may be interested in your business's finances. These may include:

- potential buyers;
- government agencies;
- banks or other financial institutions; and
- employees and consumers.

What You'll Learn

- How to **analyze** business transactions
- How to **identify** the first five steps of the accounting cycle
- How to **describe** the role of the general journal
- How to **explain** the purpose of posting
- How to **recognize** the purpose of a trial balance

Why It's Important

All businesses must record and summarize their financial transactions in the same way.

KEY TERMS

- **financial reports**
- **accounting period**
- **accounting cycle**
- **owner's equity**
- **accounting equation**
- **account**
- **accounts receivable**
- **accounts payable**
- **double-entry accounting**
- **T accounts**
- **debit/credit**
- **journal/journalizing**
- **general ledger**
- **posting**
- **trial balance**

Accounting Assumptions

When you're creating the accounting books for your business, you will make two assumptions about your business. The first is that your business will operate as a separate unit, or business entity. This means that the records and reports of your business will be kept completely separate from your personal finances. You never mix your business finances with your personal finances.

What's Your Financial ID?

DO YOU THINK LOGICALLY OR INTUITIVELY?

Which type of thinker are you—logical or intuitive? Logical thinking tends to be analytic, orderly, and consistent, sometimes based on rules or something exact. Intuitive thinking is based on insight and tends to be more approximate, symbolic, and capable of dealing with contradiction. You may have a tendency toward logical or intuitive thinking. In this quiz there aren't any right or wrong answers. Choose ten of the words below that best describe your thought processes, then write them on a separate sheet of paper.

____ abstract	____ dreamy	____ playful
____ ambiguous	____ exact	____ poetic
____ analogous	____ fantastical	____ practical
____ analytic	____ focused	____ precise
____ approximate	____ generalized	____ rational
____ conceptual	____ imaginative	____ reflective
____ constructive	____ impractical	____ specific
____ critical	____ inferred	____ speculative
____ deductive	____ literal	____ symbolic
____ detailed	____ logical	____ visionary

Scoring: Give yourself 5 points if you wrote down analytic, conceptual, constructive, critical, deductive, detailed, exact, focused, literal, logical, practical, precise, rational, reflective, or specific.

Give yourself 3 points if you wrote down abstract, ambiguous, analogous, approximate, dreamy, fantastical, generalized, imaginative, impractical, inferred, playful, poetic, speculative, symbolic, or visionary.

If you scored 30–38 points, you prefer intuitive thinking.

If you scored 42–50 points, you prefer logical thinking.

Regardless of your tendencies, try alternate types of thinking. Whenever you feel you're not communicating well, consider that the other person might be applying a different way of thinking.

The second assumption is that your business makes its financial reports in specific blocks of time. A block of time covered by an accounting report is called an *accounting period*. The accounting period can be one month or one quarter (three months), but the most common period is one year.

During this accounting period, you record all financial transactions for your business and report the results. You'll engage in activities that maintain your accounting records in an orderly manner. The activities, or steps, that help a business keep its accounting records in an orderly manner make up the *accounting cycle*.

In this chapter you'll learn the various steps of the accounting cycle. In each accounting period—whether a month, a quarter, or a year—the entire accounting cycle will be completed. You probably have heard news items such as: "Ford sales are up 4 percent over last quarter and up 6 percent from the same quarter last year." By using a set period of time, you can compare financial reports from one period to those from another period.

PREDICT

What basic assumptions will the owner of a business use to set up his or her accounting books?

The Accounting Equation

Property is anything of value that you own or control. Both people and businesses have property. You might own a CD player, a

RENTED PROPERTY Many businesses rent space from which they run their operations. *Is rented space a business asset?*

computer, clothes, a television set, or maybe a car. For a business, property could include cash, office equipment, supplies, merchandise, or vehicles. When you own an item of property, you have a legal right or financial claim to that item. In contrast, when you have control over an item, you have only the right to the use of it. A rented office is property, but a business does not have a financial claim to it. In accounting, property or items of value owned by your business are called assets.

As you may remember, your equity in a piece of property is your share of its value, or your financial claim to the property. This also applies to businesses. For example, suppose that your business owns a truck valued at $16,000. You're the owner of the business, so your equity in the truck is $16,000. If the truck is completely paid for, you're the only one with a financial claim to the truck. An owner's claim to the assets of a business is called *owner's equity*.

However, what if you still owe $3,000 to the Stratford Savings Bank for the truck? The truck is valued at $16,000, but the creditor (the bank) has $3,000 equity, while your equity is now only $13,000. Both you and the creditor have financial claims to (equity in) the asset.

*C*areers in Finance

BOOKKEEPER

There's usually no shortage of bookkeeping jobs, and you don't need a four-year degree to get started. If you're good with numbers and enjoy working with software, bookkeeping could be a satisfying occupation. Most bookkeepers maintain the financial records for companies, stores, or individuals. They classify expenses and income, verify numbers, and record the data in the correct ledger. Bookkeepers in small companies handle all financial transactions, recording debits and credits, comparing current and past balance sheets, and preparing reports for managers. They handle banking activities by filling out deposit slips and adding up checks, credit card receipts, and cash. Today most bookkeepers use timesaving accounting software to organize financial records.

Skills	Accounting, computer, math, organizational skills
Personality	Detail oriented, discreet, honest, likes working with numbers
Education	High school diploma or technical training at a community college; on-the-job training
Pay range	$20,000 to $40,000 a year, depending on experience, location, and industry

Assess If you want to go into bookkeeping, what classes should you take in high school to help prepare you?

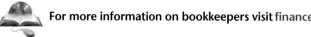

For more information on bookkeepers visit finance.glencoe.com **or your local library.**

Property = Creditor's Financial Claim + Owner's Financial Claim
$16,000 = $3,000   + $13,000

Creditors' claims to the assets of a business are called liabilities, or the debts of a business. The relationship between assets and the two types of equity (liabilities and owner's equity) is shown in the accounting equation.

Property = Creditor's Financial Claim + Owner's Financial Claim
Assets   =   Liabilities   +   Owner's Equity

The *accounting equation* (Assets = Liabilities + Owner's Equity) is the basis for keeping all accounting records in balance. The entire system of accounting is based on this equation. As your business buys, sells, or exchanges goods and services involving many business transactions, the numbers may change. However, total assets will always equal total liabilities plus owner's equity. As you learn more, you'll understand why this equation is so important.

Establishing Accounts

When you set up the books of a business, you create accounts for each of the three categories in the accounting equation: assets, liabilities, and owner's equity. An *account* shows the balance for a specific item, such as cash or equipment. You must look at your business and determine what accounts your business needs. Businesses create only the accounts they need for their type of business operation. The accounts used by one business may differ from the accounts used by another.

Chris Archer uses the following accounts for his business, Archer Delivery Service.

ASSETS	LIABILITIES	OWNER'S EQUITY
Cash in Bank	Accounts Payable	Chris Archer, Capital
Accounts Receivable		
Office Equipment		
Delivery Equipment		

Chris has established four asset accounts. The first will show all of the cash that enters or leaves the business. It's called Cash in Bank because all cash received by his business is deposited in a bank account, and all cash paid out is paid by check. In accounting, cash and checks are both considered cash transactions.

academic Connection

HISTORY

Auditors and bookkeepers could be found in ancient times. The professional accountant was first recognized in England during the 19th century. In the United States, the American Association of Public Accountants was chartered by the state of New York in 1887. The field of accounting became very important during the 20th century. Complicated tax laws and business regulations that change frequently have led to the increased need for the accountant. Today's accountant helps make decisions for the business and has a big influence on the business's success.

The second asset account is Accounts Receivable. *Accounts receivable* is the total amount of money owed to a business. Chris completed deliveries for other companies, and they owe his business money. This account represents a future value that will eventually bring cash into the business.

When Chris buys office equipment or delivery equipment, he will use these two remaining asset accounts. If he needs other accounts in his business, he can easily create them. For example, suppose that Chris buys a computer for the business. He could include it under Office Equipment, or perhaps he might create another asset account called Computer Equipment.

The only liability account listed is Accounts Payable. *Accounts payable* is the amount of money owed, or payable, to the creditors of a business. The balance owed will remain in Accounts Payable until the business pays the debt.

Finally, the owner's equity account is identified by the owner's name, Chris Archer, followed by the word "Capital." This account will report the owner's share of assets. Most businesses would have many more accounts than those presented here for Archer Delivery Service. Businesses often have accounts such as revenue or sales, utilities and other expenses, income and sales taxes, interest, merchandise, payroll, insurance, supplies, and many more.

T Accounts

When accountants analyze and record business transactions, they use a system called double-entry accounting. *Double-entry accounting* is a system of recordkeeping in which each business transaction affects at least two accounts. Remember, Archer Delivery Service has six accounts that can be used.

An efficient way to apply double-entry accounting is to use T accounts. *T accounts* show the dollar increase or decrease in an account that is caused by a transaction.

Account Name	
Left Side	Right Side
Debit	Credit

As you can see by this illustration, a T account has the account name at the top and has a left side and right side. An amount entered on the left side of a T account is called a *debit*. An amount entered on the right side of a T account is called a *credit*.

Rules of Debit and Credit

Debits and credits are used to record the increases or decreases in accounts affected by a business transaction. Under double-entry accounting, for each debit in one account (or accounts) there must be a credit of an equal amount in another account (or accounts).

The rules of debit and credit vary, depending on whether the account is an asset, a liability, or an owner's equity account. Regardless of the type of account, the left side is always the debit side and the right side is always the credit side.

Rules

- An asset account increases on the debit side and decreases on the credit side.
- Liability accounts and owner's equity accounts increase on the credit side and decrease on the debit side.

No matter how many accounts a business may have, all business transactions are analyzed in the same way: Every transaction will have debit and credit entries, and they will always be equal.

Quantity Counts

If you have to have that soda, buy it by the case. The cost per can will be less than half of what you pay at a vending machine. This is true for many other items as well.

The First Five Steps of the Accounting Cycle

This section describes the first five activities, or steps, of the accounting cycle:

1. Collect and verify source documents.
2. Analyze each transaction.
3. Journalize each transaction.
4. Post to the general ledger.
5. Prepare a trial balance.

Step 1 Collect and Verify Source Documents

When a business transaction occurs, a paper called a source document is prepared. A source document is evidence that a business transaction happened. Common source documents include check stubs, invoices, receipts, and memorandums. You must collect and check all source documents before recording anything in your business's books.

*J*esse Wells started his own lawn service business when he was a junior in high school. It wasn't long before his business grew from just mowing lawns to installing sprinkler systems and designing entire landscapes. Today, Jesse owns three commercial lawn mowers, two trucks, and has five employees. However, his business is growing so fast that Jesse describes his bookkeeping as unmanageable. He uses a receipt book to track sales. Jesse keeps a list of all his accounts payable and prides himself on paying his bills on time. Although he feels fairly confident he is completing the payroll checks correctly, he's not sure he is completing every tax form properly. This year, when he had to file his income taxes, he realized his records were in shambles. In addition, he has no way to compare his profits from year to year. In desperate need of help, Jesse turns to the experts at Standard & Poor's for advice.

STANDARD & POOR'S

Analysis: Jesse's hard work has paid off in a thriving business. Very often, such success creates its own problems. In addition to finding a solution to his current recordkeeping problems, Jesse needs to think critically about where his business is going. As his business grows, Jesse needs to devote more attention to finances, operations, and business development. It is likely that Jesse doesn't have all of the business management skills that he will need, and he may have to hire experts to assist him.

STANDARD & POOR'S

Recommendation: First, Jesse should hire an accountant to help him establish a system for keeping track of the financial aspects of his business. Once this system is set up, Jesse can record the daily entries himself or find a bookkeeper to work a few hours a week to maintain these records. From these ledger accounts, Jesse can easily calculate his net income, cash, and working capital on a monthly basis. Jesse should also ask his accountant to review his previous and current tax filings to ensure he is in compliance with tax laws. Once his financial house is in order, Jesse needs to spend some time thinking about his business goals and his role in the business. What are the prospects for future growth? What aspects of the business does he enjoy? What skills will he need to develop or acquire to grow his business? Is the sale of the business a goal? Based on his responses to such questions, Jesse can outline a two- to five-year plan.

Critical Thinking Questions

1. Why is it important for Jesse to maintain detailed financial records of his business transactions?
2. Suppose Jesse organizes his financial records and finds that costs have increased more than sales ?
3. What should Jesse do if he realizes that he probably doesn't want to be in the landscaping business two years from now?

Analyze Each Transaction

Now that you are familiar with the rules of debit and credit, analyzing transactions using T accounts is simple. Remember that every transaction must have a debit (or debits) and a credit (or credits) of an equal amount of money. Use the following steps to analyze business transactions:

1. Identify the two accounts affected.
2. Classify each of the accounts.
3. Decide whether each account is increasing or decreasing.
4. Determine which account is debited and which is credited.

Look at how Transaction #1 is analyzed using T accounts.

TRANSACTION #1

On May 5 Archer Delivery Service purchased a photocopier for $900. Check 104 was written for the full amount.

ANALYSIS

1. The accounts affected are Office Equipment and Cash in Bank.
2. Both are asset accounts.
3. The business is getting a piece of office equipment. The balance in the Office Equipment account is increasing. Cash in Bank is decreasing.
4. According to the debit-credit rules, increases in asset accounts are recorded as debits. Office Equipment is debited $900. Decreases in asset accounts are recorded as credits. Cash in Bank is credited $900.

Office Equipment		Cash in Bank	
Debit	Credit	Debit	Credit
+900	–	+	−900

Here's another example.

TRANSACTION #2

On May 7 Archer Delivery Service bought a truck for $11,000 from Gail's Auto Land. It financed the entire cost with the car dealership.

ANALYSIS

1. The accounts affected are Delivery Equipment and Accounts Payable.
2. Delivery Equipment is an asset account. Accounts Payable is a liability account. In this transaction, the business is buying a truck.

3. The balance in the account Delivery Equipment is increasing. The balance in Accounts Payable is increasing.

4. The Delivery Equipment account is debited $11,000. Accounts Payable is credited $11,000.

Delivery Equipment		Accounts Payable	
Debit	Credit	Debit	Credit
+11,000	–	–	+11,000

CONNECT

Do you keep a journal of your personal finances (in a checkbook register, for example)? Explain how business records differ from personal records.

Notice that both Transactions #1 and #2 have a debit to one account and a credit to another account. Every business transaction will have balancing debit and credit entries. This is how the system of double-entry accounting works.

Step 3 Journalize Each Transaction

Do you keep a diary or journal? Many people do. They write down the day-to-day events that they want to remember.

Businesses do the same thing. The financial events of your business are your business transactions, which you record in a journal.

KEEP ON TRUCKING Expensive equipment, such as a truck for a business, is usually financed rather than paid for in full. *What kinds of accounts in the accounting equation are affected by financing equipment?*

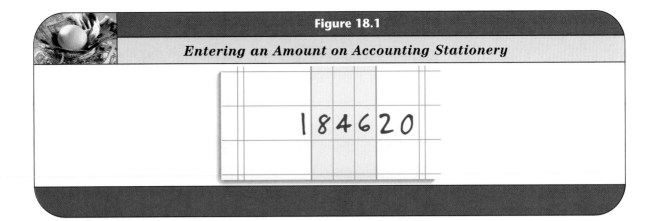

Figure 18.1

Entering an Amount on Accounting Stationery

$$1\ 8\ 4\ 6\ 2\ 0$$

You'll use T accounts to analyze the transactions, but to record the transactions, you'll use a journal. A *journal* is a record of all of the transactions of a business. Business transactions are recorded in the order in which they occur. The process of recording business transactions in a journal is called *journalizing*.

A business journal uses accounting stationery. The stationery has lined columns for recording dollar amounts. You do not use commas, decimal points, or dollar signs. For example, the amount $1,846.20 is entered as shown in **Figure 18.1**.

One of the most common accounting journals is the general journal. A general journal is an all-purpose journal in which all the transactions of a business may be recorded. When a business transaction occurs, a source document—such as a receipt or invoice—is created. Then you analyze the transaction, using T accounts, and enter it in the general journal. In the journal you record the date of

Figure 18.2

Business Transactions Entered on a General Journal

GENERAL JOURNAL   PAGE ___4___

	DATE		DESCRIPTION	DEBIT	CREDIT	
1	May	5	Office Equipment	9 0 0 00		1
2			Cash in Bank		9 0 0 00	2
3			Check 104			3
4		7	Delivery Equipment	11 0 0 0 00		4
5			Accounts Payable/Wilton Bank		11 0 0 0 00	5
6			Promissory Note			6
7						7

Figure 18.3

A General Ledger Account

ACCOUNT _____ ACCOUNT NO. _____

DATE	DESCRIPTION	DEBIT	CREDIT	BALANCE	
				DEBIT	CREDIT

the transaction, the accounts affected, and the amount of the debit and credit entries. **Figure 18.2** shows how Transactions #1 and #2 are entered in a general journal.

Step 4   Post to the General Ledger

By looking at a general journal, you can't easily see what the balance is in each of your accounts. You may want to know how much cash you have, how much your business owes in accounts payable, how much office equipment you have, and most important, whether your business is making a profit.

In order to find the balance of each account, you must transfer the amounts in the general journal to a general ledger. A *general ledger* is a book or set of electronic files that contains the accounts used for a business. Each account has its own page. Keeping accounts together in a general ledger makes information easy to find. When you need financial statements, you can take the information from the ledger and present it as well-organized reports. **Figure 18.3** shows a blank ledger page.

Next to the title "Account," you enter one of your business's account names, such as Cash in Bank. There is also a space to enter the date and a description of the entry. As you can see, the page has four amount columns. You use the first two amount columns to enter the debit or credit amounts from the general journal. You use the last two amount columns to enter the new account balance after you make an entry from the general journal.

The type of account determines which balance amount column you will use. For example, asset account balances are recorded on the debit side. Liability and owner's equity account balances are recorded on the credit side.

When you transfer amounts from the general journal to individual accounts in the general ledger, the process is called *posting*. **Figure 18.4** shows how you would post the general journal entry for May 5 to the corresponding accounts in the general ledger.

The date you record on the account in the general ledger is the date on which the transaction occurred. You may also enter a brief description of the transaction. You then transfer the debit entry of $900 from the general journal to the general ledger account called Office Equipment. Because this account had a previous balance of $1,600, it now has a new balance of $2,500. Remember that debit entries increase the balance in asset accounts.

You then record the credit entry to the general ledger account Cash in Bank. This amount is entered in the credit column. Cash in Bank is an asset account. Remember that credit entries decrease asset account balances. Thus, the balance in the Cash in Bank account decreases by $900. The new debit balance for Cash in Bank is

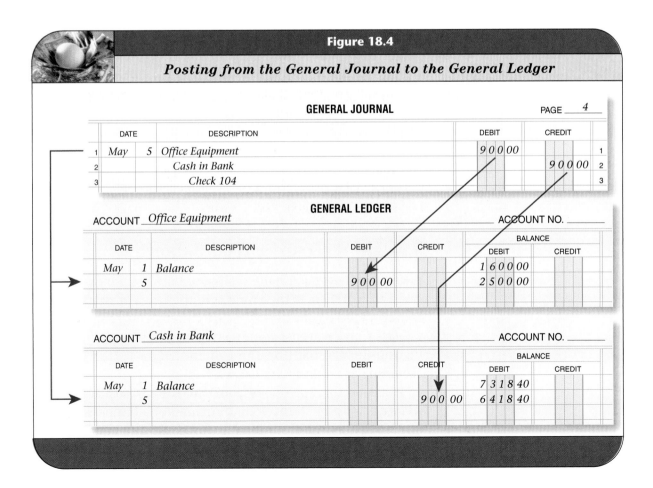

Figure 18.4

Posting from the General Journal to the General Ledger

Figure 18.5

Journal Entries Posted to a General Ledger Account

GENERAL LEDGER

ACCOUNT _Office Equipment_ _____ ACCOUNT NO. _____

DATE		DESCRIPTION	DEBIT	CREDIT	BALANCE	
					DEBIT	CREDIT
May	1	Balance			1 600 00	
	5		900 00		2 500 00	
	12		2 350 00		4 850 00	
	18			400 00	4 450 00	
	27		3 680 00		8 130 00	

$6,418.40. Both of these account balances are recorded on the debit side because they are asset accounts.

At the end of an accounting period, you'll post the figures from the general journal to the appropriate accounts in the general ledger. After all entries have been posted, the final balance for each account will appear on the general ledger. For example, at the end of the accounting period, the general ledger account for Office Equipment may look like **Figure 18.5**.

This account had a beginning balance of $1,600. Three debit entries of $900; $2,350; and $3,680 were made. Each of these entries increased the account balance. On May 18 a credit entry of $400 decreased the balance. The account called Office Equipment has a final debit balance of $8,130.

Step 5   Prepare a Trial Balance

Once you have journalized all your business transactions and posted each of them to the accounts in the general ledger, you need to know if the account balances are correct. Did you post all the amounts from the general journal to the general ledger accounts? Did you do the math on the general ledger correctly? Is the accounting equation still in balance?

To answer these questions, you'll prepare a trial balance. A *trial balance* is a list of all the account names for a business and their current balances. After you complete all posting, the total of all the debit balances should equal the total of all the credit balances. If the totals are the same, the general ledger is balanced. You can assume

Figure 18.6

A Completed Trial Balance

Archer Delivery Service
Trial Balance
For the Month Ended May 31, 20--

	Debit	Credit
Cash in Bank	2 8 9 1 00	
Accounts Receivable	1 3 7 0 00	
Office Equipment	8 1 3 0 00	
Delivery Equipment	4 2 6 0 00	
Accounts Payable		5 8 2 2 00
Chris Archer, Capital		10 8 2 9 00
Totals	16 6 5 1 00	16 6 5 1 00

that the posting is complete and that the math is correct. **Figure 18.6** shows a trial balance for the month of May 20--.

You'll notice that the accounting equation is still balanced.

Assets = Liabilities + Owner's Equity

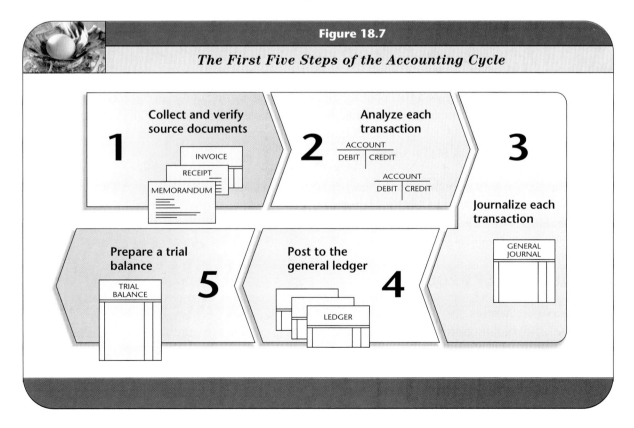

Figure 18.7

The First Five Steps of the Accounting Cycle

1 Collect and verify source documents — INVOICE, RECEIPT, MEMORANDUM

2 Analyze each transaction — ACCOUNT DEBIT | CREDIT / ACCOUNT DEBIT | CREDIT

3 Journalize each transaction — GENERAL JOURNAL

4 Post to the general ledger — LEDGER

5 Prepare a trial balance — TRIAL BALANCE

You've learned that businesses keep financial records according to an established set of principles and procedures. The steps of the accounting cycle are universal. Every business, large and small, follows GAAP guidelines.

Figure 18.7 on page 587 illustrates and summarizes the first five steps of the accounting cycle introduced in this section.

SECTION 18.1 ASSESSMENT

CHECK YOUR UNDERSTANDING

1. What tool is used to analyze business transactions in double-entry accounting?
2. Name the first five steps of the accounting cycle.
3. What is recorded in a general journal?
4. How does a general ledger help you keep your business records organized?
5. What is the purpose of preparing a trial balance?

THINK CRITICALLY

6. Suppose that you prepare a trial balance and discover that total debits do not equal total credits. What are some of the errors that you might have made?

USING COMMUNICATION SKILLS

7. **The Accounting Cycle** Dimitri teaches computer classes at a local senior citizen center. He has just been asked to teach a course on the basics of accounting for small businesses. **Develop** Write a paragraph explaining the first five steps of the accounting cycle that would help Dimitri begin a course outline.

SOLVING MONEY PROBLEMS

8. **Account Names** Jake Adams recently started Jake's Janitor Services. He cleans several of the office buildings in town. He borrowed from two creditors to purchase his cleaning equipment. **Identify** What are the account names that Jake might use in his cleaning business?

Financial Statements for a Business

To operate a business profitably, you'll need to have up-to-date financial information. You can't make decisions if you don't have the current facts. Financial statements provide this information. *Financial statements* are reports that summarize the changes that result from your business transactions during an accounting period. By preparing and analyzing these statements, you can see whether your business is on course, experiencing some difficulty, or headed for serious trouble. Preparing financial statements is another step in the accounting cycle.

Financial Statements

The primary financial statements are the income statement, also called the statement of operations and earnings, and the balance sheet. A third statement, called the statement of cash flows, is also often used. The sources of information for your financial statements are the final balances in the general ledger accounts. When you prepared your trial balance, you proved that the posting from the general journal to the general ledger was correct and complete. Now you have to report what happened during this accounting period.

You are now going to examine financial statements from a small merchandising business called the Happy House Card Shop. A *merchandising business* is a business that buys goods, marks them up, and sells them to customers. The Happy House Card Shop sells a variety of cards, gift wrapping, and small gifts that it buys from wholesalers or distributors. Many of the stores in your neighborhood are probably merchandising businesses.

Income Statement

At the end of an accounting period, you want to know how much money your business made or lost. You also want to know how much money you took in from sales and where the money went. This information is reported on your income statement. An *income statement* is a report of the net income or net loss for an accounting period. An income statement for a merchandising

What You'll Learn

- How to **identify** items included on an income statement
- How to **explain** the purpose of a balance sheet
- How to **recognize** the importance of a statement of cash flows

Why It's Important

You need current financial statements that analyze your financial position in order to make sound financial decisions about your business.

KEY TERMS

- financial statements
- merchandising business
- income statement
- cost of merchandise sold
- gross profit on sales
- net income
- balance sheet
- statement of cash flows
- cash inflows
- cash outflows

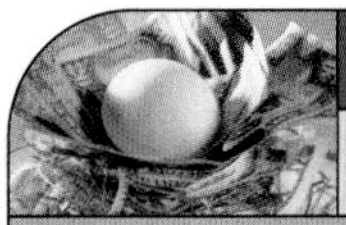

Figure 18.8

Income Statement

HAPPY HOUSE CARD SHOP
Income Statement
For the Year Ended December 31, 20--

Revenue:		
Sales		292,619 (A)
Cost of Merchandise Sold:		
Merchandise on Hand Jan. 1	83,744	
Plus Merchandise Purchased	205,813	
Merchandise Available for Sale	289,557	
Minus Merchandise Still on Hand	93,281	
Cost of Merchandise Sold:		196,276 (B)
Gross Profit on Sales		96,343 (C)
Operating Expenses:		
Advertising Expense	2,734	
Insurance Expense	487	
Maintenance Expense	3,551	
Miscellaneous Expense	762	
Rent Expense	18,500	
Salaries Expense	26,931	
Supplies Expense	1,024	
Utilities Expense	4,107	
Total Operating Expenses		58,096 (D)
Net Income		38,247 (E)

business has five sections: revenue, cost of merchandise sold, gross profit on sales, operating expenses, and net income (or loss). The amounts entered on the income statement will be the ending balances in the accounts in the general ledger. **Figure 18.8** shows an income statement for Happy House Card Shop, prepared by owner Sheila Henry.

REVENUE You'll notice that the beginning of the statement reports the total sales (A), or revenue, for the period. Happy House earned $292,619 in sales for the year ending December 31, 20--. This is the total amount of money the business earned from selling merchandise.

COST OF MERCHANDISE SOLD Next, the cost of the merchandise sold (B) is calculated and reported. The *cost of merchandise sold* is the amount of money the business paid for the goods that it sold to customers. To arrive at this amount, Sheila would first determine the cost of merchandise in the store at the beginning of the accounting period. In this case, $83,744 was on hand. Then she would add the cost of the additional merchandise Happy House purchased during the year, which was $205,813. This means that the store had a total of $289,557 in merchandise available to be sold.

After counting her inventory, Sheila determined that she still had $93,281 in merchandise in the store. This means that the cost of the merchandise sold was $196,276.

PROFIT Sheila would then subtract the cost of the merchandise sold ($196,276) from the amount earned from sales ($292,619) to arrive at (C), the gross profit on sales ($96,343). The *gross profit on sales* is the profit made from selling merchandise before operating expenses are deducted. This is the profit Sheila made by marking up her merchandise and selling it.

NET INCOME *Net income* is the amount of revenue that remains after expenses for the accounting period are subtracted from the gross profit on sales. To calculate the net income for the period, Sheila would subtract the total operating expenses (D–$58,096) from the gross profit on sales (C–$96,343). For this period, Happy House Card Shop reported a net income (E) of $38,247.

Analyzing the Income Statement

You can see that Happy House did well. It made a profit. However, it is a good idea to compare the figures on this income statement to those on last year's statement. A comparison of income statements for Happy House is shown in **Figure 18.9**. By reviewing the changes, Sheila will have a better idea of how well her business is doing.

From **Figure 18.9** you can see that sales increased by 3.10 percent from last year. Depending on where the business is located and on

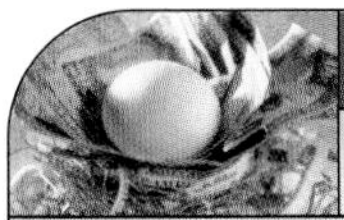

Figure 18.9

Comparison of Income Statements

HAPPY HOUSE CARD SHOP
Comparative Income Statement
For the Year Ended December 31, 20--

	Previous Year	Current Year	Dollar Change	Percent Change
Sales	283,834	292,619	+8,785	+3.10%
Cost of Merchandise Sold	186,283	196,276	+9,993	+5.36%
Gross Profit on Sales	97,551	96,343	-1,208	-1.24%
Total Operating Expenses	61,277	58,096	-3,181	-5.19%
Net Income	36,274	38,247	+1,973	+5.44%

general economic conditions, this may be good. Notice that the net income rose by 5.44 percent. This could be due to the fact that the business reduced total operating expenses by 5.19 percent. Sales rose, but the net income rose at a greater rate. This is an example of good financial management.

Another common method of analysis is to show figures on an income statement as a percentage of sales. Based on the present income statement and last year's statement from Happy House, this analysis is shown in **Figure 18.10**.

Last year the cost of merchandise sold was 65.63 percent of total sales. This year the cost of merchandise increased to 67.08 percent of total sales. Sheila Henry paid more for her merchandise but did not increase her prices at the same rate.

The gross profit on sales decreased from 34.37 percent to 32.92 percent. Happy House sold more merchandise but lowered its percentage of profit. If it were not for a drop in expenses this year, the business would have reported a lower net income. This analysis provides the owner of Happy House with information that she needs to make decisions regarding the store's pricing.

Balance Sheet

The other primary financial statement of a business is a balance sheet. A *balance sheet* is a report of the balances of all asset, liability,

RESPOND

Based on this information, do you think Happy House should raise its prices next year? Explain your answer.

Figure 18.10

Comparison of Income Statements as a Percentage of Sales

	Previous Year		Current Year	
	Amount in Dollars	Percent	Amount in Dollars	Percent
Sales	283,834	100.00%	292,619	100.00%
Cost of Merchandise Sold	186,283	65.63%	196,276	67.08%
Gross Profit on Sales	97,551	34.37%	96,343	32.92%

Figure 18.11

Balance Sheet

HAPPY HOUSE CARD SHOP
Balance Sheet
For the Year Ended December 31, 20--

ASSETS

Cash in Bank	25,372	
Accounts Receivable	9,201	
Merchandise Inventory	93,281	
Supplies	5,285	
Office Equipment	12,187	
Display Equipment	47,883	
TOTAL ASSETS		193,209

LIABILITIES

Accounts Payable	56,846	
Sales Tax Payable	3,621	
Payroll Taxes Payable	2,749	
TOTAL LIABILITIES		63,216

OWNER'S EQUITY

Sheila Henry, Capital		129,993
TOTAL LIABILITIES + OWNER'S EQUITY		193,209

and owner's equity accounts at the end of an accounting period. The main purpose of the balance sheet is to present a business's financial position by reporting the assets of a business and the claims against those assets (creditor's claims and owner's claims). It reports what the business owns, owes, and is worth on a specific date. It's like taking a financial photo of your business on the last day of the accounting period. This is your present financial situation. The balance sheet for Happy House Card Shop is shown in **Figure 18.11**.

You learned in Section 18.1 that the basic accounting equation must always be in balance. The balance sheet represents the basic accounting equation.

Assets = Liabilities + Owner's Equity

Notice that a balance sheet consists of three sections: an asset section, a liability section, and an owner's equity section. On the Happy House balance sheet, the total assets ($193,209) equals the total liabilities ($63,216) plus the owner's equity ($129,993). This means the accounting equation is still in balance.

Analyzing the Balance Sheet

To analyze these figures you would compare the current amounts on the balance sheet with figures from last year, as shown in **Figure 18.12**.

By examining the numbers and percentages, you can see that changes have taken place. The business bought additional display equipment and office equipment during the year. This is shown in the increased balances in the Office Equipment and Display Equipment accounts. However, more money is owed to creditors because the balance in Accounts Payable has also increased.

The balance sheet is an important financial statement, but to make wise decisions you should compare the financial data to a

INTERNATIONAL FINANCE **Falkland Islands**

What has a bullet-shaped body, tentacles, and a large eye set on each side of its short head? No, it's not your worst nightmare. It's a squid, a marine creature whose ancestors evolved half a billion years ago. Increasingly popular on the world's menu, squid can be bought fresh or frozen. A food you either love or hate, squid helps support the economy of the Falklands, two islands just east of the southern tip of South America. Every year foreign trawlers pay Falklanders millions of dollars in licensing fees to fish the islands' waters. Squid accounts for 75 percent of their catch. Here's a snapshot of the Falkland Islands.

Geographic area	4,700 sq. mi.
Population	2,758
Capital	Stanley
Language	English
Currency	pound
Gross domestic product (GDP)	$60.3 million
Per capita GDP	$26,000
Economy	Industry: fishing license fees, wool and fish processing, tourism. Agriculture: fodder, vegetable crops, sheep, dairy products. Exports: wool, hides, meat.

Port Stanley, East Falkland, Falkland Islands

Thinking Critically

Compare Three ounces of squid has 78 calories, 1.2 grams of fat, and 198 milligrams of cholesterol. Find a food nutrition chart in your library and compare these figures with three ounces of hamburger. Which food is more nutritious? What would happen to the Falklands' economy if more people started eating more nutritious food?

For more information on the Falkland Islands visit finance.glencoe.com or your local library.

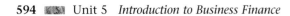

Figure 18.12

Comparison of Balance Sheets

HAPPY HOUSE CARD SHOP
Comparative Balance Sheet
For the Year Ended December 31, 20--

	Previous Year	Current Year	Dollar Change	Percent Change
ASSETS				
Cash in Bank	22,743	25,372	+2,629	+11.56%
Accounts Receivable	8,338	9,201	+863	+10.35%
Merchandise Inventory	95,026	93,281	-1,745	-1.84%
Supplies	4,631	5,285	+654	+14.12%
Office Equipment	8,958	12,187	+3,229	+36.05%
Display Equipment	41,720	47,883	+6,163	+14.77%
TOTAL ASSETS	**181,416**	**193,209**	**+11,793**	**+6.50%**
LIABILITIES				
Accounts Payable	51,119	56,846	+5,727	+11.20%
Sales Tax Payable	3,506	3,621	+115	+3.28%
Payroll Taxes Payable	2,921	2,749	-172	-5.88%
TOTAL LIABILITIES	**57,546**	**63,216**	**+5,670**	**+9.85%**
OWNER'S EQUITY				
Sheila Henry, Capital	123,870	129,993	+6,123	+4.94%

previous balance sheet. Remember, the financial statements provide the information, but you must analyze and interpret them and make recommendations based on that information.

Statement of Cash Flows

Both income statements and balance sheets provide vital financial information, but neither document shows how the cash position of the business changed during the period. You'll want to know how much cash is available during business operations.

You may remember that your personal cash flow is the money that actually goes in and out of your wallet and bank accounts. In a business, cash flow also refers to the amount of cash that you have available at any given time.

Suppose that your school has a big dance coming up on Friday. All of your friends are going and will probably go somewhere to eat after it's over. You'll need cash for Friday night, but you won't get your paycheck from your job until Saturday. In this example, money

Figure 18.13

Statement of Cash Flows

HAPPY HOUSE CARD SHOP
Statement of Cash Flows
For the Year Ended December 31, 20--

Cash Flows from Operating Activities		
Cash Receipts from:		
Sales to Customers	292,619	
Interest from Savings	1,923	
Total Cash Receipts from Operations		**294,542**
Cash Payments for:		
Purchase of Merchandise	205,813	
Operating Expenses	58,096	
Interest Expense	9,821	
Taxes	18,183	
Total Cash Payments for Operations		**291,913**
Net Cash Flows from Operating Activities		**2,629**

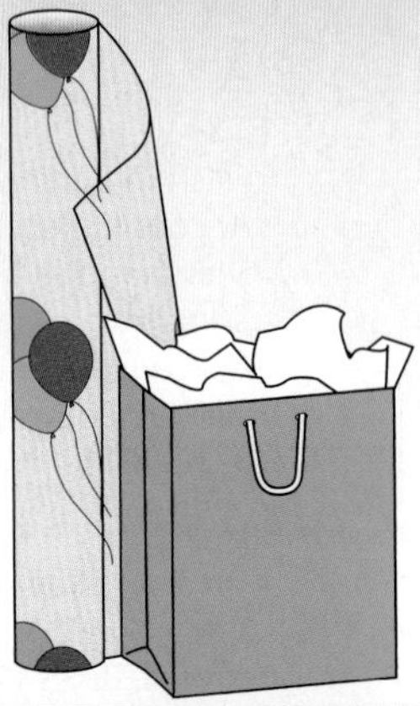

needs to go out for the dance before money comes in from your job. You have a "cash crunch" problem.

Businesses are often faced with similar problems. Unfortunately, if a small business experiences a cash crunch situation, it could have serious problems. Good cash control and management means that sufficient cash is available for operating the business on a daily basis and for emergencies.

A *statement of cash flows* is a document that reports how much cash your business took in and where the cash went. It explains why the Cash in Bank account either increased or decreased during the accounting period.

Cash flows include both *cash inflows*, or cash that enters a business, and *cash outflows*, or cash that exits a business. Cash inflows may include sales and interest earned from investments or savings. Cash outflows may include operating expenses, merchandise purchases, supplies, and interest and taxes paid. **Figure 18.13** is a statement of cash flows for Happy House Card Shop.

Analyzing the Statement of Cash Flows

Happy House has a positive cash flow. The cash inflows ($294,542) are greater than the cash outflows ($291,913) for the period. During the year, more cash entered the business than was paid out. The difference is $2,629.

When your business has negative cash flows, you will probably experience a lack of available cash. You may not be able to pay your bills or buy goods to resell. The business will not grow. Your statement of cash flows can be a major consideration when you want to borrow money. Potential investors and lenders want to see cash flowing into your business in a constant, positive manner.

A Computerized Accounting System

Most businesses use some type of accounting software to record and report their business transactions. With today's relatively low cost of computers and software, automation of accounting procedures is available to businesses of all sizes.

Even for an automated system, you still need to collect and keep your source documents. Each business transaction must be separated into its debit and credit parts. However, you'll enter the transaction

$AVVY SAVER

Accounting for Your Money

1. Put all receipts in labeled folders and file them in alphabetical order.
2. Keep a budget and review it weekly.
3. Balance your checkbook monthly.
4. Be aware of—and meet—all tax-filing deadlines.
5 Use a financial software program to track your finances.

ALL THE WORLD'S A STAGE Theatrical companies must pay for production costs well before cash in ticket sales is received. *What kind of cash flow would they experience before ticket sales begin?*

Income Statements

Dakota's gardening business now includes gardening for 22 homes and gardening and planting for three commercial properties. She's considering hiring Rashelle for an hourly fee to work with her so she can expand the business. To see if she can afford to hire Rashelle, she's prepared an income statement.

Dakota's Gardening
Income Statement for the Month Ended July 31, 2003

Revenue

Regular gardening fees	$3,460	
Charge for plantings	180	
Charge for trimming trees	300	
Total revenue		$3,940

Operating Expenses

Buying plantings	90	
Truck loan	150	
Equipment: new tree pruner	75	
Gas expense	25	
Insurance expense	35	
Total expenses		375
Net income		$3,565

In reviewing six months of income statements, Dakota felt she could afford paying Rashelle, especially if she picked up some new accounts.

Apply In your workbook or on a separate sheet of paper, choose a service business that you might like to operate. Determine what you would charge for your service. Based on your fee and services, determine what your monthly revenue and expenses would be. Using the same guidelines as shown above, prepare an income statement. Would you want to hire and supervise help or would you prefer to work alone?

in the computer system by using account numbers rather than inputting the account name. You still need to enter the amounts.

When all transactions are entered, you can tell the program to post all amounts to the appropriate general ledger accounts. Computerized posting is faster and eliminates many of the errors that you might make doing it manually. Once the posting is completed, the computer will print your trial balance and financial statements.

The basic accounting principles you've learned are the backbone of every business. All businesses use the same practices, which help them analyze their financial position and make decisions.

QUESTION

Why is it important to understand basic accounting procedures, even if you are using accounting software to manage your accounts?

SECTION 18.2 ASSESSMENT

CHECK YOUR UNDERSTANDING

1. What items are included on an income statement of a merchandising business?
2. What is the purpose of a balance sheet?
3. Why is the statement of cash flows important to a business?

THINK CRITICALLY

4. Describe how it is possible for a business to have made a profit during the most recent accounting period but not have enough money to pay its employees this week.

USING MATH SKILLS

5. **Gross Profit** Damien is the student manager of Panther's Pen, the store on his school campus. During the fall semester, sales (or revenue) totaled $5,420, and the cost of merchandise sold was $3,500. During the spring semester, sales were $4,890, and the cost of merchandise sold was $3,060.

   Apply What is the gross profit on sales for each semester? What is the percentage of gross profit to sales? Did profits improve from the fall semester to the spring semester?

SOLVING MONEY PROBLEMS

6. **Sharing Financial Information** Sylvia worked her way through college at a health food store. She learned about the various aspects of operating a business. When she graduated, she opened her own store, Sylvia's Smoothies. Now she is ready to add a partner to her business.

   Analyze What type of financial information might Sylvia need to share with potential partners?

CHAPTER 18 ASSESSMENT

CHAPTER SUMMARY

- T accounts can be used in double-entry accounting to analyze which accounts are affected by a business transaction.
- The first five steps of the accounting cycle are to collect and verify source documents, analyze each transaction, journalize each transaction, post amounts to the general ledger, and prepare a trial balance.
- The general journal is used to record all transactions as they take place.
- Posting to the general ledger allows you to see the balances in each account.
- To determine whether all of your account balances are correct, you should prepare a trial balance.

- An income statement reports the net income or net loss for an accounting period. An income statement for a merchandising business has five sections: revenue, cost of merchandise sold, gross profit on sales, operating expenses, and net income (or loss).
- The balance sheet reports the balances of all asset, liability, and owner's equity accounts for the accounting period.
- The statement of cash flows shows how much cash your business has available at a certain time. It reports how much your business took in and where this cash went.

Understanding and Using Vocabulary

You are going to hire someone to analyze your business's financial records. Using at least 15 of the key terms, create a list of questions you would ask during the interview process. Role-play the interview with a partner.

financial reports	double-entry
accounting period	accounting
accounting cycle	T accounts
owner's equity	debit
accounting equation	credit
account	journal
accounts receivable	journalizing
accounts payable	general ledger

posting
trial balance
financial statements
merchandising business
income statement
cost of merchandise sold

gross profit on sales
net income
balance sheet
statement of cash flows
cash inflows
cash outflows

Review Key Concepts

1. Name three asset accounts that might be used in a business.
2. What are the two rules of debit and credit?
3. What kinds of source documents are used by businesses?

CHAPTER 18 ASSESSMENT

4. What is the main purpose of financial statements?
5. Define cash inflows and cash outflows. Give two examples of each.

Apply Key Concepts

1. Provide examples of four assets that you might have in a retail motorcycle business.
2. For the same motorcycle dealership, analyze this transaction: On March 11 Mid-Town Motorcycles purchased three motorcycles. The store paid cash ($3,000) for one of the motorcycles and financed the others with bank loans ($6,000). What accounts should be credited?
3. What would happen if you didn't have source documents for each transaction?
4. As a business owner, how could you use the information from a comparison of income statements?
5. Prepare an example of a business cash flow problem.

 ## Problem Solving Today

T ACCOUNTS

You begin a taxi service. You obtain a loan for $150,000. On March 7 you purchase a vehicle for $25,000, paying for it with check 131.

Analyze Establish T accounts for Cash in Bank, Accounts Payable, and Transportation Equipment. Record these two business transactions in the T accounts.

 **Computer Activity** As an alternative activity, use spreadsheet software to set up T accounts for the business transaction described above.

Real-World Application

CONNECT WITH ECONOMICS

Carla was recently hired as a financial consultant by a new fitness center that offers exercise facilities and personal training. The business space is rented, and the owners purchased several pieces of exercise equipment and hired two personal trainers. Their clients either purchase memberships or pay per visit.

Give Recommendations With a partner, write a plan for the fitness center that explains the types of financial information they need to record. Describe the source documents that they might use, and suggest accounts that might be used in their general journal.

FINANCE Online

CRAZY QUILTS

Your grandmother has owned a quilt shop for 30 years. She has always recorded the financial transactions of her business by hand, but she would like to try using a computer. You offer to provide her with information about the computerized accounting systems available on the market today.

Connect Using a variety of search engines, locate information on three different computerized accounting programs. Prepare a presentation, written or oral, to show your grandmother what you found.

Managing Payroll and Inventory

STANDARD &POOR'S

Q&A

Q: I am only 16. Why should I pay Social Security and Medicare taxes? Those programs sure won't be around when I'm old enough to collect.

A: It is true that Social Security programs are projected to run low on funds around the year 2025. Under the present system, the rate of return that you would eventually receive on your contributions to these programs is much lower than what you could earn investing this money on your own. However, Congress is currently evaluating plans to ensure that Social Security will provide for future retirees. Also, Social Security and Medicare offer many other types of benefits to those who are younger than retirement age, including disability and survivors' benefits.

Managing Payroll

$\mathcal{M}$r. Lau started his own clothing business 25 years ago. Since that time his company has grown from 10 part-time workers to 120 full-time employees. Mr. Lau pays his employees well. This practice has helped him attract and keep a hardworking and loyal group of people. Salaries range from about $28,000 per year for first-year workers to as much as $75,000 for some of his senior managers. His total annual expense for employee pay is nearly $5 million. The company's profits are healthy, and Mr. Lau figures that it's worth paying more for quality employees.

It's often said that good employees are the backbone of a successful business. However, they can cost a great deal of money. In fact, payroll is generally the greatest expense of running a business. Carefully maintaining records of employees and their pay is an essential element of good financial management.

What You'll Learn

- How to **identify** the steps in managing a payroll system
- How to **describe** the methods of paying employees
- How to **distinguish** between required and voluntary payroll deductions
- How to **identify** the accounts used in recording payroll

Why It's Important

Managing payroll efficiently and accurately will enable you to run a business more effectively and profitably.

KEY TERMS

- payroll
- pay period
- gross earnings
- salary
- hourly wage
- overtime rate
- commission
- deductions
- Federal Insurance Contributions Act (FICA)
- Social Security tax
- Medicare tax
- payroll register
- direct deposit
- total gross earnings

The Importance of Payroll Records

If you own a business, a large and important part of its accounting system will involve payroll. A *payroll* is a list of employees and the payments due to each employee for a specific period of time. The specific period of time over which you pay your employees is known as a *pay period*. The two most common pay periods are weekly and biweekly (every two weeks). However, some companies pay their employees only once per month.

A good payroll accounting system ensures that employees are paid on time and have the correct amounts on their paychecks. The payroll records and reports need to be very accurate. As with other accounting functions, when you process payroll information, you must follow specific guidelines. These are known as generally accepted accounting principles (GAAP). In addition to following

GAAP procedures, state and federal governments issue strict guidelines for paying employees and reporting payroll information.

You have two major goals when setting up a payroll system. Your system should: 1) collect and process all information needed to prepare and issue payroll checks and 2) maintain payroll records needed for accounting purposes and for preparing reports to government agencies.

Every payroll system has some common tasks or steps. All are important and must be done carefully, accurately, and regularly. If you pay your employees every week, you'll complete all of these tasks weekly. These tasks or steps include:

What's Your Financial ID?

STOCKING UP ON KNOWLEDGE

Whether you plan to work for a company or imagine running your own business someday, here's a chance to test yourself on some business basics. Write your answers on a separate sheet of paper. After you finish studying the chapter, take the quiz again to see how much you learned.

1. After federal, state, and local taxes are subtracted from a paycheck, the amount of money left is called _____.

   a. gross pay   c. salary
   b. net pay   d. wages

2. The various amounts of money that are subtracted from an employee's paycheck are called _____.

   a. taxable incomes c. withholdings
   b. co-payments   d. deductions

3. The agency that collects federal taxes and oversees the federal income tax system is called the _____.

   a. Social Security Administration
   b. Internal Revenue Service
   c. Big Brother
   d. U.S. Treasury

4. A fixed amount of money that is paid to an employee for each pay period is called _____.

   a. wage   c. commission
   b. salary   d. allowance

5. The system of physically counting merchandise on hand is called _____.

   a. spot-checking inventory system
   b. unit control system
   c. point-of-sale inventory system
   d. periodic inventory system

6. The number of times a business sells its inventory in a given period of time is called _____.

   a. margin   c. unit control
   b. markup   d. inventory turnover

1. Calculating gross earnings
2. Calculating payroll deductions
3. Preparing payroll records
4. Preparing paychecks
5. Recording payroll information in your accounting records
6. Reporting payroll information to the government

Calculating Gross Earnings

The first step in a payroll system is to calculate the total earnings of all your employees for the pay period. The total amount of money an employee earns in a pay period is called *gross earnings*. The calculation of gross earnings depends on how you're paying each employee. You're probably not going to pay all employees the same way. Three of the most common methods of paying employees are salary, hourly wage, and salary plus commission.

Salary

A *salary* is a fixed amount of money paid to an employee for each pay period, regardless of the number of hours worked. For example, Catherine Boggs is the manager of the shoe department at Dickinson's Department Store. She earns a fixed weekly salary of $530 even though she may work 40 hours one week and 44 hours another week. Salaries are a typical method of payment for managers, supervisors, and certain occupations, such as teaching.

Hourly Wage

If you work for a local business after school and on the weekends, you probably receive an *hourly wage*, a specific amount of money paid per hour to an employee. Most temporary and part-time jobs, such as after-school and summer jobs for students, pay an hourly wage. Many full-time jobs, such as entry-level retail jobs, also pay an hourly wage.

Sean McCormick, for instance, works at a sporting goods outlet on weekday afternoons for $7.25 per hour. Last week he worked 20 hours, and his gross earnings were $145 ($7.25 × 20 = $145). This week he had already worked 20 hours by the end of the day on Wednesday. Sean's gross earnings vary from week to week because he works different amounts of time each week.

Employers often use time cards or a time clock to keep track of when hourly employees begin and end work each day. They use this

CONNECT

If you are currently employed, look at a recent paycheck stub and compare your gross earnings to the amount you were actually paid. What accounts for the difference?

academic Connection

MATH

When you get your paycheck, it is important that you review it carefully. You should check to see how much you earned and the amounts that have been deducted. Using your last paycheck stub, calculate the percentage deducted for each of the following:

- Federal income tax
- Social Security tax
- Medicare tax
- State tax
- Any voluntary deductions

(If you currently do not have a job, use the paycheck stub in **Figure 19.3** on page 613 for your calculations.) Then compare the percentages among your classmates. Are they similar? Explain why or why not.

information to determine the total hours each employee worked during a pay period. At the end of each period, the employer checks the information on time cards or time sheets for accuracy. If the information is incorrect, paychecks will be inaccurate. That's a problem for both employees and employers.

Overtime Pay

According to state and federal laws, hourly wage employees generally are paid extra when they work overtime, or more than 40 hours in a pay week. The *overtime rate*, the amount paid above the normal rate, is usually 1.5 times the employee's regular hourly wage. For example, Kelly Robinson's regular hourly wage is $7.40. If she works more than 40 hours in a given week, her overtime rate for the extra hours is $11.10 ($7.40 × 1.5 = $11.10).

Suppose that Kelly worked more than 40 hours last week. To calculate her gross earnings, you would multiply her regular hourly wage by 40 hours. Then you would multiply the overtime rate by the number of overtime hours. By adding the results of these calculations, you can figure out her gross earnings for the week.

Careers in Finance

PURCHASING AGENT

Would you like to be able to buy everything from stationary to pet supplies, computers to clothes, toys to new furniture? Purchasing agents handle those kinds of purchases for all types of companies. They receive bids or prices from vendors and then determine which one can provide the best product at the best price and in the most timely manner. Purchasing agents follow up on orders to see that everything is delivered as promised. They deal with almost every aspect of a business and may be involved in the planning stages of major projects. Purchasing agents are responsible for spending a company's money wisely.

Skills	Analytical, communication, computer, decision making, math, organizational, negotiation, research, sales ability
Personality	Able to cope with stress, good judgment, honest, likes working with people and numbers, tactful
Education	Bachelor's degree or high school diploma, experience in the field
Pay range	$23,000 to $70,000 a year, depending on experience, business, and location

Critical Thinking What are some of the problems a purchasing agent might encounter?

For more information on purchasing agents visit finance.glencoe.com **or your local library.**

Example: Kelly worked 43 hours this week. If her regular hourly wage is $7.40, and her overtime wage is $11.10, what are her gross earnings for the week?

Formula: $\left(\begin{array}{c}\text{Hourly} \\ \text{Rate}\end{array} \times \begin{array}{c}\text{Regular} \\ \text{Hours}\end{array}\right) + \left(\begin{array}{c}\text{Overtime} \\ \text{Rate}\end{array} \times \begin{array}{c}\text{Overtime} \\ \text{Hours}\end{array}\right) = \text{Gross Earnings}$

Solution:
$$(\$7.40 \times 40) + (\$11.10 \times 3) = \text{Gross Earnings}$$
$$\$296 + \$33.30 = \$329.30$$

Kelly's gross earnings for the week are $329.30.

Paying overtime can be very expensive for your business. You shouldn't allow employees to work overtime unless you have a very good reason. Typically, employees may work extra hours during holiday sales or other busy periods. They may also work overtime to cover for other employees who are sick or on vacation. Remember, controlling payroll costs is an important aspect of good financial management.

Commission

A *commission* is an amount of money paid to an employee based on a percentage of the employee's sales. The more the employee sells, the more he or she is paid. Paying commissions to sales employees is a way to encourage them to increase their sales.

It's very common for employers to pay sales employees a salary plus commission. For example, Olivia Chun is paid a weekly salary of $150 plus a 5 percent commission on all merchandise she sells. This week she recorded sales of $3,725. Olivia's commission for the week is $186.25 ($3,725 × 5% = $186.25). Her gross earnings for the pay week are $336.25 ($150 + $186.25 = $336.25).

Calculating Payroll Deductions

The first time you received a payroll check, you were probably surprised to see that the amount on the check was less than you expected. Various amounts that are subtracted from an employee's gross earnings are called *deductions*. Some deductions are required by local, state, or federal law. Others are voluntary deductions. These are amounts that employees choose to have withheld from, or taken out of, their gross earnings. The calculation of these deductions is the second step in a payroll system.

NINE TO FIVE All employees are paid, but not all in the same manner. Some receive a salary, some are paid an hourly wage, and some earn a salary plus commission. *What does it mean to work on salary plus commission?*

Deductions Required by Law

As an employer, you're required by law to deduct certain payroll taxes from the gross earnings of all employees. These include federal income tax, Social Security tax, and Medicare tax. In many states additional taxes are withheld for local and state income taxes. Employers deduct these taxes from employees' paychecks and forward the amounts to the appropriate government agency.

FEDERAL INCOME TAX Most people pay income tax to the federal government each year. This tax is based on their total income for the year. To ensure that people will have the money to pay these taxes, the government requires employers to withhold an amount of money from employees' paychecks each pay period. This money is sent to the government and is applied to each employee's federal income tax.

After calculating gross earnings, employers use tax tables supplied by the Internal Revenue Service (IRS) to determine the amount of federal tax to withhold from each employee's paycheck. To use the tables, employers must know how many allowances each employee is claiming. An allowance is an adjustment to the tax withheld from your paycheck. The more allowances you claim, the less tax will be withheld. It is based on your marital status and on whether you are supporting other people with your money. A single person could claim an allowance of zero or one. A married person with two children could claim an allowance of four. **Figure 19.1** shows an IRS tax table.

Suppose that Eric Gaus has weekly gross earnings of $235 and claims one allowance. According to the tax table, the amount withheld for federal income tax is $20. When you file your federal income tax return, if you had too much withheld from your pay, the government will refund you the excess amount. If you had too little withheld, you'll have to send the additional amount you owe to the IRS.

FICA TAXES In addition to federal income tax, employers also collect Social Security taxes for the federal government by deducting them from your paycheck. The 1935 *Federal Insurance Contributions Act (FICA)* established the present Social Security system. Social Security taxes are often referred to as FICA taxes. The FICA taxes pay for programs that provide income to certain individuals:

Figure 19.1

Internal Revenue Service Tax Table

SINGLE Persons—**WEEKLY** Payroll Period

If the wages are		And the number of withholding allowances claimed is—										
At least	But less than	0	1	2	3	4	5	6	7	8	9	10
		The amount of income tax to be withheld is—										
125	130	11	4	0	0	0	0	0	0	0	0	0
130	135	12	5	0	0	0	0	0	0	0	0	0
135	140	13	5	0	0	0	0	0	0	0	0	0
140	145	14	6	0	0	0	0	0	0	0	0	0
145	150	14	7	0	0	0	0	0	0	0	0	0
150	155	15	8	0	0	0	0	0	0	0	0	0
155	160	16	8	1	0	0	0	0	0	0	0	0
160	165	17	9	1	0	0	0	0	0	0	0	0
165	170	17	10	2	0	0	0	0	0	0	0	0
170	175	18	11	3	0	0	0	0	0	0	0	0
175	180	19	11	4	0	0	0	0	0	0	0	0
180	185	20	12	4	0	0	0	0	0	0	0	0
185	190	20	13	5	0	0	0	0	0	0	0	0
190	195	21	14	6	0	0	0	0	0	0	0	0
195	200	22	14	7	0	0	0	0	0	0	0	0
200	210	23	15	8	0	0	0	0	0	0	0	0
210	220	25	17	9	2	0	0	0	0	0	0	0
220	230	26	18	11	3	0	0	0	0	0	0	0
230	240	28	20	12	5	0	0	0	0	0	0	0
240	250	29	21	14	6	0	0	0	0	0	0	0
250	260	31	23	15	8	0	0	0	0	0	0	0
260	270	32	24	17	9	2	0	0	0	0	0	0
270	280	34	26	18	11	3	0	0	0	0	0	0
280	290	35	27	20	12	5	0	0	0	0	0	0
290	300	37	29	21	14	6	0	0	0	0	0	0
300	310	38	30	23	15	8	0	0	0	0	0	0
310	320	40	32	24	17	9	1	0	0	0	0	0
320	330	41	33	26	18	11	3	0	0	0	0	0
330	340	43	35	27	20	12	4	0	0	0	0	0
340	350	44	36	29	21	14	6	0	0	0	0	0

PAYING UNCLE SAM Depending on the number of allowances you claim, your employer will withhold a certain amount from your paycheck each pay period for federal income tax. *What is the purpose of withholding this money?*

- The old-age and survivors' benefit programs provide income to retired persons and the spouse and dependents of a deceased worker.
- The disability insurance program provides income to people with disabilities and their families.
- The Medicare program provides health insurance benefits for people 65 or older, certain people with disabilities, and people of any age who have permanent kidney failure.

FICA includes two types of tax: Social Security tax and Medicare tax. *Social Security tax* finances the federal programs that provide retirement, disability, and life insurance benefits. *Medicare tax* is the tax that finances part of the Medicare program.

All employees pay FICA taxes based on rates established by the U.S. Congress. The rates can change at any time. The present FICA tax rates are 6.2 percent for Social Security and 1.45 percent for Medicare. The money that is collected goes to the Social Security Administration, where it is put into a trust. It is then distributed to people presently collecting Social Security and Medicare benefits.

Go Figure...   **FICA DEDUCTION**

Example: What is the FICA deduction for Alex Calligros if his gross earnings for the week are $380?

Formula: $\left(\begin{array}{c}\text{Gross}\\\text{Earnings}\end{array} \times \begin{array}{c}\text{Social}\\\text{Security}\\\text{Tax}\end{array}\right) + \left(\begin{array}{c}\text{Gross}\\\text{Earnings}\end{array} \times \begin{array}{c}\text{Medicare}\\\text{Tax}\end{array}\right) = \text{FICA Deduction}$

Solution:
$$(\$380 \times 6.2\%) + (\$380 \times 1.45\%) = \text{FICA Deduction}$$
$$\$23.56 \qquad + \qquad \$5.51 \qquad = \$29.07$$

The amount deducted from Alex's paycheck for FICA taxes is $29.07.

As an employer you use the FICA rates to calculate how much to withhold from the taxable gross earnings of each employee for each pay period. Multiply gross earnings by the Social Security tax, and then multiply gross earnings by the Medicare tax. Add these two figures to determine the FICA deduction.

STATE AND LOCAL INCOME TAXES Many states and cities tax the earnings of people who live or work within their boundaries. In some states the taxes are simply a percentage of gross earnings. In other states, the amount owed is based on tax tables similar to the federal withholding tables issued by the IRS. Where you work or live determines whether and how state or local taxes are taken from your gross earnings.

Voluntary Deductions

Many employers deduct other amounts of money from employees' paychecks. These deductions are voluntary, meaning that the employer will deduct these amounts only if you request it. If you don't want the money deducted, it remains in your paycheck. However, once you request a voluntary deduction, it's withheld from each paycheck until you ask your employer to stop taking it out. Some common voluntary deductions include:

- Health or life insurance premiums
- Union dues
- Contributions to charities
- Pensions and other retirement plans
- Direct deposits to credit union or bank

A popular voluntary payroll deduction is a contribution to a 401(k) plan for retirement, which you learned about in Chapter 15. Many employees contribute a portion of their gross earnings to accounts in a company 401(k) plan. The funds in a 401(k) plan are tax-deferred, meaning that you don't have to pay taxes on the money that accumulates in your 401(k) plan until you withdraw it.

BTR, Inc
11432 South Letter St
Dater, CA 94432-3224

EARNINGS STATEMENT			Period Ending:	06/24
Social Security Number: 343-44-0927			Pay Date:	06/30

WALTER R. STEVENS
84432-AB SERUS DRIVE, SO.
DATER, CA 94432

Earnings	rate	hours	this period	year to date
Regular	6.18	56.00	346.08	
Other Earnings	6.18	14.00	86.52	
Gross Pay			$432.60	5,407.56

Deductions	Statutory		
	Federal Income Tax	-17.29	192.35
	Social Security Tax	-22.53	279.47
	Medicare Tax	- 5.27	65.36
	CA State Income Tax	- 2.59	31.52
	Other		
	Checking	-313.69	3,912.87
	United Way	-2.00	26.00

DISAPPEARING ACT Many people are surprised to see how much money is deducted from their gross earnings. *What are some of the items that you might see listed on the stub attached to your paycheck?*

Preparing Payroll Records

The third step in a payroll system is to prepare payroll records. Federal and state laws require all businesses to keep accurate payroll records. Employers are expected to:

- calculate earnings and deductions correctly;
- distribute employee paychecks on time;
- keep accurate payroll records;
- pay all taxes owed to government agencies on time; and
- file all required payroll reports to government agencies on time.

In order to fulfill these obligations, your business will need an efficient system for collecting, recording, and summarizing payroll information.

Preparing the Payroll Register

After collecting information for the pay period, you'll record the data on a payroll register. The *payroll register* is a document that summarizes information about employee earnings and deductions for each pay period. **Figure 19.2** shows an example of a completed payroll register for Ezra's Sport Clothes.

Notice that a payroll register has three main sections pertaining to money: Earnings, Deductions, and Net Pay. The earnings section records the regular pay, overtime pay, and gross earnings of each employee for the pay period. The deductions section of the payroll register lists and totals the various required and voluntary deductions withheld from each employee. The number of columns varies from business to business. The net pay section records the amount that remains after the total deductions are subtracted from gross earnings. For Ezra's Sport Clothes the total net pay for this week's payroll is $1,338.31.

Preparing Paychecks

Once you check the accuracy of the payroll register, you'll prepare a payroll check for each employee. This is the fourth step in a payroll system. The amount on each payroll check—often referred to as take-home pay—should equal the net pay listed for each employee. Along with the check you'll give each employee a written or printed explanation, showing how you calculated his net pay. The stubs attached to payroll checks provide this explanation and serve as a record for employees. An example of a paycheck that lists gross earnings, deductions, and net pay is shown in **Figure 19.3.**

Figure 19.2

Completed Payroll Register for Ezra's Sport Clothes

PAYROLL REGISTER

PAY PERIOD ENDING May 18   20 --   DATE OF PAYMENT May 18

	EMPLOYEE NUMBER	NAME	MAR. STATUS	ALLOW.	TOTAL HOURS	RATE	EARNINGS			DEDUCTIONS							NET PAY	CK. NO.	
							REGULAR	OVERTIME	TOTAL	SOC. SEC. TAX	MED. TAX	FED. INC. TAX	STATE INC. TAX	HOSP. INS.	UNION DUES	TOTAL			
1	3	Drummond, R.	S	0	37	7.80	288 60		288 60	17 89	4 18	35 00	5 77		5 00	67 84	220 76	186	1
2	7	Feld, D.	M	2	41	7.40	296 00	11 10	307 10	19 04	4 45	14 00	6 14	12 00		55 63	251 47	187	2
3	4	Monsalves, D.	S	0	33	8.10	267 30		267 30	16 57	3 88	32 00	5 35	7 00		64 80	202 50	188	3
4	9	Simon, J.	S	1	28	7.40	207 20		207 20	12 85	3 00	15 00	4 14		5 00	39 99	167 21	189	4
5	11	Turner, J.	S	0	42	8.20	328 00	24 60	352 60	21 86	5 11	52 00	7 05	7 00	5 00	98 02	254 58	190	5
6	6	Wyman, B.	M	2	39	7.60	296 40		296 40	18 38	4 30	14 00	5 93	12 00		54 61	241 79	191	6
24																			24
25																			25
						TOTALS	1683 50	35 70	1719 20	106 59	24 92	162 00	34 38	38 00	15 00	380 89	1338 31		

PREPARING PAYROLL   A payroll register summarizes information on employee earnings and deductions for each pay period. ***What other information is recorded on the register?***

Figure 19.3

Completed Payroll Check and Stub

Ezra's Sport Clothes
155 Gateway Blvd.
Sacramento, CA 94230

186

91-182
1721

Date_____ May 18 _____ 20 --___

Pay to the
Order of_____ Ryan Drummond _____ $ 220.76 _____

Two hundred twenty dollars and 76/100 _____ Dollars

❖ *American National Bank*
SACRAMENTO, CALIFORNIA

Agnes Werman

⑈⑈⑊⑉⑈⑂⑈⑈⑈⑉⑊⑈⑈⑊ 085 015 11890644⑈ 186

Employee Pay Statement
Detach and retain this statement.

186

| Period Ending | Earnings | | | Deductions | | | | | | | Net Pay |
	Regular	Overtime	Total	Social Security Tax	Med. Tax	Federal Income Tax	State Income Tax	Hosp. Ins.	Union Dues	Total	
5/18	288.60		288.60	17.89	4.18	35.00	5.77	–	5.00	67.84	220.76

PAYDAY The amount on each payroll check—often called "take-home pay"—should equal the net pay listed for each employee on the payroll register. *What were Ryan Drummond's gross earnings for the period ending May 18? What was his net pay?*

Direct Deposit

Instead of issuing paychecks, many businesses now offer direct deposit of employee earnings. With *direct deposit*, net pay is deposited automatically in an employee's designated bank account. As an employer you don't have to prepare a paycheck if you offer direct deposit. However, you must still give your employees a written record of their payroll information.

Employees and employers generally like direct deposit. Employees don't have to go to the bank to deposit their paychecks, they don't risk misplacing or losing a check, and funds are usually available faster. Employers can reduce the expenses of paper and labor costs in processing checks.

Automated Payroll Preparation

Today almost all businesses use some type of automated system to prepare payroll records. Computer-generated records provide an efficient and accurate system. Computers are affordable, and a variety of software packages is available for preparing payroll records and other business operations.

All information on employees, such as hourly wages or salaries, allowances, and voluntary deductions, is stored in the computer. Tax charts and percentages are updated yearly and stored in the computer as well. At the end of each pay period, the only information the employer has to enter is the number of hours each employee worked. The computer then produces the completed payroll register and paychecks for all employees. Direct deposit amounts can also be sent automatically to the appropriate banks.

Recording Payroll Information in Your Accounting Records

Once you complete the payroll register and prepare individual paychecks, the payroll must be recorded in the accounting system of your business. This is the fifth step in the payroll process. In recording the payroll, you're only recording the total amounts for the pay period. The individual amounts for each employee have already been recorded on the payroll register.

The Salaries Expense Account

Each pay period, you pay out a certain amount of money to your employees in wages or salaries. The amount you pay to all employees before any deductions are taken out is called *total gross earnings*. This is a basic operating expense of your business. You record the total gross earnings in a general ledger account titled "Salaries Expense." On the payroll register illustrated in **Figure 19.2** on page 612, the total gross earnings for the period are $1,719.20.

Deductions Become Liabilities

The amount you deduct from employee earnings for Social Security, Medicare, and other taxes or payments is subtracted from total gross earnings. This money does not belong to your company. You must pay it to the proper agencies or organizations on behalf of your employees. Therefore, all deductions taken from employees' gross earnings immediately become liabilities of your business.

In Chapter 18 you learned that in setting up your accounting system you create only the accounts that your business needs. You classified these accounts as assets, liabilities, and owner's equity. The

CHECK IT OUT This teacher likes the convenience of being paid by direct deposit. *What are some other reasons that a company might pay its employees by direct deposit?*

liabilities of your business are identified in the account title by the word "payable."

Based on the deductions shown on its payroll register in **Figure 19.2,** Ezra's Sport Clothes has the following liability accounts:

- Social Security Tax Payable
- Medicare Tax Payable
- Employees' Federal Income Tax Payable
- Employees' State Income Tax Payable
- Hospital Insurance Premium Payable
- Union Dues Payable

These items remain liabilities until your business makes the required payments to the government, insurance companies, local unions, and any other agencies or organizations.

INTERNATIONAL FINANCE   Australia

What's the world's most popular gemstone? It's made into jewelry, it's the symbol of love, and it's associated with engagements and April birthdays. If you said the diamond, you're right. Diamonds are mined on every continent except Europe and Antarctica. Diamonds are weighed in carats, a word derived from carob seeds, which were used to balance scales in ancient times. Each year the world's diamond mines yield more than 100 million carats. (One carat equals 0.007 of an ounce.) Australia produces the most, about one-third of the world's supply. Since diamonds are the hardest natural substance known, industry buys those with flaws to cut, drill, and grind other hard materials. Here's a snapshot of Australia.

Geographic area	966,153 sq. mi.
Population	18,981,000
Capital	Canberra (pop. 298,200)
Language	English, indigenous languages
Currency	Australian dollar
Gross domestic product (GDP)	$394 billion
Per capita GDP	$21,400
Economy	Industry: mining, industrial and transportation equipment, food processing, chemicals, steel.
	Agriculture: wheat, barley, sugarcane, fruits, cattle, sheep, poultry.
	Exports: coal, gold, meat, wool, alumina, iron ore, wheat.

Australia produces many of the world's diamonds.

Thinking Critically

Calculate The largest diamond ever discovered weighed 3,106 carats. How much did this diamond weigh in pounds. How many pounds of diamonds are mined worldwide each year?

For more information on Australia visit finance.glencoe.com or your local library.

Cash in Bank

After salary expenses and deductions have been recorded, the last account to be affected by payroll is Cash in Bank. Cash in Bank is the account that records all of the cash that enters or leaves the business. For the pay period shown in **Figure 19.2**, the cash account will be reduced by the total amount of net pay, which is $1,338.31. Your cash account balance will be reduced further as you make payments on your payroll liabilities.

Employer's Payroll Taxes

The amounts in the various payroll liability accounts of your business represent the taxes your employees paid on their earnings. The state and federal governments also require employers to pay additional taxes that are based on the total taxable gross earnings each pay period. This money goes toward benefits such as Social Security and unemployment and disability insurance.

Employer's Share of FICA Taxes

Federal law requires that the employer match the total amount deducted from employees' paychecks for Social Security and Medicare. In other words, if your employee pays $25, you must pay an additional $25. In **Figure 19.2** the total Social Security tax deducted from the total gross earnings for the pay period ending May 18 was $106.59. As the employer, Ezra's Sport Clothes must match this amount ($106.59) and send the government a check totaling $213.18 ($106.59 + $106.59 = $213.18). Employers also have to match Medicare deductions with an equal amount. As an employer you must match and pay Social Security tax and Medicare tax for every pay period.

Federal and State Unemployment Taxes

The employer pays both federal and state unemployment taxes. The maximum federal unemployment tax is 6.2 percent on the first $7,000 of an employee's annual wages. State unemployment tax rates and maximum taxable amounts vary among states. Employers may deduct up to 5.4 percent of the state unemployment taxes from federal unemployment taxes. Most employers, therefore, pay a federal tax of 0.8 percent (6.2% − 5.4% = 0.8%) of taxable gross earnings.

To calculate the amount to pay, you would multiply the total gross earnings for the pay period by the federal tax rate. Then multiply the

KEEPING TRACK A store like Borders bookstore employs many people working in many different areas of the business. *How do accurate payroll records help employers manage their business expenses?*

total gross earnings for the pay period by the state tax rate. Finally, add the two figures to calculate the total amount of taxes to be paid.

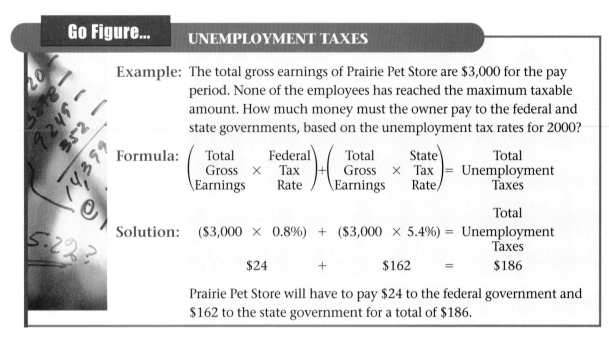

Go Figure...   **UNEMPLOYMENT TAXES**

Example: The total gross earnings of Prairie Pet Store are $3,000 for the pay period. None of the employees has reached the maximum taxable amount. How much money must the owner pay to the federal and state governments, based on the unemployment tax rates for 2000?

Formula:
$$\left(\begin{array}{c}\text{Total}\\\text{Gross}\\\text{Earnings}\end{array}\times\begin{array}{c}\text{Federal}\\\text{Tax}\\\text{Rate}\end{array}\right)+\left(\begin{array}{c}\text{Total}\\\text{Gross}\\\text{Earnings}\end{array}\times\begin{array}{c}\text{State}\\\text{Tax}\\\text{Rate}\end{array}\right)=\begin{array}{c}\text{Total}\\\text{Unemployment}\\\text{Taxes}\end{array}$$

Solution:
$$(\$3,000\times0.8\%)+(\$3,000\times5.4\%)=\begin{array}{c}\text{Total}\\\text{Unemployment}\\\text{Taxes}\end{array}$$
$$\$24\quad+\quad\$162\quad=\quad\$186$$

Prairie Pet Store will have to pay $24 to the federal government and $162 to the state government for a total of $186.

Reporting Payroll Information to the Government

The amount of money your business owes government agencies must be paid according to strict guidelines. Both the federal and state governments expect prompt payment along with the proper forms and reports. You'll need to file a variety of forms to the different levels of government. Reporting information about payments to the government is the sixth and last step in the payroll process. Current and accurate payroll information is essential in filing the reports and making the necessary payments.

RESPOND

Imagine that you are the owner of a local deli. What strategies would you use to manage payroll expenses?

Payroll Accounting in Financial Management

Accurate payroll records are essential for controlling business expenses. Good payroll records can pinpoint the labor cost for different areas of your business. They'll also indicate how much of the total gross earnings were spent on overtime. Although overtime is justified in many cases, it may also be a sign of poor use of employees.

Payroll is often the biggest expense of running a business. Therefore, it's very important to analyze carefully the payroll information of every pay period. Payroll costs can dramatically reduce your profits. However, payroll is also an area where you can reduce expenses. Good financial management requires constant review of your payroll system.

SECTION 19.1 ASSESSMENT

CHECK YOUR UNDERSTANDING

1. List the main steps in managing a payroll system.
2. What are the three most common methods of paying employees?
3. Name three required payroll deductions and three voluntary payroll deductions.
4. What are the accounts used in recording payroll?

THINK CRITICALLY

5. What might be some of the advantages and disadvantages of paying someone a salary instead of an hourly wage?

USING MATH SKILLS

6. **Eagle Earnings** Danielle is the payroll manager at Eagle Amos, a retail business that specializes in camping and hiking gear. She needs to determine the weekly gross earnings for several employees. Hourly employees earn overtime at a rate of 1.5 times the regular hourly rate and no commission. Salaried employees earn a 4 percent commission on their sales.

   Shari earns $6.75/hour and worked 44 hours.
   Rolf earns $7.35/hour and worked 40 hours.
   Litisha earns a salary of $185/week and had sales totaling $1,150.

   Calculate Help Danielle with the calculations. Which employee earned the most money this week?

SOLVING MONEY PROBLEMS

7. **Growth Spurt** Alicia runs a pool cleaning service and has almost 200 clients. Her business is growing very quickly. Now Alicia must decide whether to continue paying overtime each week to her employees or possibly hire another employee or two.
   Assess What advice would you give to Alicia? Choose the most cost-effective decision for her business.

Managing Inventory

Felix Martinez owns a small bookstore in San Diego that specializes in materials about travel in the United States and other countries. Business has been very good lately. One of Felix's most challenging tasks is deciding what books to buy and keep in stock for customers. He reviews his stock regularly to see which books are sold and which ones remain on the shelves. The decisions he makes in purchasing books can have a significant impact on his cash flow and profits.

When you own a business, one of the major drains on the financial resources of your company is the purchasing of merchandise, the items you buy with the intent to resell to customers. The amount of merchandise you have on hand at any particular time is known as inventory. Inventory is often the largest asset of a business.

Establishing an Inventory System

In order to control the purchase and sale of merchandise for your business, you must establish an inventory control system. This system tracks the quantity and cost of merchandise purchased, the merchandise in stock, and the merchandise sold to customers. Properly tracking the flow of merchandise gives you the up-to-date information you need to make management decisions. Essential items of information include:

- the amount of merchandise sold in each accounting period,
- information about which items are selling well, and
- information about which items are not selling well.

Figure 19.4 on page 620 illustrates the various stages of merchandise in a retail business.

Tracking and controlling inventory is also a major function of your accounting system. You can't make good financial decisions without accurate and current inventory information.

What You'll Learn

- How to **describe** the methods of determining inventory quantity
- How to **calculate** inventory using various costing methods
- How to **analyze** inventory turnover

Why It's Important

Maintaining adequate quantities of merchandise in inventory enables a business to meet the needs of its customers and manage cash flow more efficiently.

KEY TERMS

- **perpetual inventory system**
- **point-of-sale terminal**
- **periodic inventory system**
- **specific identification method**
- **first-in, first-out method (FIFO)**
- **last-in, first-out method (LIFO)**
- **inventory turnover**

PREDICT

Why is it important for a business to manage inventory effectively?

Importance of Controlling Inventory

Because the purchase of merchandise often requires large amounts of money, it has a great impact on your cash flow. Therefore, it's essential that you maintain the proper level of inventory. Your goal is to have enough merchandise to meet customer demand but not to overstock items.

If your inventory is too large, you may have purchased the wrong items or the wrong quantity of items. As a result, cash may not be available for operating expenses, expansion activities, or emergencies. You'll also be paying more than necessary for storage. To get rid of excess inventory, you may have to sell it at a loss—for less than you paid for it.

If your inventory is too low, customers won't have enough choices of merchandise. They may shop elsewhere, in which case you lose sales. With fewer sales, your business receives less cash. This situation has a negative effect on your cash flow.

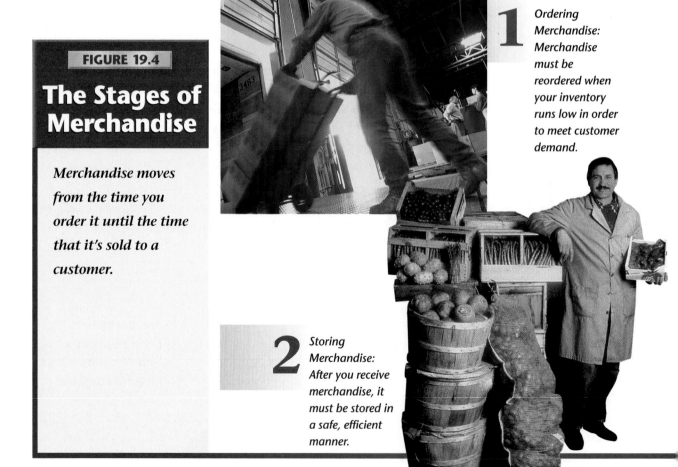

FIGURE 19.4

The Stages of Merchandise

Merchandise moves from the time you order it until the time that it's sold to a customer.

1 *Ordering Merchandise: Merchandise must be reordered when your inventory runs low in order to meet customer demand.*

2 *Storing Merchandise: After you receive merchandise, it must be stored in a safe, efficient manner.*

Can you remember how you felt when you went to a store to buy something and the store was out of that item? Disappointed customers often do not return to such a store. Satisfied customers, on the other hand, go back to businesses where they find the items they want, when they want them. Therefore, maintaining an appropriate level of inventory is a crucial element of good business management.

Determining How Much Inventory You Have

At certain points in each accounting period you may need to determine how much merchandise you have in stock. You'll also need to calculate the value of the merchandise. How do you calculate the quantity of merchandise on hand at a given point?

Two accounting methods are used to determine how much merchandise you have in inventory: the perpetual inventory system and

3 *Displaying Merchandise: Merchandise must be displayed in an appealing way that will attract customers.*

4 *Selling Merchandise: Sales of merchandise bring in cash for your business and also reduce your inventory, which must be replenished by reordering.*

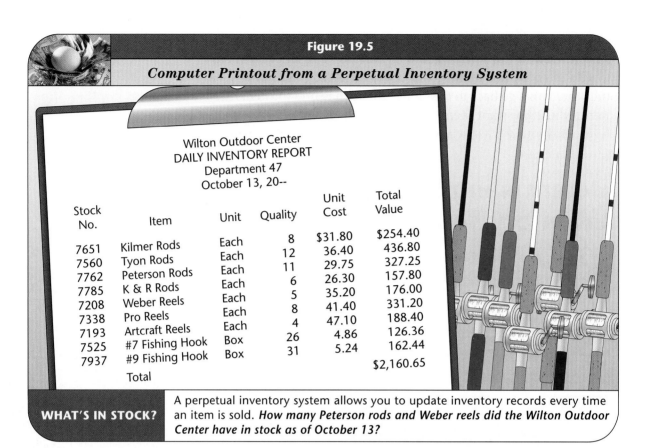

Figure 19.5

Computer Printout from a Perpetual Inventory System

Wilton Outdoor Center
DAILY INVENTORY REPORT
Department 47
October 13, 20--

Stock No.	Item	Unit	Quality	Unit Cost	Total Value
7651	Kilmer Rods	Each	8	$31.80	$254.40
7560	Tyon Rods	Each	12	36.40	436.80
7762	Peterson Rods	Each	11	29.75	327.25
7785	K & R Rods	Each	6	26.30	157.80
7208	Weber Reels	Each	5	35.20	176.00
7338	Pro Reels	Each	8	41.40	331.20
7193	Artcraft Reels	Each	4	47.10	188.40
7525	#7 Fishing Hook	Box	26	4.86	126.36
7937	#9 Fishing Hook	Box	31	5.24	162.44
	Total				$2,160.65

WHAT'S IN STOCK? A perpetual inventory system allows you to update inventory records every time an item is sold. *How many Peterson rods and Weber reels did the Wilton Outdoor Center have in stock as of October 13?*

the periodic inventory system. Both of these systems report the quantity of merchandise available for sale to customers.

The Perpetual Inventory System

A *perpetual inventory system* is a system that keeps a constant, up-to-date record of merchandise on hand. Every time an item is sold, the item is deducted from the inventory.

A perpetual inventory system allows you to determine the quantity you have on hand and the cost of the items at any time. By having current, up-to-date information, you can reorder items whenever the quantity becomes low. Then you avoid loss of sales from not having the goods your customers want.

Before the introduction of computers, this type of inventory system was impossible for most businesses to use. It was just too difficult to keep track of a large quantity of items being bought and sold. Today, however, many businesses use electronic cash registers, called *point-of-sale terminals*. These terminals are linked to a centralized computer system that keeps track of sales.

You have probably bought an item in a store where the associate passes an electronic gun or scanner over the bar code of the item you are buying. The scanner reads the bar code, you hear a beep, and the item's price appears on the screen of the point-of-sale terminal. Sales tax is automatically calculated when the items are entered. The sales slip you receive from the store lists the items you just purchased along with their prices.

In addition to recording the prices of items, point-of-sale terminals also identify the items and remove them automatically from the inventory records. When a particular item reaches a predetermined low point, the purchasing manager reorders the item so that the business doesn't run out of it. With such an automated system, businesses know the number of items sold and the number still on hand at any time. An example of a computer printout of a daily inventory report is shown in **Figure 19.5**.

It's difficult, but not impossible, for businesses that do not use computers to use a perpetual inventory system. Usually these businesses sell large items, such as cars or furniture. They usually have fewer items in stock, and they generally don't sell many items within a certain time period. As a result, it's possible for them to keep track of inventory with index cards or inventory sheets that list the items in stock. When the business sells an item, someone pulls the index card for that item from an inventory box or removes the item from an inventory sheet. Because very few items are sold each day, it's possible to maintain a noncomputerized perpetual inventory system.

The Periodic Inventory System

The other common system used to keep track of the quantity of merchandise on hand is a periodic inventory system. With a *periodic inventory system*, inventory records are updated only after someone makes an actual physical count of the merchandise on hand. You don't change inventory records every time you purchase or sell something. You count everything you have and update your inventory only after everything is counted.

Perhaps you've worked in a store and helped take inventory. If not, you may have seen a sign in a store window that read "Closed for Inventory." Businesses take a physical count of merchandise at least once a year. For most businesses the process of identifying and counting all items of merchandise is very time consuming. Therefore, inventory is usually counted when the quantity of merchandise is at its lowest point. If you have a seasonal business, this is after your peak

SCAN IT! Many stores use point-of-sale terminals and scanners to record sales. *What is the advantage of using this technology?*

CASE STUDY

Javia Novella runs Banner Dot Com. Her company designs and creates digital advertising for Web pages. Last year sales exceeded $12.5 million. Banner Dot Com employs 15 people, who live all over the United States. One of the Web designers even lives in France. Javia isn't sure how to handle payroll for her growing company. How should she handle deductions for those employees who live in states with a state income tax? Is there a special way to handle payroll for international employees? Javia plans to hire additional employees from Asia, Europe, and South America during the next two years and increase business in overseas markets. Because she is so confused, Javia turns to the experts at Standard & Poor's for advice.

STANDARD &POOR'S **Analysis:** Running a nationwide business involves additional challenges, and an international business becomes even more complex. Because Javia is able to conduct almost all aspects of her business electronically through the Internet, she will avoid many of the costs and challenges that usually come with expansion. Still, she will need to clearly understand the legal, financial, and tax aspects of each state and foreign market in which she operates.

STANDARD &POOR'S **Recommendation:** Javia should consider hiring people to work on a contract basis rather than employees. For employees she needs to withhold state and possibly local income taxes, and she needs to file the appropriate forms with her payment to each state. Javia can hire a company that offers payroll services to process this paperwork for her. For payments to her foreign workers, she can open a checking account with a financial institution that specifically provides international settlement services to small businesses. Javia will need to create service agreements that are legally binding under the laws of each country in which she does business. She will also need to file any forms required by customs and collect and remit sales and income taxes that may be imposed by international trade agreements. If she hires contract workers outside the United States, she will be subject to fewer labor laws in each country. Many foreign countries maintain trade offices that can provide Javia with information about laws in their countries.

Critical Thinking Questions
1. What do you think would be the greatest challenge in expanding a business abroad?
2. How can Javia control the risk of losing money due to a change in foreign currency rates?
3. How might a global e-commerce firm's business differ from a manufacturing company's?

sales period. In a ski shop, for example, the peak sales period is usually November through March. You would probably take inventory in May or June, when there is less merchandise to count. After taking the physical count, you can order new merchandise for the next year.

Today many businesses use electronic equipment when taking a physical inventory. An employee simply enters the stock number of each item and the quantity in stock into a handheld computer. When the physical count is complete, he or she prints an up-to-date record of the inventory items.

Even if a business uses a perpetual inventory system, it must conduct a periodic inventory at least once a year to check the accuracy of inventory records. Errors can be made in entering inventory data when you purchase merchandise. Errors can also be made at point-of-sale terminals when your business sells merchandise. Items can be lost or stolen or identified incorrectly. A periodic physical count ensures that accounting records are accurate and agree with what your business actually has in stock.

Determining the Cost of Inventory

You've determined the quantity of merchandise on hand. Now you need to calculate the cost of that merchandise. In other words, the inventory must be assigned a value. You could do this fairly easily if the cost of every item were always the same. However, that's seldom the case.

For instance, Heather Martin buys certain items for her pet store several times within a single inventory period. Often the cost of these items changes during that period. Heather might buy a specific brand and size of dog food for $9 per bag in March. She might pay $12 for the same dog food in June. How can she appropriately determine the cost of the remaining bags of dog food she still has on hand? To answer this question, businesses use one of several inventory costing methods approved by GAAP guidelines. All of these methods calculate a value for inventory on hand.

The Specific Identification Costing Method

Under the *specific identification method*, the exact cost of each item is determined and assigned to that item. The actual cost of each item is obtained from the invoice. This is the most accurate costing method. It is commonly used by businesses that sell a small number of items at high prices. These businesses include appliance stores, car dealerships, and furniture stores. Because every item must be researched, this costing method is not practical for most businesses. You'll use it only if you have few items to inventory and the cost is easy to look up.

The First-In, First-Out Costing Method

If you cannot determine the exact cost of every item in your inventory, you'll have to make an estimate. One method of estimating cost is the first-in, first-out method (FIFO). The *first-in, first-out method (FIFO)* of assigning cost assumes that the first items purchased (first in) are the first items sold (first out). It also assumes that the items the business purchased most recently are the ones on hand at the end of the period.

Matthew Lee owns a small neighborhood grocery store. One of his best-selling items is milk. Because milk is perishable, the employees stock the shelves with the milk that was purchased first. As that milk is sold, later purchases are added at the back of the shelves. The first in are the first out.

Here's an example of how the FIFO method works for Lamar's House of Music.

HOW MANY? HOW MUCH? Counting inventory and determining its value is an important task for all businesses. *Why is it important to count merchandise and assign it a value?*

TROY LASER DISC PLAYER—MODEL #875

Date	Description	Units	Cost		Total
Feb. 4	Beginning Inventory	9	$250	=	$2,250
May 12	Purchase	20	253	=	5,060
July 7	Purchase	10	258	=	2,580
Sept. 15	Purchase	12	263	=	3,156
Nov. 9	Purchase	10	265	=	2,650
	Total	61			$15,696

After taking a physical inventory, the employees at Lamar's House of Music discover that there are 12 laser disc players still in stock. Using the FIFO method, they assume that the 12 remaining players are the last ones the business purchased, because the "first in" are the "first out." They calculate the cost of the ending inventory as follows:

Nov. 9:   10 units @ $265 = $2,650
Sept. 15:   2 units @ $263 =   526
Cost of ending inventory = $3,176

The Last-In, First-Out Costing Method

Another method for calculating the value of your ending inventory is the last-in, first-out method (LIFO). The *last-in, first-out method (LIFO)* of assigning cost assumes that the last items purchased (last in) are the first items sold (first out). It also assumes that the items purchased first are still on hand at the end of the period.

For example, the Stratford Stone Company sells loose stone to contractors. When new stone arrives, it's deposited on top of the existing stone. As the stone is taken from the top of the pile, the first stones sold are the last delivered. The physical flow of the company's product, therefore, is "last-in, first-out."

If the employees at Lamar's House of Music use the LIFO method for calculating the cost of laser disc players, they would assume that the last players purchased were sold first. The earliest players are still in stock. This could happen if they pushed older items to the back of the shelves. Using the LIFO method, they would calculate the cost of ending inventory as follows:

Feb. 4:	9 units @ $250 =	$2,250
May 12:	3 units @ $253 =	$ 759
	Cost of ending inventory =	$3,009

Choosing a Costing Method

The cost of the ending inventory will vary, depending on which costing method you use. Notice that the inventory at Lamar's House of Music is valued at $3,176 using the FIFO method but at $3,009 using the LIFO method. The inventory would be valued at a different amount if the store used the specific identification method.

Businesses choose the inventory costing method that seems best for the particular type of business. Once a business chooses a method, however, it must use that method consistently. Consistent reporting helps owners and creditors compare financial reports from one accounting period to another.

Analyzing Inventory Turnover

In order to evaluate the performance of your business, you'll need to analyze current inventory information and compare it to data from previous accounting periods.

QUESTION

What can inventory turnover tell you about your business?

One type of analysis—called the *inventory turnover*—is the number of times you sell your inventory in a given time period. To calculate the inventory turnover, divide the cost of the merchandise sold in a given time period by the average inventory. (The average inventory is the value of beginning inventory plus the value of ending inventory, divided by 2).

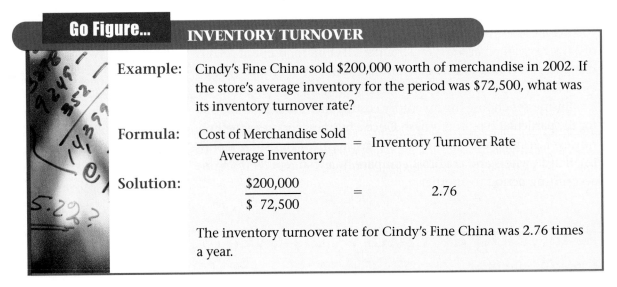

Go Figure... **AVERAGE INVENTORY**

Example: Cindy's Fine China had an inventory valued at $65,000 as of January 1, 2002, and an inventory valued at $80,000 as of December 31, 2002. What was the store's average inventory for 2002?

Formula:
$$\frac{\text{Value of Beginning Inventory} + \text{Value of Ending Inventory}}{2} = \text{Average Inventory}$$

Solution:
$$\frac{\$65,000 + \$80,000}{2} = \$72,500$$

The store's average inventory for 2002 was $72,500.

After you have determined the average inventory for a particular time period, you can calculate the inventory turnover. To do so, divide the cost of merchandise sold during that time period by the average inventory.

Go Figure... **INVENTORY TURNOVER**

Example: Cindy's Fine China sold $200,000 worth of merchandise in 2002. If the store's average inventory for the period was $72,500, what was its inventory turnover rate?

Formula:
$$\frac{\text{Cost of Merchandise Sold}}{\text{Average Inventory}} = \text{Inventory Turnover Rate}$$

Solution:
$$\frac{\$200,000}{\$72,500} = 2.76$$

The inventory turnover rate for Cindy's Fine China was 2.76 times a year.

A high inventory turnover rate means that your business has money tied up in inventory for shorter periods of time. As a result, your financing, storage, and insurance costs are reduced, which benefits your business. On the other hand, a low rate may mean that sales were lower than expected or that too many items were in inventory and remained unsold.

The inventory turnover is used to determine the number of days that merchandise is in stock. You calculate this figure by dividing the number of days in a calendar year (365) by the turnover rate.

Go Figure... NUMBER OF DAYS IN STOCK

Example: The inventory turnover for Cindy's Fine China was 2.76 in 2002 and 3.25 in 2001. How many days did the merchandise remain in stock each year?

Formula:
$$\frac{365 \text{ Days}}{\text{Turnover Rate}} = \text{Number of Days in Stock}$$

Solution:
$$\frac{365}{2.76} = \text{about 132 days} \qquad \frac{365}{3.25} = \text{about 112 days}$$

Merchandise remained in stock for about 132 days in 2002 and about 112 days in 2001.

If you find that your merchandise remains in stock for an increasing amount of time from one year to the next, you should investigate the reasons and decide whether or not to change your purchasing practices.

Payroll, Inventory, and Cash Flow

Blood flows through your body, keeping you healthy, active, and alive. Without a steady flow of blood, your body would not function properly and you would eventually die. Cash has a similar effect on a business. Cash flows through the business, giving it the financial resources it needs to operate in a healthy and profitable manner. If there is a negative flow of cash through the business, it might experience difficulty in daily operations. Cash is not available for paying bills, restocking merchandise, or expanding the business. A negative cash flow experienced over a period of time often results in the death of many businesses.

Keeping Track of Inventory

Janine is helping with inventory at her mother's jewelry store, The Silver Parrot. She's been working on birthstone pendants. After she counted them, she looked up how many were on order. Then she filled in the number to order, based on the guideline of always keeping at least five in stock.

Description	Number in Stock	Number on Order	Number to Order
January	2	3	0
February	5	0	0
March	0	3	2
April	0	3	2
May	1	3	1
June	4	3	0
July	3	3	0
August	3	0	2
September	2	0	3
October	4	0	1
November	2	3	0
December	1	3	1

Calculate Before the new product were ordered, Janine's mother decides to change the guideline to always keep 15 of each pendant in stock, rather than five. In your workbook or on a separate sheet of paper, calculate how many additional birthstone pendants Janine should order.

Payroll and inventory are two financial areas that have great influence on your cash flow and thus on the life of your business. If the inflow of cash is not sufficient to meet the demanding needs of payroll and inventory, financial problems may result. Payroll expenses must be kept to a minimum, and merchandise must be purchased with careful analysis of present and future sales markets. Careful recording, monitoring, and analysis of data involving payroll and merchandise is essential for a positive cash flow and the ability to make sound financial decisions. A successful business carefully monitors its cash flow and constantly analyzes its payroll and inventory costs.

SECTION 19.2 ASSESSMENT

CHECK YOUR UNDERSTANDING

1. Explain the difference between the perpetual inventory system and the periodic inventory system.
2. Name the various costing methods used to calculate inventory.
3. Which is better for a business—a high rate or low rate of inventory turnover? Explain your answer.

THINK CRITICALLY

4. When and why should a business conduct a physical count of its inventory?

USING COMMUNICATION SKILLS

5. **Inventory Analysis** Jerry's Junkyard sells used parts for Japanese cars. Recently Jerry hired you to analyze his current inventory information. Last year his inventory turnover rate was 16.67. This year the rate has dropped to 12.5.
   Evaluate In groups of two or three, discuss possible causes for the change in Jerry's inventory turnover rate. Then offer Jerry some suggestions. What might he do to increase his turnover rate?

SOLVING MONEY PROBLEMS

6. **Inventory Control** Aurora is planning to open a small art gallery in New York City, featuring artwork from new and emerging artists in Latin America. As she gets ready to establish her inventory system, she realizes that she'll have many decisions to make regarding how to track and control her inventory.
   Choose Decide which inventory system Aurora's art gallery should use. Explain why. Also, which costing method should Aurora use, and why?

CHAPTER 19 ASSESSMENT

CHAPTER SUMMARY

- Managing a payroll system involves the following steps: calculating gross earnings and payroll deductions, preparing payroll records and paychecks, and recording payroll information in accounting records and reports for the government.

- Three of the most common methods of paying employees are salary, hourly wage, and salary plus commission.

- The payroll deductions required by law include federal income tax, FICA taxes, and state and local income taxes (depending on where you work or live).

- Some employees request voluntary payroll deductions.

- The accounts used in recording payroll include Salaries Expense, liability accounts, and Cash in Bank.

- Two methods of accounting are used to determine how much merchandise you have in inventory: the perpetual inventory system and the periodic inventory system.

- The specific identification method; the first-in, first-out method (FIFO); and the last-in, first-out method (LIFO) are three accounting methods used to determine the cost of inventory for a business.

- The inventory turnover rate provides one measure by which to evaluate the performance of a business.

Internet zone

Understanding and Using Vocabulary

Imagine that a business is advertising two job openings: one for someone who can process payroll and the other for someone who will manage inventory. Working with a partner, write a series of questions for the job candidates. Interview each other, taking turns playing the two roles.

payroll
pay period
gross earnings
salary
hourly wage
overtime rate
commission

deductions
Federal Insurance
    Contributions Act
    (FICA)
Social Security tax
Medicare tax
payroll register

direct deposit
total gross earnings
perpetual inventory
    system
point-of-sale terminal
periodic inventory
    system

specific identification
    method
first-in, first-out
    method (FIFO)
last-in, first-out
    method (LIFO)
inventory turnover

Review Key Concepts

1. Describe the process of calculating gross earnings for an employee who is paid an hourly wage.
2. What are FICA taxes?
3. Why is the money deducted from your employees' gross earnings a liability to your business?

CHAPTER 19 ASSESSMENT

4. What is the purpose of an inventory control system?
5. Discuss the three methods of calculating the value of inventory on hand.

Computer Activity As an alternative activity, use a spreadsheet program to design a sample payroll register.

Apply Key Concepts

1. Why would inaccurate paychecks be a problem for both an employer and an employee?
2. Is it acceptable to run a business that does not report payroll information to the government? Explain your reasoning.
3. Predict the consequences of not paying an employee's voluntary deductions.
4. Think about a retail store where you shop frequently. Explain whether or not you feel that the store is able to maintain the proper level of inventory.
5. Why is it difficult for some businesses to use a perpetual inventory system?

 ### *Problem Solving Today*

PAYROLL CONSULTANT

You've just been hired to design a new payroll system for Lasertronics Corporation. The company offers health insurance and a retirement plan that require contributions from both the company and its employees.

Design Write a memo to the owner of Lasertronics describing the payroll system you plan to set up for the company. Be sure to describe how you'll collect and process all the information needed to prepare paychecks and reports. Describe the accounting procedures you will follow.

Real-World Application

CONNECT WITH LANGUAGE ARTS

Marla works for a family-owned bicycle shop that uses a manual inventory system. The shop has a computer, which it uses for accounting and other tasks, and the owner feels that it's time to computerize the inventory. Marla intends to contact several businesses to get information.

Think Critically Help Marla create a list of five questions she could ask about computerized inventory systems.

FINANCE *Online*

KNOW THE CODE

Point-of-sale terminals and bar coding are integral parts of a perpetual inventory system. Imagine that you own a small business. You want to find out more about how these tools can help you manage your inventory more efficiently.

Connect Using a variety of search engines, look for information about how bar codes function in an automated inventory system. Specifically, find the following information:

1. What are the advantages of bar coding?
2. What equipment is necessary to use bar coding to manage inventory?
3. How much does an automated inventory system cost?

Get a Financial Life!

CASE STUDY

A Business Is Born

Overview

Karla and David Farnier have two children: Eva, age 23, and Jack, age 22. Eva and Jack graduated from college without any debt—thanks to smart planning, saving, and investing by their parents. While they were in college, they worked and started saving their own money for a retail store they would open together someday. Eva and Jack have written their business plan for Party Town, where they will sell party decorations, paper goods, balloons, and games. Now it's time to begin finalizing their plan.

Resources

- Assorted magazines and newspapers
- Internet
- Portfolio (ring binder or file folder)
- Public or school library
- Word processor

Procedures

 Step A THE PROCESS

Eva and Jack are aware that having a strong financial background will be crucial to the success of their business. Therefore, they have asked you for some assistance with the financial operations of their business—accounting, payroll, and inventory management.

1. Eva and Jack are ready to hire a bookkeeper. They have asked you to help them choose the right employee. Make a list of the skills and characteristics the new employee should have. Write a newspaper ad for the position.

2. Set up a recordkeeping system for Eva and Jack. Include the following: the accounting period, the list of accounts they might use, the source documents they should maintain, and the computer software you would recommend. Then ask a local businessperson to review your recommendations and make suggestions as needed.

3. Investigate the various ways in which workers can be paid—hourly wage, salary, commission, and piecework (per job). Create a list of the advantages and disadvantages of each type of pay, from both employees' and employers' point of view. Make a recommendation to Eva and Jack about how they should pay their employees.

4. Recommend an inventory management system for Party Town, and explain your reasoning. If possible, research a similar store in your community and learn about the inventory management system it uses. Provide as many details as possible.

5. Identify a total of at least ten books, magazines, newspapers, and Web sites that could be used by someone who was interested in starting a business. The resources should focus primarily on accounting, payroll, and inventory management.

UNIT 5

Step B   CREATE YOUR PORTFOLIO

As you work through the process, save the results so that you can refer, review, and refine. Create a portfolio with four sections to showcase the information that you collected in Step A.

1. Section 1 should include the newspaper ad you created for the bookkeeper position as well as a description of the recordkeeping system you designed.

2. Section 2 should include your views on the advantages and disadvantages of the various ways in which workers can be paid and your recommendation to Eva and Jack.

3. Section 3 should describe the inventory management system that you recommended. If you were able to gather research from a store in your community, place it in this section.

4. The last section will be a bibliography of the resources that you identified.

Step C   APPLYING TECHNOLOGY

The globalization of the marketplace, advances in technology, and the downsizing of the workforce are trends that are transforming the workplace and the worker. Technology is providing ways for people to work anytime and anyplace. The workers of tomorrow must have strong technical skills and be willing to update those skills as the technology changes. People who are flexible and technically savvy will be successful.

1. Research an emerging technology and its impact on the workplace. Some suggested topics include: computers, artificial intelligence, e-books, video telephones, global positioning equipment, video conferencing, palmtop computers, and voice and eye recognition.

2. Contact a vendor who sells the products you selected to research. Find out how much they cost and what the projected sales are for the next year. If possible, ask the vendor to come to your class to demonstrate the products.

3. Create a poster, brochure, or other visual aid about your selected technology. Include the features and benefits of the product.

4. Write a two-page paper outlining your predictions for the ways in which technology will affect the workplace and the economy in the years to come.

UNIT 6

ORGANIZATION AND FINANCIAL PLANNING

*U*nit 6 explains the importance of wise financial planning and selecting the appropriate form of business. The next three chapters will describe the different forms of business ownership, how a financial plan is created, and strategies for pricing, costing, and growth.

READING STRATEGIES

To get the most out of your reading

- ■ **PREDICT** what the section will be about.
- ■ **CONNECT** what you read with your own life.
- ■ **QUESTION** as you read to make sure you understand the content.
- ■ **RESPOND** to what you've read.

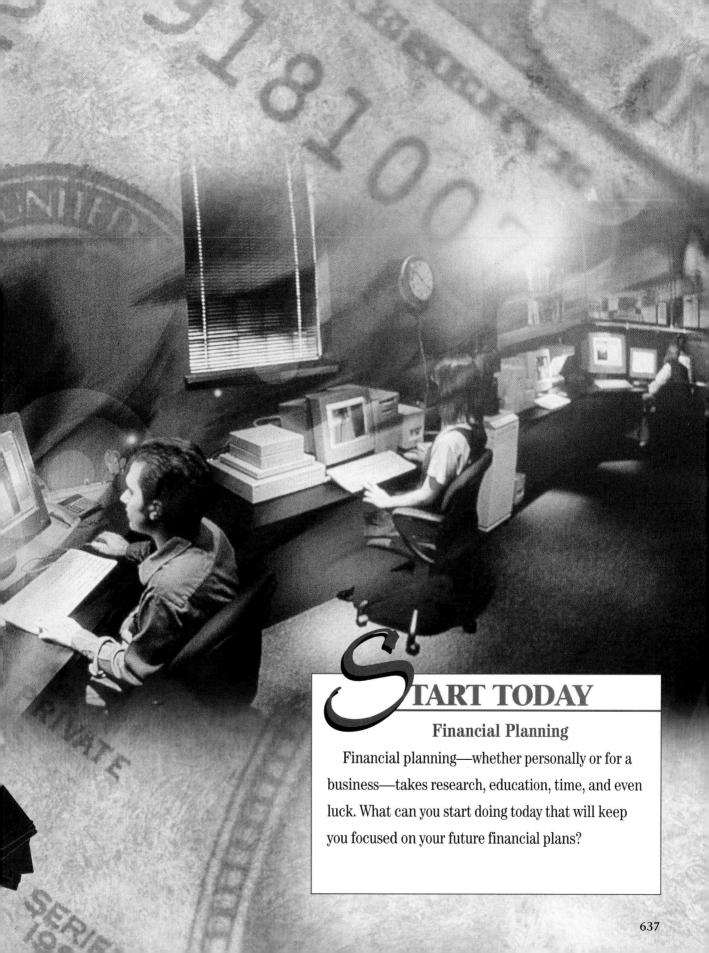

START TODAY

Financial Planning

Financial planning—whether personally or for a business—takes research, education, time, and even luck. What can you start doing today that will keep you focused on your future financial plans?

Types of Business Ownership

STANDARD
&POOR'S

Q&A

Q: Why would I want all the hassles of setting up a corporation? I think a sole proprietorship is the only way to go—you get to keep all the profits for yourself.

A: Each type of corporate structure offers certain advantages and disadvantages. Net income from a sole proprietorship is taxed at personal income tax rates, while a corporation's profits are taxed at lower, corporate tax rates. Also, an individual sole proprietor has unlimited personal liability for the business, while shareholders of a corporation have limited liability.

The Sole Proprietorship and the Partnership

oe Cartesano often stops by Wheels for Trails, a small bike shop in his town. An avid mountain biker, Joe likes to admire the many models of mountain bikes in the shop. He also dreams of opening a shop of his own someday. Joe visits Wheels for Trails so often that he has become well acquainted with the two people who work there regularly—an elderly man and a young woman. For a long time he thought that the man owned the shop. Recently, however, he was surprised to learn that the man and woman are actually business partners.

Is there a successful small business in your town or neighborhood? Perhaps it's a hair salon, a video store, or a local restaurant. Have you ever asked yourself who owns that business? As Joe Cartesano found out, you can't always determine the ownership of a business by its size or success. The salon may be owned by one person, the video store by partners, and the restaurant by several people.

Business Ownership Organization

When you start a business, you'll have a choice as to how the ownership is legally organized. Business ownership can take one of three legal forms: sole proprietorship, partnership, or corporation. It's important to select the form that best suits your needs and those of your business. This section will describe the first two forms of business ownership and examine the advantages and disadvantages of each one.

What You'll Learn

- How to **identify** the advantages and disadvantages of a sole proprietorship
- How to **explain** the differences between general and limited partners
- How to **identify** the advantages and disadvantages of a partnership

Why It's Important

Selecting the proper form of organization for your business can be an essential factor in its success.

KEY TERMS

- sole proprietorship
- Employer Identification Number (EIN)
- unlimited liability
- limited life
- partnership
- partnership agreement
- general partner
- agency power
- limited partner

The Sole Proprietorship

The word "sole" means "single" or "one." The word "proprietor" means "owner." A *sole proprietorship*, therefore, is a business owned by one person. This is the oldest and most common form of business ownership. More than 75 percent of all businesses in the United States today are organized as sole proprietorships. Although many people think of corporations when they think about business in the United States, the sole proprietorship is still the backbone of American business.

Most sole proprietorships are small business operations owned by an entrepreneur. Many provide services, such as auto repair, house cleaning, carpentry, or plumbing. They generally operate out of

PREDICT

What are the advantages and disadvantages of owning a business as a sole proprietorship?

What's Your Financial ID?

WHAT KIND OF BUSINESS WOULD YOU START?

You could start a business for virtually any activity. In this quiz use your imagination to the fullest. Just for fun, review the following list of businesses and choose five that you could imagine owning. Write your answers on a separate sheet of paper.

_____ a. car repair
_____ b. photographic studio
_____ c. veterinary clinic
_____ d. rock group
_____ e. gourmet coffee shop
_____ f. graphic artist studio
_____ g. newsletter or other publishing enterprise
_____ h. computer software

_____ i. biotechnology lab
_____ j. bed-and-breakfast inn
_____ k. architectural firm
_____ l. medical care
_____ m. hair salon
_____ n. tutoring service
_____ o. detective

What do your choices say about you?

- If you selected **b, d, f, g,** or **k,** you're probably **artistic**. Your strongest interests are in the creative arts or working in a field that requires originality and imagination.

- If you selected **e, j, l, m,** or **n,** you're probably **social**. You enjoy helping others and working closely with people.

- If you selected **a, c, h, i,** or **o,** you're probably **investigative**. You like the challenge of making decisions and coming up with innovative solutions.

- Were your selections from one category—artistic, social, or investigative—or from a combination of categories? Look to see if you have stronger interests in one area over another. Which types of daily activities do you prefer—artistic, social, or investigative?

BACKBONE OF AMERICA Small businesses have traditionally been the backbone of the American economy. *Can you name any small businesses that have started in your area recently?*

homes, small offices, and storefronts. Although some sole proprietorships become quite successful, many eventually fail. In all cases, however, the owners of sole proprietorships are pursuing their dream of running their own business.

Debbi Fields, for example, had a dream of selling cookies. She created a highly successful business—Mrs. Fields Cookies. John Johnson wanted to start a magazine. He borrowed $500 from his family and created the successful *Ebony* magazine. Even some major corporations got their start as risky ventures by entrepreneurs. Corning would not exist without Amory Houghton, and there would be no Colgate-Palmolive without the determination of William Colgate. All of these people started their businesses as sole proprietorships.

Advantages of the Sole Proprietorship

Organizing your business as a sole proprietorship has several advantages. The most important is that you have total freedom to do as you want with your business. You're the boss! You make all the decisions. However, besides giving you total control, this form of business organization has other advantages.

EASY TO SET UP If you want to start a small business, a sole proprietorship is the easiest form of business organization to set up. Although local and state governments require some paperwork, you can usually complete this without much difficulty.

In many cases you can organize a sole proprietorship merely by obtaining a license to do business from your local or state government. You may also need to obtain a state sales tax number because you may be required to collect sales tax on any items you sell to customers.

If you're planning to operate under a business name other than your own name, you'll have to apply for a Certificate of Doing Business Under an Assumed Name. This is also referred to as a DBA, which stands for "doing business as." For example, Ms. Jontos wants to start a personalized wedding planning service. She has decided to call her business Time to Remember. In order to operate legally under this business name, Ms. Jontos will need to get a DBA certificate.

If you intend to hire one or more employees to work in your business, you'll need to get an Employer Identification Number. An *Employer Identification Number (EIN)* is assigned by the Internal Revenue Service, and the government uses the number for income tax purposes. Many sole proprietors hire managers and several employees. Some large companies organized as sole proprietorships have hundreds of employees.

Careers in Finance

GENERAL CONTRACTOR

Whenever a dream home is built, an office building is constructed, or a kitchen is remodeled, a general contractor oversees the project. Being one's own boss and seeing ideas and plans materialize make general contracting a satisfying job. Contractors estimate costs, make bids, order supplies, and hire and coordinate work crews and subcontractors. They're responsible for large sums of other people's money, which they use to pay bills, subcontractors, and other laborers. Contractors must be able to read blueprints and diagrams and make sure projects are finished on time, meeting building codes and standards. Most general contractors enjoy building something that will last for years.

Skills	Accounting, communication, decision making, management, math, negotiation, organizational, problem solving, time management
Personality	Able to see the big picture, independent, likes working with people and building things
Education	High school diploma or associate degree in building construction; experience in the field; must pass contractor's license exam
Pay range	$30,000 to $100,000 plus a year, depending on experience, location, and company

Identify What are some of the ways that contractors use math skills on a daily basis?

For more information on general contractors visit finance.glencoe.com or your local library.

Although starting a sole proprietorship takes some effort, it's still the easiest form of business organization to set up. Because a minimal amount of documentation is required, the cost of organizing a sole proprietorship is also low.

OWNER HAS TOTAL CONTROL As a sole proprietor you can run your business as you wish. This is a great advantage because you don't have to convince partners or other people that your business decisions are sound. You can choose what merchandise to sell or services to provide, what prices to charge, and what hours you'll work. As the sole owner of your business, you make all management and financial decisions.

OWNER KEEPS ALL PROFITS With a sole proprietorship, when your business makes a profit, you get to keep all of it (after you pay taxes). As your business grows and becomes more successful, you'll receive larger profits. A sole proprietorship allows you alone to reap the rewards of your hard work and determination.

FEW GOVERNMENT REGULATIONS Another benefit of operating as a sole proprietorship is that you don't have to complete and file many forms and reports with the state and federal governments. Although there may be some government regulations regarding your particular business, most sole proprietorships experience little government red tape.

PROFITS TAXED ONLY ONCE A business organized as a sole proprietorship does not pay income taxes as a company. You, the owner, must declare the profits of the business on your personal income tax return. Your tax is computed on your total income for the year. If you operate your business full-time, any profits you make will be counted as taxable income. If your business is only part-time and you also have a full-time job, your taxable income will include both income from your job and the net income from your business.

Common Cents

Shop by Phone

Instead of driving from store to store, use your telephone to see if a store has the item that you're looking for and to compare prices. You'll save gas and time.

Disadvantages of the Sole Proprietorship

With most choices people make in the world, there always seems to be a good side and a bad side. Although organizing your business as a sole proprietorship has some definite advantages, this form of business organization also has several drawbacks.

LIMITED CAPITAL When you start a sole proprietorship, the only source of working capital, other than money you borrow, is your own money. Generally, no one else helps you finance the business. Moreover, the amount of cash available to you is often limited. In Chapter 17 you learned the importance of adequate funding and the need to maintain a positive cash flow in a business. Without a

sufficient amount of money to establish the business, begin operations, and expand, you could have serious difficulties.

UNLIMITED LIABILITY A major disadvantage of a sole proprietorship is that if your business is not successful, you're responsible for all losses. Known as *unlimited liability*, this responsibility means that if the business owes money, you may have to pay the debts out of your personal assets. In other words, if your business is unsuccessful, you could lose your car, home, savings, and other assets. If your business's financial situation is very bad, you may be forced to declare personal bankruptcy.

Starting any new business involves a high risk. More than half of all businesses fail within five years after being established. If your business fails, your personal financial position and credit rating could be seriously damaged. Careful financial management of your business is essential.

LIMITED HUMAN RESOURCES An advantage of a sole proprietorship is that you're the only decision maker in the business. Unfortunately, being the only one in charge can also be a disadvantage. When you're the sole owner, you can't rely on other individuals to help carry the load.

People have limited knowledge and talents. Perhaps you know a lot about a certain product or service, but your basic business skills are weak. For example, if you start a painting business, you may have skills in painting, be able to identify different types of paint, and know the proper way to apply paint to different surfaces. At the same time, you may have limited experience in pricing, recordkeeping, or advertising.

Poor decisions in purchasing, accounting, or marketing can ruin your business, even when you have a lot of knowledge about your product or service. Two or three heads are better than one because each person brings different talents and skills to the business.

LIMITED LIFE A sole proprietorship has a *limited life*, which means that when the owner leaves the business or dies, the business ceases to exist. Your business also legally ends if you sell it to someone else. In that case a new business is created in the name of the new owner.

The Partnership

When starting a business with other people, you may choose to form a partnership. A *partnership* is a business owned by two or more persons. These partners voluntarily agree to operate the business, for profit, as co-owners. When a partnership is formed, a special legal agreement is drawn up. Known as a *partnership agreement*, this written document basically states how the partnership will be organized. The agreement usually includes the following information:

- Names of the partners
- Name and nature of the business
- Amount of investment by each partner
- Duties, rights, and responsibilities of each partner
- Procedures for sharing profits and losses
- How assets will be divided when and if the partnership is dissolved

In a partnership you and your co-owners decide how to divide profits and losses from the business. You'll also outline the duties and responsibilities of each partner. All partners must agree to the conditions stated in the partnership agreement. The purpose of this written document is to prevent later disagreements among the partners.

Partnerships account for only about 7 percent of all businesses in the United States today. However, some large corporations began as partnerships. For example, in 1876 an icebox maker named Abram Anderson started a partnership with a fruit merchant named Joseph Campbell. Their small partnership eventually grew to become the Campbell Soup Company.

General Partners and Limited Partners

Within the category of partnerships there are two basic types of partners. In many partnerships all partners are general partners. *General partners* have decision-making authority, usually take an active role in the operation of the business, and have unlimited liability for all losses or debts of the partnership. Every partnership has one or more general partners.

All general partners have what is known as agency power. *Agency power*, also known as mutual agency, means that any partner has the right to sign contracts that are legally binding on the partnership. For example, suppose that Dylan, Juanita, and Charles form a partnership to make bookcases. Dylan goes to Clinton Wood Products and signs a contract to purchase wood from that company. Dylan acted on behalf of the business, and the partnership is legally obligated under this contract.

A partnership can also add limited partners. *Limited partners* rarely take an active role in decision making or in running the business. Their liability in the partnership is limited to the amount of

YOU'RE THE BOSS In a sole proprietorship the owner makes all the decisions and takes all the responsibility. One person can't be knowledgeable and skilled in everything, however. *In what areas do you think small business owners are probably most lacking in skill and knowledge?*

their investment in the business. Suppose, for example, that Chris Clark is a limited partner in Low Country Furniture, with $25,000 invested in the business. Chris won't be involved in running the business. Moreover, her financial liability is limited to her $25,000 investment. If the business fails, that's the most she can lose.

Advantages of the Partnership

Many of the advantages of forming a partnership are similar to the advantages of a sole proprietorship. However, instead of being the sole decision maker in a business, you now share decision making with your partners. More people can mean more ideas and more money.

EASY TO SET UP A partnership, like a sole proprietorship, is relatively easy to set up. Although some paperwork is required, it's generally minimal. You may need to obtain certain local or state business permits or licenses. For some types of business operations, you must also know and follow various government regulations.

The most important legal document of a partnership is the partnership agreement. It's essential that all the terms and conditions of the partnership are clearly stated in this written document. Taking care to make the agreement as complete and clear as possible will help you to avoid problems of interpretation as the partnership grows.

MORE SKILLS AND KNOWLEDGE In a sole proprietorship the skills and knowledge needed to operate the business are the responsibility of one person. With a partnership, on the other hand, the various partners can contribute different skills and experience. One person may have previous experience running a similar type of business. Another might have extensive business or accounting training. A third partner might have excellent sales and marketing skills. The pooling of talent and knowledge is an advantage that partnerships have over going it alone.

For example, in 1872 dry goods merchant Levi Strauss received a letter from one of his customers, a Nevada tailor named Jacob Davis. Davis had been making overalls for miners and had come up with a way to strengthen the pants by adding rivets to the seams. He wanted to patent his idea but couldn't afford the $68 he needed to file the papers. He wrote to Strauss to suggest that they hold the patent together. When Strauss teamed with Davis in 1873, Levi jeans became a reality.

AVAILABLE CAPITAL Several individuals generally bring more money to a business venture than one person acting alone with only personal assets. Moreover, if additional cash is needed to maintain or expand business operations, it's generally easier to raise capital when several people are working to do so.

Obtaining bank financing is often easier when more than one individual is responsible for the loan. Banks may also be more willing to loan greater sums of money to partnerships than to a sole proprietorship because the risk is shared among the partners.

The credit ratings of your partners are very important. Be careful about entering a partnership agreement with anyone who has a questionable credit rating. The ability of all partners to borrow money may be an important factor in the success or failure of your business.

PARTNERS HAVE TOTAL CONTROL When you form a partnership, the operation of the business is the sole responsibility of the general partners, who can do as they want. However, the partners are also responsible for the success or failure of the business.

PROFITS TAXED ONLY ONCE Like a sole proprietorship, a partnership is not taxed as a business. Therefore, it does not owe state or federal income taxes. The partnership agreement states how the profits of the partnership are to be divided. Each partner must pay personal income taxes to the state and federal government, based on the share of the profits he or she receives. Thus, business profits are taxed only once.

Disadvantages of the Partnership

A number of problems can arise when several people own and operate a business. While partnerships ease some of the problems associated with sole proprietorships, they still have disadvantages.

PROFESSIONAL PARTNERSHIPS Partnerships are quite common among professional groups, such as architects, lawyers, and accountants. *Can you name groups of people in other occupations that might tend to form partnerships?*

UNLIMITED LIABILITY Earlier in this section you learned that the owner of a sole proprietorship has unlimited liability. The same holds true for the general partners in a partnership. If the partnership loses money or has financial problems, each co-owner is personally responsible for all of the debts of the business. In other words, if your partnership fails and the debts of the business cannot be covered by its assets, you and your partners are responsible for paying the bills out of your own personal assets.

Suppose that two friends ask you to join them in forming a partnership. You have a large amount of personal assets. Your two partners have very few assets. If the business fails, you could end up being personally responsible for the majority of the business debts. You

STANDARD &POOR'S

CASE STUDY

*J*ulia is a stay-at-home mom with two children. Like many young couples, she and her husband, Dave, struggle with their bills. Before choosing to stay home, Julia was an editor for a publishing company. She is now looking for a home-based business and is thinking of starting an editing service. She has also been researching other businesses over the Internet and in the newspaper. There appear to be many opportunities. One recent ad offered the following, *"Need people eager to earn $2,000 to $3,000 per month part-time from home. Training provided. This is the chance to start the business you have always wanted."* Julia is skeptical and thinks it sounds too good to be true. However, she wants a professional opinion, so she turned to the experts at Standard & Poor's for advice.

Analysis: Families with young children often must make a choice between foregoing income so that one or both parents can care for the children at home, or earning more money but also paying child-care expenses. Julia is right in being skeptical of the advertisement she saw. Many home-based employment opportunities are low-paying "piece-work" jobs–assembling wooden toys for example. Working at home can be rewarding, but Julia needs to consider that starting a business often requires a great deal of time.

Recommendation: Julia and Dave should think critically about any business opportunity that requires them to invest money to get started. If Julia is interested in an advertised opportunity, she should ask for a written agreement from the company and review it with an attorney before making any investment. She should ask to speak with other investors in this type of business. Julia can also check to see if complaints against the company have been filed with her local Better Business Bureau. Finally, Julia and Dave need to be realistic about how much time Julia will be able to devote to developing a business. She will need to identify how many hours she is available to work.

Critical Thinking Questions

1. Why should Julia be skeptical of advertisements that sound too good to be true?
2. If Julia starts her own editing service, what type of business ownership should she choose?
3. How could Julia find clients for her editing service?

could even lose everything you own. It's very important to choose your business partners carefully. Know the personal financial position of each partner. Remember, each partner has unlimited liability for the entire business, not just part of it.

In 1975 two young men named Bill Gates and Paul Allen entered a partnership. Although personal computers were only a new, up-and-coming product at the time, they decided to form a company to produce computer software. Today their company, Microsoft, is a major corporation. Bill Gates and Paul Allen are two of the wealthiest people in the world.

CONNECT

Imagine that you and a few of your friends want to open a business selling memorabilia for your high school class. Describe how your different skills might complement each other.

Microsoft is a partnership that turned into one of America's greatest success stories. Most partnerships, however, never come close to this level of achievement. Many have very little success and eventually fail. Entering a partnership involves large financial risks.

DISAGREEMENT AMONG PARTNERS It's great to share the responsibility for running a business with others. Unfortunately, when several people are involved in managing a business, they may not always agree on important business decisions. A common reason for failed partnerships is that the partners have serious conflicts about how the business should operate, and they allow the business to suffer from these conflicts financially.

PROFITS MUST BE SHARED Perhaps hard work and determination on your part are the crucial factors in the success of the business. Nevertheless, you still must share the profits with your partners. The way in which you and your partners divide the profits of the business is outlined in the partnership agreement.

LIMITED LIFE The life of a partnership depends on the willingness and ability of the partners to continue in business together. Like a sole proprietorship, a partnership has a limited life. Partnerships can end for a number of reasons. Perhaps a partner dies or decides to retire or withdraw from the partnership

because of illness or for some other reason. The partners may disagree and decide to end their partnership, or they may decide to add new partners. In such instances the original partnership dissolves. The remaining partners, along with any new partners, should then draw up a new partnership agreement, which will create a new business.

SECTION 20.1 ASSESSMENT

CHECK YOUR UNDERSTANDING

1. As a sole proprietor, you can run your business as you wish. Why is this an advantage?
2. What is the difference between a general and a limited partner?
3. Name several disadvantages of a partnership.

THINK CRITICALLY

4. In your opinion, what is the most important element of a partnership agreement? Explain your reasoning.

USING COMMUNICATION SKILLS

5. **Perturbed Partners** Lawrence and Tyrell are partners in a small retail business. They sell hats and T-shirts from a kiosk in a shopping mall. Recently they've been thinking about selling other items as well, but they haven't been able to agree on what items to add to their product line. Their disagreements have caused the business to suffer financially.
   Advise What advice might you offer Lawrence and Tyrell to help them work out their differences? What solutions would you suggest? Write down your suggestions.

SOLVING MONEY PROBLEMS

6. **Business Ownership Decisions** Pamela owns a pet-sitting business. People hire her to take care of their pets when they go out of town. As part of her service, Pamela will also bring in her clients' mail and water their plants. Her business is booming, and she needs to make some critical decisions about its future.
   Critical Thinking Help Pamela decide what to do now. Should she expand her business? Add employees? Take on a partner? Make sure that you evaluate the advantages and disadvantages of each suggestion you offer.

The Corporation

June Lee has an importing business in Seattle that she started seven years ago as a sole proprietorship. Since then her company, East Meets West, has been growing steadily, and it is now quite successful. June is at a point where she would like to expand the business, perhaps by opening branches in other cities such as San Francisco, Chicago, and New York. However, expansion requires more investment and involves much greater risk. June wonders whether it might be time to form a corporation. You learned earlier in the chapter that the organization of sole proprietorships and partnerships is similar and that both have advantages and disadvantages. Both also have unlimited liability for owners such as June Lee. Corporations are set up very differently from sole proprietorships or partnerships. They provide owners with a certain amount of financial protection.

What Is a Corporation?

You've heard the word "corporation" and can probably name a number of large corporations, such as IBM, General Motors, Hershey Foods, Sony, Hewlett-Packard, Motorola, Xerox, and Goodyear. What is a corporation? What makes it different from a sole proprietorship or a partnership?

A *corporation* is a business organization that operates as a legal entity separate from its owners and is treated by law as if it were an individual person. A corporation can do everything that a sole proprietorship or a partnership can do: own property, buy and sell merchandise, pay bills, and make contracts. It can also sue others and be sued. Although only about 20 percent of businesses in the United States are organized as corporations, they produce about 90 percent of the total business revenue in the nation.

Starting a Corporation

In forming a corporation, you're creating a legal entity. This involves a much more complex process than starting either a sole proprietorship or a partnership.

What You'll Learn

- How to **summarize** the process of forming a corporation
- How to **describe** two types of corporations
- How to **discuss** the advantages and disadvantages of a corporation

Why It's Important

This form of business ownership is a driving force in the American economy.

KEY TERMS

- corporation
- articles of incorporation
- corporate charter
- corporate bylaws
- going public
- board of directors
- limited liability company (LLC)
- franchise

CORPORATE POWER Corporations produce about 90 percent of all business revenue in the United States. *Why do you think this is the case?*

Paperwork and Documents

The first thing you must do to create a corporation is to file an application with the state for permission to operate. The application to operate as a corporation is called the *articles of incorporation*. On the application you'll need to include such information as your corporate name and the type of business in which the corporation will be involved.

When the state approves your application, it issues a corporate charter. A *corporate charter* is a license to operate a corporation. The charter is an official registration of your corporation. It states the purpose of your business and spells out the laws and guidelines under which it will operate. It also officially allows you to do business under your corporate name.

In addition to the articles of incorporation, you'll have to write a set of corporate bylaws. *Corporate bylaws* are the rules by which a corporation will operate. Items in the bylaws will include how you'll elect directors of the corporation and when stockholders will meet. The corporate bylaws can be changed or amended by the stockholders of the corporation at any time.

Issuing Stock

The ownership of a corporation is divided into units called shares of stock. These shares of stock are bought by people who become known as stockholders. Stockholders are the legal owners of the corporation. If you buy even one share of stock in Xerox, for example, you're legally considered to be an owner and have all the rights of ownership. Each stockholder receives a stock certificate, a document that acts as proof of ownership. Small corporations may have only a few stockholders. Larger corporations, such as Kodak and GTE, have thousands.

CLOSELY HELD CORPORATIONS A closely held, or private, corporation is one whose shares are owned by a relatively small group of people and are not traded openly in stock markets. In many cases there are only three or four stockholders. Many small and family businesses are organized as closely held corporations.

PUBLICLY HELD CORPORATIONS A publicly held, or public, corporation is one that sells its shares openly in stock markets, where anyone can buy them. Most of these corporations trade their stock on an exchange, such as the New York Stock Exchange or the American Stock Exchange. Almost all major corporations, such as Black & Decker, Intel, and American Express, are publicly held.

GOING PUBLIC A closely held corporation can be opened to the general public if the stockholders decide in favor of this move. When a corporation decides to sell its stock on the open market, it is said to be "*going public*."

Advantages of the Corporation

Establishing your business as a corporation has a number of advantages over a sole proprietorship and a partnership.

Easy to Raise Capital

A major advantage of corporations is their ability to sell stock. If the corporation needs money for growth, expansion, or other purposes, additional shares of stock can be sold to raise the necessary funds. If a large amount of capital is needed to start a business, it often begins as a closely held corporation rather than a partnership. Examples are an automobile dealership, a restaurant, or an amusement park.

Limited Liability

A great advantage to the stockholders, or owners, of a corporation is that they have limited liability. This means that if the corporation has debts or financial problems, they are liable only for the amount of their investment.

Consider the following example. You own $20,000 worth of stock in the Family Fun Restaurant. The restaurant is not successful and goes out of business while owing thousands of dollars to its creditors. As a stockholder, you can lose up to $20,000, or the amount of your investment, to help repay these debts. You're not personally responsible for any debt beyond that amount, however. Unlike a sole proprietorship or a general partnership, a corporation leaves your personal assets protected. You're not legally responsible for all the debts that the corporation owes.

Continued Life

When a sole proprietor retires, dies, or sells his or her business to someone else, that business ceases to exist. Each time partners enter or leave a partnership, a new partnership must be created. In

WHO OWNS THAT TEAM? Professional sports teams are operated under all forms of business ownership. The Indiana Pacers are privately owned. Some, such as the Boston Celtics, are public corporations. *What would happen if such a sports team experienced a change in owners?*

a corporation, however, a change in owners does not end the legal operation of the business. Stockholders may enter or leave at any time without affecting the existence of the corporation. Its legal status continues indefinitely.

Separation of Ownership and Management

In most publicly held corporations the owners do not run the business. Instead they elect a *board of directors*, a group of individuals who are responsible for overseeing the general affairs of the corporation. Corporate officers and professional managers are hired to make day-to-day decisions in running the business. Other specialists, such as lawyers and accountants, advise the professional managers. By separating management from ownership, the corporation can take advantage of the skills, knowledge, and experience of various individuals to ensure that the business will be run successfully.

In smaller, closely held corporations, the owners often act as the managers who run the business. The separation of ownership and management usually does not occur until a company grows large and goes public. Apple Computer, for example, was established originally as a partnership managed and run by its co-owners, Steve Jobs and Steve Wozniak. In order to expand, they later formed a closely held corporation. After it became a publicly held corporation, the company hired professional managers and other specialists to run the business.

Disadvantages of the Corporation

Although the corporate form of ownership has a number of advantages, it also has several disadvantages.

Complicated and Expensive to Establish

Earlier in the chapter you read that sole proprietorships and partnerships are fairly easy to set up. In contrast, a great deal of work is required to create a corporation. If you want to set up a corporation, you'll be faced with many forms to complete, reports to file, and laws and regulations that you must follow. Forming a corporation requires time and effort.

As a result of the great amount of work and organization required, forming a corporation also costs a large amount of money. Among the many costs you'll face in creating a corporation are legal

RESPOND

Consider the responsibilities of owning and managing a large auto-parts store. Why might it be beneficial to separate the management from the ownership in this instance?

Iceland
North Atlantic Ocean
NORWAY

A rugged island of extremes, Iceland sits alone in the North Atlantic, its back to the Arctic Circle. Glaciers cover 10 percent of the island. Volcanoes, geysers, and hot springs dot its rugged landscape. Resourceful Icelanders make the best of their harsh environment. Glacial rivers supply them with both cold water and cheap hydroelectric power, while volcanoes and hot springs provide geothermal heat for their homes and hot water. Even on chilly nights, bathers can take a dip in one of Iceland's many naturally heated pools. They have their pick: "hot pots," or round pools with underwater benches; Jacuzzi-like pockets; or shallow, circular pools where, according to one visitor, "people recline like fish on a tray." Here's a snapshot of Iceland.

Bathers enjoy a geothermal spa in Reykjavík, Iceland.

Geographic area	39,769 sq. mi.
Population	277,000
Capital	Reykjavík (pop. 105,000)
Language	Icelandic
Currency:	krona
Gross domestic product (GDP)	$571 billion
Per capita GDP	$21,000
Economy	Industry: fish processing, aluminum smelting. Agriculture: potatoes, turnips, cattle, fish. Exports: fish, fish and animal products, aluminum.

Thinking Critically

Evaluate List several reasons why Iceland's geothermal energy is better than energy from fossil fuels.

For more information on Iceland visit finance.glencoe.com or your local library.

---

fees, licensing costs, filing fees, the cost of issuing stock certificates, and general administrative costs.

Slow Decision Making

A major disadvantage of the corporation is the slowness of the decision-making process. In sole proprietorships and partnerships only a few people determine how the business is run. As a result, decisions can be made rather quickly. In corporations, however, especially large ones, many different people may study the issues and discuss and debate them before making a decision. The process can be slowed even further if disagreements occur. As a result of the slow decision-making process, corporations often cannot respond quickly to issues or situations that affect their business.

Taxes

Another major disadvantage of a corporation concerns taxes. Because a corporation is a separate legal entity, it must pay state and federal income tax on its profits. As you learned earlier in the chapter, partnerships and sole proprietorships pay no income taxes as businesses.

If the profits of the corporation are distributed to the stockholders as dividends, the money is taxed again. Stockholders must report the dividends they receive from corporations as part of their personal taxable income. As a result of this tax policy, the profits that corporations earn are taxed twice—once as corporate profits and a second time as stockholder dividends.

Limited Liability Company

The government is now allowing a new form of business ownership, known as a limited liability company. A *limited liability company (LLC)* is a business that operates and is taxed as a partnership but has limited liability for the owners. It thus combines some advantages of the partnership and the corporation. In an LLC the liability of the owners is limited to their investments. The profits are taxed only once.

Most states now allow the creation of LLCs, and they're becoming very popular. The Internal Revenue Service approves of this new form of business organization as long as the company is small. It is not intended for large business operations.

Franchise

A franchise is not a form of business ownership, but it's important to understand its legal status. A *franchise* is a contractual agreement to sell a company's products or services in a designated geographic area. Franchises are very popular in fast-food businesses—McDonald's, Subway, Burger King, Wendy's, and Taco Bell are all franchises.

If you start a franchise, you first organize your business as a sole proprietorship, partnership, corporation, or LLC. You then purchase a franchise from a corporation such as Burger King. This is known as

QUESTION

Why would a business want to pay thousands of dollars to become part of a franchise?

OWNING A FRANCHISE Many fast-food businesses are franchises. *What do you think are some of the advantages of purchasing a franchise from a corporation?*

a parent corporation. You're now licensed to open a Burger King restaurant (for example), and the franchise is an asset of your business.

Smaller franchises may cost only a few thousand dollars, while large ones such as McDonald's and Midas Muffler cost hundreds of thousands of dollars. The next time you dine under McDonald's golden arches, remember that the establishment is actually a business organized under one of the three forms of business ownership. However, the business is also a franchise and has paid a franchise fee to McDonald's.

Which Form of Ownership Is Best?

No magic formula exists for deciding which form of ownership is the best. You must consider carefully the advantages and disadvantages of each. Then you can decide which one is best for your

Setting Up a Partnership

Mary has been teaching yoga classes at a health club for the past three years. She feels she now has enough experience to open her own yoga studio. Since she's concerned about costs and responsibilities, she spoke with one of the other yoga instructors, Tony, about starting a yoga business together. Tony thinks it's a great idea!

Location: One of Tony's friends works at an art gallery, which has a peaceful environment and ample floor space. Mary spoke with the owner of the gallery and negotiated using the gallery weekday evenings and Saturday and Sunday mornings. Mary and Tony agreed to pay the gallery owner 25 percent of all class fees.

Competition: The only yoga classes presently being offered in the area are at the health club where they both work.

Start-up Costs: Mary and Tony must purchase 25 yoga mats at $10 per mat. They also will have insurance costs of $1,200 per year, plus $150 in fees and licenses. They will contribute an equal amount of money from their personal savings to open the business.

Schedule: They decide to begin their business with eight classes per week: one each weekday evening, two classes on Saturday morning, and one on Sunday morning. Each class will be one hour in length. They agree that each of them will teach four classes a week and cover for the other during illness or vacation.

Responsibilities: Mary took responsibility for maintaining accounting records and paying bills. Tony is responsible for advertising and promotion.

Revenue: They decide to charge $15 per class. They project the weekend classes might bring in 25 students at each class ($375). Weekday classes might average 5 to 10 students ($75–150). Mary and Tony agree to share revenue and expenses equally.

Creating the Partnership: To establish a legal partnership, they drew up a written document outlining the organization of the business, responsibilities of each partner, and division of profits and losses.

Analyze   What kind of business would you start with a partner? With another student, discuss how you would share responsibilities if you started a partnership together. What ways might you finance the business? What skills and character traits do each of you have that might complement each other in a partnership?

1 A hobby such as fly-fishing could turn into an ideal **sole proprietorship**. An avid fisherman could offer his or her services as a fishing guide or instructor.

2 Some businesses may be too large for only one person to operate. A sports camp, for example, might be a good enterprise for a **partnership**, whose owners contribute different talents.

FIGURE 20.1

Having Fun!

Perhaps you've thought about opening a business that would allow you to combine your love of a certain sport, interest, or hobby with a business opportunity. Such a business can take different forms of ownership.

3 Some businesses are organized as **closely held corporations**. The owners may be a group with a common interest, such as kayaking.

4 Walt Disney World is part of the Walt Disney Company, a **publicly held corporation** with thousands of stockholders.

particular business and personal needs. Many people feel that a small start-up business is often best established as a sole proprietorship or a partnership. These forms of ownership are easy to establish. If the business is successful, you can consider creating a corporation to allow opportunities for gaining increased capital and limited liability.

Figure 20.1 illustrates the different forms of ownership that a business might take.

SECTION 20.2 ASSESSMENT

CHECK YOUR UNDERSTANDING

1. Explain the differences among the articles of incorporation, a corporate charter, and corporate bylaws.
2. What is a closely held corporation? What is a publicly held corporation?
3. What are the advantages and disadvantages of a corporation?

THINK CRITICALLY

4. What effect might a large increase in the number of stockholders have on a corporation?

USING MATH SKILLS

5. **Issuing Stock** Terrance and several partners own a dry cleaning business that operates as a closely held corporation. They want to go public and sell stock, hoping to raise enough capital to expand the business.
   Calculate If the initial offering of their stock sells for $29.50 per share, how many shares of stock will they have to sell to raise $1 million?

SOLVING MONEY PROBLEMS

6. **Limited Liability?** Beverly Echo-Hawk is the sole proprietor of All Wet, a raft rental company that operates on the Colorado River. She used the $35,000 she had in savings to establish the business. However, competition from other companies with newer, better equipment has resulted in net losses for All Wet. Beverly also owns $33,000 worth of stock in a corporation that is being managed poorly. Beverly fears that the corporation will go out of business within the next several months.
   Analyze Which investment poses a greater financial risk to Beverly? Why?

CHAPTER 20 ASSESSMENT

CHAPTER SUMMARY

- The benefits of a sole proprietorship include ease of creation; total control of the business by the owner; few government regulations; and the business's tax status. Also, the owner keeps all the profits.

- Sole proprietorships have several disadvantages, including limited capital, unlimited financial liability for the owner, limited human resources, and limited life.

- General partners have decision-making authority, usually take an active role in the operation of the business, and have unlimited liability. Limited partners rarely take an active role in decision making or running the business, and they have limited liability.

- Partnerships have a number of advantages: ease of creation; the varied skills and experience of the partners; the ability to obtain capital; total control by the general partners; and their tax status.

- The disadvantages of partnerships include unlimited liability for the general partners, possible conflicts and disagreements, the requirement to share profits, and limited life.

- Forming a corporation involves obtaining a corporate charter, writing corporate bylaws, and issuing stock.

- The two types of corporations are the closely held corporation and the publicly held corporation.

- The advantages of a corporation include ease of raising capital, limited liability, continued life, and separation of ownership and management.

- A corporation has several disadvantages, including the work and amount of money needed for establishment; slow decision making; and the tax liability.

Internet zone

Understanding and Using Vocabulary

Imagine that you want to open a business. Using at least ten of the following terms, write a letter to a friend asking for advice on the legal form of ownership you should establish for the business.

sole proprietorship
Employer Identification Number (EIN)

unlimited liability
limited life
partnership
partnership agreement
general partner
agency power
limited partner
corporation

articles of incorporation
corporate charter
corporate bylaws
going public
board of directors
limited liability company (LLC)
franchise

CHAPTER 20 ASSESSMENT

Review Key Concepts

1. Discuss the advantages and disadvantages of sole proprietorships.
2. What is the likelihood that new businesses will succeed?
3. Why might a partnership be more beneficial than a sole proprietorship?
4. Describe the difference between a closely held corporation and a publicly held corporation.
5. What is the role of the board of directors in a publicly held corporation?

Apply Key Concepts

1. "Being sole proprietor of a business is better than being a regular employee in a company." Do you agree or disagree with this statement? Why?
2. Why do so many new businesses fail?
3. Brook's Books operates as a sole proprietorship. The owner is considering taking on a partner. Write a paragraph about the advantages and disadvantages of this idea.
4. If you were a corporate owner, would you prefer your business to be a closely held or a publicly held corporation? Explain why.
5. What problems might arise if the board of directors of a corporation did not have the appropriate knowledge and experience?

? Problem Solving Today

HOME REPAIR HOTLINE

You want to start a home repair and maintenance business. After doing some research, you've discovered that there is a great market for

these services. You believe that the business will be more successful if you have partners.

Analyze List the steps you would take to organize your business as a partnership. Include a description of the skills, talents, and experience your partners should bring to the business.

Computer Activity As an alternative activity, create a flyer advertising your business and the services it offers.

Real-World Application

CONNECT WITH SOCIAL STUDIES

Gil has been operating a small computer consulting business for several years. The business is growing, and he would like to provide computer programming services to large companies. Gil would like to set up his business as a corporation, but he knows nothing about how that is done.

Conduct Research Find out the procedures that Gil would need to follow to set up a corporation in your state. What forms would he have to complete and what fees would he have to pay?

FINANCE *Online*

FRANCHISING FEVER

Sandi wants to purchase a franchise. Help her conduct research on the types of franchises that are available.

Connect Using a variety of search engines, locate the following information on two different kinds of franchises:
1. Initial investment needed
2. Location requirements
3. Management expertise needed

CHAPTER 21

Developing a Financial Plan

STANDARD &POOR'S

Q&A

Q: I don't understand why a financial plan is so important. The financial projections are just guesses. Why should I bother spending so much time making financial predictions that might not come true?

A: It's true that financial forecasts often have to be revised. However, a financial plan is essential to understanding what will make a business profitable, how much cash will be needed to operate the business, and the future value of the business. Once created, the financial plan should be updated regularly.

Identifying Required Capital

*A*fter attending cooking school, Ivan decided that he wanted to open a gourmet grocery store. He had learned a lot about the business while working as a manager at a similar establishment. For several weeks now he has been carrying out a very important task—developing a financial plan for his new business.

In Chapter 16 you learned that an overall business plan consists of three essential parts: a strategic plan, a marketing plan, and a financial plan. Although the development of sound strategic and marketing plans is important, their success often depends on the quality and accuracy of your financial plan. If you run out of funding, you probably won't be able to achieve the goals set forth in your strategic and marketing plans.

Sound financial planning is necessary for all businesses—especially new business ventures. Whether you run a small grocery store or a large international corporation, the growth and profits of your business depend largely on the quality of your financial management. A good financial plan will not guarantee a successful business, but a poorly constructed financial plan will usually result in a failed business. **Figure 21.1** on page 667 shows how wise financial planning can help you make your business dream a reality.

What You'll Learn

- How to **identify** start-up capital
- How to **estimate** operating capital
- How to **analyze** projected financial statements
- How to **explain** the need for reserve capital

Why It's Important

The first aspect of a financial plan is to determine how much capital you'll need. The future financial picture of your business is reported in projected financial statements.

KEY TERMS

- start-up capital
- operating capital
- financial forecasting
- projected financial statements
- fixed expenses
- variable expenses
- reserve capital

Elements of a Financial Plan

A financial plan is often considered the most important part of an overall business plan. Without adequate cash, your business may not survive.

An effective financial plan enables you to determine required capital. (Remember that capital is the money you'll need to establish your business, operate for the first few months, and expand as your business increases.) The process of determining required capital will include identifying and analyzing the assets and costs that are involved in starting a new business. Once you've identified these items, you'll assign an estimated dollar value to each one.

A financial plan also addresses the various sources of funding you'll use to acquire or purchase the needed items, as discussed in Chapter 17. In addition, the plan outlines how you'll record, summarize, and report the finances of your business.

This section will examine the process of determining required capital.

What's Your Financial ID?

ARE YOU A PERSUADER?

Your personality can help guide your future. On a separate sheet of paper write ten of the following character traits that best describe you and find out if you're a persuader, a communicator, or an individualist.

_____ a. I like meeting people.
_____ b. I'm friendly.
_____ c. I try to avoid conflict.
_____ d. I like to spend time alone.
_____ e. I like to talk.
_____ f. I'm sensitive.
_____ g. I'm interested in other people.
_____ h. I'm upbeat.
_____ i. I'm enthusiastic.
_____ j. I like to be active.

_____ k. I have perseverance.
_____ l. I'm persuasive.
_____ m. I let other people do what they want.
_____ n. I'm cautious.
_____ o. I'm ambitious.
_____ p. I like to feel in control.
_____ q. I like to plan.
_____ r. I like organization.

_____ s. I like to be the center of attention.

Score 3 points for each of these character traits: **a, b, e, g, h, i, j, k, l, o,** or **s.**

Individualist: If you scored 6–12 points, you might enjoy a career and hobbies that give you independence.

Communicator: If you scored 15–21 points, you enjoy activities where you're a team player working toward a common goal.

Persuader: If you scored 24–30 points, consider a career in sales or another field where you can influence people.

1 Analyze your needs and costs. Research the supplies your business will need and the fees and costs you'll have to pay to get started.

2 Secure funding. Your plan will describe how each business expense will be paid. Financial institutions will consider the quality of your financial plan before agreeing to loan money to your business.

3 Plan your process. In your financial plan you'll show how you'll record, summarize, and report your business's finances once you get started.

FIGURE 21.1

Creating a Business

Creating a new business requires lots of preparation and hard work. Good financial planning will help you succeed. If your financial plan is thorough and realistic, your business should have the money it needs to prosper and grow.

4 Prepare for opening. A good financial plan will ensure that you have money to cover all the supplies and preparation necessary to open your business.

Determining Required Capital

The first aspect of a financial plan is to determine how much capital you'll need. You may be shocked at the amount of money that is required to start a business and ensure its success. The purpose of a financial plan is to give you a realistic idea of what you'll need. The quality of your financial plan will affect not only the success of your business but also your ability to qualify for financing. A clear, concise, and realistic financial plan will give lenders confidence in your business knowledge and skills.

Required capital is divided into three types: start-up capital, operating capital, and reserve capital. To begin a financial plan, you'll need to analyze carefully all three types of required capital and estimate the amount of each.

PREDICT

Why is carefully estimating start-up capital so important to a new business?

Start-Up Capital

The first type of required capital is *start-up capital*—the money required to start your business. Sufficient start-up capital is essential to the survival of a new business.

Establishing a business is an expensive and risky venture. Some new businesses thrive, but many fail. The U.S. Department of Commerce reports that most small businesses that fail close in the first 18 to 30 months of operation. The most common reason for these business failures is insufficient start-up capital. If money is not available to purchase needed merchandise or pay current bills, the business will not survive.

Start-up capital is divided into two basic categories. The first category is the capital required to purchase the assets you'll need to start your business. Before you can open the doors of your business, you'll need to buy various items. These items might include equipment, display racks, and inventory.

The second category of start-up capital is start-up costs—the costs or fees involved in establishing your business. Start-up costs may include permits, legal and accounting fees, and security deposits. Some start-up costs are onetime expenses, such as permits, legal fees, and deposits for telephone service. Other costs are continuing expenses, such as rent, maintenance, and insurance.

Save, Don't Charge

Spending money is easy, especially when you have a credit card. Resist the temptation to use your card to buy something you want but can't really afford. Instead, be patient and save up for that special item.

Identifying Required Assets

Some assets are common to all new and established businesses. These are the items that most businesses need in order to operate. Other assets are unique to specific types of businesses or to certain geographic areas.

In preparing a financial plan you'll need to identify both types of assets. Be sure to record the types and quantities of items. To start, list the assets that are commonly needed by businesses. Such assets might include:

- office furniture, such as desks and file cabinets;
- computer hardware and software;
- display cases or shelves;
- store equipment, such as copiers and cash registers;
- inventory of merchandise;
- transportation or delivery equipment;
- store and office supplies;
- carpeting and lighting; and
- security and communication systems.

LARGE CAPITAL INVESTMENTS Some businesses, such as a furniture store, require a great deal of start-up capital. *Can you name other types of businesses that require large amounts of capital to begin operating?*

Next, list any assets you'll need that may be unique to your particular type of business or to your geographic area. Such assets might include:

- unique pieces of production or repair equipment;
- special types of display equipment;
- special electronic, security, or maintenance equipment; and
- required health or safety equipment.

When you make these lists, it's a good idea to observe similar established businesses, read trade journals, and consult with vendors in the industry. This will give you a better idea of what assets you'll need for your business.

Identifying Start-Up Costs

Next, you must identify and list the start-up costs for your business. This is often a complex task. You have to identify the start-up costs involved in most businesses and determine which of these costs you should include. You must also become familiar with required

local and state licenses, permits, and fees. Local trade associations, banks, and the Small Business Administration can help you identify these costs. Some common start-up costs include:

- business insurance,
- legal and professional fees,
- licenses and permits,
- banking and credit card fees,
- marketing and advertising costs,
- rent and utilities security deposits,
- remodeling and renovation costs, and
- maintenance and repair expenses.

Be sure to include any type of cost that you feel you may encounter in starting up your business. Unidentified costs are a serious problem to entrepreneurs who are beginning new businesses. Too often, unexpected or hidden costs consume start-up funds. If that happens, money may not be available for other needed items.

Assigning Costs to Identified Items

Once you've identified your required assets and start-up costs, you must estimate how much you'll have to pay for each item. Be careful to assign a realistic dollar value to each required asset and start-up cost. If you underestimate, you may have to reduce costs in other areas, and you may not have enough cash to pay for essential items. If this occurs often, your business may face a serious cash flow problem.

Play it safe by estimating on the high side. For example, suppose that your business will need a fax machine. You determine that the machine will cost between $400 and $600. When you assign costs to your required assets, you should use the $600 amount. If you pay only $525 for the fax machine, you can apply the additional budgeted amount ($75) to other costs.

The final step in calculating how much money you'll need to launch your business is to prepare a statement of required start-up capital. For example, Amanda Woodland is opening a new business called The Silver Lining Gift Shop. Amanda's statement of required start-up capital is shown in **Figure 21.2**.

Amanda realizes that there will be unexpected costs and other small items to purchase, but she thinks that she has identified all major required assets and start-up costs. After listing the items, she realizes that she'll need approximately $90,000 in start-up capital. If Amanda had not researched and analyzed all her costs carefully,

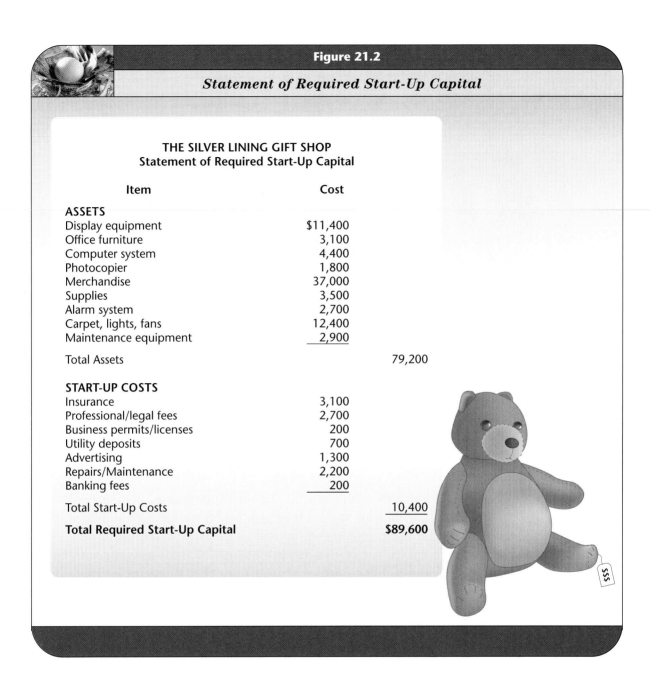

Figure 21.2

Statement of Required Start-Up Capital

THE SILVER LINING GIFT SHOP
Statement of Required Start-Up Capital

Item	Cost
ASSETS	
Display equipment	$11,400
Office furniture	3,100
Computer system	4,400
Photocopier	1,800
Merchandise	37,000
Supplies	3,500
Alarm system	2,700
Carpet, lights, fans	12,400
Maintenance equipment	2,900
Total Assets	79,200
START-UP COSTS	
Insurance	3,100
Professional/legal fees	2,700
Business permits/licenses	200
Utility deposits	700
Advertising	1,300
Repairs/Maintenance	2,200
Banking fees	200
Total Start-Up Costs	10,400
Total Required Start-Up Capital	**$89,600**

she probably would have guessed that she could start her gift shop
with much less than $90,000.

Operating Capital

After you determine how much capital you'll need to start your
business, you must address the second type of required capital. This
is called *operating capital*—the amount of capital needed to operate a business for the first few months or years.

HIT OR MISS? It's impossible to know for sure how successful your business venture will be. *What individuals or groups might you consult for reliable advice?*

Although the sale of your products or services will generate revenue, this money is often not sufficient to cover business expenses and expansion plans. You'll need to purchase additional merchandise and increase sales to keep your business running. Cash must also be available to carry out your strategic and marketing plans.

As part of your financial plan, you must estimate your operating capital—a process that is often called *financial forecasting*. This future financial picture of your business is reported in *projected financial statements*—statements that predict the financial position of a business in the months and years to come. The projected financial statements will include income statements, balance sheets, and statements of cash flows.

Projected Income Statement

As you learned in Chapter 18, an income statement for a merchandising business reports revenue, cost of merchandise sold, gross profit on sales, operating expenses, and net income (or loss). This type of financial statement usually reports what happened in the previous accounting period.

In contrast, a projected income statement is your estimate of the way in which income amounts will change over the next few months or years. You create this statement before you even begin business operations. Similar to a financial road map, this statement reveals where you hope your business will be in the future.

Estimating figures for a projected income statement can be a challenge. You must analyze all information regarding revenue and expenses for your type of business. You can obtain such information from trade associations, vendors, local business organizations, and government agencies such as the Small Business Administration and the Bureau of the Census. The information from these sources is based on facts and averages. However, to create figures for your projected income statement, you'll have to apply that information to your business and make educated guesses.

It is better to estimate projected revenues on the low side and to estimate projected expenses on the high side. This approach will allow some flexibility in the event that sales don't reach your expectations or that expenses are higher than you had originally estimated. If you project yearly sales of between $130,000 and $150,000, use the $130,000 amount. If you estimate your heating bill somewhere between $3,000 and $4,000, use the $4,000 amount.

FIXED EXPENSES Expenses are often classified as fixed or variable. *Fixed expenses* are expenses that remain the same regardless of business activity. These might include rent, insurance, or interest on a loan. Fixed expenses are fairly easy to project because they remain constant, or fixed, for a stated length of time. For example, no matter how much your business earns from sales in a particular month, you still pay the same amount in rent for the duration of your lease.

VARIABLE EXPENSES *Variable expenses* are expenses that may vary, or that can be adjusted, depending on sales. Such expenses might include the costs of supplies, advertising, wages, and sometimes utilities. For example, if sales are lower than you predicted, you could purchase fewer supplies or reduce the hours that your employees work. It is more difficult to project variable expenses.

Some variable expenses, such as maintenance and repairs, have nothing to do with sales. These also cannot be projected accurately. When your computer or cash register no longer works, you must

PRICEY PROMOTIONS Promotions are a variable expense that increases or decreases depending on the success of the business. *Can you name a promotional activity that recently took place at a local store?*

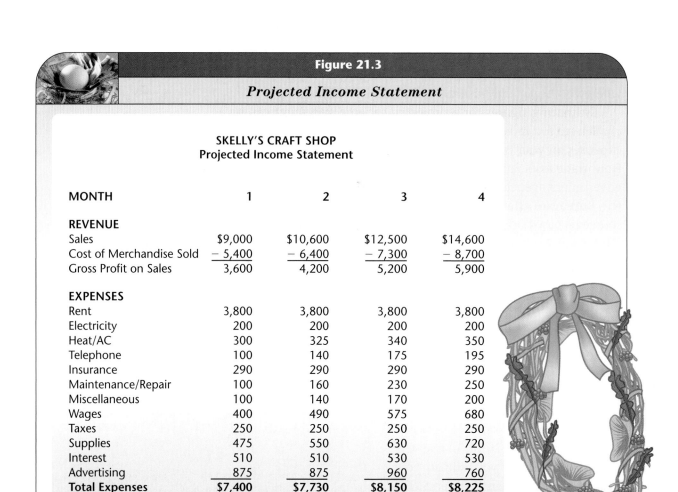

Figure 21.3

Projected Income Statement

SKELLY'S CRAFT SHOP
Projected Income Statement

MONTH	1	2	3	4
REVENUE				
Sales	$9,000	$10,600	$12,500	$14,600
Cost of Merchandise Sold	− 5,400	− 6,400	− 7,300	− 8,700
Gross Profit on Sales	3,600	4,200	5,200	5,900
EXPENSES				
Rent	3,800	3,800	3,800	3,800
Electricity	200	200	200	200
Heat/AC	300	325	340	350
Telephone	100	140	175	195
Insurance	290	290	290	290
Maintenance/Repair	100	160	230	250
Miscellaneous	100	140	170	200
Wages	400	490	575	680
Taxes	250	250	250	250
Supplies	475	550	630	720
Interest	510	510	530	530
Advertising	875	875	960	760
Total Expenses	$7,400	$7,730	$8,150	$8,225
Net Income/<Loss>	<$3,800>	<$3,530>	<$2,950>	<$2,325>

RESPOND

List at least two factors that make it common for even a well-planned business to operate at a loss for the first several months.

have it repaired or replaced. The principal characteristic of variable expenses is that they change with business conditions and other situations.

Figure 21.3 shows a projected income statement for Skelly's Craft Shop for the first four months of operation. You can see that the statement is projecting losses in each month. This is not unusual for a new business. In fact, it's common for a new business to go for several months or even a year without reporting a profit. Notice, however, that the estimated loss for Skelly's Craft Shop decreases each month. With continued good financial management, it is likely that profits will be reported in the near future.

Figure 21.4 shows a projected income statement for Skelly's Craft Shop for the first five years of operation. It provides a long-range view of business activity. Although the amounts are only estimates, if they are projected realistically, they may indicate the potential success of the business.

Notice that by the end of the second year, the craft shop anticipates a profit. If all goes according to projections, the business should be doing quite well within five years. This is good news for the business as well as important information for banks or other financial institutions that might provide funding to the owner.

Figure 21.4

Projected 5-Year Income Statement

SKELLY'S CRAFT SHOP
Projected 5-Year Income Statement

YEAR	1	2	3	4	5
REVENUE					
Sales	$172,000	$224,600	$258,500	$298,000	$370,000
Cost of Merchandise Sold	-103,200	-125,400	-147,100	-167,000	-205,000
Gross Profit on Sales	68,800	99,200	111,400	129,000	165,000
EXPENSES					
Rent	45,600	47,300	48,200	51,800	55,000
Electricity	4,600	4,800	5,000	5,200	5,600
Heat/AC	3,500	3,900	4,400	4,700	5,000
Telephone	1,200	1,400	1,600	1,800	2,200
Insurance	3,500	3,600	3,700	3,800	4,000
Maintenance/Repair	1,200	1,600	2,300	2,500	2,800
Miscellaneous	1,000	1,400	1,700	1,900	2,200
Wages	4,800	6,100	7,200	8,000	9,900
Taxes	2,900	3,500	3,900	4,200	7,600
Supplies	4,900	5,500	6,300	7,000	7,900
Interest	5,800	5,400	5,000	4,800	4,100
Advertising	5,900	5,100	4,300	4,000	5,000
Total Expenses	$84,900	$89,600	$93,600	$99,700	$111,300
Net Income/<Loss>	<$16,100>	$9,600	$17,800	$29,300	$53,700

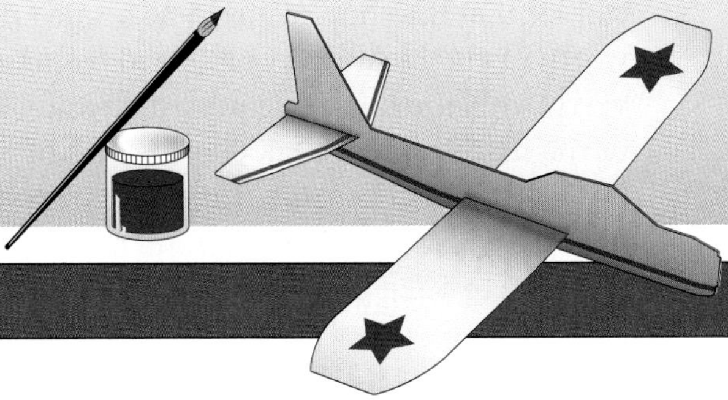

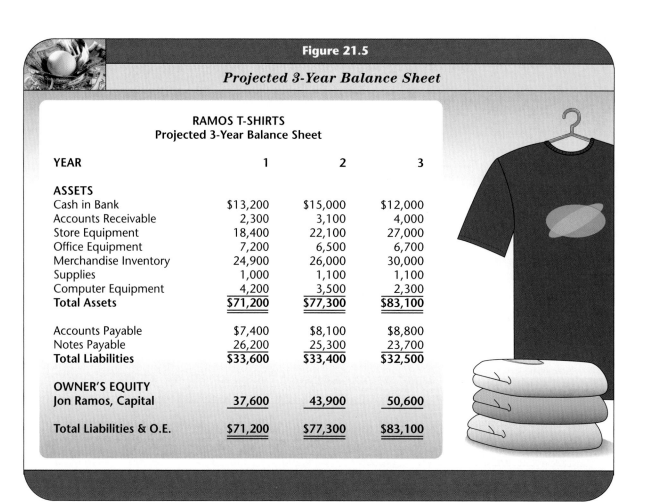

Figure 21.5

Projected 3-Year Balance Sheet

RAMOS T-SHIRTS
Projected 3-Year Balance Sheet

YEAR	1	2	3
ASSETS			
Cash in Bank	$13,200	$15,000	$12,000
Accounts Receivable	2,300	3,100	4,000
Store Equipment	18,400	22,100	27,000
Office Equipment	7,200	6,500	6,700
Merchandise Inventory	24,900	26,000	30,000
Supplies	1,000	1,100	1,100
Computer Equipment	4,200	3,500	2,300
Total Assets	$71,200	$77,300	$83,100
Accounts Payable	$7,400	$8,100	$8,800
Notes Payable	26,200	25,300	23,700
Total Liabilities	$33,600	$33,400	$32,500
OWNER'S EQUITY			
Jon Ramos, Capital	37,600	43,900	50,600
Total Liabilities & O.E.	$71,200	$77,300	$83,100

Projected Balance Sheet

Financial institutions will also want to see a forecast of the overall financial position of your business. You provide this with a projected balance sheet. On a projected balance sheet you estimate the future assets, liabilities, and worth of your business one year, three years, or five years from now. A projected balance sheet for Ramos T-Shirts is shown in **Figure 21.5**.

By reviewing the projected balance sheet for Ramos T-Shirts, you can see that the shop seems to be headed in the right direction. The worth of the business is projected to increase over the next three years, with the owner's equity increasing from $37,600 at the end of the first year to $50,600 at the end of the third year. You'll also notice that in this same three-year period, assets are predicted to increase ($71,200 to $83,100), and liabilities are predicted to decrease ($33,600 to $32,500).

Projected Statement of Cash Flows

In Chapter 18 you learned that a statement of cash flows reports how much cash your business took in and where the cash went. This document shows how the cash position of the business changed during an accounting period.

Many consider the projected statement of cash flows to be the most important projected financial statement. When you prepare a projected statement of cash flows, you analyze the amount of cash that you anticipate will be available for your business in the future. Will you have sufficient cash if your business operates on its projected path? Remember, success and growth depend on available cash.

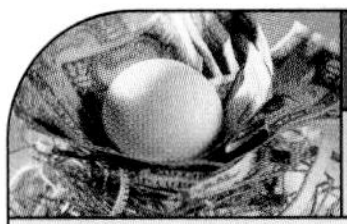

Figure 21.6

Projected Statement of Cash Flows

WESTPORT SPORTING GOODS
Projected Statement of Cash Flows

	APRIL	MAY	JUNE
CASH RECEIVED			
Sales	$30,400	$34,100	$35,900
Accounts Receivable	3,100	3,300	3,600
Interest	170	175	180
Total Cash Inflow	$33,670	$37,575	$39,680
CASH DISBURSED			
Rent	$4,600	$4,600	$4,600
Utilities	1,300	1,375	1,420
Supplies	450	450	460
Advertising	2,800	3,000	3,700
Bank Charges/Fees	220	250	270
Interest	3,400	3,300	3,200
Telephone	510	530	540
Maintenance	950	1,075	1,100
Credit Card Fees	390	425	460
Payroll	9,200	10,100	10,300
Taxes	4,800	6,000	7,300
Delivery Charges	1,040	1,260	1,290
Miscellaneous	520	600	600
Insurance	675	675	675
Total Cash Outflow	$30,855	$33,640	$35,915
NET OPERATING CASH FLOW	2,815	3,935	3,765
BEGINNING CASH BALANCE	5,860	8,675	12,610
ENDING CASH BALANCE	$8,675	$12,610	$16,375

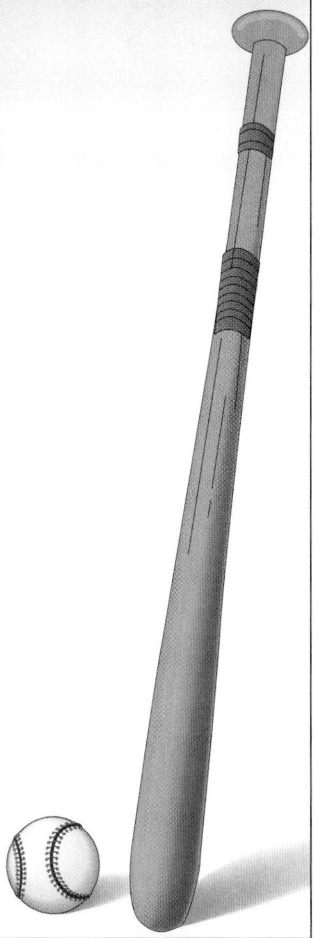

CASH ONLY When merchandise is delivered to a store, payment for the items must sometimes be made in cash. *What types of small businesses might have deliveries every day that require cash payments?*

Figure 21.6 on page 677 shows a projected statement of cash flows for Westport Sporting Goods for a period of three months. You can see that the business predicts a positive cash flow for the three-month period. In other words, more money is shown coming into Westport Sporting Goods each month than is shown going out. Realize that these three months—April, May, and June—are probably a particularly high sales period for a sporting goods store. Therefore, such a positive cash flow might not be consistent throughout the entire year.

Reserve Capital

The third type of capital is called *reserve capital*—money that is set aside for unexpected costs or opportunities. Reserve capital is like keeping a little cash in a personal savings account. If and when you need money, it's there.

When emergencies arise, reserve capital is often a lifeline for small businesses. Unexpected costs can occur at any time. Usually, you'll have to take care of them immediately. Examples of unexpected costs include repair bills and the expense of replacing broken equipment or lost or damaged merchandise. Without immediate access to cash to pay such costs, your business could face a serious financial problem.

Reserve capital is also needed to take advantage of business opportunities. Suppose that a competitor is going out of business and has offered you inventory at a great price. You can use cash from your reserve fund to take advantage of this opportunity. In such a situation cash must be available immediately, or the opportunity is lost. Good financial planning includes taking advantage of business opportunities when they arise.

In addition, business owners use reserve capital to expand and grow their businesses. For example, you might use cash from the reserve fund to buy new lines of merchandise, to expand or renovate

INTERNATIONAL FINANCE Qatar

Oil—we probably never give it much thought. By keeping our homes warm and our cars running smoothly, oil helps maintain the quality of our lives. In Qatar its discovery in the late 1930s changed the lives of an entire population. Once a nation of camel herders, fishermen, and pearl divers, Qatar now enjoys one of the highest per capita incomes in the Arab world. Oil rules the country's economy and workforce. Foreign laborers make up more than 70 percent of the population. Because Qatar's oil reserves will not last much longer, the development of natural gas resources is under way. Qatar has the world's largest natural gas field, almost half the size of the country. Here's a snapshot of Qatar.

Qatar is a small country in the Middle East.

Geographic area	4,247 sq. mi.
Population	541,000
Capital	Doha (met. pop. 339,471)
Language	Arabic, English
Currency	riyal
Gross domestic product (GDP)	$11.2 billion
Per capita GDP	$16,700
Economy	Industry: crude oil production and refining. Agriculture: fruits, vegetables, poultry, fish. Exports: petroleum products, fertilizers, steel.

Thinking Critically

Apply Supplies of oil and natural gas aren't limitless. Name some alternative sources of energy that people can use. What can you do to help conserve energy sources?

For more information on Qatar visit finance.glencoe.com or your local library.

Angelo has been working for Appleburg Locksmith for the past six years. In addition to installing and repairing locks, his duties include purchasing and inventory control. He also dispatches the locksmiths to job sites. He recently completed his degree in business and is certified as a professional locksmith. Angelo is ready to open his own business. At first, Angelo will be the only employee. He plans to have a mobile office in his truck and offer commercial and residential lock installations. He also wants to provide a 24-hour emergency service. The business plan Angelo has written doesn't have a very detailed financial plan. Angelo already owns his truck, and he figures his start-up costs will be minimal. However, he is starting to think he should make an effort to estimate his revenues and expenses for the next few months. Angelo is not sure where to begin, so he turns to the experts at Standard & Poor's for advice.

Analysis: Angelo's new business venture has a very good chance of success. He has both professional training and hands-on experience running a locksmith business. His business plan requires only a small initial investment of capital, so that he has little to lose if his business doesn't develop as quickly as he hopes.

Recommendation: Angelo does need to create a forecast of his business's financial results. He can start by estimating the start-up capital that he will need to invest in his business. This may include purchasing equipment for his truck, and the cost of tools, business cards, advertising, and insurance. Angelo should also estimate his monthly sales and expenses for a 12-month period. From this forecast, he can estimate his cash balances for each month. Angelo can expect that, initially, his operating expenses and advertising costs will exceed his sales. If so, he should plan on funding his business expenses from his own savings for a few months. Angelo can also calculate the break-even point for his business. Angelo should consider how long it might take before his sales volume reaches the break-even point and whether he has enough savings to support his business during that period. Once Angelo's business is up and running, he will want to compare his actual financial results with his forecast. He should be prepared to revise his forecast each month.

Critical Thinking Questions

1. Where can Angelo obtain start-up capital if his initial expenses are more than he had anticipated?
2. What factors are likely to be critical to the success of Angelo's business?
3. What unexpected events might cause Angelo to need more money than he had planned?

your facilities, or to purchase more up-to-date equipment. Such forward-thinking investments allow your business to develop and become financially successful.

The amount of capital set aside in a reserve fund will vary from business to business. Many businesses set up this fund as a line of credit at the bank. You should not use your reserve capital for the normal operation of your business. It should be used only for unexpected costs and worthwhile business opportunities.

SECTION 21.1 ASSESSMENT

CHECK YOUR UNDERSTANDING

1. Name the two categories of start-up capital.
2. How can you estimate the amount of operating capital you'll need to run a business?
3. How can you obtain the financial information you need to create a projected income statement?
4. Why is reserve capital necessary?

THINK CRITICALLY

5. Why is a sound financial plan critical to the success of a business?

USING COMMUNICATION SKILLS

6. **Projected Financial Statements** Theo and Cole have an opportunity to start a business selling sunglasses on the beach. Theo knows it's very important to develop a written financial plan for the new business. Cole, however, says that as long as they know what's going on, they don't need to take the time to create projected financial statements. He says that such statements are just estimates anyway.
Present a Point of View How would you help Theo convince Cole that developing a written financial plan and creating projected financial statements will give their business a better chance to succeed?

SOLVING MONEY PROBLEMS

7. **Identify Start-Up Costs** Jana plans to turn her love of basketball into a business by offering summer basketball camps for children, one-on-one training for high school players, and skills assessment for college players. Jana is ready to create a financial plan for her business.
Analyze Help Jana identify the required assets and start-up costs for her business.

A Financial Plan Cricket Lane Flowers

Molly Singer wants to start her own business. For the past five years she has worked at King Point Florist, a local flower and garden store. During that time Molly learned to create fresh flower arrangements, fruit and gourmet baskets, and dried flower displays. She has read several books on floral design and has received numerous compliments on her arrangements.

Because of her work at the florist shop, Molly has experience in purchasing flowers and arrangements, advertising, pricing, sales procedures, and recordkeeping. She has taken several business courses at the local community college and attended two seminars on running a small business.

Molly now feels that she is ready to open her own florist business. She realizes that running her own business will be very different from working for someone else. She is a little nervous about the challenges she'll face as a business owner. However, she is confident that she has the knowledge and skills she needs to operate a successful flower shop.

Molly has decided to call her new business Cricket Lane Flowers. After researching locations and potential markets for a shop, she has found a small store that will fit her needs. It's located on a main street with a steady traffic flow and high visibility. No other flower shops are in the area, but there are several small businesses nearby that seem to attract customers. The store is in good condition, the rent is reasonable, and the required painting and decorating should be affordable.

Business Plan for Cricket Lane Flowers

With some preliminary research completed, Molly is ready to create her business plan for Cricket Lane Flowers. As you've already learned, her overall business plan should consist of three parts: a strategic plan, a marketing plan, and a financial plan. This section will provide brief summaries of Molly's strategic and marketing plans as well as all elements of her financial plan.

The Strategic Plan

For her strategic plan Molly researched the local flower market, identified the competition, and decided on the line of flowers and services that her shop will provide. After careful analysis, she set the following short-term and long-term goals.

Short-term goals:
- Rent a store in a good location.
- Secure a good telecommunication system.
- Computerize all accounting functions.
- Increase sales by 5 percent or more each month during the first year.
- Utilize all local advertising outlets.

Long-term goals:
- Increase sales by 30 percent or more in each of the first three years.
- Show a profit by the end of the second year.
- Expand inventory to include fruit and gift items.
- Develop business clients.

Molly's strategic plan also outlines the steps she'll take to achieve each of her short-term and long-term goals.

IN FULL BLOOM Molly will need more than a good location to make her dream of a thriving flower shop come true. *What else will Molly need to build a successful new business?*

The Marketing Plan

In her marketing plan Molly analyzed the competition, identified advertising outlets, developed promotional activities, and established an advertising and promotion budget for Cricket Lane Flowers. The success of her sales goals depends on an effective and efficient marketing plan. At her previous job Molly purchased advertising space in local and regional newspapers and magazines. Therefore, she is familiar with the process. Molly has decided to spend $2,000 each month for the first three months to advertise her business.

The Financial Plan

With her strategic and marketing plans completed, Molly is ready to develop her financial plan. As you may recall, the success of her strategic and marketing plans depends on the quality and accuracy of her financial plan.

Before preparing a financial plan, Molly must be sure that she has set realistic goals for herself and her business. She knows that although her figures are only estimates, they must be attainable. Also, although every business owner wants to make money quickly, Molly realizes that it will take time to earn a profit.

Background Information

To help start her business, Molly has saved money over the past five years, and her brother and sister have both offered to loan her some money. She'll need to borrow additional funds, but she is confident that she'll qualify for loans because of her well-established credit history. She has financed two cars and repaid her student loans. In addition, Molly uses her credit cards wisely and makes payments on time.

Molly has decided to organize her new business as a sole proprietorship. Although she'll have unlimited liability, this form of ownership is easier and less costly to establish than others. She has consulted with an attorney and an accountant, both of whom have given her valuable information and guidance.

Molly's accountant has set up a *chart of accounts*—a list of all the general ledger accounts that a business will use. This chart of accounts will provide Molly with a framework for recording and reporting her business transactions. The accountant also set up an accounting software program so that all accounting procedures for the business can be carried out on a computer.

Elements of the Financial Plan

Molly's financial plan includes the following reports:

- Statement of Required Start-Up Capital
- Projected 12-Month Income Statement
- Projected 12-Month Statement of Cash Flows
- Projected 3-Year Income Statement
- Projected 3-Year Statement of Cash Flows
- Projected 3-Year Balance Sheet

Molly's complete financial plan for Cricket Lane Flowers appears on the following pages. By reading and analyzing her projected financial statements in **Figures 21.7** through **21.12**, you'll get a good picture of how she expects her business to develop over the next few months and years.

CRICKET LANE FLOWERS
FINANCIAL PLAN
Prepared by MOLLY SINGER

BUSINESS OBJECTIVE: To open and operate a financially successful flower shop.

REQUIRED CAPITAL:

Start-Up Capital	$89,000
Operating Capital	12,000
Reserve Capital	15,000
Total Required Capital	$116,000

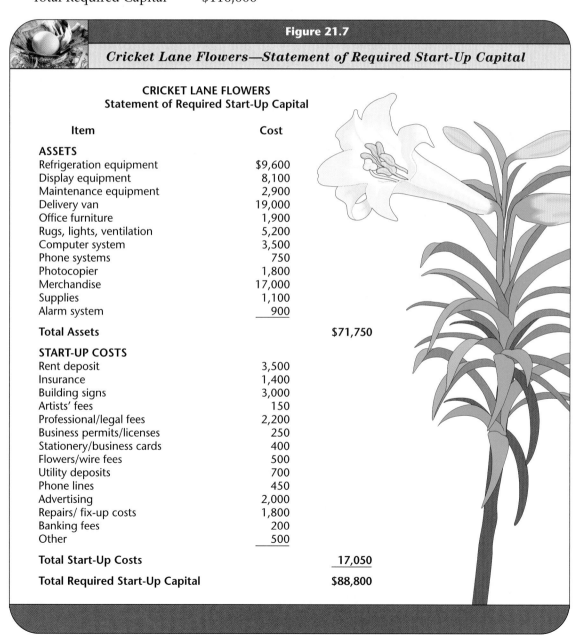

Figure 21.7

Cricket Lane Flowers—Statement of Required Start-Up Capital

CRICKET LANE FLOWERS
Statement of Required Start-Up Capital

Item	Cost
ASSETS	
Refrigeration equipment	$9,600
Display equipment	8,100
Maintenance equipment	2,900
Delivery van	19,000
Office furniture	1,900
Rugs, lights, ventilation	5,200
Computer system	3,500
Phone systems	750
Photocopier	1,800
Merchandise	17,000
Supplies	1,100
Alarm system	900
Total Assets	$71,750
START-UP COSTS	
Rent deposit	3,500
Insurance	1,400
Building signs	3,000
Artists' fees	150
Professional/legal fees	2,200
Business permits/licenses	250
Stationery/business cards	400
Flowers/wire fees	500
Utility deposits	700
Phone lines	450
Advertising	2,000
Repairs/ fix-up costs	1,800
Banking fees	200
Other	500
Total Start-Up Costs	17,050
Total Required Start-Up Capital	$88,800

Figure 21.8

Cricket Lane Flowers—Projected 12-Month Income Statement

CRICKET LANE FLOWERS
Projected 12-Month Income Statement

	1	2	3	4	5	6
REVENUE						
Sales	$11,000	$12,000	$13,300	$14,800	$15,400	$16,100
Cost of Merchandise Sold	4,900	5,300	5,850	6,500	6,800	7,400
Gross Profit on Sales	6,100	6,700	7,450	8,300	8,600	8,700
EXPENSES						
Rent	3,500	3,500	3,500	3,500	3,500	3,500
Electricity	180	180	185	185	185	185
Heat/AC	340	375	390	395	395	370
Telephone	130	140	175	205	225	225
Insurance	480	480	480	480	480	480
Maintenance/Repair	100	130	150	150	150	155
Miscellaneous	100	140	160	180	180	180
Wages	350	400	475	500	500	600
Taxes	250	360	400	450	475	490
Supplies	460	530	590	620	640	640
Interest	680	680	680	680	680	680
Advertising	2,000	2,000	2,000	1,800	1,700	1,500
Other	100	100	100	100	100	125
Total Expenses	$8,670	$9,015	$9,285	$9,245	$9,210	$9,130
Net Income/<Loss>	<$2,570>	<$2,315>	<$1,835>	<$945>	<$610>	<$430>

Figure 21.9

Cricket Lane Flowers—Projected 12-Month Statement of Cash Flows

CRICKET LANE FLOWERS
Projected 12-Month Statement of Cash Flows

	1	2	3	4	5	6
CASH RECEIPTS						
Cash Sales to Customers	$10,100	$11,300	$12,700	$14,100	$14,900	$15,400
Accounts Receivable	300	600	700	900	700	1,100
Total Cash Receipts	$10,400	$11,900	$13,400	$15,000	$15,600	$16,500
CASH PAYMENTS						
Purchase of Merchandise	4,400	4,800	5,600	6,600	7,100	7,700
Operating Expenses	7,740	7,975	8,205	8,115	8,055	7,960
Interest Expense	680	680	680	680	680	680
Taxes	250	360	400	450	475	490
Accounts Payable	200	300	450	500	600	700
Total Cash Payments	$13,270	$14,115	$15,335	$16,345	$16,910	$17,530
NET CASH FLOW	<$2,870>	<$2,215>	<$1,935>	<$1,345>	<$1,310>	<$1,030>

Figure 21.8

(continued)

	7	8	9	10	11	12
REVENUE						
Sales	$16,500	$17,200	$18,600	$20,100	$21,900	$23,000
Cost of Merchandise Sold	7,900	8,300	9,100	9,900	11,400	12,000
Gross Profit on Sales	8,600	8,900	9,500	10,200	10,500	11,000
EXPENSES						
Rent	3,500	3,500	3,500	3,500	3,500	3,500
Electricity	185	190	190	190	200	200
Heat/AC	370	350	340	340	350	360
Telephone	225	240	240	250	250	250
Insurance	480	480	480	480	480	480
Maintenance/Repairs	160	160	160	175	175	175
Miscellaneous	180	190	190	190	190	190
Wages	600	700	700	800	800	900
Taxes	525	595	615	640	660	675
Supplies	660	670	670	670	680	680
Interest	680	680	680	680	680	680
Advertising	1,200	1,200	1,200	1,400	1,500	1,500
Other	125	125	125	125	130	130
Total Expenses	$8,890	$9,080	$9,090	$9,440	$9,595	$9,720
Net Income/<Loss>	<$290>	<$180>	$410	$760	$905	$1,280

Figure 21.9

(continued)

	7	8	9	10	11	12
CASH RECEIPTS						
Cash Sales to Customers	$15,100	$16,000	$17,000	$18,600	$19,500	$21,000
Accounts Receivable	1,400	1,500	1,600	1,700	1,900	2,500
Total Cash Receipts	$16,500	$17,500	$18,600	$20,300	$21,400	$23,500
CASH PAYMENTS						
Purchase of Merchandise	6,700	7,400	8,000	8,800	9,200	10,300
Operating Expenses	7,685	7,805	7,795	8,120	8,255	8,365
Interest Expense	680	680	680	680	680	680
Taxes	525	595	615	640	660	675
Accounts Payable	800	900	1,000	1,300	1,400	1,600
Total Cash Payments	$16,390	$17,380	$18,090	$19,540	$20,195	$21,620
NET CASH FLOW	$110	$120	$510	$760	$1,205	$1,880

Negative Cash Flow for the 12-Month Period   <$6,120>

Figure 21.10

Cricket Lane Flowers—Projected 3-Year Income Statement

CRICKET LANE FLOWERS
Projected 3-Year Income Statement

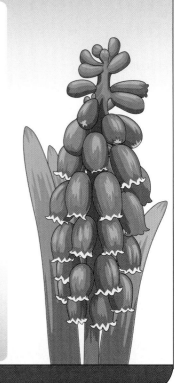

YEAR	1	2	3
REVENUE			
Sales	$199,900	$260,000	$338,000
Cost of Merchandise Sold	95,350	122,000	159,000
Gross Profit on Sales	104,550	138,000	179,000
EXPENSES			
Rent	42,000	42,000	43,500
Electricity	2,255	2,800	3,000
Heat/AC	4,375	5,400	5,700
Telephone	2,555	3,000	3,100
Insurance	5,760	6,000	6,300
Maintenance	1,840	2,500	4,000
Miscellaneous	2,070	2,400	2,700
Wages	7,325	11,200	17,000
Taxes	6,135	8,200	10,000
Supplies	7,510	8,000	9,500
Interest	8,160	9,300	9,700
Advertising	19,000	15,000	14,000
Other	1,385	2,000	2,000
Total Expenses	**$110,370**	**$117,800**	**$130,500**
Net Income/<Loss>:	**<$5,820>**	**$20,200**	**$48,500**

Figure 21.11

Cricket Lane Flowers—Projected 3-Year Statement of Cash Flows

CRICKET LANE FLOWERS
Projected 3-Year Statement of Cash Flows

YEAR	1	2	3
CASH RECEIPTS			
Cash Sales to Customers	$185,700	$241,000	$300,000
Accounts Receivable	14,900	21,500	30,000
Total Cash Receipts	$200,600	$262,500	$330,000
CASH PAYMENTS			
Purchase of Merchandise	86,600	136,000	168,000
Operating Expenses	96,075	100,300	111,000
Interest Expense	8,160	9,300	9,700
Taxes	6,135	8,200	10,000
Accounts Payable	9,750	15,000	30,000
Total Cash Payments	$206,720	$268,800	$328,700
NET CASH FLOW	**−$6,120**	**−$6,300**	**+$1,300**

Figure 21.12

Cricket Lane Flowers—Projected 3-Year Balance Sheet

CRICKET LANE FLOWERS
Projected 3-Year Balance Sheet

YEAR	1	2	3
ASSETS			
Cash in Bank	$13,000	$15,000	$19,000
Accounts Receivable	2,900	3,500	4,500
Display Equipment	8,000	7,500	7,000
Refrigeration Equipment	9,000	8,400	8,000
Delivery Equipment	17,500	14,000	11,000
Office Equipment	9,100	8,200	7,500
Computer Equipment	3,000	2,100	1,400
Merchandise Inventory	21,000	28,000	31,000
Supplies	500	450	600
Total Assets	$84,000	$87,150	$90,000
LIABILITIES			
Accounts Payable	8,400	10,100	12,800
Notes Payable	30,000	30,000	30,000
Total Liabilities	$38,400	$40,100	$42,800
OWNER'S EQUITY			
Molly Singer, Capital	45,600	47,050	47,200
Total Liabilities & O.E.	**$84,000**	**$87,150**	**$90,000**

Sources of Capital

Cash from Owner	$30,000
Personal Loans	6,000
Short-Term Commercial Loan (SBA Guaranteed)	30,000
Home Equity Loan	50,000
Total Available Capital	$116,000

The funds from the first three sources of capital will be invested immediately in the business. The amount of the home equity loan will be used in the initial operation of the business.

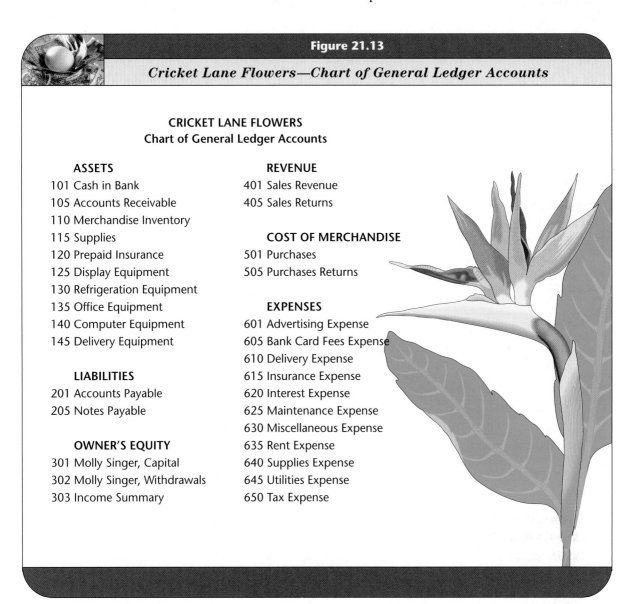

Figure 21.13

Cricket Lane Flowers—Chart of General Ledger Accounts

CRICKET LANE FLOWERS
Chart of General Ledger Accounts

ASSETS
101 Cash in Bank
105 Accounts Receivable
110 Merchandise Inventory
115 Supplies
120 Prepaid Insurance
125 Display Equipment
130 Refrigeration Equipment
135 Office Equipment
140 Computer Equipment
145 Delivery Equipment

LIABILITIES
201 Accounts Payable
205 Notes Payable

OWNER'S EQUITY
301 Molly Singer, Capital
302 Molly Singer, Withdrawals
303 Income Summary

REVENUE
401 Sales Revenue
405 Sales Returns

COST OF MERCHANDISE
501 Purchases
505 Purchases Returns

EXPENSES
601 Advertising Expense
605 Bank Card Fees Expense
610 Delivery Expense
615 Insurance Expense
620 Interest Expense
625 Maintenance Expense
630 Miscellaneous Expense
635 Rent Expense
640 Supplies Expense
645 Utilities Expense
650 Tax Expense

CONNECT

Imagine that ten years from now you want to open your dream business. What would that business be, and how would you raise the start-up capital to make your dream a reality?

Accounting Procedures

Molly's accountant created a Chart of Accounts for Cricket Lane Flowers. Molly will use these accounts to record all transactions for her business. **Figure 21.13** shows the accounts she will use.

Molly's accountant also recommended purchasing a software program to maintain Cricket Lane's accounting records, so all accounting procedures will be computerized. By using a software program, Molly will spend less time maintaining her accounting records and will have more time to run her business.

Molly will be responsible for entering all business transactions. At the end of every month, the computer system will generate a trial balance along with financial statements and reports. Both Molly and her accountant will analyze Cricket Lane's monthly income statement, statement of cash flows, and balance sheet.

By comparing these financial statements with statements from previous months, Molly's accountant will be able to evaluate the financial progress and position of her business. If a financial problem is identified, her accountant will make recommendations as to what Molly needs to do to correct the problem. It's only by careful and constant financial analysis that Molly can be assured her business

Careers in Finance

CONTROLLER

In the business world, controllers literally control all aspects of a company's accounting, including financial reports, income statements, balance sheets, statements of cash flow, and annual reports. Controllers need to have many years of experience in accounting or financial management. They often develop accounting procedures, and oversee the accounting, payroll, audit, and budget departments of a company. They may also have additional duties, depending on the type of industry. For example, a controller for a sports team withholds fines and association dues from the players' paychecks, but he or she also gets to meet the players and go to the games.

Skills	Accounting, analytical, communication, computer, decision making, management, math, organizational, problem solving
Personality	Able to see the big picture, discreet, flexible, good judgment, likes working with people and numbers, tactful
Education	Bachelor's degree or master's in accounting, finance, or business; Certified Public Accountant certification; MBA also recommended
Pay range	$47,000 to $138,000 plus a year, depending on experience, location, and company

Critical Thinking Why does a controller need analytical and problem-solving skills?

 For more information on controllers visit finance.glencoe.com or your local library.

Your Financial Portfolio

Start with a Plan

Three brothers, Collin, Kyle, and J.C., plan to start a house painting business. All of them have experience painting, and they have identified plenty of work in an area downtown that is being renovated. They want to know how much start-up capital they'll need to get their business going and keep it going until it is solidly established.

Start-up Costs

Onetime costs:

Equipment: 3 ladders	$305
Paint sprayers	120
Rollers, brushes, drop cloths, and other supplies	
(ongoing supplies will be expensed per job)	250
Down payment for van	$3,000
Total onetime costs	**$3,675**

Continuing costs (monthly):

Insurance	$120
Cell phone	25
Van loan	625
Van maintenance and gas	100
Total monthly costs	**$870**
Total continuing expenses for a year	**10,440**
Total start-up costs	**$14,115**

Identify Start-up costs depend on the type of business, the size of the business, and the amount and kind of inventory and operating expenses. Give an example of the following types of business: service, retail, manufacturing. Which might be the most expensive for start-up costs? Why?

is growing according to her projections outlined in Cricket Lane's financial plan.

At the end of each quarter or year, her accountant will also see that all required local, state, and federal reports are submitted to the appropriate agencies.

SECTION 21.2 ASSESSMENT

CHECK YOUR UNDERSTANDING

1. What reports did Molly include in her financial plan?
2. Refer to Molly's projected 12-month income statement in **Figure 21.8**. When does Molly predict that she'll begin to show a positive net income?
3. As you can see from **Figure 21.9**, Molly is projecting a negative cash flow of $6,120 for the first 12-month period during which she is in business. How did she arrive at this conclusion?

THINK CRITICALLY

4. Summarize the steps that Molly has taken to ensure that her financial plan will be efficient and effective.

USING MATH SKILLS

5. **Positive Predictions** One of Molly's long-term strategic goals is to increase sales by 30 percent or more in each of the first three years of business. As Molly reviews her projected income statements for the next three years, she knows that she made the best guess estimates for both revenue and expenses. Molly believes that she'll meet or maybe even exceed her goals.

   Apply Using **Figure 21.10**, calculate what Molly's projected sales would be in the second and third year if they increased 35 percent from each previous year. How might a 35 percent increase in sales impact Molly's projected expenses?

SOLVING MONEY PROBLEMS

6. **Start-Up Capital** According to **Figure 21.7**, Molly will need $71,750 to purchase assets for Cricket Lane Flowers. If the bank denies her application for the short-term commercial loan of $30,000, she won't have enough money for all the assets that she has identified as necessary to begin operations.

   Advise How might Molly revise her list of assets and still have what she'll need to begin to operate her business? Explain your reasoning.

CHAPTER 21 ASSESSMENT

CHAPTER SUMMARY

- Start-up capital includes both the capital required to purchase assets for a new business and any costs or fees involved in establishing a business.

- As part of your financial plan you must estimate your operating capital, a process that is often referred to as financial forecasting. This future financial picture of your business is reported in projected financial statements.

- A financial plan will include projected income statements, projected balance sheets, and projected statements of cash flows.

- Reserve capital is money that is set aside to pay for emergencies or unforeseen expenses, to take advantage of business opportunities as they arise, and for expansion and growth of the business.

- The success of your strategic and marketing plans depends on the quality and accuracy of your financial plan, including the following reports: Statement of Required Start-Up Capital, Projected 12-Month Income Statement, Projected 12-Month Statement of Cash Flows, Projected 3-Year Income Statement, Projected 3-Year Statement of Cash Flows, and Projected 3-Year Balance Sheet.

Internet zone

Understanding and Using Vocabulary

For each of the following terms, write a sentence that describes the association between the term and the process of preparing to open a business.

start-up capital
operating capital
financial forecasting
projected financial statements
fixed expenses
variable expenses
reserve capital
chart of accounts

Review Key Concepts

1. What three aspects of starting and operating a business are addressed in a good financial plan?
2. What are the three categories of required capital?
3. Why is sufficient start-up capital essential to the survival of a new business?
4. What is the difference between fixed expenses and variable expenses?
5. How does a projected income statement differ from a projected balance sheet?

CHAPTER 21 ASSESSMENT

Apply Key Concepts

1. Does Molly's financial plan address the three aspects of establishing and operating a business? If so, how?
2. How much money does Molly plan to hold in reserve? What might Molly do if she decides that she needs more reserve capital?
3. Do you think Molly has correctly estimated the start-up capital required for Cricket Lane Flowers? Why or why not?
4. Review the projected 12-month income statement in **Figure 21.8**. Name three expenses that are fixed and three that are variable.
5. Review the projected three-year balance sheet in **Figure 21.12**. At the end of the third year, will the assets of the business be higher or lower than at the end of the first year? What about the liabilities? What do you think this might mean for Cricket Lane Flowers?

 Problem Solving Today

RESERVE CAPITAL

Choose a business that you would like to own. Imagine that you've set aside some reserve capital for your new business, and now you want to develop a plan of action for some possible emergency situations. For example, what will you do if a flood damages your store?

Invent Think of three different "what if" scenarios that could happen to your business. List the scenarios and their possible solutions.

Computer Activity As an alternative activity, use Internet search engines to help you find possible solutions to the emergency scenarios on your list. For instance, you might search under "flood victim relief" to find what type of assistance is available to small businesses damaged by flooding.

Real-World Application

CONNECT WITH ECONOMICS

Molly had a difficult time preparing her projected 12-month statement of cash flows for Cricket Lane Flowers. The experiences she had when she worked at King Point Florist helped in making estimates. However, Molly realizes that she can't fully predict the impact that outside influences might have on her business.

Think Critically Describe how inflation, low unemployment, and a worldwide drought might affect Molly's business. What other economic conditions might affect Cricket Lane Flowers?

CONSULTANTS

Molly wants to prepare a list of trade associations, vendors, local business organizations, and government agencies that she can consult.

Connect Using a variety of search engines, help Molly prepare this list.
1. What are some trade associations that Molly might want to join?
2. Locate three online vendors that Molly could use in her business.
3. Find two local business organizations in your state that she might contact.
4. Identify two government agencies that Molly could ask for assistance.

CHAPTER 22

Pricing, Costing, and Growth

STANDARD &POOR'S

Q&A

Q: It sure seems like you have to know a lot of math formulas in order to set a price for a product you want to sell. Isn't there any easier way? I'm not that good at math.

A: In many cases, your selling prices should be close to what your competitors charge. You'll need to make sure, however, that your business will be profitable at those prices. For many businesses, profit margins are often only in the 10 percent to 15 percent range. For each $1 in sales, the business gets to keep 10 cents—making accurate pricing essential.

Merchandise Pricing and Costing

What You'll Learn

- How to **calculate** selling price
- How to **identify** variable and fixed costs
- How to **determine** effective pricing

$\mathcal{T}$onya decided to make a new shoulder bag for herself. She purchased a plain black cloth bag, some fabric paints, unusual buttons, and sewing supplies. She decorated the bag with bright paints, a pattern of buttons, and fabric scraps. When Tonya's friends saw her new bag, they thought it was great. Tonya's friend Monica asked how much she would charge to make a similar bag. Tonya didn't know what to say! She realized that she had no idea what her bag had actually cost to make.

Tonya could not determine a reasonable selling price for Monica's bag without first carefully analyzing the costs. If she merely guessed at a price, she might discover later that the bag cost more to make than the amount for which she had sold it.

Pricing is the process of assigning a selling price to a good or service. You must price goods and services appropriately for your business to succeed. If you set prices too high, customers may buy from your competition—or not buy at all. If you set prices too low, you may not be able to cover your costs and operating expenses.

Many factors influence the prices of goods and services. Pricing decisions must take into account costs, competition, and economic conditions. To make sound pricing decisions, a business owner must consider the goals of pricing.

Why It's Important

Effective pricing and costing are essential to a business's financial success.

KEY TERMS

- pricing
- product cost-plus pricing
- markup
- manufacturing business
- product costing
- cost behavior
- variable costs
- direct materials
- direct labor
- fixed costs
- contribution margin
- break-even point

Goals of Pricing

Every business owner wants to set effective prices that yield large profits. Most businesses have three goals that act as guidelines for effective pricing. The goals are:

- to obtain a given share of the market,

- to generate sales that produce a specific profit, and
- to meet competitors' prices.

In establishing prices, a business may have to prioritize these goals. For example, suppose that a primary goal of your new outdoor sportswear business is to match your competitors' prices. You must remember that if you set your prices too low, you may not generate enough profit for your business to succeed. Suppose that the primary goal of your business is to increase profits. You can achieve your objective by selling more items at the current price or by selling the same number of items at a higher price. However, if you raise prices to increase profits, you may no longer meet competitors' prices. As a business owner you must decide which pricing goals are most important.

What's Your Financial ID?

CREATIVE THINKING

Successful businesses rely on a constant stream of ideas and people with the courage to present them. Do you have a lot of good ideas? Here's an opportunity to test your creative thinking. Write your answers on a separate sheet of paper.

1. Do you look for ideas?
   Often   Sometimes   Rarely

2. Do you sometimes play devil's advocate as a way to stimulate others?
   Often   Sometimes   Rarely

3. Do you challenge the rules?
   Often   Sometimes   Rarely

4. Do you ask "what if" questions?
   Often   Sometimes   Rarely

5. Can you motivate yourself and do what it takes to set your ideas in motion?
   Often   Sometimes   Rarely

6. Do you use impractical ideas as stepping-stones to new ideas?
   Often   Sometimes   Rarely

7. Do you express silly ideas?
   Often   Sometimes   Rarely

8. Do you challenge assumptions?
   Often   Sometimes   Rarely

Scoring: Give yourself 5 points for each "often," 3 points for each "sometimes," and 0 points for each "rarely."

Beginner: If you scored 0–10 points, consider playing around with new ideas and presenting them. Ideas can be fun!

Explorer: If you scored 11–20 points, you're willing to stretch yourself.

Creator: If you scored 21–30 points, your input will be welcome on any team.

Brainstormer: If you scored 31–40 points, you take the lead in risky ideas that may result in big rewards.

Pricing in a Merchandising Business

All the financial procedures you have learned so far have involved merchandising businesses. A merchandising business buys goods, marks them up, and sells them to customers such as a retail store. Establishing selling prices in this type of business is relatively simple.

Retail Pricing Methods

A retail business sells goods or services to the final user, the consumer. One pricing method commonly used by retail businesses is product cost-plus pricing. In *product cost-plus pricing* you determine an item's selling price by adding the invoice cost of the item (how much the business paid for the item) to a certain percentage of that cost. This added amount is called markup. *Markup* is the difference between the cost of an item to a business and the selling price of the item. This markup must cover all of the business's expenses and allow for a profit.

Luggage World is a retail store that sells a wide variety of travel bags and suitcases. As merchandise is received, the store manager prices all bags with a 70 percent markup. Suppose that the Presidential Bag has an invoice cost of $48. The manager calculates the selling price as follows:

What factors would make pricing
in a manufacturing business
more complicated than in a retail
business?

Purchase cost	$48.00
Plus markup ($48.00 × 70%)	+33.60
Selling price	$81.60

If you cannot sell an item or a line of merchandise at a particular markup, you may have to lower the selling price or discontinue stocking the item. The decision to mark up items a certain percentage will depend on such factors as economic conditions, competition, or the season of the year.

Suppose that you purchase sweatshirts for your outdoor sportswear shop at $12 per shirt and price each one with a markup of 60 percent ($12 × 60% = $7.20). The retail price of each sweatshirt is $19.20 ($12 + $7.20 = $19.20). However, if your competitors are selling the same sweatshirts for $17.99 each, you'll probably have difficulty selling your sweatshirts with a 60 percent markup. If you lower your price to be competitive, you may not earn enough profit to cover your expenses. If you can't purchase the same sweatshirts from another supplier at a lower cost, you may need to consider selling a different line of sweatshirts.

The percentage of markup will vary depending on the line of merchandise you are selling. Usually stores that sell very few items

EXPENSIVE ITEMS A jewelry store will have only a few potential customers each day and will actually sell merchandise to only a small percentage of them. *Why does a jewelry store have to set high prices on its merchandise?*

in a day, such as expensive jewelry stores, have higher markup percentages than stores that sell many items in a day, such as music stores. Regardless of the product, the markup must cover expenses and generate a profit for the business.

Costing and Pricing in a Manufacturing Business

Not all businesses simply purchase items, mark them up, and resell them to customers. Some businesses produce new merchandise. These businesses are called manufacturing businesses. A *manufacturing business* buys raw materials or processed goods and transforms them into finished products.

If Tonya decides to sell hand-decorated shoulder bags to her friends, her business will be a manufacturing business. She purchased a plain bag and decorated it, using paints, buttons, and sewing

CHIEF FINANCIAL OFFICER

Do you want to rise to the top? A chief financial officer (CFO) heads all the financial departments in a company. You'll find CFOs in almost every industry, from entertainment and health to banking and insurance. CFOs have the vital responsibility of establishing the financial policies for their company, and they report directly to the president of the company. CFOs study the cash flow, make decisions about raising operating funds, analyze their company's investments, and evaluate its financial state. Besides knowledge of accounting, CFOs need to know federal and state laws and regulations and often must understand international trade as well.

Skills	Accounting, analytical, communication, computer, decision making, math, problem solving, long-range planning
Personality	Able to see the big picture, able to cope with stress, flexible, good judgment, independent, likes working with people and numbers, tactful
Education	Bachelor's or master's degree in accounting, economics, finance, or business administration; Certified Public Accountant certification
Pay range	$62,000 to $300,000 a year, depending on experience, location, and company

Research Think of a major corporation that interests you. Using the library or the Internet, find the name of the CFO of that corporation.

 For more information on chief financial officers visit finance.glencoe.com **or your local library.**

materials to create a desirable new item. Tonya will have to consider the cost of the materials and labor that went into the production of her first bag before she can determine an appropriate price for similar bags. Determining costs and pricing in a manufacturing business is more complicated than it is in a retail business.

Product Costing

Manufacturing businesses must analyze all costs involved in creating their products—a process called *product costing.* Only by product costing can you establish a selling price that is both competitive and profitable for your business.

Product costing will help Tonya decide whether or not she can sell hand-decorated bags for a reasonable price. She may find that her costs for the first bag were fairly low and that she can make and sell similar bags at a profit. On the other hand, she may discover that making the first bag was quite expensive. To cover all costs, she may have to set a very high selling price. The price may be so high that no one is likely to buy the bags. After examining her costs, Tonya may decide that the bags are not worth making.

THEY'RE HOT! Items that are in great demand, such as barbecues during warm weather, rarely go on sale during the summer months. *What might be the reason for this?*

CASE STUDY

Jim Britt opened Britt's Bagels 12 years ago. At that time, Britt's was the only bagel shop in town, and business was great from the very first day. After a couple of years, Britt's began serving breakfast. When the coffee craze started sweeping the United States, Jim began serving a variety of coffees and cappuccinos. Jim always seemed to recognize the trends and adapted his business accordingly.

This year, for the first time, Jim's sales did not meet expectations, and his profits were less than in previous years. Three other bagel stores opened in town—franchised operations with national name recognition. Coffee no longer seems to be as trendy as before. Jim is concerned about his business, but he isn't sure what to do next. He turned to the experts at Standard & Poor's for advice.

STANDARD &POOR'S **Analysis:** Jim's situation is not unique. He has worked hard over the years and has been rewarded with a successful business. Now, however, he is finding that his business is shrinking rather than growing, and he's not sure why. Jim needs to understand precisely the factors that are affecting his business. Jim may be losing some customers to competitors, but he also may be offering products yielding a very low profit. After analyzing his business operations, Jim needs to develop a plan to rejuvenate Britt's Bagels.

STANDARD &POOR'S **Recommendation:** Jim has many years of financial records that he can evaluate in order to understand what is happening to his business. He can start by analyzing how his revenues and costs have changed in recent years. He should prepare an analysis showing the percent of his revenues and costs attributed to each type of product during the last several years. Perhaps gourmet coffee sales were highly profitable, but as coffee sales fell, Jim's profits declined even more. Next, Jim needs to evaluate whether his bagel business and breakfast services are profitable. If his bagel sales are declining, he may be losing customers to the competition. If so, Jim's business may still be profitable, but it may continue to shrink unless he implements new strategies.

Critical Thinking Questions

1. Name some aspects of Jim's competition that he should analyze.
2. What should Jim do if he finds that, excluding coffee sales, his business is only marginally profitable?
3. What changes could Jim make in his business to help Britt's Bagels compete with the other bagel businesses in town?

*I*n this high-tech century, most of us recognize abbreviations like PC (personal computer); www (World Wide Web); and the latest in home entertainment, DVD (digital videodisk). In India, IT (information technology) is an abbreviation that's worth billions. Fueled by the country's development of new software and the Internet, IT has rocketed the Indian economy to one of the fastest growing in the world. It's a foothold India intends to keep. Each year the country's universities produce 65,000 computer scientists—more than double that of the U.S. Although nearly 40 percent of India's citizens live in poverty, IT's expansion promises a better future. The Minister of Information Technology vows to take the future to India's villages, to the poor, and in the language of the common people. Here's a snapshot of India.

Geographic area	1,269,346 sq. mi.
Population	986,611,000
Capital	New Delhi (pop. 301,000)
Language	Hindi, 14 other official languages, English
Currency	rupee
Gross domestic product (GDP)	$1.534 trillion
Per capita GDP	$1,600
Economy	Industry: textiles, chemicals, food processing, steel, transportation equipment. Agriculture: rice, wheat, oilseed, cotton, cattle, water buffalo, fish. Exports: gems and jewelry, clothing, engineering goods.

A computer programmer in Bangalore, India

Thinking Critically

Analyze Most of the Indian population lives in villages, and farms for a living. List some of the ways information technology might improve their lives economically.

For more information on India visit finance.glencoe.com or your local library.

Classifying Costs

Whether you are the manager of a large business, such as General Electric, or a small business, such as a local bakery, you need complete information about costs to make smart financial decisions. You must identify your costs and determine—as production factors or sales change—what costs will increase, what costs will decrease, and what costs will remain the same.

Cost behavior is the way a cost changes in relation to a change in business activity. For instance, as your business makes more items, some costs may increase, such as the costs of additional materials or labor. Other costs remain constant and are not influenced by the number of items you produce or the volume of sales. These costs could include rent, taxes, utilities, and insurance. In analyzing cost behavior, you'll usually classify costs as variable or fixed.

Variable Costs

Variable costs are costs that change in direct proportion to the activity level of production. This means that if production increases, these costs will increase. If production decreases, your variable costs will decrease.

To understand cost behavior, consider the example of Windy River Creations. Wayne and Naomi are Native Americans who want to start a small business producing handmade Native American jewelry. They intend to buy metal bands, beads, leather, and other materials and make items to sell to area stores. They have rented a small shop, purchased a few pieces of equipment, bought materials and supplies, and hired two local artists to make the jewelry.

Windy River has identified three variable costs. These are the direct materials used to make the jewelry, the direct labor to create the jewelry, and the supplies used in processing the jewelry.

Direct materials are the raw materials used to make a finished product. For Windy River's jewelry these materials include metal, beads, leather, pins, packaging, and other items. Wayne and Naomi plan to produce five pieces of jewelry, one of which is called the Sunset Bracelet. The direct materials needed to produce the bracelet cost $4.30.

Direct labor is the work required to convert raw materials into a finished product. To determine the cost of direct labor, multiply the amount of time spent to produce the item by the employee's hourly wage. Wayne and Naomi are paying their employees $12 per hour. It takes approximately 15 minutes (0.25 hours) to make the Sunset Bracelet. Therefore, the cost of direct labor per bracelet is $3 (0.25 × $12 = $3).

Wayne and Naomi now know that the cost of materials and labor needed to make the bracelet is $7.30 ($4.30 direct materials plus $3 direct labor). They must also take into account the cost of the supplies that will be consumed in the production process. This cost could include polish, wire, solder, glue, and finishing spray. Wayne and Naomi estimate that the cost of the supplies for one bracelet is $0.35. This brings the total variable cost per bracelet to $7.65, illustrated as follows:

Direct materials	$4.30
Direct labor	3.00
Supplies	0.35
Total variable cost	$7.65

As more units are made, the variable cost assigned to each unit remains the same, but the total variable cost for the business increases. When fewer units are made, total variable costs decrease. The table below shows how the total variable cost for Windy River increases or decreases depending on the number of Sunset Bracelets made.

	Unit Variable Cost				Total Variable Cost
7 Bracelets	$7.65	×	7	=	$53.55
10 Bracelets	$7.65	×	10	=	$76.50
18 Bracelets	$7.65	×	18	=	$137.70

Fixed Costs

Rent, insurance, taxes, salaries, and some utilities are examples of fixed costs. *Fixed costs* are costs that remain constant even if the activity or production level changes. The total fixed cost remains the same regardless of the number of units produced.

For example, Wayne and Naomi pay $700 per month to rent the shop that Windy River occupies. Regardless of the number of bracelets produced in a month, the fixed cost of rent will remain at $700. Remember, the selling price of the bracelets must exceed all fixed costs plus all variable costs in order for Windy River to make a profit.

LABOR INTENSE Many manufacturing companies use robots to assemble products. *What are some advantages to using robots instead of human beings?*

Selling Price

Wayne and Naomi plan to mark up the variable costs by approximately 70 percent in order to cover the fixed costs and show a profit. The total monthly fixed costs for the business are $1,400. Windy River is selling five types of jewelry, so each type must cover one-fifth, or 20 percent, of the fixed costs per month. Therefore, each type of jewelry must cover $280 in fixed costs per month ($1,400 × 20% = $280).

If the variable costs total $7.65 for each bracelet and a 70 percent markup is added, the selling price of the bracelet will be $13 ($7.65 + ($7.65 × 70%) = $13). Wayne and Naomi must determine whether this markup is sufficient. To do so, they'll have to figure out how many bracelets they must sell to cover both fixed and variable costs.

The Contribution Margin

The *contribution margin* is the amount of money that the sale of a particular product contributes toward the payment of fixed costs and the profit of a business. The contribution margin equals total sales minus total variable costs. For example, if a product has sales of $13,000 and has variable costs totaling $7,000, it has a contribution margin of $6,000. This is the product's contribution to covering the fixed expenses and future profits.

Sales	$13,000	
Minus variable costs	−7,000	
Contribution margin	$ 6,000	(Amount to be applied to fixed expense)

The Break-Even Point

The *break-even point* is the point at which total sales equal total costs (variable and fixed costs). It represents the sales that a business must achieve to break even, or cover all costs. At the break-even point, there is neither a profit nor a loss.

Calculating the break-even point helps you predict how changes in costs and sales will affect the profit earned by your business. You can also use the break-even analysis to determine how many units of a product must be made and sold to cover expenses.

For example, suppose that you wanted to calculate how many units of the Sunset Bracelet Wayne and Naomi would have to sell to break even, or cover all costs. Represent the number of units needed to break even by a variable such as n. On the left side of the equation, multiply unit sales price by n. On the right side of the equation, multiply the unit variable costs by n, then add the total fixed costs. Solve for n.

Go Figure...   **BREAK-EVEN POINT**

Example: Windy River sells each Sunset Bracelet for $13. The unit variable cost for the bracelet is $7.65. The amount of total fixed costs that sales of the Sunset Bracelet are expected to contribute is $280. How many units of the Sunset Bracelet must Windy River sell to break even?

Formula: Break-Even Sales = Variable Costs + Total Fixed Costs
Unit Sales Price × n = (Unit Variable Costs × n) + Fixed Costs

Solution:
$$\$13.00n = \$7.65n + \$280$$
$$\$13.00n - \$7.65n = \$280$$
$$\$5.35n = \$280$$
$$n = \$280 \div \$5.35$$
$$n = 52.3, \text{ or } 53 \text{ bracelets}$$

To break even, Windy River must sell 53 Sunset Bracelets each month.

RESPOND

What adjustments will Wayne and Naomi have to consider if sales of the Sunset Bracelet do not meet the break-even point?

Break-even sales are the sales, expressed as a dollar amount, that a business must make to cover all costs. Break-even sales for the Sunset Bracelet are $689 (53 bracelets × $13 = $689) per month. The following calculations show the accuracy of the math.

	TOTAL	UNIT
Sales (53 × $13)	$689.00	$13.00
Less variable costs (53 × $7.65)	−$405.45	−$7.65
Contribution margin	$283.55	$ 5.35
Less fixed costs	−$280.00	
Net income	$ 3.55	

Fortunately for Wayne and Naomi, Windy River has been averaging sales of 70–80 bracelets per month for the past few months, exceeding their break-even point. At the present rate of sales, the bracelet's contribution margin is covering its share of fixed costs and is contributing to a net income for the business.

By substituting different numbers in the break-even equation, Wayne and Naomi can analyze the impact on profits from changes in sales price, costs, and sales volume. What if only 45 bracelets are

TOO MANY ITEMS When a store is overstocked with certain items, they must be sold quickly to increase the amount of cash available for the purchase of new merchandise. *Can you name other reasons why a store might discount a certain item?*

sold? What if the variable costs increase by $2? How much profit is reported if 75 bracelets are sold?

Such questions are an important part of financial analysis. As a business owner you must anticipate changes in the market and be prepared with alternative plans if the changes actually occur. These techniques of examining financial possibilities and being prepared for changes help keep your business growing.

SECTION 22.1 — ASSESSMENT

CHECK YOUR UNDERSTANDING

1. What are the basic goals that businesses use as a guideline for setting prices?
2. Describe the difference between variable and fixed costs.
3. What is the purpose of calculating the break-even point?

THINK CRITICALLY

4. What would happen if a retail business sold its products to consumers for the price it paid for them?

USING MATH SKILLS

5. **Break-Even Point** Dorothy sells mirrors at weekend craft shows for $75 each. She makes the mirror frames out of colored pieces of glass and ceramic tile. The mirrors are very popular; Dorothy actually has more orders than she can fill.
   Apply Help Dorothy figure out how many mirrors she has to sell to break even. Dorothy estimates that her variable costs are $25 and her fixed costs are $1,000.

SOLVING MONEY PROBLEMS

6. **Establishing Retail Prices** Cookie Cutter's is a retail store that sells a variety of kitchen gadgets and gifts. Today is your first day on the job there, and you've been asked to price the food processors that have just arrived. The manager has told you that all products have a 65 percent markup. The invoice price of one food processor is $72.
   Calculate Figure out what the selling price of each food processor will be.

Planning for Growth

What You'll Learn

- How to **describe** common forms of business growth
- How to **discuss** profit planning
- How to **calculate** target profit
- How to **calculate** margin of safety

Why It's Important

To be successful, a business needs to make a profit but also must grow.

KEY TERMS

- **target profit**
- **target sales**
- **margin of safety**

CONNECT

Can you recall a business in your neighborhood that has expanded? Did that expansion seem to be successful or not?

The key to all successful business operations is growth. Businesses, whether they are small sole proprietorships or large corporations, are much like people. They must grow and mature to achieve success. A business that does not grow often finds itself far behind its competition.

Forms of Business Growth

Business growth can come in many forms and can be measured in many ways. It may include increases in the number of customers, sales, share of the market, employees, lines of merchandise, and (of course) profit. These are important aspects of the growth of any business as well as indicators of success. However, growth should be carefully planned and directed. Sound financial planning is essential in making decisions regarding expansion.

Every aspect of your business does not need to grow every year. For a business, bigger does not necessarily mean better. If a business grows too rapidly or in the wrong area, serious financial problems may result.

Carefully planning growth to correspond with the business's short-term and long-term goals is essential to financial success. Your short-term goals for the business reflect the areas in which you will concentrate your efforts. One year you may place an emphasis on increasing customers; the following year, you may explore new lines of merchandise. As one of your target areas grows, others may also increase and grow. For example, if you concentrate on increasing your number of customers this year, your sales—and hopefully your profits—will also report increases. Primary growth in one area often leads to secondary growth in other areas.

Customers

Adding new customers usually causes a rise in sales. More sales usually result in greater profits. Increasing the number of customers is always a primary goal in business. Acquiring new customers is often a result of two factors: effective advertising and promotions and referrals by satisfied customers. Potential customers must know where the business is located, and they must believe that buying goods and services from your business will be a positive experience. Although you may have control over your advertising and marketing programs, you have little or no control over customer referrals. Satisfying your customers' needs is the key to building a solid customer base.

Sales

Growth in sales is also a major business goal. When sales increase, however, you must be capable of handling the larger volume so that you continue to satisfy your customers. If sales grow too quickly, and you don't have the appropriate number of employees, the quality of your customer service may suffer seriously. In addition, you must be sure that you have sufficient merchandise to offer.

Market Share

Another measurement of growth is the business's share of the existing market. If your business held approximately 15 percent of the potential market last year, and this year your market share has risen to 19 percent, you have achieved positive growth. This is evidence that your business is staying competitive, probably through effective advertising and promotions.

QUESTION

What factors would you want to consider when deciding whether or not to hire more employees?

Employees

As your market share grows and your sales increase, you must maintain an appropriate number of employees. The need to hire more employees to accommodate your customers is a sign of positive growth. However, merely adding employees does not mean positive growth if the additional employees are not utilized in the proper manner. Payroll is a major expense of your business.

Lines of Merchandise

When expanding to a new line of merchandise, you must carefully analyze the potential market and estimate the profits to be made. Expanding for the sake of expansion does not mean positive growth. The new line should assure a new sales market and good profits. Unfortunately, many small businesses experience financial success only to expand to new areas of merchandise or services that prove unprofitable.

$AVVY SAVER

Book Bargains

1. Search for Internet book sites that offer discounts.
2. Look for sales; most bookstores have discount tables.
3. Browse used bookstores for books in good condition.
4. Ask your parents; they may have some great books they read at your age.
5. Trade books with or borrow books from friends.

Profits

One of the key indicators of the success of your business is the rate of growth of your profits. To make a profit is the reason you are in business. Profits must grow for your business to survive. However, planning for increased profits is often easier said than done. Businesses may approach profit in several ways.

Profit Planning

Business managers frequently evaluate cost and profit data to determine how to maximize profits. They use break-even analysis to test possible changes and to determine how those changes might affect future profits. Using the results of their analysis, managers forecast sales and plan financial activities for their business.

Setting a Target Profit

An important part of the planning process is setting goals. One common goal is to increase the amount of net income, or profit. The amount of net income that a business sets as a goal is called the *target*

HOW MANY CAN YOU SELL? Stores are always faced with the problem of realistically predicting how many items can be sold. *What problem could result from stocking too many soccer balls?*

profit. For example, you may want to expand to a new line of merchandise or possibly open another outlet or store. In order to fulfill these objectives, you'll need to generate a given amount of profit.

Suppose that Wayne and Naomi want to earn a profit of $500 per month over the next six months on sales of the Sunset Bracelet. Assuming that the selling price and costs remain constant, how many bracelets would they need to sell to achieve this target profit? The target profit equation is as follows:

Target Profit = Variable Costs + Fixed Costs + Profit

Using the above equation, you can calculate how many units a business must sell to reach its target profit. Represent the number of units needed to achieve the target profit by a variable such as n. On the left side of the equation, multiply the unit sales price by n. On the right side of the equation, multiply the unit variable costs by n. Then add fixed costs and the required profit. Solve for n.

Go Figure...   TARGET PROFIT

Example: Windy River sells each Sunset Bracelet for $13. The unit variable cost for the bracelet is $7.65. The amount of total fixed costs that sales of the Sunset Bracelet are expected to contribute is $280. The target profit is $500 per month. How many units of the Sunset Bracelet must Windy River sell to reach its target profit?

Formula: Target Profit = Variable Costs + Fixed Costs + Profit

Unit Sales Price $\times n =$ (Unit Variable Costs $\times n$) + Fixed Costs + Profit

Solution:

$$
\begin{aligned}
\$13n &= \$7.65n + \$280 + \$500 \\
\$13n - \$7.65n &= \$280 + \$500 \\
\$5.35n &= \$780 \\
n &= \$780 \div \$5.35 \\
n &= 145.7, \text{ or } 146 \text{ bracelets}
\end{aligned}
$$

Windy River would have to sell 146 Sunset Bracelets to achieve its target profit.

Windy River has been selling about 70 to 80 bracelets per month, and sales have risen approximately 10 percent per month. By increasing current sales by approximately 10 percent a month for the next six months, *target sales* (the number of units you need to sell to reach your target profit) would be about 124 bracelets per month by the sixth month.

Assuming present sales are 70 per month, projected sales would be as follows:*

Month	1	77
	2	85
	3	94
	4	103
	5	113
	6	124

*Assumes 10 percent increase in current sales per month.

As shown on page 713, Windy River would have to sell 146 bracelets per month to reach its target profit of $500. Wayne and Naomi decide that this is an unrealistic expectation at the present time. After examining the current market, they conclude that a target profit of $400 is more realistic. Using the target profit calculation, they determine that they must sell 128 bracelets each month to achieve the goal of $400 profit per month.

SHORT DEMAND Items such as seasonal clothes and CDs have a short selling period. Tastes in music and clothes change, and new items come out every day. *Can you name any other products that have a very short selling period?*

Margin of Safety

When you're analyzing target sales and profits, you should consider what will happen if you don't reach your target. Your margin of safety will indicate the amount by which sales can drop before the business experiences a loss. The *margin of safety* is the target sales minus the break-even sales. A high margin of safety suggests a minimal risk that sales will fall below the break-even point. Wayne and Naomi would calculate the margin of safety for the Sunset Bracelet as follows:

Target sales (to achieve a profit of $400)	$1,664.00	128 bracelets
Less break-even sales	−689.00	−53 bracelets
Margin of safety	$975.00	75 bracelets

The margin of safety is $975, or 75 bracelets. This means that sales can drop by this amount below target sales before the business experiences a loss on this item. For Windy River this target sales amount is a fairly safe venture.

Planning and Growth

As you project your business's financial prospects, you must analyze carefully where you will spend your profits. Growth is important, but only if it is carefully analyzed, planned, and controlled. Sound planning will usually result in successful growth; poor planning could drive you out of business.

You may always have limited funds to invest for business growth. Careful planning and financial analysis should provide you with the knowledge you'll need for intelligent investment decisions and well-planned, controlled growth. The guidelines suggested below will not guarantee successful decisions, but ignoring them could result in business failure. These general guidelines are as follows:

- Make sound financial decisions when setting short-term and long-term goals.

CONTROLLED EXPANSION Expanding your business is good, but you shouldn't expand too rapidly. *Can you name a business in your area that expanded but then had financial problems?*

Business Expansion Is More Than Magic

Under the name of Morgan the Magnificent, Victor Morgan has been performing magic since he was eight years old. Now that he's 16, he wants to branch out from school events and birthday parties for friends and family to perform professionally. He already has his own Web site and a performance video. To expand the business, he wrote down strategies and actions he could take.

- Make a flyer and a cover letter I can send out to follow-up phone calls.
- Contact a public relations agency and offer to do free performances in exchange for their helping me get publicity.
- Call the local newspaper and ask if someone could write an article about me.
- Contact the human resources department of local companies to let them know I'm available to perform at employee functions and holiday parties.
- Contact local chambers of commerce to find out when they are having street fairs or crafts fairs.
- Contact local stores that sell or rent party supplies. Ask if I can post a flyer and if they can recommend me if anybody is looking for an entertainer.
- Contact wedding planners to see if they would recommend me to be part of the wedding entertainment.
- Stop by ice cream stores to find out if I can post a flyer.

Analyze Pick a business in your town. On a separate sheet of paper list eight strategies and actions that could improve or expand the business.

- Set realistic financial targets.
- Control expenditures and costs.
- Analyze financial statements frequently.
- Analyze your competition.
- Evaluate current economic conditions.
- Maintain a reserve fund for unexpected expenses, changes in economic conditions, or other unexpected events.

SECTION 22.2   ASSESSMENT

CHECK YOUR UNDERSTANDING

1. Describe the common forms of business growth.
2. Explain how setting a target profit is related to profit planning.
3. How is target profit calculated?
4. How is margin of safety calculated?

THINK CRITICALLY

5. Explain why business growth merely for the sake of growth is not wise.

USING COMMUNICATION SKILLS

6. **Business Growth** Lil owns an independent rug store in a small town. The Rug Rack has been open for about a year, and business has been very good. Currently she sells new and antique rugs as well as home decorating magazines. Lil thinks that it is time to add a new line of merchandise and expand her customer base.

   Recommend Suppose that you write an advice column for small business owners. What guidance might you give Lil regarding the goals she has set for The Rug Rack?

SOLVING MONEY PROBLEMS

7. **Achieve Target Profit** You have been hired by Windy River Creations as a financial consultant. After analyzing the company's cost and profit data, you predict that it will earn a profit of $600 per month within the next six months on the Sunset Bracelet. Assume that the bracelet will continue to sell for $13 and that the costs will remain constant.

   Apply Figure out how many bracelets Windy River will need to sell in order to achieve this target profit.

CHAPTER 22 ASSESSMENT

Understanding and Using Vocabulary

Knowing these terms will help you speak the language of a smart business owner. Write a brief paragraph about pricing, costing, and growth, using at least seven of these terms.

pricing
product cost-plus
  pricing
markup
manufacturing
  business

product costing
cost behavior
variable costs
direct materials
direct labor
fixed costs

contribution margin
break-even point
target profit

target sales
margin of safety

Review Key Concepts

1. Describe the difference between product cost-plus pricing and product costing.
2. What are direct materials and direct labor?
3. How is the contribution margin determined?
4. How is the margin of safety determined?
5. What are the general guidelines for business growth?

CHAPTER 22 ASSESSMENT

Apply Key Concepts

1. Roland sells wrought-iron plant stands in his gift shop. He purchases the plant stands for $18 and applies a markup of 40 percent. What is the retail price of each plant stand?
2. Give three examples of direct materials that might be used to produce leather purses.
3. If the leather purse sales total $36,000 and have variable costs of $14,500, what is the contribution margin?
4. If target sales for a new snakeskin purse are $3,479 and break-even sales are calculated at $2,109, what is the margin of safety? Do you think that this would be a safe venture? Why or why not?
5. How might you prioritize the guidelines for business growth? Explain your reasoning.

? Problem Solving Today

PRICING IN A MANUFACTURING BUSINESS

You plan to begin manufacturing futons. You have done market research, written a business plan, and selected vendors from whom you will buy raw materials. You now need to set prices for your futons. You will be selling two different lines.

Explain Describe what you must consider in pricing your futons.

Computer Activity As an alternative activity, use a word processor to write a letter to local department stores that might carry your futons. Include in the letter a description of your futon lines and reasons why they should purchase futons from you.

Real-World Application

CONNECT WITH MATH

Debra just started working in the accounting department of a company that manufactures blue jeans. One of her first tasks is to determine the variable costs of producing one pair of jeans. The raw materials used to make the jeans cost $8 per pair. The cost of direct labor to convert the raw materials into one pair of jeans is $11. In addition, supplies cost $3 per pair.

Calculate Help Debra determine the variable cost for one pair of jeans. Then figure the variable costs for 50, 100, and 250 pairs of jeans.

FINANCE *Online*

PET PROJECT

You own a pet accessory store in your town. Some of the items you sell are dog and cat food, collars, leashes, pet beds, and grooming products. Because this is a very competitive market, you try hard to stay on top of current market prices and trends that might affect your business.

Connect Use a variety of Internet search engines to find the following information:
1. Competitors in your local market
2. Internet competitors
3. Trends in the pet supply industry that might affect your pricing strategy

Get a Financial Life!

CASE STUDY

Business Growth and Decision Making

Overview

Two years ago, Eva and Jack Farnier opened a retail store called Party Town. They sell a wide variety of party decorations, paper goods, balloons, and games. The business has been a success so far—Eva and Jack have been able to meet their expenses each month. Now they want to grow their business. They are interested in carrying a new line of merchandise in order to expand their share of the market.

Resources

- Crayons, markers, colored pencils
  - Internet (optional)
  - Portfolio (ring binder or file folder)
  - Public or school library
  - Publication software (optional)
- Spreadsheet software (optional)
- Word processor

Procedures

Step A **THE PROCESS**

Eva and Jack need help making a decision about what additional merchandise they should carry.

1. Recommend a new product or line of merchandise that you think Party Town should carry. (Examples might include costumes, piñatas, or party favors.) Create a flyer, poster, or other visual aid describing the new product line to the public.

2. Imagine that Party Town is located where you live. Research the competition (other party stores, discount department stores, and toy stores), either by looking through the yellow pages or by visiting a store or stores. Describe Party Town's competition in your community. Does the competition carry the new product or line of merchandise you recommended? If so, how much does the merchandise sell for? If the competition does not carry the product, try to find out why.

3. Eva and Jack also plan to sell balloon bouquets that they will make in their store. The direct materials will cost $5.25, the direct labor per bouquet is $6, and the supply costs will be about $0.85. Assume that Party Town plans to mark up the bouquets by 80%. Figure out the selling price of each bouquet. If the fixed costs are $300, determine how many balloon bouquets Eva and Jack must sell to break even.

4. Help Eva and Jack set a target profit for the balloon bouquets. How many bouquets must they sell in order to achieve the target profit? Calculate the margin of safety for this product.

5. Schedule an interview with a business owner in your community. Before the interview, create a list of seven to ten

questions about running a successful business and possible expansion strategies.

Step B CREATE YOUR PORTFOLIO

As you work through the process, save the results so that you can refer, review, and refine. Create a professional-looking portfolio of the expansion recommendations you will present to Eva and Jack.

1. The first page should be a title page, with the following information centered:
   Business Growth and Decision
      Making
   Presented to Eva Farnier and Jack
      Farnier, Owners,
   Party Town
   By (Your Name)

2. The first section should include your flyer, poster, or other visual material describing the new product or line of merchandise that you have recommended to Eva and Jack.

3. Section 2 should present your research about the competition in your community.

4. Section 3 should include the selling price, break-even point, target profit, and margin of safety for the balloon bouquets. Be sure to show your calculations.

5. The last section will detail the questions and answers from the interview you conducted with the local business owner.

Step C THE INTERNET

The Internet is often called the Information Superhighway. Almost anything you want to know can be found on the Internet. It provides a vast communication network for people from all over the world. Students and employees must learn to use all the available information ethically and legally.

1. Write a definition for the term "ethics."

2. Many employers have a formal policy that defines the acceptable and unacceptable uses of the Internet in the work environment. Write a policy that Eva and Jack might put in place for their employees.

3. Research one legal issue that can arise when an employee uses the Internet. Some suggested issues include Internet plagiarism, viruses, employers being able to access employees' e-mail, and employees accessing the Internet for personal use during work time. Write a one- to two-page paper on the legal issue you researched.

4. The Internet contains an enormous amount of information. Many people assume that just because something appears on the Internet, it is factual. However, this is not always the case. As a class, develop a list of ways to be sure that the information you access and use is accurate.

Appendix: Math Skills Builder

WRITING NUMBERS AS WORDS AND ROUNDING NUMBERS

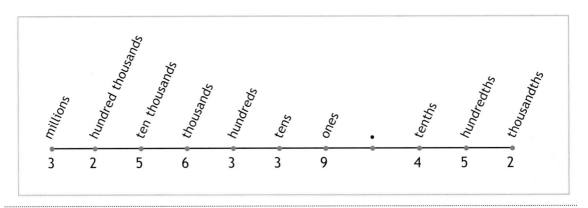

The place-value chart shows the value of each digit in the number 3,256,339.452. The place-value chart can help you write numbers.

EXAMPLE

482
8.557
$39.45

SOLUTION

four hundred eighty-two
eight and five hundred fifty-seven thousandths
thirty-nine and forty-five hundredths dollars
or thirty-nine and $^{45}/_{100}$ dollars

Place value is also used in rounding numbers. If the digit to the right of the place value you want to round is 5 or more, round up by adding 1 to the number in the place value. Then change all the digits to the right of the place value to zeros. If the number is 4 or less, round down by changing all the numbers to the right of the place value to zeros.

EXAMPLE

Round 4765 to the nearest hundred.

SOLUTION

4765   A. Find the digit in the hundred place. It is 7.

4765   B. Is the digit to the right 5 or more? Yes.

4800   C. Add 1 to the hundreds place. Change the digits to the right to zeros.

EXAMPLE

Round 0.843 to the nearest tenth.

SOLUTION

0.843   A. Find the digit in the tenth place. It is 8.

0.843   B. Is the digit to the right 5 or more? No.

0.8   C. Do not change the tenths digit. Drop the digits to the right.

WRITING NUMBERS AS WORDS AND ROUNDING NUMBERS

Dollar and cents amounts are often rounded to the nearest cent, or the hundredths place.

EXAMPLE	$26.7443	**SOLUTION**	$26.74
	$683.1582		$683.16

PROBLEMS

Write as numbers.
1. three thousand four hundred ninety-nine
2. one hundred eleven and $^{32}/_{100}$ dollars
3. two hundred six and eighty-eight thousandths

Write in word form.
4. 572
5. 2.897
6. $325.10

Round to the nearest place value shown.

7.	ten thousand	327,975	11.	one	28.91
8.	thousand	816,777	12.	tenth	86.379
9.	hundred	26,312	13.	hundredth	5.5787
10.	ten	6336			

Round 23,793,611 to the place value shown.
14. millions
15. ten millions
16. thousands
17. hundreds
18. ten thousands
19. hundred thousands

Round to the nearest place value shown.

20.	cent	$87.2671	23.	ten dollars	$5,982
21.	ten cents	$213.432	24.	hundred dollars	$12,785
22.	one dollar	$671.98			

APPLICATIONS

25. As an accountant for the advertising agency of Phillips & Phillips, Marcia Strasser writes many checks. Write each check amount in words.
    a. $27.83
    b. $121. 77
    c. $569.14
    d. $8,721. 65

26. Juan Sanchez, an inventory clerk for a lumber yard, often rounds inventory figures for easier handling. Round the number from the inventory list to the nearest ten.
    a. grade 1 oak   519 ft.
    b. grade 2 oak   795 ft.
    c. grade 1 pine   323 ft.
    d. grade 2 pine   477 ft.

ADDING AND SUBTRACTING DECIMALS

When adding decimals, write the addition problem in vertical form. Be sure to line up the decimal points. When adding amounts with different numbers of decimal places, write zeros in the empty decimal places.

EXAMPLE $15.27 + 16.39 + 36.19$

SOLUTION
```
  15.27
  16.39
+ 36.19
------
  67.85
```

EXAMPLE $58.2 + 3.97 + 8 + 123.796$

SOLUTION
```
   58.2          58.200
    3.97           3.970
    8.             8.000
+ 123.796      + 123.796
               --------
                193.966
```

When subtracting decimals, write the subtraction problem in vertical form. Be sure to line up the decimal points. When subtracting amounts with different numbers of decimal places, write zeros in the empty decimal places.

EXAMPLE $78.63 - 42.41$

SOLUTION
```
  78.63
- 42.41
------
  36.22
```

EXAMPLE $149.9 - 28.37$

SOLUTION
```
  149.9         149.90
-  28.37       - 28.37
               -------
                121.53
```

Adding and subtracting amounts of money is just like adding and subtracting decimals. The decimal point separates the dollars and cents. Remember to put a dollar sign in the total.

EXAMPLE $74.99 + 8.76

SOLUTION
```
  $74.99
  + 8.76
  ------
  $ 83.75
```

EXAMPLE $750 - 43.29

SOLUTION
```
  $750.00
  - 43.29
  -------
  $706.71
```

PROBLEMS

1.
```
  19.87
  32.24
+ 27.55
```

2.
```
  4.377
  6.829
+ 2.707
```

3.
```
    8.3
   12.78
+ 322.437
```

4.
```
   46.65
    3.5
+ 125.397
```

5.
```
$  2.77
  35.96
+ 10.37
```

6. $22.19 + 47.75 + 13.88 + 19.85$
7. $0.78 + 9.82 + 36.242 + 37.4$
8. $6.7 + 27.81 + 653.47 + 5.5$
9. $54.32 + 0.37 + 2.5 + 0.797$
10. $\$6.22 + \$53.19 + \$.33 + \$7.85$
11. $\$4.78 + \$12.50 + \$22 + \$17.10$

12.
```
  3.75
- 2.18
```

13.
```
  376.55
 - 27.42
```

14.
```
  468.47
- 233.55
```

15.
```
  367.05
- 219.87
```

16.
```
 $363.27
 - 79.14
```

ADDING AND SUBTRACTING DECIMALS

17. $547.7 - 127.6$ 18. $76.99 - 3.87$

19. $695.13 - 428.1$ 20. $3076 - 2205.50$

21. $\$300 - \$5.75$ 22. $\$445.19 - \$175.76$

APPLICATIONS Complete the sales receipts by finding the subtotals and the totals.

23.

Date 6/1/--	Auth. No. 86430	Identification	Clerk DL	Reg./Dept.	☑ Take ❑ Send
Qty	Class	Description		Price	Amount
1		dress			77 | 98
1		jacket			85 | 99
2		hosiery		12.99 ea	25 | 98

a. Freight charges will be included with your invoice at the time of shipping. You will be billed the published rates from UPS, US Postal Service.

CUSTOMER SIGNATURE X _Shelley Turner_

b. Sales Slip

Subtotal	?
Tax	13 | 30
Total	?

24.

Date 3/14/--	Auth. No. 42	Identification	Clerk JR	Reg./Dept.	☑ Take ❑ Send
Qty	Class	Description		Price	Amount
1		couch			599 | 95
1 pr		draperies			279 | 88

a. Freight charges will be included with your invoice at the time of shipping. You will be billed the published rates from UPS, US Postal Service.

CUSTOMER SIGNATURE X _Betty Clark_

b. Sales Slip

Subtotal	?
Tax	57 | 19
Total	?

Complete the bank deposit slips by finding the subtotals and the total deposits.

25.

		DOLLARS	CENTS
CASH	CURRENCY	72	00
	COINS		
CHECKS	LIST SEPARATELY 95-76	413	12
	98-11	25	00
	95-13	211	10
a.	SUBTOTAL	?	
⟳	LESS CASH RECEIVED	50	00
b.	TOTAL DEPOSIT	?	

a.

b.

26.

		DOLLARS	CENTS
CASH	CURRENCY	23	00
	COINS	7	44
CHECKS	LIST SEPARATELY 85-76	175	66
	88-11	23	33
		12	87
a.	SUBTOTAL	?	
⟳	LESS CASH RECEIVED	75	00
b.	TOTAL DEPOSIT	?	

a.

b.

27.

		DOLLARS	CENTS
CASH	CURRENCY		
	COINS	4	75
CHECKS	LIST SEPARATELY 57-12	25	95
	57-10	38	11
a.	SUBTOTAL	?	
⟳	LESS CASH RECEIVED	25	00
b.	TOTAL DEPOSIT	?	

a.

b.

28. You are a cashier at a coffee shop. Compute the correct change for each of the following orders.

	Customer's Order	Customer Gives You	Change
a.	$8.76	$10.00	
b.	$12.94	$15.00	
c.	$9.30	$10.50	
d.	$16.11	$20.00	
e.	$5.57	$5.75	
f.	$22.02	$25.00	
g.	$7.12	$7.15	
h.	$3.33	$5.00	
i.	$28.04	$30.04	
j.	$6.12	$10.25	

MULTIPLYING AND DIVIDING DECIMALS

When multiplying decimals, multiply as if the decimal numbers were whole numbers. Then count the total number of decimal places in the factors. This number will be the number of decimal places in the product.

EXAMPLE

$$
\begin{array}{r}
18.7 \leftarrow \text{factor} \\
\times\,0.34 \leftarrow \text{factor} \\
\hline
748 \\
561 \\
\hline
6358 \leftarrow \text{product}
\end{array}
$$

SOLUTION

$$
\begin{array}{r}
18.7 \leftarrow \text{1 decimal place} \\
\times\,0.34 \leftarrow +\text{2 decimal places} \\
\hline
748 \\
561 \\
\hline
6.358 \leftarrow \text{3 decimal places}
\end{array}
$$

If the product does not have enough digits to place the decimal in the correct position, you will need to write zeros. Start at the right of the product in counting the decimal places and write zeros at the left.

EXAMPLE

$$
\begin{array}{r}
0.63 \\
\times\,0.05 \\
\hline
315
\end{array}
$$

SOLUTION

$$
\begin{array}{r}
0.63 \leftarrow \text{2 decimal places} \\
\times\,0.05 \leftarrow +\text{2 decimal places} \\
\hline
0.0315 \leftarrow \text{4 decimal places}
\end{array}
$$

When multiplying amounts of money, round the answer to the nearest cent. Remember to put a dollar sign in the answer.

EXAMPLE

$$
\begin{array}{r}
\$2.25 \\
\times\,1.5 \\
\hline
3.375
\end{array}
$$

SOLUTION

$$
\begin{array}{r}
\$\,2.25 \leftarrow \text{2 places} \\
\times\,1.5 \leftarrow +\text{1 place} \\
\hline
\$3.375 \leftarrow \text{3 places}
\end{array}
$$

$\$2.25 \times 1.5 = \$3.375$
$= \$3.38$
rounded to the nearest cent

When multiplying by 10, 100, or 1000, count the number of zeros. Then move the decimal point to the right the same number of spaces.

EXAMPLE

8.32×100

SOLUTION

$8.32 \times 100 = 8.32 = 832$ 100 has 2 zeros; move decimal 2 places.

PROBLEMS

1. $\begin{array}{r} 18.3 \\ \times\,2.5 \\ \hline \end{array}$
2. $\begin{array}{r} 27.5 \\ \times\,8.2 \\ \hline \end{array}$
3. $\begin{array}{r} 56.8 \\ \times\,0.33 \\ \hline \end{array}$
4. $\begin{array}{r} 88.1 \\ \times\,0.23 \\ \hline \end{array}$

5. $\begin{array}{r} 0.57 \\ \times\,0.14 \\ \hline \end{array}$
6. $\begin{array}{r} 0.88 \\ \times\,0.07 \\ \hline \end{array}$
7. $\begin{array}{r} 0.93 \\ \times\,0.04 \\ \hline \end{array}$
8. $\begin{array}{r} 0.323 \\ \times\,0.005 \\ \hline \end{array}$

9. $\$17.85 \times 15.5 = \$276.675 =$
10. $\$25.24 \times 6.3 = \$159.012 =$
11. $\$18.15 \times 6.5 = \$117.975 =$
12. $\$14.98 \times 8.7 = \$130.326 =$

13. $33.8 \times 10 =$
14. $55.399 \times 100 =$
15. $0.518 \times 1000 =$
16. $532.788 \times 10,000 =$

MULTIPLYING AND DIVIDING DECIMALS

APPLICATION

17. Below are partial payroll records for Fanciful Flowers. Complete the records by calculating gross earnings (hourly rate x hours worked), Social Security tax (gross earnings × 0.062), Medicare tax (gross earnings × 0.0145), federal income tax (gross earnings × 0.15), and state income tax (gross earnings × 0.045). Round each deduction to the nearest cent. Find the total deductions and subtract from gross earnings to find the net pay.

	Employee	Hourly Rate	Number of Hours	Gross Earnings	Social Security Tax	Medicare Tax	Federal Inc. Tax	State Inc. Tax	Total Deductions	Net Pay
a.	M. Smith	$8.25	24	198.00	12.28	2.87	29.70	8.91	53.76	144.24
b.	R. Nash	$9.15	33	301.95	18.72	4.38	45.29	13.59	81.98	219.97
c.	C. Young	$7.75	15	116.25	7.21	1.69	17.44	5.23	31.57	84.68
d.	D. Cha	$9.15	30	274.50	17.02	3.98	41.18	12.35	74.53	199.97

When dividing decimals, if there is a decimal point in the divisor, you must move it to the right to make the divisor a whole number. Move the decimal point in the dividend to the right the same number of places you moved the decimal point in the divisor. Then divide as with whole numbers.

$$\begin{array}{r} 140 \leftarrow \text{quotient} \\ \text{divisor} \rightarrow 6\,\overline{)840} \leftarrow \text{dividend} \end{array}$$

EXAMPLE

$$3.44\,\overline{)15.5488}$$

SOLUTION

$$3.44\,\overline{)15.5488}$$

$$\begin{array}{r} 4.52 \\ 344\,\overline{)1554.88} \\ -1376 \\ \hline 1788 \\ -1720 \\ \hline 688 \\ -688 \end{array}$$

Add zeros to the right of the decimal point in the dividend if needed.

EXAMPLE

$$0.42\,\overline{)0.147}$$

SOLUTION

$$0.42\,\overline{)0.147}$$

$$\begin{array}{r} 0.35 \\ 42\,\overline{)14.70} \quad \text{zero added} \\ -126 \\ \hline 210 \\ -210 \end{array}$$

When the dividend is an amount of money, remember to place the dollar sign in the quotient and round the answer to the nearest cent.

EXAMPLE

$$48\,\overline{)\$95.12}$$

SOLUTION

$$\begin{array}{r} \$1.981 \\ 48\,\overline{)\$95.120} \end{array}$$

$\$95.12 \div 48 = \$1.98$ rounded to the nearest cent.

MULTIPLYING AND DIVIDING DECIMALS

When dividing by 10, 100, or 1000, count the number of zeros in 10, 100, or 1000 and move the decimal point to the left the same number of places.

EXAMPLE

$15{,}213.7 \div 1000$

SOLUTION

$15{,}213.7 \div 1000 = 15213.7$ 1000 has 3 zeros;
$= 15.2137$ move decimal 3 places

PROBLEMS

Round to the nearest hundredth or the nearest cent.

18. $2.7\overline{)11.61}$

19. $1.3\overline{)7.67}$

20. $6.2\overline{)44.02}$

21. $0.3\overline{)1.62}$

22. $.05\overline{)1.47}$

23. $.04\overline{)28.4}$

24. $8.3\overline{)46.99}$

25. $3.4\overline{)178.3}$

26. $88\overline{)\$356.68}$

27. $45\overline{)\$42.79}$

28. $15\overline{)\$87.32}$

29. $14.1\overline{)7.823}$

APPLICATIONS

30. Your family is looking into buying a late model, used car. Calculate (to the nearest tenth) the gas mileage for the following types of cars.

	Type of Vehicle	Miles	Gallons of Fuel	Miles per Gallon
a.	Subcompact	631	17.8	
b.	4-door sedan	471.4	16.6	
c.	Minivan	405.1	18.2	
d.	Compact	512.2	15.7	
e.	SUV	298.1	23.2	

FRACTION TO DECIMAL, DECIMAL TO FRACTION

Any fraction can be renamed as a decimal and any decimal can be renamed as a fraction. To rename a fraction as a decimal, use division. Think of the fraction bar in the fraction as meaning "divide by." For example, $5/8$ means "5 divided by 8." After the 5, write a decimal point and as many zeros as are needed. Then divide by 8.

EXAMPLE Change $3/8$ to a decimal.

SOLUTION

$$
3/8 \rightarrow
\begin{array}{r}
0.375 \\
8\overline{)3.000} \\
-24 \\
\hline
60 \\
-56 \\
\hline
40 \\
-40 \\
\hline
\end{array}
$$

EXAMPLE Change $1/5$ to a decimal.

SOLUTION

$$
1/5 \rightarrow
\begin{array}{r}
0.2 \\
5\overline{)1.0} \\
-10 \\
\hline
\end{array}
$$

If a fraction does not divide evenly, divide to one more decimal place than you are rounding to.

EXAMPLE Change $5/7$ to a decimal rounded to the nearest hundredth. (Divide to the thousandths place.)

SOLUTION

$$
5/7 \rightarrow
\begin{array}{r}
0.714 = 0.71 \\
7\overline{)5.000} \\
-49 \\
\hline
10 \\
-7 \\
\hline
30 \\
-28 \\
\hline
2 \\
\end{array}
$$

EXAMPLE Change $2/7$ to a decimal rounded to the nearest thousandth. (Divide to the ten thousandths place.)

SOLUTION

$$
2/7 \rightarrow
\begin{array}{r}
0.2857 = 0.286 \\
7\overline{)2.0000} \\
-14 \\
\hline
60 \\
-56 \\
\hline
40 \\
-35 \\
\hline
50 \\
-49 \\
\hline
1 \\
\end{array}
$$

To rename a decimal as a fraction, name the place value of the digit at the far right. This is the denominator of the fraction.

$$0.83 = {}^{83}/_{100}$$

3 is in the hundredths place, so the denominator is 100.

$$0.007 = {}^{7}/_{1000}$$

7 is in the thousandths place, so the denominator is 1000.

Note that the number of zeros in the denominator is the same as the number of places to the right of the decimal point. The fraction should always be written in lowest terms.

$$0.25 = {}^{25}/_{100} = {}^{1}/_{4}$$

$$3.375 = 3\, {}^{375}/_{1000} = 3\, {}^{3}/_{8}$$

FRACTION TO DECIMAL, DECIMAL TO FRACTION

Change the fractions to decimals. Round to the nearest thousandth.

1. $2/5$ 2. $5/6$ 3. $4/9$ 4. $7/10$

5. $9/25$ 6. $115/200$ 7. $1/7$ 8. $13/40$

9. $4/15$ 10. $5/12$ 11. $11/16$ 12. $1/4$

Change the fractions to decimals. Round to the nearest hundredth.

13. $1/8$ 14. $5/9$ 15. $33/35$ 16. $12/25$

17. $7/20$ 18. $2/25$ 19. $15/16$ 20. $2/9$

21. $3/7$ 22. $3/4$ 23. $1/6$ 24. $31/32$

Change the decimals to fractions reduced to lowest terms.

25. 0.275   26. 0.3   27. 0.15   28. 0.8

29. 1.125   30. 0.117   31. 0.32   32. 2.5

33. 44.755   34. 0.005   35. 5.545   36. 0.2

37. Stock prices have traditionally been quoted as dollars and fractions of a dollar. Change the stock prices to dollars and cents. Round to the nearest cent.

Stock	Price
a. AdobeSy	$61\,5/16$
b. AirTran	$4\,15/32$
c. CNET	$50\,3/4$
d. ETrade	$20\,1/4$
e. Omnipoint	$112\,5/8$
f. Qualcomm	$142\,1/16$
g. WebLink	$17\,13/16$
h. Winstar	$70\,23/32$

38. Individual bowling averages in the Southern Community League are carried to the nearest hundredth. Convert the decimals to fractions reduced to the lowest terms.

Name	Average
a. B. Taylor	220.13
b. J. Scott	217.02
c. T. Anfinson	216.97
d. G. Ingram	212.08
e. D. Ingram	210.50
f. B. Jordan	209.25
g. G. Maddux	207.88
h. A. Jones	205.15

PERCENT TO DECIMAL, DECIMAL TO PERCENT

Percent is an abbreviation of the Latin words *per centum*, meaning "by the hundred." So percent means "divide by 100." A percent can be written as a decimal. To change a percent to a decimal, first write the percent as a fraction with a denominator of 100, then divide by 100.

EXAMPLE Change 31% to a decimal.   **EXAMPLE** Change 17.3% to a decimal.

SOLUTION $31\% = {}^{31}/_{100} = 0.31$ **SOLUTION** $17.3\% = {}^{17.3}/_{100} = 0.173$

When dividing by 100, you can just move the decimal point two places to the left. When you write a percent as a decimal, you are moving the decimal point two places to the left and dropping the percent sign (%). If necessary, use zero as a placeholder.

EXAMPLE   **SOLUTION**

   A.   31% $31\% = 31. = 0.31$ ◄——— Drop % sign.
                     ———— Move decimal 2 places.

   B.   7% $7\% = 07. = 0.07$ ———— Insert a zero as a placeholder.

To write a decimal as a percent, move the decimal point two places to the right and add a percent sign (%).

EXAMPLE   **SOLUTION**

   A.   0.31 $0.31 = 0.31 = 31\%$ ◄ Add % sign.
                     ———— Move decimal 2 places.

   B.   0.07 $0.07 = 0.07 = 7\%$

   C.   2.5 $2.5 = 2.50 = 250\%$

   D.   0.008 $0.008 = 0.008 = 0.8\%$

PROBLEMS

Write as decimals.

1. 35%   2. 22%   3. 68%   4. 30%

5. 49.2%   6. 88.7%   7. 11.5%   8. 92.9%

9. 322%   10. 526%   11. 663%   12. 275%

13. 9%   14. 5%   15. 4%   16. 12%

17. 7.03%   18. 9.02%   19. 2.0725%   20. 3.0843%

Write as percents.

21. 0.75   22. 0.17   23. 0.44   24. 0.26

25.	0.06	**26.**	0.07	**27.**	0.01	**28.**	0.02
29.	0.003	**30.**	0.009	**31.**	0.0045	**32.**	0.0029
33.	3.12	**34.**	4.14	**35.**	6.007	**36.**	5.000
37.	0.1	**38.**	0.5	**39.**	325.5	**40.**	0.2015

APPLICATIONS

41. The percent changes in retail sales were reported as a decimal in the October issue of *Retail Monthly* magazine. Change the decimals to percents.

Retail Sales		
	Month	**Change**
a.	February	0.012
b.	March	0.006
c.	April	0.013
d.	May	0.038
e.	June	0.043
f.	July	0.011
g.	August	0.022

42. The commission rate schedule for a stockbroker is shown. Change the percents to decimals.

Commission Rate Schedule		
	Dollar Amount	**% of Dollar Amount**
a.	$0 – $2,499	2.3%, minimum $30
b.	$2,500 – $4,999	2.0%, minimum $42
c.	$5,000 – $9,999	1.5%, minimum $65
d.	$10,000 – $14,999	1.1%, minimum $110
e.	$15,000 – $24,999	0.9%, minimum $135
f.	$25,000 – $49,999	0.6%, minimum $175
	$50,000 and above	negotiated

43. During the National Basketball Association season, the teams had these won–lost records. The Pct. column shows the percent of games won, expressed as a decimal. Change the decimals to percents.

EASTERN CONFERENCE
Atlantic Division

	W	L	Pct.	GB
a. Miami	28	16	.636	-
b. New York	27	17	.614	1
c. Philadelphia	25	21	.543	4
d. Boston	21	25	.457	8
e. Orlando	21	26	.447	8 $1/2$
f. New Jersey	17	29	.370	12
g. Washington	15	31	.326	14

WESTERN CONFERENCE
Midwest Division

	W	L	Pct.	GB
p. San Antonio	30	16	.652	-
q. Utah	27	17	.614	2
r. Minnesota	25	18	.581	3 $1/2$
s. Denver	21	22	.488	7 $1/2$
t. Houston	19	27	.413	11
u. Dallas	18	27	.400	11 $1/2$
v. Vancouver	12	32	.273	17

Central Division

	W	L	Pct.	GB
h. Indiana	29	15	.659	-
i. Milwaukee	26	21	.553	4 $1/2$
j. Charlotte	24	20	.545	5
k. Toronto	24	20	.545	5
l. Detroit	22	23	.489	7 $1/2$
m. Cleveland	19	26	.422	10 $1/2$
n. Atlanta	17	26	.395	11 $1/2$
o. Chicago	9	34	.209	19 $1/2$

Pacific Division

	W	L	Pct.	GB
w. L.A. Lakers	34	11	.756	-
x. Portland	34	11	.756	-
y. Sacramento	28	16	.636	5 $1/2$
z. Seattle	29	18	.617	6
aa. Phoenix	26	18	.591	7 $1/2$
ab. Golden State	11	32	.256	22
ac. L.A. Clippers	11	34	.244	23

44. How many teams have won more than 75% of their games? _____
Who are they? _____

45. How many teams have won more than 50% of their games? _____

46. How many have won less than 30% of their games? _____

FINDING A PERCENTAGE

Finding a percentage means finding a percent of a number. To find a percent of a number, you change the percent to a decimal, then multiply it by the number.

EXAMPLE 30% of 90 is what number?

SOLUTION

$30\% \times 90 = n$ — In mathematics, *of* means "times" and *is* means "equals."
— Let n stand for the unknown number.

$0.30 \times 90 = n$ Change the percent to a decimal.

$27 = n$ Multiply.

$30\% \text{ of } 90 = 27$ Write the answer.

EXAMPLE The delivery charge is 8% of the selling price of $145.00. Find the delivery charge.

SOLUTION

$8\% \times \$145.00 = n$
$0.08 \times \$145.00 = n$
$\$11.60 = n$
$8\% \times \$145.00 = \$11.60 \text{ delivery charge}$

EXAMPLE The student had 95% correct out of 80 questions. How many answers were correct?

SOLUTION

$95\% \times 80 = n$
$0.95 \times 80 = n$
$76 = n$
$95\% \times 80 = 76 \text{ correct}$

PROBLEMS

Find the percentage.

1. 25% of 60
2. 45% of 80
3. 40% of 30
4. 33% of 112

5. 58% of 420
6. 50% of 422
7. 3% of 100
8. 2% of 247

9. 110% of 65
10. 7% of 785
11. 1% of 819
12. 4% of 19.5

13. 185% of 95
14. 200% of 720
15. 135% of 860
16. 120% of 3.35

17. 4.5% of 50
18. 1.25% of 300
19. 33.3% of 80
20. 67.2% of 365

Round the answer to the nearest cent.

21. 7% of $35.78
22. 6.5% of $80
23. 10% of $93.20
24. 5.5% of $135

25. 4.25% of $65.00
26. 2.75% of $115
27. 125% of $98
28. 7.5% of $150

29. 0.3% of $450
30. 0.15% of $125
31. 8.2% of $19.89
32. 5.25% of $110.15

FINDING A PERCENTAGE

32. The following items appeared in a sales flyer for a major department store. Calculate the amount saved from the regular price as well as the sale price for each item. Round to the nearest cent.

		Amount Saved	Sale Price
a.	Save 25% on juniors knit shirts. Reg. $18.		
b.	Save 30% on women's dresses. Reg. $69.99		
c.	Save 20% on men's shoes. Reg. $135.		
d.	Save 25% on all nursery cribs. Reg. $119.99		
e.	Save 25% on all boxed jewelry sets. Reg. $19.99		
f.	Save 30% on family athletic shoes. Reg. $59.99		

33. Student Sean Hu received these test scores. How many answers were correct on each test?

	Subject	Test Score	Number of Items	Correct Answers
a.	Math	90%	80	
b.	English	70%	90	
c.	Science	80%	110	
d.	Spanish	90%	50	
e.	Government	85%	100	

34. Sales taxes are found by multiplying the tax rate times the selling price of the item. The total purchase price is the selling price plus the sales tax. Find the sales tax and total purchase price for each selling price. Round to the nearest cent.

	Selling Price	Tax Rate	Sales Tax	Total Purchase Price
a.	$14.78	4%		
b.	$22.50	5%		
c.	$3.88	6%		
d.	$95.85	6.5%		
e.	$212.00	7.25%		
f.	$85.06	8.25%		
g.	$199.99	7.455%		

AVERAGE (MEAN)

The average, or mean, is a single number used to represent a group of numbers. The average, or mean, of two or more numbers is the sum of the numbers divided by the number of items added.

EXAMPLE   Find the average of 8, 5, 3, 7, and 2.   Add to find the total.

SOLUTION $\dfrac{8 + 5 + 3 + 7 + 2}{5} = \dfrac{25}{5} = 5$ Divide by the number of items.

EXAMPLE   Find the average of 278, 340, 205, and 235.

SOLUTION $\dfrac{278 + 340 + 205 + 235}{4} = \dfrac{1058}{4} = 264.5$

EXAMPLE   Find the average of 4.3, 7.1, 1.5, 3.2, and 6.4. Round to the nearest tenth.

SOLUTION $\dfrac{4.3 + 7.1 + 1.5 + 3.2 + 6.4}{5} = \dfrac{22.5}{5} = 4.5$

EXAMPLE   Find the average of $12, $35, $19, $23, $11, and $21. Round to the nearest dollar.

SOLUTION $\dfrac{\$12 + \$35 + \$19 + \$23 + \$11 + \$21}{6} = \dfrac{\$121}{6} = \$20.17 = \$20$

PROBLEMS

Find the average for each group.

1. 3, 5, 7, 9, 11
2. 25, 40, 35, 50
3. 211, 197, 132
4. 416, 310, 344, 430
5. 4.4, 2.9, 3.7, 1.8, 6.5
6. 3.6, 7.1, 4.8, 4.7, 6.3, 5.3
7. $23, $21, $25, $24, $26
8. $98, $87, $79, $85, $88, $91

Find the average for each group. Round to the nearest hundredth or cent.

9. 8.1, 8.6, 7.7, 9.2, 5.5, 6.9, 7.3
10. 3.3, 5.8, 4.6, 2.8, 3.4, 5.2
11. $31.70, $33.91, $36.17, $33.85
12. $4.37, $3.74, $4.90, $5.74, $6.11
13. $55.78, $44.20, $43.95, $34.36

14. $121.19, $115.08, $135, $129.05, $111.88

15. Ben Agars had bowling scores of 187, 154, and 130. What was his average?

16. Kelley O'Reilly's tips from being a waitress were $5.00, $5.50, $4.75, $3.00, $4.50, $2.00, $5.75, and $4.50. What was her average tip?

17. Last year, Michael Legato's telephone bills averaged $66.12 a month. What was his total bill for the year?

18. Mark Purdue recorded his math test scores this quarter. What is his average?

Test Number	1	2	3	4	5	6	7	8
Score	65	77	81	79	90	86	92	98

19. What does he need on the next test to have an average of 85?

20. If Mark got a 97 on test 9 and 100 on test 10, what would be his average?

APPLICATIONS

21. As captain of the school golf team, Erica Samuelson has to complete this form after each game. Help her by computing the total and the average for each golfer. She also computes the total and the team average for each game. Round to the nearest whole number.

	Golfer	Game 1	Game 2	Game 3	Total	Average
a.	Samuelson	86	78	75		
b.	Haas	80	81	70		
c.	Sutherland	82	77	71		
d.	Beck	80	66	73		
e.	McCarron	78	81	82		
f.	Total					
g.	Team average					

ELAPSED TIME

To find elapsed time, subtract the earlier time from the later time.

EXAMPLE

Find the elapsed time for Kaitlin Harper who worked from:

A. 4:30 P.M. to 11:45 P.M.   B. 5:15 A.M. to 10:33 A.M.

SOLUTIONS

$$
\begin{array}{r}
11:45 \\
-\ 4:30 \\
\hline
7:15
\end{array}
= 7 \text{ hours } 15 \text{ minutes}
$$
written as 7 h: 15 min

$$
\begin{array}{r}
10:33 \\
-\ 5:15 \\
\hline
5:18
\end{array}
= 5 \text{ hours } 18 \text{ minutes}
$$
written as 5 h: 18 min

You cannot subtract 45 minutes from 30 minutes unless you borrow an hour and add it to the 30 minutes. Remember that 1 hour = 60 minutes.

EXAMPLE

Find the elapsed time from 2:50 P.M. to 9:15 P.M.

SOLUTION

$$
\begin{array}{r}
9:15 \\
-\ 2:50 \\
\end{array}
=
\begin{array}{r}
8:15\ +\ :60 \\
-\ 2:50 \\
\end{array}
=
\begin{array}{r}
8:75 \quad \text{borrowed 1 hour} \\
-\ 2:50 \\
\hline
6:25 \quad = 6 \text{ h: } 25 \text{ min}
\end{array}
$$

To find elapsed time when the time period goes past noon, add 12 hours to the later time before subtracting.

EXAMPLE

Find the elapsed time from 6:00 A.M. to 3:15 P.M.

SOLUTION

$$
\begin{array}{r}
3:15 \\
-\ 6:00 \\
\end{array}
=
\begin{array}{r}
3:15\ +\ 12:00 \\
-\ 6:00 \\
\end{array}
=
\begin{array}{r}
15:15 \\
-\ 6:00 \\
\hline
9:15 \quad = 9 \text{ h: } 15 \text{ min}
\end{array}
$$

EXAMPLE

Find the elapsed time from 10:35 P.M. to 3:12 A.M.

SOLUTION

$$
\begin{array}{r}
3:12 \\
-\ 10:35 \\
\end{array}
=
\begin{array}{r}
15:12 \\
-\ 10:35 \\
\end{array}
=
\begin{array}{r}
14:12\ +\ :60 \\
-\ 10:35 \\
\end{array}
=
\begin{array}{r}
14:72 \\
-\ 10:35 \\
\hline
4:37 \quad = 4 \text{ h: } 37 \text{ min}
\end{array}
$$

PROBLEMS

Find the elapsed time.

1. From 2:30 P.M. to 6:35 P.M.
2. From 1:18 P.M. to 7:25 P.M.
3. From 4:40 A.M. to 8:57 A.M.
4. From 3:33 a.m. to 10:47 A.M.
5. From 3:15 A.M. to 5:20 A.M.
6. From 1:25 P.M. to 9:05 P.M.
7. From 7:35 P.M. to 11:12 P.M.
8. From 8:43 A.M. to 11:30 A.M.
9. From 6:00 A.M. to 3:30 P.M.
10. From 10:30 A.M. to 6:45 P.M.
11. From 5:45 A.M. to 9:16 A.M.
12. From 1:45 A.M. to 7:05 A.M.
13. From 6:10 P.M. to 8:08 P.M.
14. From 3:28 A.M. to 11:16 A.M.
15. From 2:27 P.M. to 9:11 P.M.
16. From 3:56 P.M. to 10:22 P.M.

17. From 12:07 A.M. to 7:25 A.M.
18. From 12:35 P.M. to 6:45 P.M.
19. From 8:10 A.M. to 4:45 P.M.
20. From 7:45 A.M. to 5:30 P.M.
21. From 7:00 A.M. to 3:00 P.M.
22. From 8:30 A.M. to 5:00 P.M.
23. From 7:30 A.M. to 4:10 P.M.
24. From 8:23 A.M. to 5:04 P.M.
25. From 5:45 A.M. to 2:15 P.M.
26. From 7:43 A.M. to 4:21 P.M.
27. From 8:45 P.M. to 1:18 A.M.
28. From 9:47 A.M. to 7:08 P.M.
29. From 11:27 P.M. to 4:11 A.M.
30. From 5:55 P.M. to 1:55 A.M.

APPLICATIONS

31. Jack Keegan worked from 7:15 A.M. to 5:00 P.M. How long did he work?

32. Elena Diaz took a bus that left Cincinnati at 5:45 P.M. and arrived in Cleveland at 1:10 A.M. How long was the trip?

33. National Delivery Service (N.D.S.) ships hundreds of packages across the United States every day by air freight. Below is an N.D.S. air freight schedule. Calculate the total transit time for each shipment. (Note that all times given are Eastern Standard Time; therefore, time zones do not need to be taken into account.)

	Shipped From	Shipped To	Departure Time	Arrival Time	Total Transit Time
a.	Chattanooga, TN	Atlanta, GA	7:35 A.M.	8:20 A.M.	
b.	Chicago, IL	Houston, TX	8:10 A.M.	12:57 P.M.	
c.	Los Angeles, CA	New Orleans, LA	8:35 A.M.	2:17 P.M.	
d.	New York, NY	Cleveland, OH	5:25 P.M.	7:25 P.M.	
e.	Boston, MA	Phoenix, AZ	11:45 A.M.	7:28 P.M.	
f.	Atlanta, GA	Miami, FL	7:07 A.M.	9:00 A.M.	

READING TABLES AND CHARTS

To read a table or chart, find the *column* containing one of the pieces of information you have. Look across the *row* containing the other piece of information. Read down the column and across the row. Read the information you need where the column and row intersect.

Shipping Costs

Not Over (lbs)	Zone 2 & 3	Zone 4	Zone 5	Zone 6	Zone 7
1	$4.00	$4.00	$4.00	$4.00	$4.00
2	$4.00	$4.00	$4.00	$4.00	$4.00
3	$5.10	$5.10	$5.10	$5.10	$5.10
4	$6.20	$6.20	$6.20	$6.20	$6.20
5	$7.30	$7.30	$7.30	$7.30	$7.30
6	$8.60	$8.90	$9.10	$9.45	$9.70
7	$8.70	$9.30	$9.70	$10.40	$10.90
8	$8.80	$9.70	$10.30	$11.35	$12.10
9	$8.90	$10.10	$10.90	$12.30	$13.30
10	$9.00	$10.50	$11.50	$13.25	$14.50

EXAMPLE What is the cost to ship a 6-lb package to Zone 5?

SOLUTION
a. Find the Zone 5 column. b. Find the 6-lb row.
c. Read across the 6-lb row to the Zone 5 column. The cost is $9.10.

To classify an item, find the row that contains the known data. Then read the classification from the head of the column.

Men's Body Measurement

Size	S	M	L	XL	XXL
Neck	14–14 $1/2$	15–15 $1/2$	16–16 $1/2$	17–17 $1/2$	18–18 $1/2$
Chest	34–36	38–40	42–44	46–48	50–52
Waist	28–30	32–34	36–38	40–42	44–46
Reg. Sleeve	32–33	33–34	34–35	35–36	36–37
Tall Sleeve	33–34	34–35	35–36	36–37	37–38
Height	Reg. 5′8″– 6′	Tall 6′1″–6′4″			

Talls: Measure 2″ longer overall, 1″ at sleeves

EXAMPLE What size shirt should a man with a 42-inch chest order?

SOLUTION
a. Find the row for the Chest measurements. b. Read across the row to 42–44.
c. Read the size at the head of the column (L). A man with a 42-inch chest should order a size L, which stands for large.

PROBLEMS

Use the shipping chart above to find the cost to ship each package to the indicated zone.
1. 3 lb, Zone 3
2. 4 lb, Zone 7
3. 9 lb, Zone 4
4. 2 lb, Zone 6
5. 6 lb, Zone 2
6. 5 lb, Zone 5
7. 1.5 lb, Zone 5
8. 6.4 lb, Zone 7
9. 8.2 lb, Zone 3
10. 7.1 lb, Zone 6
11. 5.8 lb, Zone 4
12. 9.3 lb, Zone 3

Use the size chart on the previous page to determine what size to order. In-between sizes should order the next size up.

13. Shorts—waist 33
14. Shirt—chest 37
15. Jacket—chest 47
16. Pants—waist 43
17. Sweater—chest 43
18. Shirt—height 6'2", sleeves 36

APPLICATIONS

19. Use the shipping chart on the previous page to determine the maximum amount a package can weigh.

	a.	b.	c.	d.	e.	f.
Shipping Zone	2	5	7	3	6	4
Shipping Cost	$7.30	$4.00	$13.30	$8.90	$7.30	$5.10
Maximum Weight						

Use the Federal Income Tax Table to find the amount of tax withheld in questions 20–25 and the amount of wages earned in questions 26–31:

Federal Income Tax Table
MARRIED Persons—WEEKLY Payroll Period

If the wages are—		And the number of withholding allowances claimed is—							
At least	But less than	0	1	2	3	4	5	6	7
		The amount of income tax to be withheld is—							
$480	$490	$63	$56	$50	$44	$38	$32	$25	$19
490	500	64	58	52	45	39	33	27	21
500	510	66	59	53	47	41	35	28	22
510	520	67	61	55	48	42	36	30	24
520	530	69	62	56	50	44	38	31	25
530	540	70	64	58	51	45	39	33	27
540	550	72	65	59	53	47	41	34	28
550	560	73	67	61	54	48	42	36	30
560	570	75	68	62	56	50	44	37	31
570	580	76	70	64	57	51	45	39	33
580	590	78	71	65	59	53	47	40	34
590	600	79	73	67	60	54	48	42	36
600	610	81	74	68	62	56	50	43	37
610	620	82	76	70	63	57	51	45	39
620	630	84	77	71	65	59	53	46	40

	20.	21.	22.	23.	24.	25.
Income	$491.77	$501.07	$617.30	$525.00	$600.00	$531.13
Allowances	2	1	3	0	4	6
Amount Withheld						

	Number of Allowances	Tax Withheld	Wages At least	But less than
26.	5	$47		
27.	2	$71		
28.	3	$53		
29.	1	$62		
30.	4	$38		
31.	0	$76		

CONSTRUCTING GRAPHS

A **bar graph** is a picture that displays and compares numerical facts in the form of vertical or horizontal bars. To construct a vertical bar graph, follow these steps:

a. Draw the vertical and horizontal axes.
b. Scale the vertical axis to correspond to the given data.
c. Draw one bar to represent each quantity.
d. Label each bar and the vertical and horizontal axes.
e. Title the graph.

Metropolitan Statistical Areas
Population (in millions)

Chicago, IL	8.6
San Francisco, CA	6.6
Philadelphia, PA	6.0
Detroit, MI	5.3

EXAMPLE Construct a vertical bar graph of the given data.

SOLUTION

a. Draw vertical and horizontal axes.
b. Scale the vertical axis.
c. Draw one bar to represent each quantity.
d. Label each bar and the vertical and horizontal axes.
e. Title the graph.

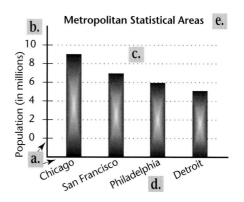

A **line graph** is a picture used to compare data over a period of time. It is an excellent way to show trends (increases or decreases). To construct a line graph, follow these steps:

a. Draw the vertical and horizontal axes.
b. Scale the vertical axis to correspond to the given data.
c. Label the axes.
d. Place a point on the graph to correspond to each item of data.
e. Connect the points from left to right.
f. Title the graph.

Percentage of Women in the Total Workforce

1950	29.6%
1960	33.4%
1970	38.1%
1980	42.5%
1990	45.8%
2000	47.5%

EXAMPLE Construct a line graph of the given data.

SOLUTION

a. Draw the vertical and horizontal axes.
b. Scale the vertical axis.
c. Label the axes.
d. Place a point to correspond to each item of data.
e. Connect the points from left to right.
f. Title the graph.

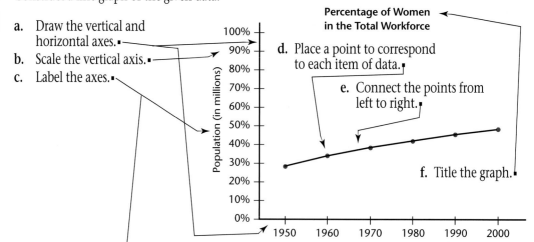

CONSTRUCTING GRAPHS

1. Construct a vertical bar graph of the given data.

   Wrenn's Department Store
   Total Sales by Department (in thousands)

Housewares	122
Men's Clothing	145
Women's Clothing	160
Appliances	183
Electronics	214

2. Read the vertical bar graph.

   a. Of the metropolitan areas listed, which is projected to have the largest population in 2033?

   b. Which of the metropolitan areas listed is projected to have the smallest population in 2033?

   c. What is Chicago's projected population for 2033?

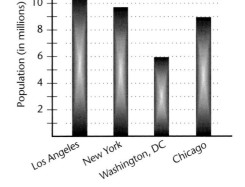

3. Construct a line graph of the given data.

   Tollhouse Industries Stock

Month	Average
Jan.	16.50
Feb.	17
Mar.	16.25
Apr.	15
May	17.50
June	18

Here are abbreviations and conversions for units of measure in the customary measurement system.

Length	Volume	Weight
12 inches (in) = 1 foot (ft)	2 cups (c) = 1 pint (pt)	16 ounces (oz) = 1 pound (lb)
3 ft = 1 yard (yd)	2 pt = 1 quart (qt)	2000 lb = 1 ton (t)
5280 ft = 1 mile (mi)	4 qt = 1 gallon (gal)	

Here are symbols and conversions for units of measure in the metric system.

Length	Volume
1000 millimeters (mm) = 1 meter (m)	1000 milliliters (mL) = 1 liter (L)
100 centimeters (cm) = 1 m	**Mass**
1000 m = 1 kilometer (km)	1000 grams (g) = 1 kilogram (kg)

To convert from one unit of measure to another, use the conversions lists above.

   When converting to a smaller unit, multiply.

EXAMPLE

SOLUTION

Convert 5 feet to inches.

Use 12 in = 1 ft

5 ft: 5 × 12 = 60

5 ft = 60 in

Convert 4 meters to centimeters.

Use 100 cm = 1 m

4 m: 4 × 100 = 400

4 m = 400 cm

When converting to a larger unit, divide.

EXAMPLE

SOLUTION

Convert 6 pints to quarts.

Use 2 pt = 1 qt

6 pt: 6 ÷ 2 = 3

6 pt = 3 qt

Convert 6500 grams to kilograms.

Use 1000 g = 1 kg

6500 g: 6500 ÷ 1000 = 6.5

6500 g = 6.5 kg

PROBLEMS

Make the following conversions.

1. 12 yd to feet
2. 8 gal to quarts
3. 9 lb to ounces
4. 2 ft to inches
5. 3 lb to ounces
6. 5 L to milliliters
7. 2.4 km to meters
8. 24 pt to cups
9. 3.6 kg to grams
10. 99 in to yards
11. 15 qt to gallons
12. 66 oz to pounds
13. 18 qt to gallons
14. 24 oz to pounds
15. 7000 g to kilograms
16. 60 cm to meters
17. 2200 mL to liters
18. 350 cm to meters
19. 29 kg to grams
20. 17.3 L to milliliters
21. 522 g to kilograms
22. 10.122 mL to liters
23. 72 cm to millimeters
24. 432.2 cm to meters
25. 1 yd 7 in to inches
26. 5 ft 7 in to inches
27. 3 qt 1 pt to pints
28. 6 lb 9 oz to ounces
29. 4 gal 1 qt to quarts
30. 3 yd 1 ft 5 in to inches
31. 5 gal 3 qt 1 pt to pints
32. 3 m 57 cm 29 mm to millimeters

APPLICATIONS

33. How many quarts will a 6-gallon bucket hold?

34. How many milliliters will a 2-liter bottle hold?

35. How many cups of coffee does a 4-quart coffeepot hold?

36. How many cups of hot chocolate will a 1.5-gallon thermos jug hold?

37. How many inches long is an 8-yard roll of aluminum foil?

38. Strawberries are sold in 1-pint containers. How many pints must be purchased to have enough for a recipe that calls for 3 cups?

39. James Jones knows that his jogging stride is about 1 meter long. The jogging trail he uses is 4.2 kilometers long. How many strides does it take him to go around the trail once?

40. The cafeteria receives 49 cases of milk each day. Each case contains 24 half-pint cartons. How many gallons of milk are received each day?

41. A soft drink is sold in 355 mL cans. How many liters are in a six-pack?

42. Katie Karanikos baked a chocolate layer cake weighing 1.5 kilograms. How many 75-gram servings can be cut from the cake?

43. Joan Baird ordered baseboard molding for the rooms of a new house. Joan needs to complete this chart to determine the total number of feet of molding needed. How much molding is needed?

Length	Width	2 lengths	+ 2 widths	= Perimeter
12 ft	10 ft	24 ft	+ 20 ft	= 44 ft
11 ft	8 ft	22 ft	+ 16 ft	=

	Length	Width
a.	11 ft	19 ft
b.	12 ft	12 ft 2 in
c.	15 ft	16 ft 8 in
d.	11 ft 8 in	12 ft 2 in
e.	12 ft 10 in	16 ft 10 in
f.	16 ft 9 in	24 ft 3 in
g.	9 ft 4 in	10 ft
h.		Total

PROBLEM SOLVING: USING THE FOUR-STEP METHOD

The problem-solving process consists of several interrelated actions. The solutions to some problems are obvious and require very little effort. Others require a step-by-step procedure. Using a procedure such as the four-step method will help you to solve word problems.

The Four-Step Method

Step 1:	Understand	What is the problem? What is given? What are you asked to do?
Step 2:	Plan	What do you need to do to solve the problem? Choose a problem-solving strategy.
Step 3:	Work	Carry out the plan. Do any necessary calculations.
Step 4:	Answer	Is your answer reasonable? Did you answer the question?

EXAMPLE

The Gordons own several rental homes that need replumbing. It will take 2 plumbers 5 days to do the work. Each plumber works 8 hours a day at $33 per hour. How much will the project cost?

SOLUTION

Step 1:	Given	2 plumbers, 5 days, 8 hours, $33 per hour
	Find	The cost per day for 1 plumber. The cost per day for 2 plumbers. The cost of 2 plumbers for 5 days.
Step 2:	Plan	Find the cost per day for 1 plumber, then multiply by the number of plumbers, and then multiply by the number of days.
Step 3:	Work	8 hours per day $\times$ $33 per hour = $264 per day for 1 plumber 2 plumbers $\times$ $264 per day for 1 plumber = $528 per day for 2 plumbers 5 days $\times$ $528 per day for 2 plumbers = $2640 for 2 plumbers for 5 days
Step 4:	Answer	It will cost $2640 for 2 plumbers for 5 days.

PROBLEMS

Identify the plan, work, and answer for each problem.

1. It takes 3 electricians 10 days to rewire some apartment buildings. Each electrician earns $37.50 per hour and works 7½ hours per day. How much will the rewiring cost?

2. Eric Cortez makes a car payment of $227.15 every month. His car loan is for 5 years. How much will he pay in 5 years?

3. Jessica Henderson and Kyle Casey spent a total of $213.58 on their prom date. Dinner cost $60.12. How much did everything else cost Jessica and Kyle?

4. Marcus Johnson purchased 2 shirts at $38 each, a belt for $19.50, jeans for $29.50, shoes for $89.99, and 3 pairs of socks at $6.99 a pair. How much did Marcus spend?

5. A contractor is building 5 new homes. It will take 4 carpet layers 3 days to install the carpet for all 5 homes. The carpet layers work 8 hours per day and earn $18.00 per hour. How much will it cost for the carpet installation?

6. The same 5 new homes will each have a foyer measuring 12 feet by 12 feet. Wood parquet floors for each foyer cost $55.30 per square yard. What is the cost of the wood parquet floors for the foyers in all 5 homes?

7. Beth Anderson charges $2.50 per page for typing rough drafts and an additional 75¢ per page for changes and deletions. A manuscript had 318 pages, of which 165 pages had changes and deletions. What was the total cost of typing the manuscript?

8. Fred Woo is paying $53.50 per month for a computer. The total cost of the computer was $855.99. How long will it take Fred to pay for the computer?

9. Mitch Elliot rode his bicycle on a 3-mile path. Approximately how many rotations did Mitch's 26" bicycle wheels make on this path? (Hint: The circumference of a circle is approximately 3.14 times the diameter and a mile = 5280 feet.)

10. Nicole and Joseph Conti drove to St. Louis, a distance of 781 miles. Their car gets 22 miles per gallon of gasoline. Gasoline costs them $1.36 per gallon. How much did Nicole and Joseph spend for gasoline on their trip?

11. Joy and Ernie both live in Columbus, Ohio. Joy drove due north for 3 hours at 60 miles per hour. Ernie drove due south for 2 hours at 65 per hour. How far apart were they after their trip?

12. Cindee Adams bought 3 boxes of cereal at $2.79 each, a roll of paper towels for 88¢, and 10 pounds of chicken at 65¢ a pound. How much change would Cindee get back from $20?

13. Thelma Wicker's pound cake is 30 cm long. She slices each cake into 2 cm slices. Thelma is serving 115 people for lunch. How many pound cakes will she need to bake?

PROBLEM SOLVING: IDENTIFYING INFORMATION

Before you begin to solve a word problem, first read the problem carefully and answer these questions:

- What are you asked to find?
- What facts are given?
- Are enough facts given? Do you need more information than the problem provides?

Some word problems provide more information than is needed to solve the problem. Others cannot be solved without additional information. Identifying what is wanted, what is given, and what is needed allows you to organize the information and plan your solution.

EXAMPLE Jonathan Klein is a lab technician at Laminates, Ltd. He earns $25.20 per hour. He is single and claims 1 withholding allowance. Last week he worked 40 hours at the regular rate and 4 hours at the weekend rate. He is 28 years old. Find his gross pay for last week.

SOLUTION

A. Wanted: Jonathan Klein's gross pay for last week
B. Facts given: $25.20 hourly rate
                                    40 hours worked at regular rate
                                    4 hours worked at weekend rate
C. Additional facts needed: Weekend rate

This problem cannot be solved.

EXAMPLE Martha Henderson, age 43, runs 3 miles every day. How many miles does Martha run in a week?

SOLUTION

A. Wanted: Number of miles run in 1 week
B. Facts given: Runs 3 miles every day
C. Additional facts needed: None

This problem can be solved. Multiply the number of miles run per day (3) by the number of days in 1 week (7). The answer is 21 miles.

PROBLEMS

Identify the wanted, given, and needed information. If enough information is given, solve the problem.

1. Kelly Jenkins bought a new car with a $4500 down payment and monthly payments of $375. How much did Kelly pay, in total, for her new car?

2. The Great Outdoors is having a sale on sports equipment. The Yosemite dome tent is priced at $99, the GlacierPoint mountain bike is $69, and Shenandoah in-line skates are $49. What is the total cost of the Yosemite dome tent and Yellowstone backpack?

3. Lisa Smith paid $175 each way to fly round-trip from Atlanta to Denver. Brittany Cruz paid $335 for the round-trip fare. Who paid more? How much more?

4. The Northside Fruit Farm pays pickers $1.50 per pound to pick blueberries, which are packed in one-pint baskets and sold at market for $2.25 per pint. How many pint baskets need to be sold to pay one worker one day's wage?

5. Tyler Fulgum paid $95 each for two tickets to a concert. He paid for the tickets with four $50 bills. How much change did he receive?

6. How much would four sets of towels cost if they were 25 x 20 inches and priced at three for $9.99?

7. Bill Hale bought a boneless shoulder roast with a $20 bill. He received $3.17 in change. How much did Bill pay per pound for the roast?

8. The party platter cost $65, beverages cost $35.77, and party supplies cost $18.13. Brandon and his friends agreed to share the total cost of food, beverages, and supplies for the party equally. How much did each pay?

9. Dana Edwards is 5 feet 2 inches tall and weighs 108 pounds. She grew 3 inches in the past year. How tall was she last year?

10. Greg Jones has finished 55 of the 60 math problems on his test. It is now 11:20 A.M. The 1-hour test started at 10:30 A.M. What is the average number of minutes he can spend on each of the remaining problems?

11. A two-drawer file cabinet and a box of files cost $110. What is the cost of the file cabinet?

12. A designer fragrance gift set is on sale for 40% off its original retail price of $65. If the retailer discounted it an additional 10% of the sale price, what would the final sale price be?

13. Matthew Travino sells stereo equipment and receives a weekly salary of $300 plus a 5% commission on sales. Last week his gross pay was $660. What is the dollar amount of stereo equipment sold by Matthew last week?

14. Darien Dromboski was shopping for coffee makers. The Javamaker model was $11.43 more than the BestBrew model and the Coffee Time model was $4.95 less than the BestBrew. How much more than the cost of the Coffee Time was the Javamaker?

PROBLEM SOLVING: USING MORE THAN ONE OPERATION

Some problems require several operations to solve. After deciding which operations to use, you must decide the correct order in which to perform them.

EXAMPLE The cash price of a new car is $22,885. Marcie Cunningham cannot pay cash, so she is making a down payment of $3300 and 60 monthly payments of $385 each. How much more does it cost to buy the car this way?

SOLUTION

A. Given: Cash price of $22,885
                    $3300 down + 60 payments of $385 each

B. Multiply: To get total of payments
                    60 × $385 = $23,100

   Add: $3300 to total payments
                    $3300 + $23,100 = $26,400

   Subtract: Cash price from total payments
                    $26,400 − $22,885 = $3515

It cost $3515 more to buy the car this way. In this example, the order of operations is very important; that is, multiply, then add, then subtract.

EXAMPLE Juan Perez bought 2 gallons of milk costing $2.69 per gallon. He gave the cashier a $20 bill. How much change did he receive if there was no sales tax?

SOLUTION

A. Given: Bought 2 gallons of milk at $2.69 per gallon, no sales tax
                    Gave cashier $20.00

B. Multiply: To get total cost
                    2 × $2.69 = $5.38

   Subtract: To find change
                    $20.00 − $5.38 = $14.62

Juan received $14.62 in change. In this example, the order of operations is multiply, then subtract.

PROBLEMS

Give the sequence of operations needed to solve the problems, then solve.

1. Your entertainment budget for the month is $50. If you spent $18.50 at the movies, $12 for tickets to a college basketball game, and $11.75 at a concert, how much is left in your entertainment budget?

2. Steve Sorrells works 9 hours a day 5 days a week. So far this year, he has worked 540 hours. How many weeks has he worked?

3. The Parent/Teacher Organization (PTO) sells soft drinks and popcorn at home basketball games. Last week they sold 225 cups of soft drinks at $1.00 per cup and 185 bags of popcorn at 75¢ per bag. What were the total sales?

4. Gerry Hanson pays his electric bills through a payment plan of $65 per month regardless of usage. At the end of one year, he is billed for the difference if his usage is more, or sent a refund if his usage is less. His usage for the last three months was $62, $64.35, and $68.20. Is he over or under his payment plan schedule so far this year? By how much?

5. Daniel Dalton sold 16 watermelons for $5 each, 20 for $4 each, and 30 for $3 each. He makes 50% commission for each watermelon he sells. How much money did Daniel make?

6. Henry Mack has a new job as an insurance adjuster and has read 272 pages of a 512-page training manual. It took him two days to read through the remaining pages. If he read the same number of pages each day, how many pages did he read each day?

7. Leah Mattison worked 40 hours for $7.25 per hour. She worked 5 hours for $18.13 an hour. How much money did Leah earn?

8. In one month, the Bowens spent $95.78, $112.13, $98.66, and $124.33 for groceries. Their monthly food budget is $450. How much money do they have left to spend for food?

9. The temperature in the greenhouse is 25 degrees Celsius at 9:00 A.M. If the temperature increases 1.5 degrees every hour, what will the temperature be at 3:00 P.M.?

10. Daryl Harden walks 3 miles round-trip to work 5 times a week. How far will he walk in one year?

11. Zach McCain assembled a total of 788 circuit boards in 4 days of work. During the first three days, he assembled 201, 196, and 198, respectively. How many did he assemble the last day?

12. In a one-month reading contest at school, Rick Gonzalez earned 3 half-point certificates, 5 one-point certificates, and 4 two-point certificates. How many points did he earn for the month?

13. The Athens Historical Society sold 1245 $5 tickets as a fund-raiser. Prizes were a $2,000 handmade quilt, 4 framed prints that cost $500 each, and 10 books that cost $25 each. How much money did the Historical Society make?

14. Drew Young sold candy bars at school to raise money for a band trip. He sold 47 $1-candy bars. If his sales totaled $68 dollars, how many $3-candy bars did he sell?

15. Spencer Baird bought 2 sweatshirts for $15.75 each and 2 T-shirts for $8.50 each. How much change did he receive from a $50 bill?

16. Josey Chandler saved $550. After she earned an additional $125, she spent $320 for a chair, $50 for a rug, and $30 for a lamp. How much money did Josey have left?

PROBLEM SOLVING: WRITING AN EQUATION

A word problem can be translated into an equation that is solved by performing the same mathematical operation (adding, subtracting, multiplying, or dividing) to both sides. Solving the equation then leads to the solution of the problem.

To set up the equation, look for words in the problem that suggest which of the four mathematical operations to use.

Words	Symbol	Operation
The total, how many in all, the sum, plus	+	Addition
The difference, how much more, how much smaller, minus	−	Subtraction
The total for a number of equal items, the product	×	Multiplication
The number left over, the quotient	÷	Division

EXAMPLE

In 40 hours at your regular rate of pay plus 10 hours of double time (twice your regular rate of pay), you earn $855. What is your regular rate of pay?

SOLUTION

Use the letter x to stand for your regular rate of pay.

$40x + 10(2x) = \$855.00$

$40x + 20x = \$855.00$

$60x = \$855.00$ (Divide each side by 60.)

$x = \$14.25$

EXAMPLE

A rectangle with a perimeter of 64 mm is 25 mm long. What is the width of the rectangle?

SOLUTION

Let w equal the width of the rectangle.

$w + 25 + w + 25 = 64$

$2w + 50 = 64$ (Subtract 50 from both sides.)

$2w = 14$ (Divide both sides by 2.)

$w = 7$ mm wide

PROBLEMS

1. The sum of 2 consecutive numbers is 47. What is the smaller number?

2. One brand of computer scanner can read 83 documents per hour while a second scanner can read 97 documents per hour. How many hours will it take to read 900 documents?

3. A jar of mayonnaise costs 97¢. The mayonnaise costs 55¢ more than the jar. How much does each cost?

4. A robot travels 36 meters around the edge of a rectangular assembly room. If the rectangle is twice as long as it is wide, how long is each side?

5. A football field is 100 yards long and has a distance around of 308 yards. How wide is it?

6. Ed and Maria Zavala-Waterman make monthly payments of $845 on their $120,000 mortgage. They will have paid $184,200 in interest when their mortgage is paid off. For how many years is their mortgage?

7. Carol Austin had gross earnings of $804.86 last week. She earns $10.25 per hour plus a 4.5% commission on all sales. She knows she worked 40 hours last week but can't remember her total sales. What were her total sales?

8. Luis Rivera earns $8.10 per hour plus double time for all hours over 40 per week. How much did Luis earn for working 48 hours last week?

9. Sandy Brubaker has 4 Guernsey cows and 3 Holstein cows that give as much milk in 5 days as 3 Guernsey and 5 Holstein cows give in 4 days. Which kind of cow is the better milk producer, the Guernsey or the Holstein?

10. The Maren Manufacturing Company building is 6 times as old as the equipment. The building was 40 years old when the equipment was purchased. How old is the equipment?

11. The sum of 3 consecutive odd numbers is 33. What are the 3 numbers?

12. Ingram, Inc. stock sells for $23\,^3/_4 a share. The Morrison Brokerage Company charges a flat fee of $45 for every transaction. How many shares could you buy for $900?

13. Keesha is working with fabric that is twice as long as it is wide. It is $6^1/_2$ yards long. How wide is it?

14. If the fabric were 4 yards, 6 inches wide, how long would it be?

15. Tom, Darren, and Kerry have a combined weight of 600 pounds. Kerry weighs 15 pounds more than Darren, while Darren weighs 15 pounds more than Tom. How much does each man weigh?

Glossary

account A record that shows the balance for a specific item, such as cash or equipment. (p. 535)

account executive A licensed individual who buys or sells securities for clients; also known as a stockbroker. (p. 293)

accounting A systematic process of recording and reporting the financial position of a business. (p. 535)

accounting cycle The activities, or steps, that help a business keep its accounting records in an orderly manner. (p. 575)

accounting equation An equation (Assets = Liabilities + Owner's Equity) that is the basis for keeping all accounting records in balance. (p. 577)

accounting period A period of time covered by an accounting report. (p. 575)

accounts payable The amount of money owed, or payable, to the creditors of a business. (p. 578)

accounts receivable The total amount of money owed to a business. (p. 578)

actual cash value One of two methods insurance companies use to determine claim settlements, under which the payment is based on the replacement cost of an item minus depreciation. (p. 427)

adjustable-rate mortgage (ARM) A mortgage with an interest rate that increases or decreases during the life of the loan; also known as a variable-payment mortgage. (p. 222)

adjusted gross income (AGI) A person's gross income after certain reductions have been made, such as contributions to an IRA or interest on a student loan. (p. 384)

agency power The right of business partners to sign contracts that are legally binding on the partnership; also known as mutual agency. (p. 645)

allowance An adjustment to the tax withheld from an employee's paycheck, based on his or her marital status and whether he or she is supporting other people with his or her money. (p. 386)

amortization The process of reducing the balance of a loan, such as a mortgage, every time a payment is made. (p. 222)

annual percentage rate (APR) The cost of credit on a yearly basis, expressed as a percentage. (p. 166)

annual percentage yield (APY) The amount of interest that a financial institution would pay on a $100 deposit for one year. (p. 139)

annuity A series of equal regular deposits. (p. 24) A contract purchased from an insurance company that provides for a sum of money to be paid to a person at regular intervals for a certain number of years or for life. (p. 495)

appraisal An estimate of the current value of a property. (p. 228)

aptitudes The natural abilities that people possess. (p. 35)

arbitration A process in which a conflict between a customer and a business is resolved by an impartial third party whose decision is legally binding. (p. 109)

articles of incorporation The application to operate as a corporation. (p. 652)

assets Any items of value that people own, including cash, property, personal possessions, and investments. (p. 66)

assigned risk pool All the people who cannot get automobile insurance; some of these people are assigned to each insurance company operating in the state. (p. 437)

assisted-living facility (ALF) A residence complex that provides personal and medical services for the elderly. (p. 483)

automatic teller machines (ATMs) Computer terminals that people can use to withdraw cash from their bank accounts, make deposits, and transfer money from one account to another; also known as cash machines. (p. 126)

balance sheet A financial statement that lists the items of value that a person owns, the debts that he or she owes, and his or her net worth; also called a net worth statement. (p. 66) For a business, a report of the balances of all asset, liability, and owner's equity accounts at the end of an accounting period. (p. 592)

bank reconciliation A report that accounts for the differences between a person's bank statement and his or her checkbook balance. (p. 147)

bankruptcy A legal process in which some or all of the assets of a debtor are distributed among his or her creditors because the debtor is unable to pay his or her debts. (p. 189)

bearer bond A bond that is not registered in the investor's name. (p. 310)

bear market Situation that occurs when investors are pessimistic about the economy and sell stocks, causing the value of individual stocks and the stock market as a whole to decrease. (p. 286)

beneficiary A person named to receive the benefits from an insurance policy. (p. 465) A person named to receive a portion of someone's estate. (p. 500)

blue-chip stock A stock that is considered a safe investment and generally attracts conservative investors. (p. 278)

Blue Cross A medical organization that provides private health insurance with hospital care benefits. (p. 454)

Blue Shield A medical organization that provides private health insurance with benefits for surgical and medical services performed by physicians. (p. 454)

board of directors A group of individuals who are responsible for overseeing the general affairs of a corporation. (p. 655)

bodily injury liability Insurance that covers injuries caused by an automobile accident for which the insured was responsible. (p. 431)

bond indenture A legal document that details all of the conditions pertaining to a particular bond issue. (p. 308)

break-even point The point at which total sales equal total costs (variable and fixed costs). (p. 707)

budget A plan for using one's money in a way that best meets one's wants and needs. (p. 75) For a business, a formal written statement of expected income and expenses for a future period of time. (p. 537)

budget variance The difference between the budgeted amount and the actual amount that one spends. (p. 79)

bull market Situation that occurs when investors are optimistic about the economy and buy stocks, causing the value of many stocks and the value of the stock market as a whole to increase. (p. 286)

business credit card A credit card that is issued to a business rather than to an individual. (p. 565)

business plan A written outline of a new business venture that describes all aspects of the business. (p. 524)

▬▬▬ C

cafeteria-style employee benefits Benefits programs that allow workers to choose the benefits that best meet their personal needs. (p. 50)

call feature A feature that allows a corporation to buy back bonds from bondholders before the maturity date. (p. 308)

capital The money a person needs to establish a business, operate for the first few months, and expand the business. (p. 551)

capital gain The profit from the sale of an asset such as stocks, bonds, or real estate. (p. 262) The profit that results from the sale of shares in a mutual fund for a higher price than the shareholder paid for them. (p. 342)

capital gain distributions Payments made to shareholders that result from the sale of securities in a mutual fund's portfolio. (p. 342)

capitalization The total amount of stocks and bonds issued by a corporation. (p. 279)

capital loss The sale of an investment for less than its purchase price. (p. 263)

career A commitment to work in a field that is interesting and fulfilling. (p. 31)

cash flow The money that actually goes into and out of a person's wallet and bank accounts. (p. 70) The amount of cash that is available to a business at any given time. (p. 540)

cash inflows Cash that enters a business. (p. 596)

cash outflows Cash that exits a business. (p. 596)

cash value The accumulated savings from a whole life insurance policy. (p. 468)

certificate of deposit (CD) A savings alternative in which money is left on deposit for a stated time period (ranging from a month to five or more years) to earn a specific rate of return. (p. 133)

chart of accounts A list of all the general ledger accounts that a business will use. (p. 684)

claim Request for payment from an insurance company to cover a financial loss. (p. 417)

class-action suit A legal action on behalf of all the people who have suffered the same injustice. (p. 111)

closed-end credit A one-time loan that is paid back over a specified period of time and in payments of equal amounts. (p. 157)

closed-end fund A mutual fund with a fixed number of shares that are issued by an investment company when the fund is first organized. (p. 328)

closing A meeting of the seller, the buyer, and the lender of funds, or the representatives of each party, to complete a real estate transaction. (p. 224)

closing costs Fees and charges for which a seller and buyer are responsible when a real estate transaction is completed; also known as settlement costs. (p. 225)

codicil A document that explains, adds, or deletes provisions in a person's existing will. (p. 505)

coinsurance The percentage of medical expenses a policyholder must pay in addition to the deductible amount. (p. 443)

collateral A form of security to help guarantee that a creditor will be repaid. (p. 168)

collectibles Items that appeal to collectors and investors, such as rare coins, works of art, antiques, stamps, rare books, sports memorabilia, rugs, Chinese ceramics, and paintings. (p. 366)

collision Type of insurance that covers damage to the insured's car when it is involved in an accident. (p. 433)

commercial bank A for-profit corporation that offers a full range of financial services, including checking, savings, and lending. (p. 129)

commercial debt financing Borrowing money from a bank or other financial institution to fund a business. (p. 558)

commercial finance company A firm that loans money only to businesses. (p. 566)

commercial loan A loan taken out to finance a new or ongoing business. (p. 558)

commercial property Land and buildings that produce lease, or rental, income. (p. 354)

commission A fee charged by a brokerage firm for the buying and/or selling of a security. (p. 294) An amount of money paid to an employee based on a percentage of the employee's sales. (p. 607)

common stock Type of stock that provides the most basic form of corporate ownership and entitles the owner to voting privileges. (p. 251)

compounding The process in which interest is earned on both the principal—the amount that was deposited—and any previously earned interest. (p. 137)

consumer A person who purchases and uses goods or services. (p. 17)

consumer credit The use of credit for personal needs. (p. 153)

consumer price index (CPI) A measure of the changes in prices for commonly purchased goods and services in the United States. (p. 79)

contribution margin The amount of money that the sale of a particular product contributes toward the payment of fixed costs and the profit of a business. (p. 706)

conventional mortgage A mortgage that offers the buyer a fixed interest rate and fixed schedule of payments. (p. 222)

convertible bond A bond that an investor can trade for shares of the corporation's common stock. (p. 308)

cooperative A nonprofit organization owned and operated by its members for the purpose of saving money on the purchase of certain goods and services. (p. 99)

cooperative education A program that allows students to enhance classroom learning with work related to their majors and interests. (p. 43)

copayment A flat fee that a person pays every time he or she receives a medical service covered under his or her health insurance. (p. 450)

corporate bond A corporation's written pledge to repay a specified amount of money along with interest. (p. 252)

corporate bylaws The rules by which a corporation operates. (p. 652)

corporate charter A license to operate a corporation. (p. 652)

corporation A business organization that operates as a legal entity separate from its owners and is treated by law as if it were an individual person. (p. 651)

co-signing Agreeing to be responsible for loan payments if the borrower fails to make them. (p. 183)

cost behavior The way a cost changes in relation to a change in business activity. (p. 704)

cost of merchandise sold The amount of money a business paid for the goods that it sold to customers. (p. 590)

coverage The protection provided by the terms of an insurance policy. (p. 411)

cover letter The personal letter that is presented to a potential employer with a résumé. (p. 46)

credit An arrangement to receive cash, goods, or services now and pay for them in the future. (p. 153) An amount entered on the right side of a T account. (p. 578)

creditor An entity (bank, finance company, credit union, business, or individual) to which money is owed. (p. 153)

credit rating A measure of a person's ability and willingness to make credit payments on time. (p. 172)

credit union A nonprofit financial institution that is owned by its members and organized for their benefit. (p. 129)

current yield The annual dividend paid by an investment divided by the investment's current market value, expressed as a percentage. (p. 287)

cyclical stock A stock whose market value tends to reflect the state of the economy. (p. 279)

D

debenture A bond that is backed only by the reputation of the issuing corporation rather than by its particular assets. (p. 307)

debit An amount entered on the left side of a T account. (p. 578)

debit card A card, issued by a financial institution, that allows people to withdraw money or to pay for purchases from their checking or savings accounts. In addition, the card allows access to an automatic teller machine for other purposes; also known as a cash card. (p. 126)

debt collectors Businesses that collect debts for creditors. (p. 188)

deductible The set amount that the policyholder must pay per loss on an insurance policy. (p. 415)

deductions Various amounts that are subtracted from an employee's gross earnings, such as federal income tax or Social Security tax. (p. 607)

deed The official document transferring ownership of a home from seller to buyer. (p. 225)

default To be unable to make payments on a loan. (p. 224)

defensive stock A stock that remains stable during periods of economic decline. (p. 279)

deficit The situation that occurs if a person spends more than he or she earns or receives. (p. 73)

defined-benefit plan A pension plan that specifies the benefits that a person will receive at retirement age, based on his or her total earnings and years on the job. (p. 489)

defined-contribution plan A pension plan that consists of an individual account for each employee, to which the employer contributes a specific amount annually; sometimes called an individual account plan. (p. 488)

demand The amount of goods and services that people are willing to buy. (p. 14)

demographic trends Ways in which groups of people change over time. (p. 37)

direct deposit The practice of automatically depositing net pay in an employee's designated bank account. (p. 613)

direct investment A real estate investment in which the owner holds legal title to the property he or she has purchased. (p. 352)

direct labor The work required to convert raw materials into a finished product. (p. 705)

direct materials The raw materials used to make a finished product. (p. 705)

disability income insurance Type of insurance that provides regular cash income when a person is unable to work because of a pregnancy, a nonwork-related accident, or an illness. (p. 461)

discretionary income The money left over after a person has paid for the essentials—food, clothing, shelter, transportation, and medication. (p. 72)

diversification The process of spreading one's assets among several different types of investments to lessen risk. (p. 254)

dividend income The cash dividends that a person receives from investments. (p. 384)

dividends Distributions of money, stock, or other property that a corporation sometimes pays to stockholders. (p. 251)

double-entry accounting A system of recordkeeping in which each business transaction affects at least two accounts. (p. 578)

double indemnity A rider to a life insurance policy that pays twice the value of the policy if the person covered by the policy is killed in an accident. (p. 471)

down payment A portion of the total cost of an item that must be paid at the time of purchase. (p. 97)

E

earned income The money a person receives for working. (p. 383)

earnest money A portion of the purchase price of a home paid by the buyer to the seller to show that the buyer's offer is serious. (p. 218)

earnings per share A corporation's net, or after-tax, earnings divided by the number of outstanding shares of common stock. (p. 288)

economics The study of the decisions that go into making, distributing, and using goods and services. (p. 14)

economy The ways in which people make, distribute, and use goods and services. (p. 14)

emergency fund Money that can be accessed quickly for an immediate need. (p. 239)

Employer Identification Number (EIN) A number assigned to a business by the Internal Revenue Service and used by the government for income tax purposes. (p. 642)

endorsement The signature on the back of a check of the payee, the party to whom the check has been written. (p. 144) An addition of coverage to a homeowners insurance policy. (p. 424)

endowment Life insurance that provides coverage for a specific period of time and pays an agreed-upon sum of money to the policyholder if he or she is still living at the end of the endowment period. (p. 469)

entrepreneur An individual who follows his or her dreams by assuming the risk of starting a new business. (p. 549)

equity The value of a home less the amount still owed on the money borrowed to purchase it. (p. 210)

equity capital Money that a business gets from its owners in order to operate. (p. 251)

escrow account An account in which money is held in trust until it can be delivered to the designated party. (p. 218)

estate Everything a person owns. (p. 499)

estate planning The process of creating a detailed plan for managing personal assets so that a person can make the most of them while he or she is alive and ensure that they are distributed wisely after his or her death. (p. 499)

estate tax A tax collected on the value of a person's property at the time of his or her death. (p. 381)

excise tax A tax collected by federal and state governments on specific goods and services. (p. 381)

exclusion An amount of income that is not included in a person's gross income and is not subject to taxes; also called tax-exempt income. (p. 384)

executor Someone designated to perform the tasks involved in carrying out a person's will. (p. 504)

exemption A deduction from a person's adjusted gross income for that person, his or her spouse, and qualified dependents. (p. 385)

F

face value The dollar amount that a bondholder (the person who owns a bond) will receive at the bond's maturity. (p. 305)

family of funds A group of mutual funds managed by one investment company. (p. 334)

Federal Insurance Contributions Act (FICA) The 1935 act that established the present Social Security system. (p. 609)

Federal Reserve System The central banking organization of the United States; also known as the Fed. (p. 15)

finance charge The total dollar amount a person pays to use credit. (p. 160)

financial forecasting The process of estimating a business's operating capital. (p. 672)

financial leverage The use of borrowed funds for investment purposes. (p. 360)

financial plan The part of a business plan that outlines not only how a person will get money to create and operate a business but also how he or she will maintain the company's financial operations and business records. (p. 525)

financial planner A specialist who is trained to offer specific financial help and advice. (p. 259)

financial reports Documents that summarize the results of financial transactions affecting a business and report its current financial position. (p. 573)

financial responsibility law A law that requires drivers to prove that they can pay for damage or injury caused by an automobile accident. (p. 431)

financial statements Reports, such as an income statement and balance sheet, that summarize the changes that result from a company's business transactions during an accounting period. (p. 589)

first-in, first-out method (FIFO) A method of estimating the cost of inventory that assumes that the first items purchased (first in) are the first items sold (first out). (p. 626)

fixed costs The costs that remain constant even if the activity or production level of a business changes. (p. 706)

fixed expenses The expenses that remain the same regardless of business activity. (p. 673)

401(k) plan A pension plan in which employees set aside a portion of their salary from each paycheck to be deducted from their gross pay and placed in a special account; also known as a salary reduction plan. (p. 489)

franchise A contractual agreement to sell a company's products or services in a designated geographic area. (p. 657)

fraud Dishonest business practices that are meant to deceive, trick, or gain an unfair advantage. (p. 105)

free enterprise system A system in which people are free to choose what they buy, what they produce and sell, and where they work. (p. 523)

future value The amount an original deposit will be worth in the future, based on its earning a specific interest rate over a specific period of time. (p. 22)

G

general ledger A book or set of electronic files that contains the accounts used for a business. (p. 584)

generally accepted accounting principles (GAAP) A standard set of guidelines used in recording and reporting financial changes in a business. (p. 537)

general obligation bond A bond that is backed by the full faith and credit of the government that issued it. (p. 317)

general partner A business partner who has decision-making authority, takes an active role in the operation of the business, and has unlimited liability for all losses and debts of the partnership. (p. 645)

gift tax A tax collected on money or property valued at more than $10,000, given by one person to another in a single year. (p. 382)

goals The things a person wants to accomplish, such as getting a college education, buying a car, or starting a business. (p. 5)

going public Deciding to sell a corporation's stock on the open market. (p. 653)

good A physical object that is produced and can be weighed or measured. (p. 13)

government bond The written pledge of a government or a municipality to repay a specified sum of money plus interest. (p. 252)

grace period A time period during which no finance charges will be added to a person's credit card account. (p. 160)

gross earnings The total amount of money an employee earns in a pay period. (p. 614)

gross profit on sales The amount of profit a business made from merchandise sales before operating expenses are deducted. (p. 591)

growth stock A stock issued by a corporation whose potential earnings may be higher than the average earnings predicted for all the firms in the country. Stocks issued by these corporations generally do not pay dividends. (p. 279)

guardian A person who accepts the responsibility of providing children with personal care after their parents' death and managing the parents' estate for the children until they reach a certain age. (p. 504)

H

handyman's special A home that is priced lower because it needs repairs and improvements. (p. 197)

hazard Anything that increases the likelihood of loss through some peril. (p. 413)

health insurance A form of protection that eases the financial burden people may experience as a result of illness or injury. (p. 443)

health maintenance organization (HMO) A health insurance plan that directly employs or contracts with selected physicians and other medical professionals to provide health care services in exchange for a fixed, prepaid monthly premium. (p. 454)

heirs The people who will have the legal right to a person's assets when he or she dies. (p. 497)

home equity loan A loan based on the difference between the current market value of a home and the amount still owed on the mortgage. (p. 224)

homeowners insurance Coverage that provides protection for a person's residence and its associated financial risks, such as damage to personal property and injuries to others. (p. 420)

hourly wage A specific amount of money paid per hour to an employee. (p. 605)

household inventory A list or other documentation of personal belongings, with purchase dates and cost information. (p. 422)

I

impulse buying The act of purchasing items on the spur of the moment. (p. 100)

income Money that a person receives, such as a paycheck from a job, an allowance from parents, or interest earned on a savings account. (p. 71)

income dividends The earnings a mutual fund pays to shareholders. (p. 342)

income statement A report of the net income or net loss for an accounting period. (p. 589)

income stock A stock that pays higher-than-average dividends compared to other stock issues. (p. 278)

income tax return A form on which a person reports how much money he or she received from working and other sources and the exact taxes, if any, that the person owes. (p. 383)

indebtedness The condition of being deeply in debt. (p. 189)

indirect investment A real estate investment in which a person, known as a trustee, is appointed to hold legal title to a property on behalf of an investor or group of investors. (p. 355)

individual retirement account (IRA) A retirement savings plan created especially for an individual. (p. 490)

inflation The general rise in the level of prices for goods and services over time. (p. 16)

informational interview A meeting with someone who works in a person's area of interest and who can provide practical information about the career or company that person is considering. (p. 44)

inheritance tax A tax collected on the property left by a person in his or her will. (p. 381)

initial public offering (IPO) The sale of stock by a company to the general public for the first time. (p. 292)

insolvency The condition that occurs when someone's liabilities are greater than his or her assets. (p. 68)

insurance Protection against possible financial loss. (p. 411)

insurance company A risk-sharing business that agrees to pay for losses that may happen to someone it insures. (p. 411)

insured A person or persons protected by an insurance policy. (p. 411)

insurer A risk-sharing business that agrees to pay for losses that may happen to someone it insures. (p. 411)

interest The price that is paid for the use of another's money. (p. 18) A periodic charge in exchange for the use of credit. (p. 155)

interest income The interest a person receives from banks, credit unions, and savings and loan associations. (p. 383)

interest inventories Tests that help people to identify the activities they enjoy the most and match their interests, likes, and dislikes with various kinds of work. (p. 35)

internship A position in which a person receives training by working with people who are experienced in a particular field. (p. 42)

intestate Without a valid will. (p. 501)

inventory Merchandise a business has on hand. (p. 538)

inventory turnover The number of times a business sells its inventory in a given time period. (p. 628)

investment-grade bonds Bonds that are issued by financially stable companies or municipalities. (p. 323)

investment liquidity The ability to buy or sell an investment quickly without substantially affecting its value. (p. 250)

itemized deduction A specific expense, such as mortgage interest, that a person deducts from his or her adjusted gross income. (p. 384)

J

job Work that a person does mainly to earn money. (p. 31)

journal A record of all of the transactions in a business. (p. 583)

journalizing The process of recording business transactions in a journal. (p. 583)

K

Keogh plan A retirement plan specially designed for self-employed people and their employees; also known as an H.R.10 plan or self-employed retirement plan. (p. 495)

L

landlord A person who owns a rental property. (p. 203)

large cap stock The stock of a corporation that has issued a large number of shares of stock and has a large amount of capitalization. (p. 279)

last-in, first-out method (LIFO) A method of estimating the cost of inventory that assumes that the last items purchased (last in) are the first items sold (first out). (p. 627)

lease A legal document that defines the conditions of a rental agreement between a tenant and a landlord. (p. 206)

legal aid society One of a network of community law offices that provides free or low-cost legal assistance. (p. 111)

liabilities The debts that a person owes. (p. 67)

liability The legal responsibility for the financial cost of another person's losses or injuries. (p. 418)

lifestyle The way a person chooses to spend his or her time and money. (p. 197)

limited liability company (LLC) A business that operates and is taxed as a partnership but whose owners have limited liability. (p. 657)

limited life A situation in which a business ceases to exist when the owner leaves or dies. (p. 644)

limited partner A partner who rarely takes an active role in decision making or in running the business and whose liability is limited to the amount of his or her investment in the business. (p. 645)

limit order A request to buy or sell a stock at a specified price. (p. 297)

line of credit The maximum amount of money a creditor has made available to someone. (p. 158) An arrangement in which bank customers can borrow a certain amount of money from the bank immediately. (p. 560)

liquid assets Cash and items that can be quickly converted to cash. (p. 66)

liquidity The ability to easily convert financial resources into cash without a loss in value. (p. 11)

living will A document in which a person states whether he or she wants to be kept alive by artificial means if he or she becomes terminally ill and unable to make such a decision. (p. 505)

load fund A mutual fund in which a person pays a commission every time he or she purchases shares; also known as an "A" fund. (p. 329)

LowDoc Program A program introduced by the Small Business Administration that allows businesses applying for loans of less than $150,000 to submit a one-page application with a small amount of documentation. (p. 564)

M

managed care A term that refers to prepaid health plans that provide comprehensive health care to their members. (p. 454)

manufacturing business A business that buys raw materials or processed goods and transforms them into finished products. (p. 701)

margin of safety Target sales minus break-even sales; indicates the amount by which sales can drop before the business experiences a loss. (p. 715)

marketing plan The part of a business plan that outlines how a person will promote his or her business to increase customers and sales in order to make a profit. (p. 525)

market order A request to buy or sell a stock at the current market value. (p. 295)

market value The price at which a property could be sold. (p. 67)

markup The difference between the cost of an item to a business and the selling price of the item. (p. 699)

maturity date The date when a bond reaches its face value. (p. 305)

mediation The attempt by a neutral third party to resolve a conflict between a customer and a business through discussion and negotiation. (p. 109)

Medicaid A medical assistance program offered to certain low-income individuals and families. (p. 459)

medical payments coverage A type of homeowners insurance that pays the costs of minor accidental injuries to visitors on a homeowner's property. (p. 423) A type of automobile insurance that applies to the medical expenses of anyone who is injured while in the insured's automobile, including the insured. (p. 432)

Medicare A federally funded health insurance program available to people over 65, certain people with disabilities, and people of any age who have permanent kidney failure. (p. 457)

Medicare tax The payroll tax that finances part of the Medicare program. (p. 610)

mentor An experienced employee who serves as a teacher and counselor for a less experienced person. (p. 52)

merchandise Goods bought with the intent to resell to customers. (p. 538)

merchandising business A business that buys goods, marks them up, and sells them to customers. (p. 701)

minimum monthly payment The smallest amount a person can pay on a credit card bill and remain a borrower in good standing. (p. 169)

mobility The ability to move easily from place to place. (p. 200)

money management A person's method of planning to get the most from his or her money. (p. 59)

money market account A savings account in which the interest rate varies as market rates change. (p. 134)

mortgage A long-term loan extended to someone who buys property. (p. 220)

mortgage bond A bond that is backed by assets of a corporation, also known as a secured bond. (p. 307)

municipal bond A security issued by a state or local (town, city, county) government to pay for its ongoing activities; sometimes called a "muni." (p. 317)

mutual fund An investment alternative in which investors pool their money to buy stocks, bonds, and other securities based on the selections of professional managers who work for an investment company. (p. 253)

N

negative cash flow The condition that occurs when a business spends more money than it receives; also known as a cash crunch. (p. 540)

negligence The failure to take ordinary or reasonable care to prevent accidents from happening. (p. 413)

net asset value (NAV) The amount one share of a mutual fund is worth. (p. 328)

net income The income a person receives (from sources such as take-home pay, allowance, gifts, and interest on bank accounts). (p. 165) The amount of revenue that remains after expenses for the accounting period are subtracted from the gross profit on sales. (p. 591)

networking A way of making and using contacts to get job information and advice. (p. 44)

net worth The difference between the amount that a person owns and the debts that he or she owes. (p. 66)

no-fault system The system under which drivers who are involved in accidents collect money from their own insurance companies. (p. 434)

no-load fund A mutual fund in which the investor pays no commission. (p. 329)

O

odd lot A quantity of fewer than 100 shares of a stock. (p. 298)

open dating A method of indicating the freshness or "shelf life" of a perishable product, such as milk or bread. (p. 100)

open-end credit The ability to borrow money for a variety of goods and services up to a limit set by the company issuing the credit. (p. 158)

open-end fund A mutual fund with an unlimited number of shares that are issued and redeemed by an investment company at the investors' request. (p. 328)

operating capital The amount of capital needed to operate a business for the first few months and years. (p. 671)

operating costs The ongoing expenses that a person expects to have operating a business. (p. 552)

opportunity cost The possibilities that a person gives up when he or she makes one choice instead of another; also known as a trade-off. (p. 10)

overdraft protection An automatic loan made to customers by a financial institution if the customers write checks for more money than they have in their accounts. (p. 142)

over-the-counter (OTC) market A network of dealers who buy and sell the stocks of corporations that are not listed on a securities exchange. (p. 293)

overtime rate An amount paid above the normal rate, usually 1.5 times the employee's regular hourly wage. (p. 606)

owner's equity An owner's claim to the assets of a business. (p. 576)

P

participation certificate An investment in a group of mortgages that have been purchased by a government agency. (p. 358)

partnership A business owned by two or more persons. (p. 644)

partnership agreement A written document that states how a partnership will be organized. (p. 645)

par value An assigned (and often random) dollar value that is printed on a stock certificate. (p. 276)

pay period The specific period of time over which a business pays its employees. (p. 603)

payroll A list of employees and the payments due to each employee for a specific period of time. (p. 603)

payroll register A document that summarizes information about employee earnings and deductions for each pay period. (p. 611)

penny stock A stock that typically sells for less than $1 a share, although it can sell for as much as $10 a share. (p. 280)

pension plan A retirement plan that is funded at least in part by an employer. (p. 50)

peril Anything that may possibly cause a loss. (p. 413)

periodic inventory system A system in which inventory records are updated periodically after someone makes an actual physical count of the merchandise on hand. (p. 623)

perpetual inventory system A system that keeps a constant, up-to-date record of merchandise on hand. (p. 622)

personal financial planning The way people spend, save, and invest their money so that they can have the kind of life they want as well as financial security. (p. 5)

personal financial statements Documents that provide information about a person's current financial position and present a summary of that person's income and spending. (p. 66)

personal property floater Additional property insurance that covers the damage or loss of a specific item of high value. (p. 422)

point-of-sale terminal An electronic cash register linked to a centralized computer system that keeps track of sales. (p. 622)

point-of-sale transaction The use of a debit card to purchase an item or a service at a retail store, in a restaurant, or elsewhere. (p. 127)

point-of-service plan (POS) A health care plan that combines features of both health maintenance organizations (HMOs) and preferred provider organizations (PPOs). (p. 456)

points Extra interest charges that a home buyer must pay in order to get a lower rate of interest on a mortgage. (p. 220)

policy An insurance contract that is purchased. (p. 411)

policyholder The purchaser of an insurance policy. (p. 411)

portfolio All the securities held by an investor. (p. 294)

posting The process of transferring amounts from the general journal to individual accounts in the general ledger. (p. 585)

potential earning power The amount of money a person may earn over time. (p. 33)

power of attorney A legal document that authorizes someone to act on another person's behalf. (p. 506)

precious gems Rough mineral deposits (usually crystals) that are dug from the earth by miners and then cut and shaped into brilliant jewels. (p. 364)

precious metals Valuable ores, such as gold, platinum, and silver. (p. 362)

preemptive right The right of current stockholders to buy any new stock that a corporation issues before the stock is offered to the general public. (p. 274)

preferred provider organization (PPO) A group of doctors and hospitals that agree to provide specified medical services to members at prearranged fees. (p. 456)

preferred stock Type of stock that gives the owner the advantage of receiving cash dividends before common stockholders receive any. (p. 252)

premium A fee paid by a policyholder to an insurer. (p. 411)

present value The amount of money a person would need to deposit now in order to attain a desired amount in the future. (p. 24)

price-earnings (PE) ratio The price of one share of stock divided by the corporation's earnings per share of stock outstanding over the last 12 months. (p. 289)

pricing The process of assigning a selling price to a good or service. (p. 697)

primary market A market in which an investor purchases securities from a corporation through an investment bank or some other representative of the corporation. (p. 292)

principal The amount of money that is deposited in a savings account and on which interest is paid. (p. 21) When referring to a loan, the amount borrowed. (p. 168)

private corporation A corporation whose shares are owned by a relatively small group of people and are not traded openly in stock markets; also called a closely held corporation. (p. 272)

private financing Borrowing money from family or friends. (p. 558)

private investor A person outside an entrepreneur's circle of friends and relatives who provides funding because he or she is interested in helping the entrepreneur's business to succeed. (p. 566)

private mortgage insurance A special policy that protects a lender in case the home buyer cannot make payments, or cannot make them on time. (p. 219)

probate The legal procedure of proving a will to be valid or invalid. (p. 503)

product costing The process of analyzing all costs involved in creating products. (p. 702)

product cost-plus pricing A pricing method in which an item's selling price is determined by adding the invoice cost of the item (how much the business paid for the item) to a certain percentage of the cost. (p. 699)

profit The amount of money earned over and above the amount spent to keep a business operating. (p. 523)

projected financial statements Statements that predict the financial position of a business in the months and years to come. (p. 672)

property damage liability Automobile insurance that applies when the insured damages the property of others; although the damaged property is usually another car, the coverage also extends to buildings and to equipment such as street signs and telephone poles. (p. 433)

prospectus A document that discloses information about a company's earnings, its assets and liabilities, its products or services, and the qualifications of its management. (p. 264) A report that provides potential investors with detailed information about a particular mutual fund. (p. 331)

proxy A document that transfers a stockholder's voting rights to someone else. (p. 273)

public corporation A corporation that sells its shares openly in stock markets, where anyone can buy them; also called a publicly held corporation. (p. 273)

R

rate of return The percentage of increase in the value of your savings from earned interest. (p. 137)

real estate Land that a person or family owns plus anything that is on it, such as a house or any other building. (p. 67)

rebate A partial refund of the price of a product. (p. 101)

refinance To take out a new mortgage at a lower interest rate. (p. 224)

registered bond A bond that is registered in the owner's name by the company that issues the bond. (p. 310)

registered coupon bond A bond that is registered in the owner's name for the face value only and not for interest; it comes with detachable coupons, and anyone who holds the coupons can collect the interest on the bond. (p. 310)

renters insurance A type of insurance that covers the loss of a tenant's personal property as a result of damage or theft. (p. 209)

replacement value One of two methods insurance companies use to determine claim settlements, under which the payment is based on the full cost of repairing or replacing an item. (p. 427)

reserve capital An amount of money set aside by a business for unexpected costs or opportunities. (p. 678)

reserve fund Money that can be made available for future expansion of a business. (p. 554)

résumé A one- or two-page summary of a person's education, training, experience, and job qualifications. (p. 46)

retained earnings A company's profits that are reinvested, often to fund expansion or research and development. (p. 249)

revenue bond A municipal bond that is repaid from the income generated by the project it is designed to finance. (p. 317)

rider A document attached to an insurance policy that changes the terms of the policy by adding or excluding specified conditions or altering its benefits. (p. 471)

risk The chance of loss or injury. (p. 413)

round lots One hundred shares or multiples of 100 shares of a particular stock. (p. 298)

S

safe-deposit box A small, secure storage compartment that can be rented in a bank, usually for $100 a year or less. (p. 63)

salary A fixed amount of money paid to an employee for each pay period. (p. 605)

savings and loan association (S&L) A financial institution that traditionally specialized in savings accounts and mortgage loans; today S&Ls also offer many of the same services as commercial banks, including checking accounts, business loans, and investment services. (p. 129)

secondary market A market for existing financial securities that are currently traded among investors. (p. 292)

second mortgage A loan based on the difference between the current market value of a home and the amount still owed on the mortgage; also called a home equity loan. (p. 556)

secured loan A loan that is backed by collateral. (p. 560)

securities All of the investments, including stocks, bonds, mutual funds, options, and commodities, that are traded—bought and sold—on securities exchanges or the over-the-counter market. (p. 271)

securities exchange A marketplace where brokers who represent investors meet to buy and sell securities. (p. 292)

security deposit An amount of money paid to the owner of a rental property by a tenant to guard against any financial loss that the tenant might cause. (p. 208)

selling short Selling a stock that has been borrowed from a brokerage firm and that must be replaced at a later date. (p. 299)

serial bonds Bonds issued at the same time that mature on different dates. (p. 309)

service A task that a person or a machine performs for someone else. (p. 13)

service contract A separately purchased agreement offered by the manufacturer or distributor to cover the costs of repairing an item. (p. 102)

service industries Industries that provide services for a fee. (p. 39)

simple interest Interest computed only on the principal. (p. 168)

sinking fund A fund to which a corporation makes deposits for the purpose of paying back a bond issue. (p. 308)

Small Business Administration (SBA) An independent agency of the federal government that offers assistance to people who are starting small businesses and to those who want to expand existing businesses. (p. 563)

Small Business Investment Companies (SBICs) Private investment firms that work with the SBA to provide longer-term funding for small businesses. (p. 567)

small cap stock A stock issued by a company with a capitalization of $150 million or less. (p. 280)

small claims court A court that deals with legal disputes that involve amounts below a certain limit. (p. 110)

Social Security tax Tax that finances the federal programs that provide retirement, disability, and life insurance benefits. (p. 610)

sole proprietorship A business owned by one person. (p. 640)

specific identification method An inventory costing method in which the exact cost of each item is determined and assigned to that item. (p. 625)

speculative investment A high-risk investment made in the hope of earning a relatively large profit in a short time. (p. 243)

standard deduction An amount set by the IRS on which no taxes are paid. (p. 384)

standard of living A measure of quality of life based on the amounts and kinds of goods and services a person can buy. (p. 32)

start-up capital The money required to start a business. (p. 668)

start-up costs The costs of setting up a business. (p. 552)

statement of cash flows A document that reports how much cash a business took in and where the cash went. (p. 596)

stock split A process in which the shares of stock owned by existing stockholders are divided into a larger number of shares. (p. 275)

stop-loss A provision that requires a policyholder to pay all costs up to a certain amount, after which the insurance company pays 100 percent of the remaining expenses, as long as they are covered in the policy. (p. 447)

stop order A type of limit order to sell a particular stock at the next available opportunity after its market price reaches a specified amount. (p. 298)

stop-payment order A request that a financial institution not cash a particular check; financial institutions charge a fee for this service. (p. 144)

strategic plan The part of a business plan that outlines a person's business goals and the steps he or she will take to achieve them. (p. 524)

sublet To have a person other than the original tenant take over a rental unit and payments for the remaining term of the lease. (p. 206)

subordinated debenture An unsecured bond that gives bondholders a claim to interest payments and assets of the corporation only after all other bondholders have been paid. (p. 307)

supply The amount of goods and services available for sale. (p. 14)

surplus Extra money that can be spent or saved, depending on a person's financial goals and values. (p. 72)

syndicate A temporary association of individuals or business firms organized to perform a task that requires a large amount of funds. (p. 355)

T

T accounts A tool to show the dollar increase or decrease in an account that is caused by a transaction. (p. 578)

take-home pay The amount of income left after taxes and other deductions are taken out of a person's gross pay; also called net pay. (p. 71)

target profit The amount of net income that a business sets as a goal. (p. 712–713)

target sales The number of units that a business needs to sell to reach its target profit. (p. 713)

taxable income A person's adjusted gross income less any allowable tax deductions and exemptions. (p. 384)

tax audit A detailed examination of a person's tax return by the IRS. (p. 403)

tax credit An amount subtracted directly from the amount of taxes a person owes. (p. 385)

tax deduction An expense that a person is allowed to subtract from his or her adjusted gross income to arrive at his or her taxable income. (p. 384)

tax-deferred income Income that will be taxed at a later date. (p. 262)

tax-exempt income Income that is not taxed. (p. 262)

tax liability The total amount of taxes a person owes. (p. 381)

tenant A person who pays for the right to live in a residence owned by someone else. (p. 203)

term insurance Type of insurance that provides protection against loss of life for only a specified term, or period of time; sometimes called temporary life insurance. (p. 467)

time value of money The increase in an amount of money as a result of interest or dividends earned. (p. 21)

title insurance Type of insurance that protects a home buyer in the event that problems with the title are found in the future. (p. 225)

total gross earnings The amount a business pays to all employees before any deductions, such as Social Security and Medicare taxes,

Social Security and Medicare taxes, are taken out. (p. 614)

total return A calculation that includes the annual dividend as well as any increase or decrease in the original purchase price of the investment. (p. 287)

transaction Any activity that has an effect on the financial situation of a business. (p. 535)

trends Developments that mark changes in a particular area. (p. 33)

trial balance A list of all the account names for a business and their current balances. (p. 586)

trust An arrangement in which a designated person, known as a trustee, manages assets for the benefit of someone else. (p. 502)

12b-1 fee A fee that an investment company charges to help pay for marketing and advertising a mutual fund; the fee is calculated on the value of the fund's assets. (p. 330)

U

umbrella policy A policy that supplements the basic personal liability coverage in a homeowners insurance policy; also called a personal catastrophe policy. (p. 423)

uninsured motorist's protection Insurance that covers the insured and his or her family members if they are involved in an accident with an uninsured or hit-and-run driver. (p. 433)

unit pricing The use of a standard unit of measurement to compare the prices of packages that are different sizes. (p. 101)

unlimited liability A situation in which the owner of a business is responsible for all debts incurred by the business and may have to pay them out of his or her personal assets. (p. 644)

unsecured loan A loan that does not require collateral from the borrower. (p. 560)

V

values The beliefs and principles a person considers important, correct, and desirable. (p. 7)

variable costs Costs (such as labor and materials) that change in direct proportion to the activity level of a business's production. (p. 705)

variable expenses Business expenses (such as rent, utilities, and insurance), that may vary or can be adjusted depending on sales. (p. 673)

venture capital firm A company that provides private funding for small businesses that need a substantial amount of immediate cash. (p. 567)

vesting The point at which an employee becomes eligible to receive the employer's pension plan contributions that he or she has gained, even if the employee leaves the company before retiring. (p. 489)

W

warranty A written guarantee from the manufacturer or distributor that specifies the conditions under which a product can be returned, replaced, or repaired. (p. 102)

whole life insurance A permanent life insurance policy for which one pays a specified premium each year for the rest of one's life. (p. 467)

will The legal document that specifies how a person wants his or her property to be distributed after his or her death. (p. 501)

withhold To take out Social Security and income tax payments from an employee's paycheck and send the money to the IRS. (p. 382)

Y

yield The rate of return, usually stated as a percentage, earned by an investor who holds a bond for a certain period of time. (p. 325)

Z

zero-coupon bond A bond that provides no interest payments and is redeemed for its face value at maturity. (p. 311)

zoning laws Regulations that limit how property in a given area can be used. (p. 214)

Index A

Index B

Common Cents

Finance Online

Photo Credits

Cover photography by: Doug Armand/Stone 234; Ron Chapple/FPG 636; Zigy Kaluzny/Stone 520; Cheryl Maeder/ FPG 376; Johnathon Nourok/ PhotoEdit 02; Jon Riley/ Stone 118; David Young-Wolff/Stone Cover

Alan Abramowitz/Stone 427; AFP CORBIS 286, 296(tl), 308, 418, 551, 567; Glen Allison/Stone 252, 424; Tony Anderson/ FPG 317; Bruce Ayers/Stone 100, 111, 238(br), 311, 442, 451, 455, 487; Paul Avis/FPG 15; David Ball/Stone 366; Davis Barber/PhotoEdit 350; Bettman/CORBIS 182(br), 183(bl); Walter Bibikow/FPG 18; Victoria Blackie/Stone 484(cr); Mike Blank/ Stone 16; Leland Bobbe/Stone 578; Ed Bock/The Stock Market 239(l); Andrea Booher/Stone 660(tl), 700; D. Boone/CORBIS 615; Daniel Bosler/Stone 553; Dugald Bremner/Stone 35; Michelle Bridwell/PhotoEdit 61; Robert Burke/Stone 602; Jan Butchofsky-Houser/CORBIS 607; Peter Cade/Stone 714; Jeff Cadge/Image Bank 620(lr); Jose Carrillo/ PhotoEdit 43; C/B Productions/The Stock Market 499; Ron Chapple/FPG 58, 572; Chris Cheadle/Stone 530(br); Paul Chesley/Stone 497; Paul Chmielowiec/The Stock Market 239(r); Ken Churnus/ FPG 174; Gianni Cigolini/Image Bank 363(tl); Ralph A. Clevenger/CORBIS 491; Tessa Codrington/ Stone 160; Stewart Cohen/Stone 97, 667(t); Connie Coleman/ Stone 641; Cosmo Condina/Stone 332; Joe Cornish/Stone 638; Will Crocker/Image Bank 363(c); Pauline Cutler/Stone 67; Robert E. Daemmrich/Stone 384; Tomas del Amo/Index Stock Imagery 532; David De Lossy/Image Bank 623, 494, 536; Kate Denny/ PhotoEdit 130(c), 530(tr); Marry Kate Denny/ Stone 324; Mark Douet/Stone 238(c); Laura Dwight/ PhotoEdit 648; Wayne Eastep/Stone 07; Paul Edmondson/ Stone 554; Andrew Errington/Stone 08(br); Amy Etra/ PhotoEdit 297, 530(tl), 678, 699; Farmhouse Productions/ Image Bank 344; Jon Feingers/The Stock Market 273, 496, 561; Al Ferguson/PhotoEdit 215; Myrleen Ferguson/ PhotoEdit 285; Ken Fisher/Stone 217(tl), 667(bc); Fisher/ Thatcher/Stone 211, 696; Owen Franken/ CORBIS 660(tr); Tony Freeman/PhotoEdit 105, 612; Rich Frishman/Stone 30; Jose Galvez/PhotoEdit 528; Michael Girard/International Stock 529; Lynn Goldsmith/CORBIS 673; Sylvain Grandadam/ Stone 667(b); Spencer Grant/PhotoEdit 88, 404(c), 616, 621(l), 670; Jeff Greenberg/PhotoEdit 559; Nick Gunderson/ Stone 462; Charles Gupton/The Stock Market 09(l), 157; Charles Gupton/Stone 540; Ernst Haas/Stone 680; David Hanover/Stone 205, 236; Will Hart/PhotoEdit 33, 256; Chip Henderson/Stone 49; Walter Hodges/Stone 565, 620(c); Gary Holscher/Stone 527; Ed Honowitz/Stone 99; Kevin Horan/ Stone 658; Hulton-Deutsch Collection/CORBIS 182(bl); Rich Iwasaki/Stone 410; Donald Johnston/Stone 26; Chris Jones/ The Stock Market 381; Mark Junak/Stone 25; Ray Juno/The Stock Market 270; Wolfgang Kaehler/CORBIS 448; Kaluzny/ Thatcher/Stone 22(t/b); Zigy Kaluzny/Stone 479, 484(tl);

Bonnie Kamin/PhotoEdit 93(bl), 130(bl); Chuck Keeler/ Stone 621(r), 652; Kelly-Mooney Photography/CORBIS 597; Paul Kenward/Stone 279, 526; Mitch Kezar/Stone 196, 539; Michael Krasowitz/FPG 80(bl), 614; Richard Laird/FPG 249; Rich LaSalle/Stone 575; Ken Lax 38(cr); David Leach/Stone 164; Julie Lemberger/CORBIS 461; Les Gibbon Cordaiy Photo Library Ltd./CORBIS 656; Mark Lewis/Stone 293, 357; Norman Y. Lono/New York Times Pictures 548; Adam Lubroth/ Stone 706; John Lund/Stone 20(cl); Patricia Martinez/ PhotoEdit 404(t); Chuck Mason/International Stock 177; Karen Huntt/Mason CORBIS 582; Peter Mason/Stone 436; Francis G. Mayer/CORBIS 365; Patti McConville/Image Bank 129; Michael Melford/Image Bank 353; Jordan Miller Photography 243; Benn Mitchell/Image Bank 363(br); Mason Morfit/FPG 280; Warren Morgan/CORBIS 318; NC State Univ., Center of Universal Design 484(b); Lance Nelson/The Stock Market 212; Joseph Nettis/Stone 447; John Neubauer/ PhotoEdit 660(b); Michael Newman/PhotoEdit 93(c), 135, 283, 404(b); Chris Noble/Stone 245; John Olsen/ The Stock Market 667(tc); Lambert Osrlam/Image Bank 183(br); Tony Page/Stone 435, 708; Jose Pelaez/The Stock Market 295, 469, 501; Steven Peters/Stone 669; Picture Finders Ltd. Leo de Wys/Stock Photo Agency 556; Larry J.Pierce/Image Bank 470; Paul Redman/Stone 217(tr); Donovan Reese/Stone 378; Ken Reid/FPG 356; Reuters Newmedia, Inc/CORBIS 383, 294, 296(tr), 296(cr); Tamara Reynolds/Stone 14; Mark Richards/ PhotoEdit 624; Jon Riley/ Stone 09(r), 38(bc), 152, 219, 508, 580; Joel Rogers/Stone 660(c); Marc Romanelli/Image Bank 92(cr); Elena Rooraid/PhotoEdit 217(c); David Rosenberg/ Stone 264; Andy Sacks/Stone 328, 476; Jane Sapinsky/The Stock Market 645; Chuck Savage/ The Stock Market 564, 626, 715; Neil Selkirk/Stone 296(c); Jed & Kaory Share/Stone 127; Richard Shock/Stone 45; Timothy Shonnard/Stone 91; Juan Silva/Image Bank 4, 126, 392; Stephen Simpson/FPG 672; Frank Siteman/Stone 08(c), 423, 428, 664; Frank Siteman/ PhotoEdit 92(bc); Don Smetzer/ Stone 09(b), 522; Adam Smith/ FPG 414; Steve Smith/FPG 10(tl); Lee Snider CORBIS 334; Joseph Sohm/Stone 120; Joseph Sohm/CORBIS 278; Paul Souders/CORBIS 82; Brian Stablyk/Stone 702; Strauss/Curtis/ The Stock Market 459; Stephen Studd/Stone 221; Superstock/Superstock 52, 78, 80(bc), 83, 103, 170, 594; Telegraph Colour Library/FPG 513; Syme Thayer/FPG 34(cr); The Purcell Team/CORBIS 141; Arthur Thevenart/CORBIS 679; Wes Thompson/The Stock Market 558; Arthur Tilley/FPG 38(tc); Bob Torrez/Stone 217(tc); David Tumley/CORBIS 367; Penny Tweedie/Stone 38(tl); Terry Vine/Stone 530(c), 592; Ron Watts/CORBIS 296(b); Roland Weber/Masterfile 107; Adrian Weinbrecht/Stone 683; David Wells/The Image Works 704; Caroline Wood/Stone 40; Young-Wolff/PhotoEdit 81, 131(cl), 131(br), 181, 187; Ziggy and Friends,Inc./Universal Press Syndicate 106